Irish America

The Historical Travel Guide
Volume 1

Revised and Expanded Edition

United States

Northern Atlantic States
District of Columbia
Great Lakes Region

and

Canada

Richard Demeter

Cranford Press • Pasadena, California

#3977654

Irish America
The Historical Travel Guide
Volume 1

Published by
Cranford Press
500 Cliff Drive
Pasadena, California 91107

Revised and Expanded Edition

Library of Congress Catalog Card Number: 97-94450

ISBN 0-9648253-3-3

Printed in the United States of America

Dedication

To the memory of
my mother
Catherine Coughlin Demeter
and
my grandparents
Leo and Mary (Kelly) Coughlin
and
my great-grandparents
Patrick and Mary (Sullivan) Coughlin,
who emigrated from County Cork, Ireland,
and were married in Philadelphia in 1884

¶ Front Cover Photograph:

The Irish Brigade Monument
Antietam National Battlefield, Maryland

Dedicated in the fall of 1997, this ten-foot-high memorial honors the Irish Brigade, which suffered almost 500 casualties while repulsing the Confederate advance into Maryland in September 1862. The bronze on the front depicts the Irish Brigade on the battlefield, while a bust of Thomas Francis Meagher, the brigade's commander, adorns the back.

¶ Back Cover Photograph:

The Irish Famine Memorial
Cambridge, Massachusetts

This strikingly modern statuary group is part of the first monument of its kind in the United States to remember the victims of the Great Famine. The statue depicts a man holding a child as he prepares to leave Ireland, presumably for America. The monument was unveiled in July 1997 by Irish President Mary Robinson.

Contents

Acknowledgments

I wish to acknowledge my use of the research facilities at the Huntington Library in San Marino, California, the Family History Center in Salt Lake City, Utah, and the Presbyterian Historical Society in Philadelphia, Pennsylvania.

I also wish to acknowledge the following individuals from whom I obtained some of the information and photographs contained in this volume: Marcia Anderson, Minnesota Historical Society, St. Paul, Minn.; Matt Armentrout, Parks and Recreation Department, Harbor Beach, Mich.; Julia Sniderman Bachrech, Chicago Park District, Chicago, Ill.; Michael Baker, London Regional Art and Historical Museums, London, Ont.; Ed Becker, Becker Funeral Home, Mount Olive, Ill.; Linda Bernier, Canadian Heritage, Quebec, Que.; Donna Bjorkquist, St. Paul Public Libary, St. Paul, Minn.; Robin Bodo, State Historic Preservation Office, Dover, Del.; Anita Bologna, *Waterbury Republican-American*, Waterbury, Conn.; Mary Breister, Fond du Lac County Historical Society, Fond du Lac, Wis.; John Brennan, University of Delaware, Newark, Del.; Chuck Bridges, Saint Mary's University, Halifax, N.S.; Rev. Leonetta Bugleisi, Beverly Unitarian Church, Chicago, Ill.; Wanda Burch, Johnson Hall State Historic Site, Johnstown, N.Y.; Michael Casarella, Charles Dawson Historical Center, Purchase, N.Y.; Jennifer Chrisman, Carrollton, Ill.; Kathy Christo, Historical Society, Union Township, N.J.; Linda Cobon, Canadian National Exhibition Archives, Toronto, Ont.; Patrick Colman, Minnesota Historical Society, St. Paul, Minn.; Joe Cook, National Capital Region Land Records, National Park Service, Washington, D.C.; Connie Cooper, Historical Society of Delaware, Wilmington, Del.; Father Arthur Coyle, St. Patrick's Catholic Church, Lowell, Mass.; Becky Crabb, Lake County Parks and Recreation Department, Lowell, Ind.; Paul Curran, Milford, Mass.; Bruce David, Kane, Pa; Karen Deller, Cullom-Davis Library, Bradley University, Peoria, Ill.; Sandy Dively, Derry Presbyterian Church, Hershey, Pa.; Larry Dohey, Archives of the Roman Catholic Archdiocese, St. John's, Newf.; Erin Dornstauder, Fort Walsh National Historic Site, Maple Creek, Sask.; John Dumville, Division for Historic Preservation, Montpelier, Vt.; Carol Durand, Whistler House Museum of Art, Lowell, Mass.; Donna Falso, Cranston Print Works, Cranston, R.I.; Louise Fox, National Historic Sites Directorate, Hull, Que.; Lucille Fragomeni, Moira River Conservation Authority, Belleville, Ont.; Melissa Frownfelter, Henry Ford Estate-Fair Lane, Dearborn, Mich.; John Galvin, Historic Madison, Inc., Madison, Ind.; Phil Germann, Historical Society of Quincy and Adams County, Quincy, Ill.; Rodie Ghezzi, Free

Public Library, Philadelphia, Pa.; Dolores Godlesky, St. Peter's Episcopal Church, Perth Amboy, N.J.; Graphic Arts Department, Chicago Police Department, Chicago, Ill.; Gay Grant, Gardiner, Me.; Kathy Harrison, Gettysburg National Military Park, Pa.; Susan Henzel, Hagley Museum and Library, Wilmington, Del.; Allan Hiltz, Ross Farm Museum, New Ross, N.S.; Father Joseph Hindelang, Our Lady of Victories Eucharistic Shrine, Boston, Mass.; Hugh Holden, Paterson Free Public Library, Paterson, N.J.; Wendy Hubley, Library of Parliament, Ottawa, Ont.; Sheila Johnson, Woodstock Museum, Woodstock, Ont.; Marilyn Jones, Ronald Reagan Home Preservation Foundation, Dixon, Ill.; Mary Karnes, Donegal Presbyterian Church, Mt. Joy, Pa.; Mabel Kelly, Sprague Mansion, Cranston, R.I.; Thomas J. Kelly, Constable Hall, Constableville, N.Y.; Duryea Kemp, Ohio Historical Society, Columbus, Ohio; Bonnie Kersten, Glen View Area Historical Society, Glen View, Ill.; Kathie Kidman, Parkwood Estates and Gardens, Oshawa, Ont.; Brenda Klinkow, McCord Museum of Canadian History, Montreal, Que.; Bob Kuhnz, Fond du Lac County Historical Society, Fond du Lac, Wisc.; Joseph Landry, Cardinal Spellman Philatelic Museum, Weston, Mass.; Joan Lenihan, Ross Farm Museum, New Ross, N.S.; Jim Leonard, Peterborough Museum, Peterborough, Ont.; Vivian Lescisin, Oshawa Public Library, Oshawa, Ont.; Michele Lord, Southington Public Library, Southington, Conn.; Captain South Lynn, Kennedy Farmhouse, Samples Manor, Md.; Steve Macheky, Dowling House, Galena, Ill.; Linda MacIver, Boston Public Library, Boston, Mass.; Michael Maloney, Embassy of Ireland, District of Columbia; Mary K. Mannix, Howard County Historical Society, Elliott City, Md.; R. S. Manuel, Penticton Museum & Archives, Penticton, B.C.; Irene Martin, Toledo/Lucas County Public Library, Toledo, Ohio; Ken Mather, Historic O'Keefe Ranch, Vernon, B.C.; Jean Matheson, National Archives of Canada, Ottawa, Ont.; Margot McAloon-Parker, Charlotte County Archives, St. Andrews, N.B.; Kathleen McAuley, Edgar Allan Poe Cottage, New York City; Mary McClure, St. Joseph's Catholic Church, Brooklyn, Mich.; Amy C. McKay, St. Paul's Church, Halifax, N.S.; David McKean, St. Patrick's Catholic Church, Lowell, Mass.; Edith McKitrick, Grace Church, New York City; Lindsey Moir, Glenbow Museum, Calgary, Alba.; Gladys Murray, Centre County Library and Historical Museum, Bellefonte, Pa.; Sheila Naticchiona, St. Peter's Catholic Church, Pleasantville, N.J.; Betsy Noble, Amherst Public Library, Amherst, N.H.; Nancy Noble, Portsmouth Public Library, Portsmouth, N.H.; Julie Nolan, Richmondtown Restoration, Staten Island, N.Y.; Marie North, State Historical Society, Madison, Wis.; Glenor Nowell, Gardiner Public Libray, Gardiner, Me.; James O'Donnell, Covington, Ohio; Joan O'Mara, Pharmacy Hall, St. John's, Newf.; Ed Patton, Western New York Irish Famine Commemoration Committee, Buffalo, N.Y.; Joan Pellikka, Jervis Public Library, Rome, N.Y.; Sister Marie Michael Power, Sisters of Mercy, St. John's, Newf.; Sue Prifogle, Rushville Public Library, Rushville, Ind.; Father Gilbert

Rahrig, St. Joseph's Catholic Church, Howell, Mich.; Catherine Rankin, City Planning and Development Office, Madison, Wis.; Reverend James Reisner, First Presbyterian Church, Elizabeth, N.J.; Jean Rentmesiter, Galloway House, Fond du Lac, Wis.; John Reynolds, Georgetown University, Washington, D.C.; Pat Richards, Fair Haven Public Library, Fair Haven, Vt.; Scott Robson, Nova Scotia Museum, Halifax, N.S.; Ralph Rourke, Hall of Fame for Great Americans, Bronx Community College of the City University of New York, New York City; Julie Saetre, Conner Prairie, Fishers, Ind.; Audrey Samson, Spring Garden Road Memorial Public Library, Halifax, N.S.; Karen Schwartz, Free Library, Philadelphia, Pa.; Kitty Schwarzbach, Public Library, Canonsburg, Pa.; Dorothy Sinclair, The Peoria Historical Society, Peoria, Ill.; Julia Sniderman Bachrech, Chicago Park District, Chicago, Ill.; Marie Soucy, St. Patrick's Catholic Church, Lowell, Mass.; Terry Sprague, Quinte Conservation, Belleville, Ont.; Charlotte Stewart, Public Archives and Records Office, Charlottetown, P.E.I.; John Stone, Kearny Cottage Historical Society, Perth Amboy, N.J.; Cindy Stouffer, Cyclorama Library, Gettysburg, Pa.; Monica Sullivan, U.S. Military Academy, West Point, N.Y.; Dr. Shawqi Tabia, Catholic University of America, Washington, D.C.; Ethel Thieling, Hastings, Minn.; Cheryl Thompson, Dawson City Museum and Historical Society, Dawson City, Yukon; Margaret Troy, Lawrence Public Library, Lawrence, Mass.; Greg Tucker, National Shrine of the Immaculate Conception, Washington, D.C.; Carolyn Vlielander-Marx, Chatsworth, Ont.; Bill Von Bank, Historic Murphy's Landing, Shakopee, Minn.; Daryll Watson, Galena Historical Society Museum, Galena, Ill.; Monica Wawryk, Fort Walsh National Historic Site, Maple Creek, Sask.; Lillian Weedmark, Bulkley Valley Museum, Smithers, B.C.; Sandy Wiessinger, Logan County District Library, Zanesfield, Ohio; Bonnie Wilson, Minnesota Historical Society, St. Paul, Minn.; Jim Winterer, University of St. Thomas, St. Paul, Minn.; Scott Wolfe, Galena Public Library District, Galena, Ill.; Mary Woods, The Boston Irish Famine Memorial Inc., Braintree, Mass.; and Harold Wright, Heritage Resources, St. John, N.B.

Grateful acknowledgment is also made to P. J. Kenedy & Sons, in association with R. R. Bowker, for permission to reprint from "Breakfast with Hercules Mulligan" by Shaemus O'Sheel.

Introduction

During the past three years people of Irish descent have been commemorating the 150th anniversary of the Great Famine. In the United States and Canada the commemoration has spurred a variety of historical works, dramatic productions, and memorial events. In July 1997, for example, an Irish Famine Monument was unveiled in Cambridge, Massachusetts, and another was dedicated the following month in Buffalo, New York. An impressive Famine Memorial was completed this June in downtown Boston, and an equally grand one is planned for Philadelphia.

During these commemorative years increasing numbers of the 48 million Americans and Canadians of Irish ancestry have learned about the significant influence which their ancestors had in the development of their respective countries. These Irish descendants became increasingly aware, for instance, that the Irish presence in North America began long before the middle of the nineteenth century, when thousands of Irish emigrants fled the famine that ravaged their native land. In fact, from the beginning of British colonization in North America during the seventeenth century, Irish men and women in significant numbers were among the early settlers.

When Irish emigration reached its peak during and just after the famine years in the mid 1800s, the émigrés continued to find refuge in America and Canada, although their Catholicism and appalling poverty and wretchedness caused many native-born residents to oppose their admission. Quite naturally, many of these newcomers faced a hostility which earlier Irish immigrants had not experienced, and while engaged in the backbreaking business of building America and Canada they usually lived and worked under the most oppressive conditions. But most of the newcomers survived the struggle and took their place in the fabric of the larger society, their many contributions serving as woof to the texture and contours of the larger culture's warp.

By 1877 Nicholas Flood Davin could boast of the role of the Irish in the history of Canada. "The Irishman was here as early as the others," Davin declared. "[H]e fought against the wilderness as well as others; his arm was raised against the invading foe as well as that of others; and when a man who was not Irish lifted the standard of revolt [in 1837] and another who was not Irish betrayed his country and his flag, who more faithful, who more heroic, than the countrymen of [Robert] Baldwin and [James] Fitzgibbon in putting down that rebellion? . . . The Irishman has played so large a part in Canada that his history could not be written without, to some extent, writing the history of Canada . . . ." By the beginning of the next century, naturalized Irish Americans and their children could boast as proudly as the Dublin-born musician Victor Herbert: "I do not wish to brag about the achievements of the Irish race, but is it not a fact that on every page of the World's history and particularly the history of this country, you will find the names of some of the most illustrious sons of Erin, and have we not in generous measure helped to build up this wonderful country since its earliest development?"

Like its predecessor, this revised and expanded edition of *Irish America: The Historical Travel Guide (Volume 1)* serves a threefold end. The book is first of all a geographical guide to landmarks associated with historical figures of Irish and Irish-American descent. As such, it includes approximately 800 such sites in three areas of the United States: the northern Atlantic states, the District of Columbia, and the Great Lakes region. The book is also a source of biographical and anecdotal information about those figures and is a chronicle of the tribute paid those men and women by later generations.

The most prominent features of this expanded edition are the addition of eighty-four more photographs and the inclusion of a 100-page section on Canada. This latter addition provides information about 200 sites connected with men and women of Irish birth or ancestry who played significant roles in the history of Canada, both while it was a British colony and since its independence. This portion of the book also contains extensive biographical information about those figures.

Although this work naturally includes landmarks associated with Irish and Irish Americans and Irish Canadians well known to a general audience, its emphasis is on the hundreds of others whose Irish ancestry is not known to most readers or whom the Muse of History has overlooked. In all, this work mentions 750 individuals of Irish birth or descent. Because a significant number of these historical figures are mentioned more than once, the reader should consult the index to find multiple listings. In subsequent references to the name, or when an individual's Irish ancestry might be unclear to the reader, I have placed an asterisk in front of the name.

This sesquicentennial year is an appropriate time to proclaim the deeds of the many Irish immigrants and their descendants whose lives added so much to the fabric of life in the United States and Canada. I hope that this revised and expanded volume of *Irish America: The Historical Travel Guide* will make these deeds better known and will inspire an appreciation of their importance.

Richard Demeter
Pasadena, California
June 1998

Landmarks of Irish America

United States

Connecticut / 17

Delaware / 25

District of Columbia / 35

Illinois / 77

Indiana / 107

Maine / 120

Maryland / 130

Massachusetts / 158

Michigan / 213

Minnesota / 224

New Hampshire / 241

New Jersey / 250

New York / 273

Ohio / 357

Pennsylvania / 375

Rhode Island / 435

Vermont / 450

Wisconsin / 455

Canada

Alberta / 463

British Columbia / 470

Manitoba / 483

New Brunswick / 485

Newfoundland / 496

Nova Scotia / 509

Ontario / 523

Prince Edward Island / 546

Quebec / 551

Saskatchewan / 570

Yukon and
Northwest Territories / 573

CONNECTICUT

CLINTON

¶ **Abraham Pierson Statue,** in front of Morgan High School.

This monument by the Irish-born sculptor Launt Thompson honors the first president of Yale, the Reverend Abraham Pierson, who taught the college's first students in his home in Clinton. A replica of the statue stands on the old Yale campus in New Haven, Connecticut.

Thompson was born in Queens County, Ireland, in 1833 and came to America with his widowed mother when he was fourteen. His interest in drawing grew as he studied anatomy in preparation for a career in medicine, but he abandoned such plans in favor of studying with a local sculptor. Nine years later Thompson opened his own studio in New York and proceeded to produce medallion heads and portrait busts that earned him membership in the National Academy of Design. He was noted for his colossal statue of Napoleon I, which was shown at the 1867 Paris Exposition.

In addition to the *Rocky Mountain Trapper* and busts of James Gordon Bennet Sr., Edwin Booth, William Cullen Bryan, and Samuel F. B. Morse, Thompson sculpted statues of General John Sedgwick (West Point, N.Y.), General Ambrose Burnside (Providence, R.I.), and General Winfield Scott (Washington, D.C.). His statue of a bewhiskered Admiral Samuel Du Pont long stood in Du Pont Circle in the nation's capital but is now located in Rockford Park in Wilmington, Delaware.

HARTFORD

¶ **Mark Twain House,** 351 Farmington Avenue.

The turrets and verandas on this orange and black brick mansion resemble the smokestacks and fan decks of a Mississippi steamboat, fitting features for the home of riverboat pilot Samuel Clemens (Mark Twain). The famous author, who was descended through his mother from Irish stock (Caseys), lived here for seventeen years. In his autobiographical *Life on the Mississippi*, Twain wrote: "Give an Irishman lager for a month, and he's a dead man. An Irishman is lined with copper, and the beer corrodes it. But whiskey polishes the copper and is the saving of him."

§ Open Monday-Saturday 9:30-5, Sunday noon-5. Closed Tuesday November, January-May and January 1, Easter, Thanksgiving, and December 24-25. Fee. Phone: 860-493-6411.

MIDDLEBURY

¶ **French and Irish Soldiers Monument,** Rochambeau Heights, near the juncture of Artillery Road and Break Neck Hill Road.

This memorial was erected in 1904 to commemorate the encampment here in June 1781 of 6,000 French and Irish troops on their march from Newport, Rhode Island, to Yorktown, Virginia. These troops played a decisive role in assuring the American victory against the British at Yorktown that October.

In his remarks at the dedication of the monument, Dennis Tierney of the American-Irish historical Society pointed out that the French army contained a large number of Irish troops, especially in the Dillon and Walsh regiments of the Irish Brigade. The former regiment was under the immediate command of Count Arthur Dillon, a member of an originally Irish family that had settled in France at the end of the seventeenth century.

A similar repatriation had occurred thousands of times before, beginning in 1607 when the English defeated Irish rebels under the command of the earls of Tyrconnell and Tyrone. The defeat of the Catholic monarch James II at the battle of the Boyne in 1690 only added to the "Flight of the Earls" from Ireland. By the beginning of the eighteenth century, an estimated quarter million Irish mercenaries had offered their services to various monarchs on the Continent.

Earlier in its career Dillon's regiment had taken part in an attack on British-held Savannah (1779) and in the capture of Tobago and St. Eustache (1780). After the war he returned to France, where he was placed in command of a division of the French army and played a prominent role in the battles of Valmy and Verdun. Although he led his troops under the tricolor of the French Republic, he was suspected of being a royalist and was guillotined in April 1794, during the Reign of Terror.

MIDDLETOWN

¶ **Thomas Macdonough Burial Site,** Riverside Cemetery, on the south side of St. John's Square.

The famous Irish-American naval commander Thomas Macdonough is among those buried here. (See Odessa, Delaware, and Plattsburgh, New York.)

NEW BRITAIN

¶ **New Britain Museum of American Art,** 56 Lexington Street.

Among the museum's 5,000 paintings and sculptures are works by Thomas Hart Benton, Mary Cassatt, *John Singleton Copley, Winslow Homer, Gilbert Stuart, and *James McNeill Whistler. (See Copley Square, Boston, and Whistler House Museum of Art, Lowell, Massachusetts.)

§ Open Tuesday-Friday, 1-5, Saturday 10-5, Sunday noon-5. Closed January 1, Easter, July 4, Thanksgiving, and December 24-25 and 31. Fee except Saturday 10-noon. Phone: 860-229-0257.

NEW HAVEN

¶ **Defenders' Monument,** at the junction of Davenport, Congress, and Columbus avenues.

Designed by James Edward Kelly, this memorial was erected in 1911 in honor of the New Haven citizens and Yale students who helped repulse British invaders in 1779. The monument consists of three bronze statues of representative colonial figures: a student, a farmer, and a merchant.

Kelly was born in New York City in 1855 to Irish parents. His first significant sculpted work was a statuette called *Sheridan's Ride*, which depicted *General Philip Sheridan as he raced astride his steed to rally his men during the battle of Cedar Creek in Virginia in 1864. Kelly also created sketches of other Civil War officers as well as a variety of bas-reliefs and busts. Among the portrait busts were those of Admiral Dewey, Count Rochambeau, *Theodore Roosevelt, and Admiral Sampson. Kelly also designed five panels on the Monmouth battle monument in Freehold, New Jersey.

The Irish-American's other major works are the Soldiers' and Sailors' Monument (Troy, N.Y.), the Sixth New York Cavalry Memorial (Gettysburg, Pa.), the Barbara Fritchie medallion (Frederick, Md.), the *William McKinley Memorial (Wilmington, Del.), and equestrian statues of General William Sherman, *Colonel Theodore Roosevelt, Caesar Rodney, and Fitz-John Porter (the last two in Wilmington, Del.). After designing a monument for the Seneca chief Red Jacket at Buffalo, New York, he was adopted into the tribe with the name *Ga-Nos-Qua* ("Worker in Stone"). He was also known as the "Sculptor of American History."

¶ **Father McGivney Burial Site,** St. Mary's Church, 5 Hill House Ave.

The church is a popular destination for pilgrims who annually visit the tomb of Father Michael McGivney, the founder of the Knights of Columbus, the international Catholic fraternal order.

One of thirteen children born to Irish immigrants in Waterbury, Connecticut, the teenage McGivney worked in a brass mill there before pursuing the priesthood. After attending St. Mary's Seminary in Baltimore, he was ordained by *Cardinal James Gibbons in 1877. The new priest's first assignment was at St. Mary's Church in an anti-Catholic area of New Haven. (Residents objected to the "aristocratic avenue being blemished by a Roman Catholic edifice.")

While at St. Mary's, McGivney proposed the creation of a mutual aid society of Catholic laymen pledged to the ideals of charity, fraternity, and patriotism. By creating such an organization, he also hoped to counter the influence of the generally anti-Catholic Masons. He and a dozen parishioners founded the fraternal order in 1882. Two years later McGivney was named pastor of St. Thomas Church in Thomaston, Connecticut, where he died in 1890 of tuberculosis and pneumonia at the age of thirty-eight. So large was the number of mourners accompanying the priest's body to Waterbury for burial that four additional cars had to be added to the train. A newspaper account at the time described the funeral procession as the largest ever seen there. McGivney's remains were reinterred in St. Mary's Church in 1982, the centennial year of the Knights' founding. (See Waterbury, Connecticut.)

¶ **Knights of Columbus Grand Council Museum,** 1 Columbus Plaza.

This museum was built as a tribute to *Father Michael McGivney, the founder of the Knights of Columbus. The museum presents exhibits about the organization's many activities as well as about McGivney and his two brothers, each of whom served as the Knights' national chaplain.

At first the Knights aroused the suspicion of the Catholic hierarchy, chiefly because of its oath and secret rituals, but it soon received official approbation. The organization later used its influence to help make Columbus Day a national holiday. In 1989 the Knights had 2.5 million members and donated $85 million to charitable causes. By 1996, however, membership had dropped to 1.5 million in the United States, Canada, Mexico, the Philippines, and several other countries. (See Waterbury, Connecticut.)

§ Open Monday-Friday 8-4:30, weekends by appointment. Phone: 203-772-2130.

¶ **Soldiers' and Sailors' Monument,** East Rock Park, 1.5 miles northeast of the Green, at the end of Orange Street.

Dedicated in 1887, this 112-foot-high granite memorial is the work of Alexander Doyle and honors the memory of American casualties in the Revolution, the War of 1812, and the Mexican War.

Born in Steubenville, Ohio, in 1857, of presumably Irish ancestry, Doyle became familiar with monument making through his father, who was employed in the quarrying business. The younger man later studied sculpture in Italy, initially while living there with his parents and then when he returned on his own to study at the national academies in Rome, Florence, and Carrara. After establishing himself in New York City, he quickly earned a reputation as a sculptor of monuments. An Indiana newspaper once opined that at the age of thirty-five Doyle had created more public monuments than any other American sculptor and that 20 percent of such monuments in the United States were the product of his hand and chisel. Rather surprisingly for American artists of his time, he was a member of no American art societies and exhibited none of his work at American art shows. Yet he was an honorary member of the Royal Raphael Academy in Urbino,

Italy.

Doyle also designed the Francis Scott Key monument (Frederick, Md.) and statues of *Henry Grady (Atlanta, Ga.), *Sergeant William Jaspar (Savannah, Ga.), *Horace Greeley (New York City), General Philip Schuyler (Saratoga, N.Y.) and General James Garfield (Cleveland, Ohio). Four of his most significant works are in New Orleans: the marble statue *Calling the Roll* and statues of *Margaret Haughery, General Albert Sidney Johnson, and General Robert E. Lee.

¶ Yale University, Old Campus, bounded by Chapel, High, Elm, and College streets.

• Berkeley College, on the northeast corner of Elm and High streets, is named for George Berkeley, the seventeenth-century Irish missionary and Yale benefactor.

• Calhoun College, on the northwest corner of Elm and College streets, is named for *John C. Calhoun, an 1804 Yale graduate and a vice president of the United States.

• The statue of the Reverend Abraham Pierson, on the west side of the old campus, is a replica of the statue by *Launt Thompson in Clinton, Connecticut [*q.v.*].

• John Trumbull's famous painting *The Surrender of Lord Cornwallis at Yorktown*, in the University Art Gallery, includes Major General Charles O'Hara among the officers. The Irishman's long service in the British army suffered a stain when Cornwallis ordered him to be his stand-in and officially surrender his sword to the victorious Americans. (See Yorktown, Virginia, in *Irish America*, Volume 2.)

• The Eugene O'Neill Collection, Yale University Library, was founded in 1931 by Carlotta Monterey O'Neill, the Irish-American playwright's third wife. It includes photographs, notes, and manuscripts of plays.

NEW LONDON

¶ Eugene O'Neill Memorial Theater Center, 305 Great Neck Road, west on U.S. 1 in Waterford.

The center is named for *Eugene O'Neill and recognizes his literary achievements: forty-five plays, four Pulitzer prizes (for *Beyond the Horizon, Anna Christie, Strange Interlude,* and *Long Day's Journey into Night*), and the Nobel Prize for Literature in 1936. The center is open year round for theater study and offers a program of summer performances.

§ Phone: 860-443-5378 or 443-1238.

¶ Monte Cristo Cottage, 1.5 miles south of U.S. 1 at 325 Pequod Avenue.

This boyhood home of Eugene O'Neill was named for his Irish-born

Monte Cristo Cottage, the boyhood home of Eugene O'Neill.

father's best known role as the Count of Monte Cristo in the play of the same name. The house has been restored to its appearance as described in *Ah, Wilderness* and *Long Day's Journey into Night*, both of which are set in the house. Visitors can view O'Neill memorabilia, the research library, and the multimedia presentation.

Much has been made of the biographical and autobiographical nature of *Long Day's Journey into Night*. Although the name of the family in the play is Tyrone, O'Neill's allusion is to Ireland's County Tyrone (*Tir-Eoghan* or *Tir-Owen*), the ancestral home of the O'Neills. The character James Tyrone is unmistakably the author's famous actor-father (James O'Neill), while Edmund, one of the grown sons in the play, is the playwright himself, named for the real-life brother who died in infancy. Mary Tyrone, the mother in the drama, is clearly intended to be the author's own mother, Mary (Quinlan) O'Neill.

The play frequently refers to the small room upstairs in Monte Cristo where she secluded herself and sought relief through morphine. Her flight from the house in a half-crazed state and her attempt to throw herself into the nearby river are immortalized in a scene in the play. This episode captures Eugene's real-life discovery of his mother's addiction, which she blamed on the "cheap quack" whom her husband had hired and who gave her the medicine as a sedative after Eugene's birth. Following these revelations, the young O'Neill finalized his break with Catholicism and religion in general. The next Sunday, as he and his father descended the stairs at Monte Cristo headed for church, the son announced that he never intended to go to mass again.

O'Neill had few favorable comments about New London. His remark that "It wasn't a friendly town" probably understated the disdain which the town's elite showed his family because of his father's shanty-Irish roots and his career as a traveling actor. The author once told a friend that he hoped to return one day to New London in order to shock the bourgeois sentiments of its elite with a "flock of painted whores, hiring a tally-ho of six horses, and having the girls ride up State Street and throw dimes to the crowd." He developed a more favorable view of the town, however, when he learned that traveling salesmen rated its red-light district as the best between New York and Boston.

O'Neill's attitude toward Ireland was equally ambivalent. Although he was proud of his Irish ancestry, he spoke critically of the "Old Sod" in front of his father. The playwright frequently alluded to his O'Neill roots and relished the story of "Red" O'Neill. According to the legend, during a boat race "Red" cut off his hand and threw it in onto the shore in order to be the first to "touch" land and thereby win the large tract of property that was the object of the contest. On one occasion O'Neill the playwright confided that "One thing that explains more than anything about me is the fact that I'm Irish."

§ Open Memorial Day-Labor Day, Tuesday-Sunday 10-5. Schedule varies after Labor Day through mid October. Fee. Phone: 860-443-0051.

SOUTHINGTON

¶ **Rochambeau Monument,** French Hill.

Like a similar memorial in Middlebury, Connecticut, this nine-foot-high monument commemorates the encampment here of 6,000 French and Irish troops on their way from Rhode Island to Virginia, where they helped force the British to surrender at Yorktown in 1781. Although originally dedicated in 1912, the memorial was rededicated in 1971 as part of celebrations marking the 350th anniversary of Connecticut's founding.

On the front of the monument is a bronze bas-relief of Count Rochambeau, the commander-in-chief of the French and Irish troops sent to help the Americans defeat the British during the Revolution. The art work was done by *James Edward Kelly. (See Defenders' Monument, New Haven.) On the reverse – beneath an Irish harp, a fleur-de-lis, and an American flag – are the names of the officers under the French general's command, one of whom was *Count Arthur Dillon of the Irish Brigade.

WATERBURY

¶ **Father McGivney Statue,** Grand and Meadow streets.

This ten-foot-high bronze statue honors *Father Michael McGivney, the Waterbury native who founded the Knights of Columbus. The memorial was dedicated in 1957. (See Father McGivney Burial Site, St. Mary's Church, New Haven.)

Statue of Fr. Michael McGivney, founder of the Knights of Columbus.
(Photo courtesy of the Waterbury Republican-American.*)*

DELAWARE

LEWES

¶ **Fisher-Martin House,** 120 King's Highway, at Savannah Road.

Although now the Lewes Chamber of Commerce and Visitor's Bureau, this clapboard structure dates from the 1730s, when it was purchased by the Reverend James Martin, a Presbyterian minister of Scotch-Irish descent and the founder of the Coolspring Presbyterian church.

§ Open Memorial Day-Labor Day, Monday-Friday 10-4, Saturday-Sunday 10-2. Phone: 302-645-8073.

¶ **Fisher's Paradise,** 624 Pilottown Road. Private.

This house was built in the early eighteenth century by Major Henry Fisher, an Irish immigrant and probably the first physician of note in Delaware. Because the house was patterned after an English country seat, Fisher's neighbors called it "a paradise."

After coming to this area from Waterford, Ireland, in 1725, Fisher was the only professionally trained physician in Sussex County. His successful practice sometimes took him to Kent County, Maryland, to offer diagnoses in serious cases. He repeatedly turned down offers to transfer his practice to Philadelphia. During the Revolution he informed George Washington that the British fleet had been sighted off Cape Henlopen headed for the Chesapeake. The Continental Congress responded by authorizing Fisher to raise a company of 100 men.

According to tradition, Caesar Rodney, one of Delaware's delegates to the Continental Congress, was a guest at Fisher's house in July 1776 when he received a letter from *Thomas McKean begging him to come to Philadelphia to vote for independence. It was from here that Rodney set out, arriving just in time to vote for the Declaration of Independence. Tradition tells how the daughter of the Tory postmaster in town had intercepted the letter to Rodney and how a Negro maid in the Tory's household informed Rodney about the note.

MT. CUBA

The name of this small town northwest of Wilmington came from Cuba Rock, part of a 250-acre estate which William Penn's daughter sold to Cornelius Hallahan, an Irishman who had come to America in 1730. The first Catholic religious services in Delaware are said to have been held in his house.

NEWARK

❡ **Kells,** 318 South College Avenue.

Now the Y.W.C.A., this stone building with two large square towers was built between 1910 and 1920 by Everett Johnson to house his newspaper, the *Newark Post*. Johnson named the building for the Book of Kells, the famous copy of the Gospels produced in the eighth century at the monastery of Kells in Ireland.

❡ **University of Delaware.**

Some of the buildings on the campus date from the early 1840s, remnants of the original academy on this site. Although that academy was founded in 1743 in New London, Pennsylvania, by the Reverend Francis Alison, it was moved to Newark in 1765. The academy was the predecessor of Delaware College, now the University of Delaware.

A native of Donegal, Ireland, Alison was a Presbyterian minister who had attended the University of Glasgow before coming to America in 1735. While ministering at New London, he bemoaned the fact that, as Ezra Stiles wrote, "there was not a College, nor even a good Grammar School in four provinces, Maryland, Pennsylvania, Jersey, and New York." Once his academy was established, Alison taught not only the classics but also logic, metaphysics, geography, and "other arts and sciences." Hailed by Stiles as "the greatest classical scholar in America, especially in Greek" and by Ben Franklin as "a Person of great Ingenuity and Learning," Alison seems to have possessed only one pedagogical weakness – "proneness to anger." Among the graduates of his academy were Thomas McKean, George Read I, and Charles Thomson, all men of Irish ancestry who played a major role in the history of their respective colonies.

§ The visitor center is at 196 South College Avenue. Tours Monday-Friday 10, 11:30, and 2; Saturday 10 and 11:30. Phone: 302-831-8123.

NEW CASTLE

❡ **George Read II House and Garden,** 42 The Strand.

This Federal-style house was originally built between 1797 and 1804 by George Read II, the son of one of the Irish-American signers of the Declaration of Independence. Following a fire that gutted the house in 1824, his son – George Read III – restored it and hosted the Marquis de Lafayette here when the famous Frenchman made his triumphal tour of the United States.

George Read II served for thirty years as U.S. district attorney in Delaware and owned a large cotton plantation in Mississippi. He is buried in the graveyard of Immanuel Episcopal Church in New Castle.

§ Open March-December, Tuesday-Saturday 10-4, Sunday noon-4; rest of the year, Saturday 10-4, Sunday noon-4. Closed holidays. Fee. Phone: 302-322-8411.

*The Federal-style house built by George Read II, the son of one
of the Irish-American signers of the Declaration of Independence.*

❡ Immanuel Episcopal Church, Market and Harmony streets.

The present structure was completed in 1710. Among the famous residents of Delaware buried in the church cemetery are *George Read I and his son, George Read II. The elder Read – the only signer of both the Declaration of Independence and the Constitution – married the widowed daughter of George Ross, the rector of the church.

❡ Stoneham, on the northeast corner of 9th and Washington streets. Private.

Now less than an acre, Stoneham (or Stonum) is the only remaining residence associated with George Read I, who purchased it in the 1750s. The original two-story building with an interior chimney was built about 1730.

Read was born in Maryland in 1733 to an Irish father and a Welsh mother. As a youngster he received part of his education at New London, Pennsylvania, from the *Reverend Francis Alison. After studying law in Philadelphia, Read was admitted to the bar at the age of nineteen and established his law office in New Castle at 22 The Strand, a cobblestone street near the river. He served in the colony's legislature for fifteen years and was attorney general and a delegate to the Continental Congress. Although he originally voted against adopting the Declaration of Independence, he signed the document the following August 2.

While serving as the acting president of Delaware immediately following its independence from Britain, he strove relentlessly to raise troops
and provisions during the Revolution. He expressed his frustration in a
letter to General Washington in 1778: "My situation is rather an unlucky
one, in a government very deficient in its laws, and those greatly relaxed
in their execution, and a Legislature as yet incomplete, and not disposed
to unite and give aid to the executive authority." Read was later a delegate
to the Constitutional Convention and was elected to the U.S. Senate. He is
depicted in the heroic painting *The Signing of the Declaration of Independence* by John Trumbull, now in the Rotunda of the U.S. Capitol.

℧ **Thomas McKean Law Office,** 22 The Strand. Private.
    Located among other eighteenth-century townhouses, this site served
as the law office of Thomas McKean, a delegate to the Continental Congress and the son of emigrants from County Tyrone, Ireland. (See Caesar
Rodney Monument, Wilmington, Delaware.)

℧ **William Penn Statue,** 2nd Street, near the Old Town Hall.
    Following his conversion to the Society of Friends (Quakers) while
living in Ireland, William Penn welcomed his coreligionists to his New
World colony, which originally included what is now Delaware. When
Penn arrived in New Castle in October 1682, among the 100 passengers
aboard his ship was at least one group of Irish Quakers from Enniscorthy
in County Wexford – Dennis Rochford, the surviving members of his family, and his two servants. (Rochford's two daughters died en route.)
    Rochford had joined the Society of Friends in Ireland in 1662. Seven
years later he was arrested for attending Quaker services in Dublin, and
the next year he was jailed in Wicklow for the same offense. Beginning in
1675, he and his family lived in England, where he operated a grocer's
shop. A year after his arrival in America, the Irishman was elected to represent Chester County in the Pennsylvania Assembly.

ODESSA

℧ **Macdonough House,** 2 miles north on State 13. Private.
    This was the birthplace in 1783 of Commodore Thomas Macdonough,
the victor of the battle of Plattsburgh in 1814 and the grandson of a Protestant who had emigrated from County Kildare, Ireland, in 1730. (See
Plattsburgh, New York.)

WILMINGTON

℧ **Caesar Rodney Monument,** Rodney Square, bounded by Market,
King, 10th, and 11th streets.

The equestrian statue on this monument was sculpted by *James Edward Kelly in tribute to Caesar Rodney, who rode through the night to Philadelphia, arriving just in time to vote for the Declaration of Independence in July 1776. (See Defenders' Monument, New Haven, Connecticut.) The bas-relief on the pedestal shows Rodney being greeted by Thomas McKean, the Irish American who had urged Rodney to hasten to Philadelphia.

McKean was born in 1734 in New London, Pennsylvania, to parents from County Tyrone, Ireland. He was a member of the Friendly Sons of St. Patrick and the first president of the Hibernian Society for the Relief of Immigrants from Ireland. Trained as a lawyer, he was as outspoken a foe of the Stamp Act as he was an ardent supporter of independence from Britain. While attending the Stamp Act Congress in New York in 1765, he helped prepare an address to the House of Commons outlining the colonial position on taxation without representation. When various other delegates to the Stamp Act Congress refused to sign that assembly's proceedings, McKean criticized those members so severely that Timothy Ruggles, the president of the Congress, challenged the Irishman to a duel. Although McKean accepted, Ruggles failed to appear on the "field of honor" the next morning. While passing through New Jersey on his way home, McKean declared that that colony's representative had likewise failed to support the actions of the Stamp Act Congress, a charge that brought McKean another challenge to a duel. (History repeated itself when the

This bronze relief depicts Caesar Rodney's arrival in Philadelphia to join Thomas McKean (left) in voting for independence.

second challenger had second thoughts and declined to attend his own affair.)

McKean gained deserved fame for his later role in precipitating a "midnight ride" as important as Paul Revere's. When, as a delegate to the Continental Congress, McKean's vote for independence was negated by *George Read, his colleague from Delaware, McKean dispatched a messenger to New Castle to urge Caesar Rodney, the third delegate from that colony, to come to Philadelphia to break the tie. Rodney arrived just in time to vote for the resolution in favor of independence on July 2, 1776. (His arrival and reception by McKean are depicted in a bronze relief on the monument.) McKean most likely signed the Declaration sometime after January 18, 1777, and seems to have been the first to dismiss the later popular impression that that document was signed on July 4. Following independence from Britain, he presented one of the drafts from which the Delaware state constitution was written. (A probably apocryphal account says that "He retired to his room . . . , sat up all night, and having prepared [the draft] without a book or any assistance whatever, presented it at 10 o'clock next morning.")

After 1777 McKean had the distinction of holding public office in both Delaware and Pennsylvania. In the former state he served as an assemblyman, acting president, and congressman, while in the latter he was chief justice of the supreme court for two decades. According to William Cobbett, one of McKean's harshest contemporary critics, the chief justice tried to ensure his own election to higher office by indiscriminately giving the oath of citizenship to Irish settlers he encountered while riding circuit. Cobbett also charged that McKean tried to enlist the Irish vote by claiming that he was a Catholic.

Whatever the truth of these charges, there is no doubt that after his election as governor McKean removed his political enemies from office. He described this policy to Jefferson as a preference for "real republicans" and justified it on the grounds that "it is not right to put a dagger in the hands of an assassin." His political opponents continued their attacks, however, accusing him in 1806 of nepotism. One hostile newspaper published the names of twelve relatives that the governor had appointed to office and referred to them as "The Royal Family," singling out McKean's oldest son as the "heir apparent."

¶ **Coffee Run Mission Site,** southeast of Hockessin off State 48.

Just within the entrance to the cemetery is a small chapel marking the site of St. Mary's Church, originally a log structure built in 1772 and the first Catholic church in the state. The church was also the residence of Father Patrick Kenny when the Dublin-born priest came to this area sometime after 1804. From here he ministered to five other missions in Delaware, Maryland, and Pennsylvania. Kenny is buried in the graveyard.

In 1812 Kenny built the two-and-a-half-story stone house on this site. Besides ministering to the spiritual needs of the faithful in and around Wilmington, he supported himself by farming. In a diary entry for January 30, 1823, he reported an explosion at the nearby Du Pont powder mill: "John Kelly, only 2 months from Ireland where he left his wife and 7 children [-] Dead. Also Wm Duffy and Wm Delany – all catholics. 4 Irish Cath wounded." On other occasions he recorded trenchant remarks about his hired hand, Patrick Haw. Seemingly irritated by the latter for some unknown gaffe, the priest described Haw as an "Irish Indian Savage, Drunkard, Egg & cider sucker." An 1827 entry illustrates the depth of the priest's embarrassment about his handyman: "Mr Patrk Haw brought home Drunk in Moses M–'s cart – This Moses M– is as smooth an enemy to Catholics as any violent puritan in America – He was proud of his freight – to the great scandal of my house and place." In another incident, when Haw was bled following a drunken spree, he bragged that his blood was so thick that "it would not come out."

¶ **Du Pont Statue,** Rockford Park, south of Rockford Tower, at the junction of Tower Road and West 19th Street.

This statue of Admiral Samuel Du Pont is the work of *Launt Thompson and stood in Du Pont Circle in Washington, D.C., from 1884 to 1920. During the Civil War, Du Pont commanded a squadron of seventy-five vessels at the capture of Port Royal, South Carolina. (See Clinton, Connecticut.)

¶ **Hagley Museum and Library,** 3 miles north on State 52 and then 0.5 mile north on State 141.

The museum occupies 230 acres of the original explosives factory established in 1802 by Eleuthère Irénè Du Pont, a French immigrant who came to America to manufacture a better and less expensive explosive powder. The property includes a machine shop, a cotton-spinning shop, the ruins of twenty-one powder mills, and Eleutherian Mills (the Georgian mansion built by Du Pont in 1803). A restored workers' community includes the Brandywine Manufacturers' Sunday School, built in 1817 with donations from Du Pont as a school for his workers and their children and the Gibbons House, where John Gibbons, an Irish foreman at the works, lived with his wife and four children.

Although Du Pont's first workers were French, he gradually replaced them almost exclusively with Irish immigrants. Du Pont hired his first Irish workers in 1803, in many cases paying for their passage to America. Yet he had strong reservations about their abilities: Nevertheless, he must have succeeded in training them to his satisfaction because by 1839 only a small number of his employees were of other nationalities.

One of the Irish workers in the Du Pont mills that year was John Gibbons, a seventeen year old from Derry, Ireland, who had begun work at the mills for $17.50 a month. During his first few months on the job, he used part of his wages to repay William McCarrow the $43 passage for himself and Mary Anne Gibbons, probably a sister who had accompanied him to America. John at first probably lived in the workmen's dormitories, although by 1841 he was renting a row house opposite the Squirrel Run factory. By 1850 he was earning $24 a month; seven years later he was the foreman at the Hagley Yard.

As foreman he appears to have been entitled to live rent free in what is now called the Gibbons House, although at the time it was referred to as "the 3rd house from the old school house." According to the 1870 Census, Gibbons lived here with his wife, Catherine, and their four children: Charles, Maggie, John, and William. In 1873, to mark his thirty-five-year tenure with the mills, Gibbons was presented with a gold watch by Henry Du Pont, the founder's son. Gibbons continued to serve as foreman until his death in 1885, at which time he was earning $55 a month.

Some years later one of Gibbons's sons became involved in an unfortunate incident that would probably have shamed his father. After being laid off from his carpentry job with the company, the twenty-eight-year-old William was part of a group of disgruntled employees who burned down a number of the Du Pont family's barns. Following his arrest, Gibbons was found guilty of arson and received fifteen lashes.

Another aspect of the Du Ponts' connection with the Irish is found in the story of Eleuthère Du Pont's great-grandson Maurice. While visiting

The Gibbons House, home of an Irish foreman at the Du Pont explosives factory.

Queenstown, Ireland, Maurice fell in love with Margery May Fitz-Gerald, variously described as a barmaid and a housekeeper at a hotel there. Maurice stubbornly insisted that he wouldn't leave Queenstown until she agreed to marry him. Once she consented, however, he returned to America alone, never mentioned the engagement to his family, and only returned to Queenstown for the wedding in Cork in October 1889. The *Wilmington Evening Journal* described the nuptials as "the sensation of two continents," while a Chicago paper claimed that the bride's "beauty and virtue [were] her only dowry."

§ The museum is open March 15-December, daily 9:30-4:30; rest of the year, Saturday-Sunday 9:30-4:30. Closed Thanksgiving and December 25 and 31. Fee. Phone: 302-658-2400.

¶ John McKinly Burial Site, Wilmington and Brandywine Cemetery, on the north side of Delaware Avenue, between Madison and Adams streets.

Buried here is Dr. John McKinly, the first president of Delaware after its independence from Britain. Born in Ireland in 1721, McKinly was elected president in February 1777 under the state's first constitution. He was later seized from his home in Wilmington by the British, who held him until September 1778, when Congress arranged for his exchange. His remains were reinterred here in 1922 after their removal from the burial ground of the Old First Presbyterian Church.

The slab on his original grave was inscribed thus: "This monument is dedicated to the memory of John McKinly, who was born in the Kingdom of Ireland on the 24th of February, 1721, and died in this town on the 31st of August, 1796. He settled early in life in this country, and, pursuing the practice of physic, soon became eminent in his profession. He served in several important employments and particularly was the first person who filled the office of President of the State after the Declaration of Independence. He died, full of years, having passed a long life usefully to the public and honorably to himself."

¶ St. Joseph's-on-the-Brandywine Catholic Church, 10 Barley Mill Road.

The original church on this site was built by the Du Ponts in 1841 for their Irish employees. Although generally supportive of these Catholic immigrants, the Du Ponts were occasionally exasperated by the religious wrangling that marred local Church-State relations. In 1852, for example, St. Joseph's parish priest, *Father John Walsh, attacked the state-supported public school system for its failure to provide financial support to Catholic schools. He once publicly ripped the pages dealing with Martin Luther and Sam Adams from a textbook used in the public schools. Alexis Du Pont commented that the local Catholics' objection to the public schools had taught him to give preference to Protestants when vacancies occurred among his employees. Nevertheless, a later Du Pont served as a trustee of St. Joseph's Church – although he was not a Catholic – and publicly declared his opposition to the Know-Nothing movement because of its proposed "proscription of all foreigners and particularly the poor oppressed Irish Catholics."

DISTRICT OF COLUMBIA

In 1791 President George Washington requested Pierre Charles L'Enfant to design plans for the new federal city. One of the commissioners whom Washington appointed to oversee the surveying of the proposed city on the Potomac River was Daniel Carroll of Duddington, a member of the famous Maryland family which traced its roots to the high kings of Ireland.

Before long, L'Enfant committed a serious faux pas involving two of the city's most influential proprietors. As he proceeded to lay out the streets, the Frenchman discovered that two houses obstructed his plan. Dismissive of the fact that one of the structures belonged to Carroll, L'Enfant announced that the houses must be demolished. Carroll's subsequent letter to Washington revealed that the designer had taken matters into his own hands – literally, it seems: "Major L'Enfant has proceeded with his hands to the demolishing of my building, which he has in great measure effected, having entirely destroyed the roof, and thrown down the greater part of the upper story, in fine the building is ruined. This appears to be the most arbitrary act ever heard of." Washington responded by warning L'Enfant in the future "to touch no man's property without his consent, or the previous order of the Commissioners." Nevertheless, L'Enfant continued to run afoul of the commissioners and the president and was dismissed in February 1792.

Following L'Enfant's departure, Andrew Ellicott took his place as surveyor of the District, and James Reed Dermott, a native of Ireland, was later selected as Ellicott's assistant. Almost immediately, though, the two were at loggerheads, Ellicott charging that Dermott had taken L'Enfant's plan of the city, and Dermott confiding that he intended to take Ellicott's job. Although the Irishman claimed that there were inaccuracies in Ellicott's survey of the city, Ellicott feared that his assistant had stolen some documents in order to make it impossible for him to prove the inaccuracies. Ellicott, in turn, feared that the inaccuracies had been Dermott's, a suspicion supported by his other assistants' complaints about having to make so many corrections because of Dermott's "deliberate, nefarious designs," caused apparently by his malicious removal of stakes. One of the assistants revealed that Dermott had "declared that he had put the affairs of the city into such a train, that they should never be set right again."

Events took an even more unpleasant turn when one of Ellicott's brothers placed an advertisement in a Georgetown newspaper seeking Dermott's apprehension for the theft of L'Enfant's plan. Under a headline customarily used to seek a horse thief – "SIX DOLLARS REWARD: STOP THE THIEF" – Ellicott described the alleged thief as "a native of Ireland, well made, about five feet ten inches high, has a remarkably red face, an impudent brazen look, dark-coloured hair, which he commonly wears tied behind. Whoever shall take up the said thief, and commit him to any jail in the United States, so that he may be brought to condign punishment, shall receive the above reward."

As things turned out, the commissioners expressed to President Washington their confidence in Dermott. They believed that the accusations against him were intended to free Ellicott from blame for a mistake of his own which had thrown the survey off – from a few inches in some places to many feet in others. After Ellicott's departure from the city, the commissioners asked Dermott "to lay off squares into lots, [and] to plot the squares" and then to prepare a plat of the city. From this request came Dermott's so-called "Tin Case Map," the plan of the city that President Adams sent to Congress for approval.

¶ Abraham Lincoln Statue, Judiciary Square, D Street, between 4th and 5th streets, N.W.

This life-size statue of Abraham Lincoln is by Lot Flannery, a native of Limerick, Ireland, and a sculptor who had known the slain president. The monument was dedicated in 1868 on the third anniversary of Lincoln's death.

Although Flannery's permanent address was in Washington, D.C., he studied and traveled in Europe and completed commissions in New York City, New Orleans, and St. Louis. In the 1860s he directed one of Washington's largest stonecutting operations. His other notable works are a statue of Stephen Douglas in St. Louis, the Arsenal Monument in the Congressional Cemetery in Washington, D.C., and busts of Benjamin Franklin and General John Logan.

¶ The Adams Monument, Rock Creek Cemetery, Section E, Rock Creek Church Road and Webster Street, N.W.

Commissioned by Henry Adams for the grave of his suicide wife, this memorial is the most unusual one in the cemetery. The monument consists of a shrouded bronze figure by *Augustus Saint-Gaudens seated upon a boulder and backed by a polished granite block. Saint-Gaudens referred to it as *The Mystery of the Hereafter* and *The Peace of God that Passeth Understanding*. (See Cornish, New Hampshire.)

After *President Theodore Roosevelt referred to the statue as that of a woman, Henry Adams wrote to him: "After March 4, should you allude to my bronze figure, will you try to do St. Gaudens the justice to remark that his expression was a little higher than sex can give. As he meant it, he wanted to exclude sex, and sink it in the idea of humanity. The figure is sexless." Homer Saint-Gaudens said that his father "occasionally explained" the figure "as both sexless and passionless" and that both a man and a woman had posed for it.

§ Cemetery open daily 7:30-dusk. Phone: 202-829-0585.

§ Anderson House, 2118 Massachusetts Avenue, N.W.

This former private residence is the headquarters, library, and museum of the Society of the Cincinnati, the oldest hereditary military society in North America. Founded in 1783 as the result of a proposal by *Henry Knox, George Washington's chief of artillery, the organization was originally limited to American and French commissioned officers who had served for at least three years during the Revolution. Ten of Washington's generals were Irish natives: Richard Butler, Edward Hand, William Irvine, William Maxwell, Stephen Moylan, John Patton, Griffin Rutherford, John Shee, Walter Stewart, and William Thompson.

The major objectives of the Society of the Cincinnati were to promote the ideals of the Revolution, to maintain the officers' *esprit de corps*, and to offer assistance to officers and family members when needed. The society was named for the Roman general Lucius Quinctius Cincinnatus, the prototypical citizen-soldier who served his country in time of military need but returned to his civilian status immediately afterwards. Membership in the order is hereditary, passing originally only from father to son but now to the oldest male collateral descendant if no direct descendant exists. With a membership of about 2,600 today, the society emphasizes historical research and the endowment of scholarships.

§ Museum open Tuesday-Saturday 1-4; closed major holidays. Library open by appointment Monday-Friday 10-4. Phone: 202-785-2040.

§ Andrew Jackson Equestrian Statue, Lafayette Square, across Pennsylvania Avenue from the White House.

This statue of Andrew Jackson, the son of an immigrant from northern Ireland, was the first equestrian statue made in the United States. The bronze was cast in 1853 by Clark Mills from cannon captured by the former president in the War of 1812. Mills at first turned down the request to do such a work, since he had never seen Jackson or an equestrian statue. Nevertheless, he produced a miniature based on a Virginia thoroughbred which he had trained to rear in such a way that its hind feet were under the center of its body. Mills spent two more years creating a plaster model. After erecting his own foundry, he succeeded in casting the body of the horse but only after five attempts. Mills was commissioned to erect an identical statue in New Orleans. It was finally cast in 1856, but only after he had suffered two disasters: the destruction of his studio by a tornado and the loss of his foundry to fire.

In March 1829 an estimated 20,000 people had arrived in Washington to attend Jackson's inauguration. While conservatives compared this event to the "inundation of the northern barbarians into Rome," Jackson's supporters followed their hero as he returned on horseback to the White House from his inauguration at the Capitol. At the White House the "President after having been *literally* nearly pressed to death and almost suffocated and torn to pieces by the people in their eagerness to shake hands with Old Hickory, had retreated through the back way. . . . Cut glass and china to the amount of several thousand dollars had been broken in the struggle to get the refreshments. . . . Ladies fainted, men were seen with bloody noses and such a scene of confusion took place as is impossible to describe – for those who got in could not get out by the door again but had to scramble out of windows. . . . [I]t was the People's day, and the People's President and the People would rule." To draw some of the crowd outside the White House, attendants placed tubs of liquor across the street in Lafayette Square. (See Waxhaw, North Carolina, in *Irish America*, Volume 2.)

¶ **Andrew Mellon Memorial Fountain,** Constitution and Pennsylvania avenues, N.W.

Built at a cost of $300,000, this fountain is a memorial to Andrew Mellon, the industrialist, financier, and secretary of the treasury who created and endowed the National Gallery of Art.

Mellon was of Scotch-Irish stock, his grandfather Thomas having come to Pittsburgh, Pennsylvania, from County Tyrone, Ireland. After entering the family banking business in 1873, the younger Mellon soon became known for his ability to identify and finance promising ventures, among them the Aluminum Company of America. He also played an important role in the creation of the Gulf Oil Corporation and the Union Steel Company. At one time he was either a director or an officer of more than sixty corporations. Although by 1920 he was president of the Mellon National Bank, he was little known nationally when President Warren G. Harding chose him as his secretary of the treasury.

In his new position Mellon pursued policies designed to lower taxes and to reduce the national debt. He believed that reduced tax rates would bring prosperity to American business and that the fruits of this prosperity would, in turn, "trickle down" to the working classes. In addition, he rejected the use of the tax code for social engineering: "I have never viewed taxation as a means of rewarding one class of taxpayers or punishing another." In general, Congress lowered federal tax rates, although not to the extent Mellon had sought. Toward the end of the decade he had reduced the national debt by a third (to $16 billion) and the budget by half (to $3.5 billion).

√ The ancestral cottage from which Thomas Mellon emigrated in 1818 at the age of five is located in the Ulster-American Folk Park, County Tyrone, Ireland. The park, promoted through the generosity of the Mellon family of Pittsburgh, Pennsylvania, chronicles the eighteenth-century emigration of 250,000 Ulster Scots (known in the United States as Scotch Irish).

¶ **Basilica of the National Shrine of the Immaculate Conception,** on the campus of Catholic University of America, 4th Street and Michigan Avenue, N.E.

As early as 1848, proposals were made to build in the District of Columbia a Catholic church which would rival any in Europe. Initial steps were not taken, however, until 1913, when *Bishop Thomas Shahan, the rector of Catholic University, sought the support of Catholic women throughout the country. The cornerstone was laid in 1920 by *Cardinal James Gibbons, the archbishop of Baltimore. Although construction of the crypt was finished by 1931, construction of the upper church was postponed because of the Depression and World War II. In 1953, however, the John McShain Company of Philadelphia was awarded the contract to construct the upper church. The basilica was dedicated six years later by *Cardinal Francis Spellman of New York.

Incorporating features of both Byzantine and Romanesque architecture, the basilica is 465 feet long and 238 feet wide at the transept. The dome is 90 feet in diameter and rises 237 feet above the crossing, while the campanile is 329 feet high.

The chief designer for the basilica project was Charles Maginnis, a native of Londonderry, Ireland. He received his early education at Cusack's Academy in Dublin, where he won the Queen's Prize in mathematics. After coming to the United States in 1885, he secured employment in several Boston architectural firms until he became a partner in the firm of Maginnis, Walsh & Sullivan in 1898. He specialized in ecclesiastical and collegiate architecture and designed structures in those genres in twenty states and in Canada, Cuba, and Mexico. Some of the more famous of the many commissions which his firm accepted were the buildings on the new Boston College campus, sixteen buildings on the University of Notre Dame campus, and the chapel at Trinity College in Washington, D.C. He was honored with a gold medal from numerous associations, including the American Institute of Architects, the American Irish Historical Society, and the Eire Society of Boston.

• To the left of the main entrance to the upper level of the basilica is the Chapel of Our Lady, Queen of Ireland. The chapel was dedicated in 1980 as a gift of *John McShain, whose company had constructed the upper church. His family's coat of arms is above the entrance. In the center of the chapel is a statue of the Madonna and Child beneath a Waterford Crystal chandelier. The mosaic on the south wall incorporates the symbols of the four evangelists used in the Book of Kells, while the north wall depicts St. Patrick and ships sailing from Ireland, a representation of the influence of Irish missionaries throughout the world.

• Bishop Thomas Shahan, who is buried in the crypt of the National Shrine, was born in Manchester, New Hampshire, to Irish immigrants. Prior to his ordination he attended the Sulpician College in Montreal and

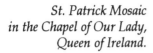

St. Patrick Mosaic
in the Chapel of Our Lady,
Queen of Ireland.

the North American College in Rome. He completed graduate work at the University of Berlin and at the Sorbonne and the Institut Catholique in Paris in preparation for a professorship of church history and patrology at Catholic University of America in Washington, D.C. Besides contributing to numerous Catholic periodicals, he was associate editor of the original *Catholic Encyclopedia,* for which he wrote more than 200 articles and rewrote or translated more than a hundred others. He also wrote six books, one entitled *St. Patrick in History.*

¶ **Blaine Mansion,** off DuPont Circle at 2000 Massachusetts Avenue and 20th Street, N.W. Private.

This imposing structure was built in 1881 for James G. Blaine, a prominent political figure of Irish ancestry who served as Speaker of the House of Representatives and secretary of state under President Benjamin Harrison. (See Augusta, Maine.).

¶ **Blair House and Blair-Lee House,** Pennsylvania Avenue, near the White House.

These adjoining townhouses constitute the President's Guest House and are used to accommodate official state visitors. Blair House was the home of President Harry Truman and his family in the summer of 1945 and again during the renovation of the White House during most of Truman's elected term of office.

Built in 1824 by a Washington physician, what is now known as the Blair House was purchased in 1836 by Francis Blair Sr, a journalist from Kentucky and a descendant of an eighteenth-century Scotch-Irish immigrant. Blair, who had come to Washington to establish the *Globe*, the official mouthpiece of the Jackson administration, was still living in the city on the eve of the Civil War. Just before that conflict erupted, he built the adjoining townhouse for his daughter.

¶ **Cannon Building,** Independence Avenue, between New Jersey Avenue and 1st Street, S.E.

One of five office buildings used by members of the House of Representatives, the Cannon Building recalls the career of Joseph Cannon, known for his arbitrary rule as Speaker of the House from 1901 to 1911.

Cannon was born in 1836 in North Carolina, where his paternal grandfather, a native of Ireland, had settled after immigrating to Quebec shortly after the American Revolution. Upon his admission to the bar, Joseph served as an Illinois state prosecutor from 1861 to 1868. In his memoirs he related an incident in which he was asked to prosecute Abraham Lincoln's stepmother for theft, a charge to which she had confessed. Suspicious that the original complainants had made the charge to embarrass the president politically, the young prosecutor interviewed Mrs. Lincoln himself. The accused readily admitted taking a piece of calico from the village store but stressed her intention of returning the swatch after seeing whether it matched some goods she had purchased earlier. Convinced that the woman was telling the truth, Cannon entered into an agreement with the judge to "wipe the charge and the confession off the records" and reprimanded the complainants for what he called their disgraceful conduct. The prosecutor admitted that what he had done was quite illegal but ended his memoir about the incident with the remark: "There are times when a judicial officer may take some liberties with the strict letter of the law in the interest of justice, and certainly this was a time."

Thus schooled in skirting the law, Cannon ran for and was elected to Congress as a Republican in 1872, beginning an almost uninterrupted tenure of fifty years in the House. For his coarse speech and vulgar manners, he became known as "foul-mouthed Joe" and "the Hayseed Member from Illinois," although later in his career he was called "Uncle Joe." His half century in Congress was remarkably devoid of any important legislation which bore his imprint, and he is chiefly remembered for the power he wielded as Speaker of the House. By selecting the committee on rules himself and by refusing, during House sessions, to recognize any member who had not previously obtained his permission to speak, he ruled the House with an iron fist. Despite three bipartisan attempts to curtail his power, he retained his office until 1911, when the Democrats came to power.

¶ Cardinal Gibbons Statue, 16th Street and Park Road.

This statue of James Gibbons, the archbishop of Baltimore and the second American cardinal, was erected by the Knights of Columbus and was dedicated in 1932.

Born in Baltimore of Irish immigrants from County Mayo, Gibbons spent five years of his childhood in Ireland before returning to his native city, where he studied for the Catholic priesthood. At the time of his appointment as bishop of North Carolina, he was the youngest of the 1,200 Catholic bishops throughout the world.

Following his consecration as archbishop of Baltimore in 1877, Gibbons banished from the public mind the belief that Catholicism was incompatible with American institutions. Since the nation's capital was at that time within his archdiocese, he made the acquaintance of each president from Jackson to Harding and developed strong friendships with Cleveland, Roosevelt, and Taft. He was also perhaps the first Catholic prelate in America to throw his influence behind observance of Thanksgiving Day by the Catholic community.

Gibbons's subsequent appointment as the nation's second cardinal drew enthusiastic public praise because of his thorough identification with

Statue of Cardinal James Gibbons.

American ideals. He, in turn, attributed the success of the Catholic Church in America to the liberty found in a country "where the civil government holds over us the aegis of its protection, without interfering with us in the legitimate exercise of our sublime mission as ministers of the gospel of Christ." He later drew additional support from the Catholic working classes of America when he intervened to prevent the Vatican from condemning the fledgling Knights of Labor on the erroneous grounds that this early labor union was a secret organization that required it members to take an oath. In 1911, on the twenty-fifth anniversary of his elevation to the cardinalate, he was feted at public ceremonies in Baltimore and eulogized by President Taft and *Theodore Roosevelt, both of whom praised his patriotism and civic virtue.

¶ **Catholic University of America,** 4th Street and Michigan Avenue, N.E.
    Following the appointment of *Bishop Thomas Shahan as rector of Catholic University in 1909, he oversaw an ambitious development program that resulted in the construction of John K. Mullen Memorial Library, Martin Maloney Chemical Laboratory, Cardinal Gibbons Memorial Hall, and McMahon Hall of Philosophy.
    • McMahon Hall was named for Monsignor James McMahon, a native of Ireland who was educated at the Sulpician seminaries in Paris and Montreal before being ordained in New York City sometime after 1843. Dedicated in 1895, the granite building was named for McMahon because he had donated $400,000 worth of real estate to the university.
    • A bronze bust of John Boyle O'Reilly, the famous Irish nationalist, editor, and author, is in the university's collection.
    In 1896, when the Ancient Order of Hibernians endowed a chair in Celtic languages and literature at the university, some members of the Catholic hierarchy objected. Four years earlier *Bishop Bernard McQuaid of Rochester had reminded Irish Catholics that the bishops of Baltimore, New York City, and Philadelphia had condemned organizations like the Hibernians because of their alleged secrecy and condonation of violence. "That the Molly Maguires of Pennsylvania and the A.O.H. are even one and the same society cannot be denied," McQuaid charged. "This fact was demonstrated beyond gainsay at the trials of the Molly Maguires for brutal murders. This new University Chair ought to be labeled the 'Murderers' Chair.'" McQuaid later changed his opinion about the Hibernians.

¶ **Congressional Cemetery,** G and 18th streets, S.E.
    • Among the many gravesites here are those of *Mathew Brady, the famous Civil War photographer, and Thomas Fitzpatrick, the Irish-born trapper, scout, and Indian agent. (See Daniel, Wyoming, in *Irish America,* Volume 2.)

• A marble monument marks the original grave of *Governor George Clinton. His remains were moved to the graveyard of the Reformed Church in Kingston, New York, in 1911. (See Kingston, New York.)

• The Arsenal Monument by *Lot Flannery adorns the grave of twenty-one women who were killed in the explosion of the Washington Arsenal in 1864.

ℐ Convent of the Visitation, P and 35th streets, N.W.

In 1797 Alice Lalor, a native of County Kilkenny, Ireland, formed in Philadelphia what later became the first American branch of the Visitation Nuns. When the group's sponsor, *Father Leonard Neale, moved to Georgetown in 1799, the women came with him and eventually established their community in a building of their own on this site.

At first these "Pious Ladies," as they were known, followed a rule similar to that of the Jesuits, but they later adopted the Visitation rule. Lalor (Mother Teresa) led the community for twenty years. The free school for girls which she founded was the genesis of the present school affiliated with the Visitation Convent.

ℐ Corcoran Gallery of Art, 17th Street and New York Avenue, N.W.

The gallery was established in 1859 by William Corcoran, whose Irish-born father had immigrated to America in 1783, eventually settling in Georgetown and serving as that community's magistrate and postmaster.

Between 1837 and 1840 Corcoran established a reputation in the brokerage and banking industries. So successful was the banking firm of Corcoran & Riggs that in 1847 he completely paid off – with interest – the balance of a $24,000 indebtedness incurred by the bankruptcy of an earlier enterprise. The following year Corcoran & Riggs received 87 percent of a $16 million bond issue by the United States government. When Corcoran successfully placed $5 million of those bonds in London, the resultant rise in their market price assured his fortune.

Following his retirement in 1854, Corcoran devoted his time to art collecting and philanthropy. To house a collection of European paintings which he had begun acquiring on a trip to the Continent in 1849, he commissioned James Renwick Jr. to design a gallery in the Second French Empire style. Construction at the museum's original site – Pennsylvania Avenue and 17th Street – began in 1859. When the museum was completed after the Civil War, Corcoran hosted a gala ball, for which the main picture gallery was lighted by 280 gas jets suspended from the ceiling. Two years later Corcoran created a $900,000 endowment for the museum and donated his own private collection, valued at $100,000. When the museum became too small for its 700 works, a new Corcoran Museum was built at 17th Street and New York Avenue. In 1925 the gallery received a bequest of European paintings and decorative arts from *Senator William Clark of Montana. In 1964 the old gallery was renamed the Renwick.

Among the works in the Corcoran Gallery of Art are a portrait of the museum's founder by Charles Loring Elliott; portraits of the French statesman François Guizot and U.S. presidents *Chester A. Arthur, *James Buchanan, Millard Fillmore, and *Andrew Jackson, all by the Irish-American artist George Healy; and a bust of the Irish poet Thomas Moore by *Jerome Connor.

§ Open Wednesday-Monday 10-5 (also Thursday 5-9). Closed January 1 and December 25. Fee. Phone: 202-639-1700.

Jerome Connor was born in County Kerry, Ireland, in 1876 and as a young child came to America with his family. Because his parents were so poor, he was forced at age thirteen to earn his own living. After working successively as a sign painter, a machinist, and a stonecutter, he lived and worked in a craftsman colony near Buffalo, New York, where he did metal work, plaster casting, and sculpture. After opening his own studio in Syracuse, he received his first major commission – a marble memorial to Walt Whitman. He later set up a studio in the nation's capital.

Connor was a strong advocate of the Irish independence movement and in 1921 exhibited a portrait bust of *Eamon De Valera, the president of the Irish Free State, at the Philadelphia Exhibition of Fine Arts. Four years later he returned to Ireland to work on a memorial County Cork to the victims of the *Lusitania* sinking, which had occurred off Cobh on May 7, 1915. While occupied on this project for fourteen years, he completed a series of relief portraits of the Cabinet members of the Irish Free State government. He died in Dublin in 1943 and was buried in Mount Jerome Cemetery in that city.

His three other works in the District of Columbia are the *Nuns of the Battlefield Memorial* and statues of *Bishop John Carroll and *Robert Emmet.

¶ Decatur House, 748 Jackson Place.

This three-story brick townhouse was designed for Commodore Stephen Decatur, the popular hero of the War of 1812. Decatur, whose maternal grandparents were Irish, lived here a little more than a year before being killed in a duel with a fellow naval officer in 1820. Only five years before, Decatur, the scourge of the Tripolitan pirates, had proclaimed the toast, "Our country! In her intercourse with foreign nations may she always be in the right; but our country, right or wrong!"

§ Open Tuesday-Friday 10-3, Saturday-Sunday noon-4. Closed January 1, Thanksgiving, and December 25. Fee. Phone: 202-842-0920.

¶ Dumbarton Oaks, 1703 32nd Street, N.W.

Until 1826 this Georgian mansion was occupied by Vice President John C. Calhoun, the son of an immigrant from County Donegal, Ireland.

Considerably altered and enlarged since then, the house is now an art museum and center of medieval studies owned by Harvard University. The mansion is surrounded by fifteen acres of formal gardens.

§ Open Tuesday-Sunday 2-5. Closed holidays. Phone: 202-339-6409.

¶ **Edmund Burke Statue,** Massachusetts Avenue, at 11th and L streets.

This monument honors Edmund Burke, the famous Dublin-born orator who championed the cause of the American Revolution while he was a member of the British Parliament. He was also advocated the independence of Ireland and the extension of civil rights to Catholics.

Statue of Edmund Burke.

¶ **Embassy of Indonesia** (formerly the Walsh-McLean House), 2020 Massachusetts Avenue, at 21st Street, N.W.

The embassy was originally built as the private residence of Thomas Walsh, an Irishman from County Tipperary who had made a fortune from gold mining in Colorado during the 1890s. After extracting approximately $23 million worth of gold from his Camp Bird Mine, he sold the concern to a British company for $5.2 million. (See Ouray, Colorado, in *Irish America*, Volume 2.)

Walsh and his wife subsequently moved to Washington, D. C., and took their place among both the *nouveaux* and the *vieux riches*. While traveling in Europe, Walsh met King Leopold II of Belgium, who tried to interest the American in investing in the Congo and promised to visit the him when he attended the St. Louis Exposition in 1903. After returning to America, Walsh purchased this piece of real estate on Massachusetts Avenue and proceeded to spend $835,000 in the construction of the sixty-room mansion and another $2 million on furnishings. One of the Walshes' parties was attended by 325 guests, who consumed 480 quarts of champagne, 288 fifths of scotch, 40 gallons of beer, and 36 bottles of liqueur. Walsh later joined King Leopold in various mining operations in the Congo and died in the nation's capital in 1909.

Before his death, however, Walsh had acquired a reputation for foolish generosity to his daughter, Evalyn. When the young girl complained that having to walk to school in Washington was "trying for my dignity," she asked her father to hire a horse and carriage. Within days the doting father presented her with a blue victoria, a pair of matched sorrels, and a coachman decked out in a silk hat. Some years later he gave his dear Evalyn a $100,000 wedding gift when she married Edward McLean, whose father owned the *Washington Post*. Walsh also succumbed to Evalyn's desire that he purchase the 44.5-carat Hope Diamond for her. As it turned out, though, the curse attached to the $154,000 investment had tragic consequences for Evalyn: her eight-year-old son was killed in a car accident, another son died after a lengthy stay in a sanitarium, her daughter died because of a drug overdose, she herself became addicted to morphine, and her adulterous, alcoholic husband went insane.

Embassy of Indonesia, former home of the Irish mining magnate Thomas Walsh.

¶ **Embassy of Ireland,** 2234 Massachusetts Avenue, N.W., at Sheridan Circle.

This limestone structure built in the Louis XVI style dates from 1909, when it was erected as a private residence according to the plans of William Penn Cresson, a prominent Washington architect. The building was occupied by a series of eight owners until the death in 1948 of Margaret Good Van Clief, the widow of a well-known industrialist, horse-breeder, and yachtsman. The Van Cliefs' two sons sold the property to the Irish government in 1949. The former residence became the Irish Legation the following year.

The story of how the legation was later raised in status to an embassy began with a remark made to President Harry Truman by Mary Cummings. A native of County Roscommon, Ireland, Cummings was the well-known hostess of the Nineteen Twenty-five F Street Club, a private and fashionable establishment in Washington, D.C., frequented by the city's elite. While Truman was a guest at the club in the winter of 1950, Cummings approached the president and posed the following question: "If Afghanistan and Pakistan and some others I could mention have Ambassadors here, why not Eire?" Truman replied that he would take her suggestion under advisement, and a short time later he announced that the governments of Ireland and the United States were raising each other's legation to the level of an embassy.

Although the role played by Mary Cummings in these diplomatic developments went unmentioned by the official White House announcement, she continued to wield an unofficial influence. This time she suggested to the president that he appoint George Garrett, the U.S. minister to Ireland since 1947, the first American ambassador to Ireland. Again Truman considered the Irishwoman's proposal and soon submitted Garrett's name for Senate confirmation.

A native of La Crosse, Wisconsin, Garrett was of mixed Irish, Scotch, and English ancestry. He attended Cornell University and the University of Chicago and from 1912 to 1917 was vice president of the Du Pont National Bank in New York City. During World War I he served as a lieutenant in the aviation section of the Signal Corps. Prior to his appointment as minister to Ireland, he was a partner with Merrill, Lynch, Pierce, Fenner and Beane. He was also a founder of the Nineteen Twenty-five F Street Club.

The Irish government greeted President Truman's announcement with the appointment of John Hearne as the first Irish ambassador to the United States. Hearne said that in coming to America he was confident of the "gracious good will and the cordial cooperation" of the United States and added that the elevation of the two countries' missions was a matter of "exceptional importance in the long story of Irish American friendship." Hearne had previously served twelve years as High Commissioner in Canada.

§ Phone: 202-462-3939.

¶ **Freer Gallery of Art,** 1200 Jefferson Drive, S.W.

Modeled after a Florentine palace, this museum exhibits art work from

Asia and the Middle East as well as paintings by Winslow Homer, John Singer Sargent, and *James McNeill Whistler. The Whistler collection includes more than a thousand of his oils, watercolors, pastels, and prints. The gallery's Peacock Room, which Whistler decorated with gold and turquoise peacocks, was designed for an English merchant.

§ Open daily 10-5:30. Closed December 25. Phone: 202-357-2700.

¶ **George Meade Memorial,** The Mall, Pennsylvania Avenue and 3rd Street, in front of the U.S. District Court.

This monument honors General George Meade, the Union commander at the battle of Gettysburg and the great-grandson of an emigrant from County Kerry, Ireland. A gift of the state of Pennsylvania, this eighteen-foot-high monument features Meade at the front of a circle of allegorical figures representing Chivalry, Energy, Fame, Loyalty, Military Courage, Progress, and War.

At the outbreak of the Mexican War, Meade was engaged in designing and constructing lighthouses in the Delaware Bay with the U.S. Army's Corps of Topographical Engineers. He subsequently saw service in the battles of Palo Alto and Resaca de la Palma and participated in the siege of Vera Cruz. After the war he returned to his engineering duties in the Delaware Bay until he was sent to Florida, where he first made surveys

George Meade Memorial.

and maps of the reefs but later served in the war against the Seminoles.

With the eruption of the Civil War, Meade was appointed brigadier general of volunteers, initially to defend Washington, D.C., from an expected Confederate assault. During the later battle of Glendale, he sustained wounds that caused him medical problems for the rest of his life. As one bullet hit his arm, another pierced his body just above the hip joint, indented his liver, and exited near the spine. Nevertheless, he continued to direct his troops from atop his mount until loss of blood forced him to retire from the engagement. Following service at Second Bull Run, Antietam, and Chancellorsville, he was unwillingly appointed commander of the Army of the Potomac.

¶ **Georgetown University,** 37th and O streets, N.W., Georgetown.

Georgetown, the first Roman Catholic college in the country, was founded in 1789 by John Carroll, the first bishop of the United States and a member of the distinguished Irish Catholic family of Maryland. A bronze seated statue of the bishop by *Jerome Connor is located in front of Healy Hall. (The sculptor added a stack of books under the bishop's chair when undergraduates took delight in placing chamberpots under the statue.)

• Healy Hall is named after Father Patrick Healy, the first African-American Jesuit in the United States and the first African American to

Statue of John Carroll at Georgetown University.

become the president of a Catholic university. The son of an Irish immigrant and a mulatto slave in Georgia, Healy was graduated from Holy Cross College in Worcester, Massachusetts, in 1850. After entering the Jesuit Order, he taught at Holy Cross for six years before going to Europe to continue his education, first in Rome and then in Louvain and Liège, Belgium, where he completed a doctorate in philosophy.

Following his ordination, Healy returned to Georgetown University to serve in a variety of capacities, finally being named its president in 1874. Besides updating its curriculum and better integrating the main campus with the institution's medical and law schools, he expanded the university's facilities. He planned and supervised the construction of a major new building – today's Healy Hall – in Belgian Gothic. The four-story structure – 312 feet long and 95 feet wide at the pavilions – was completed in 1879. The massive building's spire is the highest point in the District of Columbia. Healy is buried near the hall.

• The Georgetown Astronomical Observatory on the campus was created by Father James Curley, a pioneer astronomer and the observatory's first director. A native of County Roscommon, Ireland, Curley had arrived in the United States in 1817. After working for the next ten years as either a bookkeeper or a mathematics instructor, he joined the Society of Jesus and was ordained in 1833. He taught mathematics and astronomy at Georgetown for forty-eight years.

During that time Curley also planned and supervised the building and furnishing of the observatory, which was completed in 1844. The structure's three-story main building is sixty feet long and thirty feet wide and is surmounted by a rotary dome. Its transit instrument is seven feet long and has a 4.5-inch object glass, while the equatorial telescope in the dome has a 4.8-inch object glass with magnification powers of from 25 to 400. One of Curley's first undertakings following completion of the observatory was to determine the meridian of Washington D.C. (His computation was later found to be more accurate than the government's.) In 1852 he wrote the *Annals of the Astronomical Observatory of Georgetown College*, describing the facility and its instruments.

J James Buchanan Statue, Meridien Hill Park, 16th Street and Florida Avenue, N.W.

The funds for this monument to *President James Buchanan were provided by his niece, Harriet Lane, who served as the bachelor's hostess during his years in the White House. (See Mercersburg, Pennsylvania.)

J James Hoban Burial Site, Mt. Olivet Cemetery, opposite the National Arboretum.

In May 1863 the body of James Hoban, the Irish-born architect of the White House, was exhumed from the graveyard of St. Peter's Catholic

Church and reinterred here. For many years it was customary for the Washington Chapter of the American Institute of Architects to lay a wreath on their earlier colleague's grave. (See White House, District of Columbia.)

James Hoban Burial Site (left) and Statue of John Barry.

John Barry Statue, Franklin Park, 14th and K streets, N.W.

This bronze statue honors the memory of Commodore John Barry, the "Father of the American Navy" and a native of County Wexford, Ireland. The likeness depicts the Irishman with a great cape around his shoulders and a cocked hat on his head. His right hand grasps the hilt of his sword. On the face of the pedestal is the goddess Victory, standing with sheathed sword on the prow of a vessel, an eagle in her right hand and a laurel in her left.

The statue is the work of John Boyle, who was born in New York in 1851 to parents of Irish descent. After his father's death, the boy supported his mother as a stonecutter and later studied at the Pennsylvania Academy and the Ecole des Beaux-Arts in Paris. At the Columbian Exposition in 1891-92 and in Buffalo ten years later, he received recognition for three statuary groups: *The Savage Age, East and West,* and *Tired Out,* the last an intimate bronze of a mother and her two children.

John Barry was born in Ireland in 1745 but left his native land for America at the age of fourteen. Until 1776 he was employed in various capacities in the Philadelphia merchant marine, serving as captain at age twenty-one and eventually becoming an influential shipmaster and ship-owner. In 1774 he was the captain of *The Black Prince*, a ship owned by *John Nixon, who two years later was the first to read the Declaration of Independence in public.

Following the start of hostilities with Britain, Barry achieved fame as a naval commander for the aborning nation. In January 1776 he was placed in command of the *Lexington*, the first regular cruiser to put to sea under the authority of the Continental Congress. On April 17 the *Lexington* became the first vessel so commissioned to capture a British warship in actual battle. Barry's was also the first vessel flying the new striped American flag to capture an armed British ship. The Irishman's reputation was further enhanced when he refused a bribe from the British. During the war General Howe had offered Barry up to 20,000 guineas and command of the best British frigate if he abandoned the American cause. Barry replied that he had devoted himself to the cause of his adopted land and that neither wealth nor the promise of command over the whole British fleet would tempt him from continuing to serve her.

In the last year of the war, Barry was appointed commander of the frigate *Alliance*. During a subsequent engagement with two British vessels, he was wounded in the shoulder and was forced below to tend to his injury. After his ship's colors had been shot away, one of his men asked him if he would surrender. "No," the captain replied. "If the ship can't be fought without me, I will be brought on deck." A reenergized crew and a favorable wind allowed the *Alliance* to pound the enemy with a broadside, soon forcing the two British vessels to surrender. In 1794 President Washington named Barry the senior captain of the United States Navy, an appointment which led to Barry's honorific as "Father of the American Navy." That same year he was placed in charge of the *United States*, one of the six frigates recently authorized by Congress, being "of all the naval captains that remained . . . the one who possessed the greatest reputation for experience, conduct, and skill."

In his speech at the dedication of the Barry statue, *President Woodrow Wilson made some pointed remarks, probably to those Americans of Irish descent whose anti-British stance was contrary to his foreign policy. "John Barry was an Irishman," said the president, "but his heart crossed the Atlantic with him. He did not leave it in Ireland. And the test of us all . . . is whether we will assist in enabling America to live her separate and independent life, retaining our ancient affections, but determining everything that we do by the interests that exist on this side of the sea. Some Americans need hyphens in their names, because only part of them have come over. But when the whole man has come over, heart and thought and all, the hyphen drops of its own weight out of his name. This man was not an Irish-American; he was an Irishman who became an American." (See Independence Hall, Philadelphia.)

¶ The John F. Kennedy Center for the Performing Arts, Rock Creek Parkway, at the end of New Hampshire Avenue, N.W.

This sprawling arts center is the only official memorial in honor of President John F. Kennedy in the nation's capital. The complex includes the Grand Foyer the Eisenhower Theater, the Opera House, the Concert Hall, the Terrace Theater, the Theater Lab, the American Film Institute Theater, three restaurants, and a library. A seven-foot-high bronze bust of Kennedy is located in the Grand Foyer, while the center's river façade is carved with many of the slain president's quotations.

§ Free tours daily 10-1 except January 1 and December 25. Phone: 202-416-8341.

¶ John F. Kennedy Houses, Georgetown.

During his fourteen years in the U.S. Congress, John F. Kennedy lived in four rented Georgetown houses, all now privately owned. (Two of those addresses are 1528 31st Street, N.W., and 1400 43rd Street, N.W.) The first house in which he and his new bride, *Jacqueline Bouvier, lived was a two-story, white brick house at 3271 P Street, N.W. The couple's last residence before the White House was an eighteenth-century red brick townhouse at 3307 N Street, N.W. A plaque on the side wall of the townhouse was a gift from the members of the Washington press corps in gratitude for the hospitality shown them by the Kennedy family.

¶ John Rawlins Statue, Rawlins Park, 18th and E streets, N.W.

This bronze statue commemorates General John Rawlins, an officer of Scotch-Irish descent who served as aide-de-camp to *General Ulysses S. Grant during the Civil War.

The two men had met while living in Galena, Illinois, where Rawlins had helped organize the 45th Illinois Infantry soon after the fall of Fort Sumter. During the war he not only was an advisor to Grant but also helped moderate the general's fondness for drink. When the war was over, Rawlins sought the dry climate of the western plains in the hope that it would alleviate his tubercular condition. He accordingly accompanied the chief engineer of the Union Pacific Railroad to Salt Lake City, over the eastern route of the proposed transcontinental railroad. Rawlins' name was later given to a town in Wyoming which had grown up at one of their camp sites.

¶ Library of Congress, off Independence Avenue, across from the Capitol.

The bronze statues of Plato and Sir Francis Bacon in the library are the work of *John Boyle. (See John Barry Statue, District of Columbia.)

§ Jefferson Building open Monday-Saturday 10-5:30; Madison Building open 8:30 a.m.-9:30 p.m., Saturday 8:30-6. Phone: 202-707-8000.

¶ Mathew Brady Photo Studio, 627 Pennsylvania Avenue, N.W. Private.

Beginning in 1859, the upper floors of this four-story structure housed the studios of the famous photographer Mathew Brady, a native of upstate New York who described himself as the son of an Irishman. Some of the 3,500 photographs which he and his assistants took during the Civil War are now in the National Archives.

Brady opened his first studio in New York City in 1842, while he was only nineteen. For four consecutive years he won a silver medal for his daguerreotype entries at the annual American Institute exhibit, and in 1849 he was awarded the first gold medal ever presented for that genre. He subsequently earned recognition at the New York and London world fairs. About 1855, however, he abandoned the daguerreotype for the wet-plate process known as photography.

At the commencement of the Civil War, Brady persuaded President Lincoln and the head of the Secret Service to let him and his assistants accompany Union troops into battle. Invariably seen wearing a linen duster and a broad-brimmed flat hat, Brady frequently risked his life to remain close to his "What-is-it" Wagon, which he used as a dark room. In the general panic at the first battle of Bull Run, the wagon was overturned, although Brady was able to retrieve some of his wet plates. A writer for *Humphrey's Journal* acknowledged Brady's ability to capture and convey the horrors of the battlefield: "His are the only reliable records at Bull's Run. . . . His pictures, though perhaps not as lasting as the battle pieces on the pyramids, will nonetheless immortalize those introduced in them. Brady has shown more pluck than many of the officers and soldiers who were in the fight. He went – not exactly like the [Irish] 'Sixty-Ninth,' stripped to the pants – but with his sleeves tucked up and his big camera directed upon every point of interest on the field. . . . [I]t is certain that [those who took flight] did not get away from Brady as easily as they did from the enemy. He has fixed the cowards beyond the possibility of a doubt." Impoverished by the panic of 1873, Brady found temporary financial relief when the U.S. Government purchased 2,000 of his photographs for $25,000. He continued as a photographer in Washington until he was struck by a vehicle and died the next year.

Some of Brady's photographic assistants were fellow Irish Americans. One of them, T. C. Roche, went on to develop bromide photographic papers, while another, Stephen Horgan, invented a procedure that allowed photographs to be printed on paper from copper and zinc plates. Some of the other men – D. F. Barry, Alexander Gardner, T. J. Hines, V. T. McGillycuddy, John Moran, and Timothy O'Sullivan – served as photographic chroniclers of America's westward expansion by participating in various military and scientific expeditions.

¶ **National Archives,** Constitution Avenue, between 7th and 8th streets, N.W.

Exhibition Hall in the archives building displays the three founding documents of the American Republic: the Declaration of Independence, the Constitution, and the Bill of Rights.

Of the fifty-five delegates to the Constitutional Convention in 1787, eight who signed the Constitution were of Irish birth or descent. Their respective positions or proposals at the convention are summarized below:

• Pierce Butler of South Carolina was a champion of a strong central government, although he defended the rights of the South with regard to slavery and was the author of the fugitive slave clause in the Constitution. He opposed taking too many powers from the states, granting the National Legislature the power to veto state laws, and granting citizenship to foreigners without a long residence in the country. He also favored vesting the power to make war in the Executive, preferred the election of the Executive by electors chosen by the state legislatures, and insisted that black slaves should be included equally with whites in determining a state's representation "in a Government which was instituted principally for the protection of property."

• Daniel Carroll of Maryland seconded a motion that the presidential electors be chosen by lot from the National Legislature but later moved that the president be elected "by the people." He also argued that the senators should not be paid by their states because the Senate was "to represent and manage the affairs of the whole" nation.

• Thomas FitzSimons of Pennsylvania was an advocate of a strong national government and opposed giving the National Legislature the power to tax exports but favored granting such a power "when a proper time may call for it."

• James McHenry of Maryland proposed that the National Legislature be forbidden from passing bills of attainder and ex post facto laws

• William Paterson of New Jersey proposed a national government giving equal representation for each state and a federal judiciary consisting of a supreme court appointed by the Executive. He also insisted that black slaves should not be represented in the general government since slaves were not represented in the states in which they resided.

• George Read I of Delaware proposed that the existing state boundaries be abolished and redrawn into thirteen regions of approximately the same population and geographical area. He argued in favor of a national government which would eventually subsume the individual states and reduce them "to the mere office of electing the National Senate." He also expressed his hope that "the objects of the Genl. Govt. would be much more numerous than seemed to be expected by some gentlemen, and that [those objects] would become more & more so."

• John Rutledge of South Carolina opposed using population as the basis of a state's representation in the House but instead believed that such representation be proportionate to the taxes paid by the inhabitants of each state. He also expressed his opinion that the National Legislature would not sit more than six or eight weeks per year and favored a single Executive elected by the Senate, although he opposed giving him "the power of war and peace." He moreover proposed the "supremacy clause" – the constitutional provision that acts of Congress and treaties made under its authority "be the supreme law of the respective States."

• Richard Dobbs Spaight of North Carolina proposed that the House of Representatives be chosen by the state legislatures and that the tenure of the National Executive and members of the House be seven years.

§ Open April-Labor Day, daily 10-9; rest of the year, daily 10-5:30. Closed December 25. Phone: 202-501-5000.

¶ **National Gallery of Art,** Constitution Avenue, between 3rd and 7th streets, N.W.

The gallery was created by Congress in response to the donation by *Andrew Mellon of his personal art collection. When the museum opened in 1941, its holdings consisted of 126 paintings and twenty-six pieces of sculpture from the Mellon Collection, valued at $35 million. Following the Russian Revolution, Mellon purchased twenty-one masterpieces from the Hermitage collection of Catherine the Great for $10 million. He later paid $1.166 million for Raphael's *Alba Madonna*, reputedly the highest price ever paid for a piece of art prior to that time.

In addition to the gift of his art collection, Mellon provided the nation with securities sufficient to construct a $15 million building and to establish a $15 million endowment for the gallery. Since its creation, the museum has acquired several other private collections, including the 375 paintings and 18 sculptures of the Kress Collection. (See Andrew Mellon Memorial Fountain, District of Columbia.)

§ Open Monday-Saturday 10-5, Sunday 11-6. Closed January 1 and December 25. Phone: 202-737-4215.

¶ **National Portrait Gallery,** F and 8th streets, N.W.

The Hall of Presidents – at the west end of the second floor – contains portraits of all the U.S. presidents, including the eighteen with Irish or Scotch-Irish strains in their ancestry: Andrew Jackson, James K. Polk, James Buchanan, Andrew Johnson, Ulysses S. Grant, Chester A. Arthur, Grover Cleveland, Benjamin Harrison, William McKinley, Theodore Roosevelt, Woodrow Wilson, John F. Kennedy, Lyndon Johnson, Richard Nixon,

Jimmy Carter, Ronald Reagan, George Bush, and Bill Clinton. The portraits of James Buchanan, Abraham Lincoln, Franklin Pierce, and John Tyler were done by *George Healy, the nation's most prolific portrait painter.

The Gallery also contains Healy's paintings of Orestes Brownson, Henry Clay, *William Corcoran, John Crittenden, Abraham Lincoln, *Cardinal John McCloskey, Albert Myer, George Peabody, William T. Sherman, and Daniel Webster, as well as a self-portrait.

The Meserve Gallery (#212) displays modern prints of famous nineteenth-century Americans made from the original negatives of *Mathew Brady. The Meserve collection contains more than 5,000 glass-plate negatives, most of them made by Brady. Probably the most unusual is the "cracked plate" photograph of Abraham Lincoln – the result of a negative which broke during printing.

§ Open daily 10-5:30. Closed December 25. Phone: 202-357-2700.

¶ National Presbyterian Church, 4101 Nebraska Avenue, N.W.

One of the windows in the Chapel of the Presidents depicts the Reverend Francis Makemie, the Irish-born founder of Presbyterianism in America. (See Westover, Maryland.)

¶ Navy Museum, in Building 76 at the Washington Navy Yard, 9th and M streets, S.E.

The museum surveys the history of the U.S. Navy from Revolutionary times. Among the exhibits are a gun deck section and a foremast fighting top from the U.S.S. *Constitution*; a statue of *Commodore John Barry, the "Father of the American Navy"; and the destroyer U.S.S. *John Barry* (commissioned in 1956 and decommissioned in 1982).

§ Open Memorial Day-Labor Day, Monday-Friday 9-4, Saturday, Sunday, and holidays 10-5; rest of the year, Monday-Friday 9-5, Saturday, Sunday, and holidays 10-5. Closed January 1, Thanksgiving, and December 24-25. Phone: 202-433-6897. The U.S.S. *Barry* is open March-October, daily 10-5; rest of the year, daily 10-4. Closed Thanksgiving and December 25. Phone: 202-433-3377.

¶ New York Avenue Presbyterian Church, 1313 New York Avenue, N.W.

This church was founded in 1803 by a group of Scotch-Irish dissenters. A window in the sanctuary depicts *Francis Makemie, *William Tennent, the Neshaminy Log College, and Princeton College – all associated with the history of Presbyterianism in America.

§ Office open Tuesday-Friday 9-5, Sunday 9-1. Guided tours available after the Sunday worship service. Phone: 202-393-3700.

¶ Nuns of the Battlefield Memorial, on a triangular plot between M

Street and Rhode Island Avenue, N.W.

This memorial was dedicated in 1924 by the Ancient Order of Hibernians in honor of the Catholic nuns – many of them Irish – who served as military nurses during the Civil War. The central bronze panel relief depicts nuns in various types of religious garb, while an inscription above describes their heroic work: "They comforted the dying, nursed the wounded, carried hope to the imprisoned, gave in His name a drink to the thirsty." The dedicatory inscription below reads: "To the memory and in honor of the various orders of sisters who gave their services as nurses on battlefields and in hospitals during the Civil War." The memorial was designed by *Jerome Connor. (See Corcoran Gallery of Art, District of Columbia.)

When the *Nuns of the Battlefield Memorial* was dedicated, fewer than a score of Civil War nuns were still alive. Irish-born Sister Mary Madeleine O'Donnell of the Sisters of Mercy was the only Civil War nun to make the journey to the nation's capital to witness the unveiling. She represented the twenty religious communities that had provided volunteers during the national conflict.

Prior to 1860, American nuns had established twenty-eight hospitals throughout the country. At the outbreak of hostilities, these nuns were the only organized group of women experienced in both nursing and hospital management. As a result, they were sought out by military officials as hospital volunteers. At least 20 percent of all military nurses were reli-

Nuns of the Battlefield Mermorial near St. Matthew's Cathedral.

gious sisters – nearly 600 volunteers from more than a dozen religious congregations. A large number of the volunteers from many of these religious orders were Irish born or of Irish descent.

One of the most famous of the Irish-born volunteers was Eliza Maria Gillespie, known in religious life as Mother Mary of St. Angela or simply Mother Angela. Although she was born in Pennsylvania, her mother was from County Donegal, Ireland, and had come to America around 1777. During an almost thirty-year tenure as superior of the Sisters of the Holy Cross in the United States, Mother Angela was a pioneer in Catholic education and medical nursing. Besides establishing several academies, providing teachers for parish schools, and editing a series of Catholic textbooks, she founded a number of hospitals. During the Civil War this "Angel of Mercy" supervised the work of her congregation in military hospitals at Cairo, Louisville, Memphis, Mound City, Paducah, and Washington, D.C.

Of more than eighty volunteer nurses from the Sisters of the Holy Cross, fifty-one were Irish born. One of them, Sister de Sales O'Neill of County Cork, left a telling portrait of Mother Angela in an account recalling the day after the battle of Fort Donelson in February 1863: "Mother Angela was assisting the chief surgeon on the lower floor. It was a deliberate and difficult operation and the life of the soldier depended largely upon the accuracy of the surgeon, whose head and that of Mother Angela, on opposite sides, were bent over the poor lad who had fought under the Stars and Bars. Suddenly from above heavy liquid drops fell upon the white coif of Mother Angela who, true to her Celtic strain, did not quiver. Another, and still another, drop after drop, came faster and faster. At last, the final stitch had been taken and the two heads, that of the surgeon, and of the Sister, rose simultaneously, and not til then did the doctor know that a stain of blood, trickling through the open chinks of the upper floor, had fallen steadily upon the devoted head of Mother Angela, who stood before the surgeon with head, and face, and shoulders, and back bathed in the blood of some unknown soldier."

Mary Livermore of the Sanitary Commission provided eloquent testimony about the work done by Mother Angela's nuns. Livermore found that the surgeons at the military hospital in Cairo were so impressed by the quality of Catholic nursing that they were prejudiced against nurses of any other faith. She went on to write that "The world has known no nobler and more heroic women than those found in the ranks of the Catholic Sisterhoods." Yet she sympathized with the sick soldiers who disliked the nuns' "great headgear" – which she described as "a cross between a white sunbonnet and a broken-down umbrella."

While Mother Angela personified the good works of the Sisters of the Holy Cross, the Sisters of Charity had their own "Florence Nightingale." Born in Limerick, Ireland, and educated at the Ursuline Academy in

Charlestown, Massachusetts, Sister Anthony (née Mary O'Connell) had entered the Sisters of Charity in 1835. Like other members of her community, she served as a nurse on Civil War battlefields or in hospital camps. She and her fellow nuns – thirty of the thirty-seven were Irish born – transported boat loads of wounded soldiers up the Ohio River and accompanied others on flat cars from Cumberland to the District of Columbia. About their work Sister Anthony wrote: "At Shiloh we ministered to the men on board what were properly known as floating hospitals. We were often obliged to more further up the river, being unable to bear the terrific stench from the bodies of the dead on the battlefield. This was bad enough, but what we endured on the field of battle while gathering up the wounded is beyond description. At one time there were 700 of the poor soldiers crowded in one boat." A glowing tribute to Sister Anthony is preserved in a soldier's diary: "Amid this sea of blood she performed the most revolting duties for those poor soldiers. She seemed like a ministering angel, and many a young soldier owes his life to her care and charity. Happy was the soldier who, wounded and bleeding, had her near him to whisper words of consolation and courage. She was reverenced by Blue and Gray, Protestant and Catholic, alike; and we conferred on her the title of the 'Florence Nightingale of America.' Her name became a household word in every section of the North and South."

¶ **Oak Hill Cemetery,** Georgetown, 30th and R streets, N.W.

This sloping cemetery was established in 1848 on land purchased by *William Corcoran, the founder of the Corcoran Gallery of Art in the District of Columbia. Besides Corcoran, *Peggy O'Neale Eaton and *James G. Blaine are buried here. Blaine's grave is surmounted by a Celtic cross.

Two memorable monuments in the cemetery are the work of *Alexander Doyle: the statue and pedestal over the grave of Bishop William Pinkney and the portrait bust and pedestal that mark the grave of John Howard Payne, the author of "Home, Sweet Home!"

Payne was originally buried in Tunis, where he had died in 1852 while serving as U.S. consul there. Thirty-one years later, however, his body was reinterred in Oak Hill Cemetery, thanks to Corcoran's efforts. In making the bust of Payne for his tomb, Doyle worked from a photograph taken by *Mathew Brady, which showed that the famous song composer had a beard. After the bust was completed, an official at the cemetery was erroneously informed that Payne had never had a beard, whereupon he ordered his stonemason to remove the beard.

¶ **Octagon House National Historic Landmark,** 1799 New York Avenue.

While the Executive Mansion was being rebuilt following its burning by the British in 1814, this Federal-style house (which is actually hexagonal in shape) served as the presidential residence.

Here *Dolley Madison lived with her "darling little husband," five-foot-four-inch President James Madison, and continued her tradition of beginning each year with an open house. One observer at the festivities of January 1, 1815, wrote that the First Lady wore "a robe of rose-colored satin, trimmed with ermine, with gold chains and clasps around her waist and arms, and a white satin turban upon her head, whence sprang a tiara of white ostrich plumes."

§ Open Tuesday-Sunday 10-4. Closed January 1, Thanksgiving, and December 25. Fee. Phone: 202-638-3221.

¶ O'Neill Building, 300 New Jersey Avenue, S.E.

This House office building bears the name of *Thomas "Tip" O'Neill, the Speaker of the House of Representatives from 1977 to 1987. (See O'Neill Building, Boston, Massachusetts.)

¶ Robert Emmet Statue, Massachusetts Avenue and 24th Street, N.W.

Designed by *Jerome Connor soon after the 1917 Easter Uprising in Dublin, this statue was located elsewhere in the city until it was erected here in 1966. The seven-foot-high bronze statue honors the famous Irish Protestant patriot who led an unsuccessful insurrection of United Irishmen in his native land in 1803. Emmet's body is turned toward the Irish Embassy two blocks away.

The pedestal displays the coat of arms of the United Irishmen and is inscribed with extracts from Emmet's final speech before his execution: "I wished to procure for my country the guarantee which Washington procured for America . . . . I have parted from everything that was dear to me in this life for my country's cause. . . . When my country takes her place among the nations of the earth, *then*, and not until then, let my epitaph be written . . . ."

Duplicates of this statue stand in Golden Gate Park in San Francisco, St. Stephen's Green in Dublin, and Emmetsburg, Iowa.

¶ Robert Kennedy Memorial, Department of Justice courtyard, 10th Street.

A portrait bust of Robert Kennedy, U.S. attorney general for his brother, President John F. Kennedy, stands atop a slender pedestal. The chipped left corner of the pedestal symbolizes a life cut short by his assassination in 1968.

¶ Ronald Reagan Building, 14th Street between Constitution and Pennsylvania avenues.

After the Pentagon, this three-million-square-foot government office building is the nation's largest, an incongruous tribute to Ronald Reagan, known for his speeches against the size and scope of the federal government.

¶ St. Matthew's Cathedral, 1725 Rhode Island Avenue, N.W.

Although this Renaissance church was erected in 1893, its congregation dates from 1840. The initial money to build this church came from the sale of property donated by *Father William Matthews, the first native-born American to be ordained a Catholic priest in the United States. The church is noted for its frescoes, mosaics, marble work, and faceted-art glass windows. An inscription in the floor recalls that the cathedral was the site of funeral services for President John F. Kennedy in November 1963.

§ Open daily 6:30-6:30. Phone: 202-347-3215.

¶ St. Patrick's Church, between 10th and F streets, N.W.

Completed in 1884, the present church is located near the site of an earlier St. Patrick's, the first Catholic church in the country to be named for the Irish saint. That earlier church had been built on land purchased in 1794 by Father Anthony Caffrey, a native of Ireland. The original congregation was formed three years later and at first worshipped in a nearby house. Caffrey remained pastor of St. Patrick's until 1804, when he deeded the property to *Bishop John Carroll before returning to Ireland.

¶ Settlers of the District of Columbia Memorial, the Ellipse, 15th Street, between E Street and Constitution Avenue.

This unpretentious shaft honors the eighteen landowners or "original patentees" from whose land grants much of the District of Columbia was created.

One of these patentees was Daniel Carroll of Duddington, a member of the prominent Irish family which could trace its roots in America to 1680. His original property had been part of a land grant made by the second Lord Baltimore in 1663 and included what is now Capitol Hill. The original grant had passed to Ann Rozier, the wife of Daniel Carroll of Annapolis, the grandfather of the Duddington Daniel.

By the time the new federal city was being planned, Daniel Carroll of Duddington was one of the last private owners of his family's vast estate on Capitol Hill. On March 30, 1791, he joined the other proprietors of the land on which the new city was to be built in signing the agreement that established the District of Columbia. In 1800 a chronicler recalled: "There appeared to be but two really comfortable habitations, in all respects, within the bounds of the city, one of which belonged to Daniel Carroll [of Duddington], Esquire, and the other to Notley Young, who were the former proprietors of a large proportion of the land appropriated to the city, but who reserved for their own accommodation ground sufficient for gardens and other useful appurtenances."

Like the other proprietors of land in the area of the new capital, Daniel Carroll had originally believed that their proximity to the seat of power would make them rich. In 1837 he described the ironic results: "After nearly half a century the result is now fully known: the unfortunate proprietors are generally brought to ruin and some with scarcely enough to buy daily food for their families."

¶ **Sheridan Circle,** Massachusetts Avenue and 23rd Street, N.W.

This circle is named for General Philip Sheridan, a Union cavalry officer during the Civil War and the son of emigrants from County Cavan, Ireland. He is depicted here astride his galloping horse, Rienzi, which carried him through eighty-five battles and skirmishes. According to some accounts, when Sheridan's widow and their three daughters lived in a house across from the circle, they called out to the statue each morning with the greeting "Hello, Papa!" The fourteen-foot-high statue was designed by Gutzon Borglum and was dedicated in 1908.

Sheridan is generally regarded as the third most important Civil War Union general (after *Ulysses S. Grant and William T. Sherman). Although he attended the U.S. Military Academy, he was suspended for a year for lunging at a cadet-officer with a bayoneted rifle. During the Civil War he practically saved the army of General William Rosecrans by holding off a Confederate advance. Later, while in command of the 20th Corps of the Army of the Cumberland, he contributed to *General Grant's victory at

Statue of General Philip Sheridan in Sheridan Circle.

Chattanooga. As a result, the Union commander placed him in charge of the 10,000-man cavalry corps of the Army of the Potomac.

Grant ranked Sheridan with Napoleon and Frederick the Great as history's greatest military commanders: "As a soldier, as a commander of troops, as a man capable of doing all that is possible with any number of men, there is no man living greater than Sheridan." Yet the latter's prowess stood in contrast to his diminutive stature. At the age of thirty-three "Little Phil" weighed only 130 pounds and stood less than 5' 6".

In the last year of the war, Sheridan carried out a series of raids that prepared the way for major Union victories. In an attempt to break the Confederate communications line around Richmond, his men destroyed ten miles of railroad track, cut off telegraph communication to the city, and captured many supply trains. After promotion to command of the Army of the Shenandoah, Sheridan laid waste to the Shenandoah Valley, which had long sustained successful guerrilla campaigns against Union lines. In the spring of 1865, he led one final raid, destroying Confederate supply depots and leaving General Robert E. Lee with only one railroad line of communication with the South. Sheridan's final strategic action during the war forced Lee's evacuation of Petersburg and his retreat to Appomattox.

¶ *Spirit of St. Louis*, National Air and Space Museum, 7th Street and Independence Avenue.

It was in this fragile-looking aircraft that *Charles Lindbergh made his epochal flight from New York to Paris on May 20, 1927. Built by the Ryan Aircraft Company in San Diego, California, the plane made its 3,500-mile flight in thirty-three and a half hours. (See Charles Lindbergh House, Little Falls, Minnesota.)

Twenty-seven hours after leaving Long Island, Lindbergh approached the coast of Ireland, although at the time he was uncertain of his exact position. After sighting at first a tiny boat and than a man's head thrust through one of its portholes, the pilot closed the throttle of the plane and glided to within fifty feet of the fishing vessel. "Which way is Ireland?" Lindbergh cried out. Disappointed that he heard no response, he banked his plane and pointed it in what he hoped was the direction of Europe.

Within an hour, however, he sighted a coastline which his charts identified as Valencia and Dingle Bay, off the southwestern tip of Ireland. To his amazement he had arrived at this point two and a half hours ahead of his calculated time. He later recorded his impression of the Emerald Isle: "I've never seen such beauty before – fields so green."

§ Open daily 10-5:30. Closed December 25. Phone: 202-357-2700.

¶ **Sullivan Brothers Memorial Trees,** Capitol Plaza.

In 1951 five flowering crab apple trees were planted on the Capitol

Plaza in honor of the five *Sullivan brothers, natives of Waterloo, Iowa, who were killed during the battle of Guadalcanal in 1942. The brothers perished after their ship, the U.S.S. *Juneau*, was sunk by Japanese fire in the Solomon Islands. (See Waterloo, Iowa, in *Irish America*, Volume 2.)

¶ **Supreme Court Building,** facing the Capitol, between Maryland Avenue and East Capitol Street, N.E.

Since its creation, the Supreme Court has had seventeen members of Irish ancestry:

• John Rutledge was appointed to the first U.S. Supreme Court in 1790 but resigned the next year because of the long distances associated with circuit riding. Although President Washington returned him to the court as a recess appointment in 1795, the Senate rejected the appointment. Despondent at this rebuff, Rutledge tried to drown himself by jumping into a river in Charleston but was rescued by two slaves.

• William Paterson (1793-1806) wrote the 1795 opinion which invalidated a Pennsylvania statute because it conflicted with the federal and state constitutional protection of property. This decision was the precedent used by Chief Justice John Marshall in the *Marbury v. Madison* case, which established the right of the U.S. Supreme Court to review the constitutionality of legislative acts.

• John McLean (1830-61) traced his Scotch-Irish ancestry to the twelfth century. In 1857 he dissented from the Supreme Court's Dred Scott decision, insisting instead that Congress had the authority to exclude slavery from the territories and to free slaves voluntarily brought into free states.

• Roger Taney (1836-64) was the first Roman Catholic to sit on the court. In the Dred Scott case he ruled that the U.S. Constitution did not recognize slaves as citizens and that the Missouri Compromise of 1820 was unconstitutional because it violated the right of slave owners to take their property in slaves into the territories. During the Civil War he defied Lincoln's suspension of habeas corpus in the border states, ruling that only Congress had the power to suspend this right.

• Descended from Scotch-Irish grandparents, Samuel Nelson (1845-72) sided with the Dred Scott decision, arguing that "the law of the State is supreme over the subject of slavery within its jurisdiction." In addition, in an 1863 dissent he wrote that Lincoln had no authority to blockade Southern ports during the time between the outbreak of hostilities and the declaration of war by Congress three months later.

• John Campbell (1853-61), also of Scotch-Irish descent, voted with the majority in the Dred Scott case, although he had freed his own slaves three years before. He believed that the Union should not be jeopardized by slavery, which he said was "a transitory institution and would necessarily be modified or abrogated in the process of time."

• Edward Douglass White (1894-1921) was descended from Irish

Catholic grandparents who had immigrated to America in the 1730s. While on the court, he generally opposed intrusions by the federal government on the power of the states to regulate their own economies.

• Joseph McKenna (1898-1925) was the son of an Irish-born immigrant who operated a small bakery in an Irish neighborhood of Philadelphia. He generally concurred in opinions that supported the growth of federal power, voting, for instance, to uphold the Mann Act (extending federal power over interstate prostitution).

• Charles Evans Hughes (1910-41), whose mother was descended from northern Irish ancestors, is famous for his claim in 1926 that "The Constitution is what the Supreme Court says it is." He usually voted with conservatives on the Supreme Court to strike down much New Deal legislation, although he later reversed his voting pattern.

• James Clark McReynolds (1914-41) was the son of a wealthy surgeon and plantation owner of Scotch-Irish ancestry. McReynolds consistently opposed New Deal legislation on constitutional grounds. In a 1935 case he accompanied his dissent with the comment that "The Constitution as many of us have understood it . . . is gone." (Between 1937 and 1941 he dissented 119 times, bringing to 310 the number of dissents which he delivered during his twenty-six-year term.) Upon retirement, he said that he had tried to protect the nation but that "any country that elects Roosevelt three times deserves no protection."

• Pierce Butler (1923-39) was one of eight children of Patrick and Mary (Gaffney) Butler, who had come to America from County Wicklow after the Irish potato famine. One of the "Four Horsemen," Butler dissented when the court upheld legislation which taxed employers and employees to create old age and unemployment pensions: "The Constitution grants to the United States no power to pay unemployed persons or to require the states to enact laws . . . for that purpose."

• Owen Roberts (1930-45), the son of a Scotch-Irish mother, wrote the majority opinion which struck down the Agricultural Adjustment Act on the grounds that the Constitution did not delegate to Congress authority to regulate agricultural production.

• James Byrnes (1941-42), the grandson of Irish Catholic immigrants, generally believed in "judicial restraint," although he wrote the majority opinion using the commerce clause to strike down a California law to prevent the transportation of indigents into the state.

• Frank Murphy (1940-49) was the grandson of immigrants who had left Ireland in the late 1840s. As an ardent defender of civil liberties, he criticized the internment of Japanese during World War II and used the 14th Amendment to protect racial minorities against discrimination.

• William Brennan (1956-90) was descended from Irish immigrant parents who had come to America just before the turn of the century. Of his more than 1,250 published opinions, 400 were dissents. He helped de-

velop the use of the Fourteenth Amendment to restrict state and municipal authority. He was with the majority when they ruled that voting dis-
tricts must be approximately equal in population so as to guarantee the
principle of "one man one vote."

• Anthony Kennedy's tenure on the court since 1988 has been marked
by conservative rulings in the areas of privacy, civil rights, and criminal
law enforcement. In a speech prior to his appointment to the court, he
remarked that "An essential purpose of the criminal justice system is to
provide a catharsis by which a community expresses its collective outrage
at the transgressions of the criminal."

• Sandra Day O'Connor, the first female member of the Supreme Court,
traces her Irish ancestry to County Tipperary. (Her maiden name is reportedly a corruption of the surname O'Dea.) Appointed to the court in
1981 by *President Ronald Reagan, she has been called by the American
Bar Association Journal "arguably the most influential woman official in
the United States." Press accounts of her role in court decisions usually
describe hers as the "swing vote."

§ Open Monday-Friday 9-4:30. Closed holidays. Phone: 202-479-3000.

¶ **Theodore Roosevelt Memorial,** Roosevelt Island, Potomac River.

Located on an eighty-eight-acre wilderness island in the Potomac, this
memorial to *Theodore Roosevelt includes a seventeen-foot-high bronze
statue of the president and four huge granite slabs bearing comments he
made on nature, youth, manhood, and the state. One of the slabs records
Roosevelt's remark that "The nation behaves well if it treats the Natural
Resources as assets which it must turn over to the next generation increased
and not impaired in value." The site's location amid woodland trails and
a wide variety of trees and wildflowers highlights Roosevelt's successful
conservation efforts. (See Theodore Roosevelt Birthplace, New York City.)

§ Accessible by pedestrian bridge from the northbound lane of the
George Washington Memorial Parkway. Open daily 7-dusk. Phone: 203-
285-2598.

¶ **Trinity College,** 125 Michigan Avenue, N.E.

Located near Catholic University, Trinity College is the crowning
achievement of Sister Julia McGroarty, who conceived the idea of the
nation's first Catholic college for women and determinedly saw it through
to completion in 1900.

A native of County Donegal, Ireland, Susan McGroarty had immigrated with her parents and nine siblings to Cincinnati, Ohio. Although at
age eleven she was still unable to read, the nuns of Notre Dame de Namur
in Cincinnati provided her with sufficient education to enter that teaching
order, taking the religious name "Julia." During the next thirty-four years,
she was primarily engaged in teaching at Notre Dame schools in Massa-

chusetts and Philadelphia. Her free school for African Americans in the latter city attracted the attention and support of Katherine Drexel, the famous heiress-turned-nun who made the education of African Americans her life's work. Later, as superior of her order, Sister Julia founded fourteen convents and took steps to improve the educational standards and curriculum at the order's thirteen academies. In the last years of her life, she received the support of *Cardinal James Gibbons and the rector of Catholic University of America in the creation of Trinity College.

¶ **Tudor Place,** in Georgetown at 1644 31st Street, N.W.

This neoclassical mansion was built in 1805 for *Martha Custis Peter, the granddaughter of Martha Washington. Now a shrine to George and Martha Washington, the house contains many relics from the first president's home at Mount Vernon. Through her grandfather Daniel Parke Custis, Martha Custis Peter was descended from John Custis of Baltimore, County Cork, Ireland. (See Arlington House, Arlington, Virginia, in *Irish America*, Volume 2.)

§ Guided tours Tuesday-Friday 10, 11:30, 1 and 2:30; Saturday on the hour 10-3. Garden open Monday-Saturday 10-4 (and Sunday 12:30-4, April-May, September-October). Closed major holidays. Fee. Phone: 202-965-0400, ext. 102.

¶ **Ulysses S. Grant Memorial,** on the Mall, at 1st Street, S.W.

A seventeen-foot-high bronze equestrian figure of *General Ulysses S. Grant, believed to be the largest such statue in the world, sits atop a central pedestal surrounded by four lions, eleven horses, and eleven Union soldiers. The memorial, which took twenty-two years to complete, was dedicated in 1922, on the centenary of Grant's birth.

¶ **U.S. Capitol Building,** at the east end of the Mall.

From the beginning, Irishmen played a role in both the design and the construction of the Capitol. Although the Frenchman Pierre L'Enfant had been expected to design the Capitol as well as the President's House, when no plans were forthcoming the commissioners resorted to sponsoring a competition. One of the unsuccessful entrants was James Diamond, an Irishman whose design for the Capitol incorporated arcades, loggia, and a dome like that atop the cathedral in Florence, Italy. (Diamond was ridiculed for the outlandish rooster that adorned the dome.) Once construction got under way, several Irishmen were involved in the actual building of the Capitol. In April 1795 the commissioners contracted with *John Delahunty and the two brothers *Cornelius and Patrick McDermot Roe to do the brick and stone work on the Capitol. Five years later the Irish Catholic John Kearney was granted the commission "for the completion of the plastering and Stucco Work at the Capitol."

Two of the heroic-size paintings in the Rotunda include patriots of Irish descent in famous episodes of the Revolution: *The Signing of the Declaration of Independence* (Thomas Lynch Jr., Charles Carroll, Charles Thomson, George Read I, Edward Rutledge); and *The Surrender of Lord Cornwallis at Yorktown* (Charles O'Hara, James Clinton, Anthony Wayne, Edward Hand, and Henry Knox).

During the 1860s additional ornamentation on the Capitol was designed by Thomas Crawford, a sculptor of Scotch-Irish descent. For the House and Senate wings, he designed two bronze doors with panels illustrating scenes from the Revolutionary War and the military career of George Washington. He also designed *The Progress of Civilization* on the front pediment of the Senate, a bas-relief of a female "America" flanked by a panorama of figures representing the Indian, the pioneer, the hunter, the soldier, the merchant, the mechanic, the student, and the teacher. Crawford also designed the nineteen-foot-high female figure *Freedom* on top of the Capitol dome. He had originally intended to call this bronze figure "Armed Liberty" and place on its head a liberty cap like the type worn by freed Roman slaves. However, when Secretary of War *Jefferson Davis, a Southerner, objected to the statue's allusion to freed slaves, the artist replaced the cap with a helmet adorned with feathers and an eagle head. Crawford's plaster cast of the statue, which he modeled in Rome, was almost lost in a storm during the transatlantic voyage in 1858. After finally being cast in bronze, *Freedom* was hoisted into place in 1863.

In 1864 Congress invited each state to send the statues of two of its most notable citizens to what is now known as the National Statuary Hall Collection, housed in Statuary Hall and elsewhere throughout the Capitol. Of the ninety-one statues in the collection, twenty-three depict persons of Irish descent:

• Francis Blair Jr. (Missouri), Unionist and member of Congress who was influential in preventing Missouri from seceding;

• William Edgar Borah (Idaho), U.S. senator;

• William Jennings Bryan (Nebraska), secretary of state under Woodrow Wilson and three-time presidential candidate;

• John Burke (North Dakota), ninth governor of North Dakota;

• John C. Calhoun (South Carolina), U.S. representative and senator and secretary of war under presidents Monroe and Tyler;

• Charles Carroll of Carrollton (Maryland), member of the Continental Congress, the Maryland Senate, and the U.S. Senate, and last surviving signer of the Declaration of Independence;

• George Clinton (New York), first governor of New York, and vice president under Jefferson and Madison;

• Jefferson Davis (Mississippi), U. S. senator, secretary of war, and president of the Confederacy;

• Robert Fulton (Pennsylvania), developer of the first commercially viable steamboat;

• Wade Hampton (South Carolina), Civil War military leader;

• Sam Houston (Texas), leader in the Texas Revolution against Mexico, first president of the Texas Republic, U.S. senator, and governor of Texas;

• Andrew Jackson (Tennessee), U.S. representative and senator, state supreme court justice, victor at the battle of New Orleans, and president of the United States;

• Philip Kearny (New Jersey), Mexican War officer and Civil War commander who earned the nickname "Perfect Soldier";

• John Kenna (West Virginia), U.S. representative and senator who worked to improve navigation along the Kanawha River in his state so as to tap the area's resources;

• Samuel Jordan Kirkwood (Iowa), U.S. senator, secretary of the interior, and Civil War governor of Iowa;

• Crawford Long (Georgia), pioneer in the use of anesthesia;

• Patrick McCarran (Nevada), state supreme court justice, U.S. senator, and chief sponsor of the Civil Aeronautics Act, the Internal Security Act of 1950, and the McCarran-Walter Immigration Act;

• Ephraim McDowell (Kentucky), pioneer physician who performed the first successful ovariotomy in 1809;

• John McLoughlin (Oregon), medical doctor who became the "ruler"

*Statue of John McLoughlin
in Statuary Hall.*

of the Hudson Bay Company's vast territories west of the Rockies and who welcomed the first colonists to the Oregon Territory;

• Will Rogers (Oklahoma), famous humorist who called himself an Irish-American-Indian;

• James Shields (Illinois), officer in the Mexican War and the Civil War and the only American to represent three states in the U.S. Senate;

• George Laird Shoup (Idaho), ninth governor of Idaho;

• Edward Douglass White (Louisiana), chief justice of the U.S. Supreme Court. (See entry under Supreme Court Building.)

The statues of U.S. senators Thomas Hart Benton, *Francis Blair, and *John Kenna are the work of *Alexander Doyle, while the marble statue of the Civil War general Lew Wallace was sculpted by *Andrew O'Connor.

Born in Worcester, Massachusetts, in 1874, Andrew O'Connor learned the art of sculpture from his father, a cemetery stonecutter. During his formative years he worked successively under the tutelage of William Ordway Partridge in Chicago, Daniel Chester French in New York, and John Singer Sargent in London. Among O'Connor's most notable works are monuments to General Thomas Thomas (Purchase, N.Y.), *Theodore Roosevelt (Glen View, Ill.), and General John Johnson (St. Paul, Minn.) and statues of General Henry Lawton (Indianapolis, Ind.), Abraham Lincoln (Springfield, Ill., and Providence, R.I.), and Lafayette (Baltimore, Md.). He also produced the statue of Lincoln at the Royal Exchange in London and that of *Daniel O'Connell in Dublin.

§ Capitol open March-August, daily 9:30-8; rest of the year, daily 9-4:30. Closed January 1, Thanksgiving, and December 25. Phone: 202-225-6827.

¶ **Washington National Cathedral,** Mount St. Alban, Massachusetts and Wisconsin avenues, N.W.

• The Lee-Jackson Memorial Windows, a gift of the United Daughters of the Confederacy, commemorate episodes in the lives of *Thomas "Stonewall" Jackson and Robert E. Lee.

• Among the famous Americans buried here are *Woodrow Wilson, Helen Keller (perhaps of Irish descent), and *Annie Sullivan, Keller's teacher and almost constant companion. President Wilson's sarcophagus is decorated with a Crusader's cross, which his widow believed best symbolized his personality and political career. Wilson is the only American president interred in the capital.

§ Open first Monday in May through Labor Day, Monday-Friday 10-9; rest of the year, daily 10-4:30. Tours available Monday-Saturday 10-3:15, Sunday 12:30-2:45. Phone: 202-537-6207.

¶ **White House,** 1600 Pennsylvania Avenue.

The winner of the contest to design the President's House was the

Irishman James Hoban, who, when it came time to collect his "premium," chose the promised $500 medal rather than the cash of equal value. He was also paid 300 guineas to supervise construction of the building.

A native of County Kilkenny, James Hoban had attended the Royal Dublin Society's drawing school as a pupil of the architect Thomas Ivory. There, it seems, Hoban adopted his mentor's preference for the Palladian neoclassical style and most likely worked on the construction of various buildings in Dublin. After coming to the United States in 1785, Hoban worked first as an architect in Philadelphia and then as a "house carpenter" in Charleston, South Carolina. It is possible that he designed Charleston's old statehouse at Broad and Meeting streets as well as other buildings in the city that reflect a distinctly Irish Georgian style. He is known to have designed South Carolina's new capitol building in Columbia. (That structure was destroyed by fire in 1865.)

Although the President's House shows some internal modifications, it seems to have been modeled after Leinster House, a Palladian structure built on the outskirts of Dublin in 1745. Both houses contain eleven bays, a façade of three sections, four engaged columns, and windows with triangular and segmental pediments. Although the American house is only two stories in height, Hoban's original plan had envisioned three stories (including the ground-level basement), as is the case with Leinster House. Today Leinster House is the seat of the Irish Dáil or Parliament.

When the cornerstone of the President's House was laid in 1792, James Hoban assisted in his capacity as master of the Federal Masonic Lodge. During the ceremony a polished brass plate with the following inscription was placed beneath the cornerstone: "The first stone of the President's House was laid the 13th day of October 1792, and in the seventeenth year of the independence of the United States of America. George Washington, President. Thomas Johnson, Doctor Stewart, Daniel Carroll, Commissioners. James Hoban, Architect. Collen Williamson, Master Mason."

The distinction of being the first First Lady of Irish background to inhabit the new executive mansion belonged to *Dolley Payne Todd Madison. When the President's Mansion was torched by the British during the War of 1812, Mrs. Madison was led to safety by *Charles Carroll, who brought her to Bellevue (now Dumbarton House), one of the first houses on the heights above the river in Georgetown. The fugitive First Lady recorded that night's events: "Our kind friend, Mr. Carroll has come to hasten my departure, and is in a very bad humor with me because I insist on waiting until the large picture of General Washington is secured, and it requires to be unscrewed from the wall. This process was found too tedious for these perilous moments; I have ordered the frame to be broken, and the canvass taken out. . . ."

After the war the task of rebuilding the soon-to-be-renamed "White House" was entrusted to *James Hoban. By 1815 Hoban was regarded as the foremost builder in the District of Columbia, having constructed the original Executive Mansion, of course, as well as the Great Hotel and the Little Hotel. To the position of foreman of the Irish laborers on the job of rebuilding the executive mansion, he assigned an old friend, Nicholas Callan, an Irishman who had worked on the original structure. Hoban supervised the project until it was completed in 1829. During this postwar period he also designed and rebuilt the offices occupied by the State and War departments, additional casualties of the British invasion.

Besides enjoying a reputation as a highly respected builder, Hoban was also viewed as a civic leader. Following the District's incorporation in 1802, Hoban was elected to the city council and served as a councilman until his death. In addition, he was instrumental in establishing St. Patrick's Catholic Church, he was a founding member of the Federal Masonic Lodge, and he was the captain of the local volunteer militia. He and his wife and their ten children and nine slaves lived in a large brick row house near the President's Park (now the White House lawn). At his death in 1831, Hoban left an estate worth $60,000, much of it in the form of real estate. He was buried in the graveyard of St. Peter's Catholic Church in Washington, D.C., but in 1863 his body was reinterred in Mount Olivet Cemetery (opposite the National Arboretum).

His reputation seems not to have suffered from an episode involving *Betsy Donahue, who rented a residence owned by Hoban in the President's Park. Although the authorities usually overlooked the gambling and drinking indulged in by the workers constructing the executive mansion, those officials objected when Donahue opened a "riotous and disorderly house" in her rented building and began pulling men in off the street. Despite Hoban's testimony on her behalf, the woman was fined and the house was moved from the park.

In 1857 Congress commissioned *George Healy to paint a series of presidential portraits, each for $1,000. In all, he painted the portraits of thirteen U.S. presidents: John Adams, John Quincy Adams, *Chester A. Arthur, *James Buchanan, Millard Fillmore, *Ulysses S. Grant, Rutherford B. Hayes, Abraham Lincoln, James Madison, Franklin Pierce, *James K. Polk, John Tyler, and Martin Van Buren. Except for the portraits of Arthur, Buchanan, and Grant, the paintings are currently in the White House, as is his canvas entitled *The Peacemakers*. This large historical piece depicts a strategy meeting of President Lincoln with *General Ulysses S. Grant, General William T. Sherman, and Admiral David Porter aboard the *River Queen* at City Point, Virginia.

George Healy was born in Boston in 1813, the son of a Merchant Marine captain of Irish descent. Encouraged to develop his artistic talent by the popular Boston painter Thomas Sully, the eighteen-year-old Healy opened his own studio in the Massachusetts capital and was soon exhibiting his own works. His studio was so financially successful that he was able to spend a year studying and painting in Paris. After opening a studio in the City of Lights, he saw his reputation soar as he secured the patronage of King Louis-Philippe and other famous French political leaders. In 1855 he was recognized at the Universal Exhibition for his memorable historical canvas *Franklin Urging the Claims of the American Colonies before Louis XVI*. That same year he returned to America and established a studio in Chicago, where – regrettably – the painting of Franklin was destroyed in the Great Fire of 1871.

While in the United States, George Healy completed commissions given him by King Louis-Philippe to paint the portraits of famous American statesmen. Among those he captured on canvas for his royal patron were John Quincy Adams, Henry Clay, *Andrew Jackson, John Tyler, and Daniel Webster. He also made a copy of one of Gilbert Stuart's many portraits of George Washington. While Healy was working on the portrait of President-elect Lincoln (still *sans barbe*), the politician erupted in laughter as he read a letter from a young girl. Lincoln then remarked to Healy: "She complains of my ugliness. . . . She wishes me to put on false whiskers to hide my horrible lantern jaws. Will you paint me with false whiskers? No?" As all the world knows, Lincoln grew a beard before arriving at the White House. Healy's portrait of him was the last in which the president was clean-shaven.

Healy painted more than 700 portraits, more than the number painted by any other American artist. Among the Americans whose portraits he rendered were John James Audubon, Pierre Beauregard, *James G. Blaine, Orestes Brownson, Lewis Cass, Salmon P. Chase, Henry Clay, *William Corcoran, John Crittenden, Ralph Waldo Emerson, Nathaniel Hawthorne, Robert E. Lee, Abraham Lincoln, Henry Wadsworth Longfellow, *Cardinal John McCloskey, George McClellan, Albert J. Myer, George Peabody, David Porter, William H. Seward, William T. Sherman, Joseph Story, and Daniel Webster. Healy's most famous extant historical composition is the painting *Webster Replying to Hayne*, now in Faneuil Hall, Boston.

Approximately ten years after coming to Chicago, Healy retraced his steps to Europe and assumed a highly profitable peripatetic career. During that time he painted Pope Pius IX and Franz Liszt in Rome, King Charles I in Rumania, Louisa May Alcott in Switzerland, and Charles Goodyear in Paris. He also executed portraits of Swedish singer Jenny Lind, several members of the English nobility, and the European statesmen Otto von Bismark, François Guizot, and Louis Adolphe Thiers. While in Italy, he became the first American ever requested to contribute a self-portrait to the Uffizi Gallery in Florence.

Other works by Healy can be found in the Corcoran Art Gallery, the National Gallery of Art, the National Portrait Gallery, the Smithsonian Institution, the U.S. Capitol, the Metropolitan Museum of Art, the New York Historical Society, the Newberry Library, and the Virginia Museum of Fine Arts.

§ Self-guiding tours of the White House Tuesday-Saturday 10-noon. Tickets are required year round and can be obtained from the White House Visitor Center at E and 15th streets on tour days. Phone: 202-456-7041.

J Wilson House National Historic Landmark, 2340 S Street, N.W.

With the money he received from winning the Nobel Peace Prize, *President Woodrow Wilson purchased this house in 1921 for his second wife. Wilson never recovered from the stroke he suffered in the last year of his presidency and lived as an invalid in this twenty-three-room mansion until his death in 1924. (See Staunton, Virginia, in *Irish America*, Volume 2.)

The house contains original furnishings and Wilson memorabilia, carefully assembled and saved by his widow until her own death in 1961. One of the items on display is a miniature reproduction of the *Robert Emmet statue located near the house.

§ Open Tuesday-Sunday 10-4. Closed major holidays. Fee. Phone: 202-387-4062.

√ The home in which Woodrow Wilson's paternal grandfather lived until he left for America is still located in the village of Dergalt, near Strabane, Northern Ireland. The whitewashed thatched cottage contains some of the original furniture.

J Winfield Scott Statue, U.S. Soldiers' Home, 2nd and Upshur streets, N.W.

This bronze statue of General Winfield Scott, a hero of the War of 1812 and the Mexican War, is the work of *Launt Thompson. The ten-foot-high statue depicts "Old Fuss and Feathers" impeccably attired in his dress uniform, holding his right hand in the breast of his coat and leaning on his sword hilt with his left. (See Clinton, Connecticut.)

J Woodrow Wilson International Center for Scholars, 1000 Jefferson Drive, S.W.

Created in 1968 by Congress as the country's official memorial to the twenty-eighth president, the center seeks to commemorate Wilson's scholarship and concern for public affairs through its program of advanced research and the communication it fosters between the world of learning and the world of public affairs. In doing so, the center tries to achieve the symbiosis described by Wilson himself: "The man who has the time, the discrimination, and the sagacity to collect and comprehend the principal facts, and the man who must act upon them, must draw near to one another and feel that they are engaged in a common enterprise."

ILLINOIS

CAIRO

¶ **Magnolia Manor,** 2700 Washington Avenue.

This brick Italianate house was built in 1869 for Charles Galigher, a local milling merchant, at a cost of $75,000. In 1880 the house was the scene of a reception for *President Ulysses S. Grant and his wife after their return from a world tour.

The son of a merchant hatter of Scotch-Irish descent, Galigher – while still a teenager – began a ten-year career as the master of a steamboat in which he was part owner. He suffered a major reversal, however, after the failure of a milling venture into which he had invested his accumulated fortune of $20,000. Attempting to make a fresh start, he moved to Cairo, Illinois, and became part owner of a small flour mill, an enterprise which was immediately successful. In 1866 Galigher purchased his partners' share of the business, which within a few years was producing 50,000 barrels of flour annually. Before his mills were destroyed by fire in 1889, he had amassed a fortune of almost $500,000.

§ Guided tours Wednesday-Saturday 9-5, Sunday 1-5. Closed January 1 and December 24-25. Fee. Phone: 618-734-0201.

CARBONDALE

¶ **John Logan Statue,** Michigan Avenue and 9th Street.

This equestrian statue of John Logan, the famous Civil War general and U.S. senator, is the work of *Augustus Saint-Gaudens.

Logan, whose Scottish father emigrated from northern Ireland, commanded the 31st Illinois Volunteers during the conflict between the North and the South. After the war he orchestrated the first effort to remember the Civil War dead by decorating their graves in Woodlawn Cemetery in Carbondale in April 1867. A year later, as commander of the Grand Army of the Republic, he designated May 30 "for the purpose of strewing flowers or otherwise decorating the graves of comrades who died in defense of their country during the late rebellion, and whose bodies now lie in every city, village and hamlet churchyard in the land."

CARROLLTON

¶ **Rainey Memorial Park,** State 267 and 6th Street.

This park honors Henry Rainey, the Speaker of the House of Representatives from March 1933 until his death in August 1934. A bronze statue of Rainey depicts him holding a gavel.

Of Scotch-Irish ancestry, Rainey was elected to Congress in 1906, the first of fifteen terms in the House of Representatives. During that tenure he voted with the liberal branch of the Democratic Party, especially on issues of free silver and tariff reform. While on the Ways and Means Committee, he helped draft the Underwood Tariff Bill. Although he resigned his seat when Congress declared war in April 1917 so he could join the war effort, he withdrew his resignation at the request of *President Woodrow Wilson and subsequently helped prepare and pass the various war revenue bills. He enthusiastically supported the idea of a deep waterway linking the Great Lakes with the Gulf of Mexico, and he worked to convene an international conference on tariff reduction during the first two years of the Great Depression. When the election of Franklin Roosevelt brought a Democratic majority to the House, Rainey was elected Speaker, from which position he advanced the passage of the New Deal's legislation.

¶ Thomas Carlin Monument, Greene County Courthouse, 519 North Main Street.

This memorial outside the courthouse was erected in memory of Thomas Carlin, the founder of Carrollton and the seventh governor of Illinois. Born in Kentucky in 1789 to a father of Irish descent, Carlin was the county's first sheriff, served in the state legislature, and commanded a battalion during the Black Hawk War. While governor from 1838 to 1842, he vigorously promoted a program of internal improvements, among them the Illinois and Michigan Canal.

¶ Walnut Hall, 1 mile west on State 108. Private.

This three-story brick house fronted by Greek columns was the focal point of a 485-acre farm owned by *Henry Rainey, Speaker of the House of Representatives. During his days here the farm was open to the public as a show place and park. The house is currently being restored by its owners.

CHICAGO

¶ Art Institute of Chicago, Michigan Avenue and Adams Street.

Among the institute's many collections is a reconstruction of the Trading Room of the Chicago Stock Exchange Building. The walls and ceilings of the room are covered with intricate stencil patterns by Louis J. Millet and *Louis Sullivan. The Exchange Building, which formerly stood at 30 North LaSalle Street, was designed by Sullivan and was erected in 1894. The exchange entryway – a stone and terra-cotta arch – stands today in the nearby reflecting pool in Grant Park.

Sullivan was born in Boston, the son of an Irishman who, according to the architect, was "not even sure he was a Catholic or an Orangeman."

The father had promoted himself from a wandering minstrel to the owner of a dancing academy in London and had prospered in the same line of work after arriving in Boston in 1847. Determined upon a career as an architect, the younger Sullivan entered the Massachusetts Institute of Technology, but his study of architecture produced in him a distaste for the classical and a preference for the Romanesque revival in vogue in Boston at the time. After leaving M.I.T., he worked briefly in architectural firms in Philadelphia and Chicago before sailing for Paris with hopes of matriculating at the Ecole des Beaux-Arts. For six weeks he studied eighteen hours a day in preparation for the entrance test. After less than a year at the Beaux-Arts, however, he returned to Chicago, still without having discovered the underlying architectural law which he sought.

In 1881 he became the second half of Adler and Sullivan, a new architectural firm which soon became the second most sought after practice in Chicago. As his clientele grew, Sullivan became increasingly absorbed with answering the major question facing designers of large buildings: how to provide increased light for such structures and how to raise them to greater heights. Sullivan found his answer in what was called the Chicago School of Architecture, a movement which pioneered the use of iron and steel skeleton frames. Particularly through the Wainwright Building in St. Louis and the Gage Building in Chicago, he illustrated his discovery of the architectural principle which he had so long sought: "Form follows function." Convinced that such a modern form as the skyscraper required a new method of expression, he pointed out the incongruity of clothing such a structure in the classical accoutrements of the past. More than any other man he helped make the skyscraper America's most significant architectural contribution.

§ Open Monday-Friday 10:30-4:30 (to 8 on Tuesday), Saturday 10-5, Sunday and holidays noon-5. Closed Thanksgiving and December 25. Fee. Phone: 312-443-3600.

¶ Auditorium Building and Theater, 430 South Michigan Avenue, at Congress Street.

Built in 1889 from a design by Dankmar Adler and *Louis Sullivan, this structure originally had 136 offices, 400 hotel rooms, and a 4,200-seat auditorium. At the time of its completion, it was the city's greatest monument. Although its exterior was in the fashionable Romanesque style, its interior marked Sullivan's sharp rejection of the past. The theater's highly foliated interior decoration was an early example of Art Nouveau and of the innovative bent which earned for him the nickname "the Whitman of American architecture."

In 1946 the Auditorium Building was purchased and renovated by Roosevelt University, which maintains a collection of Sullivan memorabilia in the lobby. The theater in the complex has also been restored and was reopened in 1968.

§ Phone: 312-341-3510. For information about tours of the Auditorium Building, call 312-431-2354.

¶ **Carson, Pirie, Scott & Company Building,** State and Madison streets.

Originally built for the Schlesinger & Meyer retail store between 1899 and 1904, this structure was designed by *Louis Sullivan and is one of Chicago's fine clothing stores. The building's rounded entrance and long, horizontal windows reflect Sullivan's penchant for innovation, as does his trademark cast-iron grillwork on the exterior of the first two floors.

§ Open Monday and Thursday 9:45-7:30, and Tuesday, Wednesday, Friday, and Saturday 9:45-5:45.

¶ **Chicago Fire Academy,** 558 West DeKoven Street, between South Jefferson and West Taylor streets.

The academy's modern brick structure stands on the site of a house and a barn owned by *Patrick O'Leary and Kate O'Leary, whose cow allegedly knocked over the lantern which started the disastrous 1871 fire. In front of the academy is the *Pillar of Fire*, a huge art work of intertwined bronze flames commemorating the blaze.

The fire, which began about 9 o'clock Sunday evening, October 8, ravaged the city until the following Tuesday. In all, a 200-acre swath – covering what is now the Loop, the North Side, Sandburg Village, Old Town, and the Gold Coast – was destroyed. The conflagration left an estimated 200 to 300 people dead, 94,000 more homeless, and almost 16,000 buildings in ruins. Damage from the fire ranged from $175 million to $300 million. More people died in the conditions after the fire than from the flames.

After the conflagration Mrs. O'Leary testified that she and her husband and five children were in bed the night of the fire when they were awakened by *Daniel Sullivan, a neighbor who had spent about an hour at the O'Learys' house earlier that evening. Despite his wooden leg, Sullivan entered the burning barn and untied two of the cows before the intensity of the flames forced him to leave, but not before he caught his wooden leg between two boards. After righting himself, he rescued a calf whose back hair was on fire. By then the fire had spread to the O'Leary house, forty feet from the barn.

When Mrs. O'Leary's husband saw the fire, he led the children into the street and proceeded to throw water on the burning house until one o'clock in the morning. Although he feared that he might be blamed for starting the fire, he said that he wouldn't fault any man in America for hanging him if he had been responsible. His wife was described as "almost crazy on account of losing all her property – a barn, wagons, harness, six cows and a horse . . . . " The O'Learys' son, a later gambler known as "Big Jim," claimed that the fire had been started by local tramps smoking near the barn.

§ Open Monday-Friday 8-4, Saturday 9-1. Phone: 312-747-7239.

¶ **Chicago Historical Society,** 1601 North Clark Street.

A statue of Abraham Lincoln by *Augustus Saint-Gaudens stands on the lawn. The society's museum contains artifacts and exhibits pertaining to the Great Fire of 1871. (See Cornish, New Hampshire.)

§ Open Monday-Saturday 9:30-4:30, Sunday noon-5. Closed January 1, Thanksgiving, and December 25. Fee. Phone: 312-642-4600.

¶ **Comiskey Park Site,** 324 West 35th Street.

Until the late 1990s the nation's oldest major league baseball park was located on this site. The historic stadium was named for *Charles Comiskey, the founder of the American League and the Chicago White Sox. In 1908 Comiskey paid $15,000 for the park site's original fifteen acres between 34th and 35th streets and Shields and Wentworth streets. The White Sox played their first game in Comiskey Park on April 15, 1910. (See National Baseball Hall of Fame in Cooperstown, New York.)

¶ **Corpus Christi Catholic Church,** 49th Street and Dr. Martin Luther King Jr. Drive (formerly Grand Boulevard).

This South Side parish was founded in 1901 to serve the "Gold Coast" Irish who had built mansions along the boulevard. It was here that author James Farrell, the son and grandson of Irish Catholic working-class laborers, was born and raised and attended elementary school. This predominantly Irish neighborhood of Washington Park became the setting for Farrell's short stories and four mammoth fictional cycles that portray the Irish-American experience in Chicago between 1900 and 1930. Farrell's most famous works are the Studs Lonigan trilogy and the O'Neill-O'Flaherty pentalogy (*A World I Never Made, No Star Is Lost, Father and Son, My Days of Anger,* and *The Face of Time*).

¶ **Daley Civic Center,** 50 West Washington Street, between Dearborn and Clark streets.

Named in honor of Richard J. Daley, Chicago's last machine boss, this thirty-one-story building houses city and county offices and civil courts. An eternal flame in Hiz Honor's memory burns in the neighboring plaza.

Daley was born in 1902 to parents of Irish ancestry in the predominantly Irish area of Bridgeport on Chicago's South Side. Although he began working for the local Democratic political organization when he was only twelve, he won his first elective office as a write-in Republican. After switching parties, he continued his climb up the political ladder as state senator, chairman of the Cook County Democratic Central Committee, and finally mayor of Chicago from 1955 until his death in 1976. His power seemed almost complete when, in the last year of his tenure, the city council gave him virtual control over 40,000 government jobs when it abolished the city's civil service commission. In a nod to his heavily Irish constituency, he brought the city's St. Patrick's Day parade downtown and started the tradition of dying the Chicago River green for that annual celebration.

During the 1960 presidential campaign, Daley used his considerable clout to secure the election of Senator John F. Kennedy. After delivering the Illinois delegation's votes to the Massachusetts politician at the Democratic National Convention, Daley pressured his precinct workers to get out the vote for Kennedy on election day. When the ballots were counted, the senator had defeated Richard Nixon in Illinois by only 8,858 votes, a victory that raised suspicions of electoral fraud, particularly in Cook County (Chicago). Kennedy himself credited Daley with his victory and invited the mayor to spend a night at the White House. At the time, according to the Chicago journalist Mike Royko, Daley was, "with the single exception of the president, the most powerful politician in the country."

Although Daley's administration was known for revitalizing the city, it suffered some serious embarrassments. In response to charges of political corruption, the mayor alluded to Christ's betrayal by one of his disciples: "If our Lord couldn't have perfection, how are we going to have it in city government?" During the rioting which rocked the city following the assassination of Martin Luther King Jr. in 1968, Daley created additional controversy by his shoot-to-kill order against arsonists. Later that year he drew national attention when his police force was involved in what was later called "a police riot" against demonstrators during the Democratic National Convention. Daley emphatically defended his officers, calling the demonstrators a "lawless, violent group of terrorists." To later charges that he abused his authority while in office, Daley replied: "I don't think I am a powerful man. I'm just an ordinary mayor of an ordinary city. I'm trying to do an ordinary job."

¶ Elizabeth M. Cudahy Memorial Library, Loyola University, 6625 Sheridan Road.

Completed in 1930, this limestone structure in the Romanesque style was named for *Elizabeth Murphy, the wife of Edward Cudahy Sr., the Irish-born meatpacking magnate. (See Cudahy, Wisconsin.) Cudahy's son Michael had previously donated funds for the construction of a science hall on the Loyola campus.

¶ Graceland Cemetery, North Clark Street and West Irving Park Road.

Among the illustrious Chicagoans who lie buried beneath the cemetery's impressive statues and memorials is *Louis Sullivan, the famed architect and designer of many of the city's buildings. He designed the cemetery's bronze gates as well as the 1890 Getty Tomb, which Frank Lloyd Wright called "a symphony in stone." Sullivan's grave is marked by a monolith erected by the architects and builders of Chicago. The monument is inscribed with the following words: "By his buildings great in influence and power; his drawings unsurpassed in originality and beauty; his writings rich in poetry and prophecy; his teachings persuasive and eloquent; his philosophy where, in 'Form Follows Function,' he summed up all truth in Art, Sullivan has earned his place as one of the greatest architectural forces in America."

¶ **Grant Park,** along Lake Michigan, between Randolph Street and Roosevelt Road.

This sprawling park was named for *Ulysses S. Grant and contains several pieces of art work associated with other Irish Americans:

• the arched entryway of the 1894 Chicago Stock Exchange, built from a design by *Louis Sullivan and standing in the park's reflecting pool and

•two sculpted works by *Augustus Saint-Gaudens: a seated statue of Abraham Lincoln (across Columbus Drive at the pedestrian extension of Van Buren Street) and an equestrian statue of John Logan, the famous Illinois lawmaker and Civil War soldier (west of the Band Shell, on Michigan Avenue, at the foot of 9th Street).

¶ **Haymarket Square,** Desplaines and Randolph streets.

This was the scene of the country's most bloody labor confrontation, coming within the context of widespread agitation for an eight-hour workday.

On May 4, 1886, 2,000 people were in the square listening to labor leaders denounce alleged police brutality. At about 10:30 p.m., a large force of police led by two captains entered the square and ordered the crowd to disperse. When a bomb thrown into the ranks of the police exploded, the officers fired into the crowd, some of whom returned the gunshot. A thirty-four-year-old policeman named *Mathias Degan died almost immediately from loss of blood when a main artery was severed by a bomb fragment. Five other policemen died later of injuries, and fifty to sixty others were injured. During the battle at least two workers died and a dozen more sustained injuries. Besides Degan, four of the slain policemen had Irish names: John Barrett, Timothy Flavin, Thomas Reddin, and Michael Sheehan. Two years later a sixth Irish officer – Timothy Sullivan – died of complications caused by wounds suffered from the Haymarket incident.

¶ **Holy Trinity Orthodox Cathedral,** Leavitt Street and Haddon Avenue.

This Russian Orthodox church was designed by *Louis Sullivan, who decorated the interior with stenciled polychrome patterns and the exterior with geometric trim around the doors, windows, and roof lines.

¶ *Home,* Humboldt Park, Augusta Boulevard and Sacramento Avenue.
   This pyramidal sculpture of a miner and his child, at the east end of
the park, is the work of *Charles Mulligan.

¶ **International Harvester Company Site,** Equitable Life Assurance
Society Building, 401 North Michigan Avenue.
   The site on which the Equitable Building stands was where Cyrus
McC rmick manufactured the mechanical grain reaper which he had de-
veloped from an earlier invention by his father. McCormick traced his
ancestry to emigrants from northern Ireland. (See Steele's Tavern, Virginia,
in *Irish America,* Volume 2.)
   In 1847 the famous inventor came to Chicago to establish his enter-
prise because he believed that Illinois would be the best market and the
best transport center for his reaper. In 1902 his son merged the original
McCormick Company with several other firms to form the International
Harvester Company.

¶ **Irish-American Heritage Center,** 4626 North Knox Avenue.
   This former college building is host to a variety of musical, theatrical,
and Gaelic language activities for the Hibernophiles of the Chicago area.
The center's library features many exhibits on Ireland and Irish-American
culture.
   § Open Monday-Friday 9-5, Saturday 10-4. Phone: 773-282-7035.

¶ **Irish Castle,** 10244 Longwood Drive, at 103rd Street.
   This authentic reproduction of an Irish keep was constructed in 1886
by Robert Givins, a Chicago real estate dealer of Irish birth. He hoped to
attract home buyers into the neighborhood, which at the time was known
as Washington Heights and which he had been developing and subdivid-
ing. At its completion the structure was notable for its serrated turrets and
the dimensions of the living room: thirty-six feet long and twenty-four
feet wide (as well as high). Givins and his family lived in the "Castle"
until 1908, when it was bought by the first of a succession of owners. Since
about 1940 the structure has been the Beverly Unitarian Church.
   According to tradition, Givins conceived the idea of building this
castle-like residence while on a tour of Ireland. He was particularly taken
with an ancient ivy-covered castle which, according to some sources, stood
along the River Dee. (The object of his interest may have actually been the
ruins of Desmond Castle, a fifteenth-century tower house on a rocky islet
in the River *Deel,* at Askeaton, County Limerick.)
   Givins had an unusual talent for devising schemes to promote real
estate sales. A fellow dealer by the name of Hyde Perce described one

The Irish Castle.
(Photo courtesy of Beverly
Unitarian Church, Chicago.)

such stunt: "I recall an auction . . . where [Givens] advertised the giving away of a lot. He did so by attaching an order for a warranty deed to one of several hundred toy balloons and then setting them adrift. The finder of the lucky balloon was to be given his choice of a residence lot. Several years after this a farmer near Summit, Illinois, uncovered a small tin container while plowing his field. In it was the Givins warranty deed. He presented it to Mr. Givins and received a nice lot."

¶ **John Murphy Memorial,** the American College of Surgeons, 55 East Erie Street.

This memorial auditorium was erected in 1926 by the American College of Surgeons in honor of one of its most distinguished members, Dr. John Murphy. In the estimation of Dr. William Mayo, Murphy was "without a peer" as a teacher of clinical surgery and was "the surgical genius of our generation." A marker is located on the exterior of the building.

Murphy was born in 1857 in Appleton, Wisconsin, the son of Irish parents. After attending Rush Medical College in Chicago, he began an internship at Cook County Hospital, where he remained an attending surgeon for most of his subsequent career. Two years of graduate study in Vienna were followed by a series of medical school teaching assignments at Rush, Northwestern University, and the College of Physicians and Surgeons. He became head of the surgical staff at Mercy Hospital in 1895.

Murphy turned his early attention to abdominal surgery, becoming one of the first to investigate the cause and treatment of peritonitis after appendicitis. His invention of the Murphy Button – a device for making rapid and accurate intestinal and gastrointestinal anastomosis – permitted lifesaving operations previously thought impossible. He later devoted himself to studying the principles behind surgery of the lungs and of the nervous system.

Distinguished by his florid complexion and red beard and red moustache, Murphy was awarded many honorary degrees. In 1910 he was elected president of the American Medical Association, and six years later he was named a papal knight-commander of the Order of St. Gregory the Great. A few months before his death in 1916, he was incapacitated by attacks of angina pectoris, brought on, it was believed, by the stress of his work.

¶ *Lincoln as Railsplitter*, Garfield Park, due west of the Loop, between Kolmar and Tolman streets.

This portrayal of the sixteenth president as a youthful railsplitter was designed by Charles Mulligan. It is one of several by the Irish-born sculptor honoring the American working class.

After leaving his native County Tyrone in 1883, at the age of seventeen, Mulligan settled near Chicago, where he found work as a stonemason. He soon came under the tutelage of Lorado Taft, who made him his assistant in the sculpture department at the Art Institute of Chicago. (The young Irishman reputedly infected the night students there with his enthusiasm and radiant personality.) He also studied briefly in Paris. Even after succeeding Taft as chair of the department, Mulligan continued to carve his own works rather than give his plaster models to someone else to be rendered in stone. Nor was he averse to using mechanical aids like the pneumatic tool outfit he installed in his studio. Besides being instrumental in forming an artist colony known as the "Eagle's Nest," he was a member of several other artists' organizations as well as the Irish Fellowship Club.

Mulligan's desire to become "the prophet of hopeful, cheerful labor" is reflected in some of his earliest pieces. For the Buffalo Exposition of 1901, for instance, he produced *The Digger*, which, in its depiction of four workingmen, was a virtual paean in stone to the nation's forgotten laborers, many of them Irish. He continued to express his concern for toiling Americans with his *Miner and Child* (or *Home*) (Chicago) and his *Lincoln as Railsplitter*.

Among his many other works are the Illinois Monument (Vicksburg, Miss.), in which he depicted Lincoln, *Ulysses S. Grant, and Governor Richard Yates; *Justice and Power* and *Law and Knowledge* (a pair of entrance groups at the Illinois State House); and statues of George Rogers Clark (Quincy, Ill.), *John F. Finerty (Chicago), Abraham Lincoln (Pana, Ill.), and *William McKinley (Chicago). The statue of Finerty once stood in Chicago's Garfield Park, but its whereabouts is now unknown.

Finerty, the Chicago journalist, congressman, and president of the United Irish League of America, was born in Galway, Ireland in 1846. At the age of eighteen he immigrated to the United States and almost immediately volunteered for the Union army. During a career as a newspaper reporter, he worked for three Chicago journals – the *Republican*, the *Tribune*, and the *Times*. While on the staff of the last publication, he reported the Indian wars, including Custer's campaign against Sitting Bull in 1876. Finerty later served one term in the House of Representatives and was among the Irish who uncharacteristically supported *James G. Blaine, the Republican presidential nominee in 1884. Long active in Irish and Irish-American affairs, he served numerous times as president of the United Irish League of America and the United Irish Societies of Chicago. He was the editor of the *Chicago Citizen* and the author of *Warpath and Bivouac* and *People's History of Ireland*.

¶ *Lincoln, the Orator,* Oak Woods Cemetery, 1035 East 67th Street.
This statue of Lincoln by *Charles Mulligan seems out of place among the 6,000 Confederate soldiers buried here.

¶ **Lincoln Park,** along Lake Shore Drive, between North Avenue and Hollywood Avenue.
Two renowned statues of famous Civil War figures are located in this sprawling park:
• *Lincoln Standing Before the Chair of State* at the Dearborn Parkway entrance. This larger than life statue by *Augustus Saint-Gaudens was unveiled in 1887. In sculpting the model for this work, Saint-Gaudens used a life mask of Lincoln created by sculptor Leonard Volk before Lincoln went to Washington. As a boy, Saint-Gaudens had seen Lincoln and had later viewed him in death.
• The *General Grant Statue* on Ridge Drive overlooking Lake Shore Drive. This equestrian bronze of *Ulysses S. Grant stands on a massive stone arch and was dedicated in 1891.
The bronze statuary group *An Indian Family* by *John Boyle (along Ridge Drive) shows a male Ottawa Indian surrounded by a squaw, a papoose, and their dog. Before he started work on this piece, Boyle lived with Native Americans for two months in order to learn about their way of life. (See John Barry Statue, District of Columbia.)

¶ **McCormick Place Convention Complex,** 2301 South Lake Shore Drive, at East 23rd Street.

This massive convention and exposition center was completed in 1970 on the site of an earlier such structure destroyed by fire. Both buildings were named for *Robert McCormick (1880-1955), the editor and publisher of the *Chicago Tribune*.

A grandnephew of the famous inventor *Cyrus McCormick, Robert R. McCormick was a spokesman for Midwestern conservatism during the 1940s, a strong opponent of Franklin Roosevelt, and a leader in the isolationist movement prior to World War II. Under his management the *Tribune* led the nation in nontabloid circulation and the world in advertising revenues.

¶ **McCormick Theological Seminary,** 5555 South Woodlawn Avenue (on the University of Chicago campus).

Founded by the inventor *Cyrus McCormick, a devout Presbyterian and church leader, this theological institution is directed by the General Assembly of the United Presbyterian Church, U.S.A. Despite its Presbyterian affiliation, the seminary prepares students for the Christian ministry without regard to denomination. The seminary was originally located at 800 West Belden Avenue.

¶ **Newberry Library,** Clark, Walton, and Dearborn streets.

The library's collection of books and manuscripts relating to Irish history and culture is larger than that of any other institution in Chicago. The library also owns thirty-four portraits of famous Americans by *George Healy, among them paintings of Pierre Beauregard, *Ulysses S. Grant, Abraham Lincoln, *Philip Sheridan, and William Sherman.

§ Library services Tuesday-Thursday 10-6, Friday-Saturday 9-5. Exhibits Monday-Saturday 8:15-5:30 (to 7:30 on Monday, Friday, and Saturday). Closed major holidays. Phone: 312-255-3510.

¶ **O'Hare International Airport,** 17 miles northwest of the Loop, at Mannheim Road and Kennedy Expressway.

One of the world's busiest airports was named for *Edward "Butch" O'Hare. In 1942 this graduate of the U.S. Naval Academy was a naval aviator aboard the *Lexington* when the carrier was attacked by Japanese bombers. Single-handedly he shot down five of the nine incoming planes and damaged three others. For his bravery he was promoted to lieutenant commander and awarded the Congressional Medal of Honor. During a parade in his honor in his native St. Louis, he downplayed his heroism: "You don't have time to consider the odds against you. You're too busy throwing bullets."

O'Hare's most dramatic raid, however, occurred in September 1943 when he swooped down on the enemy's runway on Wake Island and, while dodging antiaircraft fire, destroyed two grounded planes and an approaching bomber. The following month he was reported missing in action when he was hit while leading the first group of aircraft to take off from a carrier at night and intercept Japanese attackers. It was later revealed that he had been part of an experiment to see whether fighter planes could be maneuvered into visual contact with enemy planes from a radar-equipped bomber. Before his untimely death, he had downed a total of twelve Japanese fighter planes.

In 1949 an estimated 200,000 people gathered at the site of the airport that would bear O'Hare's name for the unveiling of a plaque in his honor by his mother and his widow. The plaque depicts O'Hare in bas-relief emerging from a plane and is inscribed with the words which President Roosevelt spoke when he presented the young flier with the Medal of Honor.

Although O'Hare's father – *Edward "Artful Eddie" O'Hare – ran Al Capone's dog track in Cicero, Illinois, he was responsible for helping bring the Chicago gangster to justice. After Capone tried to bribe the jurors in his income tax evasion trial, O'Hare informed the federal court. O'Hare was gunned down many years later, not long after Capone's release from prison.

¶ Philip Sheridan Statue, Sheridan Road, Belmont Avenue, and Lake Shore Drive.

In this 1923 equestrian work by Gutzon Borglum, *General Philip Sheridan is depicted on his horse, Rienzi, after leaving Winchester, Virginia, to lead his men against a Confederate force. After the Chicago fire of 1871, Sheridan was placed in charge of keeping order in the city. (See Sheridan Circle, District of Columbia.)

¶ Police Training Academy, 1300 West Jackson.

Inside the atrium of the academy stands the Haymarket Monument, a statue modeled after an Irish policeman and dedicated to the eight police officers – six of them Irish – who died as the result of violence which erupted in Haymarket Square on May 4, 1886. (See Haymarket Square above.)

The bronze statue depicts a police officer with his right hand raised, a stance like that of Captain William Ward when, just before the bomb blast, he called out to the crowd, "In the name of the people in the State of Illinois, I command this meeting immediately and peaceably to disperse." The pedestal is inscribed with the words "The Law is Common Sense," taken from the remarks of Judge Joseph Gary when he sentenced eight alleged anarchists for the deaths of those killed in the Haymarket Riot. The statue was originally unveiled in 1889 in Union Park, where it stood for more than fifty years. After being twice damaged by bombs in the 1960s, the statue was placed in storage until it was reinstalled here in 1976

The Haymarket Monument.
(Photo courtesy of the
Chicago Police Department.)

in the presence of *Mayor Richard Daley.
    § Phone: 312-746-8310.

¶ **St. Patrick's Church,** 700 West Adams Street.
    The original St. Patrick's church on this site was erected in 1846. The present Romanesque revival structure was completed in 1856 by working-class Irish in the neighborhood. The pastor at the time was Father Dennis Dunne, a native of County Laois and the uncle of Irish-American humorist Finley Peter Dunne. Although the area surrounding the church was destroyed in the Great Fire of 1871, St. Patrick's was spared.
    The church's two towers – one Byzantine and the other Gothic – represent the different ethnic groups in the parish community. The stained glass throughout the church is the work of Thomas O'Shaughnessy, an artist of presumably Irish ancestry. The twelve nave windows are decorated with intricate Celtic interlaces (adopted from the *Book of Kells*) and with pictures of Irish saints, the foremost being St. Patrick, St. Attracta, St. Brendan, and St. Brigid. In the balcony is the triptych of Faith, Hope, and Charity, a stained-glass work of 150,000 pieces honoring Terence MacSwiney, the mayor of Cork, who died in 1920 while on a hunger strike. The top of the Faith window is adorned with a large shamrock and a large Celtic cross; the latter contains miniature paintings of Duns Scotus, the

philosopher; St. Malachi, the prophet; and St. Firgil, the geographer. At the base of the cross the spirit of MacSwiney rises out of what O'Shaughnessy called the "lurid colors of purgatory."

O'Shaughnessy was born in Medon, Missouri, in 1870, and is said to have made his first stained glass window at the age of twelve for the Chapel of the Sisters of Loretto Academy in Moberly, Missouri. The young artist came to Chicago in 1894, right after his graduation from the Fine Arts Academy in Kansas City. After setting up a commercial art studio on North State Street, he entered the Art Institute's School of Design, where he took courses with Alphonse Mucha and Louis Millet. He eventually gained a reputation as a painter, sculptor, engraver, and mosaicist.

O'Shaughnessy was a devout Catholic and a lifelong student of Irish history and art. After studying the ornamentation in the *Book of Kells* while in Dublin in 1900, he focused his attention on transmuting Celtic ornamentation into stained glass. In this pursuit he experimented for a decade before successfully producing pot metal glass whose transparency could reproduce the brilliant colors and luminous quality of the medieval illuminated manuscript. Having in effect rediscovered the fifth-century method of making stained glass – from extremely fine sands which he discovered near Ottawa, Illinois – he gave up his successful career as a commercial artist to become one of the country's best ecclesiastical stained-glass artists.

In 1911, the same year in which he perfected his pot metal glass, O'Shaughnessy persuaded the mayor of Chicago to proclaim Columbus Day as a legal holiday. His interest in the famous explorer dated from his work as a student artist in helping to save replicas of Columbus's three ships from demolition after the 1893 Columbian Exposition.

For the Century of Progress Exposition in Chicago in 1933, O'Shaughnessy received a commission to design stained glass for twenty-three windows at the Illinois Host House. Among the designs he produced were scenes depicting events in the history of Illinois, among them Father Marquette's explorations in the state, the Lincoln-Douglas debates, the opening of the Erie Canal, and the Columbian Exposition of 1893. (All the windows disappeared when the structure was dismantled.) In an interview with the Chicago *Daily News* in 1937, the artist said that, despite a promised $5,000 for his work on the Host House, he had received nothing.

Additional examples of O'Shaughnessy's stained-glass work in Chicago can be found in the Chicago Historical Society (North Avenue at Clark Street), the Madonna della Strada Chapel (6525 North Sheridan Road), and St. Stephen's Episcopal Church (3533 North Albany Avenue).

St. Patrick's Church is located in what was once the predominantly Irish neighborhood of Bridgeport, where Finley Peter Dunne was born to Irish immigrants. In 1884 the sixteen-year-old Dunne began a newspaper career that saw him work for six of the city's newspapers, first as a police and sports reporter, then as a features and editorial writer, and finally as managing editor of the *Post*. In 1890 he created the first of three Irish characters whom he used as vehicles for satire or political commentary in his columns: Colonel Thomas Jefferson Dolan; Colonel Malachi McNeery, based on the pensive real-life saloon keeper James McGarry; and Martin Dooley, the more famous derivative of the previous character.

In more than 300 weekly columns, Finley Peter Dunne used Mr. Dooley to recreate what Charles Fanning called "the first fully realized Irish ethnic neighborhood in American literature." Although on many occasions Dooley waxes nostalgic about the Great Famine and the hardships of immigration and assimilation, he also dispenses insight into the Irish character and the human condition. After opining, for example, that "f'r an impetchoos an' darin' people th' Irish is th' mos' cowardly whin it comes to mathrimony that iver I heerd tell iv," Dooley cites "Dacey th' plumber, who'd niver 'v married if he hadn't got into th' wrong buildin' whin he wint to take out a license f'r his dog, an' got a marriage license instid." Other Dooley pieces illustrate the gap between the immigrants and their more Americanized children: After scandalizing the neighborhood by wearing bloomers while riding a bicycle, Molly Donahue is sent off to confession, where she receives "a pinance th' like iv which ain't been knowed in Bridgeport since Cassidy said Charles Stewart Parnell was a bigger man thin th' pope." Dunne received national attention with the publication of *Mr. Dooley in Peace and War* and *Mr. Dooley in the Hearts of His Countrymen*, which were followed by five other volumes of "observations." One of Dooley's famous remarks was about Thanksgiving: "'Twas founded be th' Puritans to give thanks f'r bein' presarved fr'm th' Indians, and . . . we [Irish] keep it to give thanks we are presarved fr'm th' Puritans."

¶ St. Stanislaus Church, 1351 West Evergreen Ave.

This neo-Renaissance house of worship was designed by Patrick Keely and was completed in 1881 to serve a predominantly Polish parish.

Born in Kilkenny, Ireland, Keely was apparently trained by his architect father before immigrating to the United States and settling with other Irish newcomers near the Brooklyn Navy Yard. As he perfected his craft, he employed several styles: English Gothic at first, and Romanesque and Second Empire later. During a career that lasted more than four decades, Keely was the dominant figure in the field of Roman Catholic architecture in North America, designing sixteen cathedrals and an estimated 500 to 600 other churches (although explicit documentation has been found for only about 150). Among his more famous works are the Catholic cathedrals of Boston and Chicago. If his design for a Catholic cathedral in Brooklyn had been carried out, that church would have been larger than St.

Patrick's in Manhattan.

¶ William McKinley Statue, McKinley Park.

Dedicated in 1905, this statue of *President William McKinley was sculpted by *Charles Mulligan and was cast from a bronze statue of Columbus that once stood in Lincoln Park.

DIXON

¶ Ronald Reagan Boyhood Home, off Galena Street at 816 South Hennepin Avenue.

From 1920 to 1923 this two-story white frame house was the residence of young *Ronald Reagan, his older brother, and his parents. This was the first of five houses which the parents of the future president rented in Dixon between 1920 and 1939. The house features family memorabilia and a ten-minute film about Reagan's early life and later career. The president was born in nearby Tampico [*q.v.*].

Reagan's father, Jack, was born in Illinois in 1883 and was raised a Catholic by his aunts. Although he was married in a Catholic ceremony in 1904, his wife was not of that faith. This mixed marriage may explain why their older son, Neil, was raised a Catholic while their other son, Ronald, was not. As President Reagan related in his autobiography, as a youngster he occasionally defended his father's honor with his fists. It seems that some of the boy's classmates ridiculed "Dutch" because of his father's Catholicism and claimed that the local Catholic church was storing weapons to be used during a planned papal invasion of the country. When "Dutch" asked his father about this charge, Jack told his son that the story was "baloney." After some of the boy's classmates called his father a liar, "Dutch" was led "to engage some of them in hand-to-hand combat on the playground."

Although Jack Reagan dreamed of owning his own shoe store, he fell wide of the mark because of his drinking – what the neighbors politely called "a powerful thirst." After losing his job in 1931, the older Reagan actively worked for the election of Franklin Roosevelt and was rewarded with a position as head of the local welfare office. In the meantime the future president attended Eureka College, achieving considerable fame as a football player and a thespian. A career as a radio sports announcer was followed by one on the "Silver Screen," where he was known as a competent and hardworking actor, although he never achieved "superstardom."

Despite his later successful political career, Reagan never forgot his father's influence on the formation of his ideals. "Among the things he passed on to me," the president wrote in his autobiography, "was the belief that all men and women, regardless of their color or religion, are created equal and that . . . it's largely their own ambition and hard work that

Statue of Ronald Reagan.
(Photo courtesy of the
Ronald Reagan Boyhood Home
Preservation Foundation.)

determine their fate in life." The son never tired of telling the story of how his father refused to stay in a hotel when he learned that it did not accept Jews. Before angrily leaving the hotel and spending the night in his car instead, the elder Reagan retorted that the managers probably did not like Catholics either. (See Simi Valley, California, in *Irish America*, Volume 2.)

§ Open March-November, Monday-Saturday 10-4, Sunday 1-4; rest of the year, Saturday 10-4, Sunday 1-4. Closed January 1, Easter, Thanksgiving, and December 25. Phone: 815-288-3404. A visitor center is located at 810 South Hennepin Avenue.

¶ An eight-foot-high bronze statue of President Ronald Reagan stands in a park south of his boyhood home. The statue was erected in 1988 and depicts the former president holding kernels of corn in his hand – a reminder of Illinois' agricultural production.

¶ A bronze plaque at the Loveland Community Building commemorates the fact that young Ronald Reagan saved seventy-seven lives during the seven years he was a lifeguard at Lowell Park.

EQUALITY

¶ **Michael Lawler Monument,** Calhoun Street.

This memorial honors General Michael Kelly Lawler, a native of County Kildare, Ireland, who served in both the Mexican War and the Civil War. During the former conflict he was a cavalry captain, an experience which served him well when he raised the 18th Illinois Infantry at the beginning of the Civil War. Wounded at the battle of Fort Donelson, he led the attack on Vicksburg and was brevetted major general after the war. Before returning to his farm in Illinois, he followed a career as a horse trader in the South.

¶ General Lawler is buried in Hickory Hill Cemetery, two miles east on State 13.

GALENA

¶ **First Grant House,** 121 High Street. Private.

In 1860 *Ulysses S. Grant arrived from St. Louis with his wife and four children to take up residence in this brick cottage. When the Civil War broke out, this future commander of the Union army drilled recruits in Galena. Within seventeen months he was named colonel of the 21st Illinois Volunteer Regiment and brigadier general in command of the military post at Cairo, Illinois.

¶ **Galena Historical Society,** 211.5 Bench Street.

Among the items in the society's museum is Thomas Nast's life-size painting of General Lee's surrender to *Ulysses S. Grant at Appomattox. One of the officers depicted on the canvas is *General John Rawlins, Grant's aide-de-camp during the Civil War. Rawlins, who was of Scotch-Irish descent, had been a lawyer in Galena prior to the war. He later served as Grant's secretary of war.

¶ **Grant Home State Historic Site,** 500 Bouthillier Street.

After the Civil War this two-story brick Italianate house was given to *General Ulysses S. Grant by the citizens of Galena. Besides family possessions, the house displays silver and china used in the White House while Grant was president.

The former Union commander and his family lived here until 1867, when he moved to Washington, D.C., to become secretary of war for *President Andrew Johnson. He returned to the house in 1879, after two terms as president and a two-year tour of the world. He left Galena for New York City in 1881.

§ Open daily 9-5. Closed January 1, Martin Luther King Jr.'s Birthday, Presidents' Day, Election Day, Veterans' Day, Thanksgiving, and December 25. Phone: 815-777-0248 (or 3310).

❡ **Grant Park,** on the east bank of the Galena River, via the Johnson Street Bridge.

In the park stands the statue *Grant, Our Citizen,* a memorial to *Ulysses S. Grant donated by a Chicago newspaper editor.

❡ **John Dowling House,** Main and Diagonal streets.

Dating from 1826, this is reputedly the oldest house in Galena and was built by John Dowling with the help of his teenage son, Nicholas. The structure originally served as a trading post.

Although the elder Dowling was referred to as an Irishman by contemporaries and reputedly came from Dublin, nothing is known about his life in his native land. By 1824 he had arrived in St. Louis and two years later he had taken up residence in Galena. In time he became one of the largest iron dealers in the Midwest. He died on a visit to Washington, D.C., in 1843, at the age of sixty-eight. His fellow citizens memorialized him with a lengthy eulogy, part of which is printed here: "[A]ll who have been acquainted with him, will attest to the humanity, uprightness, and honesty, prominent in all his actions. Ever was he found furthering the interest of the *poor man;* and his loss will long be deplored by many who have had reason to view him as a benefactor. . . . In the social relations of life – as a husband, father and brother, he was affectionate and devoted; as an Irishman, he never forgot the land of his birth; and, as a citizen of the United States, he was warmly attached to the country of his adoption."

Nicholas Dowling seems to have become involved in his father's iron manufacturing business as early as 1829 and operated the Sligo Iron Store until 1851. During that period of time he served the city of Galena as alderman, trustee, and mayor.

§ Open Memorial Day-last weekend in October, Monday-Friday 10-4, Saturday-Sunday 10-5; rest of the year, Friday-Sunday 10-4. Fee. Phone: 815-777-1250.

❡ **J. R. Grant Leather Store Site,** 120 South Main Street.

A plaque marks the site of the leather goods shop owned by *Jesse Grant, the father of the famous Civil War commander. In 1860 the younger Grant came to Galena with his family in order to work in his father's store.

• A reconstruction of a leather store of the period is located at 211 South Main Street.

❡ **Rawlins House,** 511 Hill Street. Private.

This was the home of *General John Rawlins, aide-de-camp to *General Ulysses S. Grant during the Civil War. (See John Rawlins Statue, District of Columbia.)

❡ **Vinegar Hill Lead Mine and Museum,** 6 miles north on State 84, at

8885 North Three Pines Road.

This bitterly named mine was discovered in 1824 by *John Furlong, who christened it for the site of a skirmish against the British garrison in Wexford, Ireland, in 1798. Furlong, who had participated in the ill-fated battle, was captured by the British and impressed into military service before being sent to Canada. While there, he heard about Julien Dubuque's excursions into this part of Illinois in search of lead.

Following his escape from the British army, Furlong lived in this area for several years and purchased property in Galena soon after Illinois achieved statehood. Six years later he and three friends struck a rich vein of lead ore in what is now Vinegar Hill. Furlong's descendants worked the mine until 1934. His great-great-grandson opened the mine to tourists in 1967. Today Mark Furlong, the discover's third-great-grandson, welcomes visitors to the mine.

§ Open June-August, daily 9-5; May, September, and October, Saturday and Sunday 9-5. Fee. Phone: 815-777-0855.

❡ Although a nearby Catholic church attended by early Irish settlers no longer exists, its cemetery contains the remains of many of those pioneers.

GLENVIEW

❡ **Theodore Roosevelt Memorial,** Glenview Country Club.

Known locally as the *Boy Scout Fountain*, this memorial honors *President Theodore Roosevelt for his support of the Scouting movement and its ideals. The monument, which consists of a reflecting pool, a fountain, and a bronze statuary group of four Boy Scouts, was designed by *Andrew O'Connor. The statues of the four boys were modeled from the artist's sons.

At the dedication of the memorial on July 4, 1919, one of the speakers offered his interpretation of the memorial's emphasis on nature: "The water in the fountain is a symbol of purity. A Scout is clean. This water rushes to serve freely those who thirst. A Scout is friendly and courteous and helpful. To this fountain little birds are coming already to drink and bathe and preen their plumage. A Scout is kind to animals. And as it catches the rays of the sun and makes a joyful noise on summer days this water will remind us that a Scout is cheerful."

HIGHWOOD

❡ **Fort Sheridan,** north on Sheridan Road.

Now a 725-acre U.S. Army post, the fort is located where military troops called to Chicago after the Haymarket Riot in 1886 encamped. The following year the camp was named for *General Philip Sheridan, the famous Civil War officer who had earned a reputation for maintaining order after the Chicago fire of 1871.

LINCOLN

¶ **Lincoln Museum,** Lincoln College, 300 Keokuk.

The museum, located in the McKinstry Memorial Library, displays items and documents related to every U.S. president, including the eighteen of Irish ancestry.

§ Open February 1-mid December, Monday-Friday 10-4, Saturday-Sunday 1-4. Closed holidays. Phone: 217-732-3155 or 735-5050 ext. 295.

¶ **Mother Jones Burial Site,** United Miners' Cemetery, North Lake Street.

In 1936 a granite shaft was erected over the grave of Mary "Mother" Jones, who wished to be buried here among the miners for whose cause she had struggled for more than fifty years as a labor organizer and agitator.

After emigrating from Cork, Ireland, where she was born in 1830, Mary Harris first lived in Canada, where she received her formal education. Later, while teaching school in Memphis, Tennessee, she married an ironworker named Jones. Following his death and the deaths of their four children during a yellow fever epidemic, she returned to Chicago. Tragedy struck another bow when her possessions were destroyed in the Great Fire of 1871.

After joining the Knights of Labor, Jones spent the rest of her life in the cause of labor and the struggle against social injustice. Almost forty years later, in testimony before a congressional committee, she expressed her life's mission: "wherever a fight is on against wrong, I am always there" – in Pittsburgh during the labor riots of 1877; in Chicago during the Haymarket strike of 1886; in Birmingham during the railroad strike of 1894; in Virginia, West Virginia, and Colorado during various coal strikes between 1900 and 1913; and in New York during the street car strike of 1915-16. A West Virginia prosecutor described her as the "most dangerous woman in America," at whose arrival "20,000 contented men lay down their tools and walk out."

Jones was known for both her fiery speech and her sense of the dramatic. On one occasion she organized the striking miners' wives into a "women's army" that scared off scabs with brooms and mops. Addressing strikers in Charleston, West Virginia, in 1912, she condemned the governor for not meeting with them ("You can expect no help from such a goddamned dirty coward") and warned that if the company's security "thugs" were not dismissed, "there is going to be one hell of a lot of bloodletting in these hills." During a period of martial law in West Virginia, she was arrested and sentenced to twenty years in prison for conspiracy to commit murder. Following a congressional investigation, however, she was soon released.

Mother Jones's most dramatic effort, however, was one to build support for a federal child-labor law. In 1903 she led a march of striking Philadelphia mill workers to the home of *President Theodore Roosevelt in Oyster Bay, Long Island. Although almost all the workers soon dropped out of the 125-mile trek, Jones continued to play to the press. At Princeton University, when a professor asked her to address one of his classes, she arrived with a stooped ten-year-old boy: "Here's a text book on economics. He gets three dollars a week and his sister who is fourteen gets six dollars. They work in a carpet factory ten hours a day while the children of the rich are getting their higher education." In Paterson she said about Roosevelt: "I am going to find out if he is the President of the capitalists only or whether he is the President of the workingman, too. If he is the President of the capitalists only, he will be wiped out at the next election." When the six remaining marchers – including three children – finally arrived at Oyster Bay, they were refused admission and were informed by Roosevelt that child-labor legislation was a state responsibility rather than a federal one. Jones responded with her usual intensity: "He is a brave guy when he wants to take a gun and fight other grown people, but when those children went to him he would not see them."

PANA

℉ Abraham Lincoln Statue, Rosemont Grove Cemetery.
     This bronze statue of the martyred president was designed by *Charles Mulligan. (See *Lincoln as Railsplitter*, Chicago).

PEORIA

℉ John Flanagan House, 942 Northeast Glen Oak Avenue.
     Now the headquarters of the Peoria Historical Society, this early 1840s Federalist and Italianate structure was the home of Judge John Flanagan, an early settler in the community. The house, Peoria's oldest standing residence, displays antique tools and toys and decorative arts and textiles.
     Born in Philadelphia in 1806 to John and Jane Flanagan, the future judge studied and practiced law in that city until 1830. Sometime prior to that date, his father, formerly an ironmaker in Dublin, Ireland, succumbed to the fever, contracted while en route by ship to New Orleans. It was after this untimely event that the younger Flanagan moved to Pottsville, Pennsylvania, where he continued his legal profession and joined his brother-in-law in the coal business.

The John Flanagan House. (Photo courtesy of the Peoria Historical Society.)

Flanagan first came to the Peoria region in 1834 to settle his father's estate, which included 650 acres of land that the older man had acquired from local Indians six years before. By the end of 1837, Flanagan had brought his mother and other family members to his newly acquired property in Peoria County, where he built this house for himself and his family on a bluff overlooking Lake Peoria. He subsequently developed his property in East Bluff. As a Peoria alderman he used his influence to secure the construction of a canal to drain that section of the city. A steadfast Democrat, he supported Stephen A. Douglas in the latter's rise to political prominence in the state. Flanagan never married, believing that it was his duty to care for his invalid sister, Louise. Peoria's most prominent lawyer must have cut quite a figure as the city's most "ineligible" bachelor, known for his scrupulously neat appearance in a silk hat and a broadcloth Prince Albert.

§ Guided tours by appointment only (with three-day advance notice). Fee. Phone: 309-674-1921.

QUINCY

¶ George Rogers Clark Statue, Riverview Park, Chestnut and 2nd streets.

This statue of the famous Revolutionary War soldier was designed by *Charles Mulligan while he was the director of sculpture at the Art Institute of Chicago.

¶ John Wood Mansion, 425 South 12th Street.

Built in 1835 by Governor John Wood, this twelve-room frame house is the headquarters of the Historical Society of Quincy and Adams County.

Wood was born in New York in 1798, the grandson of Timothy Wood of Longford, Ireland, and the son of a surgeon and captain during the Revolutionary War. After heading west in 1818, he formed a partnership to raise livestock thirty miles southeast of what is now Quincy. He later bought land in this area and with the help of Irishmen Peter Flynn and James Moffatt erected a log cabin in present-day Quincy, the first white man's house in this part of the state.

Wood subsequently enjoyed a sixty-year career as the town's foremost leader, serving multiple terms as town trustee, alderman, and mayor and helping defeat a new state constitution that would have allowed settlers to bring their slaves into Illinois. From 1850 to 1854 he represented the district as a Whig in the state senate, and in 1856 he was elected lieutenant governor, succeeding to the governorship at the death of its incumbent three years later.

When a "peace convention" was held in Washington, D.C., in February 1861 in an effort to prevent the oncoming civil war, Wood was one of five delegates appointed by the governor. When war finally came, Wood

Statue of Governor John Wood in Washington Park.
(Photo courtesy of the Historical Society of Quincy and Adams County, Ill.)

was named quartermaster of the state and at age sixty-six was commissioned colonel of the 137th Illinois Volunteer Regiment. During General Nathan Forest's raid on Memphis, Wood commanded a brigade at the front.

§ Open June-August, daily 1-4; September-October and April-May, Saturday-Sunday 1-4; December, second, third, and fourth Sundays for candlelight tours. Closed November and January-March. Phone: 217-222-8212.

¶ **John Wood Burial Site**, Woodland Cemetery, South 5th Street.

¶ **John Wood Statue,** Washington Park.

This bronze statue of *John Wood, one of the founders of Quincy, was erected by the city and was unveiled on July 4, 1883.

SALEM

¶ **William J. Bryan Birthplace,** 408 South Broadway.

The "Great Commoner" – William Jennings Bryan – was born in this house in 1860 and lived here until he was nineteen, when he left to attend Illinois College in Jacksonville. Among the exhibits in the house are first editions of Bryan's books, his Spanish-American War uniform, and souvenirs of the 1896 Democratic Convention, at which he delivered his famous "Cross of Gold" speech.

Bryan's first Scotch-Irish ancestor in America was William Smith Bryan, who settled in the foothills of the Blue Ridge Mountains in Virginia in 1650. At a dinner hosted in honor of the "Great Commoner" by the mayor of Dublin in 1913, someone asked the famous American when he had dropped the "O" from his name. Bryan replied by asking the members of the audience whether they had ever heard of an O'Brian prior to the eleventh-century Irish king Brian Boru. When no one offered an answer, Bryan explained that "Bryan" had been the original name and that the "O" had been *added* by others, not eliminated by his ancestors.

As a youngster William Jennings Bryan had faced an unusual religious dilemma: whether to join his father's Baptist church or his mother's Methodist congregation. Although he compromised by attending one church on Sunday morning and the other in the afternoon, he was later converted to Presbyterianism. By his own account, however, this conversion was not the *metanoia* one would expect: "Having been brought up in a Christian home, conversion did not mean a change in my habits of life or habits of thought. I do not know of a virtue that came into my life as a result of my joining the Church because all the virtues had been taught me by my parents."

§ Open daily (except Tuesday) 1-5. Closed holidays. Phone: 618-548-

7791.

¶ William J. Bryan Memorial Park, north on State 37.

At the entrance to the park is a statue of *William Jennings Bryan by Gutzon Borglum.

SPRINGFIELD

¶ State Capitol, Capitol Street, between Spring and Second streets.

On the capitol grounds are the statues of five distinguished citizens of Illinois. The statue of Lincoln in front of a granite slab inscribed with his farewell speech to the people of Springfield is the work of *Andrew O'Connor and was unveiled in 1918. The statue of Pierre Menard, the state's first lieutenant governor, was designed by *John Mahoney.

At the entrance to the state house is a pair of allegorical works: *Justice and Power* and *Law and Knowledge*, both by *Charles Mulligan. Inside, the rotunda is adorned with statues of *Governor John Wood, Chicago mayor *Richard Daley, and *David E. Shanahan. The last politician was the son of an Irish emigrant and was a member of the Illinois House of Representatives from 1894 to 1936, the final sixteen years as Speaker.

Statue of Abraham Lincoln by Andrew O'Connor, on the grounds of the Illinois state capitol.

TAMPICO

℥ Ronald Reagan Birthplace, 111 South Main Street.

President Ronald Reagan was born in this apartment above a bakery on February 6, 1911. Nine years later his father, John ("Jack") Reagan, moved his family to Dixon, Illinois.

President Reagan's paternal line came from Ballyporeen, County Tipperary, Ireland. In 1847 his great-grandfather, Michael O'Regan, immigrated to London, where he married Catherine Mulcahy and adopted the present spelling of the family name. The couple moved to Canada with their sons in 1858 and later took up farming near Fairhaven, Illinois.

When Jack Reagan saw his son for the first time, he reputedly made the comment: "He looks like a fat little Dutchman. But who knows, he might grow up to be president some day." In his autobiography President Reagan explains that his parents had originally intended to name him "Donald" but ended up christening him "Ronald" after one of his aunts beat them to it by giving her son the name "Donald." Because Reagan never thought that "Ronald" was "rugged enough" for a boy's name, he asked people to call him "Dutch."

In 1984, when President Reagan visited Ballyporeen, he was shown his great-grandfather's 1829 baptismal record. He also hoisted a pint in a pub named after him and learned that he was distantly related to John F. Kennedy and Queen Elizabeth II. About his visit to his ancestral home, Reagan later wrote in his autobiography: "I had a flood of thoughts, not only about Michael Reagan, but about his son, my grandfather whom I had never met. I thought of Jack and his Irish stories and the drive he'd always had to get ahead; . . . What an incredible country we lived in, where the great-grandson of a poor immigrant from Ballyporeen could become president. I couldn't help but think that maybe Jack would have been proud that day."

℥ Tampico Historical Society, 119 South Main Street.

The society's museum features exhibits on local history and the life of *Ronald Reagan. The former president's birthday (February 6) is celebrated with an annual Open House.

§ Open April-October, Saturday-Sunday 1-4. Phone: 815-438-6175.

√ The Ronald Reagan Centre in Ballyporeen, County Tipperary, commemorates the birth in 1829 of the American president's great-grandfather in that small Irish community (1992 population: 319). The center, located eleven miles southwest of Caher, features videos, photographs, and other souvenirs of President Reagan's visit to Ballyporeen in 1984.

TROY GROVE

℥ "Wild Bill" Hickok State Monument, 1 block from U.S. 52.

Erected in 1929, this memorial commemorates the famous scout and lawman James Hickok, who was born here in 1837, the grandson of an Irish immigrant who had fought at Plattsburgh during the War of 1812.

Even as a youth "Wild Bill" Hickok was considered the best shot in this part of Illinois. At eighteen he headed for Kansas, where he joined the paramilitary forces intent upon bringing the territory into the Union as a free state and where he briefly served as a lawman. His first job as a stage-coach driver on the Santa Fe Trail was short lived, however, after he was attacked by a bear. Although he killed his attacker with a bowie knife, Hickok was injured so severely that he was not expected to recover. The young adventurer defied the odds, though, and recovered enough to work for the Overland Stage on the Oregon Trail. While in Nebraska in 1861, he was almost killed again, this time in a gunfight with the McCanles Gang.

With the outbreak of the Civil War, Hickok began his varied career as scout and lawman. During the war itself he served as a Union scout and was several times captured and sentenced to death as a spy but invariably escaped. After the hostilities he served as a scout and Indian fighter on the frontier for generals *Philip Sheridan, Winfield Scott Hancock, and George Custer. As deputy U.S. marshal at Fort Riley, Kansas, he was responsible for enforcing the law over a 200,000-square-mile territory. Although he killed many outlaws and recovered hundreds of stolen horses and mules, he never killed anyone except in self-defense or in the execution of his duties. His most famous act of self-defense occurred when he killed Phil Coe, the owner of a saloon and gambling house in Abilene, Kansas, where Hickok was the marshal. Although the lawman followed more peaceful pursuits for a while – touring with *William "Buffalo Bill" Cody and his troupe – he returned to the Wild West, this time to Deadwood City, North Dakota, where he was killed by Jack McCall. Hickok is buried in Mount Moriah Cemetery in Deadwood City [q.v., in *Irish America*, Volume 2].

WHEATON

¶ **Cantigny,** 3 miles west on Roosevelt Road (State 38) and then south on Winfield Road.

This 500-acre estate was formerly the property of *Colonel Robert McCormick, the editor and publisher of the *Chicago Tribune*. The property includes ten acres of formal gardens, wooded walks, and picnic facilities. Two museums are located on the property:

The First Division Museum honors U.S. military veterans, including those in the First Infantry Division (of which McCormick was a member during World War I). The museum allows visitors to experience walking through war-torn France and landing on Omaha Beach and includes an outdoor tank park.

The Robert R. McCormick Museum is the restored Georgian home of the colonel and his grandfather, an earlier owner of the *Tribune*.

§ Grounds open Tuesday-Sunday 9-dusk. Museums open Memorial Day-Labor Day, Tuesday-Sunday 10-5; February, Friday-Sunday 10-4; rest of the year (except January), Tuesday-Sunday 10-4. Closed January 1, Thanksgiving, and December 25. Parking fee. Phone: 630-668-5161.

INDIANA

BUTLERVILLE

¶ Hannah Milhous Plaque, on the south side of U.S. 50, on the east side of town.

This plaque was dedicated in 1971 by President Richard Milhous Nixon in honor of his mother, Hannah Milhous. The president's mother was a descendant of Thomas Milhous and his wife, Quakers who had come to America in 1729 from Carrickfergus, County Antrim, Ireland.

President Nixon's mother was born in 1855 on a farm near Butlerville, in a large frame house that was destroyed by fire in 1968. When Hannah Milhous was twelve years old, her family moved to Whittier, California, the Quaker colony where her son Richard was born in 1913. (See Richard Nixon Presidential Library and Birthplace, Yorba Linda, California, in *Irish America*, Volume 2.)

¶ Hopewell Cemetery, 1 mile past the Baptist Church at the west end of town.

This quaint cemetery is the final resting place of many members of the Milhous family, the maternal ancestors of *President Richard Nixon.

CONNERSVILLE

¶ John Conner Trading Post Site, indicated by a marker in front of the Moose Lodge on Eastern Avenue.

This town of about 18,000 residents grew up around the trading post established here in 1808 by John Conner. Conner's paternal grandfather was one of three brothers who had immigrated to America from County Meath, Ireland. His father, Richard Conner, was probably born in 1718 and lived in Maryland before moving to the Ohio territory. After marrying Margaret Boyer, a white woman who had grown up among the Shawnee, Richard Conner and his wife took up residence among the Christian Delaware Indians at one of the Moravian missions in Ohio. The Conners' children were born and grew up at these Indian settlements in Ohio and Michigan.

Sometime before 1800 John headed west for Indian country in what is now Indiana, where he established himself as a fur trader. During the War of 1812, he served as a guide and an interpreter for General William Henry Harrison. (Many years later Conner's granddaughter recounted how he once disguised himself as Chief Tecumseh at an Indian council. As Conner prepared and smoked a pipe and handed it to the nearest chief, however, another elder recognized the imposter and exclaimed, "You no Tecumseh – you big John Conner.") Following the incorporation of Connersville in

1813, Conner was its first sheriff and the owner of most of its first commercial ventures: a gristmill, a sawmill, a tavern, a general store, and a distillery. He also owned two farms and two town lots in Noblesville, Indiana. After his death these enterprises were maintained by his brother William.

CRAWFORDSVILLE

¶ **Ben Hur Museum,** Wallace Avenue and East Pike Street.
On the property is a bronze statue of the Civil War general Lew Wallace by *Andrew O'Connor, a replica of the artist's marble work in the rotunda of the U.S. Capitol.

It was here that Wallace wrote *Ben Hur* following his return in 1885 from Turkey, where he had served as U.S. minister. Wallace's career as lawyer, state senator, military leader, and scholar are traced through various memorabilia on display.

§ Open June-August, Wednesday-Saturday 10-4:30, Tuesday and Sunday 1-4:30. April-May and September-October, Tuesday-Sunday 1-4:30. Fee. Phone: 765-362-5769.

¶ **R. R. Donnelley and Sons Company,** John Sloan Street.
Since 1941 this factory in Crawfordsville has been the book manufacturing center of the nation's largest supplier of commercial printing services. This plant and another nearby handle the production of such world famous publications as *World Book Encyclopedia, World Book, The Holy Bible, Reader's Digest Books,* and *Time-Life Books.*

The history of Donnelley and Sons began with Richard R. Donnelley, a native of Ontario, Canada, whose parents had emigrated from northern Ireland. After serving an apprenticeship in the printing trade, the young Donnelley in 1857 accepted a managerial position with a New Orleans newspaper. Seven years later he became the managing partner of a printing firm in Chicago, which was subsequently purchased by a group of Chicago investors who hoped to create a publishing house capable of luring the western trade from the large eastern firms. The resulting merger was known as the Lakeside Publishing & Printing Co.
As the firm's new building neared completion in the Windy City, however, the structure and most of its equipment were destroyed in the Great Fire of 1871. Donnelley immediately became one of the most active leaders in the city's relief effort, obtaining permission from *General Philip Sheridan to share army rations with the city's dispossessed.

Donnelley was equally timely in finding quarters for a new printing office and headed for New York to obtain the needed heavy equipment. Upon his return he superintended the operation of his own fledgling concern while successfully reviving the Lakeside Company's fortunes, until in 1873 the two businesses were merged. The resulting giant went on to print twenty-three periodicals as well as telephone directories for various municipalities.

When Donnelley acquired complete control of the enterprise, he brought his sons into partnership with him, a move that resulted in the company's current name. By the time of his death in 1899, the family business had become the largest commercial printing and binding operation in the United States. The Lakeside Press, the company's corporate headquarters in Chicago, today prints such national magazines as *Fortune*, *Life*, and *Time*.

FISHERS

¶ **Conner Prairie Pioneer Settlement,** 4 miles south on Allisonville Road or 6 miles north of Indianapolis via I-465 exit 35.

Conner Prairie is a living-history museum that includes the Pioneer Adventure Area and Prairie Town, a reconstructed 1836 village. The oldest portion of the museum is the Conner House, a Federal-style brick residence built in 1823 by the fur trader *William Conner, whose brother had founded Connersville sometime before 1813. (See Connersville, Indiana.) Prairietown includes a schoolhouse, general store, and several workshops, while the Lily Theater presents an orientation film about the site.

William Conner had moved to this area in 1802 and constructed a log

The William Conner House. (Photo courtesy of Conner Prairie.)

cabin and trading post before marrying Mekinges, the daughter of a Delaware Indian chief. In 1818 he served as an interpreter for the negotiators of a treaty which removed Native Americans from the central part of the state to Missouri. The treaty had an unexpected effect upon Conner's marriage when his wife decided to accompany her people west, taking their six children with her.

Conner, who chose to remain in this area, later married Elizabeth Chapman, a white woman with whom he had ten more children. It was for her that he built the house on display today. He and his wife lived here until 1837, when they moved to a 150-acre farm nearer to Noblesville, a community which Conner had helped found fourteen years earlier. From there he oversaw the management of a general store, a sawmill, a gristmill, and 3,000 acres of land in four counties. He later served three terms in the state legislature.

§ Open April-November, Wednesday-Saturday 9:30-5, Sunday 11-5; also Tuesday 9:30-5 April-October. Closed Easter and Thanksgiving. Fee. Phone: 317-776-6000 or 800-966-1836.

FORT WAYNE

¶ **Anthony Wayne Monument,** on the northwest corner of Hayden Park, at Harmar Street and Maumee Avenue.

This heroic-size equestrian statue of *Anthony Wayne, the Revolutionary War general, was sculpted by *Charles Mulligan and was dedicated in 1918. Wayne established the first American fort in the area in 1794 after defeating the Miami Indians. (See Paoli, Pennsylvania.)

¶ **Historic Fort Wayne,** 211 South Barr Street.

This is a replica of the fort constructed in 1815-16 by Major John Whistler, a native of Ireland. The fort replaced an earlier one which had been saved from a siege by the Shawnee chief Tecumseh in 1812. For guidance in constructing the replica, historians and architects consulted Whistler's diagram of the fort. The four-acre site, which includes the Old Fort and the adjacent Frontier Village, features eleven wooden structures. Among those in the stockade are barracks, officers' quarters, and a hospital.

Whistler was born in northern Ireland about 1756 and as a youngster ran away from home to join the British army. During the American Revolution, he served under General John Burgoyne and was captured at the battle of Saratoga. After the war he returned to America and joined the U.S. army. In 1791 he was severely wounded in a campaign against the Indians. A dozen years later he and his infantry company were sent to the southern shore of Lake Michigan, where they constructed Fort Dearborn.

§ To verify whether the site is open, phone 219-424-3476.

INDIANAPOLIS

One of the city's ethnic enclaves was Irish Hill, a community that grew up near the Kingan and Company slaughterhouse, opened in 1862 by Samuel Kingan and Thomas Kingan, brothers from Belfast, Ireland. They were among the first to introduce mechanical refrigeration in the processing and preserving of meat on a large scale. So confident were Irish immigrants that they would find work at Kingan's that they addressed their steamer trunks to the packing plant and simply arrived there for work. The plant remained in the Kingan family until it was sold to the Hygrade Food Products Corporation in 1952.

¶ **Crown Hill Cemetery,** 700 West 38th Street.
  Among the well known figures buried here are *President Benjamin Harrison, three U.S. vice presidents, the gunman John Dillinger, and the poet James Whitcomb Riley (who mistakenly thought he was of Irish descent).

¶ **Benjamin Harrison House,** 1230 North Delaware Street, 1 mile north of Washington Street (U.S. 40).
  Except for his terms as a U.S. senator and as president of the United States, Benjamin Harrison lived in this house from 1874 until his death in 1901. The sixteen-room house contains his library, White House desk, hand-carved bed, and baby crib.
  Harrison's mother was descended from Captain Archibald Irwin, who was born in Ireland in 1772 and later settled in Franklin County, Pennsylvania. In addition, Harrison's maternal great-great-grandmother was Mary O'Caine. The future president came to Indianapolis in 1854 to practice law, a profession to which he returned after his defeat by *Grover Cleveland in the presidential race of 1892.
  § Guided tours February-December, Monday-Saturday 10-3:30, Sunday 12:30-3:30. Closed Good Friday, Easter, Memorial Day, Indianapolis 500 race day, Labor Day, Thanksgiving, and December 24-25. Phone: 317-631-1898.

¶ **Henry Lawton Statue,** Garfield Park, Raymond Street and Southern Avenue.
  This bronze statue of General Henry W. Lawton, a casualty of the Spanish-American War, was sculpted by Daniel Chester French and *Andrew O'Connor. The heroic figure was completed in Paris and depicts its subject carrying a shield.

¶ **State Capitol,** between Capitol Avenue, Washington Street, Senate Avenue, and Ohio Street.

The eight colossal marble allegorical figures in the rotunda were sculpted by *Alexander Doyle.

§ Open Monday-Friday 9-4. Phone: 317-233-5293.

LAFAYETTE

¶ **Fort Ouiatenon Historical Park,** South River Road.

This twenty-acre park on the Wabash River was created in the 1920s on what was thought to be the site of a French fort. (A replica of a French blockhouse marks the site.) From 1717 to 1760 the fort was an important fur-trading post inhabited by up to 2,000 people. The British later garrisoned the fort when Chief Pontiac unsuccessfully tried to force back white settlement after the French and Indian War. In 1765 Pontiac ended his war against the British in negotiations at the fort with George Croghan, Britain's Irish-born Indian agent. The chief symbolized his pacific intentions by hurling his tomahawk to the ground, a gesture that gave rise to the phrase "bury the hatchet."

After leaving his native Dublin, Ireland, Croghan had settled in western Pennsylvania in the 1740s and had begun to establish trading posts throughout the upper Ohio Valley. Because of his knowledge of the Iroquois and Delaware languages and customs, he was made deputy superintendent of Indian affairs by *Sir William Johnson, Britain's chief Indian agent in the region. Once, while trying to open up the Illinois country to white settlement, Croghan was attacked by Indians. He took the tomahawking he received in stride, however: "I got the stroke of a Hatchet on the Head, but my skull being pretty thick, the hatchet would not enter, so you may see a thick skull is of service on some occasions."

In 1764 Croghan was in London, seeking reimbursement for financial losses which he and other traders had experienced during the previous decade. Despite its amusing misspellings, the letter which he wrote from there to Johnson reflects its author's disillusionment with the English Establishment: "[T]he Cheefe Study of the pople in power hear att present is To Lay Heavy Taxes on the Coloneys and tis Talkt of Laying an Internal Tax on them Next Cesion of parlament. . . . The pople hear spend thire Time on Nothing Butt abuseing one aNother & Striving who Shall be in power with a view to Serve themselves and thire frends, and Neglect the publick. . . . [T]hey are all R-g-e-s (Rogues) aLike."

Like Johnson, Croghan was prominently involved in the formation of various land speculation companies. Early in his career he acquired and sold several thousand acres around Carlisle, Pennsylvania, before obtaining large tracts of land near Pittsburgh and another 250,000 acres in central New York. His most promising association appeared to be with the Grand Ohio Company, which hoped to establish Vandalia, south of the Ohio River, as the fourteenth British colony. The promise of his vast land holdings came to naught, however, with the outbreak of the Revolution, and he died in poverty.

• During the Feast of the Hunters' Moon in early October, the local residents reenact the historic gathering of traders, frontiersmen, soldiers, and Indians at the fort in the mid-eighteenth century.

§ Blockhouse open October and Memorial Day-Labor Day, Saturday-Sunday Fee. Phone: 765-476-8402.

LOWELL

¶ Buckley Homestead, 3606 Belshaw Road.

This 160-acre farm, settled by Dennis Buckley and his wife, Catherine, in 1849, has been turned into a living-history museum whose dozen buildings chronicle three periods of local Indiana history.

Having fled the Potato Famine in Ireland, the Buckleys and their four children moved to this area to be near their relatives, the Driscoll family. Despite the Buckleys' good fortune, Dennis died only two years after purchasing a seventy-nine-acre homestead. His eight-year-old son Patrick grew up to serve with the Indiana Volunteers during the Civil War, while his son John built the present house and raised grain and beef cattle.

§ Open May-October 30, grounds daily 7-dusk, buildings Saturday and Sunday 10-5 (weekdays by appointment). Fee. Phone: 219-696-0769.

MADISON

¶ Jeremiah Sullivan House, 304 West 2nd Street.

This two-story Federal-style house was built in 1818 by Jeremiah Sullivan, an early nineteenth-century justice of the Indiana Supreme Court.

Sullivan was the grandson of a distinguished Irish barrister and the son of an emigrant from Charleville, County Cork. Following his graduation from William and Mary College in Virginia, the future judge served as a captain in the War of 1812. After moving to Indiana, he became Madison's first lawyer, was elected to the state legislature, and joined the Presbyterian Church in town (although his mother was a Methodist and his father a Catholic). From 1837 to 1846 Sullivan was a justice of the state supreme court and enjoyed the distinction of suggesting the name "Indianapolis" for the state capital. Later in his life he recalled a conversation with his son, at that time a member of the state assembly: "Tommy sat with me an hour or two on Saturday night. He seems already to be disgusted with public life. He says he had seen more corruption and dishonesty during the last ten days of his life than he ever saw before. I think he has probably spoken the truth."

The elder Sullivan expressed a similar disillusionment in frequent letters, both to his son Algernon and to the Indianapolis *Republican Banner*.

The Federal-style residence of Jeremiah Sullivan.
(Photo courtesy of Historic Madison, Inc.)

After learning that Algernon had been seen attending the theater while a student in Cincinnati, Sullivan wrote to express his disappointment and sorrow and to remind his son of his Christian duty to live for the glory of God and to "use your scholarship for useful and noble purposes." As a Whig, the judge opposed the Mexican War and in mocking terms addressed the "democratic leaders who have been foisted into office by the cry of Texas glory": "The 'Halls of the Montezumas' are to be trodden by our victorious soldiery. Do not your gallant souls burn within you to be of the number who shall revel there? Or would you rather stay out of 'harm's way', and tread the Halls of the American Capitol?" After the surrender of Fort Sumter, Sullivan was more trenchant in denouncing the Southern rebels: "If ever a set of men deserved the character of thieves, murderers, and traitors, the leaders of this rebellion deserve it, and deserve the doom of thieves and traitors." Yet he saw in the growing conflict a Providential plan: "God has permitted this rebellion for wise and glorious purposes. Slavery will be destroyed, or the *system* greatly mitigated, and our country will come out of the conflict the most powerful nation on the globe." By April 1862 he was reporting to Algernon that the river towns of Indiana were being flooded with soldiers wounded at the battle of Shiloh. He

added that "A number of ladies met at our house a few days ago & made
. . . a large supply of shirts, drawers, pillow cases, mattrasses [*sic*], etc. etc.
for them."

§ Open May-October, Monday-Saturday 10-4:30, Sunday 1:15-4:30. Fee.
Phone: 812-265-2967.

NEW HARMONY

¶ **Workingmen's Institute,** 407 West Tavern Street.

When this building was constructed as a library in 1894, it was one of
a number of buildings that made up the Workingmen's Institute. That
educational enterprise had been founded in 1838 "to bring scientific and
all other useful knowledge within the reach of Manual and Mechanical
Laborers without the aid of professional men and teachers." Today this
building still serves as a public library, but it also maintains a historical
museum, an art gallery, and local archives.

That the library was ever built was due in large measure to the generosity of Dr. Edward Murphy, a successful New Harmony physician. Although born in Cork, Ireland, in 1813, he had been brought as a youngster
to Louisville, Kentucky, by a brutal man who claimed to be his uncle. After running away from his "guardian," the young Murphy came under
the tutelage of the New Harmony commune created in 1825 by Robert
Owen, the British philanthropist and social reformer. Here Murphy was
educated and unsuccessfully tried his hand at farming and haberdashery.
He subsequently attended medical school in Louisville but returned to
New Harmony to practice. From his medical practice and various investments, he acquired considerable wealth, a great portion of which he donated to the library and its art gallery. By the time of his death in 1900, he
had bequeathed not only books and Italian paintings but also $155,000.

§ Open Tuesday-Saturday 10-noon and 1-4:30. Closed major holidays.
Fee. Phone: 812-682-4806.

RICHMOND

¶ **Andrew F. Scott House,** 126 North 10th Street. Private.

This was the boyhood home of Francis MacNutt, the American diplomat, papal courtier, and author who was born here in 1863 of Scotch-Irish
ancestry.

Despite his Episcopalian upbringing and attendance at such WASP
bastions as Phillips Exeter Academy and Harvard Law School, MacNutt
converted to Roman Catholicism at the age of twenty and subsequently
announced his intention to seek ordination. While studying at the Pontifical Academy of Noble Ecclesiastics in Rome, however, he discontinued
his preparation for the priesthood and took up a diplomatic career. He

first served with the U.S. legations in Constantinople and Madrid and then with the court of Pope Leo XIII, thereby becoming the first American to hold such a position in the papal government. After ten years at the Vatican, he resigned in 1905 and spent the rest of his life at his home in the Tyrol. Of his seven books, *Letters of Cortes* and *Bartholomew de las Casas* are of particular interest to American historians. Two other works are auto-biographical – *Six Decades of My Life* and *A Papal Chamberlain*.

In 1904 MacNutt accompanied the papal legate to Ireland, on what he thought was probably the first visit to the Emerald Island by a papal rep-resentative since the time of Queen Mary Tudor in the sixteenth century. At Kingstown, when the legate prepared to impart a papal blessing to the huge crowds that had gathered at the harbor, a local clergyman with the papal entourage exclaimed, "But more than half of these people are Prot-estants! You can't give the Apostolic Blessing to Protestants – not in Ire-land!" At the clergyman's urging, the legate instead announced that he would remember the crowd in his prayers. On another occasion on that trip, MacNutt went with the legate to an evening of entertainment spon-sored by a local Gaelic language society – complete with men in kilts, women playing harps, and all singing Gaelic songs. "While this was go-ing on," MacNutt later wrote, "I told the Legate he must make a short speech and end it by shouting at the top of his lungs *Erin go bragh!* He got the three words by heart, and when he trumpeted them forth I really thought the roof would fall in on us" from the sound of the ovation he received.

RUSHVILLE

¶ **William Laughlin Monument,** County Courthouse, Main and 1st Street.

The outdoor monument on the north side of the courthouse honors Dr. William Laughlin, a man of many talents who donated the land on which Rushville is located.

Laughlin, who was born in Pennsylvania in 1778 (most likely to Irish parents), studied medicine, law, and surveying at Jefferson College in Phila-delphia. After coming to Indiana in 1816, he first taught school but then began to practice medicine and accepted a position as a government sur-veyor. Before long he had also opened a law practice and in 1818 was elected to the state legislature.

After surveying Rush County – which he named for Benjamin Rush, his college mentor and the famous signer of the Declaration of Independ-ence – Laughlin purchased land where Rushville would soon be founded. His donation of seventy-five acres became the site of the new county seat, which the commissioners named Rushville. Laughlin eventually estab-lished the town's first school, was its first teacher, and built its first water-powered grist mill.

The mill, however, proved to be Laughlin's undoing. In 1823, when Rushville was ravaged by malaria, the citizens believed that the disease had been caused by the stagnant water above Laughlin's mill dam. An enraged mob soon destroyed the mill, an act of destruction for which later citizens of Rushville hoped to atone by erecting the memorial in front of the courthouse.

SOUTH BEND

¶ **City Cemetery,** Elm Street and Colfax Avenue.

James and Mary McKinley, the grandparents of *President William McKinley, are buried here.

¶ **University of Notre Dame,** Notre Dame Avenue.

Although the Notre Dame football team is today known as "the Fighting Irish," in earlier times it was called "Catholics" and "Hoosiers." (Its opponents used derogatory terms like "Dirty Irish," "Papists," and "Damn Micks.") One of the first references to the nickname "Fighting Irish" occurred in a sports article in 1909, although the name did not become universally established until the end of the 1920s. To the charge that the nickname was inappropriate because so many of the university's students were not of Irish descent, the team's Norwegian-born coach, Knute Rockne, said, "They all have the Irish spirit, and that's what counts." (In point of fact, about 50 percent of the football players who received varsity letters from Rockne had Irish surnames.)

In 1914 the university was presented with the sword of *General Thomas Francis Meagher, at one time the commander of the Irish Brigade during the Civil War. Notre Dame's collection also includes a green flag of the Irish Brigade and the sword of *General James Shields, a hero of both the Mexican War and the Civil War.

• Corby Hall was named for *Father William Corby, the Civil War chaplain of the Irish Brigade. In front of this residence hall is a bronze statue of the former Notre Dame instructor as he gave general absolution to the soldiers at Gettysburg. This statue was dedicated in 1911 and is a copy of the original on the Gettysburg battlefield. Both works were done by the sculptor *Samuel Aloysius Murray. (Although the statue depicts Corby with his right hand raised in benediction, irreverent students at Notre Dame claimed that the priest was trying to catch a football and nicknamed the statue "Fair Catch Corby.")

• An 1890 painting of Father Corby – *Absolution Under Fire* – is located in the Snite Museum of Art on the campus. The large canvas by Paul Henry Wood, a Notre Dame student, depicts the famous scene at Gettysburg and portrays Wood as the young Zouave drummer standing nearest the priest.

Wood's promising artistic career was cut short, however, when he was killed in a fire that swept through his family's apartment in Chicago only weeks after he had completed the painting. Saddened by the death of the nineteen-year-old student, Corby traveled to Chicago to preside at the young artist's funeral.

William Corby was born in 1833 in Detroit, where his father, Daniel Corby of King's County, Ireland, had settled. When he was twenty years old, the young Corby entered the University of Notre Dame and within a year had joined the Congregation of the Holy Cross, the teaching religious order which administered the university. After his ordination he combined pastoral work with his duties as a professor and the director of the Manual Labor School at the university. When the Civil War began, Corby was commissioned chaplain of the 88th New York Infantry, one of the many Celtic units in the Irish Brigade. After the war Corby returned to Notre Dame, first assuming administrative duties there and then serving as provincial general of the Holy Cross Congregation in the United States. During his tenure at the university, he oversaw an ambitious building program, the broadening of academic offerings, and the establishment of a law school.

The sculptor Samuel Murray, meanwhile, was the son of immigrants from Cork, Ireland. He most likely learned the art of sculpting from his father, who was a stonemason. After studying art under Thomas Eakins, the young man became the famous artist's assistant and subsequently spent a half century at the Moore Institute of Arts, Sciences and Industry in Philadelphia, teaching anatomy and modeling from life. In 1894 his entry in the Philadelphia Art Club exhibition earned him a gold medal, while ten years later he was awarded a silver medal at the Louisiana Purchase Exposition in Chicago. Besides his statues of Father Corby, Murray is best known for his statue of *John Barry in front of Independence Hall in Philadelphia and the Bishop Shanahan Memorial in St. Patrick's Cathedral in Harrisburg, Pennsylvania. Murray was a member of the Friendly Sons of St. Patrick in Philadelphia.

• The Theodore M. Hesburgh Library (at the center of the east campus quadrangle) commemorates the most well-known of the university's modern presidents. The facility holds more than two million volumes and can accommodate more than half the student body.

Hesburgh, who claimed Irish descent through his mother (Anne Marie Murphy), joined the Congregation of the Holy Cross in 1934 and completed some of his undergraduate work at Notre Dame. He later received a bachelor's degree in philosophy from the Gregorian University in Rome and – two years after his ordination in 1943 – a doctorate in theology from Catholic University of America. For two years he served as chair of the religion department at Notre Dame until his appointment as executive vice president of the university in 1949. Three years later as president he undertook a campaign that resulted in improved academic standards, substantial faculty raises, and growth in the university's enrollment, endowment, and physical plant. For a time he was the Vatican representative to the International Atomic Energy Agency, and in 1970 he was appointed by *President Richard Nixon to head the U.S. Commission on Civil Rights. During his long academic career he authored several books, among them *Theology of Catholic Action, Patterns for Lifelong Learning,* and *The Challenge and Promise of a Catholic University.*

• O'Shaughnessy Hall is named for Ignatius Aloysius O'Shaughnessy, an oil company executive who donated $200,000 to the university for the creation of a fine arts foundation. The hall houses the College of Arts and Letters as well as the university's art gallery. (See O'Shaughnessy Plaza and Auditorium, St. Paul, Minnesota.)

VINCENNES

¶ **Fort Knox II,** 3 miles north on Fort Knox Road, off State 41.

Named for *General Henry Knox, George Washington's secretary of war, the original fort on this site was constructed in 1802 and served as a military outpost until 1813. The outline of the excavated fort is marked. Fort Knox was the second of three military garrisons on the Wabash River built to discourage Indian attacks against the American settlers in the region.

§ Open daily 9-5. Phone: 812-882-7472.

ZIONSVILLE

¶ **Patrick H. Sullivan Foundation Museum,** 1 block west of State 334 at 225 West Hawthorne Street.

This museum, which houses historical displays and a genealogical library, was established through the generosity of Iva Etta Sullivan, a local librarian and teacher, in honor of her great-grandfather, Patrick Henry Sullivan.

Patrick Sullivan, a native-born Virginian of Irish descent, arrived in this part of Indiana in 1824, thereby becoming the first white settler in Boone County. He later served as a county commissioner and was the father of seventeen children. Sullivan and his second wife are buried in the old Sheets graveyard, a mile southeast of Zionsville.

§ Open Tuesday-Saturday 10-4. Closed major holidays and December 25 to early January. Phone: 317-873-4900.

¶ **Patrick H. Sullivan Memorial,** on the lawn of the Hussey Library, 250 North 5th Street.

MAINE

AUGUSTA

¶ **Blaine House National Historic Landmark,** at Capitol and State streets.

From 1862 to 1893 this large Federal-style house was the residence of James G. Blaine, who served as speaker of the House of Representatives, U.S. senator, and secretary of state under presidents Garfield and Harrison. Blaine's descendants gave the house to Maine in 1919 for use as the state's executive mansion. Besides period furnishings and an art collection, the house features Blaine's restored study.

Blaine's first American ancestor was James Blaine, who had emigrated from Londonderry, northern Ireland, in 1745 and settled near Lancaster, Pennsylvania. The later Blaine was the son of Maria Louise Gillespie (an Irish Catholic) and Ephraim Lynn Blaine (a Scotch-Irish Presbyterian).

Blaine's nomination for president in 1884 by the Republican Party caused the Democrats to fear the loss of their traditional Irish allies. The Republicans first played up their candidate's roots – his Irish Catholic mother and his Irish-American cousin (Sister Angela Gillespie, a famous Civil War nurse). Blaine himself did his part, paying tribute to "the ancient faith in which my mother lived and died" and referring to Sister Angela as literally his sister. The Grand Old Party also reminded Irish voters about Blaine's generally aggressive stance toward Great Britain

The former Blaine House, now the state executive mansion.

while serving as secretary of state. In Boston, meanwhile, the Irish Land League claimed that if Blaine was elected "Ireland would be free in thirty days." And in New York a huge rally for Blaine opened with an acknowledgment of the event's historic nature: "To think of thousands of Irish Democrats assembled together to endorse the nomination of the Republican Party."

Blaine's chances of winning the Irish vote *en bloc* disappeared, however, because of a famous slur and the withering attacks of the Irish-American press. The *Irish American* labeled the Republican "the tattooed candidate, who is charged with being a renegade to the faith of his mother, and whose whole political record is a foul blot on the reputation of the Irish race for honor and probity." The paper also reminded the voters of the Republican Party's "unvarying anti-Irish proclivities." Meanwhile, while making a pro-Blaine statement, the Reverend Samuel Burchard let slip an unfortunate allusion to the Democratic Party's historical connection with saloonkeepers, Catholic immigrants, and secessionists: "We are Republicans, and don't propose to leave our party, and identify ourselves with the party whose antecedents have been RUM, ROMANISM, AND REBELLION."

§ Open Tuesday-Thursday 2-4 (unless engaged for official business). Phone: 207-287-2121.

¶ *Lady Wisdom,* State Capitol, State and Capitol streets.

The idealized statue of "Lady Wisdom" atop the dome of the state capitol was a gift of its sculptor, William Clark Noble. The twenty-foot-high copper repoussé work depicts a female figure holding a pine torch, the symbol of Maine, in her upraised right arm.

Noble, who was born in Gardiner, Maine, in 1858, was descended from an Irishman who had served as a British officer at Louisbourg, Nova Scotia, in 1744. Influenced by a biography of the Danish sculptor Thorwaldsen which he had read at age eight, Noble decided upon a career as a sculptor. To earn money to pay for art school, he became a prize fighter, boxing under the unlikely name "The Art Student" and saving $28,000 from a year's worth of prize money. After completing an apprenticeship in Boston, he began to do wax and clay modeling and decorative carvings in wood, stone, and plaster. Armed with this experience, he launched his career in Newport, Rhode Island, with commissions for interior carving and decoration.

Noble is known primarily as a sculptor, although he was also a painter of some note. Among his sculpted works are portrait busts of *William Cody, David Lloyd George, Alexander Hamilton, Nathaniel Hawthorne, Henry Cabot Lodge, Henry W. Longfellow, *John McCullough, Harriet Beecher Stowe, and *Theodore Roosevelt, and portrait reliefs of Edward Everett Hale, John Philip Sousa, and General Joseph Wheeler. His larger works include statues of *Governor Andrew Curtin (Bellefonte, Pa.); Robert Burns (Providence, R.I.); William Channing (Newport, R.I.); Bishop Phillips Brooks (New York City); Pius X, Leo XIII, and Benedict XV (the Vatican); and Thomas Jefferson, Napoleon, and *Anthony Wayne for the 1904 St. Louis Exposition.

Noble's most ambitious work, however, never came to fruition, although it brought him to financial ruin and physical collapse. For more than forty years, he had created models of a gigantic memorial to American womanhood which he hoped would be erected in the nation's capital. Envisioned as a stone monument standing 297 feet high, adorned with bronze statuary, and standing on a 300-foot oval base, the $20 million project aroused the interest of Daisy Calhoun of the Women's Universal Alliance. After working on the project for two more years and receiving only $2,000 for his efforts, Noble severed his relationship with Calhoun and attempted to obtain full compensation for his work. Instead, he ended up defending himself against Calhoun's charge of blackmail. A newspaper account described a sidelight of the resulting legal battle: "Noble had the court in gales of laughter as he mimicked Mrs. Calhoun. She wanted the model changed 'about every other day,' he said. She wanted the statues of the Arts, Science and Literature swept off the summit of the memorial, and a fifty-foot statue of herself put there, sitting on a throne, 'looking down on the poor mothers of the world.'" Although the judge dismissed the case against him, Noble was never compensated and his health was fatally ruined by the ordeal.

BANGOR

¶ St. John's Catholic Church, York Street.

This brick Gothic revival structure was designed by *Patrick Keely and was built in 1855 to serve the town's Irish community. The funds to construct the church came principally from James O'Donahue and Timothy Field, two Irishmen who had lived in Bangor before making their fortune in the California gold fields.

BELFAST

Founded in 1770, this town was named for Belfast, Ireland, by Protestant Scotch-Irish settlers who had earlier established Londonderry, New Hampshire. James Miller, a member of the group which had moved to the new site, insisted that it be named for Belfast, the place of his birth. When a dispute with the other colonists ensued, the question was decided by the toss of a coin.

DAMARISCOTTA

℧ **Matthew Cottrill House,** Main Street Historic District. Private.

This private residence is named for Matthew Cottrill, the Irish immigrant who built it after becoming one of the town's most prominent merchants. The 1802 Federal-style house was designed by Nicholas Codd, another Irishman.

Cottrill had settled in Damariscotta about 1791 and with fellow Irishman James Kavanagh had become a successful shipbuilder and exporter of lumber to the West Indies. When Father John Cheverus visited the area about 1797, he preached in one of Cottrill's barns and celebrated mass in his house. Kavanagh later fitted up one of his stores as a place of worship for the Irish Catholics in the area until a church was constructed in 1803.

Cheverus mentioned the two Irish merchants in a letter to *Bishop John Carroll in 1801, at the same time mentioning one of the disabilities that still afflicted Catholics in Puritan New England. "Last Thursday," he wrote, ". . . the judges gave us here a little specimen of their good will toward the Catholic religion and its ministers. Mr. Kavanagh, a respectable merchant, living at Newcastle [Maine], has fitted up at his own expense a small neat chapel where I officiated last year for better than three months. Moreover, the same gentleman with his partner, Matthew Cottrill, has subscribed $1000 for our new church. He thought in consequence he would be free from paying taxes to the Congregational minister of his township, but the judges of the Supreme Court now sitting in Boston declared unanimously that he must pay for the support of the said minister, [for the Massachusetts] Constitution, said they, obliged every one to contribute for the support of Protestant ministers and them alone."

GARDINER

℧ **"For Humanity" Memorial,** South Gardiner Congregational Church.

This memorial tablet to the twenty-five men of Gardiner who served in World War I was a gift of its creator, *William Clark Noble. The artist was born in Gardiner in 1858. (See *Lady Wisdom*, Augusta, Maine.)

The tablet depicts the battlefield scene of a dying soldier and a Red Cross nurse crouched beside an artillery piece. The young soldier clutches the robe of the Crucified Christ, whose image watches over the pair. Dedicated in 1923, the tablet compares the sacrifice of those who served during the war to that of Christ, who offered himself up "for humanity."

℧ **William Clark Noble Burial Site,** Mt. Hope Cemetery, Mt. Hope Cemetery River Road.

Despite his illustrious career, *William Clark Noble died a pauper and was buried in an unmarked grave. In 1983, however, a granite headstone with bronze lettering was erected over the burial site.

KENNEBUNKPORT

¶ **George Bush Home,** Walker's Point. Private.

Located on a jetty named for the former president's grandfather, this family compound is the summer home of the Bush extended family. Although George Bush's ancestry was overwhelmingly English, patrilineal fourth-, fifth-, and sixth-great-grandfathers of his were from Rathfriland, County Down, Ireland. (They bore the surname Holliday.) Another sixth-great-grandfather – William Shannon – was born in Cork about 1730 and died in Mercersburg, Pennsylvania, in 1784.

KITTERY

¶ **Fort McClary,** 2 miles east on State 103.

The original eighteenth-century fortification here was named Fort William. Considered impregnable during the Revolution, the fort was spared a British attack and was renamed Fort McClary for *Major Andrew Clary, who had fought valiantly at the battle of Bunker Hill on June 17, 1775. (See Bunker Hill Monument, Boston, Massachusetts.)

Fort McClary was garrisoned during every American military action prior to World War II. Today the fort's hexagonal wooden blockhouse, probably built in the 1840s, surmounts a cut-granite first story. Visitors can see the powder magazines, the rifleman's house, various perimeter walls, and the foundations of the original barracks.

§ Open Memorial Day-September 30, daily 9-dusk. Fee. Phone: 207-384-5160.

MACHIAS

¶ **Burnham Tavern Museum,** Main and Free streets.

In this gambrel-roofed structure Captain Jeremiah O'Brien and other local patriots gathered in June 1775 to plan the capture of the British schooner *Margaretta*. The Americans who were wounded in the battle were brought here for treatment. The museum displays photographs, paintings, and Civil War relics.

In 1770 O'Brien and his Dublin-born father had been among a group of settlers who were granted land in Machias on condition "that they build a suitable meeting house for the public worship of God and settle a learned Protestant minister and make provision for his comfortable and honorable support."

§ Open mid June-Labor Day, Monday-Friday 9-5; rest of the year, by appointment. Fee. Phone: 207-255-4432.

MACHIASPORT

¶ **Fort O'Brien,** overlooking the Machias River.

The first fortification on this site was called Fort Machias and was built soon after the beginning of the Revolution. When the fort was destroyed by the British in 1814, the site remained unfortified until the construction of Fort O'Brien in 1863. Its remaining earthworks are part of a state historic park. The fort was named for *Jeremiah O'Brien, the local hero who captured a British schooner off the coast in 1775.

§ Open daily dawn-dusk Memorial Day-

¶ **Gates House,** on State 92.

This Federal-style house displays models of the British schooner *Margaretta* and the sloop *Unity*, both of which were captured by *Jeremiah O'Brien and his brothers in the first naval encounter of the Revolutionary War. The house has a marine and genealogical library.

In June 1775 the H.M.S *Margaretta* arrived off Machiasport with two sloops to take on lumber for the British barracks in Boston. Tempers flared when Captain Moore of the 100-ton British ship refused to heed O'Brien's warning to abandon his mission. Moore raised the ante by ordering the colonials to remove the Liberty Pole which they had erected in town only a month before. When O'Brien's brother John challenged the order, Moore repeated his demand that "That liberty pole must come down or it will be my painful duty to fire upon the town." In response, a heavily armed band of forty colonials – including Jeremiah and his five younger brothers – leaped aboard the eighty-ton *Unity* and seized it. After provisioning the captured sloop with twenty shotguns, a small cannon, hay forks, and axes, the colonials gave chase to the *Margaretta*. When O'Brien ordered Moore to surrender, the British commander opened fire, killing two of the American crew. The Irishman then maneuvered his ship next to the *Margaretta* and lashed the two together, thereby making it easier to subdue the British crew. After outfitting the *Unity* with the *Margaretta*'s guns, O'Brien rechristened her *Machias Liberty*, the first American armed cruiser of the Revolutionary War. This engagement prompted the Continental Congress to create an American navy.

In subsequent years Jeremiah O'Brien's name was further immortalized by the U.S. Navy. In 1900 the torpedo boat destroyer *O'Brien* was launched at Elizabethport, New Jersey, becoming the first American vessel to be christened with an Irish name. During World War II the *Jeremiah O'Brien* was one of almost 3,000 Liberty ships built in response to the massive German sinking of Allied shipping. The *Jeremiah O'Brien* is the last surviving Liberty ship and is berthed in San Francisco, where it serves as the National Liberty Ship Memorial. (See San Francisco, in *Irish America*, Volume 2.)

§ Open mid June to mid September, Monday-Friday 12:30-4:30; rest of the year, by appointment. Fee. Phone: 207-255-8461.

NEWCASTLE

¶ James Kavanagh House, Pond Road, across from the rectory of St. Patrick's Church. Private.

This two-story Federal-style house was built in 1803 by *Nicholas Codd for James Kavanagh, a wealthy merchant and fellow Irishman. Kavanagh had earlier fitted up one of his stores as a place of worship for the Irish Catholics in the area until a church was constructed.

Bishop Cheverus mentioned Kavanagh and his Irish business partner, Matthew Cottrill, in a letter to *Bishop John Carroll in 1801, at the same time mentioning one of the disabilities that still afflicted Catholics in Puritan New England. "Last Thursday," he wrote, ". . . the judges gave us here a little specimen of their good will toward the Catholic religion and its ministers. Mr. Kavanagh, a respectable merchant, living at Newcastle [Maine], has fitted up at his own expense a small neat chapel where I officiated last year for better than three months. Moreover, the same gentleman with his partner, Matthew Cottrill, has subscribed $1000 for our new church. He thought in consequence he would be free from paying taxes to the Congregational minister of his township, but the judges of the Supreme Court now sitting in Boston declared unanimously that he must pay for the support of the said minister, [for the Massachusetts] Constitution, said they, obliged every one to contribute for the support of Protestant ministers and them alone."

¶ St. Patrick's Catholic Church, 2.5 miles north of U.S. 1 on State 215.

This oldest remaining Catholic house of worship in New England was constructed in 1803 and was dedicated five years later. It was built from a design by Nicholas Codd, who reputedly was shanghaied from Ireland expressly for the purpose. St. Patrick's is also the only Catholic church in New England to possess a bell cast by Paul Revere. A gift of *Matthew Cottrill, the bell is one of the ninety-three Revere bells which remain of the original 400.

One of the tombstones in the churchyard is that of Edward Kavanagh, whose Irish-born father was an early benefactor of the church. The son attended Collège de Montréal, Georgetown College in the District of Columbia, and St. Mary's College in Baltimore. Following the ruin of his father's business during the War of 1812, the son abandoned plans to enter the Catholic priesthood in order to revive the family mercantile and shipbuilding enterprise. He subsequently entered state politics and was the first Irish Catholic elected to a New England state legislature, the first elected to Congress from New England, and the first to be a New England governor.

§ Open daily 8-dusk. Phone: 207-563-3240.

*St. Patrick's, the
oldest Catholic church
in New England.*

NORTH WHITEFIELD

¶ St. Denis Catholic Church, State 218.

Built in 1833 to serve the Irish immigrants who had settled in this area in the early nineteenth century, this is the second oldest Catholic church in Maine and one of the oldest in New England. The earliest Irish arrivals were fishermen from Newfoundland who settled on farms in Whitefield.

PROSPECT

¶ Fort Knox State Historic Park, east on State 174 from Prospect or north from U.S. 1 west of the Waldo-Hancock Bridge over the Penobscot River.

The first of Maine's granite forts was begun during the Aroostook War, a series of disputes with Great Britain in the 1840s over the Maine-New Brunswick boundary. The fortification – in the shape of a pentagon – measures 350 by 250 feet and was named for *Henry Knox, the famous hero of the American Revolution. The fort was used as a troop training site during the Civil War and the Spanish-American War. Visitors can see original cannon, hot-shot furnaces, soldiers' quarters, powder magazines, and parade grounds. (See Boston Athenaeum, Boston, Massachusetts.)

§ Open May-October, daily 9-dusk. Fee. Phone: 207-469-7719.

THOMASTON

¶ Montpelier-The General Henry Knox Museum, High Street (State 131), near the junction with U.S. 1.

This mansion is a reconstruction of the 1795 home to which *Henry Knox retired after serving as President Washington's first secretary of war. The eighteen-room Federal-style house was designed by Boston architect Charles Bullfinch, who complied with Knox's request by incorporating such features as a flying staircase, clerestory windows, and an oval parlor.

§ Open Memorial Day-mid October, Tuesday-Saturday 10-4, Sunday 1-4. Fee. Phone: 207-354-8062 or 273-3699.

A reconstruction of "Montpelier," the 1795 home to which Henry Knox retired after serving as the first U.S. secretary of war.

YORK

¶ McIntire-Garrison House, State 91. Private.

According to local tradition, the Irish schoolmaster John Sullivan lived and worked on the McIntire farm when he first arrived in York in 1723. Sullivan's son John was the famous Revolutionary War general.

The elder Sullivan had been born in Limerick in 1691, during the siege of the city by King William. Following the Protestant victory, the young Sullivan accompanied his parents into exile in France, where he received the education that would later serve him so well in America. After returning to Ireland, however, John and his mother had a falling out over his choice of a wife. When the mother forbade the marriage, the thirty-two-year-old son decided to emigrate.

In 1723, therefore, Sullivan sailed for New England. While aboard ship, he made the acquaintance of Margery Browne, a girl of nine or ten years of age from Cork. Not until a dozen years later, however, were the two married. Tradition maintains that, when Margery was on her way to America, someone asked her what she was going to do there. "Raise governors for them," she allegedly replied, a prediction that bore fruit when her sons James and John became the respective governors of Massachusetts and New Hampshire.

After working for a while on the McIntire farm, the elder John Sullivan so impressed the local minister with his skill in seven languages that the pastor loaned him the money to cancel his passage debt and to open a school. Sullivan lived to the age of 105 and was buried in the Sullivan family plot in Durham, New Hampshire [q.v.].

MARYLAND

ADELINE

¶ **Taney Place,** 5 miles south on State 508. Private.

Built about 1750, this two-story house was where Roger Taney, the famous chief justice of the U.S. Supreme Court, was born in 1777. He was descended from Michael Taney, an indentured servant who was probably Irish and who had arrived in America in 1660.

In 1819 the house was the site of a quarrel between Michael Taney V and John Magruder over a woman. After Magruder slapped the thirty-five-year-old Taney, the master of the estate stabbed his assailant through the heart and fled into Virginia. When Taney died, his body was returned to Maryland for burial, but as the body lay in the coffin awaiting interment one of the Magruders smashed the corpse's face with a stone.

ANNAPOLIS

¶ **Charles Carroll Mansion,** Duke of Gloucester Street.

This three-and-a-half-story gabled house was the birthplace in 1737 of Charles Carroll of Carrollton, the only Catholic signer of the Declaration of Independence. Here he was married, lived during the Revolution, and entertained George Washington. Because Maryland law forbade public Catholic worship, local Catholics attended mass in the mansion's private family chapel. Nearby is St. Mary's Church, built on property deeded to the parish by Carroll's granddaughters.

Carroll was descended from a long-established Catholic family in King's County, Ireland, that traced its ancestry to that country's ancient Celtic kings. The family's first American ancestor was an earlier Charles Carroll, a friend of Lord Baltimore's who came to Maryland in 1688.

Charles Carroll of Carrollton received his early schooling at Bohemia Academy, a school in Warwick, Maryland, operated by Jesuit priests. After six years at a Jesuit institution in St. Omer, France, he spent another six years in collegiate-level studies in Rheims, Bourges, and Paris. He completed his formal education by studying law in London, although he knew that he would be ineligible for public office in Maryland because of restrictions against Catholics.

As relations between the British government and the Maryland colonists deteriorated, however, Carroll was able to play an increasingly influential role. He actively opposed the Stamp Act in 1765 and used the pseudonym "Second Citizen" in a series of newspaper articles attacking the arbitrary imposition of fees by the colonial governor. In 1774 he helped avert violence by a mob determined to prevent the unloading of tea from a brig that had arrived in Annapolis. (The ship's owner followed Carroll's advice to burn the vessel and its hated cargo.) The famous Irish-American was also elected to the extralegal Maryland convention.

Beginning in 1776, Carroll was at the center of the revolutionary struggle. He was one of several delegates appointed by the Continental Congress to persuade the Canadians to join the American colonies in their struggle against Britain. Although Congress hoped that Carroll and his cousin, the Jesuit priest John Carroll, could influence the Catholic French-Canadians to join the revolution, the embassy failed for at least two reasons. The Catholics of Quebec were traditionally hostile to their predominantly Protestant neighbors to the south, and the American invasion of Canada just months before seemed to justify the French-Canadians' suspicions. Carroll was more successful, however, in persuading the Maryland convention to instruct its delegates to the Continental Congress to vote for independence.

Carroll himself was appointed to the Continental Congress on July 4, 1776. Although unable to attend the historic vote on that date, he was among the delegates who signed the Declaration of Independence the following August. By committing treason against the British, Carroll placed his considerable wealth in jeopardy, of course. When he took up the pen to sign the famous document, one of the other delegates alluded to the precarious nature of Carroll's fortune by reportedly saying, "There goes a few millions!"

After the war Carroll continued to be an important political figure in the new nation. As a member of Maryland's first state legislature, he helped draft the state constitution and its bill of rights and opposed the confiscation of British property in the state. Although elected to the Constitutional Convention in 1789, he declined to serve. For his efforts to obtain Maryland's ratification of the completed Constitution, he was elected one of the state's first U.S. senators. A statue of him is part of the National Statuary Hall Collection in the U.S. Capitol Building [q.v.].

¶ **Roger Taney Statue,** State House, State Circle.
A seated statue of *Roger Taney, chief justice of the U.S. Supreme Court from 1836 to 1864, is located in front of the State House, the oldest in continuous use in the nation.

¶ **St. Anne's Church,** Church Circle.
Built in 1859, this is the third church on this site since the parish was founded in 1692. In the churchyard are the graves of Thomas Lynch and Charles Carroll "Barrister."

• Thomas Lynch was the grandson of the family's first American ancestor, Jonack Lynch, a native of Ireland who had come to South Carolina soon after the first settlement of that colony about 1670. From his father, Thomas Lynch inherited extensive tracts of land and early became a spokesman for colonial rights against the British Parliament and the Crown. While attending the Continental Congress, he was described by another delegate as a man who "wears the manufacture of this country, is plain, sensible, above ceremony, and carries with him more force in his very appearance than most powdered folks in their conversation. He wears his hair strait, his clothes in the plainest order, and is highly esteemed." His son was one of the Irish-American signers of the Declaration of Independence.

• Charles Carroll "Barrister" was a member of Maryland's most prominent Irish Catholic family. He is memorialized on a plaque in the church: "In Grateful Memory of Charles Carroll, Barrister. Vestryman of St. Anne's Church. Born at Annapolis the 22nd of March 1723. Died the 23 of March 1783 at his home Mount Clare. Patriot and Leader in the Cause of America's independence. Eminent Jurist and Churchman. President of the Convention of 1776 Which gave the State of Maryland its Bill of Rights and First Constitution. Honored by his Country for his outstanding Talents and Virtues. He lived to see the Attainment of his High Endeavors. He died Respected and Beloved."

§ Open daily 8-6.

¶ **St. John's College,** King George Street.

• The Carroll-Barrister House on campus was the birthplace of *Charles Carroll, nicknamed "Barrister" to distinguish him from his father, Charles, a surgeon. This 1722 structure is now used as an administration building.

• McDowell Hall was named about 1860 for John McDowell, who served as president of St. John's College for the first sixteen years of its existence.

McDowell was the grandson of an Irish immigrant who had settled in Chester County, Pennsylvania, soon after coming to America about 1715. A graduate of the College of Philadelphia, McDowell moved to Maryland in 1782 to teach and to study law. Although he engaged in a successful legal practice there, he was still attracted to teaching and, when the newly formed St. John's College offered him a professorship in mathematics, he readily accepted. He also served as the president of the fledgling institution until 1806, when he accepted a position teaching natural philosophy at the University of Pennsylvania. Although poor health forced him to return to Maryland, he declined the principalship of St. John's when it was offered to him again.

During McDowell's tenure as president of St. John's, one of its students was George Washington's step-grandson. In a letter to McDowell, the former president acknowledged that George Washington Parke Custis on occasion lacked motivation but otherwise described him as one would expect in a letter of recommendation: "From drinking and gaming he is perfectly free, and if he has a propensity to any other impropriety it is hidden from me. He is generous and regardful of the truth." The following summer Custis acknowledged that he had fallen in love with a young woman whom he would have married if she had not refused him. At the beginning of the next school year, Washington again wrote to the college president, this time urging him to act *in loco parentis*: "Prevent as much as it can be done, without too great a restraint, a devotion of his time to visitations of the families in Annapolis, which, when carried to excess or beyond a certain point, can not but tend to direct his mind from study and lead his thoughts to very different objects."

¶ **United States Naval Academy,** entrance at King George and Randall streets.

Several of the structures on the sprawling campus bear the names of famous Irish-American naval officers:

• Leahy Hall recalls the career of William Daniel Leahy, one of only five men to be named a Five-Star Fleet Admiral, the Navy's highest rank. (See Hampton, Iowa, in *Irish America*, Volume 2.)

• Macdonough Hall was named for Commodore Thomas Macdonough, the victor of the battle of Plattsburgh in 1814. (See Odessa, Delaware, and Plattsburgh, New York.)

• Mahan Hall honors Admiral Alfred Thayer Mahan, the 1859 graduate of the Academy whose most famous work was *The Influence of Sea Power upon History, 1660-1783*. Between 1886 and 1890 he was president of the U.S. Naval War College in Newport, Rhode Island [*q.v.*].

• Maury Hall bears the name of Matthew Fontaine Maury, dubbed the "Pathfinder of the Seas" for his innovations in the field of oceanography. (See Virginia Military Institute, Lexington, Virginia, in *Irish America*, Volume 2.)

Memorial Hall displays the flag which *Commodore Oliver Hazard Perry flew during his victorious engagement against a British fleet on Lake Erie in September 1813. The blue flag had originally belonged to Captain James Lawrence, whose famous words – "Don't give up the ship!" – Perry had sewn on the flag prior to his own sea battle.

§ The grounds are open daily 9-5. Closed January 1, Thanksgiving, and December 25. Tours leave the visitor center near Gate 1 at various times during the year. Fee for tour. Phone: 410-263-6933.

BALTIMORE

¶ **B & O (Baltimore & Ohio) Railroad Museum,** 901 West Pratt Street.

This museum incorporates the nation's first passenger and freight train station, the Mount Clare. The museum's thirty-seven acres exhibit more than a hundred historic rail cars (including the *Tom Thumb*) as well as various types of engines and telegraph and telephone equipment.

The station was built in 1830 on land given the Baltimore & Ohio Railroad by *Charles Carroll of Carrollton, a shrewd businessman and a major force in many of the nation's early industrial and commercial enterprises. Besides being a member of the Chesapeake & Ohio Canal Company, he was a director of the Baltimore & Ohio Railroad. In 1828, at the age of ninety-three, he performed the groundbreaking for construction of the B & O Railroad and watched as the company's first line was completed to Ellicott's Mills. (The silver spade which he used is on display in the museum.)

In May 1830 Carroll was among the passengers who made the first trip on the new railroad. The thirteen-mile ride in the horse-drawn car *Pioneer* took sixty-five minutes. The following August the first American-built steam engine – the *Tom Thumb* – ran the distance to Ellicott's Mills in seventy-five minutes, although the return trip, which was on the downgrade and included a four-minute water stop, took only sixty-one minutes. In 1844 the world's first official telegraph message was received at Mount Clare station when Samuel Morse sent the words "What God hath wrought" from the Supreme Court building in Washington, D.C.

§ Open daily 10-5. Closed Thanksgiving and December 25. Fee. Phone: 410-752-2490.

¶ Basilica of the Assumption of the Blessed Virgin Mary, Cathedral and Mulberry streets.

This is the oldest cathedral in the United States and was begun in 1806 by *John Carroll, the country's first Roman Catholic bishop. Carroll is buried in the church crypt, as is *Cardinal James Gibbons, archbishop of Baltimore from 1877 to 1921. (See Cardinal Gibbons Statue, District of Columbia.) A portrait bust of Carroll is located in the nave of the basilica.

A member of Maryland's most prominent Irish family, John Carroll was the brother of Daniel Carroll, one of the framers of the Constitution, and the cousin of Charles Carroll of Carrollton, the only Catholic signer of the Declaration of Independence. After completing his theological studies in France, Carroll was ordained a Jesuit priest about 1767. During the Revolution he was instrumental in obtaining the support of the French government for the patriot cause, a contribution which George Washington acknowledged in extremely flattering terms: "Of all men whose influence was most potent in securing the success of the Revolution, Bishop Carroll of Baltimore was the man." In 1789, a year before his consecration, he established Georgetown College as a seminary for future American candidates for the priesthood.

As the first Catholic bishop in a country that was generally hostile to and ignorant of Catholicism, Carroll argued for the use of the vernacular in the liturgy. His suggestion was based on the premise that Protestants were deprived of a proper understanding of the Catholic Church because of the use of Latin. Despite the fact that his views were attacked by the archbishop of Dublin, Carroll expressed his hope that the Church would allow the clergy in Ireland, England, and America to celebrate the liturgy in the vernacular, "for I do indeed conceive that one of the most popular prejudices against us is that our public prayers are unintelligible to our hearers. Many of the poor people, and the negroes generally, not being able to read, have no technical help to confine their attention."

Two years after Carroll's elevation to the episcopacy, the Baltimore Synod of 1791 instructed priests to read the Sunday Gospel in the vernacular and recommended the vernacular for the Our Father, the Hail Mary, and the Apostles' Creed. However, no permission was granted to use the vernacular for the mass or in the administration of the other sacraments.

§ Open Monday-Friday 7:30-5. Phone: 410-727-3564.

¶ **Carroll Park,** Washington Boulevard and Monroe Street.

This property was once part of "Georgia," the 2,300-acre plantation of Dr. Charles Carroll, whose branch of the family was Protestant due to his renunciation of Catholicism when he arrived in Maryland from Ireland in 1715. Near the center of the park is "Mount Clare," the mansion completed in 1760 as the home of Dr. Carroll's son Charles, dubbed "Barrister" to distinguish him from other men of the same name in the extended family. The house is the oldest pre-revolutionary mansion in Baltimore and contains portraits of Charles and his wife by Charles Wilson Peale.

"Mount Clare," the home of Charles Carroll "Barrister," in Carroll Park.

The estate at one time encompassed wheat fields, a grist mill, brick kilns, racing stables, and a shipyard.

§ House open Tuesday-Friday 11-3, Saturday-Sunday 1-3. Closed holidays. Fee. Phone: 410-837-3262.

¶ **Carroll Viaduct,** Gwynn's Falls near Carroll Park.

The cornerstone of this bridge – the first constructed of masonry in the United States – was laid in 1829 by *Charles Carroll of Carrollton. The viaduct, which is still in use, was built for the Baltimore & Ohio Railroad, of which Carroll was a director.

¶ **Charles Carroll Mansion,** 800 East Lombard Street.

One of six attractions known collectively as the Baltimore City Life Museums, this 1808 brick residence was the winter home of *Charles Carroll of Carrollton. Following the deaths of John Adams and Thomas Jefferson, Carroll was the last surviving signer of the Declaration of Independence. At the time of his death here in 1832 at the age of ninety-five, he was the wealthiest man in the country. The house is noted for its spiral staircase.

Two years earlier a visitor had recorded what was perhaps the secret of Carroll's longevity: "He takes a cold bath every morning in the summer, plunging headlong into it; rides on horseback from eight to twelve miles; drinks water at dinner, had never drunk spiritous liquors at any period of his life, but drinks a glass or two of madeira wine every day, and sometimes champagne and claret; takes as much exercise as possible; goes to bed at nine o'clock, and rises before day."

§ Open Wednesday-Friday 10-4, Saturday-Sunday 10-5. Closed January 1, Thanksgiving, and December 25. Fee. Phone: 410-396-3523.

¶ **Daniel Dulany Burial Site,** St. Paul's Cemetery, Lombard Street and Fremont Avenue.

Daniel Dulany was born in Annapolis in 1722 and was named for his father, a native of Queen's County, Ireland, and a descendant of the medieval O'Dulaney family. Daniel the younger was educated at Eton College and studied law at the Middle Temple in London. After three years in the Maryland legislature, he was appointed to the governor's council and later to the secretaryship of the province. His professional ability prompted *Charles Carroll to comment that Dulany was "indisputably the best lawyer on this continent."

Following Parliament's passage of the Stamp Act in 1765, Dulany published a pamphlet in which he contended that the American colonies were not – and could not realistically be – represented in Parliament and that taxation without representation violated English common law. This work was widely quoted by William Pitt when that British statesman attempted to persuade Parliament to repeal the hated tax. When relations between the colonies and the mother country turned violent, however, Dulany had no stomach for revolution and retired to his estate near Baltimore, where his continued loyalty to the Crown resulted in the confiscation of his property in 1781.

¶ **Edgar Allan Poe Burial Site,** Westminster Burying Ground, on the southeast corner of Fayette and Greene streets.

This charming cemetery contains the well-marked graves of Edgar Allan Poe and his grandfather, David Poe. The elder man had emigrated from Londonderry, northern Ireland, and settled about 1748 in Pennsylvania, where he married Elizabeth Cairnes, also of an Irish family. James McHenry, a native of northern Ireland, a signer of the U.S. Constitution, and President Washington's secretary of war, is also interred in this cemetery.

Edgar Allan Poe was so little known at the time of his death that the mourners at his funeral "filled a single carriage." Although he was originally buried in the rear of the adjoining Presbyterian Church, a campaign by Baltimore school teachers and students in 1875 raised enough money to move his body to its present location. The poet's grave is marked by a stone with his likeness on one side and a bronze plaque (given by French

Grave of Edgar Allan Poe.

admirers) on the other.

§ Open daily 8-dusk. Tours available first and third weekends April-November, Friday at 6:30 p.m. and Saturday at 10 a.m.; reservations required. Fee for tour. Phone: 410-706-2072.

¶ Edgar Allan Poe Monument, 29th Street, between Maryland Avenue and Oak Street.

This bronze statue depicts the poet *Edgar Allan Poe wearing a dressing gown and listening to the Muses. The monument contains a slightly inaccurate quotation from "The Raven": "Dreaming Dreams no Mortals Ever Dared to Dream Before." In 1930 a Poe admirer insisted that city authorities singularize the offending word "Mortals." When officials ignored his demand, he said he would remove the "s" himself on the night of May 30. Learning that police were preparing to guard the monument that night, the admirer appeared the evening before to chisel the letter from the text. Although he was arrested, the authorities did not prosecute when supporters came to his defense.

¶ Edgar Allan Poe National Historic Landmark, 203 North Amity Street.

This small three-story brick building was the home of *Edgar Allan Poe from 1832 to 1835, a period which some biographers call his "dark and mysterious years." Here he wrote "MS in a Bottle," "Berenice" (his first sensational horror story), and his only play, *Politan*. At the time, he was living with his grandmother, his aunt, his brother, and two cousins, one of whom – Virginia Clemm – he later married, although she was only thirteen years old. Fourteen years after leaving this house, Poe was found in the gutter in Lombard Street and was carried to what is now Church Home Hospital, 100 North Broadway, where he died. A marker at that location memorializes his death.

§ Open April-July 31 and September to mid December, Wednesday-Saturday 1-4. Fee. Phone: 410-396-7932.

¶ Enoch Pratt Free Library, 400 Cathedral Street, between Franklin and Mulberry.

This 1930s Art Deco library has permanent exhibits on H. L. Mencken and *Edgar Allan Poe. (See Edgar Allan Poe Burial Site above.)

¶ Fort McHenry National Monument and Historic Shrine, at the east end of Fort Avenue.

The site of the famous bombardment described in "The Star Spangled Banner," this star-shaped fort was named for James McHenry, President Washington's secretary of war when construction was begun in 1798.

Born in Ballymena, County Antrim, northern Ireland, in 1753, McHenry received a classical education in Dublin before immigrating to Philadelphia in 1771. He attended Newark Academy in Delaware and then studied medicine in Philadelphia under Dr. Benjamin Rush.

Inspired to take up arms against the British in 1775, McHenry hastened to Cambridge, Massachusetts, to enlist in the Continental Army. Because of his medical training he was at first assigned to a military hospital but he was later named surgeon to a Pennsylvania battalion. After his capture at the fall of Fort Washington, the twenty-three-year-old physician was paroled and briefly imprisoned until an exchange was completed. By May 1781 the Irishman's ability and prudence had brought him to the attention of General Washington, whose secretary he became and who later transferred him to Lafayette's staff.

At the conclusion of hostilities, McHenry pursued what became a checkered political career. Elected first to the Maryland senate and then to the Continental Congress, he was a delegate to the Constitutional Convention, where he added little to the debates but kept a private record of its proceedings. Although Adams at first retained McHenry as secretary of war, the president later dismissed him, believing that his cabinet officer was working against his reelection. McHenry denied the charge but was forced to defend himself against additional complaints of maladministration. When Congress declared war against Britain in 1812, McHenry, a staunch Federalist, opposed the conflict. Ironically, though, his son volunteered for service in the defense of Fort McHenry.

§ Open daily June-Labor Day, 8-8; rest of the year, 8-5. Closed January 1 and December 25. Fee. Phone: 410-962-4299.

¶ **Johns Hopkins Hospital,** 600 North Wolfe Street.

• The Outpatient Center – at 601 North Caroline Street – was originally known as the Brady Urological Institute, founded in 1912 with a $600,000 donation by *James Brady, the famous "Diamond Jim." Brady made the gift after receiving treatment at the Johns Hopkins Hospital for long-standing urological problems. (See Holy Cross Cemetery, New York City.)

• The Welch Library – 1900 East Monument Street – houses *Four Doctors*, an oil painting by John Singer Sargent depicting the hospital's four most prominent early physicians. The four men had been entrusted by the benefactor Johns Hopkins with the duty of carrying out his wish that the hospital advance the cause of medical science. One of the four doctors was *Howard Kelly, who was associated with the hospital from 1889 until 1919. (See Apopka, Florida, in *Irish America*, Volume 2.)

¶ **Johns Hopkins University,** off Charles and 34th streets.

The 140-acre campus of this internationally renowned private liberal arts institution was originally the estate of *Charles Carroll Jr., the son of

Charles Carroll of Carrollton, a signer of the Declaration of Independence.

§ Tours available Monday-Friday at 10, noon, and 3 (June-Labor Day) from the admissions office at 140 Garland Hall. Phone: 410-516-8171.

¶ Near the entrance to the campus is a statue of Sidney Lanier, the famous Georgia poet, whose mother was of Scotch-Irish descent. Although Lanier dreamed of pursuing music and studying at a German university, his plans were derailed by the Civil War. While serving in the conflict as a scout, he considered pursuing a literary career, but the catastrophe wrought by the war, his own worsening health, and the need for provide for his wife and children prevented him from becoming a first-rate literary figure. In 1879, however, he was named professor of English literature at Johns Hopkins University. (See Macon, Georgia, in *Irish America*, Volume 2.)

¶ One of the points of interest on the campus is "Homewood," a brick Georgian mansion built in 1809 by *Charles Carroll of Carrollton as a wedding gift for his son. Charles Carroll Jr., however, was an alcoholic whose drinking marred domestic bliss at the $40,000 mansion. The extent of the family's embarrassment about Carroll's drinking is revealed in a remark by his nephew, who wrote that "we can't get him to shoot himself, so must bear with this degradation still longer." From 1897 to 1910 Homewood was a boys' school, a fact that accounts for the graffiti-covered brick outhouse behind the mansion.

Homewood was the birthplace of John Lee Carroll, the governor of

"Homewood," the Georgian-style residence of Charles Carroll Jr.

Maryland from 1875 to 1880. This great-grandson of Charles Carroll of Carrollton grew up at the family's ancestral home, Doughoregan Manor, near Ellicott City, Maryland, and received his legal training at Harvard Law School. Although he moved to New York City in 1859 to practice law, he soon returned to his native state, both because of his father's poor health and his own Southern sympathy in the emerging sectional conflict. After his father's death he purchased Doughoregan Manor from his brother and made it his country estate.

Carroll later served two terms in the state senate and in 1875 was elected governor of Maryland despite exceptional controversy about his Roman Catholicism. Although he promoted policies designed to improve the state's commercial and agricultural interests, his reputation among the working class suffered from his intervention in a strike by employees of the Baltimore & Ohio Railroad over a wage reduction. When the strikers resorted to violence to protest the use of "scabs," the governor sent in the state militia. He was forced to call for federal troops when rioting and destruction of property began in Baltimore.

§ Homewood is located at 3400 North Charles Street. Open Tuesday-Saturday 11-4, Sunday noon-4. Fee. Phone: 410-516-5589.

¶ **Lafayette Statue,** Mt. Vernon Park, in the 500 block of North Charles Street.

This equestrian statue of the Marquis de Lafayette was sculpted by *Andrew O'Connor.

¶ **Lee and Jackson Statuary Group,** Wyman Park, at the corner of Howard Street and Park Drive.

This double equestrian memorial depicts the final meeting of Confederate generals Robert E. Lee and *Thomas "Stonewall" Jackson, just before the latter was killed at Chancellorsville, Virginia.

¶ **Patterson Park,** Eastern and Patterson Park avenues.

The original portion of this park was a gift to the city by William Patterson, a native of County Donegal, Ireland, who as a teenager had come to Philadelphia to work for the Irish shipping merchant Samuel Jackson. The foundation of Patterson's fortune was made during the American Revolution, when he sold French munitions to the rebel colonists. In the last year of the war, he was among the Baltimore merchants who gave the Marquis de Lafayette 10,000 guineas with which to obtain supplies for the Yorktown campaign.

In 1803 Patterson's eighteen-year-old daughter, Elizabeth, married Jerome Bonaparte, Napoleon's youngest brother, in a ceremony witnessed by *Bishop John Carroll. When the emperor expressed his opposition to the marriage, the couple sailed to Europe aboard the *Erin*, one of Patterson's ships, intent upon pleading their case. Although Pope Pius VII refused to grant Napoleon's demand that the marriage be annulled, the French Senate and the Maryland Assembly passed decrees of annulment. Elizabeth at first refused Napoleon's offer of $12,000 to stop referring to herself as Madame Bonaparte, but she later accepted a pension of 60,000 francs. Her tombstone in Greenmount Cemetery is inscribed with the words, "After life's fitful fever, she sleeps well."

¶ **Roger Taney Statue,** Washington Place, just north of the Washington Monument.

This statue of *Chief Justice Roger Taney is a duplicate of that in front of the State House in Annapolis.

¶ **U.S. Frigate *Constellation*,** Constellation Dock, at Pratt and Light streets, on Pier 1 in Inner Harbor.

During its heyday the *Constellation* saw action against a variety of foes: France in 1798-1800, the Tripoli pirates in 1802, the British in the War of 1812, and the Confederates in the Civil War.

In 1841 the *Constellation* came under the command of Lawrence Kearny, the newly appointed commander of the East India Squadron and a descendant of an Irish immigrant who had settled in New Jersey about 1720. At the time of his promotion, both Kearny and the ship were in Rio de Janeiro. From Rio, Kearny sailed to Table Bay, near the Cape of Good Hope, arriving there in twenty-eight days. After spending three months at Saldanha Bay – to fix the rudder – he rounded the Cape, entered the Mozambique Channel, and proceeded to Sumatra, Singapore, and finally Macao, which he reached by March 1842. (See Perth Amboy, New Jersey.)

§ The ship is currently undergoing restoration. Phone: 410-539-1797.

¶ **Walters Art Gallery,** 600 North Charles Street.

The nucleus of the gallery's 25,000 *objets d'art* was the personal collection of Henry Walters, a railroad entrepreneur in the South and the Southwest and a descendant of Scotch-Irish stock. In 1920 he enriched his museum's holdings by purchasing the Marcello Massaranti collection of Italian art for $1 million. When he died in 1931, he left his museum and its works to the city. Among the gallery's most treasured possessions is the original manuscript of the *Star Spangled Banner*.

§ Open Tuesday-Friday 10-4 (and Thursday 4-8). Closed January 1, July 4, Thanksgiving, and December 24-25. Fee. Phone: 410-547-9000.

BROOKLANDVILLE

¶ **Brooklandwood,** Falls Road. Private.

Erected in the mid 1790s, this was once the home of *Charles Carroll of Carrollton and of George Brown. A native of County Antrim, Ireland, Brown was one of the original founders and stockholders of the Baltimore & Ohio Railroad, organized in 1827 in an effort to help the port of Baltimore compete against the recently completed Erie Canal.

CAMBRIDGE

℣ Old Trinity Church, 8 miles south on State 16.

Many members of the famous Maryland Carroll family are buried in the cemetery next to the church, including *Anna Ella Carroll, an unofficial advisor to President Lincoln and the female strategist who allegedly designed the Union's successful Tennessee campaign during the Civil War. (See Kingston, Maryland.)

§ Cemetery open daily 24 hours. Phone: 410-228-2940.

ELLICOTT CITY

℣ Baltimore & Ohio Railroad Station Museum, 2711 Maryland Avenue at Main Street.

The museum is the restored first terminus of the B & O Railroad, built in 1830 at the end of the company's first stretch of track, a thirteen-mile line from Baltimore. Visitors can see the stationmaster's quarters, a waiting room, an engine house, and a freight house. The last building displays a model of the original stretch of track.

When the B & O Railroad was organized in 1827, one of its most influential founders was Alexander Brown, a native of County Antrim, Ireland, where he had been a linen auctioneer and the proprietor of a linen store in Belfast. In 1800, however, he immigrated to Baltimore with his wife and the oldest of his four sons. Almost immediately he announced in a Baltimore newspaper the opening of his linen warehouse on North Gay Street: "The subscriber, lately arrived from Ireland, has brought with him a most complete assortment of 4-4 & 7-8 wide Irish Linen, which upon examination, will be found much lower [in price] than any inspected for three years past, & which will be sold low by the box or piece for cash or good acceptance in the city on the usual credit." When his three other sons arrived in Baltimore two years later, "They landed on a hot Sunday morning in July, dressed in thick woolen Irish suits and heavy plaid stockings, and created quite a sensation among the good people of Baltimore, quietly wending their way to church. Thither their mother took them also, with a heart thankful for their safe arrival, after she had borrowed from her neighbors thinner clothing better suited to the American climate."

Although Brown had begun his American career as an importer of Irish linen, he quickly moved into the export business. At first he sent cotton and tobacco to Great Britain, but eventually he handled a full range of commodities, from champagne to indigo. In due time his sons established branches of the business in Liverpool, Philadelphia, and New York. The task of overseeing these operations as well as the movement of the family's ships and capital led quite naturally to the creation of an international merchant banking business. The firm, Alexander Brown & Sons, is the oldest banking house in the United States and is still headquartered in Baltimore. Although Brown suffered temporarily from the War of 1812, he steadfastly adhered to the principle that established his reputation for integrity: "It is essential for us in all our dealings not only to be fair but never to have the appearance of unfairness." At his death his wealth was estimated at $2 million.

§ Open Memorial Day weekend-Labor Day, Wednesday-Monday 11-4; rest of the year, Friday-Monday 11-4. Closed major holidays. Fee. Phone: 410-461-1944.

¶ **Doughoregan Manor,** 8 miles west on Manor Lane. Private.

Built about 1727, this two-story mansion was the home of *Charles Carroll of Carrollton. (Today the home belongs to Philip Carroll, a direct descendant of its earlier owner.) On either side of the manor's 300-foot façade is an ell, one containing servants' quarters and the other a Catholic chapel. The original estate of more than 13,000 acres included farm buildings and quarters for almost a thousand slaves. The estate was held intact until 1870, when all but 3,000 acres was sold.

EMMITSBURG

¶ **John Hughes Cabin,** Mount St. Mary's College.

John Hughes, a native of Ireland and the first archbishop of New York City, lived in this small log cabin in 1820 while receiving instruction at the college. In return for room and board, he worked as a gardener.

From his youth in County Tyrone, Hughes had always wanted to be a priest, but his father, a poor tenant farmer, could afford to give his son no more than a rudimentary education. About his feelings at the time, the younger Hughes said, "Many a time have I thrown down my rake in the meadow, and kneeling behind a hayrick, begged of God and the Blessed Virgin to let me become a priest." In 1817 he immigrated to America, where he worked as a laborer, a road mender, a quarry hand, and a garden digger in southern Pennsylvania.

Still intent upon priestly ordination, Hughes applied for admission to Mount St. Mary's College but was repeatedly rejected because there was no vacancy. After actually moving to Emmitsburg, he worked as a laborer on a millrace and as a mason's helper on a bridge-building project. The young man's persistence paid off at the end of 1819, when the president of the college hired him as superintendent of the institution's garden in re-

The John Hughes Cabin, where the future archbishop of New York lived while attending Mount St. Mary's College.

turn for board and instruction.

Many years later, as bishop of New York, the nation's most populous Irish diocese, Hughes condemned the clannishness of many of his flock and insisted that they adopt the predominant American culture as soon as possible. His own allegiance to his adopted country was never in doubt: "My feelings, my thoughts, have been so much identified with all that is American, that I have almost forgotten I am a foreigner." He disliked professional Irish politicians and the tendency of the Democratic party to monopolize and pander to the Irish vote.

Yet, when necessary, Hughes defended the Irish against the attacks of anti-immigrant forces. In response to the destruction of a convent in Charleston, Massachusetts, he warned that "if a single Catholic Church were burned in New York, the city would become a second Moscow." In 1844, when anti-Irish and anti-Catholic speakers announced their intention to hold a public rally, Hughes feared that the church burnings which had occurred in Philadelphia the month before might be repeated in New York. Through the Catholic press he urged Catholics to remain calm but to prepare to act in self defense if necessary. After forming cadres of between 1,000 and 2,000 men to protect each Catholic church in the city, Hughes urged the mayor to determine whether the police force had available "a company or so of artillery, and a squadron of horse" that could be used to intimidate any prospective rioters. As a result, city officials canceled the meeting.

§ The interior of the cabin can be viewed through the windows. Phone: 301-447-6122 or 301-447-6606.

√ The boyhood home of *Archbishop John Hughes is preserved in the Ulster American Folk Park in County Tyrone, Northern Ireland.

FREDERICK

¶ Barbara Fritchie House, 154 West Patrick Street.

Although Barbara Fritchie was not of Irish descent, she figured prominently in a story involving the Scotch-Irish Civil War general Thomas "Stonewall" Jackson. According to the version of the story rendered in John Greenleaf Whittier's poem "Barbara Fritchie," Jackson had ordered his men to fire on the Union flag should they encounter it on their march through Frederick in 1862. Nevertheless, the ninety-five-year-old Fritchie defiantly waved the Stars and Stripes, adding, "Shoot if you must this old gray head, / But spare your country's flag." Jackson, in turn, countermanded his order: "Who touches a hair of yon gray head / Dies like a dog! March on!"

The present structure was erected in 1927 as an exact replica of the Fritchie home destroyed by the flooding of a nearby creek.

§ Open April-September, Monday and Thursday-Saturday 10-4, Sunday 1-4; October and November, Saturday-Sunday 1-4. Fee. Phone: 301-698-0630.

¶ Evangelical Reformed Church, West Church Street.

While attending a service here before the battle of Antietam, Confederate general *Thomas "Stonewall" Jackson slept through a sermon whose sentiments were favorable to the Union. (See Clarksburg, West Virginia, in *Irish America*, Volume 2.)

¶ Mount Olivet Cemetery, at the end of Market Street.

• Near the entrance of the cemetery is a sixteen-foot monument marking the grave of Francis Scott Key, the author of the "Star Spangled Banner." The memorial was designed by *Alexander Doyle and includes a nine-foot statue of Key. The bronze standing figure depicts the composer holding the text of his famous anthem in his left hand as he points with his right arm to the Stars and Stripes atop a nearby flag pole. The monument was dedicated in 1898.

• The medallion on the monument over the grave of Barbara Fritchie, the heroine of Whittier's famous Civil War poem, was designed by *James Edward Kelly and includes a profile portrait of the heroine of Whittier's famous Civil War poem.

§ Open daily 8-dusk.

¶ Roger Taney House, 123 South Bentz Street.

From 1835 to 1864 this was the home of *Roger Taney, best known for his ruling in the Dred Scott case while he was the chief justice of the U.S. Supreme Court. Taney is buried next to his mother in St. John's Cemetery at 4th and East streets.

Taney was described by a contemporary as "a tall square-shouldered man, flat-chested . . . with a stoop that made his shoulders even more prominent, a face without one good feature, a mouth unusually large, in which were discolored and irregular teeth, the gums of which were visible when he smiled, dressed always in black, his clothes sitting ill upon him . . . . And yet, when he began to speak, you never thought of his personal appearance, so clear, so simple, so admirably arranged were his low-voiced words. . . . There was an air of so much sincerity in all he said, that it was next to impossible to believe he could be wrong.

§ Phone: 301-663-8703.

¶ Roger Taney Law Office, Court Street.

From 1801 to 1823 this building was the law office of *Roger Taney, who had come to Frederick to practice law with Francis Scott Key, whose sister he married.

Despite his ruling in the Dred Scott case that African Americans were not considered citizens under the Constitution, Taney had earlier declared his antislavery views. In defending a Methodist minister charged with inciting insurrection for delivering an antislavery sermon, Taney had said, "Slavery is a blot upon our national character[,] and every lover of freedom confidentially hopes that it will be effectually wiped away. And until that time shall came when we can point without a blush to the language held in the Declaration of Independence, every friend of humanity will seek to lighten the galling chains of slavery."

¶ Roger Taney Statue, in front of City Hall, 101 North Court Street.

A bronze bust of *Roger Taney rests on a pedestal to which is attached a plaque summarizing his career: "Chief Justice of the United States 1836-1864. Secretary of the Treasury 1833-1834. Attorney General of the United States 1831-1833. Attorney General of Maryland 1827-1831. Citizen of Frederick and Lawyer Practicing in the Frederick County Court 1801-1823. Born in Calvert County March 17, 1777. Died in Washington, D.C. October 12, 1864. Buried in St. John's Catholic Cemetery, Frederick, Md."

¶ St. John the Evangelist Church, 116 East 2nd Street.

This church was built in 1837 by Irish immigrants who labored on a nearby canal. Construction of the church was completed under the direction of *Father John McElroy, who served the parish for two decades. During that time he established a boys' school, an orphanage, a convent, a girls' free school, and a Jesuit novitiate. He later founded Boston College.

HAVRE DE GRACE

¶ **Concord Point Lighthouse,** on Concord Point.

Built in 1829, the lighthouse was first manned by Lieutenant John O'Neill, who had been rewarded with the post because of his bravery during a British raid on Havre de Grace in May 1813. His descendants served as keepers for many years after his death.

O'Neill, who was born in Ireland in 1769, had come to America at the age of eighteen. After serving under General Henry Lee in crushing the Whiskey Rebellion in western Pennsylvania, he enlisted in the American navy against the French. He operated a nail manufactory in Havre de Grace until that enterprise was destroyed when the British burned the town in 1813.

In anticipation of the British attack, about 250 American militiamen had gathered to defend the battery near the present lighthouse. When between fifteen and twenty British barges made their approach to Point Comfort, they were met with gunfire from the American position. The enemy replied with grapeshot and rockets that set fire to the town. As British landing forces advanced to seize the battery, all the militiamen but two – John O'Neill and Philip Albert – abandoned their posts. When Albert was wounded, O'Neill manned the largest gun alone, until its recoil injured his thigh. The Irishman was soon captured and spirited aboard the British frigate *Maidstone*.

In a letter to one of the British admirals, the American brigadier general Henry Miller referred to O'Neill's situation and threatened retaliation: "O'Neale has been menaced with immediate and capital punishment, as a traitor to the government of his Britannic Majesty, on the ground of his being by birth an Irishman. . . . [But], sir, in the event of O'Neale's execution, . . . I am authorized and commanded to state to your excellency, that two British subjects shall be selected by lot or otherwise, and immediately executed."

The missive had the desired effect, and O'Neill was immediately released on parole. In a letter to Colonel John Binns, he expressed the frustration which his "parole of honor" engendered in him: "[I]t grieves me to think, if the oppressors [i.e., the British] of the human race and particularly of my native country, Ireland, should come within such a distance of me as that I could be of any service to my fellow Citizens in repelling the merciless bloodhounds that I could not have the pleasure to assist in protecting my adopted country and revenging their insult, while I am their prisoner on parole."

¶ A memorial plaque erected in honor of O'Neill and surmounted by the cannon he manned during the British attack stands near the lighthouse. The bronze plaque summarizes the Irishman's heroism: "This cannon of the War of 1812 marks the site of the battery on Concord Point where John O'Neill (1769-1838) served the guns single-handedly during the British attack upon Havre de Grace, May 3, 1813, until disabled and captured. He was released from the British frigate Maidstone through the intercession of his young daughter, Matilda, to whom Admiral Cockburn gave his gold-mounted snuff-box in token of her heroism. As a tribute to the gallant conduct of her father, the citizens of Philadelphia presented to him a handsome sword."

¶ Across the street from the lighthouse are the foundational ruins of the house in which O'Neill lived while he served as lighthouse keeper from 1829 until his death in 1838.

JESSUP

¶ **Fort George Meade,** south off the Spellman Parkway.

Established in 1917 to train World War I troops, this 7,500-acre army base was named for *George Meade, the commander of Union forces at Gettysburg. (See George Meade Memorial, District of Columbia.)

KINGSTON

¶ **Kingston Hall,** on the west side of State 667. Private.

This late eighteenth-century brick mansion once belonged to Thomas King Carroll, a governor of Maryland and a member of the famous Irish-American family of Carrolls. Following his inauguration in 1830, Governor Carroll supported efforts to improve the state's educational and penal institutions and used his influence to expedite the completion of the Baltimore and Ohio Railroad. Although he worked his plantation at Kingston Hall with slaves, he opposed the "peculiar institution" and was fearful of its growth in the country. As a result, he supported the colonization of freed blacks to Africa.

Governor Carroll's daughter, Anna Ella Carroll ("Princess Anne"), was raised in her father's Protestant faith and became an outspoken champion of the anti-Catholic and antiforeign Know Nothing Party. Her most ambitious publication was *The Great American Battle*, a 365-page book praising the Know Nothings and condemning "the Papal system."

With the outbreak of the Civil War, Anna Carroll became an equally vigorous champion of the Union. When Senator John Breckinridge of Kentucky urged the border states to secede, she distributed 50,000 copies of a pamphlet in which she charged Southern leaders with having prepared for war since the 1830s. In this and two other tracts, she argued that, since secession was unconstitutional, the Confederacy was a rebel government which could be dealt with by the president rather than by Congress. During the war she authored a pamphlet in which she argued that President Lincoln possessed implied powers not directly conferred upon him by the Constitution, a position that may have influenced his decision to issue the Emancipation Proclamation as a military tactic.

Carroll also passed on to the War Department a plan for a Union invasion of the Tennessee River Valley, a strategy that would bypass the more heavily fortified Mississippi. (*General Ulysses S. Grant successfully employed the strategy, breaking Confederate power in the West through his capture of Fort Donelson and Fort Henry.) Although at first Carroll gave credit for this plan to a river pilot and amateur strategist, she later claimed that the idea was hers. For many years after the war, she unsuccessfully petitioned Congress for proper compensation for the strategy. In the 1880s she became a symbol for woman suffragists of alleged male injustice. She is buried in the graveyard of Old Trinity Church in Cambridge, Maryland [*q.v.*].

PERRYVILLE

As early as 1680 an 80,000-square-mile tract of land in this part of Maryland was known as "New Ireland." That same year Lord Baltimore, the proprietor of the Maryland colony, granted 32,000 acres of that land to George Talbot, a native of Castle Rooney, County Roscommon, Ireland. On that land was Susquehanna Manor, which Talbot renamed New Connaught. Three years later an adjoining tract of 7,000 acres – known as New Munster – was granted to a group of Irishmen, among whom was Edmund O'Dwyre of Tipperary. At about the same time, a tract called New Leinster was patented by Bryan O'Daly of County Wicklow, Ireland. In 1684 Lord Baltimore proclaimed these territories the County of New Ireland.

Although Talbot subsequently carried out the terms of his land grant, he inexplicably fell afoul of the law. As was expected of him, he brought over a hundred Irish settlers and built block houses and signal towers for protection against the Native Americans. Soon after his appointment as deputy governor, though, he precipitated a quarrel on board the *Quaker*, during which he mortally stabbed the tax collector Christopher Rousby. According to Thomas Allen, the captain of the ship, Talbot first tried to kiss him (Allen) and then "hit me a blow on the heart and a box on the ear." Talbot later approached Rousby below deck and said, "'Rousby, you son of a whore, you dog, give me your hand,' but Rousby refused unless he gave him better words. And Talbot said again, 'Rousby, you dog, give me your hand. Don't you know that I am your Governor and can do you a kindness.' Rousby answered, 'I don't value anything you can do to me.'

And with that Talbot started up and pulled Rousby's cravat to pieces. Rousby said nothing, but rose up to go, and Talbot started up and met him, and clapped him on the right shoulder with his left hand, saying, 'dear Rousby,' with his dagger under his coat in his right hand, and then stabbed him in the right breast.'" Rousby died within a half hour.

Talbot was promptly arrested and sent to Jamestown for trial, but he was soon rescued by his wife and a group of "red haired" Irishmen and taken back to Maryland. According to tradition, one of his hiding places was a cave on the Susquehanna River near Perryville, where two trained falcons brought him food until he surrendered in July 1685. At his trial in Jamestown, he tried to exonerate himself by saying that he had killed "without any manner of premeditated malice in the height of his passion for which he most heartily beg'd God and the King's pardon." Although the jury found him guilty, he was later pardoned by the King.

ROCKVILLE

¶ **F. Scott Fitzgerald Burial Site,** St. Mary's Cemetery, Veirs Mill Road and Rockville Pike.

Before his death in 1940, the famous Irish-American author requested to be buried with his Maryland ancestors in St. Mary's Catholic Cemetery in Rockville. The local bishop denied permission, however, probably because of Fitzgerald's defection from the Catholic Church. Instead, he was buried in Rockville Union Cemetery.

(When Fitzgerald was laid out in a Hollywood funeral home, one of the few people who came to pay their respects was Dorothy Parker. Rarely at a loss for the right phrase, she judged the dead author with the words he had used to describe the protagonist in his masterpiece, *The Great Gatsby*: "The poor son of a bitch.")

In 1975, after St. Mary's Cemetery had been declared a historic monument, Fitzgerald's daughter – Scottie – obtained permission to transfer his remains to the site. In a gesture of reconciliation, the archbishop of Baltimore said: "F. Scott Fitzgerald came out of the Maryland Catholic tradition. He was a man touched by the faith of the Catholic Church. There can be perceived in his work a Catholic consciousness of reality. He found in his faith an understanding of the human heart caught in the struggle between grace and death. His characters are involved in this great drama, seeking God and seeking love. As an artist he was able with lucidity and poetic imagination to portray this struggle. He also experienced in his own life the mystery of suffering and, we hope, the power of God's grace." Fitzgerald's gravestone bears the last line of *The Great Gatsby*: "So we beat on boats against the current, borne back ceaselessly into the past." (See F. Scott Fitzgerald Birthplace, St. Paul, Minnesota.)

SHARPSBURG

¶ **Antietam National Battlefield,** on State 34/65.

Here on September 17, 1862, Union forces stopped the Confederate advance into Maryland and Pennsylvania, but at a cost to both sides of 23,000 dead and wounded. Although the Irish Brigade played a conspicuous part in this victory by pushing the enemy back to its second line, one Irish regiment lost half its men while another lost a third. According to one eyewitness, "The rebels seemed to have a special spite against the [Brigade's] green flag, and five color-bearers were shot down successively in a short time.... 'Big Gleason,' ... six feet seven, sprang forward and snatched it up. In a few minutes a bullet struck the staff, shattering it to pieces; Gleason tore the flag from the broken staff, wrapped it around his body ... and went through the rest of that fight untouched."

• One of the many memorials on the battlefield is a shaft in honor of *William McKinley, who was attached to the Union commissary at the time of the battle. Realizing that the men in his brigade had eaten only a scant breakfast before the engagement, he drove a mule team loaded with food rations and hot coffee right into the thick of the fighting. For this unusual attention to duty, he was promoted to second lieutenant. Rutherford B. Hayes, a major at the time, described McKinley's action as "a thing that had never occurred under similar circumstances in any other army in the world." (See Canton and Niles, Ohio.)

• The Irish Brigade is honored with a memorial next to the observation tower overlooking the "Bloody Lane," a sunken road where the brigade suffered more than 500 casualties: 113 dead and 422 wounded. The ten-foot memorial includes two bronze sculptures embedded in Irish granite. The bronze on the front depicts the Irish Brigade – and its famous ensign – on the battlefield, while a bust of *Thomas Francis Meagher, the brigade's commander, adorns the back. (See front cover photograph.)

The inscription on one of the side panels summarizes the history of the brigade: "Formed in November 1861, the brigade was largely recruited in New York, Massachusetts and Pennsylvania. Its initial regiments were the 69th, 88th and 63rd New York State Volunteers. Other units identified as part of the brigade included the 29th Massachusetts, 116th Pennsylvania and 28th Massachusetts volunteer infantry regiments. The brigade fought in all of the major campaigns of the Army of the Potomac. It lost over 4,000 men during the war. This total is larger than the number of soldiers who served in the brigade at any single time. Eleven brigade members were awarded the Congressional Medal of Honor. Of the five officers who commanded the brigade, three were killed or mortally wounded: Colonel Richard Byrnes (Cold Harbor), Colonel Patrick Kelly (Petersburg), and Brigadier General Thomas A. Smyth (Farmville). The brigade was mustered out in June 1865."

The bronze sculpture on the front of the Irish Brigade Monument on the Antietam Battlefield.

The other side panel recounts the brigade's exploits at Antietam: "On 17 September 1862, the brigade crossed Antietam Creek (9:30 a.m.) at Pry's Ford. As it formed at the edge of a cornfield, Father William Corby, chaplain, rode along the line giving absolution to the soldiers. The 69th New York occupied the right, then the 29th Massachusetts, the 63rd and 88th New York. Crossing the cornfield, the command encountered a rail fence which was torn down under severe fire. An opposing Confederate column advanced within 300 paces of the brigade. After several volleys, the Irish Brigade charged with fixed bayonets at 30 paces. It poured 'buck and ball' into General George B. Anderson's brigade (2nd, 4th, 14th and 30th North Carolina infantry regiments), which fell back to 'Bloody Lane.' After fierce combat, its ammunition exhausted, the Irish Brigade was relieved."

Below the bust of Thomas Meagher on the back side of the monument is the following narrative: "The Irish Brigade commander was born in Waterford City, Ireland, on 23 August 1823. A well-educated orator, he joined the Young Ireland movement to liberate his nation. This led to his exile to a British penal colony in Tasmania, Australia, in 1849. He escaped to the United States in 1852 and became an American citizen. When the Civil War broke out, he raised Company K, 'Irish Zouaves,' for the 69th New York State Militia Regiment, which fought at First Bull Run under Michael Corcoran. Subsequently, Meagher raised the Irish Brigade and commanded it from 3 February 1862 to 14 May 1863. He later commanded a military district in Tennessee. After the war, Meagher became secretary and acting governor of the Montana Territory. He drowned in the Missouri River near Fort Benton on 1 July 1867. His body was never recovered."

Meagher's exploits at Antietam are the subject of a poem by James Bourke, excerpted here:

They mourn him in the land he loved,
His priceless worth, his conquering arm,
They miss him where in grace he moved –
For camp and council both have proved
His master mind to guide or charm.
And many a tale will yet be told,
By camping fires in future wars,
Of him who with his clansmen bold
Shook out the old green banners fold
To fight beneath the Stripes and Stars.

And hosts will whisper listening guests
The Southern foeman's wild refrain,
When glared he o'er the green-plumed crests,
And sprigs of green on Irish breasts –
"Here comes that damned Green Flag again!"
And hearts will fire and pulses bound
At thoughts of Antietam's day;
When hemmed by fire and foeman round,
The Irish stormed the vantage ground –
And claimed the glory of the fray.

During the dedication of the Irish Brigade memorial on October 25, 1997, Archbishop Edwin O'Brien quoted the words which Father Corby uttered at a ceremony twenty-five years after the battle of Antietam: "Oh, you of the younger generation, think what it cost your forefathers to save our glorious inheritance of union and liberty! If you let it slip from your hands you will deserve to be branded as ungrateful cowards and undutiful sons. But no! You will not fail to cherish the prize – it is too sacred a trust – too dearly purchased."

§ Battlefield and visitor center open 8:30-5 (to 6 Memorial Day-Labor Day). Closed January 1, Thanksgiving, and December 25. Fee. Phone: 301-432-5124.

SILVER SPRING

¶ Old St. John the Evangelist Church, 9700 Rosensteel Avenue.
Erected in 1894, this brick structure marks the site of the first frame church built here in 1774 by *John Carroll, the Maryland native who became the first Catholic bishop in the United States. Today the church is known as Our Lady, Queen of Poland.

In the cemetery nearby is the grave of *Daniel Carroll, the bishop's brother and one of the signers of the Constitution. The graveyard was originally part of a land grant made in the 1680s to an ancestor of the Carroll family.

Born in Upper Marlboro, Maryland, in 1730, Daniel Carroll attended a school operated by English Jesuits at St. Omer, France. In 1751, three years after returning to Maryland, he succeeded to the management of his father's vast estates and numerous slaves. Besides increasing these inherited holdings, he operated a successful mercantile business, exporting tobacco and importing manufactured goods. From the Cherokee and Catawba Indians living near his estates, he learned their language, a facility that led to his appointment as an interpreter between the colonial authorities and representatives of those two tribes.

Carroll's involvement in political affairs began in 1777, when he was appointed to a five-man advisory board to the state governor. During the 1780s he served in the state legislature and in the Continental Congress. While a member of the latter body he signed the Articles of Confederation in 1781, thereby providing the approval of the thirteenth state needed to adopt the new frame of government. When his cousin Charles Carroll declined appointment to the Constitutional Convention, Daniel served in his stead. There he advocated the direct election of the U.S. president, but, when that proposal was rejected, he supported a system of presidential electors chosen by the voters. After signing the Constitution, he helped convince his fellow Marylanders to ratify the document, which he called "the best form of government which has ever been offered to the world."

As one of his state's first representatives in Congress, Carroll played an important role in getting Congress to adopt the First Amendment. In 1791 he was one of three commissioners selected by President Washington to oversee the surveying and construction of the new capital city on the banks of the Potomac. (See District of Columbia.)

TANEYTOWN

¶ **Antrim,** 30 Trevanion Road.

Recently restored as a bed and breakfast establishment, this antebellum mansion was built in 1844 by Andrew Ege as a wedding gift for his daughter. The house, once the center of a 450-acre plantation, was named for Ege's birthplace, County Antrim, Ireland.

§ Phone: 800-858-1844.

UPPER MARLBORO

¶ **Darnall's Chance,** 14800 Governor Oden Bowie Drive.

Constructed between 1694 and 1713, this brick residence was owned for almost forty years by the prominent Darnall and Carroll families. Although the two families were cousins, they became even more intertwined through the marriage of *Charles Carroll of Carrollton to Mary "Molly" Darnall in 1768. The house is the probable birthplace of two other mem-

bers of the famous Irish Catholic family: Bishop John Carroll and his older
brother Daniel Carroll, a signer of the U.S. Constitution.

§ Open Monday-Friday 9-4, Sunday 12-4. Phone: 301-952-8010.

"Darnall's Chance," home of the Catholic branch of the Carroll family.

WARWICK

¶ **St. Francis Xavier (Old Bohemia) Church,** west on State 282, Eastern Shore.

The first Catholic congregation on this site was formed in 1704 by the
Jesuits, who by 1745 had also established Bohemia Academy. Among its
students were *John Carroll and *Charles Carroll of Carrollton. Because at
that time Catholics were denied opportunities for political and educational
advancement in Maryland, the two Carroll cousins were sent by their fathers to France, where they attended a school run by English Jesuits.

Among the priests buried in the church is Father Charles Whelan (Friar
Maurice), an Irish-born Capuchin priest who was the first pastor of St.
Peter's Church in New York City [*q.v.*], the first Catholic house of worship
in that city.

§ Mass is said here on the third Sunday of April, May, September, and
October. The rectory museum is open Sunday 12-3 (summer only). Phone:
302-378-5803 (St. Joseph Church, Middletown, Delaware).

WESTOVER

J Rehobeth Presbyterian Church, 5757 Coventry Parish.

Built in 1705-06 through the efforts of the Reverend Francis Makemie, this is the oldest Presbyterian church in the United States. A native of County Donegal, Ireland, Makemie is credited with laying the foundation of the Presbyterian Church in America. (See Temperanceville, Virginia, in *Irish America*, Volume 2.)

Following his graduation from the University of Glasgow, Makemie was ordained by the presbytery in Laggan, Ulster. Between 1683 and 1698, he served as a missionary in the American colonies – originally in North Carolina, Virginia, and Maryland but later in Barbados. During his ministry he was a well known controversialist, defending with his pen Presbyterian practices and beliefs against the attacks of Quakers and Anglicans. After settling in Accomac, Virginia, he acquired property and married the daughter of a wealthy merchant.

While visiting England in 1704-05, Makemie laid the foundation for the Presbyterian Church in America by persuading the Presbyterian and Independent ministers of London to send two of their number to America. The following year these two joined Makemie and four other ministers to form the first American presbytery, a move generally ascribed to Makemie's leadership.

At the beginning of 1707, Makemie was arrested in New York for preaching without a license from the royal governor, Lord Cornbury. After having been denied permission to preach publicly in the Dutch Church in New York City, Makemie had responded by preaching instead in a private house "though in a public manner, and with open doors." In the ensuing controversy, Cornbury called Makemie a "Jack of all Trades . . . a Preacher, a Doctor of Physick, a Merchant, an Attorney, or Counsellor at Law, and which is worse of all, a Disturber of Governments."

At his trial the embattled minister argued that "if our liberty . . . depended upon [either] a license or certificate from the Bishops of England, or the Governors of America, we should soon be deprived of our liberty of conscience secured to us [nonconformists] by [the Toleration Act]." The jury apparently agreed with Makemie's logic and acquitted him.

§ Phone: 410-957-0949.

MASSACHUSETTS

ADAMS

❡ William McKinley Monument, 92 Park Street, in front of the public library.

This eight-foot-high bronze statue of *President William McKinley rests on a pedestal decorated with reliefs depicting episodes from the former president's life: as a congressman addressing the House of Representatives, as a commissary sergeant risking his life to bring food to troops during the battle of Antietam, and as president taking the oath of office. The fourth relief is inscribed with an excerpt from his last speech, given in Buffalo, New York, just before his assassination: "Let us remember that our interest is in Concord, not Conflict, and that our real Eminence is in the Victories of Peace, not those of War." (See Niles, Ohio.)

BOSTON

❡ Ann Glover Memorial, Our Lady of Victories Shrine, 27 Isabella Street.

In the church is a plaque memorializing Ann Glover, an Irishwoman who was hanged as a witch near the site of this church on November 16, 1688. The tablet describes her as the first Catholic martyr in Massachusetts because the Puritans' notorious anti-Catholic sentiments probably were a factor in their prosecution of her.

During the summer of 1688, in a prelude to the more famous witchcraft trials of Salem, Massachusetts, four children of John Goodwin of Boston were the victims of what was believed to be demonic possession. Goodwin's thirteen-year-old daughter, Martha, was the first of the children to exhibit the customary symptoms – after she had accused the family's washerwoman of stealing linens. According to the Puritan minister Cotton Mather, the washerwoman's mother – Ann Glover – had "bestowed very bad Language" upon the Goodwin daughter. Before long, Martha was "visited with strange Fits," allegedly through the witchcraft of Glover, whom Mather described as an "ignorant and a scandalous old Woman" and whom even her husband sometimes described as a witch. Within a few weeks three other Goodwin children were seized with similar afflictions. Sometimes they would be deaf, blind, or dumb, while at other times they appeared to be swallowing their tongues. However, following a day of prayer and fasting observed specifically for the benefit of the afflicted children, the youngest was permanently freed from his torment.

In the meantime, Ann Glover was questioned by the authorities and jailed. According to Mather, she could speak only Gaelic at the trial, although she was known to speak English well. In court she said that she and her husband had been sent from Ireland to Barbados during Cromwell's time. Mrs. Glover stated that while in Barbados her husband was "scored to death and did not give up his religion [probably Roman Catholicism], which same I hold to." When asked whether she was a Papist, and when shown "an idol [statue of a saint?] that was diabolical," she said, "I die a Catholic!" Perhaps because she not could fully comprehend the questions put to her, she admitted that she had tormented the children by stroking small rag dolls that were produced during the trial. When she took up one of these dolls in court, one of the afflicted children was seized with fits.

In addition, the night after her trial Glover was heard explaining to the devil that she had confessed everything because he had deserted her. Upon examination by court-appointed physicians, Glover acknowledged her Roman Catholicism and recited the Lord's Prayer "very readily." After the doctors had declared her of sound mind, the magistrates signed her death warrant, although reluctantly. As Glover predicted from the scaffold, her death brought no cessation to the sufferings of the Goodwin children. They continued to exhibit signs of affliction for many months.

¶ **Boston Athenaeum,** 10.5 Beacon Street.

Among the library's holdings are the book collections of George Washington and General Henry Knox, the Revolutionary War hero and the first president's secretary of war. Knox was descended from a member of a Scotch-Irish congregation from Londonderry, Ireland, who had come to Boston in 1729 and established the "Church of the Presbyterian Strangers."

Many of the books in the Knox collection are from the "New London Book Store," which he opened on Washington Street (near Court Street) in 1771. In his first newspaper advertisement, he announced "A large and very elegant assortment of the most modern Books in all branches of Literature, Arts and Sciences . . . to be sold as cheap as can be bought at any place in town."

Despite Knox's support of the Patriot cause, his bookstore became "a great resort for the British officers and Tory ladies." One of these "high-tone" ladies was Lucy Flucker, the daughter of the colony's royal secretary, who, despite her family's prohibition, married the young Knox. To lure him to the Loyalist persuasion, Lucy's father tempted him with a commission in the British Army, although unsuccessfully.

§ Open Monday-Friday 9-5:30; tours available Tuesday and Thursday at 2:30. Phone: 617-227-0270.

¶ **Boston Common,** in downtown Boston, bounded by Arlington, Beacon, Park, Tremont, and Boylston streets.

Several impressive monuments with Irish or Irish-American associations are located on the Common.

• The John Barry Monument, near the information center, pays tribute to the Irish native who became known as the "Father of the American
Navy." (See St. Mary's Church, Philadelphia, Pennsylvania.)

John Barry Monument.

• Designed by *Augustus Saint-Gaudens, the Shaw Memorial (on Beacon Street, across from the State House) honors Colonel Robert Gould Shaw
and the other officers and men of the 54th Massachusetts Regiment. The
memorial, which was dedicated in 1897, depicts Shaw and his men as
they passed the State House on May 28, 1863, after receiving their regimental colors from Governor John Andrew. The back of the monument is
inscribed with the names of the men of the regiment who were decorated
for bravery.

Although Shaw and his officers were white, the enlisted men in this
regiment were all free African Americans who had volunteered to fight
during the Civil War. The 54th fought bravely during the attack on Fort
Wagner, South Carolina, on July 18, 1863, but Shaw and many of his men
were killed in the assault and were buried near the fort. In his memoir
Saint-Gaudens explained why the memorial to Shaw and his men had
taken him so long to complete: "My own delay I excuse on the ground
that a sculptor's work endures for so long that it is next to a crime for him
to neglect to do everything that lies in his power to execute a result that

will not be a disgrace. There is something extraordinarily irritating, when it is not ludicrous, in a bad statue."

In 1910, when the National Institute of Arts and Letters presented Mrs. Saint-Gaudens with its gold medal in honor of her husband's work, the ceremony included a reading of the following excerpt from Robert Underwood's poem "Saint-Gaudens: An Ode":

> So, on the traveled verge
> Of storied Boston's green acropolis
> That sculpted music, that immortal dirge,
> That better than towering shaft
> Has fitly epitaphed
> The hated ranks men did not dare to hiss!
> When Duty makes her clarion call to Ease
> Let her repair and point to this:
> Why seek another clime?
> Why seek another place?
> We have no Parthenon, but a noble frieze, -
> Since sacrifice than worship nobler is.
> It sings – the anthem of a rescued race;
> It moves – the epic of a patriot time,
> And each heroic figure makes a martial rhyme.
> How like ten thousand treads that little band,
> Fit for the van of armies! What command

The Robert Gould Shaw Memorial by Augustus Saint-Gaudens.

Sits in that saddle! What renouncing will!
What portent grave of firm-confronted ill!
And as a cloud doth hover over sea,
Born from its waters and returning there,
Fame, sprung from thoughts of mortals, swims the air
And gives them back her memories, deathlessly.

• The Boston Massacre Monument, near Oliver Wendell Holmes Walk, is a twenty-five-foot granite shaft in honor of the victims of the famous skirmish between British soldiers and taunting colonials. The shaft contains the names of the five "massacre" victims: Crispus Attucks, Samuel Maverick, Jonas Caldwell, Samuel Gray, and Patrick Carr (a native of Ireland).

In front of the shaft is a seven-foot bronze female figure holding a broken chain in her right hand and a flag in her left. An eagle beside her has just landed, while her right foot rests on a twisted crown about to fall off the plinth. Around the apex of the shaft are thirteen stars. A bronze bas-relief on the base depicts the Massacre on King (now State) Street. On the relief are two quotations: "From that Moment we may date the Severance of the British Empire" (Daniel Webster) and "On that night the Foun-

Monument to the victims of the Boston Massacre, one of whom was the Irishman Patrick Carr.

dation of American Independence was laid" (John Adams).

In a speech at the dedication of the monument in 1888, Hugh O'Brien, Boston's Irish-born mayor, said: "The Boston Massacre was one of the most important and exciting events that preceded our Revolution . . . . I rejoice . . . that the erection of the Attucks Monument on Boston Common ratifies the words of the [Declaration of Independence] that all men are free and equal; and that the memory of the martyrs whose blood was shed in the cause of liberty in 1770 will thus be preserved and honored for all time."

• Dedicated in 1877, the Soldiers' and Sailors' Monument is considered the greatest work of Martin Milmore, a native of Sligo, Ireland, where his father was a schoolmaster. The centerpiece of this Civil War memorial is a granite shaft topped by a bronze figure of "Liberty." Around the pedestal are statues representing Peace, the Sailor, the Muse of History, and the Soldier. Between the projections on which the statues stand are four bas-reliefs depicting the Battle of Fort Sumter, the Departure of the Forces for the War, the Work of the Boston Sanitary Commission, and the Return from the War.

Milmore was educated in Boston schools, learned woodcarving from his brother, and in his first effort at sculpting modeled a bust of himself with the help of a mirror. While living in Rome, he executed busts of Pius IX, Ralph Waldo Emerson, and Wendell Phillips. He was also known for his portrait busts of *Ulysses S. Grant, Abraham Lincoln, Henry Wadsworth Longfellow, *Cardinal John McCloskey, Charles Sumner, and Daniel Webster. Milmore's other larger works are the Soldiers' Monument in Roxbury, Massachusetts, the statue of General Sylvanus Thayer at the U.S. Military Academy, and the *Sphinx* in Cambridge, Massachusetts. According to Daniel Chester French, "Milmore was a picturesque figure, somewhat of the Edwin Booth type, with long dark hair and large dark eyes. He affected the artistic . . . , wearing a broad-brimmed soft black hat, and a cloak. His appearance was striking, and he knew it."

¶ Visitors to the nearby Public Gardens will be interested to know that the flower beds were introduced by William Doogue, a native of Ireland and the Superintendent of Common and Public Grounds in Boston from 1878 to 1906. After emigrating from Stradbally, County Laois, with his parents and eight siblings, Doogue had settled in Middletown, Connecticut. Following his graduation from high school in 1843, he began an apprenticeship in the nurseries of George Affleck & Company, in Hartford, where he learned the science of floriculture, horticulture, and landscape gardening. He later studied botany under a professor at Trinity College in the Connecticut capital. Doogue moved to Boston in 1856 to assume the management of the floricultural and horticultural business of Charles Copeland.

• One of the statues along Boylston Street in the Public Gardens is a

Statue of Colonel Thomas Cass in the Boston Public Gardens.

likeness of Colonel Thomas Cass, the commander of the 9th Massachusetts Infantry. The statue was dedicated in 1899 in the presence of veterans of the "Fighting Ninth." One of them, Major D. G. McNamara, said that the monument commemorated "the deeds of heroism which [Cass's] gallant regiment achieved while battling for three years on Southern soil for the preservation of the Union of the States."

Born in Ireland in 1822, Cass conducted a real estate and brokerage business after immigrating to Boston. In 1854 he became captain of a militia unit known as the Columbian Artillery Company, which by then had a largely Irish Catholic membership. The following year, however, the governor disbanded all militia companies made up of persons of foreign birth. At the outbreak of the Civil War, Cass formed the 9th Massachusetts, composed entirely of Irish immigrants from Marlborough, Milford, Salem, and Stoughton. He was killed while leading his men at the battle of Malvern Hill in Virginia on July 1, 1862. He is buried in Mt. Auburn Cemetery, Cambridge, Massachusetts.

¶ **Boston Massacre Site,** marked by a circle of cobblestones at the intersection of State and Congress streets.

On March 5, 1770, a lone British sentry outside the Customs House near this site was attacked by a gang of rowdy youths, a disturbance that attracted a growing crowd. After moving a detachment of eight Redcoats to the scene, Captain Thomas Preston (himself an Anglo-Irishman) attempted to pacify the crowd, although he told his men to load their weapons. When a bystander hit one of the soldiers with a stick, the Redcoat accidentally discharged his gun as he fell to the ground. The other soldiers immediately fired into the mob, killing four and wounding seven others. Among the wounded who later died was the Irish immigrant Patrick Carr.

On the night of the violent confrontation between Boston "ruffians" and British soldiers, Carr was living in Queen (now Court) Street in the household of his employer, a leather-breeches maker. When Carr responded to the clamor of bells announcing the initial commotion, he started to leave the house with a small cutlass hidden under his coat until a neighbor persuaded him to leave the weapon at home. By the time the Irishman approached the center of the disturbance, the "Lobster Backs" had begun firing into the crowd of taunting citizenry. As he crossed King Street, he was hit by a bullet that "went through his right hip & tore away part of the backbone & greatly injured the hip bone." A companion carried him into a nearby house and then ran for a doctor. Carr was later moved to his master's house in Queen Street. Although at least two doctors tried to save his life, the young apprentice died on March 14. Three days later – on St. Patrick's Day – Carr was laid to rest in the Old Granary Burial Ground on Tremont Street, where four of the other victims of the "Massacre" had already been buried.

At the trial of the British soldiers, several witnesses gave compelling testimony about Carr's apparent intentions on the night of the violence. Carr's landlady explained how the Irishman had originally intended to go to the scene of the disturbance carrying a concealed weapon. Dr. John Jeffries, who had gone to see Carr the morning after the "Massacre," repeated what he purported was his conversation with the wounded man: "I asked him whether he thought the soldiers would fire. He told me he thought the soldiers would fire long before. I asked him whether he thought the soldiers were abused a great deal, after they went down there. He said, he thought they were. I asked him whether he thought the soldiers would have been hurt, if they had not fired. He said he really thought they would, for he heard many voices cry out, kill them. I asked him then . . . whether he thought they fired in self-defense, or on purpose to destroy the people. He said he really thought they did fire to defend themselves; that he did not blame the man whoever he was, that shot him." In answer to the question whether he thought Carr was aware of the danger he was in at the time of the disturbance, Jeffries replied somewhat equivocally: "He was told of it. He told me also, he was a native of Ireland, that he had frequently seen mobs, and soldiers called upon to quell them." Jeffries again paraphrased Carr's assertion that the British soldiers had shown unusual patience in the face of the taunting they received. According to Jeffries, Carr claimed "that he had seen soldiers often fire on the people in Ireland, but had never seen them bear half so much before they fired in his life." In a final conversation with Jeffries, the Irishman allegedly forgave "whoever he was that shot him, he was satisfied he had no malice, but fired to defend himself."

¶ **Boston Public Library,** 666 Boylston Street, Copley Square.

This Italian Renaissance structure is noted for several pieces of art work by Irish or Irish-American artists:

• a bust of the goddess Athena and the seal of the library (with the words "Free to All"), both of them by Augustus Saint-Gaudens and located on the façade of the building;

• a medallion portrait of Robert C. Billings (a benefactor of the library) by Augustus Saint-Gaudens;

• a pair of lions by Louis Saint-Gaudens in honor of the men of two Massachusetts regiments who died in the Civil War. (The names of the campaigns and the battles in which the regiments participated are inscribed on the pedestals.)

• bronze busts of Irish natives Hugh O'Brien (Boston mayor) and John Boyle O'Reilly (journalist), both by John Donoghue

Donoghue was born in Chicago in 1853 to parents from western Ireland and attended the Chicago Academy of Design and the Ecole des Beaux-Arts. His most notable classical works are the bust *Phaedra* and the statues *Young Sophokles, Hunting Nymph, Hannibal,* and *Kypris.* While in Rome, he also modeled a colossal figure called *The Spirit,* intended for exhibition at the Chicago World's Fair. Officials refused to accept the statue, however, because they feared that it would be blown down by the elements in the Windy City. As the model for his statue *The Boxer,* Donoghue used the famous pugilist *John L. Sullivan.

§ Open October-May 30, Monday-Thursday 9-9, Friday and Saturday 9-5, Sunday 1-5; rest of the year, Monday-Thursday 9-9, Friday and Saturday 9-5. Closed holidays. Phone: 617-536-5400.

¶ **Bunker Hill Monument,** Monument Square, Charlestown.

This 221-foot granite obelisk commemorates the battle of Breed's Hill on June 17, 1775. Among the Americans who participated in the battle were 694 men with Irish surnames, among them Coughlan, Lyons, McGaffey, and Savage. In addition, seven of the American officers were natives of Ireland, five had Irish immigrant parents, and another five were of Irish descent. Seventy percent of the companies that suffered casualties had Irishmen or sons of Irishmen in them; fifty-four casualties had Irish surnames, and twenty-two were natives of Ireland. The names of the Americans killed in the battle are on the Memorial Tablets in Winthrop Square in Charlestown.

One of the unfortunate officers cut down that day was Major Andrew Clary, the son of an immigrant from County Tyrone, Ireland. During the battle Clary commanded a battalion in John Stark's New Hampshire regiment and fought valiantly, but later that day he was struck by a chance shot from a British frigate in the Charles River. The major was described as "a favorite officer, six and a half feet in height, with a Herculean form in perfect proportions, a voice like a Stentor and the strength of Ajax; ever unequalled in athletic exercise and unsubdued in single combat, whole bodies of men had been overcome by him and he seemed totally unconscious that he was not equally unconquerable at the cannon's mouth." Fifty years later, in an address to mark the laying of the cornerstone of the Bunker Hill Monument, Daniel Webster made note of Clary's valor during the battle.

Another colorful participant in the battle was the clergyman John Martin. Born in Ireland in 1750 and living in the west country until the age of seven – "speaking and hearing nothing but old Irish" – he attended a Catholic seminary in West Meath before coming to Rhode Island in 1771. During the battle on Breed's Hill, he supervised about a thousand men as they labored to finish building the entrenchments. His clerical dress and his ministrations to the dead and wounded guaranteed him no quarter, however, for the British soldiers "damned him for a clerical dog" and fired upon him as he carried off the American casualties: "The soldiers rushed on him with their bayonets, [but] he defended himself with his sword and killed his adversaries, [and then] brought off his wounded." For his bravery he was rewarded with a chaplaincy in a Rhode Island regiment. Later during the war he crossed the British lines as a spy for the Americans.

§ Open daily 9-4:30. Phone: 617-242-5641.

J Callahan Tunnel, under Boston Harbor to Logan Airport.

A frequent automotive bottleneck, this Boston landmark was opened in 1961 in honor of William F. Callahan Jr., the son of the state public works commissioner in the 1930s, 1940s, and 1950s.

The younger Callahan was a sandy-haired, six-foot-two-inch graduate of Exeter Academy and the Pennsylvania Military College, where he was a star polo player on the intercollegiate team during his senior year. During World War II, he was an infantry lieutenant with the 10th Mountain Division in the Italian Appenines, when he was killed by shrapnel from the mortars of the retreating Nazis, just north of Florence. "He was impatient to get into action," Callahan's father said about his twenty-four-year-old son. "He was afraid the war would be over before he got [into] it."

Callahan Senior was renowned for supervising the construction of the first 125 miles of the Massachusetts Turnpike in twenty-seven months and constructed most of Route 128 as well. He also seems to have pulled a fast one in changing the logo associated with the turnpike system. Originally the logo depicted the figure of Paul Revere on horseback and encircled with the words "Massachusetts Turnpike Authority." Sometime in the late 1950s, however, the logo was changed to its present image: a Pilgrim hat pierced by an arrow. According to some reputed authorities, the new logo was Callahan's way of depicting the ascendant Irish – symbolized by the arrow – piercing the Yankee hold on the state's political power.

¶ Cardinal Cushing Memorial, in a small park at Cambridge and Bowdoin streets, opposite the Saltonstall Building.

This bronze bust of Richard Cushing, the archbishop of Boston from 1944 to 1970, was erected from contributions made by the Catholic clergy of the Boston archdiocese. At its dedication in 1981, Cardinal Humberto Medeiros described his predecessor as a leader who "never lacked the common touch."

The son of a blacksmith from County Cork, Cushing was born in South Boston in 1895 and while in high school was interested in baseball and public speaking. After attending Boston College for two years, he decided

Cardinal Cushing Memorial.

to enter the seminary, motivated, he facetiously said, by the chance to become a politician. For almost two decades after his ordination he worked with the Society for the Propagation of the Faith, until his selection as auxiliary bishop of Boston in 1939.

Cushing was buoyed by the hope that the election of Pope John XXIII would lead to a new openness in the Catholic Church. In 1961 the cardinal expressed his belief that "the Church is a dynamic, not a static institution. . . . It cannot be frozen in set forms. There are essentials of its life, but beyond these there must always be innovation, enterprise, new vision." Although very interested in the issues of religious liberty and ecumenism discussed at the Second Vatican Council, he participated in the proceedings only minimally, apparently because of difficulty in understanding the Latin in which the discussions were conducted.

Cushing later broke new ground by speaking in synagogues and Protestant churches and served as a panelist in a Catholic-Protestant conference at Harvard University. In response to criticism about these actions, he replied: "I'm all for Catholics being identified with Protestants and Jews . . . in every possible friendly way. Nobody is asking them to deny their faith, and they shouldn't be asking anybody to deny their faith." In 1963, when he left to participate in the election of a successor to John XXIII, he expressed his hope that "the new Pope will be living in the twentieth . . . and not the fourteenth or sixteenth century." His own modern vision of the Church was seen in the fact that he established the first Catholic chapel at an airport and the first diocesan center for radio and television.

Through his association with the Kennedy family, Cushing became a friend and admirer of John F. Kennedy. During the latter's presidential campaign, the cardinal countered critics who charged that Kennedy would be obliged to follow Vatican policies as president. "Whatever may be the custom elsewhere," Cushing pointed out, "the American tradition . . . is satisfied simply to call to public attention moral questions with their implications, and leave to the conscience of the people the specific political decision which comes in the act of voting." Cushing gave the invocation at Kennedy's inauguration and later conducted the funeral of the assassinated president at St. Matthew's Cathedral in Washington, D. C. In 1966 Cushing bragged that he and Kennedy's father had helped the young senator defeat Hubert Humphrey in the 1960 West Virginia primary. According to the cardinal, he had identified the Protestant ministers in that state to whom Joseph Kennedy contributed money, supposedly without any political strings attached. "It's good for the Lord. It's good for the church. It's good for the preacher, and it's good for the candidate," Cushing rationalized.

¶ A plaque at 808 East Third Street in South Boston identifies Cushing's birthplace.

¶ Cardinal O'Connell Way, in the West End, north of Cambridge Street and between Blossom and Staniford streets.

William O'Connell was born in Lowell, Massachusetts [*q.v.*], the son of immigrants from County Cavan, Ireland. After graduating from Boston College, O'Connell studied for the priesthood at the North American College in Rome. Several years after his ordination in 1884, he was named rector of his Roman alma mater, in which capacity he doubled the school's enrollment and put its finances in order. After the Russo-Japanese War he was named papal envoy to the Japanese emperor, who subsequently awarded him the Grand Cordon of the Sacred Treasure. The Vatican later adopted all the archbishop's recommendations with regard to Japan: the development of a native clergy, the introduction of more religious orders, and the creation of a Catholic university in Tokyo.

After becoming archbishop of Boston in 1907 and cardinal four years later, O'Connell oversaw an administration that recorded phenomenal growth. He created 128 new parishes, introduced twenty religious communities into the archdiocese, doubled the number of elementary schools, and tripled the number of high schools. In addition, three women's colleges were founded under his auspices, enrollment at the archdiocesan seminary tripled, and Catholic charities benefited from his disbursement of a $2.5 million bequest which he had received from an American theater impresario.

In 1937 even Harvard University – founded 300 years before as a bulwark of Puritan orthodoxy – recognized O'Connell's work for the people of Boston by awarding him a doctoral degree, the first by Harvard to a member of the American Catholic hierarchy. Two years later he became the first American prelate to attend a papal conclave. (He had missed two earlier conclaves because of his inability to reach Rome within the allotted ten-day period. His protest caused Pius XI to extend the time to eighteen days.)

¶ Charlestown Navy Yard, off I-93 in Charlestown.

The U.S.S. *Constitution*, the oldest commissioned ship in the American navy, was launched near here in 1797. It earned the name "Ironsides" because of its exploits during the War of 1812.

The nickname "Ironsides" was shared with *Father William Henry Reaney, one of the first Catholic chaplains in the U.S. Navy. Reaney was appointed chaplain in 1892 and received his nickname because of his birth aboard the U.S.S. *Constitution* as it lay in New York harbor. Noted for his friendliness and Irish wit, he loved athletics of all kinds, especially boxing. He was, in fact, a sparring partner of *President Theodore Roosevelt. During his chaplaincy he served on the U.S.S. *Charleston, Baltimore,* and *Olympia.*

§ Open 9:30-dusk. Phone: 617-242-5670.

¶ **Church of the Immaculate Conception,** Harrison Avenue and Concord Street.

Designed by *Patrick Keely, this edifice was built as the collegiate church of Boston College, founded in 1863 on adjacent property by Father John McElroy, a native of Ireland. The Jesuit college, New England's first such Catholic institution, began with a faculty of six Jesuits and a student body of twenty-two. The school remained on this site until 1913, when it was relocated in Chestnut Hill, a Boston suburb.

McElroy had come to America in 1803 from Enniskillen, County Fermanagh, Ireland. After working as a bookkeeper at Georgetown College for a number of years, he joined the Society of Jesus. While a seminarian at Georgetown during the War of 1812, he witnessed the burning of the nation's capital by the British from his dormitory window. After his ordination he served as an instructor at Georgetown College and then as pastor of St. John's Church in Frederick, Maryland.

In 1846 the Irish priest was appointed by *President James K. Polk as a chaplain to the American army at Matamoros, Mexico, where he served for eleven months and earned the highest praise of General Zachary Taylor. Returning to Boston after the war, the priest foresaw the need of an institution of higher learning to serve the increasing numbers of Catholics in the city. After much effort he finally obtained the property on Harrison Avenue, in the city's South End.

¶ **Copley Square,** at Boylston and Dartmouth streets.

This expansive urban plaza was named for John Singleton Copley, America's most outstanding colonial artist and one of the world's most talented painters at the turn of the nineteenth century. His parents had emigrated from Ireland around 1736, one or two years before the birth of their famous son in Boston.

Although Copley had secured a reputation – and a commensurate income – as a Boston portrait painter before the age of thirty, he felt uncomfortable with the growing political unrest on the eve of the Revolution. (His wife's family was loyalist in its sentiments.) He therefore found it opportune to travel to London, where, during his subsequent expatriate career, he became known for his heroic-sized historical paintings. His most famous works in this genre are *The Death of the Earl of Chatham, The Siege of Gibraltar, The Arrest of Five Members of the Commons by Charles I,"* and *The Death of Major Pierson."*

Copley's own political leanings were revealed shortly after George III recognized American independence, when the artist painted the Stars and Stripes over a ship in the background of a portrait of Elkanah Watson. About the pictorial sleight of hand, Watson later wrote: "This was, I imagine, the first American flag hoisted in Old England."

¶ **Copley Studio Site,** marked with a plaque on the Somerset Club at 42 Beacon Street. Private.

Despite his permanent residence in London beginning in 1774, *John Singleton Copley continued to own the home and studio formerly on this site. Around 1800, however, he sold the property to a consortium of speculators. (See entry above.)

¶ **David Ignatius Walsh Statue,** Charles River Esplanade, near the Hatch Shell.

This imposing bronze statue commemorates the life and career of the first non-Yankee to be elected governor of Massachusetts. The curving wall behind the statue models the shape of the music shell nearby and is inscribed with the Latin motto *Non sibi sed patriae* ("Not for himself but for his country").

One of ten children born to Irish emigrants, Walsh was able to attend Holy Cross College and Boston University Law School because of the sacrifices made by his mother and older sisters, who worked in the textile mills near Leominster, Massachusetts. His attractive personality and oratorical skills soon led to a successful career in politics. In the short span of six years, he enjoyed rapid electoral advancement as lieutenant governor, governor, and U.S. senator. (With his election to the Senate in 1918, Massa-

Statue of David Walsh.

chusetts was represented by a Democrat in that house for the first time since 1851.)

Walsh's career was characterized by his commitment to reforms intended to improve the economic and social conditions of the urban, ethnic, and industrial working class. He was particularly proud of his successful efforts as governor to improve the state labor code and to create a system of university extension courses for the benefit of his blue-collar constituents. Although he supported the general goals of the New Deal, he broke with Franklin Roosevelt over the latter's "court-packing" scheme and the president's decision to campaign for a third term. While chairman of the senate naval affairs committee during the late 1930s, Walsh argued for the necessity of military preparedness, but he considered the conflict in Europe as "nothing but a clash of two forms of imperialisms" and demanded absolute neutrality on the part of the United States. Nevertheless, following the Japanese attack on Pearl Harbor, he insisted that "we must defend ourselves."

¶ **Dorchester Heights National Historic Site,** Thomas Park, Dorchester Heights, South Boston (near the intersection of Broadway and G Street).

Completed in 1902, the 215-foot monument on this site commemorates the actions taken by the Continental Army in May 1776 to dislodge the British from Boston after a yearlong siege.

Extraordinary efforts to drive out the British had begun in November 1775, when *General Henry Knox and his men began a 300-mile trek from upstate New York to Boston, dragging in the dead of winter the fifty-nine cannon they had captured at Fort Ticonderoga. On the night of March 4, 1776, American soldiers and volunteers moved the artillery into position on these heights south of Boston. Although the British launched an attack on the American position, they were unsuccessful and evacuated their troops and local Tories on March 17.

§ Open daily 9-9 in summer; abbreviated times the rest of the year.

¶ **Edward Logan Statue,** at the entrance to Logan International Airport, East Boston.

This statue by Joseph Coletti was unveiled in 1956 to honor the memory of the Massachusetts lawyer, judge, and soldier for whom Boston's busy airport is named.

The son of an Irish immigrant, Edward Logan was born in South Boston in 1875. Following his graduation (as class valedictorian) from Harvard College, he joined the 9th Massachusetts Infantry and served as a sergeant-major in the Spanish-American War. His first exposure to politics came a few years later, when, while still attending law school, he was elected to the Boston city council. Following a single term in each house of the state legislature, he was appointed justice of the South Boston municipal court. From the bench he dispensed his own mix of justice and mercy, often using his personal resources to take care of the needy families of law breakers whom he sentenced to imprisonment.

Although Logan remained a municipal judge until his death, he continued to take an active role in *affairs militaires*. Having returned to the 9th Massachusetts in 1901, he advanced to the rank of colonel. In an article for the *Boston Globe Magazine*, Peter J. Howe provided an interesting insight into his subject: "An avidly religious man, Logan felt that all his soldiers should attend religious services on Sunday, whatever denomination they were. When he found out one Sunday that many of 'his boys' weren't attending any service, he had one of his officers take them on a 25-mile hike. The next Sunday he did it again. The Sunday after that everyone was at church."

When the United States declared war on Germany in April 1917, Logan led a detachment of troops in the seizure of the interned German liner *Kronprinzessin Cecilie* in Boston harbor. He subsequently led his infantry regiment – reorganized as the 101st – through the major French campaigns, including the Marne and St. Mihiel. In 1928, after thirty-one years in the national guard, he was retired with the rank of lieutenant general, the first man in the history of the state's national guard to be so honored.

❡ Edwin O'Connor Apartment, 10 Marlborough Street, in the Back Bay. Private.

During the mid 1950s this was the address of the author *Edwin O'Connor while he was completing his masterpiece, *The Last Hurrah*. The book, one of the most popular political novels in American literature, recounts the final campaign of Frank Skeffington, an aging Irish-American party boss created in the image of Boston's real-life mayor *James Curley.

O'Connor, the son of a doctor and a school teacher, was born in Providence, Rhode Island, in 1918. At the University of Notre Dame he had originally intended to study journalism but changed his major to literature when a professor advised him: "You can learn all you need to learn about journalism in six months. English literature takes a little longer." Following his graduation he worked as a radio announcer and producer, developing what one critic called his "ability to write with his ears." It was an ability that Clifton Fadiman acknowledged about the style of *The Last Hurrah*: "I find myself remembering . . . its talk, its spate of wild, outrageous, useless talk cascading down every page, . . ." *The Oracle*, a novel about a pompous radio broadcaster, met with some acclaim but little financial success.

The Last Hurrah, however, immediately made its way to the best-seller list, although not without professional criticism. The *New Yorker* reviewer, for example, charged that O'Connor had transformed the "barbaric"

Skeffington into a "fairy godmother of widows and orphans," thereby glamorizing vices as virtues. The *New York Times* reviewer, on the other hand, opined that O'Connor "has no doubts about what Skeffington cost the city or the Irish. . . . He also makes it clear, however, that the tragedy is collective, the failure of the Irish as a whole to have the courage of their own qualities and to make better use of them." In 1958 the book was transformed into a motion picture starring Spencer Tracy as the protagonist Skeffington.

Despite the popularity of *The Last Hurrah*, it was for *The Edge of Sadness* that O'Connor won the Pulitzer Prize for fiction in 1962. Told through the eyes of Father Hugh Kennedy, a reformed alcoholic priest, the honored novel chronicled three generations of the Carmodys, an Irish-American family not unlike the Kennedys of Massachusetts. Expressing a preference for *The Last Hurrah*, a *New York Times* reviewer commented that the Pulitzer Prize had gone to the "right writer – if for the wrong book."

¶ **Faneuil Hall,** Faneuil Hall Square, Merchants Row.

The assembly hall on the second floor is dominated by the huge oil painting *Liberty and Union, Now and Forever* by *George Healy. The work depicts the famous debate which took place in the U.S. Senate on January 25, 1830, in which Daniel Webster of Massachusetts argued the issue of nullification and states' rights with Robert Haynes of South Carolina. (See White House, District of Columbia.)

In painting the huge work for King Louis-Philippe of France, Healy included either in the Senate chamber or in the gallery the most prominent politicians and members of Washington society of the day. The Irish-American artist worked on the painting for seven years, only to see his royal patron deposed in 1848. Healy later sold the work to a group of Boston businessmen, who presented it to the city in 1851.

§ Open Monday-Friday 10-5. Closed January 1, Thanksgiving, and December 25. Phone: 617-523-1300.

¶ **Granary Burial Ground,** Tremont Street.

Among those buried here the victims of the Boston Massacre (including the Irishman Patrick Carr) and James Sullivan (a governor of Massachusetts and the first Irish justice of the state's supreme court).

§ Open daily 8-4:30.

¶ **Holy Cross Cathedral,** Washington and Malden streets.

Because by 1860 the area in which the original Church of the Holy Cross was located had become increasingly commercial, *Bishop John Fitzpatrick decided to sell that church and erect the present structure at this site. The cathedral was designed by *Patrick Keely and was constructed between 1866 and 1876. It is one of the largest Gothic cathedrals in the world and one of about thirty churches which Keely designed in the Boston area.

¶ Irish Famine Memorial, Washington and School streets.

This beautifully landscaped park is dominated by a pair of larger-than-life sculptures, one of an impoverished family leaving Ireland and the other of a family filled with hope upon arriving in Boston. The work of Robert Shure, the statuary groups were unveiled in June 1998 to commemorate the victims of the Great Hunger that ravaged Ireland in the 1840s. The memorial is located a few blocks from where the Irish refugees first crowded into tenements along Boston's waterfront.

¶ James Curley Memorial, near Faneuil Hall, in the park between North and Congress streets.

This memorial consists of two life-size bronze statues of colorful Boston mayor James Curley, one of him seated on a park bench as if talking to a companion, and the other standing with his hands behind his back.

Curley, the son of immigrants from Galway, Ireland, early tried his hands at politics, sometimes showing an unappreciated independence by campaigning against his ward boss's candidate. In one electoral contest, although Curley won by 500 votes, the party bosses stole the election from him by "counting him out." Nevertheless, the determined Curley was

Statues of Mayor James Curley.

successively elected to the city council, the state assembly, the board of aldermen, the House of Representatives, the governorship, and the mayoralty.

During his four terms as mayor between 1914 and 1949, Curley was known as the "mayor of the poor" and a champion of the Irish. His administrations were marked by increased expenditures for public works, a policy whose increasing tax assessments caused many of the city's business interests to oppose him. He failed to be reelected in 1917 when a rival ward boss split the Irish vote by running two phoney candidates with Irish surnames.

Although previous Irish mayors had refrained from attacking Yankee culture and tradition, Curley lambasted the WASP Establishment. In a letter to the Harvard Board of Overseers, he exulted: "The Massachusetts of the Puritans is as dead as Caesar, but there is no need to mourn the fact. Their successors – the Irish – had letters and learning, culture and civilization when the ancestors of the Puritans were savages running half-naked through the forests of Britain. It took the Irish to make Massachusetts a fit place to live in." On another occasion he attacked wealthy Yankees as descendants of scoundrels who "got rich selling opium to the Chinese, rum to the Indians, or trading in slaves."

Despite his active campaigning for Franklin Roosevelt in 1932, Curley was disappointed in his hope of securing in return a suitable political appointment. Although the Irish American had hoped to be named secretary of the navy, F.D.R. suggested the Italian ambassadorship, adding that Curley would be the first Catholic ambassador to Rome. After asking for time to think it over, Curley sent telegrams to the King of Italy, Premier Mussolini, and the Vatican to obtain their reaction to the proposal. When the former mayor returned to Roosevelt ready to accept the ambassadorial spot, the president claimed that the appointment had run into objections from the Italian monarch. After Curley proffered the affirmative telegram from the Italian government, F.D.R. changed his story and said that it must have been Mussolini who objected. Curley called Roosevelt's bluff by producing the telegrams which expressed approval by both the Italian premier and the Holy See and then stormed out of the office. (The former Boston mayor later learned that his name had never been submitted for the position.)

ℐ James Curley Residence, 350 Jamaicaway at Moraine Street.

Mayor James Curley began construction on this brick colonial mansion – appropriately enough – on St. Patrick's Day, 1915. The twenty-one-room house is notable for its chandeliers, Italian marble fireplaces, and shamrock-decorated shutters. It was here that Curley died in 1958, just short of his eighty-fourth birthday.

During his political career Curley survived both personal tragedy and political scandal. Although he and his wife had nine children, only two survived to adulthood. In fact, in 1950 two of their children died of cerebral hemorrhage the very same day. During his first term in the state legislature, he spent sixty days in jail for impersonating someone else in a civil service exam. (Always trying to win political advantage, he said about the incident, "I did it for a friend!") Later, while mayor in the 1930s, he was charged with defrauding the city and was ordered to repay almost $43,000. Finally, after his last term as mayor, the seventy-two-year-old Curley served five months in jail for mail fraud stemming from a charge of influence-peddling in Congress.

A fictionalized version of his career is portrayed in *Edwin O'Connor's 1956 novel *The Last Hurrah*, although because of what Curley described as inaccuracies the former mayor responded in a 1957 autobiography, *I'd Do It Again*. Even one of his most outspoken critics admitted that Boston "would be a shabby place without having had him."

§ Although the house is generally not open to the public, it can be viewed by appointment. Phone 617-635-4105.

¶ **James Family House,** 131 Mt. Vernon Street, Beacon Hill. Private.

During the mid 1880s, this address was the home of Henry James Sr. and two of his children, Alice and Henry Jr. It was here that Henry Jr. wrote a dramatization of his novel *Daisy Miller*.

The family was descended from William James, a Protestant emigrant from Bailieborough, County Cavan, Ireland, who settled in Albany, New York, in 1789. According to family lore, James arrived in America with a very small sum of money, a Latin grammar, and a desire to visit one of the Revolutionary War battlefields. By 1805 he had opened five stores in Albany, from which he shipped such commodities as wheat, flax, seeds, timber, and meat to New York City. As the first president of the Albany Savings Bank, he acquired extensive holdings in upstate New York, including an interest in the Erie Canal. In 1824 he bought the village of Syracuse – a 250-acre tract with an equal number of inhabitants – for $30,000. He and three partners proceeded to drain and grade the terrain prior to promoting and selling 320 lots, some for as much as $620 apiece. The partners later purchased the Saratoga Salt Company, which was producing 400,000 bushels of course salt per year. At the time of James's death, he was one of the two or three wealthiest men in the country, having accumulated a fortune which allowed his children and grandchildren to travel and pursue intellectual interests.

The patriarch's three wives – two of Irish ancestry – bore him a baker's dozen of children, the most famous of whom was the theologian Henry James Sr. (His maternal grandparents haled from County Longford.) The otherwise prolific writer was oddly succinct about his siblings: "I have nothing to say of my [surviving] brothers and sisters, who were seven in number, except that our relations were always cordially affectionate." About his father he noted the older man's general aloofness, observing that he never "questioned me about my out-of-door occupations, or about my companions, or showed any extreme solicitude about my standing in school." Yet after Henry's right leg was amputated because of severe burns, the son noticed that his father's tenderness was such "as to give me an exalted sense of his affection." During a visit to the family's ancestral home in Ireland in 1837, Henry was "so intoxicated with the roads and lanes and hedges and fields and cottages and castles and inns that I thought I should fairly expire with delight."

Of Henry Senior's three children, Alice was the most passionately sympathetic to the Irish. She was particularly scathing about the English, who, she wrote, "are absolutely without the Irish brain cell & they have consequently a structural inability to conceive of an Irishman as having the ordinary human attributes." Most of her London friends, whom she referred to as "imbecile Unionist abortions," opposed Irish home rule. She confessed that their "hideous, patronizing, doctrinaire, all-for-Ireland's-good, little measured out globules of remedies, make my blood boil so I never speak on the subject."

¶ **John Boyle O'Reilly House,** Winthrop Street, toward the lower end of Common Street.

The last house before the fire station was once the home of John Boyle O'Reilly, the Irish-born patriot, political prisoner, author, editor, and civic leader.

¶ **John Boyle O'Reilly Memorial,** Boylston Street, near the Brookline Avenue bridge over the Back Bay Fens.

A bronze bust of John Boyle O'Reilly stands atop a tapering stone pedestal. To the rear is a female personification of Erin twining a laurel wreath and flanked by allegorical figures of her sons, Poetry and Courage (or Patriotism). Courage is depicted as a virile youth dressed like an ancient Irish warrior, while the winged figure of Poetry holds a lyre in his left hand and with his right offers Erin a leaf for her wreath. The work of Daniel Chester French, the monument was dedicated in 1896, six years after O'Reilly's death.

Born near Drogheda, Ireland, in 1844, O'Reilly became active in the Fenian movement to overthrow British rule in Ireland even while he was a member of a British regiment. When his efforts to recruit other Irish soldiers to the cause were uncovered, he was court-martialed and found guilty of conspiracy and failure to inform the authorities of "an intended mutiny." Although he was sentenced to death, that penalty was commuted to life imprisonment and finally to twenty years of penal servitude. During a two-year period he was imprisoned at six different locations throughout England. At Mountjoy Prison he wrote three poems on the walls of his cell: "The Irish Flag," "For Life," and "The Irish Soldiers." Beneath the last was scratched the remark: "Written on the wall of my cell with a nail, July 17, 1866. Once an English soldier; now an Irish felon; and proud of the exchange." In October 1867 he was transported to a penal colony in Western Australia to serve the rest of his sentence.

In 1871, however, with the help of *Father Patrick McCabe, the prison colony's chaplain, O'Reilly made his escape, ultimately to America. He first took passage on an American whaling ship commanded by Captain David Gifford, who treated him kindly during the six-month cruise to Java and who lent him twenty guineas when they separated off the Cape of Good Hope. (While still on Gifford's ship, O'Reilly was almost killed during the pursuit of a whale but was rescued by the second mate, Henry Hathaway.) At Good Hope, O'Reilly boarded another American ship bound for Liverpool, where he shipped aboard the *Bombay* as "third mate" and headed for Philadelphia, arriving nine months after his escape from Australia. In 1873 O'Reilly dedicated his first book – *Songs of the Southern Seas* – to Captain Gifford, but news of the dedication arrived two hours after his death. O'Reilly's memorial to the good captain was the poem "A Tribute Too Late."

After moving to Boston, O'Reilly began a literary career that made him one of the most popular writers and commentators on the Irish-Ameri-

John Boyle O'Reilly Memorial.

can scene. His editorial influence grew steadily, initially after he obtained a position with the *Pilot*, the most influential "Irish paper" in America, and later when he joined with *Cardinal William O'Connell of Boston to purchase that publication. Through this vehicle, as well as through his articles in the major publications of the period, O'Reilly became a spokesman for racial and religious tolerance, American patriotism, Irish nationalism, and the ideals of the Democratic Party.

Despite his support for the rights of Irish-American citizens, O'Reilly condemned sectarianism and efforts to create an Irish political party. After the 1871 Orange Riots (generally between Catholic and Protestant Irish in New York City), he thundered on the editorial page of the *Pilot*: One way to end this discord is "when Americans, tired out and indignant with her squabbling populations, puts her foot down with a will and tells them all – Germans, French, Irish, Orange – 'You have had enough now. There is only ONE flag to be raised in this country and that flag is the Stars and Stripes.'" He later urged reconciliation between Orangemen and Catholic Irish: "No matter if we do differ in religious belief: that is no reason why we should be enemies and ready to fly at each other's throat. The best Irishmen in our country's history were North of Ireland Protestants. Twine the flags – they are both Irish. The Orange is the oldest national color. Let us be sensible, friends on both sides, and not carry our island bickerings into the view of America's friendly cities." And even in the face of a growing xenophobic nativist movement, he attacked efforts to establish an "Irish" political party to counter anti-immigrant measures: "The Irishman who would proscribe a native American, and the native American who would proscribe an Irishman, are guilty of the same crime against the principles of the Constitution. . . . All that was good and beautiful in our dear native island, we should cherish forever. . . . But we cannot, as honest men, band together in American politics under the shadow of an Irish flag."

O'Reilly acknowledged, however, that most of his fellow Irish Americans joined him in their steadfast devotion to the Democratic Party. In defending this loyalty, he wrote that "Every assault on their rights as citizens in this country has come from the Republican party and its predecessors . . . ." Yet it is interesting to contrast the following excerpts of his essentially Jeffersonian Democratic creed with its modern New Deal expression: "Democracy means to us the least government for the people, instead of more or most. It means that every atom of paternal power not needed for the safety of the Union and the intercourse of the population should be taken from the Federal Government and kept and guarded by the States and the people . . . . It means antagonism to all men, classes and parties that throw distrust and discredit on the . . . common people . . . ."

An indication of the esteem in which this naturalized American was held by his contemporaries is evident in the frequency with which he was called upon to provide the appropriate patriotic sentiment on various civic occasions. Before a gathering of the Grand Army of the Republic in 1886, for example, he delivered a Memorial Day oration entitled "The Common Citizen Soldier," usually regarded as his best speech. Two years later he read his poem "Crispus Attucks" at the dedication of the Boston Massacre Monument on the Boston Common, and in 1889 he read a poem at the dedication of the Pilgrim Monument at Plymouth. He also wrote "Liberty Lighting the World" for the unveiling of the Statue of Liberty.

Following his death in 1890, O'Reilly was universally praised for his ability to foster cultural understanding. One eulogist described him thus: "Loving and loyal to the land of his adoption, and ever ready to work for her good and her glory . . . he never forgot the land of his birth; he always battled for her against scurrilous enemies, here and abroad. . . . Here he made friends for Ireland by his genius, his tenderness for oppressed humanity, his 'love for justice and hatred of iniquity' . . . ." Other eulogists emphasized his ability to abolish the old distinction between English American and Irish American: "This man, this Roman Catholic, on New England soil, in daily association with the sons of Puritans, – the sons of men who hated the Papacy as the instrument of Satan, and whose descendants have not entirely got beyond the narrowness of their forefathers, – could yet describe in fitting terms, and show the appreciation of his mind and soul for, the achievements of the founders of New England."

¶ John Fitzgerald House, 4 Garden Court Street. Private.

A marker identifies the location of the house in which *John "Honey Fitz" Fitzgerald lived with his family between 1886 and 1894. His daughter Rose – the mother of President John Fitzgerald Kennedy – was born here in 1890.

Fitzgerald's twenty-five-year political career was one of the most colorful in Boston history. Following his election to the Massachusetts Senate, he became a spokesman for the rights of the Irish and of immigrants in general. During the mayoral campaign of 1905, he promised a "Bigger, Better, Busier Boston" and raised eyebrows by conducting the city's first political motorcade and spending $120,000, twice as much as his blueblood Republican opponent.

Once in the mayor's office, Fitzgerald supported industrial development and harbor expansion and built vocational schools, public baths, and playgrounds. He permitted graft in the awarding of city contracts, however, and created such sinecures as city dermatologist and municipal tea warmer. Ever the extrovert, he attended 1,500 dances, 1,200 dinners, and a thousand meetings – all during his first term alone. Before long, his mellifluous eloquence and singing voice had earned him the nickname "Honey Fitz." In the 1910 campaign he first sang "Sweet Adeline," which eventually became his trademark.

Although he ran for a third term in 1914, he withdrew from the race because of attacks by challenger *James Curley, who threatened to expose Fitzgerald's alleged affair with a woman known as "Toodles." In a bid for the U.S. Senate two years later, Fitzgerald unsuccessfully ran against Henry Cabot Lodge; in 1952 the ex-mayor's grandson – John Fitzgerald Kennedy – won a Senate seat in a race against Lodge's grandson.

Of John Fitzgerald's six children, Rose was his favorite. After graduating from Dorchester High School (where she was elected the prettiest senior), Rose studied music at the New England Conservatory before attending the Convent of the Sacred Heart in Boston and the Manhattanville College of the Sacred Heart in New York. Although her father attempted to prevent her from marrying Joseph P. Kennedy, she was persistent and finally won her father's grudging permission. (Fitzgerald won a partial victory, however, by denying Kennedy a lavish wedding, arranging instead a private ceremony in *Cardinal William O'Connell's chapel.)

Although Rose's marriage to "the lone wolf" banker of Wall Street promised her a charmed life, it was regularly punctuated by more than its share of tragedies involving her children. The mental retardation of her daughter Rosemary was followed by the deaths of Joseph Jr. during World War II, of Kathleen in a plane crash in France in 1948, and of John and Robert at the hands of political assassins. "I just made up my mind that I wasn't going to be vanquished by anything," she once said. "If I collapsed, I knew it would have a very bad effect on other members of the family." Her life was summed up in her personal motto: "I know not age, nor weariness nor defeat."

¶ The Rose Fitzgerald Kennedy Garden, near the birthplace, contains a granite fountain inscribed with a quote from the Kennedy matriarch: "If God were to take away all his blessings and leave me but one gift, I would ask for faith."

¶ Boston continues to remember its colorful mayor in the John Fitzgerald Bridge (across the Charles River) and the John Fitzgerald Expressway (I-93 and U.S. 1 across the east end of Boston). He is buried in St. Joseph's Cemetery (990 La Grange, West Roxbury).

¶ **John F. Kennedy Statue,** State House, Beacon Street and Park Street.

A bronze life-size standing statue of President John F. Kennedy is located on the south side of the State House. The statue catches the president in his stride, with his right hand in his coat pocket.

¶ **John Glover Statue,** Commonwealth Avenue, between Clarendon and Berkeley streets.

One of several works in Boston by the sculptor *Martin Milmore, this bronze likeness of General John Glover depicts the Revolutionary War hero in a defiant stance, sword in hand and left foot on a cannon.

¶ Kennedy Federal Building, on the north side of City Hall Plaza.

Completed in 1966, this twenty-six-story structure was named in honor of John F. Kennedy, who served as a congressman from Charlestown before being elected to the U.S. Senate from Massachusetts.

¶ Louis Sullivan Birthplace, 22 Bennet Street. Private.

A bronze plaque placed here by the Boston Society of Architects and the Massachusetts State Association of Architects marks the birthplace of *Louis Sullivan. Known for his innovations in American architecture, he was the son of an Irish immigrant father who had operated a successful dancing academy in London before coming to Boston in 1847. (See Art Institute of Chicago, Chicago, Illinois.)

¶ Maurice Tobin Statue, near the Hatch Shell on the Esplanade along the Charles River.

Though less well known than his erstwhile friend and political rival James Curley, Maurice (pronounced "Morris") Tobin shared with "Hiz Honor" Irish immigrant parentage. For more than twenty-five years, Tobin was a fixture in the political constellation: state legislator, Boston School Committee member, Boston mayor, Massachusetts governor, and secretary of labor for President Truman.

Statue of Maurice Tobin.

The son of an emigrant from Clougheenofishogue, Ireland, young Tobin was said to have had the largest carrier route of any newsboy in his native Roxbury. In 1926, at the age of twenty-five, he became the youngest member of the Massachusetts House, where he campaigned to abolish the death penalty and to investigate the practices of the telephone company. (After he left office the company conveniently offered him a job.) As mayor for three terms between 1938 and 1944, Tobin tried to implement government economies, but his efforts were overshadowed by a police scandal and a wartime fuel shortage. He raised eyebrows with a speech that warned about "another struggle in the next generation" and "possible international complications" with China and India. For both eventualities he urged a high birth rate to assure "a sizable backlog of children." Later as governor (1945-46) he used his wartime emergency power to seize the Eastern Massachusetts Street Railway, thereby ending a strike by 2,000 employees that had inconvenienced more than half a million passengers. While chief executive he signed legislation authorizing the construction of the Mystic River Bridge through Charlestown, an 11,906-foot structure that was opened in 1950. Eight years later the bridge was renamed for Tobin.

The former governor's death in 1953 gave rise to a widely circulated story. On the morning of his death, so the tale ran, his widow, Helen, routinely left for church with the couple's three children. "My Maurice wouldn't want me and the children to miss mass," she said. "He was such a religious man, and I know he was spiritually prepared for this."

¶ McCormack Building, Bowdoin Street and Ashburton Place.

This state office building was named for John McCormack, the first Catholic to be elected Speaker of the U.S. House of Representatives.

McCormack was a native of South Boston, one of thirteen children born to an Irish bricklayer and his wife, themselves the children of emigrants fleeing the Irish potato famine in the 1840s. During a long career in the House of Representatives, McCormack fervently supported the New Deal and earned the nickname "the fighting Irishman" for his aggressive debating style. Because of his close ties with many Catholic clerical leaders, he was dubbed "the Archbishop" by his enemies, although many Jewish voters in his district called him "Rabbi John." Noted for his anti-Communist stance, he was appointed chairman of the first House Committee on Un-American Activities. With the election of Sam Rayburn to the speakership in 1940, McCormack served as his deputy until he himself assumed the Speaker's chair in 1962. After warning the nation about the importance of the scientific race with the Soviet Union, he sponsored the bill to create the National Aeronautics and Space Administration. He died in 1980.

¶ McGrath and O'Brien highways (State 28 through Somerville and

Cambridge).

The Somerville section of Route 28 is named for *Father Christopher McGrath (1843-1932), a native of East Boston who was sent to Somerville in 1869. Five years later he founded St. Joseph's parish there.

Once in Cambridge, Route 28 bears the name of Monsignor James O'Brien, the son of Hugh O'Brien, Boston's first Irish-born mayor. The future priest was born in Boston in 1854 and received his early education in the city's public schools. He studied for a short time at Boston College before entering St. Charles College in Ellicott City, Maryland. After completing his theological studies at St. Mary's Seminary in Baltimore, he was ordained by *Cardinal James Gibbons in 1878. Seven years later he was assigned to St. James Church, Boston. In 1891, however, O'Brien was sent to Somerville, where he consulted with Father McGrath. Armed with a $600 pledge of support from the latter cleric, O'Brien proceeded to oversee the construction of St. Catherine's Church, the second Catholic house of worship in Somerville.

J The Museum at the John F. Kennedy Library, on the campus of the University of Massachusetts, State 3/I-93 exit 14 to Morrissey Boulevard (in Dorchester).

Dedicated in 1979, the library contains many Kennedy memorabilia, including the president's rocking chair and a copy of his desk inside a replica of the Oval Office in the White House. A thirty-minute film chronicles the former president's life. The museum also commemorates the political career of *Robert Kennedy.

§ Open daily 9-5. Closed January 1, Thanksgiving, and December 25. Fee. Phone: 617-929-4523.

J Museum of Fine Arts, 465 Huntington Avenue.

The museum's galleries exhibit American, Asian, Classical, Egyptian, and European sculpture and painting. Among its sculpted pieces are works by *Thomas Crawford, including *Adam and Eve, Hebe and Ganymede, Orpheus and Cerberus, Shepherdess, Aurora, Mercury and Psyche, Pandora, Boy Playing Marbles, Children in the Wood, Dancing Jenny, Flora, Indian Hunter,* and a bust of Josiah Quincy. The museum also contains Celtic ornaments, Irish silver, works by *John Singleton Copley and *James McNeill Whistler, and the 1853 painting of Daniel Webster by *George Healy.

§ Open Monday and Tuesday 10-4:45, Wednesday-Friday 10-9:45, Saturday and Sunday 10-5:45. Closed Thanksgiving and December 24-25. Fee. Phone: 617-267-9300.

J Nichols House Museum, 55 Mt. Vernon Street.

Between 1885 and 1960 this brick mansion was the home of Rose Standish Nichols, author and pacifist and the country's first female landscape architect. The museum contains two works by *Augustus Saint-Gaudens: the bronze statue *Diana of the Crossroads* and a bronze relief of Robert Louis Stevenson.

§ Open May-October, Tuesday-Saturday 12:15-4:15; February-April and November-December, Monday, Wednesday, and Saturday 12:15-4:15. Closed July 4, Labor Day, Thanksgiving, and December 25. Fee. Phone: 617-227-6993.

¶ **Old City Hall,** School Street (next to King's Chapel).

The present building was completed in 1865 and was used until the new city hall in Government Center was opened in 1968. Today the Old City Hall serves various commercial uses.

Boston's first Irish Catholic mayor was *Hugh O'Brien. After arriving in Boston with his immigrant parents, the youngster learned the printing trade and at age sixteen set himself up as editor and publisher of the *Shipping and Commercial List*. He later served as an officer of the Franklin Typographical Society and the Charitable Irish Society.

In 1875 O'Brien launched his political career by serving the first of six terms as city alderman. Nine years later he was first elected mayor, continuing the city's tradition of businessmen-amateur politicians. By the end of his first term, his advocacy of mayoral control of the budget, limits on municipal spending and taxing, and tax incentives to attract manufacturing interests to the city had gone far to dispel Yankee mistrust of an Irish Catholic mayor. Nevertheless, he was unsuccessful in his fourth mayoral bid, partly because of opposition from the American Protective Association, which had stirred up anti-Catholic and anti-immigrant sentiment.

¶ **O'Neill Building,** Causeway Street and Lomasney Way.

This state government building was named for Thomas "Tip" O'Neill, the Speaker of the House of Representatives from 1977 to 1987.

The grandson of an immigrant bricklayer from County Cork, the young O'Neill was nicknamed for a baseball player renowned for hitting foul tips. During his senior year at Boston College, the young political aspirant narrowly lost a bid for a seat on the Cambridge City Council. Following his election to the state legislature, he became the youngest majority leader in the state's history and an advocate for the "Little New Deal," a program of social legislation on the state level.

Newly elected to the U.S. House in 1952 to replace *John F. Kennedy, O'Neill generally supported the liberal Democratic agenda. Although he almost immediately became part of the congressional power structure – thanks to House Democratic whip *John McCormack – the novice congressman never forget his ties to his constituents. His regular Saturday walks through the ethnic neighborhoods in his district became legendary and reflected his belief that "All politics is local." He generally backed

Lyndon Johnson's domestic programs but broke with the president on the Vietnam War. Following the congressional Watergate hearings, O'Neill publicly called on *President Richard Nixon to resign, fully expecting him to do so "for the good of the country" before impeachment proceedings began.

During the presidency of *Ronald Reagan, O'Neill used his influence as Speaker to oppose the conservative president's policies. Convinced of government's ability to ameliorate social ills, O'Neill opposed a balanced budget because it would "dismantle the programs that I've been working for as an old liberal." During his political wrangling with Reagan, the Speaker once called him the most ignorant man who had ever occupied the White House and referred to him as "a cheerleader for selfishness" and "Herbert Hoover with a smile."

¶ Lomasney Way is named for Martin Lomasney, the son of an Irish immigrant tailor and for thirty years the head of Boston's Democratic political machine. He once described the machine's philosophy: "I think there's got to be in every ward somebody that any bloke can come to – no matter what he's done – and get help. Help, you understand; none of your law and your justice, but help." *Mayor John "Honey Fitz" Fitzgerald later acknowledged Lomasney as his "political grandfather," from whom he had learned that "the politician who thinks he can get away from the people who made him, usually gets what is coming to him – a swift kick in his political pants."

¶ Patrick Collins Monument, Commonwealth Avenue, between Berkeley and Clarendon and streets.

This memorial to Patrick Collins, Boston's second Irish-born mayor, consists of a granite plinth flanked by allegorical female figures of Erin and Columbia and topped by a bust of Collins. The monument was dedicated in 1908 after a fund-raising campaign led by Charles Eliot, the president of Harvard University.

After accompanying his mother from County Cork to Boston in 1848, the young Collins faced harassment by his Yankee peers because of his religion and race, frequently being beaten up and once suffering a broken arm. As a youngster he held a variety of jobs, including fishmongering, farming, coal mining, and upholstering. (He even helped organize an upholsterers' union.)

While still pursuing his education, Collins began the political career that would earn him the nickname "one of Boston's greatest Irishmen." Even before his graduation from Harvard Law School, he was elected to the Massachusetts House. Later in the state senate he advocated the removal of various anti-Catholic disabilities and fought for the introduction of Catholic chaplains in jails and public hospitals. Beginning in 1901, he was elected to two successive terms as mayor of Boston. He reduced the

*Monument to Boston's
second Irish-born mayor,
Patrick Collins.*

city's tax levels and generally opposed what he called "benevolent Socialism" – excessive municipal spending and borrowing. He also served three
terms in the U.S. House of Representatives and was *President Grover
Cleveland's consul general in London.

Despite his political reliance on Boston's Irish, Collins tried to discourage ethnic politics, emphasizing the *unum* more than the *pluribus* in
the American motto. During the 1876 election he told the voters: "I kneel
at the altar of my fathers, and I love the land of my birth, but in American
politics I know neither color, race nor creed. Let me say here and now that
there are no Irish voters among us. There are Irish-born citizens, like myself, and there will be many more of us, but . . . Americans we are, Americans we will remain . . . ."

¶ St. Stephen's Catholic Church, Hanover Street, at the east end of
the Paul Revere Mall.

The present church stands on the site of the second Congregational
house of worship in the North End. In 1802 that structure was torn down
and replaced by a larger one designed by Charles Bulfinch. The Unitarian
congregation that was using the church in 1862 sold it to the Roman Catholic Archdiocese, which sought it as a place of worship for the teeming
numbers of Irish living in the area. In 1965 *Cardinal Richard Cushing
restored the church to conform to its original design by Bulfinch. Fifteen

years later Cushing was honored by the Boston Society of Architects for his leadership in the restoration effort.

• In 1863 John Fitzgerald – the future mayor of Boston – was born in a slum-tenement not far from St. Stephen's (where he was baptized). He was one of eleven children born to Irish Famine immigrants who had come to Boston in the 1840s. Fitzgerald was the first Irish boy and the first Catholic to attend Boston Latin School, where he overcame the prevailing bigotry to be chosen captain of two athletic teams and the editor of the school newspaper. His matriculation at Harvard Medical School was cut short, however, by the obligation to support his family after his father's untimely death. Fitzgerald later married *Mary "Josie" Hannon, who bore him six children. The oldest, Rose Fitzgerald, married *Joseph P. Kennedy and was the mother of President John Fitzgerald Kennedy.

• On January 22, 1995, St. Stephen's was crowded with mourners attending the funeral of Rose Fitzgerald Kennedy after her death at the age of 104.

J Soldiers' Monument, Winthrop Square, Charlestown.

This statuary group by *Martin Milmore was erected in 1876 as a memorial to the men of Charlestown who died in the Civil War.

J Trinity Church, Copley Square.

Some of the frescoes in this Romanesque church were painted by *Augustus Saint-Gaudens and John LaFarge. Although the statue of Episcopal bishop Phillips Brooks outside the church was designed by Saint-Gaudens, it was sculpted by his assistants after the artist's death.

§ Open daily 8-6. Phone: 617-536-0944.

BROOKLINE

J Holyhood Cemetery, Heath Street.

Holyhood is the final resting place of many Boston Irish, including:

• Patrick Collins, the mayor of Boston from 1901 to 1905, whose funeral was attended by 100,000 people.

• Patrick Guiney, a native of County Tipperary, Ireland, who served in thirty Civil War engagements, succeeded to command of the Ninth Massachusetts Volunteers, and was partially blinded at the battle of the Wilderness. Guiney's death in March 1877 occurred on a public street in Boston, after he had removed his hat, knelt on the pavement, and crossed himself.

• John Boyle O'Reilly, the famous editor, poet, and Irish nationalist, whose grave is marked by a huge boulder.

• James Jeffrey Roche, author, journalist, and poet.

Born in Queen's County, Ireland, Roche grew up in Canada, where his father had resettled and conducted a school. In 1883 the younger man became assistant editor of the *Boston Pilot* and seven years later succeeded to the editorship of that paper, the country's leading Catholic Irish journal. Besides contributing to the nation's major publications and producing several collections of poetry, he wrote the adventure novel *The Story of the Filibusters* and a biography of John Boyle O'Reilly, his friend and fellow Irish patriot and American citizen. He also collaborated with Douglas Hyde and Lady Gregory in preparing a ten-volume work entitled *Irish Literature*.

The huge granite memorial on Roche's grave was a gift of the John Boyle O'Reilly Club. In 1909 the monument was inscribed as follows: "A writer – he gave freely of his genius to humanity that the strong might be restrained, the weak strengthened and right might reign; a poet – patriotism, heroism and justice were the burden of his song; and author – his kindly wit and gentle satire were turned on folly and hypocrisy; and editor – his pen fought stoutly for the oppressed and persecuted of all races and creeds; a man – he never surrendered his principles to temptation, keeping his conscience clear and his mind free."

§ Phone: 617-327-1010.

¶ Kennedy National Historic Site, 83 Beals Street.

This frame house was the birthplace in 1917 of President John F. Kennedy, whose father, *Joseph P. Kennedy, had purchased it just before his marriage to *Rose Fitzgerald in 1914. (The elder Kennedy, the son of a prosperous East Boston family, had graduated from Harvard two years before and was well on his way to financial success via real estate, banking, and the stock market.) Two other Kennedy children – Rosemary and Kathleen – were born in this house. In 1966 the Kennedy family repurchased the residence, which the president's mother restored to its 1917-21 appearance. Visitors can listen to a tape recording of Rose Kennedy describing various aspects of the house as well as incidents from the family's history.

§ Tours available daily 10:45-4, mid March-November. Fee. Phone: 617-566-7937.

√ The Kennedy Ancestral Home, where President John F. Kennedy's great-grandfather was born in 1820, is located in Dunganstown, County Wexford, Ireland. One of the rooms in the original whitewashed cottage displays mementoes and photographs of the president's visit in 1963, including the wreath he laid on the graves of the leaders of the Easter Rising at Arbour Hill in Dublin.

¶ Kennedy Residence, on the northeast corner of Abbotsford and Naples roads. Private.

Joseph and Rose Kennedy moved to this house in 1921. During their six-year residence here, their children Eunice, Patricia, and Robert were born in the house.

CAMBRIDGE

¶ **Irish Famine Memorial,** Cambridge Common.

The first monument of its kind in the United States to remember the victims of the Great Famine, this strikingly modern work features two statuary groups atop a granite base. One depicts an Irish woman sitting on a rock cradling a dying child and saying farewell to the other figure, that of a man holding a child as he turns to look back before taking his leave, presumably to America. The work of the internationally known Derry artist Maurice Harron, the sculpture was unveiled in July 1997 by Mary Robinson, the president of Ireland. (See back cover photograph.)

The Irish Famine Memorial on Cambridge Common.

¶ **James Family Burial Plot,** Cambridge Cemetery, Coolidge Avenue off Mount Auburn Street (next to Mount Auburn Cemetery).

Prior to his death in 1882, Henry James Sr., the son of the Irish progenitor of the famous American family, expressed his wish to be buried with ordinary Cambridge citizens in the new municipal cemetery. In doing so, the theologian rejected the more prestigious Mount Auburn Cemetery, described by Blanche Linden-Ward as the "quintessential product of a Unitarianism that [James] considered 'not itself a religion, but rather a kind of cultural substitute for religion.'" According to Preston Brooks, James was "a mystical democrat" and "an absolute libertarian," who, like Whitman, "preferred the company of stage-drivers to that of 'our' literary men." James once described "a crowded horse-car" as the "nearest approach on earth to the joy of heaven." His interment here was followed ten years later by the burials of his children, Alice, William, and Henry Jr. (See James Family House, Boston.)

¶ John F. Kennedy School of Government, Harvard University, Boylston Street (also known as John F. Kennedy Avenue).

Following the assassination of President John F. Kennedy in 1963, the Kennedy family offered Harvard University $3.5 million if its Graduate School of Public Administration was renamed the John F. Kennedy School of Government. The Kennedy Institute later donated $10 million to a Kennedy Institute of Politics within the J.F.K. School of Government.

¶ John F. Kennedy Park adjoins the school of government named for the nation's thirty-fifth president.

¶ Longfellow National Historic Site, 105 Brattle Street.

This Georgian residence was the home of the famous American poet from 1837 until his death in 1882. Among the paintings in the house are three by *George Healy: *Fanny Appleton* (Henry Wadsworth Longfellow's wife), *Mary Appleton* (Mrs. Longfellow's sister), and *Franz Liszt*. The last portrait was done in 1868 following a visit by Longfellow and Healy to the Convent of San Francesco Romano in Rome, where the famous pianist was living at the time. Longfellow was so impressed by the inspired expression on Liszt's face as the musician held a candle to light his guests' way that he asked Healy to portray that look just as they had seen it.

§ Tours available Wednesday-Sunday 10-4:30, mid May-October 31. Fee. Phone: 617-876-4491.

¶ Massachusetts Institute of Technology.

Originally known as Boston Tech, M.I.T. had its beginnings in 1865 in downtown Boston. When the new Cambridge campus was officially opened in 1916, a domed and porticoed edifice was erected in honor of William Barton Rogers, the founder and first president of the institution.

Rogers, one of four extraordinary brothers who went on to distinguished careers in science, was born in Philadelphia in 1804, the son of an immigrant from County Tyrone, Ireland. He attended the College of William and Mary, where his father, Dr. Patrick Kerr Rogers, taught chemistry and natural history. At the age of twenty-three, the younger Rogers succeeded to his father's chair. In 1835, however, he accepted the professorship in natural philosophy at the University of Virginia. Although he remained there for eighteen years, he disliked the racial and religious bigotry and intolerance he encountered in Charlottesville. After moving to New England and marrying into a wealthy Yankee family, he became a well-known public speaker on science and its role in the educational curriculum.

In 1859 Rogers and a similarly inclined group formed the Massachusetts Conservatory of Arts and Sciences and sought incorporation from the state for the Massachusetts Institute of Technology, "having for its objects the advancement of the Mechanic Arts, Manufactures, Commerce, Agriculture and the applied sciences generally, together with the promotion of the practical education of the industrial classes. . . ." It was not until 1865, however, that the school actually opened – with fifteen students attracted by the prospect of learning "the various professions of the Mechanician, the Civil Engineer, the Builder and the Architect, the Mining Engineer and the Practical Chemist." Except for a nine-year period, Rogers served as the institute's president until 1881.

§ Tours leave from 77 Massachusetts Avenue, Monday-Friday 10 and 2 (except holidays). Phone: 617-253-4795.

¶ Mount Auburn Cemetery, 580 Mount Auburn Street.

Mount Auburn is regarded as the country's first garden cemetery and contains the graves of such illustrious Americans as Oliver Wendell Holmes, Julia Ward Howe, Henry Wadsworth Longfellow, and James Russell Lowell. Some monuments in the cemetery have an "Irish connection":

• The tombstone of the Civil War officer Thomas Cass is inscribed with the following: "In Memory of Colonel Thomas Cass, Organizer and First Commander of the Famous Ninth Regiment of Infantry and Massachusetts Volunteers. Born in Farnley, Queens County, Ireland, 1821. Mortally wounded at the Battle of Malvern Hill, Virginia, July 1st, 1862, while leading his Regiment. Died in Boston, July 12th, 1862."

• *The Sphinx* was sculpted in 1872 by the Irish-born brothers Martin and Joseph Milmore and is inscribed with the words "American Union Preserved / African Slavery Destroyed / By the Uprising of a Great People / By the Blood of Fallen Heroes."

• The cemetery chapel contains a life-size statue of the Revolutionary patriot James Otis by Thomas Crawford, the latter of Scotch-Irish descent.

§ Open June-August 31, daily 8-7; rest of the year, daily 8-5. Phone: 617-547-7105.

CHESTNUT HILL

¶ Boston College, 140 Commonwealth Avenue.

Boston College was founded in 1863 by *Father John McElroy on property in Boston's South End. The Jesuit college began with a faculty of six

Jesuits and a student body of twenty-two. In 1913 the school was relocated to its present site. The earliest buildings on campus were designed by the architect *Charles Maginnis in the English Collegiate Gothic style. Today the campus covers 200 acres on three levels.

• On the campus is the John J. Burns Library, which houses three million manuscripts and more than 100,000 rare books (including the largest archive of rare Irish books in the country). The collection also contains religious and art objects, Hibernian regalia, and stained glass windows with Irish themes. The library was created by Brian P. Burns, a business executive, attorney, and philanthropist, and is named for his father, a Boston judge and the first Irish American to join the faculty of Harvard Law School.

§ Library open Monday-Friday 9-5. Appointment recommended. Phone: 617-552-3282.

COHASSET

¶ The *St. John* Memorial, Central Cemetery, Joy Place, off North Main Street.

In 1914 the Ancient Order of Hibernians dedicated this twenty-foot Celtic cross to mark the burial place of about forty-five of the ninety-nine Irish immigrants killed in the wreck of the brig *St. John* in 1849. The monu-

The St. John *Memorial, marking the burial place of forty-five Irish immigrants killed in a shipwreck off Cohasset in 1849.*

ment was unveiled by Theresa St. John of Cohasset, the granddaughter of James St. John and Mary Cole, one of the Irish survivors.

On October 7, 1849, as the British brig *St. John*, loaded with emigrants from Galway, Ireland, approached the coast of Massachusetts, it was driven upon the rocks near Cohasset. Ninety-nine of its 121 passengers and crew members were lost. Henry David Thoreau captured the emotional impact of the incident in "The Shipwreck," a chapter in his book *Cape Cod*.

CONCORD

¶ **Walden Pond Reservation,** 0.5 mile south on State 126.

On the north shore of the pond is a replica of the cabin which Henry David Thoreau built here in 1845. In *Walden* he explained that the boards for his dwelling place had come from the shanty of James Collins, an Irishman who worked on the Fitchburg Railroad. After paying Collins $4.25 for the shanty, Thoreau tore it down and removed it to the side of the pond, where he spread the boards on the grass so the sun could bleach and warp them back into shape. Thoreau added that an Irish lad ("a young Patrick") later told him that "neighbor Seeley, an Irishman," had stolen some of the usable nails from the boards while Thoreau was busy trans-porting the wood to the new site.

§ Open daily dawn-dusk. Parking fee. Phone: 978-369-3254.

EAST BROOKFIELD

¶ **Connie Mack Birthplace,** Maple and Main streets. Private.

This was the birthplace in 1863 of baseball player *Connie Mack (né Cornelius McGillicuddy), for fifty years associated with the Philadelphia Athletics, either as manager or owner. (See Cooperstown, New York.)

FALL RIVER

¶ **Battleship Massachusetts,** off I-95 exit 5.

On exhibit is a variety of U.S. Navy vessels, including a battleship, a submarine, two PT boats, and the destroyer U.S.S. *Joseph P. Kennedy Jr.* The destroyer, named for the older brother of John F. Kennedy, was built in 1945 and saw action in the Korean War, the NASA space recovery mis-sions, and the 1962 Cuban blockade.

Joseph Kennedy Jr. was killed in 1944 while flying a top secret mis-sion across the English Channel in an attempt to destroy what was be-lieved to be the launching site of Hitler's V-1 rockets. Just before the flight, he made a phone call to a friend in London: "I'm about to go into my act. If I don't come back, tell dad . . . that I love him very much." After his death his nineteen-year-old brother Robert took his place by enlisting in the Navy and later served aboard the U.S.S. *Joseph P. Kennedy Jr.*

§ Open daily 9-5. Closed January 1, Thanksgiving, and December 25. Fee. Phone: 508-678-1100.

HULL

¶ Public Library, 9 Main Street.

The library was originally the summer home of John Boyle O'Reilly, the Irish-born patriot, author, editor, and civic leader. The Queen Anne-style house was designed by O'Reilly's wife and was built on the site of Hunter House, Hull's first parsonage (built in 1644 and razed in 1888). O'Reilly's original house had a foyer, a living room, two reception rooms, and four bedrooms. The structure was purchased by the town of Hull in 1913 to be used as its public library.

• The John Boyle O'Reilly Memorial, on the grounds of the library, was unveiled on August 10, 1917, by the author's daughter. Among the guests that day was Henry Hathaway, who had saved O'Reilly's life in an incident that occurred after the Irishman's rescue from a British penal colony in Australia. (See John Boyle O'Reilly Memorial, Boston.)

§ Phone: 781-925-2295.

The John Boyle O'Reilly Memorial Plaque in Hull.

HYANNIS

¶ **John F. Kennedy Hyannis Museum,** Town Hall Building, 397 Main Street.

This museum features five rooms of photographs capturing the life and times of the Kennedys and their friends at Hyannis. A seven-minute film describes life at the "Summer White House."

§ Open mid April-mid October, Monday-Saturday 10-4, Sunday and holidays 1-4; mid February-mid April and mid October-December 31, Wednesday-Saturday 10-4. Fee. Phone: 508-790-3077.

¶ **John F. Kennedy Memorial,** Ocean Street, on Lewis Bay.

This memorial consists of a bronze medallion of the president's profile set in a twelve-foot curved stone wall, in front of which are a fountain and pool.

¶ **Kennedy Compound National Historic Landmark.**

This five-acre property includes three large frame houses that have belonged to various members of the Kennedy family. The largest and oldest dates from 1904 and belonged to Joseph and Rose Kennedy. To the rear of the "Big House" is the two-story shingle home of John F. Kennedy, while the twelve-room house to the right belonged to Robert Kennedy.

When Joseph and Rose Kennedy's children visited their parents' estate here, they were expected to follow a strict regimen. Every morning at 7 a.m. all the children were required to report promptly on the lawn for calisthenics with their own physical education instructor. After breakfast came swimming, sailing, and tennis lessons, followed by competitions in all three sports later in the day.

§ The compound is not open to the public, although local boat tours offer a view of the summer homes.

LAWRENCE

¶ **Edward O'Leary Bridge,** near the Merrimack Falls.

Dedicated in 1935, this structure pays tribute to World War I veteran *Edward O'Leary, a native son who was severely wounded at the battle of St. Mihiel in September 1918. O'Leary had volunteered for the Great War only fifteen months before, joining Battery C, 102nd Field Artillery, 26th Division.

¶ **Father James O'Reilly Bridge,** along Union Street.

The name of this bridge honors the pastor of St. Mary's Church, where he served from 1886 to 1924. A native of Lansingburg, New York, the Augustinian priest built the Shrine of Our Lady of Good Hope on Haverhill Street in Lawrence and formed three additional ethnic Catholic congregations in that city: Syrian Maronite, Lithuanian, and Portuguese. During the 1912 textile strike in Lawrence, he proposed a protest parade by the International Workers of the World, an event that brought 40,000 marchers into the streets. A decade later he helped settle a six-month-long strike on terms favorable to the more than 20,000 textile workers who had walked off their jobs.

¶ Joseph Casey Bridge, along Amesbury Street.
Formerly known as Central Bridge, this span across the Merrimack was renamed in 1940 for *Joseph Casey, a World War I hero and a patrolman with the Lawrence Police Department. Casey died three years before the rededication, the victim of wounds received while serving in France as top sergeant of Company F, 101st Infantry, 26th Division. For his service during the war, he was twice awarded the Distinguished Service Cross.

LOWELL

¶ Cardinal O'Connell Bust, Cardinal O'Connell Parkway, Merrimack and Arcade streets, near City Hall.
A granite birdbath in the middle of the parkway is surmounted by a bust of William O'Connell, who was born in Lowell in 1859 and went on to become Boston's third Catholic cardinal. He was the youngest of the

Bust of Cardinal O'Connell.

eleven children of John and Brigid O'Connell, natives of County Cavan, Ireland.

As the Irish population of Lowell continued to increase, prejudice against them grew, particularly in the public schools. Although in 1835 the Catholic Irish population in Lowell was only 12 percent of the total, within eight years it had climbed to 20 percent." By 1861 the Irish constituted perhaps half of the town's inhabitants. According to O'Connell, his early years in the Lowell public schools in the 1860s was "a perfect torture," characterized by the feeling that his teachers held a "bitter antipathy" toward the Catholic Irish students. He added that the Irish youngsters were made to feel inferior to Protestant children of English ancestry. And he complained that, when the teachers discussed the English Reformation, they portrayed the Protestant leaders – even the bloody Cromwell – as saints, while belittling the "glorious name of Thomas More." (See Cardinal O'Connell Way, Boston.)

¶ **Irish Heritage Memorial,** Cardinal O'Connell Parkway, Merrimack and Arcade streets, near City Hall.

Erected in 1977, this stone memorial is inscribed with a tribute to the city's Irish heritage: "The Irish community of Lowell was the first ethnic group to inhabit this area. Through their efforts in every facet of city life, they helped establish Lowell as one of the most important cities of the nation."

¶ **Lowell National Historical Park,** off Lowell Connector exit 5B to 246 Market Street.

Drawn to Lowell by the prospect of harnessing the water power created by the Concord and the Merrimack rivers, a group of investors began construction of textile mills and power canals in 1822. The restored textile mills, workers' houses, and five-mile canal system in the park commemorate the city's place in the American Industrial Revolution. Guided tours by foot, trolley, and boat are offered several times daily in the summer.

§ The visitor center at 246 Market Street provides exhibits and a slide show about Lowell's industrial development. Open daily 8:30-5. Closed January 1, Thanksgiving, and December 25. Phone: 978-970-5000.

¶ Outside the visitor center is a bronze statue of a canal construction worker applying his strength to a lever in order to move a huge granite block. The statue could easily represent Hugh Cummisky or one of the many other Irishmen who labored to construct the earliest local canals.

A native of County Tyrone, Cummisky was one of the first and most successful Irish in Lowell. Having come to Lowell from Boston – where he had been the construction foreman and general supervisor on the docks in Charlestown – he became the leader of a work gang whose loyalty he could use as leverage with his Yankee employers. He and his men worked first on the Middlesex Canal (connecting Lowell with Boston Harbor), then on the Pawtucket Canal, and finally on the construction of St. Patrick's Catholic church in Lowell.

Cummisky's purchase of property at Merrimack and Lowell streets in 1830 was the first recorded land transaction with an Irishman in Lowell, and within ten years he had bought additional property on four other streets. While in Lowell, he developed friendships with the local Yankee leaders and served as town constable. In 1860 he listed himself as a "gentleman" who owned $6,000 in real estate and $1,000 in personal property.

¶ The Working People Exhibit at the Patrick J. Morgan Cultural Center, 40 French Street, features information on the daily life of the mill workers and describes the role of immigrants in the development of the city.

Because of expanded production in Lowell's textile mills, by the late 1840s the mill owners employed more than 10,000 workers. The recession of 1848, however, resulted in the dismissal of hundreds of workers, many of them Yankee women. When the economy revived, the mills hired Irish girls, who worked for whatever they could get. Harriet Hanson Robinson, who was employed in the Lowell mills between 1836 and 1848, wrote that the first Irish women worked as scrubbers and waste pickers: "They were always good natured, and when excited used their own language. . . . These women, as a rule, wore peasant cloaks, red or blue, made with hoods and several capes, in summer . . . to 'kape cool,' and in winter to 'kape warrum.' They earned good wages, and they and their children . . . very soon adapted themselves to their changed conditions of life and became 'as good as anybody.'" In 1851 the Prescott Corporation changed its recruitment practices altogether, no longer hiring Yankee women but employing Irish women exclusively, a shift that was adopted by other employers to varying degrees.

§ Open daily 1-5.

¶ **St. Patrick's Catholic Church,** 282 Suffolk Street.

The first Catholic church on this site was erected in 1831. The present structure was built at a cost of $60,000 and was dedicated in 1854. The memorial in the pavement in front of the church marks the graves of three Irish-born priests whose pastorates and the later pastorate of their younger cousin are known as the "O'Brien Dynasty" (1848-1922). A plaque in honor of the O'Briens is located in the church vestibule.

St. Patrick's is located in what during the 1820s began to be called "The Acre," one of two Irish settlements or "paddy camps" in Lowell. While "The Acre" was settled by emigrants from southwestern Ireland, the other camp – "The Half Acre" – was inhabited by Connaught Irish.

Factional tempers flared routinely between the two groups, causing one peaceful citizen to ask the mayor to help "preserve the peàce, and maintain order and quiet in the neighborhood of the Catholic Church, on Sunday." As late as 1849 Corkonians and Connaughtmen fought a sporadic three-day battle. On the last day Irish women worked "like beavers, lugging bricks & stones in their aprons for the contending parties" before the city guards put an end to the violence. Ironically, this riot occurred only hours before the arrival in Lowell of Father Theobald Mathew, the famous temperance crusader from Ireland.

That demon rum was not without influence in causing these melees never escaped the notice of hostile Yankees. On the heels of the 1849 riot, the *Lowell Tri-Weekly American* thundered: "[T]hese disgraceful riots . . . almost universally commence over a glass of liquor. *Rum* is the prime mischief-maker, and under its influence the sectional differences of the old country are magnified into huge proportions." Other anti-Irish sources that year provided unsettling statistics: More than 75 percent of the unlicensed saloons in Lowell were run by Irish, and 90 percent of the inmates in the city almshouses were Irish; the number of arrests for one month in 1848 equalled the number for a whole year in the early 1840s.

Middle-class Yankees in Lowell were also outraged by the proverbial uncleanliness of their Irish neighbors. In 1848 a Protestant minister described the frequent living arrangements of the Irish: "Their rooms are generally not ventilated at all. Some six to ten persons frequently sleep in a single room, and sometimes in one bed . . . . The . . . little uncovered ground [is] the receptacle of dirty water, rubbish, and corrupt vegetable matter; and numerous outhouses of necessity near to the windows, sometimes filling every room, and the whole neighborhood with noxious exhalations." As late as the 1880s another observer described the Lowell camps as "an Irish village, with the real Irish cabins and shanties, built of board, sod, and mud – much as can be seen in Ballyshannon" – or built of slabs, stones, and turf. Other commentators railed against the Irish custom of housing the pigs in the shanties.

¶ Whistler House Museum of Art, 243 Worthen Street.

The museum includes the birthplace of James McNeill Whistler and a gallery that displays examples of mid nineteenth- and twentieth-century American art, including etchings by Whistler.

Descended from an Irish branch of an old British family, Whistler denied that he was a native of Lowell ("I shall be born when and where I want, and I do not choose to be born at Lowell . . . ."). Instead, he claimed to have been born in St. Petersburg, Russia, where his American-born father superintended the building of the St. Petersburg-Moscow Railroad and where the youngster first took drawing lessons. After returning to the United States for his education, he spent three years at the U.S. Military

Academy before heading for Paris in 1855, never to return to America.

During his subsequent career Whistler was noted for his portraits, marine scenes, and landscapes. His most famous work – *Portrait of My Mother* (originally called *An Arrangement in Grey and Black*) – is now in the Louvre. While in London, he become known for his acerbic wit and eccentric dress. His artistic creed is summed up in his notion that a painting had "no mission to fulfill" but was a "joy to the artist, a delusion to the philanthropist, and a puzzle to the botanist." Although he disdained critics, he conceded their usefulness because "they keep one always busy . . . either fighting or proving them idiots." When art critic John Ruskin mocked him for asking 200 guineas for one particular painting – "for flinging a pot of paint in the public's face" – Whistler successfully sued him for slander, although the artist was awarded only a farthing. (See Historic Fort Wayne, Fort Wayne, Indiana.)

§ Open March-December, Wednesday-Saturday 11-4, Sunday 1-4. Closed holidays. Fee. Phone: 978-452-7641.

MARBLEHEAD

¶ **Eugene O'Neill House,** Point O'Rock's Lane at Marblehead Neck. Private.

Built about 1900, this six-room Victorian cottage was the last home of *Eugene O'Neill, where he and his third wife, Carlotta Monterey, lived from 1948 to 1951.

MILFORD

¶ **Irish Round Tower,** St. Mary's Cemetery, State 85.

This seventy-three-foot cylindrical tower was erected about a century ago through the efforts of Father Patrick Cuddihy, pastor of St. Mary's Church in Milford from 1857 until his death in 1898. Believed to be the only Irish round tower in the United States, it is modeled – say some authorities – on the tower on Devenish Island in County Fermanagh.

Cuddihy was a native of Cashel, County Tipperary, where he was born in 1809. He received his early education in Clonmel, but at the age of seventeen he was sent to St. Isadore's Convent in Rome. After studying philosophy and theology in the Eternal City, he was ordained a priest there in 1831. Upon his return to Ireland, he worked for the next two decades in Limerick, Clonmel, and Waterford and rebuilt the Franciscan church in each of the latter two cities.

Cuddihy immigrated to America in 1852 in order to work in the Boston diocese. As pastor in Pittsfield, Massachusetts, he constructed six churches and many schools throughout the western portion of the state. His subsequent tenure at St. Mary's in Milford saw the construction of the magnificent church and bell tower which still stand. Described by the historian Alfred Webb as "an Irish gentleman of the old school," Cuddihy spoke Irish and loved to sing songs in his native tongue. He was almost as fluent in other languages, reciting from Dante's *Inferno* and quoting poetry in German and Latin. At his death at the age of ninety, he was the oldest Catholic priest in the United States.

When chided by a friend about his construction of the tower in Milford, Cuddihy replied, "It may be folly – yet when you and I have passed away the Irish in America will make a pilgrimage to the Irish Round Tower at Milford." It may have been this remark that gave currency to the myth that the Milford tower was modeled after the one at Glendalough in the south of Ireland. According to Paul Curran, a Milford historian, most of Cuddihy's parishioners had roots in southern Ireland and would not have identified with a round tower patterned after one in the north. In 1996 Curran launched a $50,000 fund-raising drive to repoint the mortar in the Milford tower.

As it happened, Milford's tower has remained largely unknown to most Irish Americans, many of whom prefer to see the real thing in Ireland. According to Curran, two things happened to frustrate's Cuddihy's hope that his tower would attract many Irish-American visitors: the Wright Brothers and Aer Lingus.

*The Irish Round Tower
in Milford.*

NEW BEDFORD

¶ *Catalpa* **Memorial,** on the grounds of the Registry of Public Deeds Building, Pack and 6th streets.

This granite monument was erected in 1976 to commemorate the rescue of six Fenian prisoners from an Australian penal colony a hundred years before. The names of the Irishmen are listed on the granite stone: Richard Cranston, Thomas Darragh, Michael Harrington, Thomas Hasset, Martin Hogan, and James Wilson.

The unusual rescue was conceived by *John Boyle O'Reilly, the editor of the *Boston Pilot*. Replicating the scheme that had effected his own escape from the same prison only seven years earlier, O'Reilly and his supporters hired a New Bedford whaler, the *Catalpa*, under the command of Captain George Anthony. With the groundwork laid by two Fenian leaders who had preceded the ship to Australia, the prisoners deserted their work detail and made their way to the shore, there to await the arrival of the *Catalpa*. Although the six successfully boarded the whaleboat sent out by the larger ship, stormy weather prevented it from immediately returning to the *Catalpa*. After a storm-tossed night at sea, they sighted the American ship and gratefully boarded her.

The Fenians' escape had not gone unnoticed, however, as the arrival of the British gunboat *Georgette* proved. Even before the British ship fired a warning shot, Captain Anthony realized that he would easily be bested in a shooting match. Perhaps believing that patriotism is the last refuge of outlaws – as well as scoundrels – Anthony ordered his men to hoist the Stars and Stripes. "That's the American flag," he cried to the British officer. "I am on the high seas. My flag protects me. If you fire on this ship, you fire on the American flag." Although the captain of the *Georgette* allowed the *Catalapa* to sail on, he continued to follow the ship for some time but eventually returned to Australia. The six Fenians arrived safely in New York City in 1876. In a speech marking their return, O'Reilly said, "The Irishman who could forget what the Stars and Stripes have done for his countrymen, deserves that in the time of need that flag shall forget him."

§ Original documents and photographs associated with the *Catalpa* rescue are on display in the New Bedford Whaling Museum on Johnny Cake Hill in the historic part of town. Open daily 9-5. Closed January 1, Thanksgiving, and December 25. Fee. Phone: 508-997-0046.

NEWBURYPORT

¶ Nathaniel Tracy House, 94 State Street.

Although this structure has been the Newburyport Public Library since 1865, it dates from 1771, when it was built by *Patrick Tracy for his son

Nathaniel.

The younger Tracy was born in Newburyport in 1751 and was graduated from Boston Public Latin School and Harvard College and is said to have done postgraduate work at Yale. After his marriage to the daughter of Jeremiah Lee of Marblehead, the newlyweds moved into this brick mansion on State Street, which now houses a portrait of Tracy by Gilbert Stuart. With his brother and his brother-in-law, Tracy carried on the family's lucrative foreign trade and was soon the owner of three magnificent homes. By the early 1780s the partnership owned 110 merchant vessels and twenty-four cruising ships.

During the Revolution Tracy fitted out twenty-three merchant ships as privateers in support of the Patriot cause, the *Yankee Hero* being the first ship to be so outfitted for service by the Continental Congress. Tracy also loaned the government more than $167,000 to prosecute the war. Although his cruisers and privateers captured 120 enemy vessels (with cargoes valued at $4 million), he lost a total of thirty-three ships of his own. Ironically, the end of the war brought financial ruin to Tracy. By 1786 he was bankrupt and was forced to sell or mortgage his homes. His repeated attempts to obtain reimbursement from Congress for his wartime loans proved fruitless, and he lived the last decade of his life in retirement, dying at the age of forty-five.

¶ **Patrick Tracy Square,** opposite the Unitarian Church (26 Pleasant Street).

A historical marker in the square is dedicated to the memory of Patrick Tracy (1711-1789), "in recognition of his economic and social contributions to the welfare of Newburyport. Emigrating to Newburyport from his native home in Kilcarberry, County Wexford, Ireland, in 1745, he became a successful and wealthy owner of 54 privateers that sailed out of our port during the American Revolution and built a mansion for his eldest son, Nathaniel, in 1771, which is now the Newburyport Public Library."

PROVINCETOWN

¶ **Provincetown Playhouse,** Town Hall, Commercial Street.

This playhouse has been located in the Town Hall since 1977, when fire destroyed its predecessor, the Wharf Theater. The earlier theater, literally on the town wharf, had seen the debut of many plays by *Eugene O'Neill while he was a member of the Provincetown Players. Each summer the playhouse produces at least one of O'Neill's plays.

O'Neill's debut as a performed playwright occurred with the production of *Bound East* in the Wharf Theater in July 1916. The author incorporated in the play some of the "life experiences" he had enjoyed since leaving Princeton University during his freshman year: steamship voyages as a seaman; life as a derelict in Argentina, Liverpool, and New York; an attempted suicide; and newspaper work on the *New London Telegraph*. O'Neill appeared in the play as the second mate – with only one line. (See New London, Connecticut.)

ROXBURY

¶ **Forest Hills Cemetery,** 95 Forest Hills Avenue.

Besides being the final resting place of the Irish-American playwright Eugene O'Neill, this cemetery is noted for two memorials associated with the Irish sculptor Martin Milmore:

• The Soldiers' Monument in honor of the Civil War slain depicts a soldier resting on his rifle as he gazes on the graves of his fallen Union comrades. Milmore also designed war monuments for Boston, Charlestown, and Fitchburg, Massachusetts; Canaan and Keene, New Hampshire; and Erie, Pennsylvania.

• Milmore's grave is marked by one of the most famous pieces of sculpture in the United States – *Death and the Young Sculptor* by Daniel Chester French.

§ Phone: 617-524-0128.

SALEM

¶ **Father Theobald Mathew Statue,** Hawthorne and Derby streets, near Immaculate Conception Church.

This statue of Father Theobald Mathew, the "Apostle of Temperance," commemorates the famous Capuchin priest's visit to Salem on his tour of the United States in 1849. The statue was originally erected in 1887 on Central Street but was moved to this location in 1916.

The fourth of a family of twelve children, Mathew was born in County Tipperary in 1790. Following his ordination as a Capuchin priest, the young cleric worked among the poor in Cork, where he founded an industrial school for children and was a trustee of the city's workhouse. In 1838 he became head of the Cork Total Abstinence Society, a move that raised eyebrows because of the society's Quaker sponsorship. Within a decade six million people had taken the pledge, Father Mathew himself administering the oath to more than half the population of Ireland and another 200,000 people in Scotland and England. As early as November 1839 the Boston *Pilot* wrote: "The people flock to him in great multitudes, and the number of those whom he has induced to abandon the horrible vices of drunkenness is beyond calculation."

By 1849 Father Mathew had taken his crusade to the United States. His arrival in New York equaled the reception given Lafayette in 1824, and more than 20,000 people took the abstinence pledge during the priest's

*Statue of Theobald Mathew,
the "Apostle of Temperance."*

visit to the city. His warm reception even in Yankee Boston caused Josiah Quincy Jr. to wonder what the Puritan Fathers would say if they could see their descendants welcoming a "Papist" priest with such enthusiasm. In the nation's capital, meanwhile, the House of Representatives voted Father Mathew a seat on the floor, although slaveholding senators tried to bar the priest from their chamber. In the end the Capuchin's supporters in the Senate prevailed. During his two years in the United States, Father Mathew visited twenty-five states and gave the pledge to 600,000 people.

SPRINGFIELD

¶ *The Puritan,* State and Chestnut streets.

This imposing statue, sculpted by *Augustus Saint-Gaudens in 1885, depicts Deacon Samuel Chapin, one of Springfield's founders. The sculpture was commissioned by Chester Chapin, a sixth-generation descendant of the minister and a later president of the Boston and Albany Railroad. Since no likeness of Deacon Chapin was available to Saint-Gaudens, he sculpted the head of *The Puritan* from a bust he had made of the younger Chapin in 1881.

¶ *Titanic* **Historical Society Museum,** I-90 exit 7, 1 mile south on

State 21, 1 mile west on State 141 (Main Street) to 208 Main Street.

This museum tells the story of the ill-fated luxury liner *Titanic*, which was constructed in Belfast, Ireland, between 1909 and 1911. More than 900 feet long and as high as an eleven-story building, the *Titanic* was considered unsinkable. Yet less than five days out on its maiden voyage in April 1912, it struck an iceberg and sank in less than an hour. Of the 2,227 passengers and crew, 705 escaped in twenty rafts and lifeboats. One of the survivors of that fateful day was *Margaret Tobin Brown ("Molly" Brown), who earned the nickname "Unsinkable" after taking command of the other survivors in lifeboat number six. (See Hannibal, Missouri, and Denver, Colorado, in *Irish America*, Volume 2.)

§ Open Monday-Friday 10-4, Saturday 10-3. Closed holidays. Phone: 413-543-4770.

TEWKSBURY

¶ Anne Sullivan-Helen Keller Monument, Main Street.

Officially known as *Water*, this sculptural work by Mico Kaufman pays tribute to Anne Sullivan, Helen Keller's tireless Irish-American teacher. The memorial depicts the turning point in Keller's life when Sullivan used the manual alphabet to spell out the word "water" while pumping the liquid over the deaf and blind girl's hand. This technique was the beginning of Sullivan's effort to develop her pupil's vocabulary through continuous manual communication. Sullivan was a longtime resident of Tewksbury. (See Tuscumbia, Alabama, in *Irish America*, Volume 2.)

WESTON

¶ Cardinal Spellman Philatelic Museum, 0.5 mile north of State 30, next to the Regis College campus, at 235 Wellesley Street.

The museum houses the private stamp collection of Cardinal Francis Spellman, the grandson of Irish immigrants and the archbishop of New York from 1939 to 1967. Changing exhibits of stamps and postal memorabilia are displayed in the museum's two galleries.

In 1932 Spellman – then a monsignor – accompanied a papal legate to Ireland in connection with the International Eucharistic Congress held in Dublin. After visiting the village of Clonmel – where his paternal grandfather was born in 1831 – Spellman and the legate arrived in Dun Laoghaire to an enthusiastic greeting by more than a million souls. The Irish American later recalled that it was from this very harbor that his ancestors had emigrated, driven by famine and persecution. In an address to the Friendly Sons of St. Patrick eight years later, Spellman reminisced: "It was difficult to realize that in one hundred years I, their grandchild and great grandchild, ... through their sacrifices and patriotism and above all through their devotion to the Catholic faith, was privileged to enjoy their heritage and to return to their native land as an American with Irish blood in my veins. . . ."

One of the concerns which occupied Spellman's attention during his career was the establishment of formal diplomatic relations between the United States and the Holy See. In 1936, during a visit to the United States by Cardinal Eugenio Pacelli, the papal secretary of state, Spellman was instrumental in arranging a meeting between the Vatican dignitary and President Franklin Roosevelt to discuss the issue. A major step toward diplomatic recognition occurred three years later when the American president appointed Myron Taylor as his personal representative to Pius XII, the former Eugenio Pacelli. During the 1950s, however, opposition to full diplomatic recognition in the Senate was so great that Spellman despaired of achieving his goal. In 1958, when Senator John F. Kennedy announced his candidacy for the presidency, the Massachusetts politician opposed recognition, fearing that the issue would cost Kennedy Protestant support. Not until 1984 – during the presidency of Ronald Reagan – did the two governments establish diplomatic relations.

Spellman had first become interested in philately when he was a student at the North American College in Rome. He acquired many of the volumes in his collection as gifts from heads of government during World War II. In an address to the National Federation of Stamp Clubs, he remarked that "Stamps are miniature documents of human history . . . . They delineate cultural attainments, industrial works, domestic, civil and social life."

Soon after Spellman's appointment as archbishop of New York, the collection was moved to Regis College. Unhappily, however, in 1959 some of the stamps in the collection were stolen from the college library. Following the burglary, the collection was moved to the newly built Cardinal Spellman Museum, the gift of Mabel Gilman Corey. In 1969 another theft resulted in further loss to the collection. The following year authorities discovered that a volunteer at the museum had systematically pilfered stamps worth $40,000 over a period of years. The burglar eventually made full restitution in the form of stamps of equivalent quality and value.

Over the years the following Irish or Irish Americans have been recognized on U.S. postage stamps: Chester A. Arthur, John Barry, William Jennings Bryan, James Buchanan, Nellie Cashman, "Buffalo Bill" Cody, Grover Cleveland, George M. Cohan, David Crockett, Bing Crosby, Stephen Decatur, Father Edward Flanagan, Stephen Collins Foster, Robert Fulton, Ulysses S. Grant, Horace Greeley, Father John Harrington, Joel Chandler Harris, Benjamin Harrison, Victor Herbert, James Hoban, Sam Houston, Charles Evans Hughes, Andrew Jackson, Thomas "Stonewall" Jackson, Andrew Johnson, Stephen Kearny, John F. Kennedy, Robert Kennedy, Henry Knox, Thomas Macdonough, Edward

MacDowell, John McCormack, Cyrus McCormick, Ephraim McDowell, William McKinley, John McLoughlin, Andrew Mellon, Margaret Mitchell, Eugene O'Neill, Matthew C. Perry, Oliver H. Perry, Edgar Allan Poe, James K. Polk, George Read II, Theodore Roosevelt, Edward Rutledge, Augustus Saint-Gaudens, Philip Sheridan, Annie Sullivan, John Sullivan, and Charles Thomson.

§ Open Tuesday-Thursday 9-4, Saturday 10-4, Sunday 1-4. Phone: 781-894-6735.

WORCESTER

¶ **College of the Holy Cross,** 1 College Street.

• The Dinand Memorial Library houses the Richard O'Flynn Collection, which includes records of Irish societies, cemeteries, and military units like the Jackson and Emmet Guards.

• The Healy Building is named for James Augustine Healy, the first African-American Jesuit priest and Catholic bishop in the United States. Healy was one of ten children born to Irish immigrant Michael Morris Healy and a mulatto slave on his plantation near Macon, Georgia. Like his four brothers, the younger Healy attended Holy Cross College, where his father had enrolled them as a way of securing their emancipation.

Upon graduation James Healy pursued a career in the Catholic priesthood. After studying at seminaries in Montreal and Paris, he was ordained in the Cathedral of Notre Dame in 1854. Returning to Boston, he served first as chancellor to *Bishop John Fitzpatrick and then as pastor of Holy Cross Cathedral and St. James Church. He was especially devoted to the welfare of orphans and delinquents and succeeded in persuading public charitable and correctional institutions in Boston to permit Catholic clergy to perform religious services in them.

As bishop of Portland, Maine, Healy won the nickname "The Children's Bishop" because of his efforts against child labor abuses and on behalf of children of men killed in the Civil War. He was equally mindful of the poor and sick in his diocese, often paying their doctor bills and delinquent taxes. In addition, he was an active member of the Catholic commission for Negro and Indian missions.

Two of Healy's brothers also became priests, while two of his sisters became nuns. A third brother – Michael Healy – followed a decidedly different career path. Determined upon a life at sea, he ran away from Holy Cross as well as schools in Montreal and Belgium before his brothers let him follow his dream. After entering the U.S. Revenue Cutter Service in 1865, he was assigned to patrol the North Pacific and the Arctic, where he performed rescue operations and explored previously unknown areas. His account of these explorations was unfortunately destroyed by fire.

In 1886 Michael Healy began his career as the federal government's principal law enforcement officer in the waters around Alaska. On both the high seas and in remote coastal villages, he was revenue officer, federal marshal, grand jury, judge, and chief warden. On one occasion he helped transport reindeer from Siberia to Alaska for Eskimo faced with starvation caused by the loss of other sources of food. Among the Eskimo, in fact, he was a legend. When one of them was asked, "Who is the greatest man in America?" he replied, "Why, Mike Healy. He is the United States. He holds the power here for the whole country."

According to tradition, Healy was one of the sea captains upon whom Jack London based his fictional Captain Larsen in *The Sea Wolf*. For his wild escapades in the bars of San Franciso's Barbary Coast, Healy was called "Hell Raising Mike." And for ruthlessly crushing mutinies against other captains, he was court-martialed. Following his conviction he was demoted to the lowest grade of captain, although his later heroic efforts to rescue shipwrecked whalers in the Arctic apparently restored him to his stripes. He died in 1904, survived by his wife and only one of their eighteen children.

MICHIGAN

BEAVER ISLAND

Beginning in 1847, this island was settled by 2,600 Mormons who hoped that the island's remoteness would protect them from the usual hostility which the sect encountered. This expectation was unrealized, however, and open violence broke out between the Mormons and local inhabitants, who destroyed some of the sect's buildings.

A group of Irish fishermen from Mackinaw City later settled on the island, rebuilding the destroyed structures, establishing their base at St. James, and claiming some of the farm land. After these Irishmen received legal title to their holdings, they invited many of their friends and relatives from northern Ireland to join the settlement. Many of these later immigrants came from Aranmore Island off the west coast of County Donegal and surely must have spoken Irish.

One of these immigrants was Charles O'Donnell. While working on a railroad construction job in Toronto, he ran off with the payroll which his gang foreman had entrusted to him. The Irishman later came to Beaver Island – which he thought was remarkably like Aranmore – to help build the lighthouse known as Harbor Light. After returning to Toronto to repay the sum he had stolen, he came back to Beaver Island with his wife and as many other Irish as he could persuade.

¶ The tombstones in the cemetery attached to St. Mary's Church in St. James reveal the names of those early settlers, listed here in order of frequency: O'Gallaghers, Boyle, O'Donnell, McDonogh, Green, Floyd, McCann, McCauley, Bonner, Martin, Dunleavy, Mooney, Malloy, and O'Brien.

¶ Southwest of St. James is a log and clapboard cabin built about 1860 by an Irish settler named Philip Connelly. It was later the home of Feodor Protar, a Russian immigrant who schooled himself in medicine and offered free medical services and supplies to the inhabitants of the island.

BUCHANAN

¶ **Joseph Coveney Burial Site,** Oak Ridge Cemetery, Front Street.

The cemetery contains an unusual monument over the grave of Joseph Coveney, a native of Ireland who settled here in 1836. Because he was an atheist, the monument is inscribed with atheistic sentiments. The grave marker had to be made in England, however, because no local stonecutter would carve the inscription.

DEARBORN

❡ **Henry Ford Estate-Fair Lane,** off Evergreen Road and U.S. 12, on the campus of the University of Michigan.

Built by Henry Ford in 1915 for $2 million, this fifty-six-room mansion was the permanent home of the famous automotive pioneer and industrialist. He selected the name "Fair Lane" after the name of the street in County Cork where his maternal grandfather had been born. Now located on only 72 of the estate's original 1,369 acres, Fair Lane is owned by the University of Michigan.

Besides a powerhouse which Ford and his friend Thomas Edison devised to allow the estate to produce its own power, light, and heat, the house had a bowling alley, a heated indoor swimming pool, and a $30,000 organ. Each of the eight fireplaces in the mansion is inscribed with an appropriate epigram (e.g., "Chop your own wood and it will warm you twice."). Among the guests who stayed here were President Herbert Hoover, *Charles Lindbergh, and the Duke of Windsor.

§ Tours available April-December, Monday-Saturday at 10, 11, 1, 2, and 3, Sunday 1-4:30; rest of the year, Monday-Friday at 1, Sunday 1-4:30. Closed January 1, Easter, Thanksgiving, and December 25. Fee. Phone: 313-593-5590.

Fair Lane Mansion, the home of Henry Ford.
(From the collections of Henry Ford Estate-Fair Lane. Photographer Matthew Winquist.)

❡ **Henry Ford Museum,** Village Road and Oakwood Boulevard.

This twelve-acre museum chronicles America's transition from an agricultural society to an urban one. It also traces the life of the famous automotive pioneer through photographs, letters, and artifacts. Among the items on display are Henry Ford's 1896 Quadricycle (his first automobile) and the fifteen-millionth Model-T, constructed in 1927. The museum also displays one of the largest collections of *Eclectic Readers* by *William McGuffey.

The museum's exhibit on the American automobile displays five vehicles used by nine U.S. presidents. One of the automobiles here is the 1961 Lincoln Continental convertible in which John F. Kennedy was killed while in Dallas. This car was subsequently rebuilt with a permanent roof and armor plating that added a ton to its weight.

§ Open daily 9-5. Closed Thanksgiving and December 25. Fee. Phone: 313-271-1620, 271-1976, or 800-835-5237.

¶ **Greenfield Village,** Village Road and Oakwood Boulevard.

This eighty-one-acre complex is designed to recreate American history as a living experience rather than "book history" heavy on dates and facts. Henry Ford's experiential sense of history was summed up in the opinion that "Our history has depended more on harrows than on guns or speeches. I thought that a history which excluded harrows and all the rest of daily life is bunk . . . ."

Begun in 1920, Ford's collecting program brought to this site an unequaled array of tools, machines, and buildings from America's past, including his own birthplace. The village also contains the homes of Noah Webster and the Wright brothers as well as the birthplaces of *William McGuffey and Harvey Firestone.

• The two-story log cabin in which *William McGuffey was born in 1800 was moved here from Washington, Pennsylvania, in 1934. McGuffey's famous series of readers was used in American schools for a century. (See Oxford, Ohio.)

• The birthplace of Henry Ford is a two-story clapboard farmhouse originally located on his parents' forty-acre farm in Dearborn. The eleven-room house, where Ford lived until age sixteen, was moved to Greenfield Village in 1944. Ford's paternal grandfather, John Ford, had been a Protestant tenant farmer near Clonakilty in County Cork, Ireland. In 1847 he left his homeland for America, bringing with him his wife and their seven children. One of the sons, William, subsequently met and married the daughter of Patrick O'Hern, also a native of Cork. Their son Henry was born in 1863.

In the early 1920s this son – now a famous car manufacturer – visited Ireland to open his company's first factory outside the United States. During the visit he pledged £5,000 for the Hospital Building Fund in Cork. The next day, however, the local press reported that he had promised to donate £10,000. When officials from the hospital fund offered to correct the error with a new headline ("Henry Ford Did Not Give £10,000 to Hospital"), the American manufacturer realized that he had been "taken in" and promised to make the larger donation. His only condition was that he be allowed to choose the biblical quotation that would adorn the hospital: "I came among mine own – and they took me in."

§ Open daily 9-5. Closed Thanksgiving and December 25. Greenfield Village building interiors are closed January-March. Fee. Phone: 313-271-1620, 271-1976, or 800-835-5237.

DETROIT

¶ **Father Casey Burial Site,** St. Bonaventure Friary Chapel, 1740 Mt. Eliott Street.

On the left hand side of the chapel is the grave of Father Solanus Casey, a Capuchin priest declared "venerable" by Pope John Paul II in July 1995. Casey is the first man born in the United States to be recognized by the Catholic Church for his "heroic virtues," the first step on the road to possible canonization.

Born in a log cabin near Prescott, Wisconsin, in 1870, Bernard Casey – as he was baptized – was the son of Famine immigrants from counties Monaghan and Armagh. One of sixteen children, "Barney" dropped out of school to help support his family, working in succession as a lumberjack, a streetcar conductor, and a prison guard. Although he first entered the Milwaukee archdiocesan seminary, his difficulty with the German and Latin in which the courses were conducted forced him to leave. He encountered additional difficulties with his studies after joining the Capuchin Franciscan Order in Detroit (accepting the religious name "Solanus"). Although ordained in 1904, he was denied permission to preach and hear confessions.

After serving for fourteen years in various parts of New York, Casey was assigned to St. Bonaventure Friary in Detroit. There he tried to satisfy the needs of those who sought food and financial assistance, and he was one of the founders of the soup kitchen that now serves more than 1,000 people each day. His reputation for prophecy and healing brought busloads of people to see him. Local church authorities are investigating two possible miracles attributed to him.

Casey's cause for sainthood is being advanced by Father Michael Crosby, who wrote most of the 1,300 pages of documentation about Casey's life presented to the Vatican. According to Crosby, the Detroit priest was an ardent advocate of Irish home rule. "[He] took on a couple of bishops who were not as strong as he thought they should be in supporting Ireland," Crosby said. "He wrote very strong articles to the editor of the *Irish World* newspaper about Irish independence."

§ Open daily 8:30-5.

GROSSE POINTE SHORES

¶ **Edsel and Eleanor Ford House,** 1.5 miles east from I-94 Vernier/8 Mile exit and then 1 mile north to 1100 Lake Shores Road

Reflecting the architectural style found in the English Cotswolds, the mansion on this sixty-three-acre estate was completed in 1929 as the home of Edsel Ford, the only child of industrialist *Henry Ford. The house contains an art collection of Old Masters and Impressionist paintings.

§ Open April-December, Tuesday-Saturday 10-4, Sunday noon-4; rest of the year, Wednesday-Saturday 1-4. Fee. Phone: 313-884-4222.

HARBOR BEACH

¶ **Frank Murphy Birthplace Museum,** 142 South Huron Street.

This nineteenth-century house was the birthplace of Frank Murphy, governor of Michigan, U.S. attorney general, and associate justice of the U.S. Supreme Court.

All four of Murphy's grandparents were Irish immigrants who had fled their homeland between 1847 and 1849. His father, who at sixteen was imprisoned for his part in the Fenian invasion of Canada, settled in Harbor Beach, where he practiced law and was known for his unorthodox views, being staunchly anti-British and a follower of *William Jennings Bryan. His son Frank, meanwhile, after serving as a lieutenant in World War I, briefly studied law at Trinity College, Dublin, where he took particular interest in the Sinn Fein movement, so recently catapulted into prominence because of the 1916 Easter Uprising.

Murphy's subsequent political career was colored by the challenges caused by the Great Depression. As mayor of Detroit he complemented the city's public relief efforts with the creation of an employment agency and public housing for homeless men. When the city's resources were stretched to the limit, Murphy convened a series of mayoral conferences which sought federal aid for the nation's struggling cities. (Murphy was elected the first president of the resulting U.S. Conference of Mayors.)

Later, as governor of strike-racked Michigan, he refused to use the National Guard to expel sit-down strikers from the factories. Through his preference for negotiating, he was able to achieve peaceful settlements in six major strikes. (He once said that the sit-down strike was a "reassertion of the personality – the dignity of the offended human reasserting itself after the frightening experience of the Depression.") His refusal to use the National Guard to break up a sit-down strike in a General Motors plant in Flint caused the automobile manufacturer to recognize the United Auto Workers.

Following his appointment to the Supreme Court, Murphy was a consistent defender of civil liberties, although he was criticized for allowing his personal philosophy to influence his interpretation of constitutional law. Perhaps his most famous dissent was in the 1944 case which upheld the detention of Japanese Americans on the West Coast after the attack on Pearl Harbor.

¶ Frank Murphy is buried in Rock Falls Cemetery, just south of Harbor Beach.

HOLLY

During the late 1800s and the beginning of the twentieth century, the area off Saginaw Street in Holly was infamous for its brothels and taverns. In 1908 the town was visited by the intemperate temperance crusader Carrie Nation. After delivering a lecture on the evils of liquor, she "did a hatchet job" on some of the saloons in this part of town. Holly commemorates the appearance of this "visiting angel" during the Carry Nation Festival on the weekend after Labor Day. (See Bryantsville, Kentucky, and Belton, Missouri, in *Irish America*, Volume 2.)

IRISH HILLS

The lakes and the rolling hills of this region along State 12 thirty-five miles southwest of Ann Arbor so reminded the Reverend William Lyster of Ireland that he named the area for his native land. The region's topography can be viewed from the Irish Hills Towers, one mile west of the junction of U.S. 12 and State 124.

On Route 12 three miles west of State 50 is St. Joseph's Shrine, an enlargement of a fieldstone chapel which Irish settlers built in the 1840s. The churchyard contains the graves of those Irish pioneers and their children.

MUSKEGON

¶ **Hackley Park,** Webster Avenue between 3rd and 4th streets.

The park contains memorials to three Irish Americans: statues of Philip Sheridan and Ulysses S. Grant and a monument in honor of William McKinley. The bronze figure of McKinley was the nation's first memorial to the president after he was assassinated in 1901.

¶ **Muskegon Museum of Art,** 296 West Webster Avenue.

In addition to a European collection, the museum features the works of *James McNeill Whistler and includes the painting *Tornado Over Kansas* by *John Steuart Curry.

§ Open Tuesday-Friday 10-5, Saturday and Sunday noon-5. Closed major holidays. Phone: 616-722-2600.

NILES

❡ **Carey Mission Site,** Grant Street, on the west bank of the St. Joseph River.

The mission was founded in 1822 by the Reverend Isaac McCoy, the first Protestant missionary in this part of the state and the grandson of an Irish immigrant who had come to America in 1760. At its height the mission boasted twenty-seven buildings and provided for the instruction of seventy Native American pupils in agriculture and scholastic subjects.

During his ministry toward the Indians in this area, McCoy traveled hundreds of miles and endured the usual physical hardships of a frontier missionary as well as the unusual grief of losing five of his children while he was away. (He lost five more children at other times.) As more and more settlers and traders visited the mission, bringing with them pernicious influences (especially "demon rum"), McCoy concluded that only segregation from the white man would allow for the civilization and Christianization of the Native Americans. He accordingly waged a campaign to popularize his colonization concept and to win from Congress the creation in 1830 of the "Indian Country" in what is now Oklahoma.

OLD MISSION PENINSULA

❡ **Old Mission Church,** Grand Traverse Bay.

The present structure is a replica of the log church built here in 1839 by the Reverend Peter Dougherty, a Presbyterian missionary of most likely Irish descent who labored among the Ottawa and Ojibwa Indians in this area. Omena, on the west side of Grand Traverse Bay, was named from the Indian word *Omenah?* ("Is it so?"), which Dougherty used to reply to every statement made by a native American.

ROYAL OAK

❡ **Shrine of the Little Flower,** Woodward Avenue (State 1) and Twelve Mile Road.

Although this shrine to St. Thérèse of Liseux is noted for its 111-foot crucifixion tower (dubbed "the silo" by the irreverent), it is more well known as the site of the radio broadcasts of Father Charles Coughlin, the first pastor to use radio as a regular feature of his ministry.

Coughlin's first broadcast occurred in October 1926, a century after his great-grandfather had arrived in America and joined other Irish immigrants in building the Erie Canal. During the radio program Coughlin contrasted the message of St. Thérèse (the "Little Flower") with the racial hatred espoused by the Ku Klux Klan. When local Klan members responded by burning a cross outside the priest's original shrine, the radio preacher raised the ante, predicting that someday he and his followers would "raise a cross so high to the sky that neither man nor beast can burn it down." By 1933 Coughlin had kept his promise, as the finishing touches were added to his 111-foot tower. (The sculpted image of the crucified Christ on the tower is twenty-eight feet high, large enough, presumably, to intimidate the most zealous White Robe.)

Coughlin continued to express controversial views during the 1930s, but now against different targets. He argued, for example, that atheism and materialism had led to socialism and communism and that laissez-faire economics had led to the Depression. As the unofficial spokesman for the downtrodden, he condemned President Hoover as "the banker's friend, the Holy Ghost of the rich, the protective angel of Wall Street."

The orator-priest initially embraced Franklin Roosevelt's economic prescriptions for the country, in 1933 hailing the New Deal as "Christ's Deal" and urging support for specific elements in the president's overall program. By the middle of the decade, though, Coughlin was opposing Roosevelt's internationalism and engaging in personal vituperation against the president. He called F.D.R. a "liar," "communistic," and "Franklin Doublecross Roosevelt," adding that the difference between the Republicans and the Democrats was simply a matter of degree: "between carbolic acid and rat poison."

By now the controversial priest was noted for a singularly unpriestly oratorical style: tearing off his Roman collar in public and screaming invective and haranguing audiences. In response to Coughlin's personal attacks on President Roosevelt, *Archbishop Edward Mooney of Detroit tried to restrain the priest's inflammatory remarks. Using his authority under canon law to censor a priest's public addresses, Mooney appointed a panel to review Coughlin's radio broadcasts before delivery, although, strangely, the members of the panel were priests sympathetic to Coughlin.

§ Open Monday-Friday 6:30-3:15, Sunday 7:30-2:30. Phone: 248-541-5122.

SAULT STE. MARIE

℥ John Johnston Homestead, 415 Water Place.

The present structure incorporates features of a house completed by John Johnston in 1816 to replace a home which the Irishman had built in 1794. The original building had been destroyed in 1814 by U.S. troops retaliating against Johnston, a British subject, for his role in a successful attack on the American fort on Mackinac Island.

Johnston was born near Coleraine, County Antrim, in 1763, the son of a civil engineer who had designed and built the waterworks in Belfast. He was first educated at a school in Coleraine, but at the age of ten his mother placed him in charge of a tutor who instructed him in ancient and modern history. When the boy turned seventeen, he traveled to Belfast to assume a job superintending the water system built by his father. A dozen years later, though, he decided to emigrate. During a brief visit to New York while en route to Canada, the young Irishman caught a brief glimpse of George Washington while they both attended church in that city.

After arriving in Montreal, Johnston renewed his acquaintance with Andrew Todd, an Irish gentleman who at the time was a partner in a British fur-trading company. In May 1791 the two Irishman accompanied a trading party bound for Lake Superior. While stopping at Michilimackinac, Johnston recorded in his journal that the place was filled with goods, furs, traders, and boatmen. He later spent several months at Sault Ste. Marie before proceeding west to La Pointe, opposite the Twelve Apostles Islands in Lake Superior. Not long after establishing a trading post here, he met and married – *à la indien américain* – a Chippewa woman, the daughter of Wab-o-jeeg ("White Fisher"), a chief of the Ojibway tribe. Johnston baptized his Indian wife – giving her the name "Susan" – and later remarried her in a British rite. In 1793 the couple settled in Sault Ste. Marie, where Johnston proceeded to build a log house. It was here that Johnston lived for the next three and a half decades and where the couple's eight children were born.

When his mother died in 1804, Johnston inherited his parents' estate at Craige, near the Giant's Causeway, in County Antrim. To dispose of various legal matters involved in the inheritance, he and his daughter Jane sailed for Ireland, arriving in Cork late that autumn. After visiting friends in Dublin, Johnston left his daughter in Wexford with the intention that she should be educated by his sister there. After Johnston had proceeded north to Antrim, however, he received news that his sister had suddenly died, apparently a victim of the Irish dampness. With his plans now completely changed by the hand of fate, he decided to return to North America, but not before paying short visits to London and Liverpool.

Despite his many years on the frontier, Johnston never lost his thirst for knowledge and his strong Christian faith. During one particular winter in the Canadian wilds, for instance, he whiled away the time by reading through five volumes of the *Encyclopedia Britannica*. In addition, his correspondence frequently expressed his religious sentiments or referred to Christian duties or doctrines. Though generally tolerant, he held a special animus for religious skeptics and for faiths other than Protestant. According to his son-in-law, Johnston "looked with abhorrence upon such writers as Paine, and could not bring himself to think that the genius or talents of a Gibbon and Hume, found any adequate counterpoise to their want of faith in the Gospel of Christ." Johnston's reading of the Book of Revelation also had led him to believe that its fulfillment was about to be consummated by the downfall of "Popery" and Islam.

Johnston likewise attempted to make his domestic life a reflection of his former status in Ireland, at least as far as frontier life permitted. A description written seventy years after his death in 1828 portrayed the earlier conventionalities that had dominated the Irishman's home: "Here had gathered from away back many notable people, and here was kept up all possible of the state and ceremony of a noble house of Ireland; the presiding genius of a noble and stately woman, daughter of a noted Ojibway chief. The sons and daughters of the house were sent away to school, but trained at home in the strict conventionalities of the social life in which their father was reared. Some were sent to Ireland to be educated. On the great sideboard in the dining-room were arranged many pieces of solid silver service brought from Ireland. . . ."

Johnston's life as a successful outfitter and merchant in the fur trade was destroyed, however, by the war of 1812. At the onset of that conflict, Johnston was among a British force of 1,000 soldiers, Indians, and trappers who forced the surrender of the American fort on Mackinac Island. In the last year of the war, when an American force was sent to recapture the British position on Mackinac, Johnston gathered and provisioned a band of about 100 men for the defense of the island. His band had to flee, however, when a second American force tried to intercept it. Frustrated that they had failed to capture Johnston, the Americans sacked and pillaged the Irishman's stores and home in Sault Ste. Marie, going so far as ransacking the Johnstons' bedrooms for articles of female apparel.

Although Johnston rebuilt his home in 1815, his financial situation was so desperate that he appealed to the British government to compensate him for the losses he had incurred while fighting in its service. When this request was denied, he sold his estates in Ireland for £3,250 and with the proceeds reestablished his business. He also presented his claim to the United States government, but his role as an officer in the British service during the war made compensation by the American government out of the question. In fact, Johnston's role in the war prevented him from obtaining title to his property in Sault Ste. Marie for years after the area was incorporated into the United States. Not until 1853 – twenty-five years after his death – did Congress confirm his claim.

§ Phone: 906-635-5170 (Chippewa County Historical Society).

WHITEFISH POINT

¶ **Great Lakes Shipwreck Museum,** 11 miles north of Paradise, at 110 Whitefish Point Road.

Among the museum's collection of artifacts connected with various shipping disasters is a bell from the *Edmund Fitzgerald,* an ore carrier sunk off Whitefish Point during a storm on November 10, 1975. The museum also features a short film about the ill-fated vessel, whose sinking was the subject of "The Wreck of the *Edmund Fitzgerald,*" a song by Gordon

Lightfoot.

Known as "The Pride of the American Flag" after its christening in 1958, the 729-foot-long vessel bore the name of the president of Northwestern Mutual Life Insurance Company of Milwaukee, Wisconsin. Despite its 7,000-horsepower steam turbine, the ship went down in 500 feet of water with the loss of its entire crew of twenty-nine men.

Born in Wilwaukee in 1895, Edmund Fitzgerald was the grandson of John Fitzgerald, a native of Ireland and one of thirteen children born to William and Julia Fitzgerald of Oola, County Limerick. (Like five of his brothers, John Fitzgerald was a ship captain on the Great Lakes.) After receiving a doctorate from Yale in 1916, Edmund Fitzgerald worked for Northwestern Malleable Iron Company, Combined Locks Paper Company, and several banks in Milwaukee. Between 1933 and 1969 he served in a variety of positions at Northwestern Mutual Life: vice president, president, chairman of the board, and trustee. He died in 1986 at the age of ninety.

§ Open mid May-mid October, daily 10-6. Fee. Phone: 906-635-1742.

MINNESOTA

ELK RIVER

¶ **Oliver H. Kelley Farm,** on U.S. 10, 2.5 miles southeast, at 15788 Kelly Farm Road.

This 189-acre farm was the property of Oliver Kelley, the founder of the National Grange of the Patrons of Husbandry, formed to promote and protect the interests of the country's farmers. The large Italianate farmhouse on the property was built about 1875 and was occupied by Kelley's daughters, who operated the farm while he served with the Department of Agriculture in Washington, D.C. Today the farm is a living-history center, whose costumed interpreters demonstrate the use of nineteenth-century farming implements and practices.

Kelley, the great-grandson of an Irish immigrant who had come to America in 1755, arrived in Minnesota in 1849. He thereafter became an enthusiastic promoter of the region and hoped to attract settlers through his letters to the eastern press. Beginning in 1865, while a clerk for the Bureau of Agriculture in the nation's capital, he surveyed agricultural conditions throughout Minnesota and the South. He and six associates subsequently founded the National Grange. Although as the new organization's secretary Kelley stressed its social benefits, others hoped to use the Grange in the farmers' battle against monopolies, especially the railroads. By 1874 the organization numbered 20,000 granges, primarily in the South and Middle West.

§ Farm and interpretive center open May-October, Monday-Friday 10-5, Saturday-Sunday noon-4. Only interpretive center is open rest of the year, Saturday 10-4, Sunday noon-5. Fee. Phone: 612-441-6896.

GRACEVILLE

¶ **John Ireland Marker,** on the western end of town on the north side of State 28.

This memorial plaque commemorates the role played by Father John Ireland, a native of Kilkenny, in establishing several Irish farming communities throughout the state.

Beginning in the 1870s, just before he was elevated to the episcopacy, Ireland threw his support behind the colonization of Irish immigrants to the west. Appalled by the conditions which his fellow Irish immigrants endured in the eastern cities, he believed that these newcomers should be encouraged to adopt a rural way of life. In this way, he hoped, they would be freed from the squalor and temptations in the slums (chief of which, in his view, was Demon Rum). To help achieve this end, he became an agent for the St. Paul & Pacific Railroad, thereby becoming eligible to purchase large tracts of land relatively cheaply.

After acquiring almost 400,000 acres in the state, Ireland helped establish nine colonies – the most successful such effort conducted under Catholic auspices in the United States. Four of the new communities were christened with typically Irish names (Avoca, Clontarf, Fulda, and Iona), and four of the nine are still in existence. The settlement at Clontarf, for example, was created in 1876 by a "prohibition colony" from Pennsylvania. After arriving at Benson, Minnesota, at that time the western terminus of the Great Northern Railroad, the group trekked north to a tract of land which they named for a watering place near Dublin. In a pamphlet entitled *Invitation to the Land*, Ireland later described Clontarf as one of the "wide open opportunity-waiting spaces of the west."

The St. Paul churchman quickly learned, however, that the story of one failure could counteract a string of successes. Such seems to have been the case with the creation of the Connemara colony near Graceville. The group – composed of 300 Irish fishermen and peasants from the west coast of Ireland – arrived there in 1880. At once they were provided with clothing, two months' worth of provisions, houses already constructed, and offers of work from farmers in the local area. Despite these auspicious beginnings, the colony soon failed. To fishermen and subsistence farmers from Ireland, the cultivation of wheat on a large scale proved beyond their ability, especially the ability of the slackers and former paupers who composed a large portion of the group. Many of the colonists died that first winter because they had been too lazy to sod their shanties and to dig cellars to protect their potatoes.

Despite the extent of Ireland's achievements at resettlement, the number of Irish immigrants to the Great Plains was much lower than he had hoped. In 1898 he looked back over the history of colonization somewhat ruefully, declaring that, if greater efforts had been made during the previous decade, the western states would have been peopled by many more Catholics and "tens of thousands of Catholic families would have gained happy homes and an honorable competence upon the land, instead of having gone down to ruin in the fierce maelstrom of large cities." (See Cathedral of St. Paul, St. Paul, Minnesota.)

GRAND RAPIDS

¶ **Judy Garland Birthplace Historic House,** 2 miles south of U.S. 2 and U.S. 69 at 2727 U.S. 169S.

Judy Garland, the famous star of *The Wizard of Oz*, lived in this partially restored house until she was four years old, when she and her vaudevillian parents moved to California. Although she frequently referred to her father's Irish charm, it is unlikely that he had much Irish ancestry, if indeed any. The future entertainer's undoubted Irish roots came from her maternal grandmother, Eva Fitzgerald.

Garland, whose real name was Frances Gumm, was born in 1922 and made her theatrical debut in vaudeville at the age of two or three – encoring "Jingle Bells" seven times. At the age of thirteen she broke into motion pictures when Metro-Goldwyn-Mayer Studios offered her a contract. During the next fifteen year she appeared opposite some of the biggest names in the industry: with *Mickey Rooney in the Andy Hardy films, *Babes on Broadway*, and *Girl Crazy*; with *Gene Kelly in *For Me and My Gal*, *Summer Stock*, and *The Pirate*; and with Fred Astaire in *Easter Parade* and *Royal Wedding*. For her performance as Dorothy in *The Wizard of Oz*, she received a special award from the Academy of Motion Picture Arts and Sciences in 1939.

§ Open May-October, daily 9-5; rest of the year, by appointment. Fee. Phone: 800-664-5839.

• In late June each year Grand Rapids honors its famous daughter with the three-day Judy Garland Festival, which includes a talent show and a series of film seminars.

¶ **Judy Garland Historical Center,** Center School Heritage and Arts Center, at the junction of State 2 and U.S. 169.

One of the museums in this restored schoolhouse features memorabilia from the life and movie career of *Judy Garland. (See entry above.)

§ Open Monday-Friday 9:30-5, Saturday 9:30-4. Also open Sunday 11-4 Memorial Day-Labor Day. Fee. Phone: 218-326-6431.

HASTINGS

¶ **Ignatius Donnelly House Marker,** on the grounds of the Nininger Town Hall, 1.5 miles northwest on County 42 (Nininger Road).

A metal marker commemorates the site of Ignatius Donnelly's home, originally located just north of the town hall. Donnelly, the son of an Irish physician, was an internationally known author, orator, politician, social reformer, and prophet and lived in the Nininger house until his death in 1901.

Despite efforts to save the house and make it the centerpiece of a state park, the structure was razed in 1949, but not before the beautiful cherry paneling in Donnelly's library was saved. The library was temporarily reconstructed in 1981 as part of an exhibit in honor of Donnelly at the Minnesota Historical Society in St. Paul.

The plaque in front of the town hall reads in part: "Donnelly, a lawyer from Philadelphia, moved west to Minnesota and launched a national campaign to attract settlers to Nininger City, a promising village of more than 500 residents when it was laid out around this site in 1856. After the town melted away during the panic and depression of 1857, Donnelly turned his astonishing energy to politics, serving one term as lieutenant governor and three terms in Congress. For nearly 40 years his restless search for fair and effective social and economic institutions led him to play a role in virtually every agrarian reform movement of the late nineteenth century. In addition to his fiery campaigns on behalf of farmers and workers, Donnelly wrote several unconventional and widely read books of popular science, including *Atlantis, The Great Cryptogram, Ragnarok,* and *Caesar's Column,* in which he predicted the collapse of American society in the year 1988."

Although Donnelly was a staunch Republican while he served in Congress both during and immediately after the Civil War, he gradually turned his back on a party which he felt served privileged special interests through its support of hard-money principles and a protective tariff. In a nation faced with the tremendous upheaval brought about by industrialization, he believed that politics would increasingly become a conflict "between the few who seek to grasp all power and wealth, and the many who seek to preserve their rights as American citizens and freemen." He accordingly moved more and more to the left – from Liberal Republican to Granger to Greenbacker to Populist.

As a motivating force behind the formation of the Populist Party, Donnelly authored the preamble of that party's 1892 platform, generally regarded as the most radical ever proposed by a major party. ". . . We meet in the midst of a nation brought to the verge of moral, and political, and material ruin," he warned. "Corruption dominates the ballot-box, the legislature, the Congress, and touches even the ermine of the bench. . . . The fruits of the toil of millions are boldly stolen to build up colossal fortunes for a few . . . ." He also helped formulate and promote the party's agenda: direct election of U.S. senators, restriction of immigration, the initiative and referendum, a graduated income tax, low-interest government loans, a silver standard, and government ownership of the railroads.

Although more generally known for his political career, Donnelly earned a reputation as an iconoclastic author. In *The Great Cryptogram,* for example, he attempted to prove that the works attributed to Shakespeare were actually written by Francis Bacon. In a later novel entitled *Caesar's Column: A Story of the Twentieth Century* (1891), he described America as he envisioned it a century into the future. Writing under the pseudonym "Edmund Boisgilbert" and using the eyes of a young traveler, he depicted a nation of extreme contrasts: a world of physical comforts and technological marvels (e.g., airships and communications and transportation systems), on the one hand, and, on the other, "a degraded society . . . with the rich in complete control, the laboring classes reduced to a horrible quasi-barbaric poverty, ending in a revolution more bloody and violent than any that had preceded it." To Donnelly this "brave new world" was the result of "the reduction, by competition, of the wages of the worker to the least sum that will maintain life and muscular strength to do the work required . . . . I do not know if there is a hell in the spiritual universe, but if there is not, one should certainly be created for the souls of the men who originated, or justified, or enforced that damnable creed." (Donnelly was equally trenchant in his anticlericalism, although amusingly alliterative: "It was a black and bloody and bitter and dreadful world when the black gowns controlled it – both in Europe and America.") Elsewhere in *Caesar's Column* he pleaded "for a renewal of the bond of brotherhood between classes; for a reign of justice on earth that shall obliterate the cruel hates and passions which now divide the world." And to the churches he made some pointed suggestions: "The world to-day clamors for deeds, not creeds! for bread, not dogma; for charity, not ceremony; for love, not intellect." Although the establishment press ignored the book, by the end of the decade it had sold almost 700,000 copies in Europe and the United States.

LITTLE FALLS

¶ Charles A. Lindbergh House and History Center, 0.5 mile west on State 27 and then 1.5 miles south on Lindbergh Drive.

This is the boyhood home of the famous aviator who in 1927 made the first solo flight across the Atlantic. The complex features exhibits about three generations of the Lindbergh family. Although Lindbergh's Swedish roots are well known, his Irish ancestry through his maternal great-grandmother Emma Kissane is usually overlooked. (See *Spirit of St. Louis*, National Air and Space Museum, District of Columbia.).

§ Open May-Labor Day, Monday-Saturday 10-5, Sunday noon-4. Day after Labor Day to mid October, Saturday 10-4, Sunday noon-4. Fee. Phone: 320-632-3154.

MINNEAPOLIS

¶ Dowling Urban Environmental Center, 3900 West River Road.

Although it originally housed the Michael Dowling School for Crippled Children, this building is still named for the Minneapolis banker and lecturer whose achievements in the face of personal hardship made him a national figure.

Born in 1866 in Massachusetts, Michael Dowling was the son of an Irish immigrant journeyman carpenter. As a youngster the son supported himself by working as a Mississippi steamboat hand, as a farmer in the Northwest, and as a paperboy in Chicago. During a blizzard in Minnesota, however, extreme exposure led to the loss of both his legs, his left arm, and most of his right hand. Having in the meantime become an orphan, he was declared a public charge, although he persuaded the authorities to finance his education at Carleton College in return for dispensation from their obligation to support him.

Following his graduation from college, the young Dowling followed a variety of careers – teaching school, selling books, operating a skating rink, and serving as a school principal. He later established a weekly newspaper and was chief clerk of the Minnesota legislature and secretary of the National League of Republican clubs. In this last capacity he came to the attention of *President William McKinley, who sent him to the Philippines to report on the condition of the school system there.

After election to the Minnesota House of Representatives, Dowling served as its Speaker, although he continued to pursue a career in real estate, banking, and insurance. After World War I he visited disabled soldiers throughout the United States and England, hoping to rouse their spirits with his own life story and positive attitude. Dowling and his wife were married for twenty-five years and had three children.

¶ **Minneapolis Institute of Arts,** 2400 Third Avenue South.

Considered one of the region's finest art museums, the institute has more than 80,000 *objects d'art* from as far back as 2000 B.C. In addition to ancient Greek and Roman statuary, the museum's collection includes Italian, Dutch, and French paintings. Its American collection includes works by *John Singleton Copley, Thomas Eakins, *Georgia O'Keeffe, John Singer Sargent, Benjamin West, and Grant Wood.

§ Open Tuesday-Saturday 10-5 (also Thursday 5-9) and Sunday noon-5. Closed July 4, Thanksgiving, and December 25. Phone: 612-870-3131.

¶ **Sister Kenny Institute,** 800 East 28th Street.

This internationally known medical facility stands in tribute to Elizabeth Kenny, the Australian nurse ("sister") who revolutionized the treatment of infantile paralysis.

Born in 1886 in Southwestern Queensland, Kenny was the daughter of an Irish emigrant who had left County Kilkenny for Australia in 1862. (She described herself as "75 percent Irish, 25 percent Scotch for some balance.") After completing her nursing training, she became what was called a "bush nurse," dedicated to serving the rural population in the "outback." In 1910, while beginning her first assignment in the vicinity of Clifton, Queensland, she encountered a child suffering from an illness that completely baffled her. After wiring a description of the symptoms to the nearest doctor – who was forty miles away – she learned that the affliction was infantile paralysis.

When a number of other children began to show the same symptoms, Kenny attempted to relieve the muscle spasms, which she believed were actually contractions. To do this, she applied hot packs and began moving the children's arms and legs and massaging the muscles, all the while advising against the customary use of splints. The children responded to her treatment and soon were able to move their limbs on their own. Only later did Kenny learn that her treatment contradicted the conventional wisdom that the paralysis was caused by a sagging – rather than a contraction – of the muscles, a diagnosis which justified the use of splints to keep the strong, normal muscles from pulling the weak, affected ones out of place. Despite impressive results, Kenny continued to be ridiculed by conservatives in the medical establishment for stimulating – rather than immobilizing – the muscles.

During World War I, Kenny made fifteen round trips between Australia and Great Britain as a nurse aboard army transports. In an interesting sidelight to this wartime experience, she invented and patented a transport stretcher and a device to stabilize a wounded body while in transit. The modest royalties she received from these devices allowed her to carry on her subsequent nursing career for free. About a decade after returning to Australia, she opened a clinic, although her techniques continued to provoke violent opposition from some Australian physicians.

In 1940, however, physicians at the University of Minnesota and at the Minneapolis General Hospital invited Sister Kenny to open a clinic in Minneapolis. During her ten-year stay there she trained about forty nurses and physiotherapists in her technique and achieved a recovery rate of 85 percent among the eighty-four infantile paralysis cases she treated. In rapid succession she finally gained recognition and acceptance from the National Foundation for Infantile Paralysis and the American Medical Association. Her life was later dramatized in a motion picture produced by United Artists' and starring Rosalind Russell.

§ Phone: 612-863-4400.

NORTHFIELD

¶ **Northfield Historical Society Museum,** 408 Division Street.

The museum was formerly the First National Bank of Northfield, the target of a robbery attempt on September 7, 1876, by the James-Younger Gang. (The James brothers were of Irish descent. See Kearney, Missouri, in *Irish America*, Volume 2.) When the bandits were unable to open the safe, they shot indiscriminately into the street, killing two townspeople and wounding a third. Two of the would-be robbers were also wounded, however, when hastily armed merchants near the bank returned fire. After only seven minutes in town, the remaining six members of the gang escaped, but just ahead of a small posse. By nightfall the number of pursuers had grown to 200, and within a few days to a thousand. Although Jesse and Frank James eluded the posse, Charlie Pitts was killed and the three Younger brothers were captured and sentenced to life imprisonment.

• Each year on the weekend after Labor Day the town of Northfield celebrates the Defeat of Jesse James Day, complete with a parade, a rodeo, and a reenactment of the robbery attempt.

OWATONNA

¶ **Norwest Bank,** East Broadway and North Cedar Street.
Designed by *Louis Sullivan, this 1908 bank is regarded as one of the Chicago architect's finest structures. The local bankers who commissioned the work were impressed with Sullivan's rejection of the typical Revival architecture of the period and gave him a free hand. The one-story brick and stone bank is known for its decorative ironwork, large arched windows, and mosaic ornamentation. Its vibrantly decorated interior – largely the work of George Grant Elmslie, Sullivan's chief designer – features stained-glass windows, chandeliers, stenciled walls, and plasterwork incorporating more than 200 shades of color. (See Art Institute of Chicago, Chicago, Illinois.)

ST. PAUL

¶ **Cathedral of St. Paul,** 239 Selby Avenue.
Patterned after St. Peter's Basilica in the Vatican, this Catholic cathedral was constructed between 1905 and 1915 under the leadership of Archbishop John Ireland. The city of St. Paul commemorated the Irish-born immigrant by naming the boulevard between the cathedral and the State Capitol in his honor.

Archbishop Ireland was born in Kilkenny, Ireland, in 1838 and came to America with his parents. While still a youngster in St. Paul, he showed an aptitude for polemics, often arguing theology with the Presbyterian minister on his milk route. Following his ordination, he served in the Civil War as chaplain of the Fifth Minnesota Volunteers until he was stricken with fever at Vicksburg. As a pastor in St. Paul he campaigned against political corruption and the influence of liquor interests, going so far as to defenestrate whiskey bottles during house-to-house inspections in the Irish community. He subsequently became the leader of the temperance movement in this part of the country after three drunken men presented him with a piece of paper signed by a saloon keeper and his patrons and containing the plea, "For God's sake organize a temperance society." For his zeal in this effort, he was called the "Father Mathew of the West" and "the Consecrated Blizzard" of the Old Northwest.

Like his contemporary *Cardinal James Gibbons of Baltimore, Ireland sought to dispel the notion that Catholicism was incompatible with American institutions. In a major address during the Third Plenary Council in 1884, for example, the bishop of St. Paul insisted that "the principles of

the church are in thorough harmony with the interests of the Republic
. . . ." He later lent his influence to prevent the Vatican from officially condemning the Ancient Order of Hibernians and the Knights of Labor, although his need to do so called into question his thesis about the compat-
ibility of the Church and America's democratic ideals. Whatever the case,
his liberalism on Church-State matters, on the one hand, and his political
identification with the Republican Party, on the other, energized his enemies within the hierarchy. Despite the best efforts of *Theodore Roosevelt
and Secretary of State John Hay on his behalf, Ireland was never awarded
the red hat. (See Graceville, Minnesota.)

§ Open Monday-Tuesday and Thursday-Friday 8-6, Wednesday 8-4,
Saturday 8-8, Sunday 1-6. Phone: 612-228-1766.

⁋ **F. Scott Fitzgerald Birthplace,** 481 Laurel Avenue. Private.

This was the birthplace in 1896 of F. Scott Fitzgerald, the famous novelist whose love-hate relationship with the wealthy formed the basis of
much of his work, including *This Side of Paradise* and *The Great Gatsby*.

Fitzgerald's dual American and Irish ancestry seems to have been the
cause of the identity crisis that plagued him for most of his life. Through
his paternal forebears, Fitzgerald was descended from prominent figures
in the history of colonial Maryland. (He was named, in fact, for Francis
Scott Key, the author of the "Star Spangled Banner" and a cousin of his
paternal grandmother.) His maternal grandfather, Philip McQuillan, had
emigrated from County Fermanagh, Ireland, in 1843, settling first in Galena, Illinois, and then in St. Paul, where he operated a wholesale grocery
business and left a fortune worth more than $125,000. Yet despite this
grandfather's financial success, Fitzgerald regarded his maternal ancestry as "straight 1850 potato-famine Irish." The author's cultural schizophrenia is evident in his remark that "I am half black Irish and half old
American stock. . . . The black Irish half of the family had the money and
looked down upon the Maryland side of the family who . . . really . . . had
'breeding.' So . . . spent my youth alternately crawling in front of the
kitchen maids and insulting the great."

An example of Fitzgerald's iconoclasm occurred in St. John the Evangelist Episcopal Church in St. Paul one Christmas Eve. After "suppering
heavily" while home from Princeton in 1913, the young college student
expressed a desire to sing Christmas carols. Entering the church after the
service had begun, he swayed down the aisle until he reached the foot of
the pulpit. "Don't mind me, go on with the sermon," he said to the minister directly above his head. Fitzgerald later commented that the St. Paul
press was so eager to report his impropriety that the local papers "had the
extra out before midnight." (See Rockville, Maryland.)

⁋ **F. Scott Fitzgerald Residence,** Summit Terrace, 599 Summit Avenue. Private

In 1918 *F. Scott Fitzgerald was living with his parents in the three-story apartment at this address, on a street which he later called "a museum of American architectural failures."

It was here that the twenty-two year old worked on the final version of *This Side of Paradise* after the manuscript – originally called *The Romantic Egotist* – had been rejected twice by Scribner's. He worked on the third floor of the apartment, pinning to the curtains the chapters he intended to keep in the revision. By the end of that July he told his editor that while his earlier book had been "a tedious, disconnected casserole this is a definite attempt at a big novel and I really believe I have it." When his publisher finally accepted the manuscript, he wrote to a friend at Smith College:

> In a house below the average
> On a street above the average
> In a room below the roof
> With a lot above the ears
> I shall write Alida Bigelow ...
> Scribner's has accepted my book. Ain't I smart!

¶ Ignatius Donnelly Burial Site, Calvary Cemetery, Front and St. Albans streets, Block 32, lot 8.

A large headstone marks the graves of *Ignatius Donnelly and his wife, Katherine, and their daughter, Mary, and her husband, George Giltinan. (The Donnelly name is on the north side of the stone and is not visible from the road.) Donnelly was a prominent state and national politician, author, and social reformer. (See Hastings, Minnesota.)

¶ James J. Hill House, 240 Summit Avenue.

Constructed between 1889 and 1891, this 36,000-square-foot Victorian house belonged to James J. Hill, the founder of the Great Northern Railroad. The three-story house was built at a cost of $200,000 and has a three-story pipe organ, twenty-two fireplaces, stained-glass windows, and an art gallery.

Hill, whose ancestors had come from northern Ireland, abandoned plans to become a doctor when an accident with an arrow caused the loss of sight in one eye. After arriving in St. Paul at the age of seventeen, he found work as a clerk for a steampacket line and soon learned all aspects of the freight business. By 1867 he had contracted to supply the St. Paul & Pacific Railroad with fuel. Realizing that coal would soon replace wood as the railroad's chief fuel, he completed a survey of the nation's coal sources and markets and formed the Northwestern Fuel Company. Through his subsequent development of the Great Northern Railroad system between St. Paul and Puget Sound, he was soon on his way to gaining monopoly control of the rail freight between Chicago and the Pacific Northwest. (Between 1891 and 1906 the G.N.R. network expanded with the construction of an average of one mile of railroad per day.) By 1901 Hill and his associates had secured controlling interest in both the Northern Pacific and the Chicago, Burlington & Quincy lines.

In the administration of his railways, Hill insisted that his officers follow a simple maxim: "Intelligent management of railroads must be based on exact knowledge of facts. Guesswork will not do." While at the height of his railroad career, he was also a director of several banks, including Chase National. In the last year of his life, his friends honored him with the endowment of the James J. Hill Professorship of Transportation at Harvard University.

§ Open Wednesday-Saturday 10-3:30. Closed holidays. Fee. Phone: 612-297-2555.

¶ James J. Hill Reference Library, 80-90 West 4th Street.

Located in an Italian Renaissance building shared with the St. Paul Public Library, the Hill Library was established through a $1 million endowment created by the railroad magnate *James J. Hill. The interior of the two-story hall, which opened in 1921, is lined with Ionic columns.

¶ James Shields Statue, second floor rotunda, State Capitol, Aurora and Constitution avenues.

At the insistence of the Grand Army of the Republic, this memorial statue in honor of General James Shields was erected by the state of Minnesota in 1914.

A native of County Tyrone, Ireland, Shields enjoyed a number of distinctions: He challenged Abraham Lincoln to a duel, served in three conflicts (the Black Hawk War, the Mexican War, and the Civil War), and was the only American to represent three states in the U.S. Senate (Illinois, Minnesota, and Missouri). (See Carrollton, Missouri, in *Irish America*, Volume 2.)

After representing Illinois in the U.S. Senate at the beginning of the 1850s, the Mexican War veteran settled on his land grant in Minnesota Territory. While there, he became an energetic promoter of Irish colonization and was influential in establishing the townships of Erin, Kilkenny, Montgomery, and Shieldsville. By 1857 the last-named community had almost 300 residents, more than half of them natives of Ireland and most of the rest of Irish parentage. That same year he became one of Minnesota's first U.S. senators.

§ Capitol open Monday-Friday 9-5, Saturday 10-4, Sunday 1-4. Closed January 1, Easter, Thanksgiving, December 25. Phone: 612-296-2881.

*Statue of James Shields
in the Minnesota State Capitol.
(Photo courtesy of the
Minnesota Historical Society.)*

¶ Minnesota History Center, 345 Kellogg Boulevard West.
    The society's holdings include approximately half the volumes in the
personal library of *Ignatius Donnelly, the famous author, politician, and
social reformer. His collection originally numbered several hundred books
– 200 on Shakespeare and Bacon alone – and was housed in the cherry
paneled library of his home in Nininger, Minnesota. (See Hastings, Minnesota.) During his lifetime, the collection was one of the largest in the
state. Because Donnelly made marginal notations in many of his books, it
is possible to trace the source of his social and political ideas. Long after
Donnelly's death, however, when the house lay in disrepair, "souvenir
hunters" stripped the library of many of its fine volumes. The remaining
works – as well as the library itself – were rescued before Donnelly's house
was razed in 1949. The volumes which the historical society today pos-
sesses are in the Reserve Room and are accessible through prior arrangement.
    In 1981 the Minnesota Historical Society reconstructed Donnelly's pan-
eled library as part of an exhibit. The library was later disassembled and
today is held in storage by the historical society.
    § Open Tuesday-Saturday 10-5 (also Thursday 5-9), Sunday noon-5.
Closed January 1, Thanksgiving, and December 25. Phone: 612-296-6126.

¶ **O'Shaughnessy Plaza and Auditorium,** 143 West 4th Street.

This plaza and civic auditorium are named for Ignatius Aloysius O'Shaughnessy, an oil company executive and a benefactor of the University of St. Thomas in St. Paul.

The grandson of an Irish immigrant who had settled in Massachusetts in the 1830s, O'Shaughnessy was a 1903 graduate of St. Thomas College (the predecessor of today's university). He worked in the insurance and banking fields before creating the Global Oil & Refining Company in 1917 and serving as president of its subsidiaries, the Lario Oil & Gas Company and the Globe Pipeline Company. In addition to being a director of the First National Bank of St. Paul and a member of the Chicago Yacht Club, he was a trustee of the University of Notre Dame, a Knight of the Holy Sepulchre, and a Knight of Malta. He was noted for his benefactions of almost $1 million to three Catholic educational institutions: Notre Dame University (for the creation of a fine arts foundation), St. Thomas College (for the erection of a physical education building), and to St. Louis University in Missouri (for its library).

¶ **St. Paul Seminary,** Mississippi River Boulevard between Summit and Goodrich avenues.

This Catholic seminary was established in 1894 by *Archbishop John Ireland following a bequest by *James J. Hill. Although raised by a Baptist father and a Methodist mother, the famous railroad magnate had married Mary Theresa Mehegan, the daughter of Catholic Irish immigrants. Hill's other benefactions to the archdiocese of St. Paul were numerous and generous, including $50,000 toward the construction of the cathedral.

¶ **St. Thomas Academy,** 949 Mendota Heights Road.

This college preparatory and military academy was created in 1963 as an offshoot of St. Thomas College, originally founded in 1885 by *Archbishop John Ireland. The campus chapel is built in the style of a Byzantine basilica, and the school library contains impressive holdings of French and Celtic literature.

¶ **University of St. Thomas,** 2115 Summit Avenue.

The life of Archbishop John Ireland is commemorated in two memorials at this Catholic institution: a stained-glass window in St. James Church and a statue of the Irishman in the lower quadrangle of the campus.

At first known as St. Thomas College, this institution was founded in 1885 by Ireland, for almost two decades the archbishop of St. Paul. The property on which the college was built originally belonged to William Finn, an Irish-American soldier stationed at nearby Fort Snelling. Finn had acquired the land as a pension when he was discharged from military service after blowing off one of his fingers in a gun accident. He later sold

*Statue of Archbishop Ireland
at the University of St. Thomas.*
*(Photo courtesy of the
University of St. Thomas.)*

the property to Archbishop Ireland.

The college was initially both a seminary for the training of priests and a liberal arts institution for lay students. In 1894, however, the theological school was moved to a new site, now occupied by St. Paul Seminary. Today the St. Thomas campus boasts several buildings erected through the generosity of *Ignatius Aloysius O'Shaughnessy, a 1903 graduate of the college and a prominent oil company executive. The school's library, educational center, and athletic building and stadium bear the name of their donor. A bust of O'Shaughnessy is located in the library, while his regalia as a Knight of Malta and of the Holy Sepulchre are on display in the educational center. (See O'Shaughnessy Plaza above.)

SANBORN

¶ Sod House on the Prairie, 1 mile east of junction U.S. 71 and then 0.25 mile south on a gravel road.

These two sod houses were built in 1987 by Stan McCone to honor his Irish ancestors who lived in such houses in Tulare, South Dakota, in the 1880s. McCone's first American ancestor was Thomas McKone, who was born in County Antrim in 1827 or 1829. After settling in Clinton, Iowa, this immigrant McKone married Sarah Dunn Pierce, who had come to America after her first husband died in Ireland, reputedly from choking on a pork chop.

One of the sod houses contains a dirt floor and is simply furnished, while the other has a wooden floor, is appointed more amply, and can be rented out to bed and breakfast guests.

§ Open April-October, daily 10-5. Fee. Phone: 507-723-5138.

SHAKOPEE

¶ **Historic Murphy's Landing,** 1 mile east, at 2187 County 101E.

This eighty-eight-acre site is an outdoor living-history museum that features forty period buildings, including two farmsteads, a fur trading post, and a schoolhouse. The structures represent the various ethnic groups which settled in the Minnesota River Valley between 1840 and 1890: Czech, Danish, English, French, German, Irish, Norwegian, Polish, and Scandinavian. The site also includes sixteen Native American mounds dating from the first century B.C.

• Historic Murphy's Landing occupies the site of a nineteenth-century inn and ferry landing owned by Richard Murphy, who arrived in this area in 1853.

Presumably of Irish background, Murphy was born in Tennessee sometime between 1801 and 1804 but moved to Illinois at the age of seventeen. After serving in the Black Hawk War, he was elected to the Illinois legislature. In 1848, however, *President James K. Polk appointed him Indian subagent for the St. Peter Indian Agency in what later became the state of Minnesota. He was stationed for about four years at Fort Snelling before being transferred to the Dakota reservation agency.

After taking up this new position, Murphy moved to Eagle Creek, a small town east of Shakopee. In 1856 the state legislature granted him a fifteen-year charter to operate a ferry on the Minnesota River, a concession that prompted him to build a two-story inn to accommodate the travelers for whom he expected to play boatman. Before long, however, plans were afoot to build a bridge across the river in order to provide a direct route from Shakopee to St. Paul. According to the plan, the bridge would be built at a site near Murphy's hotel. Although at first the prospect of a bridge seemed to threaten Murphy's ferry business, he soon realized that the railroads would connect with the river at Eagle Creek, forming a juncture with the steamboat lines already there or likely to develop. As a result, he visualized the emergence of a large settlement on his very doorstep. Unfortunately, however, the rail line was not built for a decade, during which time the Shakopee landing was preferred to Murphy's. Murphy used the hotel as a home for his family and lived there until his death in 1875.

The stone inn was subsequently used for a variety of purposes, including a homeless shelter during the Depression. In 1963, however, the building was destroyed by fire, caused by either a defective chimney or faulty wiring. The twelve members of the family that lived there at the time escaped the flames but suffered the other extreme – a temperature of thirty degrees below zero. The foundations of the inn are still visible and are located near the center of Murphy's Landing Village.

• The second site in Murphy's Landing with an Irish connection is the O'Connor House, built in 1865 by an immigrant named John O'Connor.

O'Connor and his wife, Catherine, were born in Ireland in 1825 and 1835, respectively. After immigrating to the United States, they eventually made their way to Minnesota, arriving in Glendale in 1855. After service as a private in the Minnesota Volunteers for three years during the Civil War, O'Connor returned to the state but soon moved with his wife and four children to Shakopee. There in 1865 he built the house on display in Murphy's Landing Village.

At the time of its construction, the house was located on a highly desirable corner, but the value of the residence declined precipitously when the St. Paul & Sioux City Railroad ran its tracks down the middle of Second Street. Although railroad officials claimed that O'Connor had granted them permission to build the tracks in front of his house, the Irishman sued. (The result of the suit is unknown.)

The nature of O'Connor's employment or occupation remains a mystery. Since the census records give no such evidence, it has been presumed that he was a handyman who worked for his neighbors whenever he could.

The John O'Connor House. (Photo courtesy of Historic Murphy's Landing.)

With the birth of his seventh child in 1871, O'Connor and his wife must have been living a precarious existence, a conclusion justified by the fact that the Irishman mortgaged his home eight times during the next seven years. In addition, on at least two occasions the house was sold to pay off debts or back taxes, although in each case O'Connor redeemed the property. His situation must have been desperate when his wife was fined $30 for assaulting a neighbor, Anna May Hilgers.

§ Historic Murphy's Landing is open Memorial Day-Labor Day, Tuesday-Sunday 10-5; day after Labor Day-late September, Saturday-Sunday 10-5; day after Thanksgiving-end of December, Saturday-Sunday 10-4. Fee. Phone: 612-445-6900 or 445-7491.

NEW HAMPSHIRE

AMHERST

¶ **Horace Greeley Birthplace,** Horace Greeley Road.

A stone monument and plaque stand in front of the birthplace of Horace Greeley, the founder of the *New York Times* and coiner of the advice "Go west, young man." The house, which has four fireplaces, dates from about 1775.

Greeley, who was descended from Scotch-Irish stock on his mother's side, set a new standard in American journalism by replacing the usual interest in the lurid with an emphasis on social and political reform. Through his editorials he attacked slavery and economic monopolies, opposed capital punishment, supported the rights of labor, and advocated the free distribution of government lands to western settlers. The focus of his efforts was summarized in his remark that newspapers should be "as sensitive to oppression and degradation in the next street as if they were practised in Brazil or Japan."

As the slavery issue intensified during the 1850s, Greeley favored disunion rather than complicity in the extension of the "peculiar institution" into the western territories. When civil war finally came, he insisted that Congress and President Lincoln emancipate the slaves, partially in the belief that the Union could not "afford to repel the sympathies and reject the aid of Four Millions of Southern people." As war dragged on, however, he urged Lincoln to negotiate a peace with the South, arguing that "our bleeding, bankrupt, almost dying country . . . shudders at the prospect of fresh conscriptions, of further wholesale devastations, and of new rivers of human blood."

CANAAN

¶ **Soldiers' Monument,** Broad Street Park.

This traditional Civil War memorial was designed by *Martin Milmore. A duplicate stands on the town common in Peterborough, New Hampshire. (See Boston Common, Soldiers' and Sailors' Monument, Boston, Massachusetts.)

CORNISH

¶ **Saint-Gaudens National Historic Site,** off State 12A between Cornish and Plainfield.

After purchasing this summer home and studio in 1883, Augustus Saint-Gaudens remodeled it and named it "Aspet" after his father's birthplace in France. Two studios on the property display bas-reliefs, busts, portraits, and models of his statuary (including the Admiral Farragut Statue, the Adams Memorial, *The Standing Lincoln*, and *Amor Caritas*). The sculptor's grave is marked by a small Ionic temple on the property.

Saint-Gaudens was born in Dublin to a French father and an Irish mother (Mary McGuiness), but within six months of his birth his family sailed for America, eventually settling in New York City. There the young-ster first showed his artistic bent by sketching the shoemakers in his father's shop. He later studied drawing at Cooper Union and the National Academy of Design.

By 1867 Saint-Gaudens was working as a cameo cutter in Paris and attending a small art school, where, as he reported, "I modeled my first figures from the nude." Within a year he was studying sculpture at the Ecole des Beaux-Arts and startling his comrades by singing the "Marseillaise." Although he suffered from illness and financial worries after moving on to Rome, he designed *Hiawatha* there and received various commissions, among them requests for copies of busts of Demosthenes and Cicero. The hold which the Eternal City had on him at that time is evident when – once again living in New York – he would "turn on the water at the little wash-basin, let it run continuously with a gentle tinkle, and thus recall the sound of the fountain in the garden at Rome."

After returning to the United States, Saint-Gaudens received a variety of commissions. His most famous were *Admiral Farragut* (New York City), *The Puritan* (Philadelphia), *Lincoln* (Chicago), *General John Logan* (Chicago),

"Aspet," the home of the Dublin-born sculptor Augustus Saint-Gaudens.

the *Shaw Memorial* (Boston), *General William Sherman* (New York City), the *Adams Monument* (District of Columbia), and *Diana* (for the tower of the original Madison Square Garden). He was also commissioned to design statues of Robert Louis Stevenson (Edinburgh, Scotland) and Charles Stewart Parnell (Dublin, Ireland). In 1905 he created designs for several U.S. coins, including a rendering of "Liberty" for the twenty-dollar gold piece. (His model for the figure "Liberty" was Mary Cunningham, an Irish immigrant girl.)

Saint-Gaudens was a founder of the Society of American Artists, received honorary degrees from Harvard, Princeton, and Yale, and was elected to the Royal Academy. As a teacher at the Art Students' League, he advised his pupils "to develop technique and then to hide it." On one occasion, as he wended his way through a studio full of the accouterments of his "trade" – scaffolds, plaster casts, and clay models – he remarked that "People think a sculptor has an easy life in a studio. It's hard labor, in a factory."

§ Open Memorial Day weekend-October 31, grounds daily dawn-dusk, buildings daily 9-4:30. Fee. Phone: 603-675-2175.

¶ Saint-Gaudens House and Studio, Dingelton Hill and Whitten roads.

Although this two-and-a-half-story house was originally built about 1794 for Shakers in Enfield, New Hampshire, it was bought and moved to this site by *Louis Saint-Gaudens, the younger brother of the more famous sculptor Augustus Saint-Gaudens.

Louis Saint-Gaudens was born in New York City in 1854 and studied sculpture first under his brother and then at the Ecole des Beaux-Arts in Paris. After returning to the United States, he became part of the "Cornish Colony" and helped his brother in many of his works. Louis, who suffered from alcoholism, occasionally climbed a windmill on the property, pulled up the ladder after himself, and nursed a bottle of bourbon in that secluded spot.

In 1901 the younger brother exhibited at the Pan-American Exposition in Buffalo, New York. His most famous work is probably his pair of lions in the Boston Public Library, sculpted to honor the men of two Massachusetts regiments who died in the Civil War.

DERRY

Scotch-Irish Presbyterians arrived in this area in 1719, although apparently they were at first taken for Catholic Irish. In 1722 the area now occupied by Derry and Londonderry was granted to John Moor and named for the famous Ulster city. The earliest settlers cultivated potatoes – the first grown in North America – and introduced Irish linen-making. The products of this latter industry became so brazenly imitated that by 1748 the town officials ordered that the end of each quantity of cloth produced here be stamped with the words "Londonderry in New Hampshire."

¶ **Matthew Thornton House,** 2 Thornton Street. Private.

A granite boulder in front of this clapboard house memorializes Matthew Thornton, the Irish-born signer of the Declaration of Independence who bought the house in 1757.

Thornton was a native of Limerick, Ireland, and arrived in Boston in 1718. Although he was a physician in Derry from 1740 to 1778, there is little evidence about the nature of his medical practice. It is known, however, that on at least two occasions he was paid extremely large sums by the New Hampshire Assembly for rendering medical services: £25 for attending a man injured in a riot, and £94 for caring for a sick soldier.

Apparently interested in the new medical developments of his time, Thornton allowed himself to be inoculated against the small pox. He used his recovery experience as the basis of a satire on members of his profession: "Dr. Cash . . . was the [inoculator], and for a few days, visited us [but] we saw no more of him, till I paid his bill of 18 dollars. Dr. Surly came two or three times each day . . . , viewed us through his glasses, and then, with a smiling grin, softly said, 'What, no worse yet? this is but trifling to what you will feel, before all is over.' Dr. Critical Observer . . . came once in two or three days, and stayed about a minute each time. Dr. Gay . . . tripped round and sung a tune, and told us 'all would end well.' Dr. Experience, a merchant, who has had the Small Pox, visited us every day, and gave a much truer account of the Small Pox than all the doctors." Thornton's later criticism of the medical corps in the Continental Army lacked the humor of his satire but was just as biting: "An inexcusable Neglect in the Officers, want of Fidility [sic], Honour, and Humanity, in the Drs and averice [sic] in the Suttlers, has Slain ten Soldiers to the Enemies['] one, and will Soon prevent every man of Common Sense from putting his Life and Fortune in the Power of Such as Destroy both without pity and mercy."

Both before and after the Revolution, Thornton served New Hampshire in a variety of positions. In 1775 he was elected president of the provincial congress and was the chairman of the committee which drafted the state's first constitution – the first adopted by any of the thirteen former colonies. Although he was not appointed to the Continental Congress until four months after the Declaration of Independence was adopted, he was permitted to sign the document on November 19, 1776.

Some years later, while Thornton served as a state judge, an incident in his court gave rise to an amusing anecdote. According to the story, when the defense attorney found Thornton reading a book and the associate justice asleep during the trial of a particular case, the lawyer told the jury:

"Gentlemen, my unfortunate client has no hope but in *your* attention, since the Court in their wisdom will not condescend to hear this case!" Thornton replied by saying, "When you have anything to offer, Mr. _____, which is pertinent to the case on trial, the Court will be happy to hear you. Meantime I may as well as resume my reading."

¶ **Pinkerton Academy,** Pinkerton Street.

This educational institution was founded by Major John Pinkerton and Elder James Pinkerton, whose father had come from Ulster to Londonderry about 1738. In 1814 these two prosperous merchants endowed the school with $14,500 "for promoting piety and virtue, and for the education of youth in such of the liberal arts and sciences or languages as the Trustees . . . shall direct." Today the academy offers a college preparatory curriculum as well as agricultural, commercial, and scientific courses of studies to 2,600 students in grades nine through twelve.

DUBLIN

The original land grant in this area was given to William Thornton and thirty-nine other colonists about 1750. The first settler in Dublin was Thornton's brother Matthew Thornton, a native of Limerick, Ireland, and a signer of the Declaration of Independence. Many of the other early settlers were Scotch-Irish.

DURHAM

¶ **John Sullivan Memorial Bridge,** across the Bellamy and Piscataqua rivers.

This bridge on the route from Durham to Portsmouth was named for *John Sullivan, the Revolutionary War general and governor of the state. (See next entry.)

¶ **John Sullivan House,** 23 New Market Street. Private.

This eighteenth-century structure was the home of John Sullivan, who purchased it in 1764. His grave is in the cemetery behind the house. A monument in front of the house marks the site of the meetinghouse where Sullivan and a band of colonials hid the arms and gunpowder which they had seized from the British at Fort William and Mary in 1774. (See New Castle, New Hampshire.)

The son of an Irish schoolmaster, Sullivan was born in New Hampshire and studied law in Portsmouth. As relations with England worsened in the early 1770s, he was sent to both the first and the second continental congresses. Following his appointment as brigadier general in the newly formed Continental Army, he served in the siege of Boston until

The John Sullivan Monument
(with the Sullivan House
in the background).

the British evacuation on St. Patrick's Day 1776. During the battle of Long Island, however, he was captured but later released. He subsequently accompanied the American army in its retreat across New Jersey and took a prominent role in the battles of Trenton and Princeton. Although an attempt was made to suspend him for his failed expedition against the British posts on Staten Island, Washington refused to recall him.

After spending the winter of 1777-78 at Valley Forge, Sullivan was ordered to take command in Rhode Island. His siege of Newport failed, however, after the French withdrew their army and fleet to Boston, a maneuver that Sullivan regarded as desertion by his European ally. In March 1779 the American general led an expedition against the Iroquois in New York and western Pennsylvania. After receiving reinforcements, he completely routed the Iroquois and their Loyalist allies near Elmira, New York [*q.v.*].

After the war Sullivan held a variety of political posts. In New Hampshire he was a member of the state constitutional convention (1782), speaker of the Assembly (1785), governor (three times between 1786 and 1789), and chair of the state convention called to ratify the Federal Constitution (1788). With the creation of the new national government, he was appointed U.S. district judge for New Hampshire.

MERRIMACK

¶ Matthew Thornton Home and Grave, State 3 (Daniel Webster Highway).

This private residence was formerly the home of *Matthew Thornton, who purchased it in 1780 after its confiscation from a Tory who had fled the state. Three years later the legislature granted Thornton the exclusive right to ferry passengers across the river near his house. This area is still known as Thornton's Ferry. (See Derry, New Hampshire.)

Thornton's grave is located across the highway and is marked by a monument dedicated in 1892.

The Matthew Thornton House in Merrimack.

NEW CASTLE

¶ Fort Constitution, in a small park east of the town square.

Known in revolutionary times as Fort William and Mary, this fortification was the object of an attack by colonials under Major John Sullivan on December 15, 1774. During this raid and another the day before, the Americans captured five tons of gunpowder, fifteen cannon, and a large quantity of arms. Sullivan must have relished the irony of his victory when he thought of his grandfather Philip O'Sullivan, who had fled Ireland after the victory of King William III at the battle of the Boyne in 1690.

Occurring four months before the battles of Lexington and Concord, the attacks on Fort William and Mary constituted the first overt act of aggression against British authority in the colony. Some of the captured munitions were turned against the British at the battle of Bunker Hill the following spring. In a letter to John Adams in 1775, Sullivan urged Congress to declare independence from Great Britain at once: "Have we any encouragement from the people of Great Britain? Could they exert themselves more if we had shaken off the yoke and declared ourselves independent? Why, then, in God's name is it not done? Do the members of your respectable body think that [the British] will throw their shot and shells with more force than at present? . . . . Could they have treated our prisoners worse had we been in open and avowed rebellion than they do now?"

PETERBOROUGH

¶ MacDowell Colony National Historic Landmark, north on MacDowell Road off U.S. 202.

In 1896 the Scotch-Irish composer Edward Alexander MacDowell turned his sixty-acre farm here into a working retreat with the erection of a log studio to complement "Hillcrest," his farmhouse. His widow later opened the "colony" to other musicians as well as to writers and painters. Today the colony's 500-acre property consists of approximately thirty-five studios and outbuildings. Visitors are welcome at Colony Hall and can visit the library and MacDowell's grave.

Although MacDowell's initial musical training in the United States was from South American instructors, his subsequent musical preparation was decidedly European. In 1876 he was admitted to the Paris Conservatoire, but, after developing a dislike for French music, he decided to pursue his education in Germany. He was soon appointed head piano instructor at the Darmstadt Conservatory. On a later visit to Franz Liszt to play his (MacDowell's) First Piano Concerto, the American musician was so nervous that he could not ring the bell to the famous European's house. For the next two years MacDowell concentrated on composing orchestral pieces and symphonic poems.

Following his return to Boston with his new wife, MacDowell realized that he must devote his time to performance and instruction rather than composition. He was soon lionized as the foremost American composer and pianist and , as result, developed a growing clientele of piano and composition students. This increasing fame may have been influential in his appointment in 1896 to the first professorship of music at Columbia University. Although he established a male chorus and a university orchestra, he was distressed by the realization that his music classes carried no academic credit and that few of his students were prepared for the calibre of musical instruction he hoped to give them. He vainly requested that the academic world place greater emphasis on the fine arts.

After suffering a carriage accident in 1905, the forty-four-year-old musician began to show signs of mental illness. During periods of lucidity, however, he expressed his hope of turning his summer estate at Peterborough into an artists' colony. Leonard Bernstein, Aaron Copland, and Virgil Thomson were among the composers who subsequently spent time in residence here. Since 1960 the MacDowell Medal has been awarded annually to a distinguished composer, artist, or writer.

Historical marker in Londonderry, New Hampshire.

NEW JERSEY

ATLANTIC CITY

¶ **John F. Kennedy Bust,** opposite the Atlantic City Convention Center, on the Boardwalk between Mississippi and Florida avenues.

BARNEGAT LIGHT

¶ **Barnegat Lighthouse State Park,** on the north end of Long Beach Island, off Broadway Avenue.

Historic 172-foot Barnegat Lighthouse warns seafarers of Barnegat Shoals, the site of more than 200 shipwrecks. The lighthouse, known as the "Grand Old Champion of the Tides," was rebuilt in 1857-58 under the direction of *George Gordon Meade, who at the time was an engineer but who later was the Union commander at Gettysburg. Used as a lighthouse until 1927, the structure affords a fine view. (See George Meade Memorial, District of Columbia.)

§ Park open daily dawn-dusk. Lighthouse open Memorial Day-Labor Day, daily 9 am.-9:30 p.m.; October and other times in May and September, Wednesday-Sunday 9-4:30. Fee for lighthouse. Phone: 609-494-2016.

BRIDGEPORT

¶ **Commodore Barry Bridge,** over the Delaware River between Bridgeport, New Jersey, and Chester, Pennsylvania.

The bridge is named for John Barry, the Irish-born "Father of the American Navy." (See St. Mary's Church, Philadelphia, Pennsylvania.)

CALDWELL

¶ **Grover Cleveland Birthplace,** 207 Bloomfield Avenue (State 506).

Grover Cleveland, the only U.S. president to serve two nonconsecutive terms, was born here in 1837 and lived here until his family moved to Fayetteville, New York, four years later. Cleveland's maternal grandfather was Abner Neal, a Protestant of Anglo-Irish extraction who had emigrated from Ireland in the late 1700s, apparently driven from his native country because of his political activities. After settling in Baltimore, he became a bookseller and publisher of law books. One of the president's great-great-great-grandfathers was Richard Lamb of Dublin, who died in either 1736 or 1737 on his way to New England.

Perhaps because of his Irish roots, Cleveland twice offered what help he could in defense of Fenian prisoners captured during ill-fated attempts to invade Canada. After the first unsuccessful attempt – led by *John

O'Neill in May 1866 – Cleveland and some other Democratic lawyers handled the prisoners' case for free. When a similar invasion failed four years later, the Fenian prisoners were taken to Canada for trial. Because the future president was occupied with another legal case in Buffalo, he made arrangements for a friend of his to defend the Fenians without charge. After the invaders were convicted, Cleveland was among those who petitioned *President Ulysses S. Grant to commute the prison sentence.

During the presidential campaign of 1876, Cleveland became the object of attacks against his character. A Buffalo newspaper first published the insinuation that Cleveland was the father of an illegitimate son, the issue of a relationship with a widow named Mrs. Halpin. Although Cleveland never knew for sure that he was the father of the child, he agreed to take responsibility for him when Halpin claimed that Cleveland was the boy's father. When the mother began drinking while nursing the child, Cleveland indirectly took steps to have the boy committed to the care of an orphan asylum, the expenses of which Cleveland agreed to pay. After Halpin kidnapped the child, the authorities intervened and recommitted him to the orphanage, although he was later adopted by a distinguished New York family. During the campaign Cleveland's detractors titillated the voters with the jeer: "Ma, Ma, where's my Pa? Gone to the White House, Ha, Ha, Ha!"

§ Open Wednesday-Saturday 9-noon and 1-5, Sunday 1-5. Closed holidays. Phone: 973-226-1810.

Birthplace of President Grover Cleveland.

ELIZABETH

¶ Caldwell Burial Sites, First Presbyterian Church, Broad Street, south of Caldwell Place.

A seventeen-foot monument in the churchyard marks the graves of the *Reverend James Caldwell and his wife. Caldwell was the most famous colonial pastor of this church.

The inscription on the monument reads: "Sacred to the memory of the Rev. James Caldwell and Hannah his wife, who fell victims to their country's cause in the years 1780 & 1781. He was the zealous and faithful pastor of the Presbyterian Church in this Town, where by his evangelical labors in the gospel vineyard, and his early attachment to the civil liberties of his country, he has left in the hearts of his people a better monument than brass or marble."

Born in Virginia of Scotch-Irish and Huguenot descent, James Caldwell was graduated from the College of New Jersey (now Princeton) in 1759 and within two years was ordained and installed here as pastor. Because of his militancy for the Patriot cause and his service as a chaplain during the war against Britain, Loyalists called him the "high priest of the Revolution" and offered rewards for his capture.

In 1781 Caldwell met his death during an unfortunate incident with a Patriot guard, an Irishman named James Morgan. Having gone to meet an acquaintance who had arrived by boat at De Hart's Point, Caldwell went aboard the vessel to pick up a package belonging to the woman. As the minister returned to his carriage, Morgan ordered him to stop, apparently with the intention of questioning him about the package. When Caldwell failed to obey the command quickly enough, the sentry shot him through the heart. At Morgan's trial another soldier testified that he had heard the Irishman express his intention to "pop" Caldwell off whenever he had the chance, while still another soldier claimed that Morgan had been bribed to kill the parson. (See Springfield and Union, New Jersey.)

FREEHOLD

¶ Monmouth Battle Monument, Monmouth County Courthouse, Monument and Court streets.

This eighty-five-foot shaft is crowned with a representation of "Liberty Triumphant." The statue of Molly Pitcher and the five large panels on the base of the monument were designed by *James Edward Kelly. The bas-relief panels depict scenes from the battle of Monmouth in 1778: Colonel Nathaniel Ramsey defending his guns, Washington rallying his troops, Molly Pitcher at the cannon, the council of war at Hopewell, and the charge of *Anthony Wayne.

¶ **Old Tennent Church,** Main and Tennent streets.

Built in 1731 for a predominantly Scottish and Scotch-Irish congregation, this church was served during the middle of the eighteenth century
by two eminent Irish-born pastors – William Tennent and his brother John
Tennent. William, who was pastor here for forty-four years, was buried
beneath the church floor after his death in 1777.

William Tennent had come to America as a boy from his native County
Armagh with his father, a Presbyterian minister. After attending his father's
"Log College" in Neshaminy, Pennsylvania, the young man studied theology in New Brunswick, New Jersey, where he was almost buried alive.
It seems that, after intense study had broken his health, one day he fell
into unconsciousness while conversing with his brother in Latin. After his
body had become as "cold and stiff as a stake," he was prepared for burial
– but suddenly he came back to life. He later reported having experienced
a state of perfect bliss, although for a year he had no memory of his former
life. After recovering sufficiently, he succeeded his brother as pastor of the
Freehold church.

Apparently because Tennent's inattention to financial affairs had led
to some difficulties, a friend of his suggested that he find a wife "to attend
to his temporal affairs, and to comfort his leisure hours by conjugal en-
dearments." When the ingenuous minister replied that he did not know
how to go about obtaining a wife, the friend introduced him to his sister-
in-law. The two were married within a week.

HALEDON

¶ **American Labor Museum/Botto House National Landmark,**
83 Norwood Street.

During the 1913 textile workers strike in nearby Paterson, the Botto
House, the home of an Italian immigrant weaver, was the headquarters of
a monstrous labor rally. Today the house is a museum featuring exhibits
on the labor movement and immigrant life.

Among the labor agitators who addressed the thousands of strikers
who gathered here was Elizabeth Gurley Flynn, whose Irish immigrant
working-class parents had had a long association with political and social
radicalism. She recalled that she "drew in a burning hatred of British rule"
with her mother's milk and that before she was ten she knew of the great
Irish heroes – Robert Emmet, Wolfe Tone, Michael Davitt, Charles Stewart
Parnell, and Jeremiah O'Donovan Rossa. She proudly proclaimed that her
ancestors had participated in every rebellion against the British and that
her father, who lived past eighty, never mentioned the word "England"
without adding the curse, "God damn her!"

Flynn was a labor activist for almost her entire life. Even as a youngster she was closely involved with socialist activities in the Bronx and quit

high school in 1907 after joining the recently formed Industrial Workers of the World. During the next twenty years, she participated in various labor struggles, among them the free speech movement in Montana and Washington; strikes by textile workers in Lawrence, Massachusetts, and Paterson and Passaic, New Jersey; and the Mesabi Range miners' strike in Minnesota. During these crusades she became friends or associates of the major labor and radical leaders in the country, including Eugene V. Debs, *William Z. Foster, and Bill Haywood. She was even the subject of a song – "The Rebel Girl" – written in her honor by an imprisoned labor leader in Utah.

Following World War I, Flynn redirected her efforts. For the next four years, she was engaged in helping defend political and economic dissidents, many of whom had been arrested during the 1919-20 Red Scare. She was a founder of the American Civil Liberties Union and remained on its board of directors until she was expelled for being a member of the Communist Party. In 1953 she was convicted of violating the Smith Act – for advocating the overthrow of the government – and served a two-and-a-half-year prison term. Among her writings was a 1950 work entitled *Horizons of the Future for a Socialist America*.

§ Open Wednesday-Saturday 1-4; other times by appointment. Closed holidays except Labor Day. Fee. Phone 973-595-7953.

¶ West of Haledon, on State 504, is William Paterson State College, named for the famous Irish-born member of the Constitutional Convention, senator in the first Congress, and governor of New Jersey. Paterson was born in County Antrim in 1745 and was brought to America as an infant two years later.

JERSEY CITY

¶ **Frank Hague Portrait,** city council chambers, City Hall, 280 Grove Street.

Even in death the image of Jersey City's most famous party boss dominates the halls of power, reminding modern politicos that Frank Hague enjoyed a public career which spanned four decades.

Hague was born in Jersey City to immigrant parents from County Cavan, Ireland. To escape arrest for conspiracy against the British government, his father had fled to Italy, where he served in the papal army of Pius IX. The son, meanwhile, worked at a variety of jobs, one of them as a blacksmith's helper with the Erie Railroad. (He quit in short order because he disliked being "a nursemaid to locomotives.")

The young Hague made his political debut by winning the post of ward constable in 1899. Fourteen years later, sensing the mood of the public, he assumed the role of civic reformer to become one of five city commissioners from a field of ninety other candidates. As commissioner he ran a successful campaign against police corruption and laid the groundwork for his mayoral victory in 1917, the first of numerous terms as "Hiz Honor."

Hague certainly deserved his reputation as a hardfisted machine politician. He was often described as humorless and prone to personal violence. In fact, he once related an incident in which he "hauled off" and punched a doctor who had taken forty-five minutes to arrive at the scene of a fire. In addition to his clout at City Hall, he wielded great influence over both the county and state Democratic machines. From this vantage point he was able to secure the election of his candidate in six gubernatorial elections between 1919 and 1940.

The source of Hague's power, of course, was his ability to dispense patronage, initially in the form of municipal jobs and services and later through relief and public works projects sponsored by the New Deal. In return for his largess, he extracted untold millions from his "clients" as well as from the municipal treasury. Some idea of the extent of his personal corruption is evident in the $50,000 altar which he donated to St. Aedan's Church in the city – a gift worth more than six times his highest salary as mayor. Additional clues are his admission that he possessed a net worth of $8 million and a $15-million lawsuit filed by former city employees seeking the return of dues extorted by his machine. The Socialist leader Norman Thomas attributed the success of Hague's organization to the "dispensing [of] bread, circuses, and punishment."

Under Hague's charge the Jersey City police force became known for its professionalism. By 1940 his "men in blue" numbered 968, the largest number for any American city with a population between 300,000 and 400,000. His police also received the highest salary in the country. Hague once described Jersey City as "the most moralist city in America," probably because of its effective police force.

Although an incident in 1937 revealed Hague's concern for the youth of the city, the episode was later used as an example of his arrogance. When two high school students decided to attend night school so they could work during the day, the board of education denied them working papers on the grounds that they were legally required to attend day school. "That's the law," explained a school bureaucrat when the mayor ordered that the boys be issued the working papers. In response Hague retorted: "Listen, here is the law! I am the law! These boys go to work!" After coming under attack for this remark, Hague recanted, saying that "I have never desired to be the law. . . ."

In a later episode involving young miscreants, Hague was willing to allow the police a leeway that the law perhaps did not permit. "I want the policeman to be the boss – to rule with an iron hand in his handling of the boy problem. . . ," he pontificated. "[The] police officer won't offend me if he 'warms' the young hoodlums. Every time the policeman gets after him he will serve to warn the boy that crime is not being coddled or encouraged. The way to save him is not by sending him to prison but to prove to him that crime doesn't pay." The mayor's remarks on another occasion equated the insistence upon "rights" with Communist subversion: "Whenever I hear a discussion of civil rights and the rights of free speech and the rights of the Constitution, always remember you will find him [the advocate?] with a Russian flag under his coat; you never miss."

§ Open Monday-Friday, 9-4. Phone: 201-547-5150 (City Clerk).

KEARNY

¶ Philip Kearny Statue, in front of the main post office on Midland Avenue.

Like the name of this town of about 35,000 residents, this life-size statue honors the heroism of Major General Philip Kearny, whose country estate – "Belle Grove" – was formerly located in this area.

A descendant of an Irish immigrant who had settled in nearby Perth Amboy in 1720, Kearny lost his left arm in the Mexican War and was the commander of the 1st New Jersey Brigade during the Civil War. He met his death when he was shot by Confederate forces after unwittingly cross-

Statue of Philip Kearny.

ing enemy lines at Chantilly, Virginia, on September 1, 1862. The fallen Kearny was eulogized in superlative terms. The Union general John Pope described his fellow officer with unusual eloquence: "Tall and lithe in figure, with a most expressive and mobile countenance, and a manner which inspired confidence and zeal in all under his command, no one could fail to admire his chivalric bearing and his supreme courage. He seemed to think that it was his mission to make up the shortcomings of others, and in proportion as these shortcomings were made plain, his exertions and exposure were multiplied." General Winfield Scott, meanwhile, praised Kearny as "the bravest man I ever knew, and a perfect soldier." (See Arlington National Cemetery, Arlington, Virginia, in *Irish America*, Volume 2.)

LONG BRANCH

¶ **Long Branch Historical Museum,** 3 miles north at 1260 Ocean Avenue.

This was formerly the Church of the Presidents, so called because it was attended by seven U.S. presidents when they summered in this famous resort community: *Ulysses S. Grant, Rutherford B. Hayes, James Garfield, *Chester A. Arthur, *Benjamin Harrison, *William McKinley, and *Woodrow Wilson.

§ Open by appointment. Phone: 732-229-0600.

MARGATE

¶ **Lucy, the Margate Elephant,** 9200 Atlantic Avenue.

This sixty-five-foot-high wooden elephant was built in 1881 by James Lafferty, a native of Philadelphia who was born in 1856 to prosperous Irish immigrant parents. Lafferty, a real estate developer, erected the structure to attract potential buyers to his building lots. A staircase in the animal's legs leads to an observation level. The pachyderm has served as a real estate office, a residence, and a tavern.

§ Open mid June-Labor Day, daily 10-8; April-mid June and day after Labor Day-October 31, Saturday and Sunday 10-4:30. Fee. Phone: 609-823-6473.

McGUIRE AIR FORCE BASE

This Air Force facility was named for *Major Thomas McGuire, the winner of the Medal of Honor for his heroic actions in World War II. Born in New Jersey in 1920, McGuire joined the Army Air Corps in 1941 and while serving in the Pacific theater downed thirty-eight Japanese aircraft, a tally that was the second highest of any American fighter pilot during the war. McGuire was killed when his plane crushed in the Philippines in 1945 while he covered a fellow pilot under attack.

MORRISTOWN

J Kemble Estate, Tempe Wick Road, near State 202. Private.

In 1781 this mid-eighteenth-century mansion was occupied by *General Anthony Wayne, whose Pennsylvania Line was encamped in nearby Jockey Hollow with other units of the Continental Army.

J Morristown National Historic Park.

General George Washington and the Continental Army encamped in this area during the winters of 1777-78 and 1779-80. Today the park includes Washington's headquarters, a library and historical museum, Fort Nonsense, and Jockey Hollow.

Aware of the sizable numbers of Irish soldiers in his ranks, Washington in 1780 ordered that St. Patrick's Day be celebrated among his men at the Morristown encampment. He ordered "that all Fatigue and Working Parties cease for tomorrow, the 17th, a day held in particular Regard" by the Irish. The camp parole on March 16 was "Saint," and the countersign was "Patrick" or "Sheila." According to a newspaper account, "the Day was ushered in with music and hoisting of colors exhibiting the thirteen stripes, the favorite harp and an inscription, 'The Independence of Ireland.'"

Almost a year later, however, on January 1, 1781, Jockey Hollow was the scene of a mutiny by the eleven regiments of the Pennsylvania Line. Long feared by the line's commander, *General Anthony Wayne, the mutiny was sparked by long-standing grievances concerning supplies, pay, and terms of enlistment. After seizing the guns and ammunition in the camp and after refusing to heed the words of Wayne and a hundred other officers, approximately half of the line's 2,500 men headed off to Philadelphia to present their grievances to the Continental Congress in Philadelphia.

The overall composition of the Pennsylvania Line may have been reflected in the Eleventh Regiment's high percentage of Irish-born recruits: 28 percent of its sergeants and 45 percent of its rank and file. That a considerable number of Irish soldiers were involved in the mutiny can be surmised from the fact that Wayne selected two officers of Irish descent to accompany him to Princeton, New Jersey, where he hoped to negotiate with the leaders of the rebellion. One of the officers was Richard Butler, a native of Ireland, whose brother William was commandant of the Fourth Regiment and whose three younger brothers were officers in the line. The other brigade commander to go with Wayne was Walter Stewart, a Pennsylvania native of Irish descent who was so handsome that the ladies of

Philadelphia referred to him as "the Irish Beauty." Irish-born Colonel Stephen Moylan was later permitted by the mutineers to join the negotiations.

It was probably during the mutiny of the Pennsylvania Line that General Wayne was accorded his nickname, "Mad Anthony." After Wayne ordered the arrest of his trusted spy – the Irishman "Jemmy the Rover" – for disorderly conduct, the bold subordinate asked whether Wayne was "Mad" or "in Fun." When told that he would receive twenty-nine lashes for any future misconduct, Jemmy replied, "Then Anthony is mad! Farewell to you! Clear the coast for the Commodore 'Mad Anthony's' friend."

§ Open daily 9-5. Closed January 1, Thanksgiving, and December 25. Fee. Phone: 973-539-2085.

ℐ Schuyler-Hamilton House, 5 Olyphant Place.

During Washington's encampment in Morristown in 1779-80, this private residence was used as the headquarters of Dr. John Cochran, the chief physician and surgeon general of the Continental Army.

Born in Pennsylvania to immigrants from northern Ireland, Cochran had studied "physic and surgery" at Lancaster, Pennsylvania, and had served with the British medical corps during the French and Indian War. At the outbreak of the Revolution, he volunteered for the American hospital services and helped draft a plan to create military hospitals for the American troops. General Washington was so impressed with Cochran's care for smallpox victims and for his wounded men that he recommended him for the post of physician and surgeon-general in the middle department of the Continental Army. Later as the army's physician-in-chief, Cochran regularly complained of the bureaucratic delays that hampered his work. "It grieves my soul," he wrote in a private letter, "to see the poor, worthy, brave fellows pine away for want of a few comforts, which they have dearly earned. I shall wait on the Commander-in-Chief, and represent our situation, but I am persuaded it can have little effect, for what can he do? He may refer the matter to Congress; they to the Medical Committee, who will pow-wow over it awhile and nothing be heard of it."

§ Phone: 973-267-4039.

NEWARK

Three Catholic churches in Newark were designed by *Patrick Keely: St. Patrick's Pro-Cathedral (1846-50,) Washington Street and Central Avenue; St. Mary's Abbey Church (1856), High and William streets; and St. James Church (1863-66), Lafayette and Jefferson streets.

ℐ Essex County Courthouse, Springfield Avenue and Market Street.

The façade of this 1906 French Renaissance structure is adorned with eleven statues by sculptor *Andrew O'Connor. In addition to representations of Truth and Power on either side of the entrance, statues of Adam, Eve, Cain, Thais, Wisdom, Learning, Justice, Maternity, and Light adorn the cornice. (See U.S. Capitol Building, District of Columbia.)

¶ Franklin Murphy Statue, Weequahic Park, Elizabeth Avenue and Meeker Street.

Erected in honor of the thirty-eighth governor of New Jersey, this statue captures the likeness of Franklin Murphy, whose great-grandfather had emigrated from Ireland in 1756.

Born in Jersey City in 1846, Franklin Murphy was a student at Newark Academy when the Civil War prompted him to enlist in the 13th New Jersey Volunteers. During the conflict, he participated in nineteen engagements, including Antietam, Chancellorsville, Gettysburg, and Lookout Mountain.

At the end of the war, Lieutenant Murphy returned to Newark, where he subsequently followed careers in business and politics. After organizing the firm of Murphy & Company, varnish manufacturers, he introduced a pension plan and a profit-sharing system for his employees, steps that were far ahead of their time. In 1883 he was elected as a Republican to the Newark Common Council, from which position he was elected to the State Assembly two years later. Prior to his election as governor in 1901, he served as the commissioner who planned Essex County's park system and chairman of the Republican state committee. During his gubernatorial administration he applied his business experience to the management of the state's fiscal affairs and advocated enlightened labor legislation. In this regard he introduced an auditing system to monitor state expenditures, and the legislature passed the state's first primary election law, child-labor law, and workshop-ventilation law.

¶ Military Park, bounded by Broad Street, Park Place, Rector Street, and Raymond Boulevard.

In the park are a bust of *John F. Kennedy and a statue of *Major General Philip Kearny (the commander of the New Jersey volunteers during the Civil War). The pedestal of the Kennedy memorial is inscribed with an excerpt from the president's inaugural address: "Let every nation know, whether it wishes us well or ill, that we shall pay any price, bear any burden, meet any hardship, support any friend, oppose any foe, in order to ensure the survival and success of liberty. This much we pledge – and more."

¶ Monsignor Doane Statue, Doane Park, north of Military Park.

This bronze statue by *William Clark Noble honors Monsignor George

Hobart Doane, a Civil War chaplain and the rector of St. Patrick's Cathedral in Newark.

PATERSON

¶ **Andrew McBride Statue,** City Hall, 155 Market Street.

One of the three statues in front of City Hall is that of Andrew McBride, a noted physician and the mayor of Paterson during the 1913 textile workers strike in the city. The statue was erected in 1947.

A native of Paterson, McBride was the son of an ironworker from Belfast, Ireland. After receiving a medical degree from the College of Physicians and Surgeons at Columbia University, the younger McBride practiced medicine in Paterson for fifty-five years. During much of that time he was on the staff of St. Joseph's Hospital, for two years as chief of staff. With the American entry into World War I, he served in the medical corps and was in command of the hospital at Camp Dix, New Jersey, during the 1918 influenza epidemic. During that period he worked twenty hours a day and eventually developed blisters on his feet from making the rounds of the wards, which at one time housed 5,000 patients.

In 1907 McBride had resigned as county physician to run for mayor of Paterson, a position he held for three successive terms. During that tenure he superintended the expansion of the municipal park system, the erection of several fire stations and public schools, and a major building program of sewers and streets. After 1923 the former mayor was either appointed or elected to numerous state commissions. In 1931 he was elected Paterson's outstanding citizen for his exemplary civic involvement.

McBride's role in the 1913 textile workers strike, however, tarnished his reputation with the laboring classes in Paterson. When the strikers first walked off the job, they hoped that the mayor would remain neutral in the industrial dispute, as previous mayors and police chiefs had done. That possibility seemed remote, however, given the fact that McBride was a trustee of the Paterson Board of Trade, an organization dedicated to promoting the business and manufacturing interests of the city. In addition, under the city's relatively new commission form of government the police were responsible to a commission on which the city's silk manufacturers were well represented. As a result, the chief of police allowed his regular force to be augmented with sixty corporate detectives, or "specials," hired by the textile owners. In the end the mayor and the police commission allowed this combined police force to attack the strikers. A team of federal investigators later concluded that legal authority in Paterson during the strike had, in effect, been turned over to the mill owners and that the "specials" had been "clothed with the authority of the police and sheriff" and had been used "as a private army of the mill owners."

On his last birthday, in January 1945, McBride expressed his philosophy of life. "If God gives one good health and a reasonable mind and a desire to work," the venerable doctor exclaimed, "He has richly endowed that individual. Now if that person in turn fails to appreciate these gifts by sharing them with his less fortunate brothers, then he indeed misses much in life that is worth living for[, for] we are our brothers' keepers. We should bend our every effort toward helping people who really deserve and need to be helped."

Statues of Andrew McBride (left) and Dean William McNulty.

❡ **Dean McNulty Statue,** St. John the Baptist Catholic Church, 381 Grand Street.

This bronze statue in front of the church marks the grave of Dean William McNulty, Paterson's most famous churchman and philanthropist. The statue shows McNulty seated on a bench, with his head tilted, listening to a young orphan boy.

McNulty, who was born in Ballyshannon, County Down, Ireland, in 1829, was graduated from Fordham University, and was ordained a priest in 1857. During his fifty-eight-year pastorate in Paterson, he founded hospitals, orphanages, schools, and homes for the aged. After his death at the age of ninety-three, his funeral was probably the biggest public demonstration of its kind in New Jersey until that time.

❡ **Paterson Museum,** Rogers Mill, 2 Market Street.

Among the museum's exhibits are two submarines built by John Philip Holland – the shell of his original fourteen-foot submarine built in 1878 and his second thirty-foot submarine constructed three years later.

Holland was born in Liscanor, County Clare, Ireland, in 1841, where he learned English at St. Macreehy's National School. After joining the Christian Brothers, he taught at several of that religious congregation's schools in the country. While teaching in Dundalk, he pursued the study of submarine navigation, reading the works of others in the field and constructing a successful model of an underwater apparatus. Plagued by ill health, however, he sought permission to leave the Christian Brothers and subsequently immigrated to Boston in 1873.

Despite his new surroundings, Holland never abandoned his hope of perfecting a submarine boat. In 1875 he submitted a refined design to the U.S. Navy, only to have it dismissed as a "lunatic scheme of a civilian landsman." His hopes were buoyed, however, when the Irish Republican Brotherhood (also known as Fenians) offered to finance an experimental craft. In 1878 Holland tested his one-man boat in the Passaic River. (The steam-powered, fourteen-foot-long craft was recovered from the river bottom in 1927 and is now in the Paterson museum.)

Impressed by the possibility that submarine power could pose a serious threat to British naval supremacy, the Fenians commissioned Holland to build a full-size submarine. The resulting *Fenian Ram* was constructed at the Delamater Iron Company in New York City and was thirty-one feet in length, displaced nineteen tons, was powered by a one-cylinder inter-

John Holland's second submarine, familiarly known as the "Fenian Ram."

nal-combustion engine, and was equipped with an underwater cannon fired by compressed air. After its launching in 1881, the $23,000 vessel frequently sailed under New York Harbor, on one occasion remaining on the bottom for an hour. The vessel was able to dive by inclining its axis and being propelled forward by its motor rather than being pushed up and down by vertical action. The Fenians, however, were never able to make practical use of Holland's invention. For many years the *Fenian Ram* was kept in storage, but in 1916 it was placed on exhibit to raise funds for victims of the Easter Rising in Dublin that year.

Although several of Holland's plans were finally accepted by the U.S. Navy Department, they were never carried to completion because of unavailable appropriations. In 1895 the J. P. Holland Torpedo Boat Company obtained a $150,000 government contract to construct a submarine according to Navy specifications, which, however, virtually ignored Holland's ideas. The Irishman must have felt vindicated, though, when the *Plunger,* as the craft was called, was abandoned as a failure.

Finally, using private capital, Holland proceeded to build a submarine of his own. Bearing its inventor's name, the vessel was constructed in Elizabeth, New Jersey, and was launched in 1898. Measuring fifty-three feet in length and having a displacement of seventy-five tons, the *Holland* was armed with a dynamite gun and several torpedoes. Surface propulsion was provided by an internal combustion engine, while electric storage batteries and a motor provided underwater propulsion, making the *Holland* the first submarine able to cruise for any significant distance while submerged. Like the earlier *Fenian Ram*, it could dive by inclining its axis. After receiving the support of *Theodore Roosevelt, the secretary of the navy, and undergoing a series of tests, the *Holland* was finally purchased by the U.S. government, which soon ordered six more like it. Holland's Torpedo Boat Company subsequently constructed submarines for Great Britain, Russia, and Japan.

In 1910 the Japanese government honored Holland with the Mikado's Order of the Rising Sun. He died four years later, just before the submarine warfare of World War I shattered forever his hope that the submarine would be used only for peaceful purposes.

§ Open Tuesday-Friday 10-4, Saturday and Sunday 12:30-4:30. Closed holidays. Fee. Phone: 973-881-3874.

¶ **William Hughes Statue,** in front of Passaic County Courthouse, Hamilton and DeGrasse streets.

This statue was erected by citizens of the state to honor William Hughes, who represented New Jersey in the U.S. Senate from 1913 to 1918.

Born in Drogheda, Ireland, in 1872, Hughes had come to the United States as a youngster. After working in the Paterson silk mills, he followed a career in law and made a specialty of representing various unions

Statue of William Hughes.

throughout the city. In 1902 he won a seat in the U.S. House of Representatives, ironically beating the influential owner of the mills in which he had worked as a boy. In Congress he supported an eight-hour work law, antitrust legislation, and direct election of U.S. senators. During his subsequent term in the Senate, he called for railroad regulation, female suffrage, creation of a labor department, and improvement of the Passaic River. It was said of him that "Billy Hughes always spoke for 20,000,000 laboring people when he addressed the senate."

PENNSAUKEN

¶ **Peter McGuire Burial Site,** Arlington Cemetery, Cove Road (State 616), just past Bethel Park Cemetery.

A six-foot polished granite tombstone marks the grave of the Irish-American Peter McGuire, generally regarded as the "Father of Labor Day."

A wood joiner by trade, McGuire was a member of the International Workingmen's Association and the Social Democratic (later Socialist Labor) Party and helped organize the United Brotherhood of Carpenters and Joiners. He was also instrumental in laying the groundwork for the formation of the Federation of Organized Trades and Labor Unions in 1881. Eventually becoming involved in the eight-hour day movement, he went on to become one of the founders of the American Federation of Labor. He served the A.F.L. as first secretary and vice president. He is usually credited with the idea of establishing a holiday in honor of the working class.

The first Labor Day parade was held in New York City on September 5, 1882. Five years later Oregon became the first state to designate a Labor Day holiday, while the U.S. government followed suit for its employees in 1894.

PERTH AMBOY

¶ **Kearny Cottage Museum,** Hayes Park, 63 Catalpa Street.

Built in 1781, this was the birthplace and lifelong home of Lawrence Kearny, the motivating force behind efforts to open up China to American trade. The four-room museum on the first floor of the clapboard house displays such personal items as Kearny's sabre and sea chest.

Like his more famous cousin, the Civil War hero Philip Kearny, Lawrence Kearny was descended from an Irish emigrant who had settled in Perth Amboy soon after 1704. A century later, in 1807, Lawrence Kearny joined the U.S. Navy and subsequently served in a variety of capacities aboard ships engaged in protecting American shipping from piratical raids. As commander of two expeditions, for example, he captured bandit ships off Cuba and in the Mediterranean. In 1840, however, he was appointed commander of the East India Squadron and charged with protecting U.S. interests in China. (See U.S. Frigate *Constellation*, Baltimore, Maryland.)

Kearny Cottage, the birthplace of Commodore Lawrence Kearny.

From the start he made a favorable impression upon the leaders of the Middle Kingdom, particularly in his fairness and insistence that the United States "does not sanction 'the smuggling of opium' on this coast under the American flag, in violation of the laws of China." His most important role in cultivating Sino-American relations was his call that China open five of its ports to American trade as it had recently done for the British. Within a year of his request, the Chinese complied, eventually formalizing the new relation by signing the 1844 Treaty of Wanghia. During his later career Kearny served as commandant of the New York Navy Yard and mayor of Perth Amboy.

§ Open Tuesday and Thursday 2-4; last Sunday of the month 2-4. Phone: 732-826-1826.

❡ **St. Peter's Episcopal Church,** Rector and Gordon streets.

Throughout the church are wall plaques in memory of various members of the Kearny family, whose first American ancestor emigrated from Ireland in 1704. Among those honored are Philip Kearny, the famous Civil War general, and his cousin, Lawrence Kearny, the naval officer and vestryman of St. Peter's Church.

PLEASANTVILLE

❡ **Alfred E. Smith Monument,** St. Peter's Elementary School, Chestnut Street.

On the grounds is a statue of St. Thomas More, the sixteenth-century English statesman and martyr, erected in 1937 by members of the legal profession in honor of *Alfred Smith. (See Alfred E. Smith Boyhood Home, New York City.) The monument recognizes Smith's role as legislator, Catholic lay leader, governor of New York, and presidential candidate. Smith's nickname – "the Happy Warrior" – is recalled in verses from Wordsworth inscribed on the statue's base:

> Who, if he rise to stations of command,
> Rises by open means;
> And there will stand on honorable terms;
> Or else retire, and in himself possess his own desire,
> Find comfort in himself and in his cause.
> And, while the mortal mist is gathering,
> Draws his breath in confidence of Heaven's applause.
> This is the Happy Warrior;
> This is he whom every man in arms should wish to be.

PRINCETON

❡ **Grover Cleveland Burial Site,** Princeton Cemetery, 29 Greenview

Avenue.

A square monument topped by an urn-shaped finial marks the grave of former president *Grover Cleveland, who spent his last years as a lecturer and a trustee at Princeton University. His last words before his death in 1908 were: "I have tried so hard to do right." (See Caldwell, New Jersey.)

℘ **Westland,** 15 Hodge Road and Cleveland Lane. Private.

This two-and-a-half story stone residence was the home of *Grover Cleveland from 1897 until his death in 1908.

℘ **Woodrow Wilson Residences.**

During his tenure at Princeton University (1890-1910) as either professor or president, *Woodrow Wilson resided in the homes at 72 and 82 Library Place. While governor of New Jersey (1910-12) he lived at 25 Cleveland Lane. Each house is closed to the public.

℘ **Woodrow Wilson School of Public and International Affairs,** Princeton University.

Made possible by a $35 million donation in 1961, the school was named for Woodrow Wilson, a Princeton alumnus who became president of the university, governor of New Jersey, and president of the United States. Wilson's paternal grandfather was a native of Strabane, County Tyrone, Ireland. (See Staunton, Virginia, in *Irish America*, Volume 2.)

While president, Wilson saw his foreign policy toward Great Britain complicated by the failure of the Easter Rising in Dublin in 1916 and by the policy of national self-determination which he proclaimed in his Fourteen Points. Although Irish-American politicians condemned Britain for crushing the rebellion and executing its leaders, Wilson refrained from doing anything that would jeopardize the Anglo-American war effort. (Wilson's Presbyterian Scotch-Irish roots often placed him at odds with the Catholic Celtic Irish.) He did, however, suggest to the British that American public opinion would never be satisfied short of some degree of Irish independence.

While on the surface Wilson's call for self-determination seemed to encompass Irish independence, the president believed that the Irish Question was an internal matter to be resolved by the British. Once, when a delegation of Irish Americans requested to see the president in order to press the case of Irish home rule, Wilson ordered his Secret Service man to eject the delegation's leader from the building. Wilson was further embarrassed when more than 5,000 supporters of Irish freedom sent a delegation to France to state their case at the Paris Peace Conference. Although Wilson received the delegation, he admitted that his "first impulse was to tell the Irish to go to hell." Despite a resolution by the U.S. Senate requesting that the Irish-American delegates get a hearing at the Versailles conference, Wilson refused to accommodate them further, thereby causing American Hibernophiles to join forces with Wilson's enemies.

SOUTH ORANGE

¶ **Seton Hall University,** 405 South Orange Avenue.

• The McManus Collection in the McLaughlin Library contains 4,000 volumes on Irish history, politics, and literature.

• The carriage house on the campus was built in 1887 for Eugene Kelly, an Irish immigrant who became a successful merchant and investor and a patron of Seton Hall University.

A native of County Tyrone, Kelly began a career in the dry-goods business soon after his arrival in America in the 1830s. First employed with Donnelly & Company, New York City's largest dry-goods business, he quickly went off on his own, making a small fortune selling merchandise in Kentucky and St. Louis before heading for San Francisco. Although he arrived in the booming California city too late to reap the rewards of trade with the "Forty-Niners," Kelly and two other Irishmen founded what later became the leading dry-goods company on the West Coast. He and other Irish partners went on to establish a banking house, which opened a branch in New York City when Kelly returned there in 1856. Thirty-five years later the San Francisco branch became a joint-stock company known as the Donohue-Kelly Banking Company.

While living in New York, the multimillionaire devoted his energies to philanthropy and civic affairs. He served on the New York Board of Education for more than a decade, was a trustee and patron of the Metropolitan Museum of Art, and was a member of the committee that organized the dedication of the Statue of Liberty. Besides being a major benefactor of St. Patrick's Cathedral and Seton Hall College, he was one of the founders of Catholic University in America in Washington, D.C. To that last institution he donated $100,000 to endow chairs in ecclesiastical history and Holy Scripture named, respectively, for himself and his wife.

SPRINGFIELD

¶ **First Presbyterian Church,** 37 Church Mall.

A monument in front of the church commemorates the battle of Springfield on June 23, 1776, and the part played in it by the *Reverend James Caldwell, the chaplain of Dayton's New Jersey Brigade. During the battle, when the American soldiers ran out of wadding for their rifles, Caldwell broke open the church doors and began to distribute to the men copies of the Watts hymnbooks. "Now put Watts into them, boys!" he cried. The initiative of the "Soldier Parson" is immortalized in the poem "Caldwell of Springfield" by Bret Harte and in a painting by John Ward Dunsmore at Fraunces Tavern in New York City. (See Elizabeth and Union, N.J.)

Four stanzas from Harte's poem are reprinted below:

.... Stay one moment; you've heard
Of Caldwell, the parson, who once preached the word
    Down at Springfield? What, No? Come that's bad, why he had
    All the Jerseys aflame, and they gave him the name
Of the "rebel high priest." He stuck in their gorge
For he loved the Lord God and he hated King George.

He had come, you might say! When the Hessians that day
Marched with Knyphausen they stopped on their way
    At the "farms," where his wife with a child in her arms
Sat alone in the house. How it happened none knew
But God – and that one of the hireling crew
    Who fired the shot! Enough! – there she lay,
    And Caldwell the chaplain, her husband, away.

Did he bear it – what way? Think of his as you stand
By the old church today – think of him and that band
    Of militant plow boys! See the smoke and the heat
    Of that reckless advance – of that struggling retreat!
Keep the ghost of that wife, foully slain, in your view, –
And what could you, what should you, what would *you* do?

Why, just what *he* did! They were left in the church
For the want of more wadding. He ran to the church,
    Broke the door, stripped the pews, and dashed out in the road
    With his arms full of hymn books and threw down his load
At their feet! Then above all the shouting and shots,
Rang his voice: "Put Watts into 'em – Boys, give 'em Watts!"

STANHOPE

¶ Waterloo Village, off I-80 exit 25.

Although the village is now an outdoor living-history museum, it was originally the center of an ironmaking industry at Andover Iron Works. The forge was constructed by 1760 and during the Revolution was seized from its loyalist owners and turned into a major supplier of armaments for Washington's Continental Army. The property includes fourteen historic buildings and a portion of the Morris Canal, constructed by Irish laborers and opened in 1831. The canal, which allowed cargo boats to cross the state in five days, led to the development of the village, which soon boasted a grist mill, a saw mill, a stagecoach inn and tavern, and a general store. (These structures on still on the property.)

A plaque near Smith's General Store commemorates the role of the Irish in constructing the Morris Canal: "Two hundred years ago, here at Andover Forge, and throughout the state of New Jersey, the Irish settlers who formed one third of Washington's army fulfilled their vision of freedom through their participation in the Revolutionary War. Here, in peace, they contributed their skills in engineering and construction toward he creation of the Morris Canal for the economic expansion of their adopted country, using the well-developed canal experience of their homeland. Presented in the bicentennial of Waterloo to the Honorable Brendan Byrne, Governor of New Jersey, by Princess Grace of Monaco, international chairman of the Irish American Cultural Institute. Dr. Eoin McKiernan, President. Neil S. Sullivan Sr., Director. January 18, 1975."

§ Open mid April-September, Wednesday-Sunday 10-6; October-mid November Wednesday-Sunday 10-5. Closed Easter. Fee. Phone: 973-347-0900.

TRENTON

¶ **Trenton Battle Monument,** Five Points (the intersection of North Broad Street, North Warren Street, Martin Luther King Jr. Boulevard, Pennington Avenue, and Brunswick Avenue).

The thirteen-foot bronze statue of George Washington and the bust of General William Stryker on this 137-foot-high monument were sculpted by William O'Donovan.

O'Donovan was born in 1844 in what is now West Virginia and enlisted in the Confederate army at the age of eighteen. In the 1870s, after establishing a studio in New York City, he achieved recognition for his bas-reliefs and portrait busts of well known Americans, among them the bust of *Archbishop John Hughes at St. John's College, Fordham, New York. O'Donovan's many military works include equestrian reliefs of Lincoln and Grant for the Soldiers' and Sailors' Arch (Brooklyn, N.Y.), a monument to the captors of Major André (Tarrytown, N.Y.), a statue of General Daniel Morgan (Schuylerville, N.Y.), and additional statues of Washington in Newburgh, New York, and Caracas, Venezuela.

¶ **Washington Crossing State Park,** 8 miles northwest on State 29 and then northeast on County 546.

Although this park is the site of the landing by George Washington and his troops after they crossed the Delaware River from Pennsylvania on Christmas Eve 1776, the park is also the site of a less famous crossing in the opposite direction. Following Washington's defeat at the battle of Long Island, the American general was pursued by Lord Cornwallis west across New Jersey. When Washington reached Trenton on December 8, 1776, he used the boats and rafts of Patrick Colvin, the owner and operator of the only ferry between Trenton and the Pennsylvania side of the Delaware. Three and a half weeks later, the Irish Catholic Colvin helped ferry Washington and his men back across the Delaware River when they launched their surprise attack against the British at Trenton on Christmas Eve.

§ Park open Memorial Day weekend-Labor Day, daily 8-8; rest of the year, daily 8-4:30. Phone: 609-737-0623.

¶ The Ferry House, at the south end of the Continental Line in the park, belonged most likely to Patrick Colvin at the time of the crossing.

On two other occasions in his life, Colvin rendered patriotic services to George Washington. In 1781, when the general crossed New Jersey on his way to join Lafayette in Virginia, his army was again ferried across the Delaware by Colvin. Eights year later, when the newly elected president passed through Trenton on his way to New York City for his inauguration, Colvin took charge of the presidential party.

§ Ferry House open Wednesday-Saturday 10-noon and 1-4, Sunday 1-4. Phone: 609-737-2515.

UNION

¶ **Caldwell Parsonage Museum,** 909 Caldwell Avenue.

During the colonial period this was the parsonage of Connecticut Farms Presbyterian Church, which still stands a few blocks away. Among those living here in June 1780 was the family of the *Reverend James Caldwell, known as the "Soldier Parson" because of his active support of the Patriot cause during the Revolution. (See Springfield and Union, New Jersey.)

Although Caldwell's family had fled here for safety from British troops, the dangers of war followed. In the battle of Connecticut Farms that June, Caldwell's wife, Hannah, was killed by a random bullet, and the parsonage was burned by the enemy. From then on, Caldwell always preached with pistols close at hand. After he himself was killed the following year, his nine children were placed with foster parents.

§ Open the third Sunday of the month.

WESTFIELD

¶ **Gallows Hill,** Broad Street, on the northeast side of town.

Here in 1781 was hanged James Morgan, the Irishman found guilty of shooting the "Fighting Parson," the *Reverend James Caldwell.

The day on which Morgan was scheduled to be hanged for his crime was unusually cold, and when the execution was delayed he snapped at his guards, "Do your duty and don't keep me here shivering in the cold."

NEW YORK

ALBANY

¶ **Cathedral of the Immaculate Conception,** Eagle Street and Madison Avenue.

This Gothic Revival cathedral was completed in 1852 from a design by *Patrick Keely for *Bishop John McCloskey, who was born in Brooklyn in 1810, the son of immigrants from County Derry, Ireland.

§ Open Monday-Friday 6-5, Saturday and Sunday 8-6. Phone: 518-463-4447.

¶ **Dongan's Charter,** Albany County Hall of Records, 20 South Pearl Street.

Each year on the Saturday closest to July 22, the city of Albany celebrates its chartering in 1686 by Thomas Dongan, the first colonial governor of New York. The 300-year-old charter is preserved in the Albany County Hall of Records and can be viewed by special arrangement.

Although born in 1634 in Castletown, County Kildare, Ireland, Dongan grew up in France, where his father had taken his family following the fall of Charles I and the victory of the parliamentary forces in the English Civil War. After joining the Irish Regiment in France, the young Dongan served in several campaigns with the French army and eventually attained the rank of colonel.

With the restoration of the Stuarts in 1660, Dongan was recalled to England and was subsequently appointed governor of New York. In that capacity he did a creditable job protecting the interests of the Catholic proprietor (the Duke of York) and attempting to guarantee the rights of the colony's inhabitants. He successfully defended the boundaries of the colony against French incursions and cemented an alliance with the Iroquois.

Following instructions from the duke, Dongan convened in 1683 the first representative assembly ever held in New York. At Dongan's urging, this assembly later adopted "The Charter of Liberties and Privileges granted by His Royal Highness to the Inhabitants of New York and its Dependencies." When the Duke of York succeeded to the throne as King James II, however, the new monarch refused to accept Dongan's charter in every particular, although he did recognize the document's grant of religious freedom to all Christians. Three years later the governor granted a charter to Albany, the event which is recognized in the city's annual celebration.

Dongan also opened the first free common school in the colony during the British regime. Established in New York City in 1685, the school was administered by Father Henry Harrison, an Irish Jesuit. With the end of James's short reign in 1688, Dongan returned to England, where he tried to regain his ancestral home, which had been confiscated during the civil war. Following the death of his brother (the Earl of Limerick) in 1696, Dongan succeeded to the title.

§ Open Monday-Friday 9-5. Phone: 518-447-4500.

¶ **Philip Sheridan Statue,** on the grounds of the state capitol, bounded by Washington Avenue and Swan, State, and Eagle streets.

This imposing equestrian statue honors *Philip Sheridan, a cavalry commander under *General Ulysses S. Grant during the Civil War.

Although Sheridan's memoirs claim that he was a native of Albany, he actually may have been born aboard the ship which carried his parents from Ireland to America. According to one theory, he may have invented an American birth in order to be eligible for the presidency of the United States.

Statue of the Civil War commander Philip Sheridan.

AMSTERDAM

¶ **Guy Park Historic Site,** 366 Main Street (State 5) at Henrietta Street.

Now a visitor center and the office of the local chamber of commerce, this fieldstone house was built in 1766 by *Sir William Johnson for his daughter Mary and her husband, Colonel Guy Johnson, Sir William's nephew.

A native of Ireland, the colonel had come to America early in life and by 1756 was living in the Mohawk Valley. He served the British during the French and Indian War, for a time as his uncle's secretary, but more notably as commander of a company of rangers under General Amherst. This military experience served him well when, after the war, he was a colonel and an adjutant general in the New York militia. In 1762 he was appointed deputy to his uncle, who by then was British superintendent of Indian affairs in this region. When Sir William died a dozen years later, the younger man succeeded to that post.

With the coming of the Revolution, Johnson played a vital role in maintaining the loyalty of the Six Nations to the British. In the spring and summer of 1775, for instance, he secured an informal alliance with the Native Americans in the Lake Ontario region as well as in the vicinity of Montreal. The following summer, however, his efforts to achieve better military cooperation between the British and their Indian allies on the New York frontier were a failure. In August 1779 his combined British and Indian force was defeated by *General John Sullivan near Newtown (now Elmira), New York [*q.v.*]. He spent the last two years of the war at his headquarters at Niagara, from which he continued to incite the natives to depredations against frontier settlements. Like many other Loyalists, Johnson suffered the confiscation of his estates in New York and after the war went to England to press his case for compensation. A contemporary described him as "a short, pursy man, of stern countenance and haughty demeanor," adding that "His voice was harsh, and his tongue bore evidence of his Irish extraction."

§ Open Monday-Friday 8:30-4:30. Phone: 518-842-8200 (Chamber of Commerce).

AUBURN

¶ Myles Keogh Burial Site, Fort Hill Cemetery, 19 Fort Street.

Captain Myles Keogh was one of the thirty-two Irish natives who perished when the 7th Cavalry under George Armstrong Custer was annihilated by several thousand Sioux and Cheyenne at the battle of the Little Bighorn in June 1876. (See Hardin, Montana, in *Irish America*, Volume 2.) Although Keogh was originally buried on the battlefield, a month after the disastrous engagement his corpse was exhumed for interment here in Fort Hill Cemetery. The poetic inscription on his funeral monument reads:

> Sleep soldier! Still in honored rest
> Your truth and valor wearing
> The Bravest are the tenderest
> The loving are the daring.

BUFFALO

In May 1866 Buffalo was one of three staging areas for a planned invasion of Canada by the Fenians, an American offshoot of the Irish Revolutionary Brotherhood pledged to the use of force to free Ireland from British rule. To serve as their secretary of war, the Fenians had chosen General Thomas Sweeny, an Irish-born hero of the Mexican War and a Civil War infantry commander. Sweeny proceeded to plan a three-pronged invasion of Canada which the Fenians hoped would result in the capture of Canada as a bargaining chip for the independence of Ireland. (See Ridgeway, Ontario, Canada.)

¶ **Albright-Knox Art Gallery,** Elmwood Avenue, near State 198.
    This Greek Revival building is flanked by two side porches, each with four caryatids designed by *Augustus Saint-Gaudens and based on those of the Erechtheum in Athens, Greece.
    § Open Tuesday-Saturday 11-5, Sunday noon-5. Closed January 1, Thanksgiving, and December 25. Phone: 716-882-8700.

¶ **Naval and Military Park,** 1 Naval Park Cove, at the foot of Pearl and Main streets.
    Among the ships on display here is the cruiser *The Sullivans*, named in honor of the five Sullivan brothers who were killed during the battle of Guadalcanal in November 1943.
    The brothers – Albert, Madison (Matt), Joseph (Red), Francis, and George Sullivan – ranged in age from twenty to twenty-nine and were natives of Waterloo, Iowa. The five had enlisted in the U.S. Navy together in January 1942 on condition that they not be separated during the war. The brothers perished after their ship, the U.S.S. *Juneau*, was sunk by Japanese fire in the Solomon Islands. George, the eldest brother, died while trying to escape on a raft, while the other four went down with the ship. A spokesman for the Navy said that the loss of the Sullivan brothers was the heaviest blow suffered by any American military family.
    The brothers were honored by a mass at St. Patrick's Cathedral in New York City and by the announcement that a newly built destroyer would be named in their honor. In April 1943 the Sullivans' mother christened the ship in San Francisco. That same month the Sullivans' sister, Genevieve, took her brothers' place in the war effort by joining the WAVES, while their forty-three-year-old uncle, Patrick Henry Sullivan, joined the crew of the new destroyer. (See Waterloo, Iowa, in *Irish America*, Volume 2.)
    § Open April-October 31, daily 10-5; November, Saturday-Sunday 10-4. Fee. Phone: 716-847-1773.

¶ **Oliver H. Perry Statue,** central plaza.

This monument was erected in 1915 in honor of *Oliver Hazard Perry, the commander of the victorious American fleet at the battle of Lake Erie in 1813. (See Put-in-Bay, Ohio.)

❡ Theodore Roosevelt Inaugural National Historic Site, Wilcox Mansion, 641 Delaware Avenue.

Following the assassination of *President William McKinley in 1901, it was in this house that *Vice President Theodore Roosevelt took the oath of office as the twenty-sixth president of the United States. This 1838 Classical Revival house features a slide show and memorabilia related to Roosevelt and McKinley.

At the time of McKinley's assassination, Roosevelt was in Vermont but rushed to Buffalo by train. When it appeared that McKinley was recovering after surgery, the vice president left on an outing to the Adirondacks with his family. Three days later, however, after receiving a message that the president was dying, Roosevelt returned to Buffalo but arrived after McKinley's death. (See Theodore Roosevelt Birthplace, New York City.)

§ Open April-December, Monday-Friday 9-5, Saturday-Sunday noon-5; rest of the year, Monday-Friday 9-5, Sunday noon-5. Closed major holidays. Fee. Phone 716-884-0095.

❡ Western New York Irish Famine Memorial, at the foot of Erie Street.

Dedicated in 1997, the 150th anniversary of the worst year of the Great Famine, this unusual monument is dominated by a fourteen-foot-high monolith surrounded by thirty-two rough-hewn stones, one for each of Ireland's counties. The granite commemorative stones fanning out from the monolith represent the Irish Diaspora.

❡ William McKinley Assassination Site, in the middle of Fordham Drive, between Elmwood Avenue and Lincoln Parkway.

A bronze tablet marks the spot where *President William McKinley was killed as he was shaking hands with visitors to the Temple of Music at the Pan-American Exposition on September 6, 1901. The assassin – Leon Czolgosz – had approached the chief executive with a handkerchief covering the revolver in his hand. McKinley died eight days later at the Milburn House, at 1168 Delaware Avenue. (See Niles, Ohio.)

❡ William McKinley Monument, Niagara Square.

This 120-foot-high obelisk monument was dedicated in 1907 in memory of *President William McKinley. A marble lion stands at each corner of the base.

CAMBRIDGE

℘ **Philip Embury Burial Site,** Woodland Cemetery.

A monument marks the burial place of Philip Embury, the Irish-born founder of American Methodism. Under his leadership Irish immigrants erected the first Methodist church in America on John Street in New York City in 1768.

Two years later Embury moved to upstate New York, where he farmed, preached, served as a magistrate, and formed a Methodist society in the town of Ashgrove. Sixty years after his death in 1772, his remains were removed from his farm to Ashgrove, although in 1866 they were reburied in Woodland Cemetery in Cambridge.

CANAJOHARIE

℘ **Canajoharie Library and Art Gallery,** southwest off New York thruway exit 29 at Church Street and Erie Boulevard.

The museum contains watercolors and oils by such painters as *John Singleton Copley, Winslow Homer, John Singer Sergeant, and Gilbert Stuart.

§ Open Monday-Wednesday and Friday 10-4:45, Thursday 10-8:30, and Saturday 10-1:30. Closed holidays. Phone: 518-673-2314.

CANANDAIGUA

Canandaigua stands on the site of the Seneca Indian village destroyed in 1779 by *General John Sullivan. (See Sullivan Monument, Elmira, New York.)

CANASTOTA

℘ **Canastota Canal Town Museum,** 122 Canal Street.

This 1874 structure displays local memorabilia as well as items associated with the construction of the Erie Canal.

§ Open June-August, Monday-Friday 10-4, Saturday 10-1; April-May and September-October, Tuesday-Friday 11-3. Closed holidays. Phone: 315-697-3451.

℘ **Old Erie Canal State Park,** State 5/46 or I-90 exits 33 and 34.

Visitors can see portions of the old Erie Canal, including the towpath, change bridges, and aqueducts.

Conceived by Irish-born Christopher Colles and advocated by Governor DeWitt Clinton, himself of Irish descent, the canal was built between 1817 and 1825. Because the canal provided work for increasing numbers of Irish immigrants, it was called "a capital road from Cork to Utica." At the time of its completion, it stretched 350 miles from Albany to Buffalo, and almost 50,000 Irish lived along the route, most of them the men who had worked on the huge undertaking.

Three Irish workers were singled out for special recognition because of their herculean feat: finishing fifty feet of canal – including banks and towpaths – to a depth of four feet in five and a half days, for the "very liberal wages" of $1.87 per day.

§ Open dawn-dusk. Phone: 315-687-7821.

CONSTABLEVILLE

ᔕ Constable Hall, 0.5 mile east of State 26.

Completed in 1819, this Georgian mansion was the home of five generations of the Constable family and is modeled after the Anglo-Irish family's ancestral home in Dublin, Ireland. The mansion's sixteen rooms include a fireproof office, a chapel, and two wine cellars.

The stately residence was constructed by William Constable Jr., whose grandfather, a native of Dublin, was a surgeon in the British army and had come to America in the mid eighteenth century. The builder's father, William Sr., attended Trinity College in Dublin and was an aide to Lafayette during the Revolution. He later was a successful import/export merchant in New York City and was a partner in the Macomb Purchase, a 1791 real estate transaction involving the acquisition of four million acres in New York, approximately one-tenth of the state's area.

When William Constable Jr. inherited his father's vast estates, he proceeded to supervise construction of Constable Hall. To raise money for the project, he sold a large portion of his lands as well as a portrait of George Washington which his father had commissioned of Gilbert Stuart.

§ Open late May-mid October, Tuesday-Saturday and Monday holidays 10-4, Sunday 1-4. Fee. Phone: 315-397-2323.

COOPERSTOWN

ᔕ National Baseball Hall of Fame and Museum, Main Street.

Exhibits include the Ballparks Room, the Baseball Today display, the Grandstand Theater, the Great Moments Room, and the World Series Room.

When the museum was opened on June 12, 1939, *U.S. Postmaster General James Farley and seventy postal clerks were on hand to sell half a million commemorative stamps recognizing the centenary of American baseball. Among the Irish-American members of the Baseball Hall of Fame are "Duke of Tralee" Roger Bresnahan, "Mickey" Cochrane, Charles Comiskey, Ed Delahanty, Hugh Duffy, Michael "King" Kelly, "Iron Man" Connie Mack, Joseph McGinnity, and "Orator" Jim O'Rourke.

• Charles Comiskey, the son of a Famine Irish immigrant father, began his career with the Milwaukee team and went on to become the founder of the American League. In 1900 he established the Chicago White Sox, a team which he owned until his death in 1931. The team's home stadium, Comiskey Park, was named for him. His stinginess in refusing to pay for the laundry of his team's uniforms caused his players to protest by wearing their increasingly dirty uniforms for several weeks and calling themselves the "Black Sox."

• Ed Delahanty was one of five brothers in Cleveland to play for the major leagues. Between 1888 and 1903 he played for the Philadelphia Phillies and the Washington Senators and was the only player to win the batting championship in both the National and the American leagues. His career ended when he was suspended for heavy drinking. A week later he was found drowned near Niagara Falls, presumably because of a fall from a train.

• At the age of twenty-four, Connie Mack (né Cornelius McGillicuddy) parlayed his skill as a baseball player into $200 a month in the Connecticut League. He popularized overhand pitching and was one of the first catchers to take up a position directly behind the batter. After stints with the Washington Senators and the Pittsburgh Pirates, in 1901 he became manager and part owner of the Philadelphia Athletics. Over the next thirty years, his team won nine pennants, five World Series titles, and a record 3,776 wins. In 1914 and again during the Depression, falling attendance and rising salary demands from his "$100,000 infield" forced Mack to sell or release his star players, a move that caused his critics to call him a pennypincher. Nevertheless, the white-haired Mack, who always appeared in a business suit and a straw hat, was regarded as the "Grand Old Man" of baseball and was elected to the sport's Hall of Fame in 1937.

• Michael "King" Kelly did duty as catcher, shortstop, and outfielder with the Cincinnati Reds, the Chicago White Stockings, the Boston Beaneaters, and the New York Giants. His sale to Boston for $10,000 caused an uproar and earned him the nickname the "Ten Thousand Dollar Beauty." As the number one idol of his day, he achieved immortality with his base-stealing record (84) and with his base-running slide, the subject of the popular song "Slide, Kelly, Slide." Known for his disregard of the rules both on and off the field, when asked if he drank while playing, he replied, "It depends on the length of the game." Toward the end of his life, when he slid from a stretcher during his final illness, Kelly reputedly observed that "This is my last slide." At the time of his death, he was playing the lead role in *Casey at the Bat* on the Boston stage. He was the author of *Play Ball: Stories of the Diamond Field*.

• A visit to the National Baseball Hall of Fame would be incomplete without a reference to "Casey at the Bat," the classic expression of the sport's ethos. Although the poem was first recited publicly in 1888, it was not until almost a half century later that its author revealed the identity of the "Mighty Casey." According to Ernest L. Thayer, the author, the poem's slugger was named for Daniel Henry Casey, a high school classmate in Worcester, Massachusetts. When Thayer needed a name for his mythical ballplayer, he thought of the 200-pound, six-foot-two-inch teenager, who had almost beaten him up for remarks he had made in a newspaper article. Thayer described his choice of Casey's name as "a taunt thrown to the wind. God grant he never catches me." In subsequent years "Casey at the Bat" was the inspiration for one song, numerous verse parodies, three motion pictures (one starring *Michael "King" Kelly), two Disney cartoons, and an opera. Like some of the other spin-offs from the original, the opera gave Casey a personal history: He was born in Mudville in 1859 to John and Mary (O'Toole) Casey.

§ Open May-September, daily 9-9; rest of the year, daily 9-5. Closed January 1, Thanksgiving, and December 25. Fee. Gift shop. Phone: 607-547-7200.

EAST DURHAM

Nicknamed the "Irish Catskills," "Ireland's 33rd county," and the "Irish Music Capital of America," East Durham is a center of Irish and Irish-American culture. The area is host to noted musicians and athletic events, including hurling, Gaelic football, and the Irish-American Golf Open.

¶ East Durham Irish Cultural and Sports Centre.

This sixty-acre site is home to the following:

• The Irish American Heritage Museum. Located in an 1850s farmhouse, the museum boasts more than 2,000 square feet of galleries that interpret the Irish-American experience. Open Memorial Day weekend-Labor Day, Tuesday-Sunday and holidays 10-4; day after Labor Day-Columbus Day, Friday-Sunday and holidays 10-4; or by appointment. Fee. Phone: 518-634-7497 or 432-6598 in the off season.

• The John E. Lawe Memorial. A bronze bust and an inscribed plaque honor the "Champion of the Working Man," who "stood tall in the U.S. labor movement. A union man all his working life, 35 years with the Transport Workers Union of America, AFL-CIO as a dues-paying member, officer and international president (1985-1989). He was a dynamic local union leader, forceful negotiator, forward looking labor statesman and thoughtful labor spokesman. This emigrant from Kilgass, Strokestown, County Roscommon, Ireland, befriended and helped all struggling emigrant peoples. A proud Irish American (chosen Grand Marshal of New York City's 1987 St. Patrick's Day Parade), John was faithful to and supportive of both his native land and his adopted country. He was a dutiful husband, loving and protective father, an involved and much-honored community citizen, a concerned Roman Catholic gentleman. He passed this way and left it better for his passing."

• The John E. Lawe Memorial Sports Stadium, a professional playing field constructed to the same dimensions (95 x 160 yards) as Croke Park in Dublin. This field is the first of its size in North America and was dedicated on September 24, 1990.

• The Outdoor Pavilion, for performances and festival use

• The Patrick Kellegher Little League Baseball Field, home to the East Durham Little League

• The Peter J. O'Neill Library, open to the public by appointment and

• The Michael J. Quill Cultural Centre Building (under development), a performing arts and sports facility that will contain a theater, a banquet hall, exhibition space, and covered sports bleachers.

¶ National Shrine of Our Lady of Knock, on the grounds of St. Mary's Catholic Church, State 145, just south of town.

This shrine was constructed in the 1980s through the efforts of *Father Jeremiah Nunan and *Father John Mallon, the pastor of St. Mary's Church. The shrine commemorates an apparition which occurred in the small Irish village of Knock on August 21, 1879. The interior of the church is decorated with an Irish motif: stained glass windows depicting favorite Celtic saints, an altar screen resembling the church wall in Knock on which the apparition appeared, and, of course, the Irish tricolor.

National Shrine of Our Lady of Knock in East Durham.

ELMIRA

¶ **Mark Twain Burial Site,** Woodlawn Cemetery, at the north end of Walnut Street.

The grave of the famous humorist *Samuel Clemens is marked by a twelve-foot-high monument. The height is an allusion to the author's pseudonym: "Mark Twain," an expression denoting a depth of two fathoms (twelve feet) used in the riverboat trade. (See Hartford, Connecticut.)

¶ **Mark Twain Study,** on the Elmira College campus.

Built for *Samuel Clemens by his sister-in-law, this octagonal-shaped structure resembles a Mississippi riverboat pilothouse, a reminder of the author's days on the famous river. It was here that he wrote *The Adventures of Huckleberyy Finn.* (See Hannibal, Missouri, in *Irish America,* Volume 2.)

§ Open mid June-August 31, daily 9-5; rest of the year, by appointment. Phone: 607-735-1941.

¶ **Sullivan Monument,** Newtown Battlefield, 3 miles east on State 17.

The tall obelisk on this site commemorates *General John Sullivan, whose destruction of the Iroquois settlement at Newtown (now Elmira) in 1779 brought to fourteen the number of such villages which he had destroyed in an effort to crush Britain's Indian ally.

The monument reads: "Near this site, Sunday, August 29, 1779, was fought the Battle of Newtown between Continental troops commanded by Major General John Sullivan and a combined force of Tories and Indians under Colonel John Butler and Joseph Brant, avenging the massacre of Wyoming and Cherry Valley, destroying the Iroquois Confederacy, ending attacks on our settlements, and thereby opening westward the pathway of civilization."

One episode in the battle of Newtown is described in the following excerpts from "Sullivan 1779," a poem by Joseph Clarke read at the dedication of the monument in 1912:

> Thus Sullivan, with battle-flag outflung,
> Marched grimly by the banks of the Chemung;
> Vengeance his mission, a mandate to destroy:
> Death to the slinking murderers who crept
> By night upon our settlers as they slept,
> And slew them – woman, girl and boy –
> By the blazing of their log-built homes,
> Carved from the age-old wilderness
> Where the Susquehanna foams.

. . . .

The column writhes along its hard-won trail
In swelter in the noonday heat,
When a forest scout comes hurrying down
On noiseless moccasined feet.
"At the river's bend an Indian town,
A score of rough-hewn huts tricked out
With barbarous colors, blue and brown,
But none makes answer to our shout."
And Sullivan's force went death-like pale,
On his brow a deepened frown.
"Burn it to ashes; let the flames outspread
Till their fields are bare," he hoarsely said.
'Twas quickly done,
And the smoke still hung o'er the blasted vale,
When Sullivan gloomily rode ahead
In the blood-red setting of the sun.

§ Open Friday before Memorial Day-Columbus Day, daily 10-dusk.
Phone: 607-732-6067.

FAYETTESVILLE

§ **Grover Cleveland House,** 109 Academy Avenue. Private.

This was the boyhood home of *Grover Cleveland, the only U.S. president to serve two nonconsecutive terms (1887-91 and 1895-99). (See Caldwell, New Jersey.)

FORT JOHNSON

§ **Fort Johnson,** near the junction of State 5 and 67.

Now the Montgomery County Historical Society Museum, this gray stone structure was built in 1749 as the home of Sir William Johnson, his third in the Mohawk Valley. The fort contains original furnishings and displays on the Mohawk Indians and local history.

A decade earlier Johnson, a native of County Meath, Ireland, had been sent to America by his parents in the hope that such a trans-Atlantic move would break up his romance with an Irish girl. That he had his own reasons for emigrating, though, is evident in the fact that he brought a dozen Irish families with him, presumably to settle on the 14,000-acre estate of his uncle, Peter Warren, also a native of County Meath. At first Johnson worked as overseer on his relative's vast "plantation" – known as "Warrensburg" – in the Mohawk Valley. Within a year, however, the newcomer made the first of many land purchases which helped him become one of the largest property owners in the British colonies. (One grant in

"Fort Johnson," built in the eighteenth century by Sir William Johnson.

the early 1750s encompassed 20,000 acres a dozen miles west of Fort Johnson.) In settling his vast estates, he preferred German and Irish immigrants to Dutch, regarding the last as "neither laborious, industrious, nor soldiers." At the time of his death in 1774, he controlled one-fifth of the Mohawk Valley and had successfully developed the land into a network of Anglo-Irish plantations based on traditional Irish settlement patterns.

Despite his vast real estate holdings, Johnson's initial wealth derived from his lucrative fur trade with the Six Nations Indian tribes. As a trader he was on good terms with the local Native Americans, and he quickly adopted their customs and dress and learned the Mohawk language. According to local tradition, the Mohawk chief King Hendrick one day informed Johnson that he – the chief – had dreamed that he owned a coat similar to the expensive one owned by the Irishman. In accordance with Indian custom, Johnson graciously offered the coat to his Mohawk friend. A few weeks later Johnson approached King Hendrick with a similar "dream wish," pointing out to King Hendrick the many thousands of acres of land which – in a dream – the chief had granted him. Although the Mohawk gave his friend the land, he requested Johnson to dream no more.

During the French and Indian War, Johnson played a major role in asserting British dominion in the region. Rising from the rank of colonel in 1745 to major general a decade later, the Irishman succeeded in keeping the Iroquois from siding with the French during the colonial struggles that ravaged the Mohawk Valley in the 1740s and 1750s. In 1755 he and his Mohawk allies defeated a French force at Lake George [*q.v.*], where he subsequently built Fort William Henry. For his services the King made him a baronet and "Sole Agent and Superintendent" of the Six Nations.

Although Johnson occasionally pressured these tribes to grant him large tracts of land, he nevertheless had a sincere concern for their welfare and frequently protected them from more rapacious white settlers. The Indians' esteem for him is preserved in their tribute that "He never deceived us." With his adoption into the Mohawk nation, be became the first European to be allowed to speak before the Iroquois confederation's longhouse council. In fact, Johnson died while presiding over a conference of 600 Iroquois who had gathered at Johnson Hall to express their grievances against the murder of several of their brothers by encroaching white settlers. (Johnson's role in the Mohawk Valley is a prominent feature of a 1993 motion picture entitled *The Broken Chain* and starring Pierce Brosnan as the influential Irishman.)

Despite Johnson's exalted status in the Mohawk Valley, no evidence exists that he ever entered into either a sacramental or a civil marriage. By his first "wife" – a German indentured servant named Catherine Weissenberg – he had three children. Following her death at Fort Johnson in 1759, he successively took into his home two Indian women – one the niece of a Mohawk chief and the other Molly Brant, the sister of the famous Chief Joseph – with whom he had ten children. (A persistent rumor claimed that Johnson was the father of 700 Indian children.) Molly was known as "the brown Lady Johnson" and confidently presided over her "husband's" household, first at Fort Johnson and then at Johnson Hall. (See Johnstown, New York.)

§ Open mid May-mid October, Wednesday-Sunday 1-5. Fee. Phone: 518-843-0300.

FORT STANWIX

¶ **Fort Stanwix,** 112 East Park Street.

The site of this reconstructed fort was the scene of a gigantic "summit meeting" in 1768 between *Sir William Johnson and some 2,000 Native Americans. Although the resulting Treaty of Fort Stanwix was intended to keep European settlers from moving into Indian lands, it effectively granted possession to the British of large tracts of Indian land in what is now New York, Pennsylvania, West Virginia, and Kentucky – all for twenty boatloads of gifts worth about $50,000.

§ Open April-December, daily 9-5. Closed Thanksgiving and December 25. Fee. Phone: 315-336-2090.

FORT TICONDEROGA

¶ **Fort Ticonderoga,** 1 mile northeast on State 74.

In a bloodless surprise attack in 1775, the fort was seized from the British garrison by Ethan Allan and his Green Mountain Boys. That winter some of the fort's cannon were transported overland by oxcart to Boston. Two reminders of that grueling feat – performed under the command of *Henry Knox – are located on the parade ground within the fort:

• The inscription on the Knox Monument reads: "From this fortress went General Henry Knox in the winter of 1775-76 to deliver to General George Washington at Cambridge the train of artillery from Fort Ticonderoga, used to force the British Army to evacuate Boston." The bronze plaque on the monument depicts oxcarts pulling cannon through the forests.

• The Knox Gun is one of the artillery pieces which were seized from Fort Ticonderoga and which were intended to help General Washington dislodge the British from Boston. While in transit, however, this gun fell through the frozen Mohawk River, where it remained until 1800. After its recovery it stood in front of the city hall in the village of Mohawk Valley for twenty years and was fired each time local Federalists won an election. When the Democrats were finally victorious at the polls, they consigned the hated cannon to the bottom of the river. The gun was rescued once and for all just prior to World War II.

§ Open July-August, daily 9-6; early May-June 30, 9-5; September-late October, daily 9-5. Fee. Phone: 518-585-2821.

GLEN FALLS

⚓ Charles Evans Hughes Birthplace, 20 Center Street. Private.

Built about 1850, this clapboard house was the early home of *Charles Evans Hughes, New York governor, chief justice of the U.S. Supreme Court, presidential candidate, and secretary of state. Hughes was born here in 1910 to a Welsh father and an Irish mother (Mary Catherine Connelly).

GREAT NECK

⚓ F. Scott Fitzgerald House, 6 Gateway Drive. Private.

In 1922 this large colonial mansion on Long Island was rented by *F. Scott Fitzgerald, who worked on *The Great Gatsby* in a room over the garage. With his wife, Zelda, and countless weekend guests, he played the role of Trimalchio. On mornings after a typical bash, neighbors usually found him in a Bacchanalian sleep on the lawn.

HORSEHEADS

This small town of 7,000 inhabitants received its name from the 300 horse skulls which the first settlers in this region discovered in 1789. The skulls were the remains of the pack horses which had been used to transport the troops under *General John Sullivan from Pennsylvania to western New York to fight the Iroquois. Sullivan and his men had killed their starving and worn-out horses for food and left the remains behind.

INDIAN CASTLE

¶ **Indian Castle Church,** State 5S. Museum.
This clapboard house was built about 1770 by *Sir William Johnson as a mission church for the Indians in the area. The land for the church had been donated by the famous Mohawk chief Joseph Brant. Johnson was a superintendent of Indian affairs for the British in the mid 1700s.

JOHNSTOWN

¶ **Burke's Tavern,** West Montgomery and Williams streets. Private.
Built in 1765, this tavern was operated by innkeeper James Burke. The structure was moved to this site in 1788 from a nearby lot owned by *Sir William Johnson.

¶ **Drumm House,** West Green Street.
Built in 1763 by *Sir William Johnson, this was at one time the home of Edward Wall, who taught in the free school established by Johnson.

¶ **Johnson Hall State Historic Site,** 0.25 mile west off State 29 on Hall Avenue.
This Georgian mansion was built in 1763 by *Sir William Johnson. Between then and the American Revolution, it served as the center of his commercial and diplomatic relations with local Indian tribes. The house was designed by a Boston architect and although made of wood has the appearance of stone. One of the two original stone houses next to the main building displays a diorama and period exhibits. (See Fort Johnson, New York.)
§ Open mid May-October 31, Wednesday-Saturday 10-5, Sunday 1-5. Phone: 518-762-8712.

¶ **William Johnson Burial Site,** St. John's Episcopal Church, North Market and West Main streets.
The construction of the original church on this site was supervised by *Sir William Johnson, who was buried in its chancel in 1774. When that structure was burned in 1836, it was replaced by the present building. Johnson's grave is marked by a large stone memorial located on the church grounds and inscribed as follows: "Grave of Sir William Johnson, Bar-

"Johnson Hall," one of William Johnson's three homes in the Mohawk Valley.

onet, 1715-1774. His Indian name Warraghiyagey, 'He who does much business.' Founder of Johnstown, St. John's Episcopal Church, St. Patrick's Lodge 4 F. & A. M., first free school. Supt. of Indian affairs, major general British army, colonel of the Six Nations, builder of an empire."

J William Johnson Statue, near Johnson Hall State Historic Site.
    Erected in 1904, this memorial is inscribed with a tribute to *Sir William Johnson: "A man of strong character, a colossal pioneer. One of the greatest men of his time. Sole superintendent and faithful friend of the Six Nations and their allies. Their warragiyagey. Founder of Johnstown. He established here the first free school in the state. Born in Ireland, 1715. Died in Johnstown, 1774." (See Fort Johnson, New York.)

KINGS PARK

J Alfred E. Smith Sunken Meadow State Park.
    This state park along the north shore of Long Island is named for New York's famous Irish-American mayor.

KINGSTON

J George Clinton Burial Site, Dutch Reformed Church, Main Street, between Wall and Fair streets.

George Clinton, the first governor of New York after independence from Britain, is buried in the churchyard. A monument was dedicated to his memory when his remains were reinterred here after their removal from Washington, D.C.

The grandson of an immigrant from Longford, Ireland, George Clinton was first elected to the governorship in 1777. The strong political machine which he developed served him well during his seven terms in the statehouse. He was opposed to the federal constitution – because he knew it would shift power from the states – and he hoped to block its adoption by presiding over the New York ratifying convention. He abandoned his opposition, however, when the necessary nine states approved the union. When his presidential aspirations were dashed in 1808, he agreed to accept the vice presidency under James Madison, for whom, however, he showed public disdain.

LAKE GEORGE

¶ Fort William Henry Museum, Canada Street (U.S. 9).

This stockaded structure is a reconstruction of the fort built on this site in 1756 by *Sir William Johnson to protect the portage between Lake George and the Hudson River. The original fort featured prominently in *The Last of the Mohicans* by James Fenimore Cooper.

§ Open May-June and September-mid October, daily 10-5; July and August, daily 9 a.m.-10 p.m. Fee. Phone: 518-668-5471.

¶ Lake George Battleground Park, 0.5 mile south off U.S. 9.

Two monuments in this expansive park pay tribute to two prominent figures of Irish descent:

• The William Johnson and King Hendrick Monument consists of two bronze statues, one of the Mohawk chief King Hendrick and the other of *Sir William Johnson. The statues depict an episode in September 1755 when King Hendrick advised Johnson against attacking the nearby French.

After dismissing the chief's advice, Johnson sent 1,200 colonial and Indian troops to prevent the French from cutting his lines of communication with Fort Edward. When the British were repulsed in a clash with the French, the latter engaged Johnson's troops on this site but were thrown into retreat, suffering the loss of their commander and the capture of many prisoners.

• The Henry Knox Monument notes that "Through this place passed Gen. Henry Knox in the winter of 1775-1776 to deliver to Gen. George Washington at Cambridge the train of artillery from Fort Ticonderoga used to force the British army to evacuate Boston."

§ Open mid June-Labor Day, daily 9-8; early May-mid June, Saturday-Sunday 9-8. Parking fee. Phone: 518-668-3352.

*The William Johnson and
King Hendrick Monument
in Lake George Battlefield Park.*

MALONE

℘ Flanagan Hotel, Main and Elm streets.

In 1870 this hotel was the headquarters of the Fenian leaders who planned to lead their troops in the seizure of Canada to force the British to grant independence to Ireland. Although *President Ulysses S. Grant sent *General George Gordon Meade to prevent an invasion, Meade arrived too late to stop the initial incursion but was able to prevent 1,300 reinforcements from setting out from Malone.

The Fenians had been only moderately more successful four years earlier. In response to the arrival of about 2,000 Irish-American Fenians in Malone, the Canadians at that time had stationed gunboats in the St. Lawrence River and troops along the New York border. Although the Fenians crossed the international boundary on June 2, 1866, and exchanged shots with Canadian troops, the undisciplined and poorly provisioned Fenians retreated almost immediately.

MENANDS

℘ Chester A. Arthur Burial Site, Albany Rural Cemetery, Cemetery Avenue, off Broadway.

Following his death from a massive cerebral hemorrhage in 1886, former president *Chester A. Arthur was buried here next to his wife. (See Fairfield, Vermont.)

§ Open daily 8-4:

MIDDLEBURG

¶ **Timothy Murphy Monument,** Middleburg Cemetery, Huntersland Road, off State 145.

This monument marks the grave of Timothy Murphy, the Irish-American rifleman whose legendary marksmanship during the Revolutionary War earned him the nickname "Sure-shot Tim."

The inscription on the monument reads: "To the Memory of Timothy Murphy, Patriot, Soldier, Scout, Citizen, Who served in Morgan's Rifle Corps, fought at Saratoga and Monmouth, and whose bravery repelled the attack of the British and their Indian allies upon the Middle Fort, October 17, 1780, and saved the colonials of the Schoharie Valley."

NEWBURGH

¶ **George Clinton Statue,** Clinton Square, off Broadway and Bush

Statue of George Clinton.

Avenue.

This statue honors *George Clinton, a member of the Continental Congress (1775-1777), brigadier general (1777), governor of New York (1777-1795, 1801-1804), and vice president under Jefferson and Madison (1804-1812). (See Kingston, New York.)

¶ **Knox's Headquarters State Historic Site,** Quassaick Avenue (State 94) and Forge Hill Road in Vails Gate.

Built in 1754, this two-story stone structure was the home of John Ellison, a local mill operator. During the later years of the Revolutionary War, it was used as the headquarters of several American commanders. *General Henry Knox lived here in the summer and fall of 1779 until he departed to prepare for the siege of Yorktown, Virginia. He resided here again from May to September 1782, when General Washington was headquartered in Newburgh. For the next year and a half, Knox was the commander of nearby West Point. He later served as President Washington's secretary of war.

§ Open Memorial Day-Labor Day, Sunday 1-5; other times by appointment. Phone: 914-561-5498/1765.

¶ **Temple Hill Monument,** New Windsor Cantonment State Historic Site, 1 mile north of Vails Gate on Temple Hill Road.

A tall fieldstone monument was erected on this site in 1892 to honor the 7,000 American troops who were quartered here in the fall of 1782, at what was the last encampment of the Continental Army. A tablet on one of the sides commemorates the Society of the Cincinnati, an hereditary fraternal organization of Continental Army officers. The society was created here on May 10, 1783, and was based on a constitution drafted by *General Henry Knox.

§ Open mid April-October 31, Wednesday-Saturday 10-5, Sunday 1-5. Fee. Phone: 914-561-1765.

¶ **Washington's Headquarters State Historic Park,** Liberty Street, between Washington and Lafayette streets.

For sixteen months after the Revolutionary War, the Hasbrouck House on this site was General Washington's headquarters. Exhibits about the Continental Army are on display in an adjacent museum.

This six-acre park also contains the Peace Monument, erected in 1883 to mark the disbanding of the Continental Army a century before. The four bronze statues on the fifty-three-foot monument were created by *William O'Donovan and represent the four types of soldiers who served in the Revolution: artillerymen, cavalrymen, riflemen, and officers. O'Donovan's life-size statue of George Washington originally stood inside the monument but is now located in front of the museum.

§ Open mid April-late October, Wednesday-Saturday, 10-5, Sunday 1-5; rest of the year, Saturday 10-5, Sunday 1-5. Phone: 914-562-1195.

NEW YORK CITY

¶ **Admiral David Farragut Statue,** Madison Square Park, 23rd Street and Broadway.

This bronze statue by Augustus Saint-Gaudens was the Dublin-born sculptor's first major success. The work honors the commander of the Union fleet which captured New Orleans and defeated the Confederate fleet at Mobile in 1864. Farragut is depicted as a wind-buffeted figure flanked by female representations of Courage and Loyalty. The Union naval officer was famous for his command, "Damn the torpedoes, full speed ahead!"

¶ **Alfred E. Smith Boyhood Home,** 25 Oliver Street, Lower Manhattan.

A plaque on this three-story brick row house notes that Al Smith, the future governor of New York, lived here from 1909 until 1924. Despite Smith's reputation as the "quintessential Irish American," his father was of German and Italian background, while his mother – Catherine Mulvehill – was only half Irish. In 1928 Smith was the unsuccessful Democratic nominee for U.S. president, the first Irish Catholic since Charles O'Conor in 1872 to be nominated for the U.S. presidency.

¶ The nearby Alfred E. Smith Park (on Catherine Street) is adorned with a statue of the famous politician, dedicated in 1945 and showing Smith in a speaking pose behind a podium. The base of the statue is inscribed with the title of his political theme song, "The Sidewalks of New York."

¶ The Governor Alfred E. Smith Houses are located along East River Drive between the Manhattan and the Brooklyn bridges.

¶ **American Irish Historical Society,** 991 5th Avenue at 80th Street.

Since 1940 this five-story townhouse opposite the Metropolitan Museum has been the headquarters of the nation's premiere American-Irish historical society. The organization's library contains more than 30,000 volumes about Irish and Irish-American topics as well as photographs, personal items, musical instruments, and religious and art objects.

The society's headquarters is adorned with statues or portrait busts of the following Irish or Irish-American personalities: Samuel Beckett, Irish playwright and novelist; Edmund Burke, Irish statesman and orator; Charles Daley, New York justice; Thomas Davis, founder of *The Nation*; Eamon De Valera, native of New York and first president of Ireland; John Goff, New York attorney; President John F. Kennedy; William MacNeven, Irish patriot and physician; Admiral Richard Meade, first president of the

American Irish Historical Society; Daniel O'Connell, "Catholic Emancipator"; Charles O'Conor, New York attorney; William O'Donovan, sculptor; Charles Stewart Parnell, Irish political leader; Theodore Roosevelt, founding member of the American Irish Historical Society; and Wolfe Tone, Irish revolutionary. (The statue of Charles O'Conor is by *Augustus Saint-Gaudens.)

§ Open Monday-Friday 10-5 (appointment necessary). Phone: 212-288-2263.

¶ **Bayard-Condict Building,** 65 Bleecker Street, Lower Manhattan.

Erected between 1897 and 1899, this extremely ornate building is the only one in New York City designed by *Louis Sullivan and was one of the city's first skyscrapers.

¶ **Bennett Park,** between 183rd and 185th streets, Pinehurst and Fort Washington avenues, Upper Manhattan.

This was once the estate of James Gordon Bennett, the publisher of the *New York Herald*, and his wife, Henrietta Agnes Crean, a native of Ireland. The property and its house were maintained by their son, James Gordon Bennett Jr., who became chief executive officer of his father's paper in 1867.

The younger Bennett increased the *Herald*'s circulation by promoting several news exploits of his own making. One such effort was Henry Stanley's expedition to Zanzibar in search of David Livingstone. Another was Bennett's sponsorship of an expedition in search of the Northwest Passage, an unsuccessful venture which received full coverage in the *Herald*, however, through the reporting of *Aloysius MacGahan. Bennett also attracted favorable attention for the paper through the Herald Relief Fund for victims of agrarian dislocation and violence in Ireland, subscribing $100,000 to the fund himself.

¶ **Bishop Brooks Statue,** Church of the Incarnation, 209 Madison Avenue, Lower Manhattan.

This life-size statue of Bishop Phillips Brooks was sculpted by *William Clark Noble.

¶ **Broadway,** extending north from Battery Park to West 96th Street.

The "Great White Way" was first paved by Daniel Crimmins, who as a boy had worked for his Irish-born father's construction company. During his own contracting career, he constructed more than 400 buildings in the city, dug the tunnels for underground gas lines and electric wires, constructed much of the elevated-railway trackage, and built miles of viaducts and streets. He sometimes had as many as 12,000 men working for him at one time, and because of his generally good labor-management relations he was often asked to arbitrate wage disputes.

For his generosity to various charitable institutions in the city, Crimmins was named a Knight Commander of the Order of St. Gregory by Pope Leo XIII. A member of the Friendly Sons of St. Patrick and the American Irish Historical Society, Crimmins is also remembered as the author of *St. Patrick's Day – Its Celebration in New York and Other American Places, 1737-1845* (1902) and *Irish-American Miscellany* (1905).

¶ **Brooklyn Bridge,** Lower Manhattan.

One of the forces behind the building of the Brooklyn Bridge was William Kingsley, a second-generation Irishman who argued for a bridge across the East River to Brooklyn and who persuaded the engineer John A. Roebling to undertake the job.

Born in 1833 to Kilkenny emigrants living in Franklin County, New York, Kingsley was baptized William Kinsella but later changed his surname, presumably to hide his Celtic origins. After coming to Brooklyn in 1857, he formed a contacting business, which over the years paved Brooklyn's streets and built many of its reservoirs, waterworks, and sewers. At the time of his death, Kingsley was a director of the *Brooklyn Eagle*, the American District Telegraph Company, and the Metropolitan Gas Light Company. He was buried in Greenwood Cemetery in New York City.

¶ **Cardinal Hayes Place,** Pearl and Duane streets, Lower Manhattan.

This site in what was known as the "Five Points" section is named for Patrick Joseph Hayes, the fifth archbishop of New York. He was born near here in 1867 to immigrants from the vicinity of Killarney, Ireland.

Following his graduation from Manhattan College, with honors in philosophy and the classics, Hayes decided on a career with the Church. He completed his initial theological studies in Troy, New York, before doing graduate studies in theology at the Catholic University of America. The young priest enjoyed a rapid ascent up the clerical ladder, chiefly through his association with *Archbishop John Farley of New York, first as the latter's secretary and then as his chancellor.

Soon after the American entry into World War I, Hayes was given the responsibility of ministering to the spiritual needs of Catholic chaplains and personnel in the U.S. military forces. Within a year the U.S. military increased the number of its chaplains from twenty-five to almost 900. In his new position Hayes visited military bases in the United States but was prevented from going to the European front partly because of Farley's illness. About a year after succeeding Farley as archbishop, Hayes founded Catholic Charities.

Although Hayes rarely took public stands on political issues, he made an exception with regard to events in Ireland and when he believed it was necessary to uphold Catholic moral principles. In 1919-1920, for example, as guerilla war against the British was stepped up, he warned the Irish that violence would lose them American support. He not only welcomed Eamon De Valera as the president of the new "Irish Republic" but also contributed $1,000 to the Sinn Fein campaign. And, when violence accelerated, the American cardinal tried to encourage peace between the factions. On another front, meanwhile, in 1935 he spoke out against a suggestion of the American Birth Control League that families on public relief should practice artificial birth control. He also opposed an amendment to the U.S. Constitution forbidding child labor on the grounds that it was an infringement of parental rights by the federal government.

¶ Castle Clinton National Monument, Battery Park, Lower Manhattan.

Originally known as West Battery, the first fort on this site was designed by John McComb Jr. as a circular formation with walls eight feet thick. Renamed in 1815 for *DeWitt Clinton, the city's longtime mayor, the fortress was later turned into Castle Garden, featuring a fountain and a promenade. From 1855 to 1890, however, the site was an immigrant landing station, processing more than eight million newcomers to America. The station provided fair currency exchange, medical care, and information about housing, job opportunities, and travel to different parts of the country. A statuary group honoring America's immigrants stands in front of the former processing center. Today Castle Clinton is a point of departure for ferry boats to Ellis Island and the Statue of Liberty.

During the 1880s an Irish immigrant named Charlotte Grace O'Brien persuaded the Irish Catholic Colonization Society to establish a depot at Castle Garden to care for Irish immigrant women. There more than 100,000 Irish women and girls found a temporary home, employment, counseling, and a chapel.

§ Open daily 8:30-5. Closed December 25. Phone: 212-344-7220.

¶ Central Park, extending from 59th to 110th streets and from 5th Avenue to Central Park West.

Central Park contains several Irish-American landmarks of note:

• Thomas Moore Bust, 59th Street and 5th Avenue entrance. This portrait bust by Denis Sheahan pays tribute to the famous Dublin-born songwriter. After attending Trinity College, Moore avoided political involvement and instead emigrated to England, where he studied law. His extremely sentimental but popular *Irish Melodies* (1807-1834) expressed the glories of Gaelic civilization. Among his most famous melodies are "Flow On, Thou Shining River" and "The Harp That Once Through Tara's Halls."

Sheahan, born in Buttevant, County Cork, in 1843, taught art and astronomy at Yale College following his arrival in America. As a sculptor he is known for his statues of the Irish patriots Robert Emmet and Daniel O'Connell and of George Custer, Robert E. Lee, and Governor John Wise of Virginia. Sheahan also won distinction for his invention of a unique sundial that combined the functions of both a timepiece and a calendar. His sundials can be found all over the world, particularly in South America.

• Victor Herbert Bust, near the East 72nd Street entrance. This bronze bust by *Edmond Quinn honors the Dublin-born musician who wrote more than forty operettas, among them *Babes in Toyland* and *Naughty Marietta*. The memorial is located near the Guggenheim bandstand, where Herbert used to play with the 22nd Regiment. After leaving Vienna, where he had been the first cellist with the Strauss orchestra, he played in the New York Metropolitan Opera Orchestra.

Herbert became an active exponent of Irish sensibilities when he was elected president of the Society of the Friendly Sons of St. Patrick in 1914. The following year he founded the society's glee club and addressed the organization's annual meeting in especially chauvinistic terms: "I do not wish to brag about the achievements of the Irish race, but is it not a fact that on every page of the World's history and particularly the history of this country, you will find the names of some of the most illustrious sons of Erin, and have we not in generous measure helped to build up this

Bust of the Irish songwriter   *William T. Sherman Equestrian Statue*
Thomas Moore by Denis Sheahan.   *by Augustus Saint-Gaudens.*

wonderful country since its earliest development? But we have become grateful sons of the Goddess of Liberty, enjoying the blessings of Freedom denied us in our own land. Unbounded as is our loyalty to the country of our adoption . . . we are still fond lovers of that Green Isle beyond the Sea."

Following the abortive 1916 Easter Uprising in Dublin, Herbert presided at a mass meeting to protest Britain's iron-fisted crushing of the revolt. He called on the attendees to remember the "Irish martyrs of 1916" and to contribute to a fund for the families of the executed rebels. The following October he opened the Irish Relief Fund Bazaar at Madison Square Garden, taking the opportunity to pay tribute to those who died in the uprising: "Those men paid the penalty of their convictions and won for themselves imperishable fame."

On the heels of this political activity, Herbert wrote the opera that he called the effort of his life. According to its creator, *Hearts of Erin* (later known as *Eileen*) contained no traditional Irish airs but, rather, "'Irish' numbers" which he had written "in the characteristic spirit of the music of my native country." So successful was Herbert in this task that a reviewer later wrote that the composer had expressed in music the very heart of a nation. Although *Eileen* was probably inspired by events in Dublin the previous spring, the opera actually takes place during an unsuccessful rebellion in 1798. After returning from the Continent to prepare for an uprising supported by the French, the opera's protagonist, Barry O'Day, falls in love with Eileen Mulvaney. Despite the military and political rout that follows, love conquers all as the amorous pair live happily ever after. The opera concludes with the hymn "When Ireland Stands Among the Nations of the World."

• Jacqueline Kennedy Onassis Reservoir, between 86th and 96th streets.

❡ At 59th Street and 5th Avenue, just outside the entrance to Central Park, is the William T. Sherman Equestrian Statue. Designed by *Augustus Saint-Gaudens, this colossal work includes a figure of Victory carrying an olive branch before the mounted Union general, who cut a swath of destruction through Georgia during the Civil War.

❡ Charles O'Conor Birthplace Site, 129 Front Street, Lower Manhattan.

On this site in 1804 was born Charles O'Conor, the New York attorney who held the distinction of being the first Catholic nominated for the presidency of the United States.

The son of an Irish political refugee, O'Conor received the nomination in 1872 from the "Straight-Out" Democrats, a group of dissidents who had bolted the Democratic Party after its selection of *Horace Greeley as its standard bearer. His popularity with these Southerners may have been due to his earlier opposition to abolition and to his belief that slavery was a "just, benign and beneficent" institution. He had also expressed the South's fear of becoming a minority in the federal government: "If we continue to fill the halls of legislation with abolitionists, and permit to occupy the executive chair men who declare themselves to be enlisted in a crusade against slavery, . . . what can we reasonably expect from the people of the South but that they will pronounce the Constitution . . . [and] this Union . . . unendurable evil . . . ." Although O'Conor refused the nomination, he and the dissidents' vice presidential candidate, John Quincy Adams, won 29,408 votes in twenty-three states.

¶ **Charles O'Conor Portrait Bust,** Appellate Division of the New York State Supreme Court, near Madison Square Park, Lower Manhattan.

During a legal career that lasted half a century, *Charles O'Conor was recognized as the ablest lawyer in America. One of the legal cases which brought him much attention involved the defense of *Jefferson Davis following the Civil War.

In late May 1865, Northerners sympathetic to Davis contacted O'Conor to request that he serve as the former Confederate president's counsel, most likely against a charge of treason against the United States. A year later, while Davis was still imprisoned at Fort Monroe, Virginia, O'Conor petitioned the U.S. attorney general to release Davis on $1 million bail posted by Northern businessmen Cornelius Vanderbilt, Gerrit Smith, and *Horace Greeley. The request was denied, however, because Davis was still a military prisoner and thus not eligible for bail. But on May 4, 1867, the attorney successfully sought a writ of habeas corpus requesting the military authorities at Fort Monroe to remand Davis to civil authorities in the state.

When O'Conor subsequently learned that the government prosecutor was not ready to proceed with the case, he again requested bail for his client. This time Davis was released after Greeley and several others pledged $100,000 in sureties. At the end of November, O'Conor petitioned that the indictment for treason be dismissed on the theory that Davis had already been punished for his alleged crime by the provision in the Fourteenth Amendment which stripped him of his United States citizenship. The next month Chief Justice Salmon P. Chase agreed, quashing the indictment and ruling that the case could not be tried ex post facto.

Toward the end of his career, O'Conor achieved additional fame for his prosecution of the notoriously corrupt "Tweed Ring." Although he was successful in breaking up New York City's most infamous machine, he feared that his legal victory would provide no lasting protection against future corruption. O'Conor's pessimism in this regard is evident in public appeals he made soon after the Tweed litigation. In a pamphlet entitled *Democracy*, he argued that "in the main[, government] should be unfelt and unseen, or at least unperceived" and that "every positive regulation, not indispensable to the public and general welfare . . . violates the spirit of the Constitution." In an address in 1877, he said that "to be left alone by politicians and intermeddling officials is all that society needs." He warned that, while the U.S. Constitution guarantees liberty, "little, if anything, towards insuring perpetuity, or controlling the will of the popular majority, was affected by the device of a written constitution. The endurance, vigor, virtue of those fundamental principles which, in fact, are in the Constitution, depend wholly upon the intelligence and patriotism of our people."

¶ Chester A. Arthur House, 123 Lexington Avenue, Lower Manhattan.

Although this address now houses stores and apartments, it was formerly the residence of *Chester A. Arthur for most of his adult life. Following President Garfield's death in 1881 at the hands of an assassin, Vice President Arthur took the oath of office here on September 20. A bronze plaque on the building was dedicated in 1964 to mark the eighty-first anniversary of Arthur's signing of the Pendleton Civil Service Act. (See Fairfield, Vermont.)

¶ Chester A. Arthur Statue, Madison Square Park, Broadway and 23rd Street, Lower Manhattan.

Unveiled in 1899, this statue honors *President Chester A. Arthur. (See Fairfield, Vermont.)

¶ Church of the Ascension, 5th Avenue and 10th Street, Lower Manhattan.

The marble altar relief in this Gothic Revival brownstone church was created by *Augustus Saint-Gaudens.

¶ City Hall, Broadway and Park Row, Lower Manhattan.

The city hall was constructed in 1811 through the influence of New York mayor DeWitt Clinton, whose grandfather had emigrated from Ireland to America in 1731. Besides serving ten annual terms as mayor and two terms as governor, Clinton was a state legislator, a U.S. senator, and the principal advocate for building the Erie Canal. In the New York legislature, he was a spokesman for Irish immigrants and drafted the law removing franchise restrictions against Roman Catholics.

• On the east side of City Hall is a bronze seated statue of *Horace Greeley, the founder of the *New York Times* and coiner of the advice "Go west, young man." Ever the eccentric, he was known for his squeaky voice, white socks and overcoat, broad-brimmed hat, throat-whiskers, and shapeless pants.

Despite his earlier unsuccessful attempts to win political office, Greeley tried again in 1871, this time as the nominee of both the Democratic Party and the Liberal Republicans. Although the latter group supported him because of his opposition to the renomination of *President Ulysses S. Grant, he had little prospect of gaining many Democratic votes because of his frequent attacks against the Democratic Party over the years. During the campaign he was called a fool, a crank, and a traitor and was an easy object of ridicule in political cartoons of the day. He was personally hurt by the invective hurled against him and lamented that he sometimes thought he was running for the penitentiary rather than for the presidency. After carrying only six Southern and border states, he felt that he was "the worst beaten man who ever ran for high office." (See Amherst, New Hampshire.)

ℐ Christopher Colles Residence, 6 State Street.

This was the home of Christopher Colles, the Dublin-born engineer who designed New York City's water system and proposed what became the Erie Canal. He is buried in Trinity Churchyard [*q.v.*] in Lower Manhattan.

ℐ Claremont Avenue, Upper Manhattan.

This street was named for "Claremont," the mansion house of Michael Hogan, a native of County Clare, Ireland, and a wealthy New York businessman and philanthropist. The house was built in the early 1790s by George Pollock, an English linen merchant, and until 1953 stood on Strawberry Hill, north of Grant's Tomb.

Hogan, who began his career as a sea captain, first arrived in New York in 1804. With him was his wife, who was described as "a dark Indian princess" (possessed of a dowry of £40,000 in gold) and for whom he purchased Pollock's mansion. Hogan christened *la grand maison* either for his native County Clare or for the castle of his longtime friend, the Duke of Clarence, the future "Sailor King" of England, William IV. A memorial plaque in Hogan's honor is in Grace Church in Lower Manhattan. (See Michael Hogan Tablet below.)

ℐ Conference House, Hylan Boulevard, Tottenville, Staten Island.

On September 11, 1776, this structure was the site of an unsuccessful peace conference between Admiral Richard Howe (the commander of British naval forces in America) and three representatives of the Continental Congress (John Adams, Benjamin Franklin, and *Edward Rutledge). During the conference with Howe, Rutledge insisted that nothing short of complete independence would satisfy the Americans.

ℐ Dominick Lynch House, 36 Broadway, Lower Manhattan.

This was the residence of Dominick Lynch, a successful merchant and a native of Galway, Ireland, who counted eighty-four mayors of that city among his ancestors.

In 1780, while still in Ireland, Lynch opened a branch of his father's trading business in Bruges, Flanders. His subsequent wealth was based on the purchase and shipment of flax seed to Ireland and on other trade during the continental wars of the period. (It was joked that he was the only Irishman to come to America with his fortune already made.)

After arriving in the United States, Lynch became involved in a number of enterprises of varying success. With his business partner, Thomas Stoughton, he opened a commercial house in New York City, for which he provided two-thirds of the $7,500 capitalization. He subsequently invested in bank stocks, real estate, and the China trade. He also acquired a tract of 2,000 acres near Fort Stanwix on the Mohawk River in New York State. Although he originally named his property Lynchville, sometime before the turn of the century he changed the name to Rome. Over the next twenty years, he built there a woolen factory, a cotton factory, and a sawmill.

In the meantime, mutual dissatisfaction had led to a dissolution of his partnership with Stoughton in 1795. As a result of litigation that continued for two decades, however, Lynch had to pay his former partner $25,000. While living in New York City, Lynch was a generous benefactor of St. Peter's Catholic Church.

⚓ Duane Street, City Hall area.

This street was named after James Duane, the son of a prosperous New York merchant of Irish birth who arrived in New York soon after 1700. The younger Duane was a member of the Continental Congress, the first mayor of New York following the Revolution, a member of the New York state convention which adopted the Constitution, and the first federal judge of the district of New York.

⚓ Edgar Allan Poe Cottage, Poe Park, 2640 Grand Concourse and Kingsbridge Road, the Bronx.

This frame farmhouse was the last residence of any duration of *Edgar Allan Poe. Though well known when he arrived here in 1846 with his wife, Virginia, and his mother-in-law, Maria Clemm, he was impoverished. "Eddie rarely left his beautiful home," Mrs. Clemm recalled. "I attended to his literary business; for he, poor fellow, knew nothing about money transactions." Here Poe wrote his poems "Annabel Lee" and "The Bells," and here Virginia died of tuberculosis the next year. Her bed and Poe's rocking chair are on exhibit, as is a portrait bust of the author by *Edmond Quinn. The museum shows an audiovisual presentation about Poe's life. (See Edgar Allan Poe sites in Baltimore, Maryland.)

§ Open Saturday 10-4, Sunday 1-5. Closed holidays. Fee. Phone: 718-

881-8900.

Edmond Quinn, a native of Philadelphia of Irish descent, first studied art under Thomas Eakins at the Pennsylvania Academy of Fine Arts. At age twenty-five the student spent several months in Spain, where he was influenced by the work of Velazquez. He later studied modeling and sculpting in Paris.

Among Quinn's other sculpted works are a statue of John Howard (Williamsport, Pa.), the reliefs on the battle monument at King's Mountain (South Carolina), a bronze statue of Edwin Booth as Hamlet (Gramercy Park, New York City), the female figure of "Victory" for the war memorial at New Rochelle (N.Y.), and busts of Henry Clay, Cass Gilbert, *Victor Herbert, Edwin Markham, and *Eugene O'Neill. His busts of Edwin Booth, Dr. Oliver Wendell Holmes, and *James McNeill Whistler are in the Hall of Fame of New York University.

Although Quinn was said to have had a Celtic sense of humor, melancholia was evidently more predominant in his personality, for he ended his life by drowning in 1929.

¶ Edgar Allan Poe House, 45 West 3rd Street, Greenwich Village.

The famous poet lived here for a brief time and received medication for a cold at the Northern Dispensary (at Christopher Street and Waverly Place).

¶ Edgar Allan Poe Street, West 84th Street, between Broadway and Westend Avenue.

This renamed portion of West 84th Street marks the general location of the home and farm owned by *Patrick Brennan, where *Edgar Allan Poe lived in 1844 and where he completed "The Raven."

When Poe first met Brennan and his wife and their six children, he described the pair as "a hospitable agriculturalist and his consort." Poe later described their farm as "a perfect paradise," where he hoped that his consumptive wife, Virginia, would soon regain her health. As the poet revised his earlier drafts of "The Raven," he doubtless incorporated into it the statue of the goddess Athena – the "pallid bust of Pallas" – which stood above one of the doors in the Brennan home. Years later the Brennans recounted their observations about the sensitive poet: of the papers strewn over the floor of the room with the bust, of his daydreaming on a bench near the pond or at the summit of Mt. Tom, and his vigils with Virginia as they enjoyed the sunsets across the Hudson. Poe described his experience with the Brennans as "playing hermit in earnest, nor have I seen a living soul out of my family."

¶ Ellis Island, New York Harbor.

The island can be reached by ferry from Battery Park in lower Manhattan and from Liberty Park in Jersey City.

In 1890 Congress chose Ellis Island as the site of a new federal immigration center. The facility was built at a cost of $500,000 and contained a two-story processing building, a hospital, a boiler house, a laundry, and a utility plant – all constructed of wood. It also had telegraph and railroad ticket offices, a money exchange office, and an information bureau for the benefit of those seeking friends and relatives among the immigrants. Two military structures on the island were converted into dormitories for detainees.

On January 1, 1892, the Ellis Island Immigration Center formally opened to process steerage passengers coming into the country. More than twelve million immigrants – 500,000 of them Irish – were processed here before the center was closed in 1954.

• The outdoor American Immigrant Wall of Honor contains panels engraved with the names of 200,000 immigrants who arrived in the United States between 1892 and 1924.

• The Annie Moore Statue in the main building was erected in 1992 to commemorate the centennial of Ellis Island's opening and to honor the first immigrant registered at the new center. An identical statue stands in Queenstown in Cobh, County Cork, Ireland, the port from which Annie and her two younger brothers set sail.

*Statue of Annie Moore,
the first immigrant
to register at Ellis Island.*

Described as a fifteen-year-old "little rosy cheeked Irish girl," Annie Moore was among the 148 steerage passengers who arrived in New York Harbor aboard the steamship *Nevada*. On the morning of January 1, 1892, the passengers were placed aboard the immigrant transfer boat *John E. Moore*, which landed at the wharf on Ellis Island "amid a clang of bells and din of shrieking whistles."

By a prearranged plan Annie was escorted to a registry desk, where her name was the first to be registered at the new landing bureau. The next day the *New York Times* described her arrival: "When the little voyager had been registered [the superintendent] presented her with a ten-dollar gold coin and made a short address of congratulations and welcome. It was the first United States coin she had ever seen and the largest sum of money she had ever possessed. She says she will never part with it, but will always keep it as a pleasant memento of the occasion."

Annie was accompanied by her two younger brothers, Anthony and Philip. The trio had come to join their parents, Matt and Mary Moore, who had immigrated to the United States three years earlier and had left the three children with an aunt until they could earn passage money for the rest of the family. The three youngsters arrived with a single piece of baggage among them.

On June 8, 1988, the Ellis Island Restoration Commission revealed its intention to establish a computerized genealogical center on Ellis Island. The system would contain information about seventeen million immigrants obtained from the original ship manifests.

One of the guests of honor that day was Margaret O'Connell Middleton of Tucson, Arizona, Annie Moore's granddaughter. During the ceremony she returned the ten-dollar gold piece given to her grandmother when she arrived at Ellis Island. She in turn was given another gold piece by Ellis Island's superintendent in honor of the center's opening.

§ Open daily 9-5. Closed December 25. Phone: 212-269-5755 (general information) or 212-363-7772 (museum).

¶ **Emigrant Savings Bank,** 51 Chambers Street, City Hall area.

Although now used for other purposes, the building at this site was once the Emigrant Savings Bank, founded in 1817 by *William MacNeven to help Irish immigrants.

¶ **Father Duffy Statue and Square,** Broadway and West 47th Street, Midtown Manhattan.

In front of a Celtic cross stands a bronze statue of *Father Francis Duffy, the pastor of nearby Holy Cross Catholic Church. Within his parish were the slums and gangs of "Hell's Kitchen," the dance halls and burlesque houses of Times Square, and the legitimate theaters of Broadway.

Duffy is more generally known as chaplain of the "Fighting 69th"

Statue of Father Francis Duffy.

Regiment, a unit predominantly Irish since 1860, when it refused to march in honor of the visiting Prince of Wales. During World War I, the unit became the 165th Regiment of the American Expeditionary Force fighting in France. For his service on the battlefield, Duffy was awarded the Distinguished Service Cross, the Cross of the Legion of Honor, and the *Croix de Guerre*. At the time of his funeral in St. Patrick's Cathedral, he was eulogized by President Franklin Roosevelt as "a great Samaritan, a great Catholic, a great soldier."

The statue was erected in 1937 by his many friends in the theatrical profession. Among the 30,000 people at the dedication were members of the 69th Regiment band (playing "Onward, Christian Soldiers") and Irish Americans James Farley, Alfred E. Smith, and James Tunney.

¶ **Fifth Avenue,** extending north from West 8th Street to 142nd Street.

Despite conflict over social and political issues in recent years, organizers of the St. Patrick's Day Parade continue a long tradition with their annual march down Fifth Avenue. The first St. Patrick's Day Parade in New York City took place in 1779 when the Volunteers of Ireland, a regiment of Irish soldiers serving in the British army, marched in honor of the Irish patron saint. The modern parade extends from 44th to 86th streets.

¶ **Five Points,** Park, Baxter, and Worth streets, Lower Manhattan.

As early as the 1820s this area of the city had a large Irish population and may have been one of the country's earliest slums. The Five Points area was notorious for its bars, whorehouses, foul-smelling tanneries, and criminal gangs (one of them composed mostly of natives from County Kerry, Ireland).

¶ **Foley Square,** at the intersection of Duane, Lafayette, Pearl, and Centre streets, City Hall area.

The square was named for *Thomas Foley, a Tammany Hall politician known for his influence in New York state politics.

Born in 1852, Foley at age thirteen began work as a butcher's delivery boy and a blacksmith's helper but eventually opened several saloons. (His rules for such establishments forbade the admission of women and the encouragement of drunkenness by his bartenders.) In the meantime, he became a Tammany operative, first as a district captain, then as a city council member, and finally as New York County sheriff. He could have been nominated for state senator or become the outright leader of Tammany, but because he felt that he was better suited for politics rather than officeholding he declined the offers. As the unofficial head of Tammany, he was known for his generosity – and gullibility – to those in need. Angered by newspaper attacks against him by *William Randolph Hearst, Foley helped frustrate the famous publisher's attempts to win election as governor and U.S. senator.

The Tammany "kingmaker" is best remembered as being the political godfather of *Alfred E. Smith and for throwing his support behind his successful gubernatorial bid. After Foley's death in 1925, Governor Smith acknowledged his affection for his political mentor and offered the following tribute: "Tom had one great piece of advice that he gave to everyone when he started them off. He used to say: 'When anybody comes to see you about anything, tell them the truth. They won't like it at the time you tell it to them, but six months afterwards they will be your friend because they will find it out.'"

¶ **Ford Foundation Building,** 320 East 43rd Street, Midtown Manhattan.

This cube-shaped building faced with acres of glass was designed by Roche, Dinkeloo & Associates in the late 1960s.

Kevin Roche, a native of Dublin, received a bachelor's degree in architecture from the National University of Ireland in 1945. After moving to the United States, he studied at the Illinois Institute of Technology.

¶ **Fordham University,** 3rd Avenue and Fordham Road, the Bronx.

This Jesuit university was founded in 1841 by *John Hughes, New

York City's first archbishop. A statue of Hughes by *William O'Donovan is located on the lawn in front of the university buildings.

¶ Fort Clinton, McGowan's Pass, Central Park.

Named in honor of *DeWitt Clinton, the longtime mayor of the city, the fort was built to defend nearby McGowan's Pass, reputedly named for Captain Daniel McGowan, a native of Ireland and a Revolutionary War soldier who owned a farm here.

¶ Fraunces Tavern, 54 Pearl Street, at Broad.

Among the items on display in the museum is a painting by John Ward Dunsmore depicting a scene from the battle of Springfield, New Jersey, in June 1776. During the battle, when the American soldiers ran out of wadding for their rifles, the *Reverend James Caldwell – the "Soldier Parson" – broke open the doors of the Presbyterian church and began to distribute to the men copies of the Watts hymnbooks. "Now put Watts into them, boys!" he cried. (See Springfield, New Jersey.)

On December 3, 1932, Fraunces Tavern was the site of a memorial meeting to commemorate a famous breakfast which occurred here in 1783. Following George Washington's return to New York City that year, the former American commander had breakfast with *Hercules Mulligan, a haberdasher by trade who had served as Washington's personal spy during the Revolution. This historic meal was celebrated in the poem "Breakfast with Hercules Mulligan" by Shaemus O'Sheel, who read the poem at the 1932 memorial. The last twenty-one lines of the poem are quoted here:

> Over the Bowling Green they ride,
> Washington, Mulligan, side by side;
> Thus the Chieftain, in all men's view
> Proves Hercules Mulligan staunch and true.
>
> For Washington knows the Irish breed;
> They sprung to arms in the hour of need,
> Sullivan, first to strike on land,
> O'Brien, first to strike at sea,
> Knox and Moylan and Wayne and Hand,
> Barry, Magaw and Shee.
> They proved their mettle on many a field,
> First to charge and last to yield,
> In the cause of Liberty.
>
> Washington smiles and bows to his host;
> "Hercules Mulligan, here's a toast:
> If the land we have seen this day set free
> Ever shall be in danger

From foe within or stranger,
May Heaven grant, to save us then,
The hearts and the hands of Irishmen."
And the shout rings 'round the board, "Amen"![1]

With the arrival of peace and the creation of a new nation, Mulligan seems to have continued his haberdashery business, one that now boasted among its clients the new president of the United States. According to Washington's account books, between May 1789 and May 1790 he paid Mulligan £288 for tailoring services and quantities of gingham, flannel, velvet, and other materials. (See Hercules Mulligan House Site below.)

§ Open Monday-Friday 10-4:45, Saturday and Sunday noon-4. Closed major holidays except July 4. Fee. Phone: 212-425-1778.

¶ **Frawley Circle,** at the northeast corner of Central Park (110th Street).

This area is named for *James Frawley, a Tammany Hall politician, public administrator, and state senator.

¶ **General Grant National Memorial,** Riverside Drive and 122nd Street, Upper Manhattan.

*Ulysses S. Grant and his wife are buried in this circular Greek Revival tomb, the largest mausoleum in the United States. The white marble interior resembles that of Les Invalides, Napoleon's tomb in Paris, and is adorned with heroic bronze busts of five other Civil War generals, including *Philip Sheridan. Along the south façade are engraved Grant's words "Let us have peace." (See Point Pleasant, Ohio.)

Following Grant's death in 1885, his funeral procession through New York City was seven miles long and attracted a million people. His body was originally placed in a temporary vault in Riverside Park until the national memorial was completed in 1897.

§ Open daily 9-5. Closed January 1, Thanksgiving, and December 25. Phone: 212-666-1640.

¶ **George M. Cohan Statue and Square,** Broadway and West 46th Street, Midtown Manhattan.

This square is dedicated to George M. Cohan, one of America's most famous composers and musical comedy stars, an entertainer who composed more than 500 songs, helped produce about 150 plays, and either wrote or collaborated on the writing of forty plays.

When the statue in Cohan's honor was dedicated in 1959, Oscar Hammerstein II and George Jessel presided at the event. The crowd of

[1]©1997 Official Catholic Directory, published by P.J. Kenedy & Sons, New Providence, New Jersey. A member of the Reed Elsevier plc group.

Statue of George M. Cohan.

45,000 people in attendance closed the ceremonies by singing "Give My Regards to Broadway." The sides of the pedestal are inscribed with the names of Cohan's four most famous songs.

The grandson of Michael Keohane, an immigrant from County Cork, George Cohan was born into a traveling vaudevillian family and made his first stage appearance literally as an infant. As one of "The Four Cohans," the youngster acted, sang, danced, and recited in his father's sketches. His first great success was as the lead character in *Peck's Bad Boy*, a role that reputedly came naturally for the mischievous Mick. It was during these early years that he developed his trademark style – singing out of the corner of his mouth, thrusting his head forward as he strut across the stage, and ending each performance with his ingratiating *gracias*: "My mother thanks you, my father thanks you, my sister thanks you, and I thank you."

After succeeding to the role of sketch writer and business manager, Cohan formed a production partnership that produced many hits. The first success was *Little Johnny Jones*, a musical by Cohan about an American jockey accused of throwing the English Derby. Although critics were less than enthusiastic – some labeling it "flag-waving" – the public excitedly took up two of its songs – "Give My Regards to Broadway" and "Yankee Doodle Boy." (Although Cohan was born on July 3, his father invented the story that his son had been born on Independence Day, thus making him a "real live nephew of [his] Uncle Sam, born on the Fourth of July.") Other patriotic musicals followed, among them *George Washington, Jr.*, in which Cohan sang "You're a Grand Old Flag." But Cohan's greatest hit song – selling one and a half million copies – was "Over There," inspired by America's entry into World War I.

Years later President Franklin Roosevelt presented Cohan with the gold medal which Congress had voted to award him for the song. At his funeral in St. Patrick's Cathedral, the organist played "Over There" as a dirge, the first time a secular piece of music had ever been played in the Catholic cathedral.

¶ **Gramercy Park,** between 3rd & Park avenues and East 20th & East 21st streets, Lower Manhattan.

During the Dutch period this area was known as Crommessie ("small, crooked knife," for a nearby brook). A later owner of the property was *James Duane, the first mayor of New York after the Revolution. He named the area Gramercy Seat.

In the park is a bronze statue of the actor Edwin Booth as Hamlet, the work of the sculptor *Edmond Quinn and a gift of the Players' Club.

¶ **Grand Army Plaza,** Brooklyn.

Three notable monuments associated with Irish Americans are located in the Grand Army Plaza:

• The equestrian reliefs of Abraham Lincoln and *Ulysses S. Grant on the Soldiers' and Sailors' Memorial Arch are the work of *William O'Donovan. To ensure the historical accuracy of his reliefs, the artist spent weeks searching for a model horse as similar to Grant's steed as possible.

• Erected in 1965, the John F. Kennedy Memorial consists of a bronze bust of the slain president on a white marble stele.

§ Open daily dawn-dusk.

¶ **Greenwich Village,** Lower Manhattan.

This area was once the estate of Irish-born Sir Peter Warren, an illustrious naval commander during the colonial wars of the 1740s.

Born on the Warren estate at Warrenstown, County Meath, in 1703, Warren joined the British navy as a midshipman at the age of twelve and spent a dozen years cruising the West Indies and the North American coast. In 1730 he sailed to New York City as the captain of a twenty-gun frigate. Once there, he purchased "Greenwich House," a twenty-acre site on the Hudson River and the first acquisition of what grew to become a 300-acre estate now known as Greenwich Village. He later purchased 14,000 acres in the Mohawk Valley, an extensive tract managed by *William Johnson, his nephew and Britain's Indian agent in that region.

Beginning in 1745, Warren was assigned to active duty in the Anglo-French conflict. While Governor William Shirley of Massachusetts led an expedition against the French stronghold of Louisbourg on Cape Breton Island, Warren prevented an enemy supply ship from reaching the besieged fortress. In a dramatic address to the army just before Louisbourg's surrender, he said that he would rather die and be buried there than leave without capturing the city. For his efforts he was named rear admiral of the Blue Fleet and governor of Cape Breton Island. His popularity was such that a street in New York City was named for him and a tavern called the Admiral Warren was opened on Wall Street.

Warren's greatest naval victory, however, occurred when he defeated a French fleet off Cape Finisterre in 1747. This personal triumph led to knighthood, election to Parliament, and promotion to vice admiral of the White Fleet. He later led three other naval expeditions and retired with £200,000 of prize money. Following his death in Dublin, he was buried near Warrenstown and was honored with a monument in Westminster Abbey.

¶ Greenwood Cemetery, 5th Avenue at 25th Street, Brooklyn.

Opened in 1840, this beautifully landscaped cemetery is noted for its Victorian statuary, some of which includes monuments in the form of mangled railroad cars, sinking steamboats, and fire hydrants. The 500,000 graves here include those of Irish-born Marcus Daly and Lola Montez and Irish-Americans DeWitt Clinton, Horace Greeley, and William Kingsley.

• Marcus Daly, the "Copper King" who developed the Anaconda Mines in Montana. Born in Ballyjamesduff, County Cavan, Daly by 1876 was part owner of the Alice Mine in Butte, Montana. Four years later he bought the Anaconda Silver Mine and converted it to copper. (See Butte, Montana, in *Irish America*, Volume 2.)

• Born Marie Dolores Eliza Rosanna Gilbert in Limerick, Ireland, Lola Montez was notorious for her multiple marriages and numerous love affairs. She counted among her lovers the musician Franz Liszt, the novelist Alexandre Dumas, and Bavaria's King Ludwig, the last of whom she infected with syphilis and generally so dominated that his government was mocked as the *Lolaministerium*. Montez was known not only for her paramours but also for her erotic Spider Dance, a feature of her famous dance tours. But the main attraction was Montez herself, known for carrying a pistol, smoking cigars, and humiliating and assaulting men. During the last years of her life, as syphilis ravaged her body, she preached to prostitutes about the dangers of the disease. At the end she suffered from incontinence, seizures, and loss of speech.

• The memorial to DeWitt Clinton consists of a heroic-size statue atop a pedestal with bas-reliefs depicting scenes from the construction of the Erie Canal. Clinton was a major proponent of such an engineering feat,

*Statue of DeWitt Clinton
in Greenwood Cemetery.*

which employed thousands of Irish workers along its course.

• The monument to William Kingsley – one of the major advocates of building a bridge across the East River – was erected by the board of trustees of the East River (Brooklyn) Bridge and is formed of a stone from that structure.

• [See entries about Horace Greeley elsewhere.]

§ Open daily 8-4. Phone: 718-768-7300.

¶ **Hall of Fame for Great Americans,** Bronx Community College of the City University of New York, on the heights overlooking the Harlem and Hudson rivers.

A 630-foot open-air colonnade dedicated in 1901 enshrines the bronze busts of 98 of the 102 Americans inducted into the Hall of Fame. The following honorees were of Irish descent: President Grover Cleveland; Stephen Collins Foster, composer of minstrel songs and popular ballads; Robert Fulton, inventor and steamship promoter; President Ulysses S. Grant; President Andrew Jackson; Thomas "Stonewall" Jackson, Civil War general; Sidney Lanier, musician, poet, and literary critic; Edward Alexander MacDowell, pianist, composer, and music teacher; Matthew Fontaine Maury, oceanographer and naval officer; President Theodore Roosevelt; Augustus Saint-Gaudens, sculptor; James McNeill

Whistler, artist and portrait painter; and President Woodrow Wilson.

In addition, the busts of Abraham Lincoln and General William Sherman on display here are replicas of works by *Augustus Saint-Gaudens, while the likenesses of John Quincy Adams, Oliver Wendell Holmes, and James Kent were sculpted by *Edmond Quinn.

¶ **Hercules Mulligan House Site,** 218 Pearl Street, Lower Manhattan.

Hercules Mulligan was born in Coleraine, County Antrim, Ireland, in 1740 and came to America with his parents at the age of six. He was descended from an O'Mulligan of County Cavan, one of the hereditary bards of the O'Reilly family. He probably worked for the haberdashery firm of Kortright and Company in New York City before opening a clothing and tailoring business of his own in the same city. A measure of his wealth is evident in the fact that he purchased a house on this site for £1,500.

As relations between the British and their American cousins continued to deteriorate, Mulligan was extremely active in the anti-British agitation in New York City. In January 1770, three months before the Boston Massacre, he reputedly was one of the "Liberty Boys" who fought with British troops in New York. In July 1776 he and Captain Isaac Sears led the mob that destroyed the famous bronze statue of King George III on Bowling Green.

Mulligan's most famous role during the revolutionary struggle, however, was as a "confidential agent" (spy) for General George Washington. In 1779 Mulligan informed the American commander-in-chief that the British general Sir Henry Clinton intended to send 300 infantry to intercept Washington as he led his men through Connecticut on their way to Newport, Rhode Island. Mulligan later helped frustrate another attempt to seize Washington when he overheard a British officer in his shop boast that Washington would be a captive "before another day." Mulligan immediately ran to the wharf and dispatched an African American with a warning to the American general. In addition, sometime before April 1781 Mulligan warned Washington that he and the governors of New Jersey and New York were the targets of an assassination plot. In acknowledging the warning, the commander-in-chief wrote that "I shall take precautions on the occasion, as appear to me necessary." Mulligan's activities prompted the suspicion of the turncoat Benedict Arnold, who believed that the Irishman was a spy for Washington. Arnold arrested and court-martialed Mulligan but failed to secure a conviction.

¶ **High Bridge (Aqueduct Bridge),** across the Harlem River at 174th Street, Midtown Manhattan.

Erected in 1842, this bridge was designed by Father Thomas Levins, a scientist, architect, and engineer from Drogheda, Ireland.

Levins had studied at Stonyhurst College in England before joining the Society of Jesus and coming to the United States in 1822. After teaching mathematics and natural philosophy at Georgetown College in the District of Columbia for three years, he left the Jesuits but not the priesthood. In the meantime, he had earned a reputation as a theologian, a mineralogist, and a lapidary and was twice appointed to the board of examiners of cadets at the U.S. Military Academy at West Point. By 1825 he was serving in the New York City diocese, but nine years later he was suspended during a controversy with Bishop DuBois. It was probably after this unpleasantness that Levins was employed as an engineer on the Croton Aqueduct and designed High Bridge.

Sometime during his career Levins served as editor and writer for *The Green Banner*. The purpose of this early Irish newspaper was "to recreate, to instruct, and to enlighten," and its motto was "Let all the ends thou aimst at be Thy Country's, thy God's, and Truth's." Levins used the pen name "Fergus McAlpin" and took the lead in attacking the Calvinist ministers who had played a part in writing the hoax *The Awful Disclosures of Maria Monk*. Eventually reinstated to the active ministry by *Bishop John Hughes, he served as pastor of old St. Patrick's Cathedral between Mott and Mulberry streets.

¶ Holy Cross Cemetery, 3620 Tilden Avenue, Brooklyn.

Among the cemetery's "permanent inhabitants" are Irish Americans James "Diamond Jim" Brady and James Fitzsimmons and Irish native William R. Grace.

• To prepare for his new job as a railroad equipment salesman, the young James Brady bought three hand-tailored black suits and a diamond ring, the first of many "sparklers" that earned him his nickname. (In time even his garter clasps and underwear buttons were gems.) His hospitality and gregariousness brought him increasing sales commissions, which, with investments in the railroads and other speculative ventures, were the basis of his formidable fortune. (In 1896 he won $180,000 after betting that McKinley would be elected president.)

Although he never drank anything stronger than orangeade, Brady's gastronomical feats were legendary (e.g., consuming six dozen oysters for a snack). Warned by his doctor to diet and exercise, Brady went through the motions on a gold-plated, diamond-studded bicycle. After a successful kidney stone operation, he donated $220,000 to establish a urological clinic named for himself at Johns Hopkins University in Baltimore. The operation also yielded rumors: one that he had paid a widow $200,000 for her husband's stomach, and another that he could now eat only grass because of his newly implanted cow's stomach.

Whatever the case, by 1916 Brady's gastric ulcers, diabetes, heart disease, and kidney problems were so severe that he moved to Atlantic City to await death – but in a $1,000-a-week suite which reflected the grand style that was his trademark. Not long before he died, he bought a $6,400 "diamondized" pair of glasses for his dog, and in his will he remembered his friends with thirty sets of "sparklers" valued at $1 million.

• [See entries for Fitzsimmons and Grace elsewhere.]

¶ Horace Greeley Statue, Greeley Square, between West 32nd and West 33rd streets, Midtown Manhattan.

This bronze statue of *Horace Greeley, the editor of the *New York Tribune* in the mid nineteenth century, was sculpted by *Alexander Doyle.

In 1848, at a mass meeting of the Friends of Ireland in New York City, Greeley claimed that the immigration of thousands of Irish into America each year gave the United States the right to comment on Britain's policy toward its island colony. He particularly refuted the British charge that defects in the Irish character were responsible for the appalling state of the island by stressing the hard work which the Irish immigrants had contributed to America. He even questioned the very basis of Britain's claim upon Ireland: "In confessing that they know not how to make the Irish people contented, peaceful, prosperous and happy, [English] statesmen admit that they have not the ability to govern Ireland, and therefore have no moral right to persist in this attempt."

Fifteen years later an editorial in the *Tribune* commented on the upcoming gubernatorial race: "The nomination of Fernando Wood and [John] Hoffman, neither of whom has a drop of Irish blood in his veins, for Mayor of a city, three-fourths of whose Democratic voters are Irish, is an insult to the honor of the Old Sod . . . . The Irish vote in New York is enough to elect two Mayors. . . . Nominate an Irishman, elect an Irishman, and then, when you call upon him in City Hall, you've got an Irish Mayor as sure as there's never a snake nor a toad in Ireland."

¶ Hugh O'Neil Store Site, Avenue of the Americas, between 21st and 22nd streets.

In 1876, when Hugh O'Neil opened his department store formerly on this site, New York's working class customers were treated to a relatively new phenomenon – a flashy public relations-oriented salesman who was out to top all competitors' prices. Known as "The Fighting Irishman of Sixth Avenue," O'Neil lassoed his customers with loss-leaders and beat the competition by undercutting their prices and providing delivery service. (He was particularly proud of his fleet of delivery wagons.) Despite his keen mercantile sense, he was a religiously devout man beloved by his employees. He took special care that they observed their religious faith, and he let them take time off from work to attend to those duties.

¶ Hunter College, 68th Street and Park Avenue, Midtown Manhattan.

Formerly a teacher training institution, this city college was founded in 1869, largely through the influence of Thomas Hunter, a native of Ardglass, County Down, Ireland, who served as president of the school until 1902.

While still in his native land, Hunter became a teacher at age eighteen but was quickly labeled *persona non grata* because of his political views and his involvement with the "Young Ireland" movement. After writing newspaper articles supporting Irish independence and expressing his views about the Established Church and the Anglo-Irish tie, he found it prudent to leave the country. After arriving in New York City in 1850, he began a career that made his name a byword in educational circles. Not yet nineteen and possessed of little money and only a box of books, he accepted employment as a drawing teacher.

Within seven years, however, Hunter had risen to the principalship of Public School 35 and proceeded to establish the school's reputation for scholarship and discipline. He later used his influence to support adult education, teacher training programs, tenure for teachers, and an end to corporal punishment. In 1866 he created the first evening high school in New York City and eventually campaigned for the creation of secondary schools for girls in the city.

¶ **Ireland House,** 1A Fifth Avenue, Greenwich Village.

This renovated townhouse serves as the focal point of New York University's Irish and Irish-American Studies curriculum. Programs at the center include lectures, seminars, films, and performances.

Ireland House was made possible through the generosity of Lewis Glucksman, an N.Y.U. alumnus and faculty member, and his wife, Loretta Brennan Glucksman, a member of the arts and science board of overseers at the university. Mrs. Glucksman, who traces her ancestry to counties Donegal and Leitrim, was named president of the American Ireland Fund in 1995.

At the dedication ceremonies in April 1993, an honorary degree was conferred on Irish Prime Minister Albert Reynolds, while presidential medals were granted to a number of Irish personalities: actor Cyril Cusack, theatrical producer Noel Pearson, actress Geraldine Fitzgerald, author Seamus Heaney, actress Maureen O'Hara, flutist James Galway, and Sister Stanislaus Kennedy (founder of a service organization for Dublin's homeless).

§ Phone: 212-757-3318.

¶ **James Stranahan Statue,** Prospect Park, Brooklyn.

A statue of James Stranahan, the chief founder of Prospect Park, stands at the Grand Army Plaza entrance to the park. The bronze likeness was sculpted by Frederick MacMonnies and was dedicated in 1891.

Born in Peterboro, New York, Stranahan was of Scotch-Irish stock and eventually became a successful railroad contractor. He was an outspoken advocate of the Greater New York plan, a proposal that involved the loss of Brooklyn's identity and its consolidation with New York City.

¶ James Walker House, 6 St. Luke's Place. Private.

This was once the home of James "Jimmy" Walker, the *bon vivant* mayor of New York City and the son of an Irish immigrant carpenter from County Kilkenny.

Before entering politics, Walker had achieved minor success as a Tin Pan Alley songwriter, known for his lyrics to sentimental numbers like "Kiss All the Girls for Me" and "Will You Love Me in December as You Do in May?" Even after his election to the state legislature and the mayor's office, he continued to frequent the world of vaudeville, gambling casinos, and night clubs. While in the New York Assembly, he sponsored legislation for a forty-hour work week for women and children and for the legalization of Sunday baseball. He also attacked the Ku Klux Klan, Prohibition, and the censorship that accompanied the Red Scare after World War I.

His tenure as mayor (1926-1932) was generally unexceptional, except for its corruption and his affair with an English actress. An official investigation of his administration revealed at least two embarrassing facts: the existence of a safe deposit box taken out in his name and containing at one time $750,000 in cash, and his reception of $300,000 in stock profits from men who did business with the city. After being divorced by the woman for whom he had left his first wife, Walker experienced a moral and religious transformation that brought him back to Catholicism. "The glamor of other days I have found to be worthless tinsel, and all the allure of the world just so much seduction and deception," he confessed. "I now have found in religion and repentance the happiness and joy that I sought elsewhere in vain."

¶ The James J. Walker Park is located near Hudson and West Houston streets.

¶ John Finley Walk, near 81st Street, over East River Drive, Midtown Manhattan.

This promenade is appropriately named for John Houston Finley, a pedestrian *extraordinaire* whose perambulations throughout New York were legendary.

Descended from the Reverend James Finley, who had emigrated from Ireland in 1734, the latter-day Finley was born in Illinois in 1863 and lived an extremely multifaceted career. After completing graduate work in economics, history, and politics at Johns Hopkins University, he became the secretary of a state charitable organization. It was from this latter vantage point that he became an outspoken advocate of private and public efforts to provide for the ill and the needy. Named at twenty-eight to the presidency of Knox College in Galesburg, Illinois, he went on to accept, in rapid succession, the editorship of *Harper's Weekly*, a chair in politics at Princeton, the presidency of the City College of New York, and the position of state commissioner of education. In 1921 he began an association of almost two decades with the *New York Times*, eventually as editor-in-chief. In the meantime he remained active as a leader in the Boy Scouts of America, the state commission for the blind, and the Red Cross commission to Palestine and the Near East.

Finley achieved additional fame by his passion for perambulating. Believing that "a good walk clears the mind and stimulates thinking," he regularly walked to work until past seventy years of age, and every year on his birthday he walked the thirty-two-mile circuit around Manhattan Island. Once when he missed the last train from Princeton, New Jersey, he walked from there to New York City. On another occasion he covered seventy-two miles by shanks' mare in a single day. The French in the Heart of America, one of eight books which he wrote, was inspired by a long tour in which he followed – mostly on foot – the routes of the French explorers in the Great Lakes and the Mississippi River regions.

¶ **John Street Methodist Church,** 44 John Street, between William and Nassau streets, Lower Manhattan.

The present structure is located on the site of the first Methodist church in America, erected in 1768 by Irish Methodists under the leadership of Philip Embury.

Although descended from Palatine Protestants who had fled the persecution of Louis XIV, Embury was probably born in Ballingrane, County Limerick, Ireland, about 1728. As a youngster he was educated by both German and English schoolmasters and was apprenticed to a carpenter. When Methodist preachers appeared in Limerick in 1749, he was attracted by their message and three years later underwent a religious experience: "the Lord shone into my soul a glimpse of his redeeming love, being an earnest of my redemption in Christ Jesus."

In 1760 Embury joined a group of emigrants who sailed for New York. There he found work as a carpenter and as a teacher in a school on Little Queen Street. His earlier religious enthusiasm seems to have waned, however, until a friend's indignation over cardplaying by her fellow Palatines caused him to attempt their moral reformation. "Philip," said the friend, "you must preach to us, or we shall go to Hell, and God will require our blood at your hands." Embury soon took up preaching, initially in his own home and then in Wesley Chapel, the first church on this site.

§ Open Monday, Wednesday, Friday noon-4. Phone: 212-269-0014.

¶ **Josiah Porter Statue,** Van Cortlandt Park, the Bronx.

This statue of General Josiah Porter was sculpted by *William Clark Noble.

❡ Judson Memorial Church, 55 Washington Square and Thompson Street.

A marble relief on the south wall follows a design by *Augustus Saint-Gaudens, although it was executed by Herbert Adams.

❡ Margaret Corbin Commemorative Plaque, Margaret Corbin Plaza and Drive, 183rd Street and Fort Washington Avenue, Upper Manhattan.

Erected in 1909, this large stone monument bears the legend: "On this hill-top stood Fort Tryon, the northern out-work of Fort Washington. Its gallant defence against the Hessian troops by the Maryland and Virginia regiment 16 November 1776 was shared by Margaret Corbin, the first American woman to take a soldier's part in the war for liberty."

Corbin was the daughter of a Scotch-Irish pioneer in western Pennsylvania. When her husband, John Corbin, enlisted in the Pennsylvania Artillery, she accompanied him into battle, serving, most likely, as cook, nurse, and laundress for the men. At the battle of Fort Washington in 1776, Margaret took her husband's place after he was struck down by attacking Hessians. She fought with "distinguished bravery" until she in turn was

Margaret Corbin Plaque.

hit by grapeshot that tore away one of her arms. A monument marks her grave near the Old Cadet Chapel at the U.S. Military Academy at West Point [*q.v.*].

¶ **Mathew Brady Studio Site,** Broadway and Fulton Street.

A plaque marks the site of the photographic studio which *Mathew Brady established near here in 1842. He and his assistants later seared the nation's conscience with photographs of the Civil War that belied earlier romantic notions about war. (See Mathew Brady Photo Studio, District of Columbia.)

¶ **Matthew C. Perry House,** Quarters A, U.S. Naval Facility, Brooklyn.

This frame clapboard building was the residence of *Matthew C. Perry while he served as commander of the New York Navy Yard from 1841 to 1843. Perry was famous for opening up Japan to American trade in the mid 1840s. (See Newport, Rhode Island.)

¶ **McSorley's Old Ale House,** 15 East 7th Street.

Founded by *John McSorley in 1854, this famous New York watering hole has been immortalized in art (*A Mug of Ale at McSorley's* by John Sloan, 1913) and literature (*McSorley's Wonderful Saloon* by Joseph Mitchell).

¶ **Metropolitan Museum of Art,** 5th Avenue and 82nd Street.

The museum's vast collection includes *The Last Moments of John Brown* and *Jerusalem the Golden*, among the best-known works of the Irish-born painter Thomas Hovenden. The former painting is an accurate depiction of the famous abolitionist's death, as described in the second stanza of "Brown of Ossawatomie" by John Greenleaf Whittier:

> John Brown of Ossawatomie, they led him out to die;
> And lo! a poor slave-mother with her little child press nigh.
> Then the bold, blue eye grew tender, and the old harsh face
>   grew mild,
> As he stooped between the jeering ranks and kissed the
>   negro's child.

Hovenden was born in County Cork in 1840 but was orphaned at the age of six. As a teenager he served an apprenticeship to a carver and gilder, who expressed his confidence in the boy's talent by sending him to the Cork School of Design. He later studied at the National Academy of Design in New York and then at the Ecole des Beaux-Arts in Paris.

Hovenden's first painting of note was a scene from the French Revolution, depicting the efforts of a family to protect itself during the Reign of Terror by casting bullets and sharpening its swords. Known as *Breton Interior of 1793*, this work established Hovenden's reputation with a European audience. Meanwhile, his numerous depictions of African-American life betrayed an interest in that suffering race. He met an untimely death at the age of fifty-five, however, when he was killed while unsuccessfully trying to save a young girl from an oncoming railroad train.

§ Open Tuesday-Sunday 9:30-5:15 (also Friday and Saturday 5:15-8:45). Closed January 1, Thanksgiving, and December 25. Fee. Phone: 212-535-7710.

¶ Michael Corcoran Burial Site, Calvary Cemetery, Laurel Hill Boulevard, Woodside.

A new headstone erected in 1989 by the Sligo Mens' Association marks the grave of Michael Corcoran, the commander of the "Fighting 69th" New York State Militia, one of the three units which initially formed the famed Irish Brigade.

The headstone is inscribed as follows: "In Memory of Brigadier General Michael Corcoran, Irish Patriot, American Soldier, Catholic Citizen. Born at Carrowkeel, Sligo, Ireland, Sept. 21, 1827. Col. 69th N.Y. State Militia 1859-1861. Commanding the Regiment in Volunteer Service of U.S. Organizer of Corcoran's Legion N.Y. Volunteers. Died in the Service of the U.S. Dec. 22, 1863." Corcoran's wife, Elizabeth, is also buried here.

¶ Michael Hogan Tablet, Grace Church, 10th Street and Broadway, Lower Manhattan.

A memorial plaque inside the church honors Michael Hogan, an Irish sea captain, merchant, and philanthropist: "Sacred to the Memory of Michael Hogan. During many years a resident of this City. Born at Stone-Hall in the County of Clare, Ireland, September 29, A.D. 1766. In early manhood a bold and successful navigator and discoverer, in seas then almost unknown; In mature age, a prosperous merchant; The decline of life was not unmarked by vicissitudes of fortune; But prosperity did not elate, nor could adversity subdue his firm and constant spirit. Each quarter of the Globe, bore witness to his enterprise, and its success. Regretted by his friends, respected by his enemies, a life of stainless integrity closed at the City of Washington, March 26, A.D. 1833, Aetatis 67." Claremont Avenue [*q.v.*] in Upper Manhattan is named for his mansion house.

¶ Michael J. Quill Corner, on the southeast corner of Broadway and West 240th Street, the Bronx.

Dedicated in 1992, this memorial honors Michael J. Quill, the longtime president of the Transport Workers Union.

Born in County Kerry, Ireland, in 1905, Quill came from a family that actively supported the Irish Republican Army during the 1916 Irish Rebellion and the civil war that followed. As a youngster he was a member of *Fianna Eireann*, the Republican Boy Scout movement, and by age fifteen had joined the I.R.A.

In 1933 Quill immigrated to New York City, where he was one of a number of former I.R.A. members interested in organizing the transit workers there. Quill was a founder of the Transport Workers Union and served as its president for more than thirty years. By 1945 the union numbered 45,000 members in New York, Philadelphia, Chicago, and Brooklyn. Twenty years later it counted 135,000 among its ranks.

Quill usually supported the position of the Communist Party on political and labor-related issues and was a leader in some Communist-led organizations. In 1948, however, he broke with the party and thereafter purged the T.W.U.'s leadership of Communists. The longtime labor leader died in 1966, soon after calling a general strike against the New York City transit system, a move which paralyzed the city.

¶ **Moylan Place,** 125th Street, between Broadway and Amsterdam Avenue, Upper Manhattan.

This square was named for Stephen Moylan, a native of Cork, Ireland, and aide-de-camp to General George Washington during the American Revolution. (See Moylan Park, Philadelphia, Pennsylvania.)

¶ **Old St. Patrick's Cathedral,** 268 Mulberry Street, Lower Manhattan.

Consecrated in 1815, this church was the second in the United States to be dedicated to the patron saint of Ireland. Originally the largest church in the city, it remained the cathedral of the New York archdiocese until 1879, when the new cathedral on Fifth Avenue was completed.

The most historic event which occurred in Old St. Patrick's Cathedral was the final ceremony connected with the conferring of the cardinalate on *Archbishop John McCloskey, the first American Roman Catholic prelate to be so honored. The *New York Times* on April 28, 1875, described the pageantry of the installation ceremony in surprisingly sympathetic detail: "The imposition of the biretta on his Eminence, the newly-made Cardinal, was surrounded with all the elaborate pageantry which the Church of Rome mingles so frequently with its religious ceremonies. Everything that could give to the occasion, pomp, and lustre was rigidly carried out, and the ceremony was the most gorgeous ever connected with the ministrations of the Roman Catholic Church in this country. . . . The gold and scarlet decorations flashed, thurifers swung their censers, and sent up clouds of incense before the Altar, the jeweled mitres and rich vestments of the Bishops and Archbishops gave an additional lustre to the sanctuary, and the grand organ pealed through the cathedral the measures of a jubilant religion."

Earlier during his episcopacy in New York City, McCloskey had taken at least two controversial positions. Although a strong supporter of Irish nationhood, in 1866 he expressed his opposition to the violent tactics of the Fenians and warned New York Catholics against joining or supporting the revolutionary group. Later, while attending the First Vatican Council in Rome, he opposed the council's intention to promulgate the doctrine of papal infallibility. While he intellectually accepted such a doctrine, he believed that its formal definition would be ill-advised, causing a backlash of anti-Catholic sentiment throughout the world. Nevertheless, he voted for the definition in July 1870.

So highly regarded was McCloskey that following his death in 1885 the *New York Sun* editorialized: "His learning, his piety, his humility, his truly Christian zeal, earned for him universal respect which will be to-day manifested as his body is carried to the tomb. The first American cardinal has died at a time when all Christians are ready to honor his memory as that of a man who has done measureless service in the cause of religion, good morals, and humanity . . . . Protestants and Catholics will join in sincerely mourning the first American cardinal as a Christian hero lost."

¶ **Peter Cooper Statue,** Cooper Union Institute, 4th Avenue and 7th Street, Lower Manhattan.

Erected in 1897, this bronze statue by *Augustus Saint-Gaudens honors the famous inventor, manufacturer, and philanthropist who in 1859 opened an institute to provide the working people of the city with free instruction in the practical arts and sciences.

¶ **Police Academy Museum,** 235 East 20th Street, Lower Manhattan.

This museum is of interest to Hibernophiles because of its exhibits about "New York's finest." Many members of the force were Irish born, especially prior to 1859, when American citizenship became a prerequisite for the job.

As early as 1815 the city had a police marshal named *John McManus, while as late as 1888 the Irish constituted 28 percent of the city's police force even though that ethnic group comprised only 16 percent of the population. Even in 1933, 36 percent of the force was either native Irish or Irish American. Thomas Byrnes, one native-Irish officer, became nationally known for his successful investigations and for his work *Professional Criminals of America*. In 1918 Irish-born Ellen O'Grady became the country's first female deputy commissioner of police.

§ Open Monday-Friday 9-3. Closed major holidays. Phone: 212-477-9753.

¶ **Provincetown Playhouse,** 133 MacDougal Street, Greenwich Village.

This former stable is where *Eugene O'Neill began his New York stage career, when in 1917 he and others established this theater and presented many of his plays during the following decade. (See New London, Connecticut.)

¶ **Richmondtown Restoration,** east of I-278 via Richmond Road/ Clove Road exit to 441 Clarke Avenue, Staten Island.

Richmondtown Restoration is a 100-acre village that recreates 300 years of Staten Island history. On the property is the Kruser-Finlay House, purchased in 1875 by *Patrick Finlay and his wife, Catherine. Succeeding members of the family lived here until Mary Finlay donated it to the city of New York.

§ Museum open July-August, Wednesday-Friday 10-5, Saturday-Sunday 1-5; rest of the year, Wednesday-Sunday 1-5. Closed January 1, Thanksgiving, and December 25. Fee. Phone: 718-351-1611.

¶ **Robert F. Kennedy Bust,** in a park to the west of Cadman Plaza, Brooklyn.

This portrait bust of Robert F. Kennedy commemorates the slain presidential candidate, assassinated in Los Angeles in June 1968. (See Arlington National Cemetery, Arlington, Virginia, in *Irish America*, Volume 2.)

¶ **St. James Church,** 23 Oliver Street, Lower Manhattan.

Built in the 1820s to serve the Irish in the slums of the Five Points area, this church was the scene of the gathering which created the Ancient Order of Hibernians in America.

The A.O.H. was founded in 1836 to protect the Irish and their churches from anti-immigrant violence in New York City. Later during its history the organization strove to uphold the reputation of Irishmen from the "nefarious custom of criminals, pugilists, and the abandoned and submerged tenth of society adopting Irish names."

The A.O.H. also successfully fought the stereotype of the Irishman almost universally found in the American theater at the time. That image was described by Maurice Bourgeois in 1913: "The stage Irishman habitually bears the general name of Pat, Paddy, or Teague. He has an atrocious Irish brogue, perpetual jokes, blunder and bulls in speaking, and never fails to utter, by way of Hibernian seasoning, some wild screech, or oath of Gaelic origin, at every third word. . . . His hair is of a fiery red, he is rosy-cheeked, massive, and whiskey-loving. His face is one of simian bestiality, with an expression of diabolical archness written all over it. He wears a tall hat, with a clay pipe stuck in his face, an open collar shirt, a three-caped coat, kneebreeches, worsted stockings, and cockaded shoes. In his right hand he brandishes a stout blackthorn or sprig of shillelagh, and threatens to belabor therewith the daring person who will tread on the tail of his coat. For his main characteristics . . . are his swagger, his boisterousness, and his pugnacity. He is always ready with a challenge, always anxious to back a quarrel, and peerless for cracking skulls at Donnybrook Fair."

¶ The attendance of *Alfred E. Smith at St. James Elementary School across the street is commemorated by a plaque on the school door.

Smith was generally an indifferent student and preferred to perform in timely comedies and melodramas in the St. James parish hall. He was also known for his victories in speech contests and won a medal for elocution. (One of his favorite poems to recite was "Cohen on the Telephone.")

¶ **St. Malachy's Chapel,** 239 West 49th Street. Midtown Manhattan.

Located in the city's theater district, this famous chapel caters to actors and theatergoers alike. The chapel was named for a twelfth-century Irish monk who served as primate of Armagh in County Down. While on a papal mission to France, Malachy died at Clairvaux, with St. Bernard at his side.

§ Phone: 212-489-1340.

¶ **St. Mark's Church in the Bowery,** 2nd Avenue at 10th Street.

Although this historic Episcopal church is famous as the final resting place of Peter Stuyvesant, the last Dutch governor of New York, St. Mark's also has an important Irish connection. In the churchyard are buried the remains of Thomas Addis Emmet, one of Ireland's most famous political exiles, physicians, and lawyers. (See St. Paul's Chapel below.)

§ Open Monday-Friday 10-6. Phone: 212-674-6377.

¶ **St. Patrick's Cathedral,** 5th Avenue and 50th Street.

Now in the heart of Manhattan, St. Patrick's was originally dismissed as "Hughes' Folly" when it was begun by *Archbishop John Hughes on a site which critics said was too far out in the country. In 1858, when Hughes kicked off a fund-raising campaign by asking for 100 contributions of $1,000 each, he received 103 such gifts. This response allowed him to lay the cornerstone of a church which he hoped would be "worthy of God, worthy of the Catholic religion, and an honor to this great city." Dedicated in 1879, the new marble Gothic Revival cathedral took up a full city block, could seat 2,500 worshippers, and had cost $1.9 million. The church's spires and the Lady Chapel inside were added by *Archbishop Michael Corrigan.

The window over the entrance to the south transept of the church depicts eighteen scenes from the life of St. Patrick. Another window celebrating Ireland's principal patron saint is on the west wall.

Hughes and Corrigan are buried in the church, as are fellow Irish-American archbishops John Farley, Patrick Hayes, John McCloskey, Francis Spellman, and Terence Cooke.

§ Open daily 6:30 a.m.-8:45 p.m. Phone: 212-753-2261.

¶ **St. Paul's Chapel,** Broadway and Fulton Street, Lower Manhattan.

*Memorial in honor of
General Richard Montgomery,
on the façade of St. Paul's Chapel.*

Within the precincts of Manhattan's oldest house of worship are monuments in honor of three of the most famous Irish immigrants to America. A rather ornate memorial under the portico marks the grave of Richard Montgomery, while stone markers in the graveyard commemorate Thomas Addis Emmet and William MacNeven, both political exiles from their native land.

   • Richard Montgomery was born in County Donegal in 1737, the son of an Anglo-Irish father who represented Lifford in the Irish Parliament. After enlisting in the British army, the younger Montgomery served under Wolfe at the capture of Quebec in 1759. Although he sailed home after the French and Indian War, he returned to America in 1772, purchased a small estate along the Hudson River, and married into the family of Robert Livingston.

   At the outbreak of the Revolution, Montgomery sided with the patriots and was appointed brigadier general, accepting *Vox Populi* as *Vox Dei*: "The will of an oppressed people, compelled to choose between liberty and slavery, must be obeyed." Subsequently named America's first Irish general, he headed the American expeditionary force into Canada, taking Montreal on November 12, 1775, but failing in an attempted assault on Quebec on December 31. Montgomery died during the unsuccessful attempt and was denied "the poor courtesy of a coffin" by the British commander.

At the beginning of the new year, the Continental Congress ordered that a monument – the first in America to an Irishman – be erected in St. Paul's Church in memory of the fallen officer. In 1818 Montgomery's wife succeeded in obtaining possession of his remains, which were accordingly exhumed at Quebec and reburied within St. Paul's.

• Thomas Addis Emmet was born in Cork in 1764 and followed careers in both medicine and the law. After graduating from Trinity College in Dublin, he earned a doctoral degree in medicine from the University of Edinburgh and returned to the Irish capital to practice. When his brother Robert, a member of the Irish bar, was executed by the British for his part in an abortive uprising in Dublin, however, the young doctor took up the study of law.

After achieving considerable renown as a lawyer, Emmet increasingly became involved with political issues. His legal defense of a member of the United Irishmen on a charge of treason became a *cause célèbre*, all the more so when Emmet took the society's oath at the end of an impassioned speech before the court. A government informer described Emmet as "the most dangerous man in Ireland, from the standpoint of zeal, bearing, power of speech, and ability." After becoming a member of the United Irishmen's executive committee, Emmet was arrested as a conspirator in 1798 and was subsequently jailed in a number of prisons. Finally released on condition that he leave the Empire, he and his family progressed through Europe before landing in New York City in 1804.

Once in New York, Emmet was granted the right to practice law, despite strong opposition from Federalist judges and lawyers, who considered him and other refugees as "wild Irishmen come to stir up sedition." His first appearance at the New York bar was as counsel for a society that sought the freedom of African-American slaves. In 1812 he was appointed attorney general of New York, and three years later he argued the first of several cases before the U.S. Supreme Court. The most famous – *Gibbons v. Ogden* – found him matched against Daniel Webster, who later graciously remarked that his opponent had brought to America the erudition and eloquence of the Irish bar. The political *émigré* suffered a stroke while engaged in the trial of a case involving Snug Harbor, a home for retired sailors. Emmet's admirers were quick to point out that his first speech at the American bar had been in defense of a slave and that his last effort in a court of law had been on behalf of a charitable institution.

In 1832 Emmet's "sympathizing countrymen" erected the monument which stands in St. Paul's churchyard. One side of the thirty-foot obelisk is inscribed with a short tribute in Gaelic. The English translation reads: "He contemplated invaluable benefits for the land of his birth; he gave *eclat* to the land of his death; and received in return her love and admiration." On the side of the monument facing Broadway is a bas-relief medallion of Emmet, below which is an inscription in English, partially quoted here: "In memory of THOMAS ADDIS EMMET who exemplified in his conduct, and adorned by his integrity, the policy and principles of the United Irishmen – 'To forward a brotherhood of affection, a community of rights, an identity of interests, and a union of power among Irishmen of every religious persuasion, as the only means of Ireland's chief good, an impartial and adequate representation in an Irish Parliament.' For this, (Mysterious fate of virtue!), exiled from his native land. In America, the land of freedom, he found a second country, which paid his love by reverencing his genius. . . ." Below this inscription is an American eagle supported by two hands – one Irish and the other American – clasped and crossing over an unstrung Irish harp. The lengthy inscription is repeated in Latin on a third side of the obelisk. Emmet is buried in the churchyard of St. Mark's in The Bowery.

• A contemporary of Emmet's, William MacNeven was born in County Galway of a family whose ancestors had been expelled by Cromwell from their landed estates in Ulster and had been forced to settle in Connaught. Because Catholics in Ireland still suffered under educational disabilities which had not applied to the Protestant Emmet, for example, the young MacNeven moved to the Continent to study medicine at the universities of Prague and Vienna.

After returning to Dublin to begin a career in medicine, MacNeven became involved in dangerous political activities. His work as a member of the United Irishmen led to imprisonment before his release in 1802 under sentence of banishment. While in France, the Irish exile still fostered unrealistic hopes of support from Napoleon in a projected invasion of Ireland. He served in the Irish Brigade of the French army for two years before embarking for New York City, where he arrived on July 4, 1805.

From the first, MacNeven threw himself into his medical practice. After giving a series of clinical lectures at the New York Hospital, he was elected professor of obstetrics in the College of Physicians and Surgeons. During his academic tenure he published a number of scientific studies, one of them on the atomic theory of chemistry. For a time he was coeditor of the *New York Medical and Philosophical Journal and Review* and was elected to the American Philosophical Society in 1823. He subsequently established the forerunner of Rutgers Medical School.

Despite his success in America, MacNeven never wavered in his concern for Ireland and her people. To help newly arrived immigrants, he wrote and published a pamphlet with pertinent advice and joined with Thomas Emmet in establishing a free employment agency. He also created an organization called the Friends of Ireland, with which he sought American support for Catholic Emancipation in his homeland. As Emmet had supported efforts to get Congress to sell public lands in Illinois to Irish immigrants, so MacNeven promoted Texas as a place where his "poor

Irish countrymen . . . would at once possess a quantum of ground, power, and wealth, that would give them a real home, consideration, and happiness." MacNeven is buried on the Riker Farm, Astoria, Queens, New York.

§ Open Monday-Friday 9-3, Sunday 8-4. Closed holidays. Phone: 212-602-0800.

¶ **St. Peter's Church,** Barclay and Church Streets, Lower Manhattan.

Although the present church dates from 1836, it replaced an earlier structure built in 1786, the year after the first Roman Catholic congregation in New York City was incorporated.

The first pastor of St. Peter's was Father Charles Whelan (Friar Maurice), a Capuchin priest who had been born in Ireland in 1741 but who had escaped the Irish penal laws by spending much of his life in France. In 1780, however, he joined the French fleet as a chaplain and accompanied it to Newport, Rhode Island, as it prepared to assist the Americans in their revolution against Great Britain. After being imprisoned by the British for a time, he arrived in New York City in October 1784.

Whelan was immediately struck by the desperate situation of his parishioners. He lamented, for example, "That Catholics here are very poor, but very zealous, being for the most part Irish. They are not able to build a chapel, nor even to buy a place for saying Mass, only a Portuguese gentleman has allowed us a part of his house for that purpose." He later wrote to the papal nuncio in Paris about the polyglot nature of his parishioners: "It is necessary for a priest in this place to know at least Irish, English, French and Dutch, since our congregation is composed of people of these nationalities as also of Portuguese and Spaniards." After serving as pastor for two years, Whelan became a missionary in Kentucky but by 1790 had returned to New York State. He finally settled at Bohemia Manor, near Warwick, Maryland, [q.v.], where he died in 1806.

One of the earliest members and benefactors of St. Peter's parish was Dominick Lynch, a successful business entrepreneur who had immigrated to America from Galway, Ireland, in 1785. He contributed generously to the construction of the church and even sough financial support for the project from his relatives in Galway. He was also one of the five signers of the famous address to George Washington in 1790 in which he congratulated the newly inaugurated president on behalf of the Catholics of the nation. Lynch and his wife – whom he had married in Dublin before coming to New York – had thirteen children. He died in 1825 and is buried in the family vault at St. Peter's.

• One of the memorials in St. Peter's Church is a tablet commemorating the life and career of *Governor Thomas Dongan. (See Albany, New York.)

• In 1988 a plaque in honor of Father John Drumgoole was placed on the rectory of St. Peter's Church. Born in Abbeylara, County Longford,

Ireland, in 1816, the immigrant priest was known as the "Shepherd of the Homeless Newsboys." The memorial tablet is inscribed with a summary of the priest's career: "In 1871 Father Drumgoole became the resident chaplain of the Saint Vincent de Paul Newsboys' Home at 53 Warren Street near Printing House Square, the location of New York City's great newspapers. In 1881 the Mission of the Immaculate Virgin was established for homeless children on Lafayette Street. He founded Mount Loretto on Staten Island in 1852 and it became the largest child caring institution in the United States. It stands today as a monument to Father Drumgoole."

¶ **St. Raymond's Cemetery,** Tremont Avenue, between Waterbury Street and Bruckner Expressway, the Bronx. Make inquiries at Lafayette Street and Randall Road.

Two famous Irish Americans are buried here: "Typhoid Mary" Mallon and Father Francis Duffy, the chaplain of the "Fighting 69th" Regiment.

• Mary Mallon was the first known carrier of typhoid fever in the United States. Born in Ireland about 1868, she worked as a cook after coming to New York and was linked to at least six outbreaks of typhoid fever in the state. The first episode occurred in 1904, when the fever was traced to a house in Oyster Bay in which she had been a cook. Fleeing from the authorities, she was not traced until three years later, when she was found in the kitchen of a Park Avenue home. When it was proved that she was a typhoid carrier – "a human culture tube," according to one physician – she was committed to a hospital on North Brother Island.

Although Mallon was released in 1910 on condition that she never accept a job handling food again, four years later she was found working at a sanitarium in New Jersey when an epidemic broke out there. Eluding authorities once again, she was employed at a maternity hospital when twenty-five of its employees were stricken with typhoid. In 1915 she was permanently committed to a hospital, where she remained until her death in 1938. In all, she infected fifty-three people, three of whom died.

• [See Father Duffy Statue and Square in New York City.]

¶ **Shea Stadium,** 126th Street and Roosevelt Avenue, Flushing, Queens.

The home of the New York Mets, this familiar landmark is named for William Shea, the man most responsible for the return of a National League baseball team to New York City.

Of Irish and French ancestry, Shea developed an interest in baseball as a child, when his father took him to see the games of such semiprofessional New York teams as the Farmers, the Bushwicks, and the Ivanhoes. In high school, when his Spanish teacher began to give out passes to Yankee games as a way of encouraging her students to study, the young Shea's interest in the language suddenly increased. Through his zealous application he was able to attend the Yankees' games at the Polo Grounds on a regular basis, quite a treat for a youngster who had never before seen a major league game.

Shea was not without his own athletic abilities, however. In high school he played baseball and basketball and won a sports scholarship to New York University, starring on the varsity lacrosse team. (He later played with one of the best non-collegiate lacrosse teams in the country.) After playing football for only a year at N.Y.U., the young college student won a four-year scholarship in that sport to Georgetown University, a break that allowed him to pursue a fifth year of law school.

Even during his subsequent legal career, Shea managed to maintain a professional association with baseball. One of the clients of the firm for which he worked was a trustee of the Brooklyn Dodgers, and it was through this connection that Shea became acquainted with *Walter O'Malley, the future owner of the Dodgers. In the 1930s Shea became an owner of the Long Island Indians, a minor league football team that served as a farm club for the Washington Redskins.

When both of New York City's National League baseball teams (the Dodgers and the Giants) moved to California in 1957, Shea was one of the most focal critics of the decisions. "No team here ever lost money. . . ," he commented at the time. "It was simply a question of making more money. The most flagrant violation of loyalty to one's fans I've ever seen." It was in this context that the mayor of New York appointed Shea to a city committee on baseball. From that vantage point Shea formed a short-lived third major league (the Continental League), a gambit that forced the other two major leagues to agree to expand from eight to ten teams. One of the new teams thus created was the New York Mets, who began play in 1962. In short order the New York City Council authorized construction of a new stadium at Flushing Meadow, the World's Fair site, and voted to name it after Shea. The new field was completed in 1964, at a cost of $25,500,000.

¶ **Shrine of Mother Elizabeth Ann Seton,** 7 State Street, Lower Manhattan.

Originally designed in the early nineteenth century as a private residence, this Federal-style mansion was later purchased by Charlotte Grace O'Brien, an Irish immigrant, who operated it as a settlement house for Irish immigrant girls in the 1880s. Known then as the Mission of Our Lady of the Rosary, it today serves as a shrine to Mother Seton, the first American-born canonized saint of the Catholic Church.

¶ **Sixty-Ninth Regiment Armory,** 68 Lexington Avenue, between East 25th Street and East 26th Street.

Since 1906 this armory complex has been the headquarters of the legendary "Fighting 69th," a unit of the New York National Guard which from its creation in 1851 was a predominantly Irish one. Although the

69th lost its distinctively Celtic cast after World War II, it still participates in New York City's annual St. Patrick's Day Parade. The armory displays exhibits on the history of the regiment between the Civil War and World War II.

During the long history of the 69th Regiment, three personalities stand out as preeminent. One of the unit's early officers, Colonel Michael Corcoran, was court-martialed for refusing to parade his men in front of the Prince of Wales during the royal's visit to New York City. Thomas Francis Meagher, like Corcoran a native of Ireland, commanded the regiment after its incorporation into the Irish Brigade during the Civil War. The 69th's most famous chaplain was *Father Francis Duffy, who served with the unit against the Mexican outlaw Pancho Villa and on the front lines in France after the American entry into the First World War. (See Michael Corcoran Burial Site and Father Duffy Statue, New York City; Gettysburg, Pennsylvania.)

§ Open Monday-Friday 8-4. Phone: 212-532-6013.

¶ **Songwriters' Hall of Fame,** formerly at 1 Times Square.

Although the Songwriters' Hall of Fame is currently without a permanent home, its list of honorees continues to grow. In addition to the well-known Irish-American songwriters George M. Cohan and Stephen Collins Foster, the Hall of Fame includes such lesser known men of Irish heritage as Patrick Gilmore and Chauncey Olcott.

• Born in County Galway, Ireland, Patrick Sarsfield Gilmore immigrated to Canada in 1848 with a military band but soon moved to Boston. There he opened a music store and organized Gilmore's Boston Band. At the outbreak of the Civil War, he and his musicians joined the Union army. While in New Orleans in 1864, he orchestrated a music festival of several massed bands and introduced the use of cannon fire to the musical score. During the war he composed several songs reflecting the fratricidal conflict: "Freedom on the Old Plantation," "Good News from Home," "The Spirit of the North," and "When Johnny Comes Marching Home."

In 1869 Gilmore presented the first of his gargantuan concert-festivals. To accommodate a chorus of 10,000 people, an orchestra of 1,000, six bands, and an audience commensurately large, the organizers of the five-day National Peace Jubilee in Boston constructed a 50,000-seat auditorium. This triumph was followed three years later by his World Peace Jubilee, also in Boston, to which he attracted international musicians (including Johann Strauss), an orchestra of 2,000, and a chorus ten times as large. During a performance of Verdi's "Anvil Chorus," 100 Boston firemen provided accompaniment on actual anvils. After this second *tour de force*, Gilmore and his band toured the United States, Canada, and Europe. He also composed *Columbia*, a choral work which he hoped would become a new national anthem.

• Chauncey Olcott was born of Irish parents in Buffalo, New York, in 1860 and early became associated with traveling companies of entertainers and minstrel shows. While in London, he obtained an Irish romantic role in a light opera, a break that inspired him to specialize in that kind of role. Once returned to America, he began a career in a succession of sentimental Irish comedies, including *The Irish Artist* (for which he wrote both the words and the music), *Edmund Burke*, and *The Minstrel of Clare*. He introduced American audiences to "Mother Machree" and "When Irish Eyes Are Smiling" (both of which he coauthored) and "My Wild Irish Rose," a composition of his own which appeared in *Romance of Athlone*. Two of his lesser-known airs are "Sweet Iniscara" and "Kate O'Donohue."
§ Phone: 212-221-1252.

¶ **Sullivan Street,** Greenwich Village.
This street was named for *General John Sullivan, one of George Washington's most famous officers during the Revolutionary War. (See Durham, New Hampshire.)

¶ **Theodore Roosevelt Birthplace National Historic Site,** 28 East 20th Street, between Park Avenue South and Broadway, Lower Manhattan.
Built in 1922, this four-story building is a replica of the house in which Theodore Roosevelt was born in 1858 and lived until age fifteen. Five rooms in the house have been refurnished with their original contents, while Roosevelt memorabilia are on display in the museum rooms. The most impressive piece of art work in the house is an equestrian statue of Roosevelt as a Rough Rider.
Assertions of Roosevelt's Irish ancestry rest partially upon his descent from John Barnwell, who came to America from County Meath, Ireland, in 1701. On his maternal side Roosevelt was descended from John Dunwoody, who emigrated from Londonderry, northern Ireland, in 1730 and settled in Chester County, Pennsylvania, before moving with his family to Georgia.
During Roosevelt's first term in the New York Assembly, he recorded his unflattering estimation of his Irish colleagues on a legislative committee: "The Chairman is an Irishman named Murphy, . . . a Fenian; he is a tall, stout man with a swollen, red face, a black moustache . . . and has had a long experience in politics – so that to undoubted pluck and a certain knowledge of parliamentary forms he adds a great deal of stupidity and a decided looseness of ideas as regards the 8th Commandment. Next comes John Shanley of Brooklyn, an Irishman, but born in America; much shrewder than Murphy and easier to get along with, being more Americanized, but fully as dishonest; . . . a Tammany Hall gentleman named McManus, a huge, fleshy, unutterably course and low brute who was for-

merly a prize fighter, at present keeps a low, drinking and dancing saloon, and is more than suspected of having begun life as a pickpocket."

Following his election to the presidency in 1904, however, Roosevelt was much more flattering in his estimation of the Irish electorate: "One of the things I am most pleased with in the recent election is that while I got, I think, a greater proportion of the Americans of Irish birth or parentage and of the Catholic religion than any previous Republican candidate, I got this proportion purely because they knew I felt in sympathy with them and in touch with them, and they and I had the same ideals and principles, and not by any demagogic appeals about creed or race, or by any demagogic attack upon England."

§ Open Wednesday-Sunday 9-5. Closed federal holidays. Fee. Phone: 212-260-1616.

❡ Theodore Roosevelt Memorial, in front of the American Museum of Natural History, Central Park West, Midtown Manhattan.

This sixteen-foot bronze group of *Theodore Roosevelt with an Indian is one of the largest equestrian statues in the world. The figures on either side of the horse represent Africa and America. This Native American was probably the model for the profile on the Indian-head nickel.

❡ Trinity Church, Broadway at Wall Street, Lower Manhattan.

Although the congregation at this church has always been of the Anglican or Episcopal denomination, during the colonial period it was attended by many Irish Catholics because no Catholic church existed in the city until 1786. One such Irish Catholic parishioner was John Leary, who both during and after the Revolution kept a livery stable on Leary (now Cortland) Street. Known as "the jockey of the day," he wrote an article on horse breeding which appeared in the *New York Mercury* under the byline "a lover of the turf." Although Leary seems to have attended Trinity Church regularly, once a year he journeyed to Philadelphia to attend mass at a Catholic church there.

Trinity churchyard contains the graves of many Irish and Irish Americans, both the famous and the less well known. Among them are the following five:

• The first Irish person to be buried here was Catherine O'Brien, the wife of the dissolute New York governor Edward Hyde, Viscount Cornbury. O'Brien, who was born in County Clare in 1673, married Cornbury at age fifteen and accompanied him to New York when he was appointed governor of that colony in 1701. When she attended an Indian council in Albany with her husband, one of the River Indians presented her with an otter skin as a token of the tribe's high regard for her. In 1839, 133 years after her death, her coffin was discovered in the foundations of the church.

• Christopher Colles, an engineer and a gunnery instructor in the American army during the Revolution, first proposed the idea of building a canal to join the Hudson River to the Great Lakes. (The notion was taken up and successfully promoted as the Erie Canal by *DeWitt Clinton.) Colles had earlier suggested that New York City abandon its dependence on springs and wells by building a system of reservoirs and piping throughout the city. He also conceived and developed the first semaphoric telegraph system for the United States and was the author of numerous scientific essays and pamphlets.

• Robert Fulton, the famous inventor and advocate of steam navigation, is honored with an outdoor memorial erected in 1901 by the American Society of Mechanical Engineers. (His remains are interred in the Livingston family vault, Section North 7.) Fulton's American ancestor probably came from Kilkenny, Ireland, and by 1735 had settled in Lancaster, Pennsylvania. As a youngster Fulton displayed an inventive turn of mind, devising a rocket and a hand-powered paddle wheel. He later developed a "plunging boat" or submarine, which he actually demonstrated to the French government as a way to destroy British warships. With Fulton himself aboard, the underwater device reached a depth of twenty-five feet and remained submerged for four and a half hours.

Fulton is more renowned for his efforts to promote the steamboat,

Robert Fulton Memorial.

however. After building and successfully operating a prototype in France in 1802, he launched the *Clermont* in New York City five years later. The ship, 133 feet long and eighteen wide, was powered by a steam engine that turned fifteen-foot side paddle wheels. The vessel's 150-mile cruise up the Hudson River in thirty-three hours prompted Fulton to say that "The power of propelling boats by steam is now fully proved." In partnership with Robert Livingston, Fulton subsequently demonstrated the economic viability of steam navigation.

• Hercules Mulligan, the famous spy for General George Washington, was a vestryman of Trinity Church from 1784 to 1787. After his death in 1825, he was buried here in the family vault of his wife, Elizabeth Sanders.

• The inscription on one of the tombstones in the churchyard memorializes one of the city's lesser known Irish: "James Woods / a native of Ireland / who died June 3d 1801 aged 46 years / Unseen to Mankind's view / An exile of Old Erin's true / His principles was [*sic*] just and good / And for his country's freedom stood."

§ Museum open Monday-Friday 9-11:45, Saturday 10-3:45, Sunday 11-3:45. Phone: 212-602-0800.

¶ **Union Square,** Broadway and 14th Street, Lower Manhattan.

In 1865 the Fenians held a convention in Philadelphia to draft a constitution creating an Irish Republic and providing for a congress and a president. The newly elected president established an Irish government in exile at the Fenians' headquarters in Union Square. Both the American flag and the Fenian flag – the latter emblazoned with a harp and a sunburst – flew from the building.

At the center of Union Square is the Independence Flagstaff, erected in 1926 as a memorial to Tammany Hall boss *Charles Murphy. The cost of the flagpole was defrayed from the $80,000 which the Tammany machine collected during the sesquicentennial of the signing of the Declaration of Independence. Although Tammany Hall dominated the political life of the city in the nineteenth century, it reached the height of its influence under Murphy in the next. The son of Irish immigrants, Murphy was the machine's absolute boss from 1902 to 1924 and was "responsible" for electing three mayors of the city and two governors of the state. Although he welcomed to Tammany Hall anyone who sought his help, he remained publicly aloof and generally unknown to all but his associates, for he never made speeches or gave interviews and, except for an early minor appointment, never held or sought political office.

¶ The Roundabout Theater, northeast of Union Square, at 100 East 17th Street, was formerly the headquarters of the Tammany Society.

¶ **United Nations Plaza,** 1st Avenue, between 42nd and 48th streets.

Three structures along 44th Street were designed between 1976 and 1987 by the architectural firm of *Kevin Roche, John Dinkeloo & Associates: One United Nations Plaza, a thirty-nine-story building which houses offices and hotel accommodations for U.N. personnel and delegates; Two United Nations Plaza, a companion glass and metal structure; and the UNICEF Building.

Other projects in New York City by Roche, Dinkeloo & Associates are the Ford Foundation Building, the Trans World Airlines Terminal at Kennedy International Airport, the CBS Headquarters Building, one of the theaters at the Lincoln Center for the Performing Arts, four wings on the Metropolitan Museum of Art, and the redesigned Central Park Zoo.

¶ **U.S. Customs House,** opposite Bowling Green.

Completed in 1907 at a cost of $7 million, this massive structure is decorated with numerous pieces of statuary. The largest are four groups representing Africa, America, Asia, and Europe. The façade is adorned with a series of statues that stand for the major commercial centers of world history: England, France, Germany, Denmark, Holland, Portugal, Venice, Spain, Genoa, Phoenicia, Greece, and Rome. The art work representing Holland and Portugal was done by *Augustus Saint-Gaudens.

¶ **Wave Hill,** off the Henry Hudson Parkway at West 249th Street and Independence Avenue, Upper Manhattan.

Now a public garden and a cultural center overlooking the Hudson River, Wave Hill was the summer home of young *Theodore Roosevelt, whose family rented the Georgian house when he was twelve and thirteen years old. *Mark Twain, Arturo Toscanini, and Queen Mother Elizabeth were among the other famous residents or guests who stayed at the estate.

§ Open Tuesday-Sunday 9-4:30 (to 5:30 mid May-mid October). Fee. Phone: 718-549-3200.

¶ **Woodlawn Cemetery,** Webster Avenue at East 233rd Street, the Bronx.

Established in 1863, this cemetery contains the graves of more than 250,000 people, including the following Irish or Irish Americans:

• Nellie Bly, the famous journalist who traversed the world in fewer than eighty days. Born Elizabeth Cochrane in 1865, she staked out a journalistic career dedicated to exposing evils in society. (She probably used the byline "Nellie Bly" because of the reference to cleaning out a kitchen in the Stephen Foster song of the same name.) She subsequently wrote stories for the *Pittsburgh Dispatch* about working girls and the conditions they endured in the slums and the sweatshops. Her later exposé of poverty and political corruption in Mexico resulted in her expulsion from that country.

After persuading Joseph Pulitzer of the *New York World* to let her write a story based on personal experience in the city's mental asylum, she prepared herself for living among the insane by perfecting self-induced trances. So convincing were her vegetative states that she was committed to the asylum on Blackwell's Island, where four doctors agreed that she suffered from hysteria. While there, she recorded the brutal treatment and the terrible food which the patients had to endure. She herself was denied water until her throat was so parched that she could hardly talk. As the result of a grand jury investigation into her charges, the city earmarked $13 million to improve the Blackwell facility. On another occasion she committed theft in order to be arrested and jailed, the better to expose the verbal abuse and filthy conditions which women suffered in prison. The city subsequently began to provide matrons for the female prisoners.

Nellie Bly's most famous exploit was her successful attempt to best the record of Jules Verne's fictional Phileas Fogg. She set out from Jersey City in mid November 1889, provisioned with what became her trademark wardrobe: an ulster with shoulder cape, a hunting cap, a plaid cloth dress, a knapsack, and a crocodile skin traveling bag. Within a week her ship arrived in Southampton, England, and she was soon on her way to France, where she enjoyed an interview with Jules Verne himself before proceeding to Italy. At Brindisi she boarded an Indian mail steamer and sailed across the Mediterranean and through the Suez Canal to Ismailia. (In Port Said she rode a donkey through the streets of the city and described the Arab encampments there.) From Ismailia she sailed through the Red Sea to Aden before arriving in Colombo, Ceylon, on December 8. Her arrival in India was delayed, however, because the steamship from Calcutta was late. From India she sailed 2,000 miles to Singapore and then to Hong Kong, where she finally abandoned her flannel underwear for tropical muslin. After leaving Hong Kong, she visited Canton (where she picked up a monkey that was her constant companion at all subsequent press conferences) and touched at Yokohama (where her ship was hit by the monsoon). After disembarking in San Francisco on January 21, she proceeded to cross the United States by train – via Kansas City and Chicago – and arrived in New York on January 25. She had traveled a total of 24,899 miles in seventy-two days, six hours, and eleven minutes and had become a world celebrity.

Toys, clothing, games, a race horse, and a Broadway song ("Globe Trotting Nellie Bly") were named in her honor. A popular poster showed her on a tightrope, balancing a parasol, with the world at her feet. Her grave was unmarked until 1978, when the New York Press Club recognized her with an appropriate tombstone.

• Finley Peter Dunne, the Chicago journalist who filled 300 weekly columns with the observations of Martin Dooley, the fictional barkeep who chronicled the Irish neighborhood in which the author grew up. Dunne received national attention with the publication of *Mr. Dooley in Peace and War* and *Mr. Dooley in the Hearts of His Countrymen.*

• Charles Evans Hughes, New York governor, chief justice of the U.S. Supreme Court, presidential candidate, and secretary of state.

• John McCullaugh, the "First Chief of Police of Greater New York." A native of Ireland, he was first assigned as a rookie cop to a district few police would enter – Five Points, an Irish slum notorious for its bars, whorehouses, and gangs. He battled gambling, vice, and the Whyo Gang, leading the effort that finally resulted in the trial and execution of the gang's leader for killing his girlfriend.

• Edward McGlynn, a Catholic priest who was excommunicated for advocating the single-tax theories of Henry George, a social reformer who ran for mayor of New York in 1886 and 1897. One of twelve children born to Irish immigrants from Donegal, McGlynn had actively supported George, even though the reformer's major ideas had been condemned by some of the Catholic clergy as anti-Christian and destructive of the right to private property. After McGlynn openly disagreed on the issue with *Archbishop Michael Corrigan, the priest was stripped of his pastoral duties and ordered to Rome to recant. As a sign of solidarity with McGlynn, 25,000 Irish workers marched in protest, while McGlynn's refusal to travel to Rome resulted in his excommunication. As the situation simmered for the next five years, the recalcitrant priest received support from the *Freeman's Journal*, the *Catholic Herald*, the *Irish World*, and even *Cardinal James Gibbons, who defended McGlynn's right to advocate social reform. Despite McGlynn's eulogy at George's funeral, the rebel priest was reinstated in 1900.

• George McManus, the comic strip artist who struck it rich with "Bringing Up Father." Born in St. Louis, where his father, a native of County Meath, managed the Grand Opera House, McManus as a youngster showed a talent for drawing. One day when he was reprimanded by his teacher for drawing during class time, his father declined to join in the censure and instead showed his son's work to the editor of the *St. Louis Republic*. Immediately hired as a $5-a-week errand boy, McManus was soon employed to draw scenes at "hangings, murders and suicides."

While working for the *New York World* some years later, McManus tried his hand at producing comic strips, all of which, however, were short-lived, although the title of one – "Let George Do It" – entered the language. After being enticed to the *New York American*, McManus developed the husband and wife team that starred in "Bringing Up Father," a strip which became a regular feature of the Hearst paper in 1913. The storyline's appeal centered on the conflict between its antagonists as they dealt with their new circumstances after winning the Irish Sweepstakes. While Maggie, a former washerwoman, followed the allure of high society, her ex-bricklayer husband, Jiggs, continued to prefer the company of his drinking buddies at the local saloon. At its peak the strip was enjoyed by eighty million readers in forty-six countries, appeared in sixteen languages, and earned its creator $100,000 a year in royalties.

• Virginia Fair Vanderbilt, the daughter of *James Fair, one of the "Big Four" Comstock magnates who made their fortune in the Nevada gold and silver mines. She lies buried near her sister, Theresa Fair.

• George M. Cohan, Victor Herbert, and Chauncey Olcott. [See individual entries elsewhere.]

§ Open daily 9-4:30. Phone: 718-920-0500.

¶ **W. R. Grace Building,** 41 West 42nd Street, Midtown Manhattan.

W. R. Grace & Company was founded in 1865 by William R. Grace, a native of Queenstown, Ireland, who had come to America at the age of fourteen. Much of the Irishman's original fortune was made as the result of commercial agreements with Peru. As an advisor to Peruvian officials, Grace armed and equipped the country's army during the late 1870s and supplied it with munitions during its war with Chile. When the war left Peru $250 million in debt, Grace assumed that debt obligation in exchange for numerous concessions. Among the most lucrative were railroad leases and full ownership of silver mines, guano deposits, and five million acres of land containing oil and mineral deposits. For his exploitation of the country, he was dubbed the "Pirate of Peru." .

After obtaining control of a large share of the trade between the United States and South America, Grace opened branches in almost every Latin American country. In Chile he developed power companies, nitrate properties, and cotton and sugar mills. In 1892 he formed the New York-Pacific Steamship Company, the original direct steamship service between New York and the west coast of South America. He also served as president, trustee, or director of numerous financial or commercial enterprises.

Prior to his entry into New York politics, Grace earned recognition for two humanitarian gestures to his native land. In 1880, in response to a campaign by the *New York Herald*, he contributed one quarter of the cargo shipped as famine relief to Ireland. This and a related gesture cost him about $50,000. That same year Grace was elected mayor of New York City, a position to which he was reelected until 1887. During his administration he opposed the Tammany machine and attacked organized vice and patronage. In 1897 he established the Grace Foundation to provide women with skills in dressmaking, stenography, and other practical domestic arts.

OYSTER BAY

¶ **Roosevelt Bird Sanctuary,** 2 miles east on East Main Street, at Cove Road.

The grounds include a museum exhibiting plant and animal life found on Long Island as well as a memorial to *President Theodore Roosevelt, known for his early conservation efforts.

§ Open Monday-Thursday 8-4:30, Friday 8-2, Saturday-Sunday 1-4:30. Closed January 1, Thanksgiving, and December 25. Phone: 516-922-3200.

¶ President Roosevelt's grave is located in Young Memorial Cemetery, adjacent to the bird sanctuary.

¶ Sagamore Hill National Historic Site, 3 miles east, at 20 Sagamore Hill Road.

From 1885 until his death in 1919, this twenty-three-room Victorian mansion was the home of Theodore Roosevelt, who inherited a smidgen of Irish blood from two sources. (See Theodore Roosevelt Birthplace, New York City.) He had planned to name the estate "Leeholm" for his wife (Alice Hathaway Lee), but she died before construction got under way. The property was named for the Indian chief Sagamore Mohannis. While Roosevelt was president, the eighty-three-acre estate served as the summer White House. "At Sagamore," he wrote, " we love a great many things – birds and trees, and books . . . and horses and rifles, and children and hard work and the joy of life." On exhibit are Roosevelt's hunting trophies, gun collection, art treasures, and various mementos, including a bust of the president by *William Clark Noble.

§ Open May-mid October, daily 9:30-5; rest of the year, Wednesday-Sunday 9-4. Closed January 1, Thanksgiving, and December 25. Fee. Phone: 516-922-4447.

PLATTSBURGH

¶ Thomas Macdonough Memorial, South River Street, in front of City Hall.

This 135-foot obelisk honors Thomas Macdonough, the Irish-American victor of the battle of Plattsburgh in 1814. The monument is decorated with reliefs and the names of four of his ships: *Eagle, Preble, Saratoga,* and *Ticonderoga.*

Macdonough was born in Odessa, Delaware, in 1783, the grandson of an immigrant who had left Ireland in 1730. At seventeen the future hero joined the Navy and served under *Stephen Decatur against the pirates of Tripoli. During the period 1807-08 he served as first lieutenant aboard the *Wasp* on a voyage to England and on cruises along the Atlantic coast enforcing the American embargo against imports from Europe. In 1810 he was seized by a British press gang and was forced aboard a frigate. The enterprising sailor escaped by disguising himself in the clothes of a British tar. At the time, he promised himself: "If I live through this I'll make England remember the day she impressed an American sailor!" It may have been shortly after this incident that he was granted a furlough in order to make a voyage to the East Indies.

Soon after war broke out between Britain and the United States in 1812, Macdonough resumed active duty. Taking command of the American fleet on Lake Champlain in upstate New York, he was quickly frustrated in his attempt to outfit the fleet. The transportation of naval stores, weaponry, carpenters, and even seamen from the seacoast to the lake proved daunting, and the winter season arrived before he could begin operations. His hope that things would move apace in the spring proved illusory when the British captured two of his ships, thereby gaining a decided advantage. Although Macdonough finally assembled a fleet the following September, the British retreated from the lake into Canadian waters, a development that again postponed the inevitable conflict.

By spring 1814 Macdonough had constructed or somehow obtained a fleet of thirteen vessels. (See Vergennes, Vermont.) To counter the American's twenty-six-gun flagship *Saratoga* and the twenty-gun *Eagle*, the British spent the summer building additional ships of their own and with the construction of the *Confiance*, with thirty-seven guns, were on the verge of regaining the advantage. In the meantime a large British army had advanced to the vicinity of Plattsburgh. When the fateful engagement finally occurred on September 11, the battle at first raged indecisively until Macdonough positioned his ships so that they could fire both broadsides into the British. (Tradition maintains that a rooster aboard Macdonough's flagship crowed during most of the battle. The cock's alleged good luck popularized the use of the bird's image on local weather vanes.) By the time the British surrendered they had lost more than a hundred men, while the Americans suffered only fifty-seven deaths.

Macdonough's victory over the British fleet frustrated Britain's attempt to control the Great Lakes and forced the enemy's army to retreat into Canada. As a result, Great Britain could press no claim upon American territory at the peace negotiations ending the war. "This unfortunate adventure on Lake Champlain has changed utterly the atmosphere of the negotiations," commented the frustrated British colonial secretary. The American negotiators and their British counterparts signed a peace treaty that Christmas Eve.

POUGHKEEPSIE

¶ **Thomas Dongan Statue,** Mt. Carmel, at the corner of Mill and Clover Streets.

This monument honors Thomas Dongan, the Irish Catholic proprietary governor of New York from 1683 to 1687. The inscription on the pedestal describes Dongan as "one of the greatest constructive statesmen ever sent to any English colony." The rest of the inscription reads: "The

Statue of Governor Thomas Dongan in Poughkeepsie.

assembly which he created passed an act known as 'The Charter of Liberties and Privileges' which assumed the sovereignty of the people and proclaimed religious liberty, the right of suffrage, trial by jury, and no taxation without the consent of the assembly. Dongan's charter was the Magna Carta of American constitutional liberty. Many of its principles are embedded in the structure of our federal government." (See Albany, New York.)

ROCHESTER

¶ Holy Sepulchre Cemetery, 2461 Lake Avenue.

Very different monuments mark the graves of two Irish natives whose obscurity in American history belies their significance:

• Catherine De Valera Burial Site, Section 12 South, the second row from the end. The predominant name on the tombstone on this site is "Wheelwright," the surname of the Englishman whom Catherine De Valera married sometime after the birth of her son Edward (or Eamon), the first president of the Irish provisional government.

Born Catherine Coll in County Limerick in 1879, the future president's mother came to America at the age of twenty-three. While employed by a French family in New York, she met a Spaniard by the name of Vivion De Valera. Although Eamon De Valera later claimed that his parents were married in New Jersey in 1881, at least one biographer denies that any marriage took place. According to this thesis, Vivion De Valera abandoned Catherine soon before their son was born in the Child's Hospital in New York City in 1882. Whatever the case, the mother sent the youngster to Ireland when he was almost three years old. She subsequently married Charles Wheelwright, a livery driver.

Although Catherine saw her son only occasionally thereafter, she came to his defense after the British sentenced him to death for his role in the 1916 Easter Rising. Armed with his birth and baptismal certificates, she reminded the British that her son was an American citizen. The British, hoping to persuade the United States to enter the Great War on its side, prudently refrained from alienating Americans by executing De Valera. The son later visited his mother on his fund-raising visits to the United States.

• Patrick O'Rorke Burial Site, under a Celtic cross on a small hill. O'Rorke arrived in America in 1837, brought here as a one-year-old infant by his parents, both natives of County Cavan. Although the youngster later won a scholarship to Rochester University, the school's association with a Protestant sect drew his mother's disapproval and caused him to decline the stipend. The young man was subsequently appointed to the U.S. Military Academy and was graduated at the top of his class – almost literally at the outbreak of the Civil War. After seeing action in several early battles, O'Rorke was named colonel of the 140th New York, although he was only twenty-six years of age. During the battle of Gettysburg, the Irishman initially led his command up Little Round Top, but almost immediately he was shot in the neck and died. Despite his death, his men repulsed the enemy charge and captured the summit. (See O'Rorke Memorial, Gettysburg, Pennsylvania.)

℣ Irish Famine Memorial, St. John Fisher College, near the dining hall.

This marble monument honors "those millions of Irish who died as a result of The Great Famine of 1845 through 1850 whose only crime was their heritage and faith."

℣ Patrick O'Rorke Portrait Bust, in the High Falls development in the Brown's Race Historic District, between State and Platt streets.

This bust of *Colonel Patrick O'Rorke was unveiled in 1992. It is flanked by two large panels summarizing events in his life.

§ Phone: 716-325-2030.

ROME

Originally known as Lynchville, this area was settled by Dominick Lynch, whom George Washington called "the handsome Irishman." By 1786 Lynch had purchased almost 2,400 acres at Fort Stanwix, subdivided the property into village lots, and founded a settlement to which he gave his family name. The town's Dominick Street and Lynch Street were named for its founder, whose children are remembered in Depeyster, James, Jane, Jasper, and Louisa streets.

¶ **Erie Canal Village,** 3 miles west on State 49 at 5789 New London Road.

This restored 1840 community offers insights into the way of life which many Irish workers on the Erie Canal experienced. The village includes a train station, a blacksmith shop, a hotel, and a settler's cabin. The visitor center presents an audiovisual program, and a thirty-minute mule-drawn packet ride along the canal is available.

§ Open May-Labor Day, daily 9:30-5; time varies day Labor Day-January 31. Fee. Phone: 315-337-3999.

¶ **Oriskany Battlefield,** 6 miles east on State 69.

On August 6, 1777, as 600 Mohawk Valley militiamen marched to relieve Fort Stanwix, they were ambushed by a force of local Tories and Native Americans. Two hundred militiamen were killed in the six-hour battle that ensued.

The site of the bloodiest battle of the Revolution is marked by a ninety-three-foot granite obelisk erected in 1883. Two of the bronze bas-reliefs on the memorial were designed by the sculptor *William O'Donovan. One of his reliefs depicts General Nicholas Herkimer, the leader of the American troops, seated on the ground with his wounded leg extended. He seems to be emphasizing with his outstretched left arm a command to a young aide on his right side. The other bas-relief portrays hand-to-hand combat between a German-American soldier dressed in buckskins and an Indian with an uplifted tomahawk. The advancing foot of each combatant rests on the breast of a dead soldier on the ground.

§ Open Memorial Day-Labor Day, Wednesday-Saturday and Monday holidays 10-5, Sunday 1-5. Audiovisual presentation and tours available. Phone: 315-768-7224.

SARATOGA NATIONAL HISTORICAL PARK

This park commemorates the American victory over British general John Burgoyne in two battles fought in this area in September and October 1777.

• The Fraser Monument marks the spot where British general Simon Fraser fell wounded on October 7, 1777, a victim of Irish-American sharpshooter Timothy Murphy. Murphy's direct hit and Fraser's death the following morning contributed to the American victory.

• The Timothy Murphy Hibernian Monument in the Bemis Heights area honors the heroism of the soldiers of Irish descent who fought and died here for the American cause. The monument, which was erected in 1913 by the Ancient Order of Hibernians of Saratoga County, reads: "To the memory of Timothy Murphy, celebrated marksman of Col. Morgan's Rifle Corps whose unerring aim turned the tide of battle by the death of the British general Frazer on October 7, 1777, thereby adding to the world's history one of its decisive battles. In this monument is commemorated the heroic deeds of hundreds of other soldiers of Irish blood who laid down their lives on this bloody field that the union of states might be triumphant."

Born in 1751 to Irish immigrant parents living in New Jersey, Murphy had grown to manhood on the frontier of Pennsylvania's Wyoming Valley. Although unable to read and write, he was a legendary marksman during the Revolutionary War and earned the nicknamed "Sure-shot Tim." In July 1777 he joined Colonel Daniel Morgan's elite Rifle Corps. During the fighting at Saratoga the following October, Morgan entrusted Murphy and a few other sharpshooters with a special mission: "That gallant officer is General Fraser[.] I admire and honor him but it is necessary he should die[;] victory for the enemy depends on him. Take your station in that clump of bushes and do your duty." After setting his rifle in the fork

The Timothy Murphy Hibernian Monument.

of a tree, Murphy took aim at his target. Although two bullets missed
their mark (hitting Fraser's horse instead), the third struck the general,
who was removed from the field and died the next morning. Murphy is
also said to have been responsible for mortally shooting Sir Francis Carr
Clerke, General Burgoyne's aide-de-camp.

Murphy's marksmanship and its geopolitical repercussions are commemorated in a poem which its author, Joseph Clarke, read at the battle
site on July 26, 1913:

> 'Twas the brave Morgan lowered his glass,
> And pointing where Fraser stood,
> Cried, "Woodsmen say when a man must pass,
> 'He's the log that jams the flood.'
> . . . .
> One man holds back the flood of the fates
> That sweeps us on to be free;
> Let heaven open for him its gates."
> And Tim Murphy climbed a tree.
> Then Fraser fell, and the battle tide
> Flowed madly on for our cause,
> And John Burgoyne in his dandy pride
> Surrendered his king's applause;
> . . . .
> Then came the French and the war was done.
> And freedom's glory grew.
> So when we bless George Washington,
> Let us bless Tim Murphy, too

§ Open daily 9-5. Closed January 1, Thanksgiving, and December 25.
Phone: 518-664-9821.

SARATOGA SPRINGS

¶ **The Casino,** Congress Park, on Broadway (U.S. 9) between Circular
and Spring streets.

The Casino was originally known as the Saratoga Club when it was
built by John Morrissey, the founder of three earlier gambling houses in
New York City. He also built the first thoroughbred race track at Saratoga.

Brought to the United States from Ireland at three years of age,
Morrissey had spent many of his early years as a "runner," engaged to
allure newly arrived immigrants to his employer's boarding house in New
York City. He eventually joined a gang and before he was eighteen had
compiled a rap sheet for burglary, assault, and battery. His pugilistic talents were soon enlisted by the local Tammany Hall politicians, who made

him the head of the Dead Rabbits, their dependable gang of toughs. Before long, he parlayed his talent into a professional boxing career. In 1858 he won the American bare-knuckle heavyweight championship in an eleven-round bout with *J. C. Heenan. Morrissey was subsequently elected to Congress and the New York state senate.

§ Open June-September, Monday-Saturday 10-4, Sunday 1-4; rest of the year, Wednesday-Saturday 10-4, Sunday 1-4. Fee. Phone: 518-584-6920.

¶ The National Museum of Racing and Hall of Fame, Union Avenue and Ludlow Street.

The museum features exhibits, sculpture, paintings, and videos on the history of thoroughbred racing in America. The Hall of Fame honors race horses, trainers, and jockeys.

One of the famous horsemen honored in the Hall of Fame is *James "Sunny Jim" Fitzsimmons. Born in an area of New York that later became the race track of the Coney Island Jockey Club, Fitzsimmons almost literally had racing in his blood. By age eleven he had his first job around the track – mucking out stalls – but he soon took off on his own as a free-lance rider weighing eighty-four pounds. (Some years later, he spent all night shoveling clay, thereby losing eleven pounds in order to reach a qualifying weight.) By 1904 he was the leading trainer at Pimlico, and in 1906 he opened a public stable at Aqueduct, charging a mere $4 per day.

As Fitzsimmons' clientele grew – at times he was training more than fifty horses at once – so did the number of his winners. From 1906 to his retirement sixty years later, he saddled 2,275 winners, whose combined purses exceeded $13 million. He trained two winners of the Triple Crown, and Bold Ruler and Nashua were among his famous charges.

Fitzsimmons was dubbed "Sunny Jim" by George Dailey, the sports editor of the *New York World*, after an amiable and carefree comic strip character. During his eighty years in racing, Sunny Jim's only complaint was that he was never able to sleep late in the mornings. "I came into this game with nothing to give it . . . ," said the grand old man of American racing. "Racing gave me the happiest life you could want. Racing doesn't owe me a thing, but I owe the game a hell of a lot."

§ Open late July-Labor Day, daily 9-5; rest of the year, Monday-Saturday 10-4:30, Sunday noon-4:30. Closed January 1, Easter, Thanksgiving, and December 25. Fee. Phone: 518-584-0400.

SCHOHARIE

¶ Old Stone Fort Museum, 1 mile north on North Main Street; 2 miles south on State 30 from I-88 Schoharie/Central Bridge exit.

The museum is housed in the Old Stone Fort, originally built in 1772 as a Dutch Reformed church. Six years later it was fortified and enclosed by a log palisade.

In October 1780 a force of Tories and Native Americans under the command of *Sir John Johnson entered the Schoharie Valley, plundering and killing as they advanced. (Johnson was the son of *Sir William Johnson, Britain's superintendent of Indian affairs in New York) At the time, the fort was garrisoned by Americans, one of them *Timothy Murphy, the famous frontiersman, Indian killer, and marksman.

Realizing that Johnson's forces surrounded the fort, the American commander was willing to surrender and ordered one of his militiamen to exit the fort carrying a flag of truce. Murphy, however, shot the flag from the militiaman's hand rather than see the fort surrendered. When the commander ordered the other men to subdue Murphy, they refused. Encouraged in his defiance, Murphy threatened to kill anyone who tried to surrender.

The British commander had meanwhile withdrawn, believing that his artillery was incapable of breaching the walls of the fort. Murphy was only mildly reprimanded for his disobedience. He is buried in Middleburg Cemetery in Middleburg, about ten miles from Schoharie.

• A reenactment of Johnson's raid takes place here during the first weekend in October.

§ Open July-August, Monday-Saturday 10-5, Sunday noon-5; May-June and September-October, Tuesday-Saturday 10-5; Sunday noon-5. Fee. Phone: 518-295-7192.

SCHUYLERVILLE

¶ Saratoga Battlefield Monument, Burgoyne Street off State 32.

This 155-foot granite obelisk commemorates the American victory over the British in two battles fought near here in September and October 1777. The exterior niches contain statues of General Philip Schuyler, General Horatio Gates, and Colonel Daniel Morgan. The latter work was designed by *William O'Donovan.

STONY POINT

¶ Stony Point Battlefield State Historic Site, 2.5 miles northeast off U.S. 9 on Park Road.

The Patriot Soldiers Monument honors the American troops under *Brigadier General Anthony Wayne who in July 1779 captured a British garrison of 600 men posted here on the west bank of the Hudson River. "Our officers and men behaved like men who are determined to be free," said Wayne, who received a head wound during the surprise midnight assault, the last major northern battle of the Revolution. (See Paoli, Pennsylvania.)

§ Grounds open mid April-late October, Wednesday-Saturday and holidays 10-5, Sunday 1-5; check times for museum. Phone: 914-786-2521.

TAPPAN

¶ **Dutch Reformed Church,** Main Street at Old Tappan Road.
On September 29, 1780, Major John André, the captured British spy, was tried here by a tribunal of fourteen American generals (including *James Clinton, *Henry Knox, Arthur St. Clair, and the Marquis de Lafayette).

TARRYTOWN

¶ **Captor's Monument,** Patriots' Park, on U.S. 9.
Atop this monument is a bronze statue of John Paulding, one of the American soldiers who captured Major John André, the famous British spy, in September 1780. The statue is the work of *William O'Donovan.

TROY

¶ **James Connolly Memorial,** Riverfront Park, River and Front streets, near City Hall.
Erected in 1986 by the members of various trade unions, this memorial bust by the Irish sculptor Paula O'Sullivan commemorates the two years during which James Connolly lived in Troy. The memorial inscription reads: "James Connolly. Dedicated to the principles of organized labor. Born: June 5, 1868. Resident of Troy, New York: 1903-1905. Martyred for Irish freedom: May 12, 1916. 'Be Men Now or Be Forever Slaves.'"
Born in Scotland to Irish immigrants, Connolly moved to Dublin in 1896 to accept a post as secretary of the Socialist Club there. Although he proceeded to found the Irish Socialist Republican party, disagreements within its ranks caused him to sail to America and eventually settle in Troy. (He was soon followed by his wife and the four of their five children who survived the crossing.) During his eight years in the United States, he established the Irish Socialist Federation and was editor of its journal. In 1910, however, he returned to Dublin, where he helped orchestrate the massive – but unsuccessful – transport workers strike of 1913.
Although Connolly's socialist internationalism aroused the distrust of Irish nationalists, he was made commander of the Irish Citizen Army and helped prepare its members for the uprising that finally occurred in April 1916. During the fighting that erupted after Connolly and his 1,000 troops seized the General Post Office in Dublin, the commander was wounded in the ankle. When the rebels surrendered at the end of the week, Connolly was court-martialed and sentenced to death – all while he lay in

a hospital bed. On May 12 he was driven to Kilmainham Jail, where he was propped up in a chair and shot.

¶ **Soldiers' and Sailors' Monument,** Monument Square, 2nd and River streets.

This impressive monument in front of City Hall is crowned by a seventeen-foot figure of Columbia, the work of *James Edward Kelly.

U.S. MILITARY ACADEMY

The visitor center (outside Thayer Gate) is open daily 9-4:45. Closed January 1, Thanksgiving, and December 25. Phone: 914-938-2638.

¶ **Cadet Library**

The library contains memorial plaques in honor of two famous Irish Americans whose careers at West Point were eclipsed by their later achievements in less bellicose pursuits.

• *Edgar Allan Poe is commemorated with a plaque by *Augustus Saint-Gaudens and with a white marble doorway in the east hallway. Poe's name is engraved across the top of the doorway, as is an appropriate aphorism by Sir Francis Bacon: "There is no exquisite beauty without some strangeness in proportion."

Poe's career at West Point was marked by frequent absences, usually at a nearby tavern. These infractions soon led to his court-martial and dismissal in March 1831, after only eights months at the academy. Before he left, however, he sought subscriptions from the cadets to publish a book of verse. In the expectation that the poems in the volume would satirize the academy's superintendent, many of the cadets eagerly paid the seventy-five-cent subscription fee. When they saw the finished product, though, they felt that they had been deceived because it was filled with what one commentator called "sentimental rubbish."

• Near the Poe doorway is a white marble tablet by *Augustus Saint-Gaudens in honor of the famous painter *James McNeill Whistler. The tablet is inscribed with an unusual quotation: "The Story of the Beautiful is Already Complete[,] Hewn in the Marble of the Parthenon and Broidered with the Birds upon the Fan of Hokusai." Below the words is the butterfly symbol with which Whistler usually signed his works. Although Whistler excelled in drawing while at West Point, he was dismissed in his third year for failing chemistry. "Had silicon been a gas," he reportedly said, "I would have been a major general."

¶ **Cullum Hall**

Among the portrait paintings of West Point graduates on display here are those of Irish Americans George Gordon Meade ('35), Irwin McDowell

('38), John Reynolds ('41), Ulysses S. Grant ('43), Alexander McDowell Cook ('52), and Philip Sheridan ('53) as well as a portrait of William T. Sherman by *George Healy.

¶ General John Sedgwick Statue

This statue of the Civil War officer is the work of sculptor *Launt Thompson.

¶ Grant Hall and Grant Barracks

Named for *Ulysses S. Grant, Grant Hall displays a portrait of the Civil War commander as well as portraits of generals George Washington, Winfield Scott, *Philip Sheridan, and William T. Sherman.

¶ Mahan Hall

Opened in 1972, this is the newest academic building on campus and was named in honor of Dennis Mahan, a professor of engineering at the academy from 1832 to 1871.

Born in New York City soon after the arrival of his parents from Ireland, Mahan sought and obtained an appointment to the U.S. Military Academy primarily because of his interest in studying drawing there. Following his graduation from West Point in 1824, he pursued further study at the School of Application for Engineers and Artillery in Metz, France. Upon his return to the academy four years later, he was appointed professor of civil and military engineering. Because he was hampered by the unavailability of textbooks for his courses, he developed his own, some of which his students used as manuals when they commanded troops during the Mexican War and the Civil War.

At the height of his career, Mahan was a member of many scientific associations, including the National Academy of Sciences and the Geographical Society of Paris. Depressed, however, by the recommendation that he retire from the faculty at West Point, he sailed to New York to visit his doctor, but on the way he stepped over the side of the vessel and drowned.

¶ Major Sylvanus Thayer Statue

This memorial to the "Father of the U.S. Military Academy" is the work of *Martin Milmore. Thayer was the academy's superintendent from 1817 to 1833.

¶ Margaret Corbin Burial Site, West Point Cemetery, near the Old Cadet Chapel.

A stone monument adorned with a bronze bas-relief marks the grave of *Margaret Cochran Corbin, the "first woman to take a soldier's part" in the American Revolution. The bas-relief depicts Corbin manning a cannon at the battle of Fort Washington, where she took her husband's place after he was struck down by attacking Hessians. (See Margaret Corbin Commemorative Plaque, New York City.)

Following her release from the army at the end of the Revolutionary War, Corbin was awarded a sergeant's half pension as well as a ration per day and became the only woman in the Invalid Regiment, stationed at that time at West Point. Described as a "stout, red-haired, freckled-face young Irish girl, with handsome, piercing eyes," she cut a colorful figure in camp. Because she usually wore a cocked hat and an artilleryman's coat over her dress, she was nicknamed "Captain Molly," although she was also dubbed "Dirty Kate" for her slovenly attire and unwashed appearance. Following her second marriage to a man whose name is unknown, she was described as being "far advanced in her pregnancy."

In September 1782 "Captain Molly" presented a requisition for 257 gills of whiskey, which she claimed was part of her rations. An aide to *General Henry Knox wrote to General Washington expressing his belief that army regulations prohibited the issuance of whiskey to women. Washington's aide, however, authorized Knox to grant her request, although he warned about the imprudence of giving her too much of the drink. He also asked Knox how it could be "that a woman with an old, decrepit husband should be far advanced in pregnancy."

¶ Shea Stadium
This track and field stadium was named in 1958 for *1st Lieutenant Richard Shea Jr., a 1952 West Point graduate who was posthumously awarded the Medal of Honor for his heroic actions during the Korean War. Although seriously wounded in the torso and the neck while defending "Pork Chop" Hill, Shea refused five times to abandon his position but instead reorganized and led the remaining units on the hill. He and fifty other men died there, on July 8, 1953.

WESTFIELD

¶ Old McClurg Mansion, at the junction of U.S. 20 and U.S. 394.
This is the restored 1820 residence of James McClurg, a Scotch-Irish merchant and trader who hired bricklayers from Pittsburgh to build this structure in the style of an Irish manor house. Because of its ornamentation, the house was dubbed "McClurg's Folly." Today the building contains period furniture, farm implements, and a military exhibit.

McClurg's father had fled Ireland with his young family in 1798, soon after the collapse of an uprising that year. (Because he was suspected of being a leader in the revolt, the elder McClurg was spirited out of the country in an empty water barrel aboard ship. Although the family's terrier showed unusual interest in the keg while authorities searched the ship, the stowaway was not detected.) McClurg and his family first lived in Philadelphia, but they later moved to Pittsburgh, where they established that city's first iron foundry.

In 1808, however, James McClurg headed off on his own, traversing the virgin lands as far as present-day Cleveland before settling in Westfield. Here he built his brick mansion and a hotel that was considered the best west of Albany at the time. About 1831 he and two partners built a flour and grist mill in Westfield to supply the increasing numbers of settlers coming into the region. McClurg later purchased land in Chicago, Rock Island, and Racine, Illinois, and joined the Republican Party soon after its formation.

§ Open Monday-Tuesday and Thursday-Saturday 1-5. Fee. Phone: 716-326-2977.

WILTON

¶ **Grant Cottage State Historic Site,** southbound I-87 exit 17, 4 miles west to the junction of State 9 and Ballard Road, to Mount McGregor Correctional Facility.

Impoverished because of bad business investments and suffering from throat cancer, former president *Ulysses S. Grant came here in June 1885 to finish his memoirs. After working feverishly on the volume so his family would have an income, he completed the book just four days before his death on July 23, 1885. The publication of Grant's memoirs later earned almost $500,000 for his family. The cottage contains original furnishings and some of Grant's clothing.

§ Open Memorial Day-Labor Day, Wednesday-Sunday 10-4; day after Labor Day-mid October, Saturday-Sunday 10-4. Fee. Phone: 518-587-8277 or 584-4768.

YOUNGSTOWN

¶ **Old Fort Niagara,** Fort Niagara State Park, north on State 18.

Located on the site of earlier French forts dating from 1678, the fort was captured for the British by *Sir William Johnson in 1759. Today the fort includes a moat, a drawbridge, ramparts, blockhouses, and the only fortified French castle in the United States.

§ Open daily 9-4:30 (to 5:30 April-May and September-October; 6:30 in June; 7:30 in July-August). Closed January 1, Thanksgiving, and December 25. Fee. Phone: 716-745-7611.

OHIO

CANTON

¶ **McKinley Museum of History, Science and Industry,** 800 McKinley Monument Drive, N.W., off I-77 exit 106.

Named for *William McKinley, the twenty-fifth president of the United States, this museum features displays in Historical Hall and Industrial Hall, presidential memorabilia in McKinley Hall, and nineteenth-century structures in the Street of Shops. (See Niles, Ohio.)

§ Open day after Memorial Day-day before Labor Day, Monday-Saturday 9-6, Sunday noon-6; rest of the year, Monday-Saturday 9-5, Sunday noon-5. Closed holidays. Fee. Phone: 330-455-7043.

¶ **McKinley National Memorial,** 800 McKinley Monument Drive, N.W., off I-77 exit 106.

This circular stone monument – resembling both the Taj Mahal in India and Hadrian's Tomb in Rome – honors *President William McKinley. A nine-foot-high bronze statue depicts a standing McKinley – one hand holding some papers and the other in his pants pocket – delivering his last speech in Buffalo, New York, before his assassination there in 1901. He is buried here with his wife and their daughters. (See Niles, Ohio.)

§ Open Memorial Day-Labor Day, Monday-Saturday 9-6, Sunday noon-6; mid March-day before Memorial Day, and day after Labor Day-November, Monday-Saturday 9-5, Sunday noon-5. Phone: 330-455-7043.

CARROLLTON

¶ **McCook House,** in the public square.

This brick Federal-style house was the home of *Major Daniel McCook Sr., whose ten sons were dubbed the "Tribe of Dan." Both he and nine of his sons served in the Union army during the Civil War. Four of them made the supreme sacrifice, including Daniel McCook Sr., who was mortally wounded in July 1863, while trying to intercept Confederate raiders near Buffington Island, Ohio. Because McCook's five nephews also fought for the Union, the family clan was known as the "Fighting McCooks."

The McCooks' first American ancestor was an Irishman of Scottish descent who had fled Ireland in 1780 when the United Irishmen movement collapsed. He eventually settled in Canonsburg, Pennsylvania.

§ Open June-mid October, Friday-Saturday 9-noon and 1-5, Sunday 1-5. Fee. Phone: 330-627-3345.

CINCINNATI

¶ **Stephen Foster Statue,** Alms Memorial Park, Mt. Lookout district, Tusculum and Columbia avenues.

This bronze memorial to Stephen Collins Foster depicts the famous Irish-American songwriter sitting on a knoll as he gazes toward the Kentucky hills. The statue of Foster, who spent several years in Cincinnati, was a gift of Eli Lily, the founder of the pharmaceutical company that bears his name. (See the Stephen Foster Memorial Building, Pittsburgh, Pennsylvania.)

CLEVELAND

¶ **President Garfield Statue,** Lakeview Cemetery, 12316 Euclid Avenue.

This marble statue by *Alexander Doyle is located inside the chapel in the base of the James A. Garfield Monument. The memorial, which was erected in 1890, is a circular tower fifty feet in diameter and 180 feet high and is located above the grave of the slain president.

The graves of John D. Rockefeller, *Senator Mark Hanna, and Secretary of State John Hay are also located in this cemetery. Hanna, who was descended from Scotch-Irish Quakers from northern Ireland, was known as the "King Maker" because of his influence in the Republican Party at the end of the nineteenth century and the beginning of the next.

§ Cemetery open April-late November, daily 9-4. Phone: 216-421-2665.

¶ **John Carroll University,** University Heights, Warrensville Center and Fairmount Boulevard.

This Jesuit institution was founded in 1886 and was named for *John Carroll, the first Catholic bishop of the United States. (See Baltimore, Maryland.)

¶ **Mark Hanna Statue,** University Circle, spreading north, east, and south from Euclid Avenue, east of East 107th Street.

Sculpted by *Augustus Saint-Gaudens, this seated bronze statue was placed here in 1907 to honor the Cleveland native who maneuvered the nomination of *William McKinley as the Republican candidate for president in 1896. Hanna was of mixed Irish and Scotch-Irish ancestry.

¶ **Oliver H. Perry Statue,** at the northern boundary of Gordon Park.

This bronze statue of *Oliver Hazard Perry commemorates the twenty-seven-year-old naval commander who defeated the British fleet on Lake Erie during the War of 1812. (See Put-in-Bay, Ohio.)

COLUMBUS

¶ O'Shaughnessy Reservoir, 16 miles north on Riverside Drive.

Completed in 1925, this water storage site was named for *Jerry O'Shaughnessy, the former waterworks superintendent of Columbus for almost a half century.

Born in Delaware, Ohio, in 1854, O'Shaughnessy at age sixteen began work digging the foundation for one of the pumping stations in the modern water works system that the city of Columbus was then constructing. In rapid succession he was promoted through the system's ranks – "wiper of machinery," fireman, and then engineer – until in 1896 he was named superintendent. Five years prior to this appointment, he and a partner had founded an undertaking business.

During his lifetime O'Shaughnessy was very active in a variety of Catholic and Irish organizations. Besides serving as county president of the Ancient Order of Hibernians, he organized the first female auxiliary of that group. He was also a member of the Knights of Columbus and for many years was president of the Friendly Sons of St. Patrick.

¶ State Capitol, Broad and High streets.

• The capitol rotunda is decorated with plaques honoring the eight U.S. presidents who were born in Ohio, among them three of Irish ancestry: Ulysses S. Grant, Benjamin Harrison, and William McKinley,

• Outside the west entrance to the capitol is a bronze statue of *President William McKinley reading an address at the Pan-American Exposition in Buffalo, New York, in 1901. This was his last speech before he was

Statue of President William McKinley outside the Ohio state capitol. (Photo courtesy of the Ohio Historical Society.)

assassinated by an anarchist.

• On the capitol grounds is a memorial to seven Ohio statesmen and Civil War soldiers, including *Ulysses S. Grant and *Philip Sheridan. Known as the "My Jewels Monument," it includes bronze statues of the seven Ohioans around a shaft topped by the Roman aristocrat Cornelia, who said that her sons were her greatest jewels.

§ Phone: 614-752-6350.

DAYTON

¶ Patterson Homestead Museum, 1815 Brown Street.

The present structure incorporates portions of an earlier house built in 1816 by Colonel Robert Patterson, a renowned Indian fighter and a hero of the Revolutionary War. The house contains family memorabilia, while the grounds feature a variety of gardens. Patterson's surrounding estate was known as "Rubicon Farm."

Patterson claimed Irish descent through his paternal great-great-grandfather, who had emigrated from Ireland about 1700 and settled in Lancaster, Pennsylvania. The future Indian fighter was born in 1753 near Cove Mountain, Pennsylvania, but at the age of seventeen headed off on his own. In 1774 he served for six months with the Rangers against the natives on the Pennsylvania frontier, and in October of the following year he was among a group of pioneers who pressed into Kentucky. The party finally settled at the present site of Lexington, where they constructed two cabins. Patterson later represented Fayette County in the first Kentucky legislature.

In October 1776 Patterson experienced what must have been one of the most hair-raising and "sidesplitting" incidents in his frontier career. After traveling up the Ohio River from Georgetown, Kentucky, he and six companions encamped at a site then known as Hockhocking. During the night, the men were fired upon by Indians, who, according to Patterson's own account, "rushed upon us with tomahawks, as if determined to finish the work of death they had begun. . . . I saw the flash of the gun and felt the ball pass through me, but where I could not tell, nor was it at first painful. I sprang to take up [my] gun, but my right shoulder came to the ground. I made another effort, and was half bent in getting up, when an Indian sprang past the fire with savage fierceness, and struck me with his tomahawk. From the position I was in, it went between two ribs, just behind the back bone a little below the kidney, and penetrated the cavity of the body. . . . I felt the blood running and heard it dropping on the leaves all around me." After the attackers had left the scene, Patterson saw by the light of the fire that one of his companions was dead and scalped, three were wounded, and another missing. Although one of the survivors went for help, it was not until the fourth day after the harrowing incident that a rescue party arrived, but not before one of the wounded victims expired. According to Patterson's account, one of the rescuers described the survivors as "more like corpses beginning to putrify [sic] than living beings." Patterson ended his narration with the grisly recollection that "the howling of the wolves in the direction of the fatal spot whence we had so narrowly escaped with our lives, left no doubt that they were feasting on the bodies of our much lamented friends."

The closing years of the Revolutionary War served only to enhance Patterson's reputation as a fearless frontiersman. In 1778 he served with General George Rogers Clark during the latter's Illinois campaign, commanding the advance guard and being among the first to enter the captured town of Kaskaskia. During his subsequent career as an Indian fighter, he held command in the major campaigns in the Old Northwest: captain under Clark against the Shawnees on the Little Miami and Mad rivers, second in command to Daniel Boone at the battle of Lower Blue Licks, and colonel both on Clark's second expedition into the Miami country and on Logan's campaign against the Shawnees.

In the meantime, Patterson had married Elizabeth Lindsay, with whom he had nine children, all born, it seems, while the couple lived in Lexington. Their youngest child – Jefferson Patterson – married Julia Johnston, one of fifteen children born to *Colonel John Johnston and his wife. (See Piqua, Ohio.) In 1804 Patterson left Kentucky to purchase a large tract of land ("Rubicon Farm") south of Dayton. Before building the brick structure which survives today, he lived in the log cabin already on the property. It was from here that he set out once more to serve in one final campaign: as quartermaster during the War of 1812. He was later among the original proprietors of Cincinnati, Ohio, and owned one third of that settlement when it was first laid out. He died there in 1827.

§ Open April-December, Tuesday-Friday 10-4, Sunday 1-4; rest of the year, by appointment. Closed major holidays. Phone: 937-222-9724.

¶ **William McKinley Statue,** Cooper Park, East 3rd and St. Clair streets.

This eighteen-foot bronze statue behind the Dayton Public Library depicts *President William McKinley in a speaking pose.

DEFIANCE

¶ **Fort Defiance Site,** Defiance City Park.

Stones, earthworks, and plaques mark the site of Fort Defiance, constructed in 1794 while *Major General Anthony Wayne campaigned against the Indians in the area.

When Wayne and his troops first arrived at this site in August 1794, he referred to it contemptuously as "the grand emporium of the hostile Indians of the West." The fort received its name from Wayne's challenge:

"I defy the English, the Indians and all the devils in hell to take it."

DETROIT

℧ Ulysses S. Grant House, Michigan State Fair Grounds, State Fair and Woodward avenues.

After returning from the Mexican War, *Ulysses S. Grant lived in this house (originally located on East Fort Street) while he was company commander and quartermaster of the Detroit Barracks. Grant once described the two-story cottage as "a neat little house [with] a double parlor, a dining room, one small bedroom and kitchen in the lower level. There is a nice upstairs and a garden filled with the best kind of fruit."

§ The house can be viewed from the outside during the Fair (the last week before Labor Day).

FORT RECOVERY

℧ Fort Recovery State Memorial, on State 49 at State 119.

The centerpiece of this nine-acre site is a replica of the fort and stockade built here in 1793 by *General Anthony Wayne. The fort's museum has exhibits on the Indian Wars of the 1790s.

The construction of Fort Recovery was part of Wayne's effort to "recover" this area from control of the Indians, who had decisively defeated an American army under General Arthur St. Clair in 1791. It was not until three years later that Wayne avenged this defeat with his victory at Fallen Timbers, after which the Native Americans signed the Treaty of Greenville.

§ Museum open June-August 31, daily noon-5; May and September, Saturday and Sunday noon-5. Fee. Phone: 419-375-4649.

FREMONT

℧ Memorial Monument, Birchard Library Park, 423 Croghan Street.

Besides honoring the soldiers and sailors of Sandusky County who gave their lives in America's wars, this monument marks the grave of *Major George Croghan. (See Lafayette, Indiana.)

In 1813 the twenty-one-year-old Croghan was in command of 150 American soldiers at Fort Stephenson (now Fremont) when they fought off an attack by 400 British soldiers and 300 of their Indian allies. Near the monument is the single cannon which the Americans used against their foes in that engagement.

§ Park open daily dawn-dusk.

GEORGETOWN

❡ Ulysses S. Grant Boyhood Home, 219 East Grant Avenue.

When *Ulysses S. Grant was a year old, his family moved to Georgetown, where his father built this white brick Federal-style house. His father's tannery is located across the street, while the two-room schoolhouse which the young boy attended is on South Water Street. Among the Grant memorabilia on display in the schoolhouse is a picture of West Point which Grant drew in 1840 and which he signed "H. U. Grant" – "H" for "Hiram." (He adopted the name "U. S. Grant" after a bureaucrat's error on his army commission.)

§ Open Monday-Saturday 9-1 and 2-5. Closed Holidays. Phone: 937-378-4222.

GIBRALTAR ISLAND

❡ Perry's Lookout

Located on an eminence at the eastern end of this island in Put-in-Bay, this lookout is reputedly where *Commodore Oliver H. Perry kept watch as a British naval squadron moved into the bay in 1813. Perry's subsequent victory at Put-in-Bay is commemorated by a nearby monument built in 1866.

JAMESTOWN

❡ Dean Family Farm, 5 miles northwest off U.S. 35 on Ballard Road. Private.

This farm, home to eight generations of the Dean family, was first tilled about 1812 by *Daniel Dean, an Irish immigrant and pioneer settler in this area.

LISBON

❡ McCook House, Market Street.

Now a tavern, the McCook House was formerly the home of *Robert McCook, whose two sons and fifteen grandsons were known as the "Fighting McCooks" because of their service in the U.S. armed forces. All but one of the clan saw action in the Civil War, thirteen as officers: two generals, four major generals, one major, two colonels, two lieutenants, and two naval commanders. McCook's son John also lived here with his sons, in later life known as the "Tribe of John."

The member of the tribe who had perhaps the most varied career was Edward McCook. While only sixteen, the young adventurer followed the lure of the gold rush as far as Colorado, where he later practiced law and became a leader in the organization of that territory. Although he saw action on several fronts during the Civil War, he was best known for preventing the reinforcement of troops in Atlanta by destroying Confederate transport trains and cutting the rail lines to the south of the Georgia capital.

After the war McCook acted at various times as military governor of Florida, U.S. minister to Hawaii, and territorial governor of Colorado. As governor he encouraged railroad construction, organized a school system, and was instrumental in building Denver's water system. He also paved the way for the development of mineral resources and agricultural lands in the state by removing the Ute Indians to Utah. By the end of his life he was the largest real estate owner and taxpayer in Colorado. His first wife was Mary Thomson, the granddaughter of Charles Thomson, the Irish-born secretary of the Continental Congress during the 1770s.

MASSILLON

¶ **Four Chaplains Memorial Viaduct,** on State 172 (over the Tuscarawas River) on the west side of town.

Two bronze plaques on either end of the viaduct commemorate the heroism of the four chaplains – one Catholic, one Jewish, and two Protestant – who gave up their life jackets to soldiers aboard the sinking U.S.S. *Dorchester* in 1943. The four clergymen were Father John Patrick Washington, Rabbi Alexander Goode, Reverend Clark Poling, and Reverend George Fox. Father Washington was born in Newark, New Jersey, in 1908, the oldest of either seven or nine children born to Irish immigrant parents. (See Falls Church, Virginia, and Bottineau, North Dakota, in *Irish America*, Volume 2.)

MOUNT VERNON

¶ **Daniel Emmett Birthplace,** Senior Citizens' Center, at the juncture of Martinsburg, Newark, and Granville roads (State 583, 13, and 661).

It was here that Daniel Emmett, the composer of "Dixie," was born in 1815. His immensely popular tune was premiered in New Orleans in 1861 and was soon adopted as the war anthem of the Confederacy.

Before finally settling in Ohio, Emmett's Irish pioneer ancestors had crossed the Blue Ridge and the Allegheny mountains. As a youngster he was introduced to music by his mother, and it was probably while working in his father's blacksmith shop that he composed the song "Old Dan Tucker." After learning how to read and write, however, he was apprenticed to a printer and for a time worked for the *Western Aurora* newspaper in Mount Vernon.

At seventeen Emmett joined the army as a fifer but was soon discharged when he was found to be underage. Evidently intent upon making a mark in the musical field, he organized in 1842 the Virginia Minstrels, whose striped calico shirts, white trousers, and blue calico coats were of his own design. For a dozen years this group enjoyed phenomenal success popularizing African-American music. In 1857, however, Emmett joined the Bryant Minstrels, for whom he composed "Dixie." Some of his other Civil War songs were "The Road to Richmond," "Walk Along, John," and "Here We Are, or Cross Ober Jordan."

¶ Emmett is buried in Mound View Cemetery, off Wooster Road (State 3).

NEWARK

¶ **Ohio and Erie Canal Monument,** 3 miles south on State 79.

This monument commemorates the canal's ground-breaking ceremonies, which occurred here on July 4, 1825, with *DeWitt Clinton, the governor of New York and the "Father of the Erie Canal," officiating.

Many of the thousands of spectators who attended the ceremony barely heard the speeches because they were distracted by the flies and the tramping of cavalry horses near the rostrum. One wag commented that "it was all right to have the horses in front of the speaker's stand, for they cannot read and we can."

NEW LEXINGTON

¶ **J. A. MacGahan Burial Site,** Maplewood Cemetery, Swigart Street.

This is the final resting place of Januarius Aloysius MacGahan, a war correspondent and the master of nine languages, who was born near here of Irish parents in 1844. The monument over his grave is inscribed with his name and the honorific "Liberator of Bulgaria."

After studying law and foreign languages in St. Louis, MacGahan traveled to Europe, where he improved his linguistic skills while living in Paris, Brussels, and Germany. At the outbreak of the Franco-Prussian War in 1870, he sent back vivid descriptions of the conflict for the *New York Herald*, including reports about the Paris Commune and his own capture and release. After spending some time in the Crimea, he became a favored figure with the Czar's court. Probably because of that popularity, he risked defying the Russian prohibition against newspaper coverage of a military expedition against the Khanate of Khiva. For twenty-nine days he and two companions eluded the Czar's Cossacks in a pursuit of almost a thousand miles. Although finally captured, he was allowed to stay with the campaign.

MacGahan was later instrumental in achieving Bulgarian independence. His reports to the *London Daily News* verifying rumors about Turkish massacres of Bulgarians indirectly led to Russia's declaration of war against Turkey in 1876. A year later, with the Turks defeated and Bulgaria independent, MacGahan was proclaimed that country's liberator. Following his death in 1878, he was buried in Bulgaria until his body was brought to the United States and reinterred in Maplewood Cemetery in 1884.

At the unveiling of the monument over MacGahan's grave in 1911, Svetozar Tonjoroff, his Bulgarian eulogist, referred to him as the "patron saint of Bulgaria." The speaker also described one of the massacres which MacGahan had reported in the press: After about 4,000 Bulgarian villagers had sought refuge in a church, the Turkish commander besieging the village offered amnesty to any of the men who laid down their weapons. When the Bulgarian men in the village surrendered themselves and their arms, the Turks reneged on their promise and proceeded to torch the church and the women and children still inside. "[T]he most enduring monument to MacGahan . . . is to be seen on every map of Europe . . . ," Tonjoroff said, "[and] is builded of indestructible materials in the heart and soul of every Bulgarian, for all time. That monument is Bulgaria itself – free, with its face toward the light, marching steadily to the fulfillment of its destiny . . . ."

NILES

¶ **William McKinley Birthplace Site,** 36 South Main Street.

Although the building at this address is now a bank, a marker in the entranceway notes that *President William McKinley was born on this site in 1843. None of his personal residences survives today.

¶ **National McKinley Birthplace Memorial,** 40 North Main Street.

This huge neoclassical memorial to William McKinley is located close to the spot where the twenty-fifth president was born in 1843. The monument consists of a colonnaded porch called the Court of Honor, at the center of which is a statue of McKinley surrounded by figures of his political associates. The attached museum displays items connected with McKinley's life and career.

Of Scotch-Irish ancestry, McKinley was descended from James MacKinlay, who had accompanied William III to Ireland and fought with the Presbyterian king at the battle of the Boyne in 1690. David McKinley, a son of James known as "the weaver," was the first of the future president's ancestors to immigrate to America. This great-great-great-grandfather of the president was born in northern Ireland (probably County Antrim) about 1705 and immigrated to York County, Pennsylvania, about 1743.

A century and a quarter later, during the Civil War, William McKinley served with the 23rd Ohio Regiment. (See Sharpsburg, Maryland.) After coming to Canton, Ohio, in 1867 to begin practicing law, he entered politics, serving in Congress for fourteen years and as governor of Ohio for four. Elected president in 1896 and again in 1900, he was assassinated by

Leon Czolgosz, an anarchist, in Buffalo on September 6, 1901. McKinley's last words were, "Goodbye all. It is God's will. His will, not ours, be done."

§ Open Monday-Thursday 9-8, Friday and Saturday 9-5:30; also Sunday 1-5 (September-May only). Phone: 330-652-1704.

The neo-classical National McKinley Birthplace Memorial.
(*Photo by Justine Hill and courtesy of the National McKinley Birthplace Memorial.*)

OXFORD

¶ **William McGuffey Monument,** Miami University, Campus Avenue.

Located in the courtyard of McGuffey Hall, this monument includes a bust of McGuffey and a group of young children reading a book.

McGuffey, a Presbyterian minister of Scotch-Irish background, was famous for his *Eclectic Readers,* the first of which he wrote and saw published while he was a professor of philology and foreign language at Miami University. Over the next seventy years, eight publishers issued 160 editions of his works, whose sales reached a phenomenal 122,000 copies.

McGuffey became a champion of public education and an educational reformer whose *Readers* were second only to the Bible in their influence upon nineteenth-century America. Possessed of a prodigious memory, he could recite entire books of the Scriptures by heart. When preaching, he always spoke without text, and he claimed that he had given 3,000 sermons without ever writing a single one. His educational career included the presidency of three Ohio institutions of higher learning – Miami, Cincinnati, and Ohio universities – and a professorship at the University of Virginia.

Through the use of maxims, anecdotes, essays, and stories, McGuffey's

Readers reflected an unambiguous moral code. Besides biblical excerpts the textbooks contained selections by Beecher, Rousseau, Webster, Jefferson, Irving, Grimké, Phillips, Channing, Longfellow, Lord Bacon, Addison, Bryant, Byron, Milton, and Shakespeare. Whatever the vehicle, these nineteenth-century "Books of Virtues" tried to inculcate in their young readers the virtues of piety, charity, patriotism, kindness, honesty, and gratitude. One story, for instance, put forward John Jones for emulation because "he did not love to play so much that he could not work." Another described Truthful George, whose offer to pay for a window he had broken brought him a partnership with a grateful merchant. And while laziness, drunkenness, and gambling were inevitably condemned in the readers, thrift, perseverance, and industry were praised: "If we strive, 'tis no disgrace, / Though we may not win the race; / What should you do in that case? / Try, Try Again."

❡ **William McGuffey Memorial Museum,** Miami University, Spring and Oak streets.

From 1833 to 1836 this two-story brick house was the home of *William McGuffey. Today the museum contains a variety of McGuffey memorabilia, including a large collection of *McGuffey's Readers* and *Spellers* as well as his octagon desk with swivel top.

§ Open Saturday and Sunday 2-4. Phone: 513-529-1809 or 2232.

PIQUA

❡ **Piqua Historical Area State Memorial,** 1.25 miles north off State 66, at 9845 North Hardin Road.

Besides an Indian museum and a canal boat ride, one of the attractions of the park is the Johnston farm and Indian agency. The farm property was originally staked out in 1811 by John Johnston, a native of Ballyshannon, Ireland, whose parents had immigrated to Pennsylvania in 1786. The three-story brick Georgian residence in which Johnston lived until sometime in the 1840s has been restored, and the original outbuildings on the property have been reconstructed.

In the early 1790s Johnston served as supplymaster for *General Anthony Wayne during the campaign against the Native Americans of northwest Ohio. Beginning in 1802, he served as an Indian agent for the U.S. government and then from 1812 to 1829 for the state of Ohio. He acted as paymaster and quartermaster during the War of 1812 and was influential in weaning significant Indian support away from Chief Tecumseh. (Johnston was also known for hosting on his property as many as 6,000 Indians at a time.) In the early 1840s he negotiated the removal of the Native Americans from the state and was the author of *An Account of the Indian Tribes of Ohio.* He was a founder of Kenyon College and Miami University.

§ Open Memorial Day-Labor Day, Wednesday-Saturday 9:30-5, Sunday and holidays noon-5; day after Labor Day-October 31, Saturday 9:30-5, Sunday noon-5. Fee. Phone: 937-773-2522 or 800-752-2619.

The Ohio farmhouse of John Johnston, a native of Ballyshannon, Ireland.
(Photo courtesy of James O'Donnell.)

POINT PLEASANT

¶ **Ulysses S. Grant Birthplace,** State 52 and 232.

Ulysses S. Grant, the famous Civil War general and eighteenth president of the United States, was born in this white frame cottage in 1822. The house contains memorabilia connected with the Grant family, among them the general's cradle, Bible, and West Point trunk.

Grant's great-great-grandfather was William Simpson, born in northern Ireland about 1710. Simpson seems to have emigrated from Derigna, near Ballygawley, County Tyrone, in 1738 and died in Buckingham, Pennsylvania, twenty-six years later.

§ Open April-October 31, Wednesday-Saturday 9:30-noon and 1-5, Sunday noon-5. Closed major holidays. Fee. Phone: 513-553-4911.

¶ **Ulysses S. Grant Memorial Bridge,** on U.S. 52.

Built in 1925-26, the bridge is marked by stone pillars mounted with Civil War guns. A bas-relief of *President Grant is on one of the pillars.

POLAND

¶ **McKinley House,** 6 miles south on State 170 at 210 Main Street.

This was the residence of *William McKinley while he was a student in town here. In 1861 he enlisted in the Union army at a local stagecoach inn called the Sparrow Tavern.

POMEROY

¶ **Buffington Island State Monument,** 20 miles southeast on State 24.

This four-acre park is on the site of one of the few Civil War battles that took place in Ohio. In the park is a monument to *General Daniel McCook Sr. – one of the famous "Fighting McCooks" – who was killed during that engagement in July 1863. (See Carrollton, Ohio.)

PUT-IN-BAY

¶ **Perry's Victory and International Peace Memorial,** South Bass Island in Lake Erie.

The victory of *Commodore Oliver H. Perry at the battle of Lake Erie is commemorated by a 352-foot-high Doric column of granite topped by a bronze urn. The actual battle site ten miles to the northwest can be seen from the observation deck.

The son of Christopher Perry and his Irish wife, Oliver Hazard Perry joined the Navy in 1799 at the age of fourteen. He first saw action in the West Indies during the naval war with France and then in the Mediterranean during the war with Tripoli. From 1807 to 1809 he was engaged in the construction of gunboats, a fleet of which he commanded while trying to enforce the American embargo. When the United States declared war against Britain in 1812, he was assigned the task of creating an American fleet to challenge British control of Lake Erie. From his headquarters at Erie, Pennsylvania, he spent the spring and summer of 1813 supervising the building, equipping, and manning of ten vessels, the largest of which were the *Lawrence* and the *Niagara*, each 480 tons burden. Having made the *Lawrence* his flagship, Perry sailed up the lake to Put-in-Bay and reconnoitred the British fleet of six vessels at the Detroit River.

The fateful battle was finally joined on September 10, 1813. In preparation for the encounter, Perry ordered that a battle flag with the motto "Don't give up the ship" – attributed to the dying Lawrence – be unfurled from his flagship. Early in the conflict, however, the *Lawrence* was virtually destroyed by the *Detroit*, with a loss of eighty-three of her 103 men. Perry quickly transferred to the *Niagara*, which subsequently broke through the British line after a fifteen-minute barrage forced the limeys to surrender. Perry lost twenty-seven killed to the enemy's forty-one, although each side had about ninety-five wounded. The victorious American sent his famous message to General William Henry Harrison: "We have met the enemy, and they are ours. Two ships, two brigs, one schooner, and one sloop." (His dispatch to the secretary of the navy – similar to Nelson's report after the battle of the Nile – is less well known: "It has pleased the Almighty to give to the arms of the United States a signal victory over their enemies on this lake.") Perry's achievement won control of Lake Erie for the Americans and made possible Harrison's invasion of Canada. Harrison's victory at the battle of the Thames effectively ended the War of 1812 in the Northwest.

§ Accessible by passenger/auto ferry from Catawba and Port Clinton (April-November); by plane from Port Clinton (year-round). Open mid June-Labor Day, daily 10-7; rest of the year, daily 10-5. Closed November to late April. Fee for elevator. Phone: 419-285-2184.

SOMERSET

The Somerset Historic District contains three sites associated with General Philip Sheridan, the famous Civil War cavalry officer whose victory over General Robert E. Lee at Five Forks led to the latter's surrender at Appomattox. Sheridan's parents were emigrants from County Cavan, Ireland. (See Sheridan Circle, District of Columbia.)

¶ **Philip Sheridan Boyhood Home,** 114 Sheridan Avenue (State 13).
As a youngster in Somerset, Philip Sheridan had two teachers, one of them the itinerant Irishman Patrick McNaly. Sheridan recalled that McNaly resorted to whipping every student in the class if he could not discover the "guilty mischief-maker." The famous officer later acknowledged the importance of his early education by saying that it was "the little white schoolhouse of the North [that] made us superior to the South."
It was from Somerset that the young Sheridan set out for West Point in 1848. Although he found that his Catholicism and Famine-Irish background were distinct handicaps, it was his Irish temper that almost ended his plans to pursue a military career. The unfortunate incident occurred at the beginning of his senior year, when a cadet sergeant began to berate Sheridan during a parade march. Provoked by the verbal harassment, Sheridan cursed the sergeant ("God damn you, sir, I'll run you through") and lunged at him with his bayonet. Perhaps because he missed his intended target, Sheridan was suspended from the academy for only a year. During that time he returned to Somerset.

¶ **Sheridan House,** 417 South Columbus Street. Private.
Sheridan built this house for his parents.

¶ **Sheridan Statue,** in the town square (U.S. 22 and State 13).

SPRINGFIELD

This city had its origins in a sawmill and gristmill erected soon after 1800 by *Simon Kenton, a scout and spy who participated in the major campaigns against the Indian tribes in the Old Northwest. Here in 1807 Kenton and other settlers in Springfield met with the Indian chiefs Tecumseh, MacPherson, and Roundhead to reaffirm their mutual desire for peace in the area.

STEUBENVILLE

¶ **Edwin Stanton Statue,** in front of the courthouse, 301 Market Street.
This eighteen-foot monument to President Lincoln's secretary of war was sculpted by *Alexander Doyle. The statue, which depicts Stanton making a speech at the courthouse, was a gift of the artist to Steubenville, where both he and Stanton were born.

¶ **"Fighting McCooks" Monument,** town center.
This memorial honors *Daniel McCook and *John McCook and their fifteen sons, known as the "Fighting McCooks" because of their service in the U.S. armed forces. All but one of the clan saw action in the Civil War, thirteen as officers. (See Carrollton and Lisbon, Ohio.)

¶ **Union Cemetery,** 1720 West Market Street.
Among those interred here are the *Reverend Joseph Ruggles Wilson (the father of Woodrow Wilson) and three of the *"Fighting McCooks" (Anson, George, and Francis McCook).

TOLEDO

¶ **Fallen Timbers Monument,** off State 24 on Jerome Road.
This memorial commemorates the 1794 victory of *General Anthony Wayne over local Native Americans. As a result of their defeat, the Indians relinquished their rights to most of the land in the vicinity.

¶ **James Steedman Statue,** Riverside Park, Summit and Galena streets.
This statue of the Union commander General James Steedman was sculpted by *Alexander Doyle.

¶ **Wildwood Manor House,** 5 miles northwest, at 5100 West Central Avenue, in the Wildwood Preserve Metropark.
Constructed in the 1930s, this Georgian mansion was the home of Rob-

ert Stranahan Sr., the cofounder of Champion Spark Plug Company. The manor house features seventeen baths, sixteen fireplaces, more than fifty rooms, and a solarium that overlooks the formal gardens.

Stranahan was a cousin of Frank Stranahan, reputedly the first white settler in Fort Lauderdale, Florida, and the grandson of an immigrant from County Antrim, Ireland. (See Fort Lauderdale, Florida, in *Irish America*, Volume 2.)

§ Open Wednesday-Sunday and holidays noon-5 (also Wednesday 5-8, June-August). Closed January 1, Thanksgiving, early December, and December 25. Phone: 419-535-3050.

URBANA

¶ **Simon Kenton Burial Site,** Oakdale Cemetery, south on U.S. 36.

This is the grave of Simon Kenton, the scout and famous Indian fighter who once saved Daniel Boone's life. The grave is marked by a monument erected in 1884 and adorned by the heads of an Indian chief, a panther, a fox, and a bear.

Born in Virginia in 1755 to an Irish father and a Scotch mother, Kenton at age fifteen fled across the Alleghenies after mistakenly thinking that he had killed the suitor of a young girl whose affections he had sought. For a time, as the unofficial guardian of white settlers coming into Kentucky via the Ohio River, he protected them against Indian attacks. During subsequent campaigns against the Native Americans, he was the friend and companion of Daniel Boone, whose life he saved during an Indian attack on Boonesborough. On several other occasions Kenton was in the service of General George Rogers Clark, at least once as captain of a retaliatory force that burned Indian huts, forts, and crops.

During his lifetime Kenton was a frequent captive of the Shawnee. His captors forced him to suffer the gauntlet eight times and condemned him to death three times, although he was invariably rescued. On one occasion he was tied to the stake for twenty-four hours, only to be released to run a mile-long gauntlet between two rows of 600 savages. During that particular trial he was knocked down, severely beaten, and again imprisoned.

In 1778 Kenton was brought captive to Wapatomica, a Shawnee village near present-day Zanesfield. There he was forced to run the gauntlet and was painted black in preparation for his expected immolation at the stake. While he awaited death, he was recognized by Simon Girty, a white man with whom he had scouted on Lord Dunmore's expedition but who had turned renegade and was then living with the Indians. Girty interceded on behalf of his former comrade, obtained his release, and took him home, where he washed his wounds and gave him new clothes.

¶ **Simon Kenton House Site,** 10 miles south on U.S. 68.

The log manor house which *Simon Kenton built on this site in 1803 was located near a spring where, twenty-two years earlier as an Indian captive, he had stopped to take a drink.

WARREN

According to local boosters, two of the most famous musical compositions of *Stephen Collins Foster may have had their genesis in Warren. Foster is said to have begun writing "Jeanie with the Light Brown Hair" while staying at the Austin House, a local stagecoach inn, while a stroll along the Mahoning River supposedly provided the inspiration for "My Old Kentucky Home."

YOUNGSTOWN

¶ **The Butler Institute of American Art,** 524 Wick Avenue.

In addition to works by the Irish-American artist John Singleton Copley, the museum's permanent collection includes major canvases by Mary Cassatt, Thomas Eakins, Winslow Homer, Frederic Remington, and Benjamin West.

§ Open Tuesday-Saturday 11-4 (also Wednesday 4-8 p.m.), Sunday noon-4. Closed holidays. Phone: 330-743-1107.

ZANESFIELD

¶ **Zane-Kenton Monument,** Sandusky Street.

This sixty-ton boulder was dedicated in 1914 to frontiersmen Isaac Zane and *Simon Kenton. (See Urbana, Ohio.)

¶ Kenton's farm, cabin site, and original grave are located off State 33. In 1865 his remains were removed to Urbana, Ohio [q.v.].

PENNSYLVANIA

ALLENTOWN

¶ **George Taylor House and Park,** 4 miles north off U.S. 22 at Lehigh and Poplar streets, Catasauqua.

Constructed in 1768, this house was the home of George Taylor, one of the three Irish-born signers of the Declaration of Independence. The restored house features a museum and a walled garden.

Taylor, who was born in northern Ireland about 1716, came to Pennsylvania twenty years later and first worked for an ironmaker named Savage at his mill near Easton, Pennsylvania. Because the young Irishman was not physically strong enough to continue his first job of shoveling coal, he was soon put in charge of the enterprise's bookkeeping. After Savage's death Taylor came into possession of the mill by marrying his former master's widow.

With his election to the Pennsylvania legislature in 1764, Taylor began a political career that brought him much influence. He bitterly opposed the colony's royal government and became an outspoken critic of the Stamp Act and the closure of Boston harbor by the British. In 1775 he called for the creation of an intercolonial congress and a declaration of independence from Britain as soon as possible. Although he was not a member of the Continental Congress when it voted for independence, he was appointed to that body two weeks later to replace one of the five Pennsylvania del-

Home of George Taylor, an Irish-born signer of the Declaration of Independence.

egates who had opposed independence. Taylor signed the Declaration of Independence the following August.

§ Open June-October 31, Saturday and Sunday afternoon; other times by appointment. Phone: 610-435-4664.

BELLEFONTE

¶ **Andrew Curtin Statue,** in front of the courthouse, Allegheny and High streets.

This statue by *William Clark Noble honors *Andrew Curtin, the popular Civil War governor of Pennsylvania, who was born here in 1815. The house in which Curtin was born no longer exists, and his home during his adult life is now the Elks Club on High Street.

Curtin's father, an immigrant of Scotch-Irish stock, came to this area in 1800 from County Clare, Ireland, and engaged in the manufacture of iron in nearby Milesburg [q.v.].

BETHEL

¶ **Miller House,** Manse Drive.

This stone and masonry house was erected by James Miller on the site of a log structure built about 1763 by his Irish ancestor, immigrant Oliver Miller. The first shot fired in the Whiskey Rebellion of 1792 occurred here.

BRYN MAWR

¶ **Harriton House,** 1 mile north of U.S. 30 on Morris Avenue, 0.5 mile west on Old Guelph Road, and then north on Harriton Road.

Originally called "Bryn Mawr," the 700-acre Harriton estate was bought by Richard Harrison in 1719, although the two-story stone house on the property had been built fifteen years earlier. Title eventually passed to Harrison's daughter, Hannah, who in 1774 married Charles Thomson, the secretary of the Continental Congress. With the creation of the new federal government in 1789, Thompson retired to Harriton.

Thomson had been born in County Derry, Ireland, in 1729. Ten years later his widowed father left Ireland with his six children but died on shipboard and was buried at sea off the Delaware Capes. After stripping the orphans of their valuables, the captain of the ship put the children ashore at New Castle, Delaware. Before long the young Thomson had taken the first steps in an academic career. He attended the academy of *Dr. Francis Alison in New London, Pennsylvania, and then conducted a private school for several years. He was so intent upon studying Greek that he walked sixty miles from Philadelphia to Amboy, New Jersey, to meet a British officer who was regarded as the foremost Greek scholar in America at that

"Harriton House," the home of Charles Thomson.

time. Through his acquaintance with Benjamin Franklin, he became a teacher at the Philadelphia Academy and later at the William Penn Charter School.

During his lifetime Thomson acquired a reputation for accuracy and fairness. On one occasion a group of Quakers asked him to record in short hand the events surrounding the signing of the Treaty of Easton in 1756. His unofficial record was accepted by the head of the Delaware tribe when the chief disputed the accuracy of the official minutes taken by the governor's representative. A year later the Indians adopted Thomson into their tribe and gave him a name meaning "man who tells the truth." His subsequent reputation for accuracy while secretary of the newly assembled Continental Congress earned him immortality in the saying, "Here comes the truth; here is Charles Thomson!"

Although at first his appointment as secretary to Congress was considered temporary, Thomson served for fifteen years. Predictably, he left a record of how he was asked to accept the undertaking while on his honeymoon in Philadelphia in 1774: "I . . . followed the messenger myself to the Carpenters' Hall, and entered Congress. Here was indeed an august assembly, and deep thought and solemn anxiety were observable on their countenances. I walked up the aisle, and standing opposite to the President, I bowed, and told him I waited his pleasure. He replied, 'Congress desire the favor of you, sir, to take their minutes.' I bowed in acquiescence, and took my seat at the desk." (History does not record his wife's opinion about the interrupted honeymoon.) During his tenure with Congress, he recorded the birth of a new nation and enjoyed the honor – with John Hancock – of signing the first copy of the Declaration of Independence transmitted to the world. (The original document was in Thomson's hand.) Following his resignation in 1789, Thomson retired to Harriton. For the next twenty years he devoted himself to translating the Septuagint and the New Testament, publishing in 1815 a synopsis of the four Gospels. He died in 1824 at the age of ninety-five and was buried at Harriton.

§ Open Wednesday-Saturday 10-4; other times by appointment. Closed holidays. Fee. Phone: 610-525-0201.

¶ In 1838 the promoters of North Laurel Hill Cemetery in Philadelphia conceived the idea of obtaining the remains of distinguished individuals like *Charles Thomson and his wife as a method of attracting patronage. Although Thomson's heirs objected to the scheme, one of his nephews gave his approval. When a farmhand unexpectedly came upon the exhumers at their ghoulish work, they quickly threw the supposed bodies of Thomson and his wife into a wagon and headed posthaste for the new cemetery. Although some doubt remains about the identity of the reburied corpses, a sixteen-foot obelisk in honor of Thomson marks the new grave site. (See North Laurel Hill Cemetery, Philadelphia.)

CANONSBURG

¶ **Log Academy,** East College and Central streets, in front of the Canon-McMillan Middle School.

Erected in 1780 by the Reverend John McMillan, this log cabin college is the oldest school building west of the Allegheny Mountains. The school was the forerunner of Jefferson College, which subsequently merged with Washington College, now located in Washington, Pennsylvania.

The son of Irish immigrant parents who had settled in Chester County, Pennsylvania, McMillan was a graduate of the College of New Jersey (now Princeton) and had been ordained in 1776. Because of the onset of the war with Britain, however, it was not until two years later that his wife joined him in this part of the state.

Although he later described the generosity of his parishioners in helping him build and furnish the cabin in which he and his bride lived, he confessed that "Sometimes indeed we had no bread for weeks together, but we had plenty of pumpkins and potatoes and all the necessaries of life; as for luxuries, we were not concerned in them." Despite the cabin's privations, it was here that McMillan gave instruction in Greek, Latin, and theology from 1782 to 1791. Although in that latter year he turned over his students to the newly created Canonsburg Academy, he continued to teach theology to its graduates. In later years he served as professor of divinity and vice president of Jefferson College. During his long career he reputedly trained at least 100 students for the ministry. Until his death in 1833, he continued to wear the knee breeches, buckled shoes, and cocked hat of an earlier generation.

CARLISLE

¶ **Carlisle Barracks,** 1 mile north on U.S. 11.

The barracks once housed the Carlisle Indian School, established in 1879. Jim Thorpe, the winner of the pentathlon and decathlon in the 1912 Olympics, was one of the 6,000 Indians who attended the school. Thorpe was of mixed Irish, French, and Native American ancestry.

§ Open late May-early September, daily 10-1. Closed federal holidays. Phone: 717-245-3152.

¶ **Jim Thorpe Monument,** in the courthouse square (High and Hanover streets).

¶ **William Thompson Burial Site,** Old Carlisle Graveyard, on East South Street.

In addition to the grave of Molly Pitcher, famous for her heroism at the battle of Monmouth, this cemetery contains the grave of the Irishman William Thompson. The burial site is marked by a graceful Celtic cross.

Born in County Meath in 1736, Thompson had been a surveyor and justice of the peace in Carlisle before serving in the French and Indian War as a captain of dragoons. When news of the battle of Bunker Hill reached Pennsylvania, he was placed in command of a battalion of riflemen raised in the southeastern counties of the colony. Dressed in white rifle shirts and round hats, the privates were noted for the accuracy of their aim, and many of them stood more than six feet in height. (The predominantly Irish character of the unit is evident in the fact that, of its 731 men, 361 were natives of Ireland and 171 others had Irish surnames.) With the Irishman Edward Hand as his lieutenant colonel, Thompson marched his men to Boston, becoming the first military commander to arrive from the south.

After his promotion to brigadier general in March 1776, Thompson was ordered to Canada with 2,000 men, but he was captured near Three Rivers. Upon his exchange and return to Pennsylvania, he charged *Thomas McKean, then a member of Congress, with hindering his exchange. So hateful were Thompson's words about McKean that Congress declared him "guilty of an insult to the honor and dignity of this house." Although Thompson appeared before Congress and apologized, McKean brought suit for libel and was awarded £5,700 in damages. His point having been made, McKean declined the award.

CHAMBERSBURG

This town of 17,000 people was named for Benjamin Chambers, one of four brothers who had come to Pennsylvania from County Antrim, Ireland, between 1726 and 1730. Soon after their arrival, they settled in what is now Dauphin County, where they set up a mill. Benjamin and his brother Joseph later founded what became Chambersburg, while one of the other brothers moved to Cumberland County and the fourth settled near Shippesburg.

CLARK

J Tara, I-80 exit 1N, then 7 miles north on State 18 to State 258. Phone: 412-962-3535 or 800-782-2803.

Built in 1854, this Greek Revival mansion is now an inn whose name is an allusion to the Southern plantation created by *Margaret Mitchell for *Gone With the Wind*. Each room in the modern Tara is named after a character from the famous novel. (See Atlanta, Georgia, in *Irish America*, Volume 2.)

CONCORDVILLE

J Newlin Mill Park, 1.5 miles east on U.S. 1.

This 150-acre park preserves the home and mill operation of Nathaniel Newlin, an Irish immigrant who was a leader in local commercial and political affairs. The property includes Newlin's restored gristmill (1704) and a miller's house erected by Nathaniel Newlin III in 1739 .

Newlin had emigrated from County Tyrone in 1683, accompanying his English father (Nicholas) and Irish mother (Elizabeth Paggett) as they fled to escape further persecution because of their Quakerism. After buying 500 acres from William Penn, Nicholas Newlin settled in Concordville and built a sawmill. He was elected to the Provincial Council and later served as a justice of the local court. By the time of his death in 1699, he had acquired almost 750 acres in Concord and Birmingham townships.

Nathaniel Newlin, meanwhile, gradually came to own almost 9,000 acres in Concordville and elsewhere. During his fourteen terms as a representative of Chester County in the Pennsylvania Assembly, he worked with the governor to obtain passage of a law that granted Pennsylvania Quakers the same legal rights enjoyed by their coreligionists in England. He also drew up legislation prohibiting the sale of rum to the Indians and threw his support behind the creation of a government loan office authorized to issue £15,000 of paper money in an effort to overcome a widespread recession. During his political career he also served as a justice of the peace, an assessor, and a tax commissioner. His contribution of £8 toward the construction of the Quaker meetinghouse in Concordville was the congregation's largest subscription. He was placed in an embarrassing position with his fellow Quakers, however, when he was required to pay a £10 fine because of his daughter's fornication.

§ Open March-September, daily 9-dusk; rest of the year, daily 8-5. Nature trails, picnicking, and trout fishing. Fee. Phone: 610-459-2359.

The Newlin Gristmill in Concordville.

COUDERSPORT

This small town of 3,000 people was founded by John Keating, an Irish mercenary who had served as a captain of the Irish Brigade in the French army. After coming to America in 1792, Keating became involved with land speculators and their colonization efforts along the Susquehanna River. It was during this time that he managed the Ceres Land Company, which owned 300,000 acres in this part of the state. Keating granted fifty acres to each of the first fifty settlers in the Coudersport area.

EASTON

¶ **Parsons-Taylor House,** on the northeast corner of 4th and Ferry streets. Private.

This two-story stone house was occupied by George Taylor, one of the Irish-born signers of the Declaration of Independence. After 1763 he began to live here much of the time in order to be closer to his ironworks. Taylor and his wife had two children, although he had five illegitimate children by his housekeeper. He died in this house in 1781. (See Allentown, Pennsylvania.)

§ Phone: 610-258-1612 (Chamber of Commerce).

ERIE

¶ **Oliver H. Perry Monument,** Presque Isle State Park, 5 miles north on Peninsula Drive (State 832). Accessible by ferry.

This monument marks the area where *Oliver H. Perry built the fleet that successfully engaged the British in the Anglo-American contest for control of Lake Erie in September 1813. (See Put-in-Bay, Ohio.)

§ Park open daily 5 a.m.-dusk. Beaches open Memorial Day weekend-Labor Day. Phone: 814-833-7424.

¶ **Reconstruction of the U.S. Brig *Niagara*,** 164 East Front Street.

The U.S. Brig *Niagara* was the small wooden vessel to which *Oliver H. Perry moved when his flagship was rendered indefensible during the battle of Lake Erie. The only original part of the reconstructed ship is a long section of the keel, recovered when the ship was raised from Misery Bay in 1875. (See Put-in-Bay, Ohio.)

§ Open Memorial Day weekend-September 30, Monday-Saturday 9-5, Sunday noon-5. Fee. Phone: 814-871-4596.

¶ **Wayne Memorial Blockhouse,** State Soldiers' and Sailors' Home, 560 East 3rd Street.

This replica of the blockhouse in which *Anthony Wayne died in 1796 was erected as a memorial to the Revolutionary War general. Although his body was originally buried at the foot of the flagpole here, it was reinterred in Radnor, Pennsylvania, in 1809. (See Paoli, Pennsylvania.)

§ Open daily. Visitors can obtain key from the Soldiers' and Sailors' Home. Phone: 814-871-4531.

FORT WASHINGTON

¶ **Hope Lodge,** Pennsylvania Turnpike exit 26S to Pennsylvania Avenue and then 3 blocks to 553 Bethlehem Pike.

After the battle of Germantown in 1777, this mansion was the headquarters of *John Cochran, the surgeon-general of the Continental Army. (See Schuyler-Hamilton House, Morristown, New Jersey.)

§ Open Tuesday-Saturday 9-4, Sunday noon-4. Closed holidays. Fee. Phone: 215-646-1595.

GETTYSBURG

¶ **Ancient Order of Hibernians Memorial,** St. Francis Xavier Catholic Church, 22 West High Street.

A tablet in front of the church portrays *Father William Corby granting absolution to the Irish Brigade on July 2, 1863, the second day of the battle of Gettysburg.

¶ **Dobbin House Tavern,** 89 Steinwehr Avenue.

Although the Dobbin House is now a restaurant, it was originally built in 1776 as the home of the Reverend Alexander Dobbin, a native of Londonderry, northern Ireland. Dobbin had come to this area to assume the pastorate of the Rock Creek Presbyterian Church. The house, built on a 300-acre tract which he had bought, served as the dwelling for his increasingly large family – ten children born to his first wife (Isabella Gamble, a native of County Down, Ireland) and nine children already born to his second wife.

To supplement his salary as a minister, Dobbin opened a "Classical Academy" in his home. This school was both a seminary and a liberal arts college, the only one of its kind west of the Susquehanna River. Among his students Dobbins was known not only for his scholarship in Latin, Greek, and Hebrew but also for his skill in biblical interpretation and criticism. He had a personal library of 300 volumes.

§ Phone: 717-334-2100.

The eighteenth-century home of the Reverend Alexander Dobbin.

GETTYSBURG NATIONAL MILITARY PARK

The country's most revered battlefield is crossed by thirty-one miles of
marked avenues, three observation towers, and more than 1,300 statues,
monuments, and markers. The park roads are open daily 6 a.m. to 10 p.m.

¶ **Father Corby Statue,** South Hancock Avenue.
    Dedicated in 1910, this statue depicts *Father William Corby in the act
of granting general absolution to the members of the Irish Brigade just
before they set out to help occupy Little Round Top on July 2, 1863. The
statue was designed by the sculptor *Samuel Aloysius Murray. A replica
of the statue stands on the campus of Notre Dame University in South
Bend, Indiana [*q.v.*].
    With the outbreak of the Civil War, Father Corby had been commis-
sioned chaplain of the 88th New York Infantry, one of the many Celtic
units in the Irish Brigade. In that capacity he participated in all the campaigns of the Army of the Potomac, seeing service most notably at the
battles of Antietam, Fredericksburg, Chancellorsville, Gettysburg,
Spotsylvania, and Petersburg. He is best remembered for granting general absolution to the members of the Irish Brigade at Gettysburg.
    The scene was later described by St. Clair Mulholland, himself a na-

Statue of Father William Corby
as he granted absolution
to the Irish Brigade.

tive of County Antrim, Ireland, and at the time a major in the brigade: "As a large majority of the brigade were Catholics, the Chaplain of the brigade, Rev. William Corby, proposed to give a general absolution to all the men before going into the fight. While this is customary in the armies of Catholic countries in Europe, it was perhaps the first time it was ever witnessed on this continent. . . . Father Corby stood on a large rock in front of the brigade. Addressing the men, he explained what he was about to do, saying that each one could receive the benefit of the absolution by a making a sincere act of contrition and firmly resolving to embrace the first opportunity to confess his sins, urging them to do their duty, and reminding them of the high and sacred nature of their trust as soldiers and the noble object for which they fought. . . . The brigade was standing at 'Order arms!' As he closed his address, every man, Catholic and non-Catholic, fell on his knees with his head bowed down. Then stretching his right hand toward the brigade, Father Corby pronounced the words of absolution . . . ."

Father Corby is remembered in these excerpts from "A Miracle of War" by Smith Johnson:

> With spirits ardent, undismayed,
> With flags uplifted toward the sky,
> There stands brave Meagher's old brigade
> Those noble laurels ne'er will fade
> Upon the page of history.

> "All forward, men!" No, pause a while –
> Dead silence follows like parade
> At "order arms," for 'long the file
> There moves a priest with holy smile –
> The priest of Meagher's old brigade.

> All eyes were toward him reverent turned,
> For he was known and loved by all,
> And every face with fervor burned,
> And with a glance his mission learned –
> A mission of high Heaven's call.

> Then spake the priest: "My comrades, friends,
> Ere long the battle fierce will surge,
> Ere long the curse of war descends –
> At such a moment God commends
> You from the soul all sin to purge.
> "Kneel, soldiers; lift your hearts to God,
> In sweet contrition crush the pride
> Of human minds; kneel on the sod
> That soon will welter in your blood –

Look up to Christ, who for you died."

And every man, whate'er his creed,
Kneels down, and whispers pass along
The ranks, and murmuring voices plead
To be from sin's contagion freed
And turned from path of mortal wrong.

Across the vale the gray lines view
The priest and those who, kneeling now,
For absolution humbly sue
And joining hearts, the gray and blue,
Together make the holy vow.

¶ **1st New Jersey Brigade Monument,** in the woods off Hancock Avenue 0.25 mile south of the Pennsylvania Monument.

The west side of this memorial is adorned with a likeness of *Philip Kearny, who commanded the 1st New Jersey Brigade during the Civil War. A plaque notes that Kearny's brigade fought in all the important battles of the war and that its force of 13,805 men included the 10th, 23rd, and 40th regiments of New Jersey Volunteers. (See Kearny, New Jersey; Arlington National Cemetery, Arlington, Virginia, in *Irish America*, Volume 2.)

Portrait bust of Philip Kearny on the 1st New Jersey Brigade Monument.

¶ **George Meade Headquarters,** Taneytown Road.

This one-and-a-half-story farmhouse was the headquarters of *General George Gordon Meade, who had been given command of the Army of the Potomac only five days before the battle. Although he was driven from the house by artillery fire on the afternoon of July 3, 1863, the Union troops under his command successfully repulsed the Confederate drive. (See George Meade Memorial, District of Columbia.)

After evacuating his headquarters, Meade was confronted by an angry civilian who complained that his house was being used as a hospital and that his property was littered with amputated limbs. When the citizen expressed his intention to seek reimbursement from the government, Meade rebuked him: "Why, you craven fool, until this battle is decided, you do not know, neither do I, if you will have a government to apply to. . . . If I hear any more from you, I will give you a gun and send you to the front to defend your rights." After the battle Meade was named brigadier general in the regular army.

¶ George Meade Equestrian Statue, Hancock Avenue.

The bronze plaque on the pedestal summarizes George Meade's military career and bears the words of recognition which Congress used to honor Meade "for the skill and heroic valor which, at Gettysburg, repelled, defeated and drove back, broken and dispirited, beyond the Rappahannock, the veteran army of the Rebellion."

¶ Irish Brigade Monument, Sickles Avenue, the Loop.

Designed by *William O'Donovan, this memorial was dedicated on July 2, 1888, the twenty-fifth anniversary of the Irish Brigade's participation in the battle of Gettysburg. O'Donovan, ironically, had been a corporal in the Confederate army at Gettysburg and had seen earlier action against the Irish Brigade in engagements from Bull Run to Appomattox.

The memorial, in the shape of a Celtic cross, specifically honors the 63rd, 69th, and 88th New York regiments, which initially formed the Irish Brigade. The five medallions on the cross represent the three regiments, New York State, and Ireland. (The Irish Brigade later included the 28th Massachusetts and the 116th Pennsylvania infantries.) During the fighting at Gettysburg, three Irish companies helped capture Little Round Top.

A plaque on the reverse side of the monument recalls that the three New York regiments were under the command of Colonel Patrick Kelly at Gettysburg and numbered only 240 of their original 3,000 men. A native of County Galway, Kelly was – according to W. L. D. O'Grady, a member of the 88th New York – dark complected and possessed of "probably the finest war-horse in the United States." O'Grady's memoir was especially flattering of Kelly's horsemanship: "His [Kelly's] favorite charger, 'Faugh-a-Ballagh' . . . would 'negotiate' the most formidable stone-wall, fence, or brook with his 'wetterweight' [sic] master on his back like a colt – a frequent performance which never failed to start the Brigade cheering. It was the one thing where the light-heartedness of the boy showed in Col. Kelly, for he was habitually a grave man, a man of few words, gentle, kind, unassuming, feeling his responsibilities in fullest measure, and with a disciplined bravery that would send his men, himself at the head, to storm the very gates of hell . . . ." The day before his death during the

The Irish Brigade Monument.

assault on Petersburg in June 1864, Kelly remarked about the loss of some domestic pets and – in an allusion to his swarthy complexion – predicted his own demise: "I've lost my black horse, and my black dog, and now they'll have 'the little black man.'"

At the dedication of the monument, William Collins read his poem "In Memory of the Fallen Dead of the Irish Brigade." Stanza VI is reprinted here:

> Here, on the field of Gettysburg, where treason's banner flew:
> Where rushed in wrath the Southern gray to smite the Northern blue;
> Where'er that blue, by valor nerved, in seried ranks was seen
> There flashed between it and the foe the daring Irish Green!
> And never yet, on any land, rushed forth to Freedom's aid
> A braver or more dauntless band than Ireland's brave Brigade.
> Pause on their graves! 'Tis holy dust ye tread upon to-day –
> The dust of Freedom's martyred dead, whose souls have passed away!

The Irish Brigade had been organized and first commanded by Thomas Francis Meagher, a native of Waterford, Ireland, who had escaped to America from a British penal colony in Tasmania in 1852. He had been banished to that remote part of the British empire for his involvement in the failed Irish rebellion of 1848. After his arrival in New York City, he studied and practiced law and was made editor of the *Irish News*, a position from which he became the spokesman for the "Young Ireland" movement in America.

At the onset of the Civil War, Meagher organized a company of Zouaves, which was later incorporated into the Irish 69th Volunteers. In the winter of 1861-62, he organized and commanded the Irish Brigade, whose banner boasted an Irish harp, a wreath of shamrocks, and the Gaelic motto "They shall never retreat from the charge of lances." The brigade fought in thirty-six engagements or campaigns during the war, including Fair Oaks, Antietam, Fredericksburg, Chancellorsville, Gettysburg, and Appomattox. (See Irish Brigade Monument, Sharpsburg, Maryland; see Helena, Montana, in *Irish America*, Volume 2.)

√ A commemorative tablet on the Granville Hotel in Waterford, Ireland, marks the site of Meagher's birthplace in 1823. The tablet refers to Meagher as the "Illustrious '48 Patriot" and contains his famous remark "With My Country I Leave My Memory."

¶ James McKay Rorty Memorial, Cemetery Hill.
This monument honors not only its Donegal-born namesake but also the other members of Battery B of the First New York Light Artillery. Rorty was killed while helping repulse Pickett's Charge.

¶ John Buford Statue, Stone Avenue and U.S. 30 (west of Gettysburg).
Erected in 1895, this statue of the Union general John Buford is the work of *James Edward Kelly.

¶ John Reynolds Monuments
Three memorials at Gettysburg honor General John Fulton Reynolds: a granite shaft on Reynolds Avenue, about 400 yards west of the road; an equestrian statue in the National Cemetery (by *James Edward Kelly); and an equestrian statue on the Chambersburg road.

The grandson of an Irish immigrant who had come to America in 1762, Reynolds was a graduate of the U.S. Military Academy and had been breveted for gallantry at Monterrey and Buena Vista during the Mexican War. Between that conflict and the Civil War, his tours of garrison duty were interrupted by an overland expedition to Salt Lake City and participation in the campaigns against the Rogue River Indians in Oregon and the Mormons in Utah. On the eve of the Civil War, he was named commandant of cadets at West Point, where he was also a tactics instructor. During the war Reynolds was placed in command of the I Army Corps of the Army of the Potomac. If his plan to attack the enemy's left flank at Chancellorsville had been adopted, the victory might have gone to the

Union. In the face of General Lee's expected incursion into the North, Reynolds was ordered to occupy Gettysburg. There, on the first of the three-day struggle that followed, he was killed by a sharpshooter as he led the Second Wisconsin Regiment near the Chambersburg road.

¶ 9th Massachusetts Volunteers Monument, on the north slope of Big Round Top.

A gift of the Society of the Ninth Regiment, this memorial was dedicated in 1885 and marks the center of the position which the Irish regiment held during the battle of Gettysburg.

¶ 116th Pennsylvania Infantry Monument, Sickles Avenue, the Loop.

The work of J. Henderson Kelly, this unusual memorial was dedicated in 1889 and depicts a dead soldier lying near a shattered stone wall, his rifle and cap nearby. Commanded by *Major St. Clair Mulholland, the 116th Pennsylvania – with approximately sixty-six men – was one of the smallest infantry regiments in the Army of the Potomac.

Mulholland later expressed the feelings which Gettysburg would ultimately arouse in Americans: "The field is fast becoming the National Mecca, and year after year the number of visitors to the ground increases until tens of thousands of Americans annually make a pilgrimage to the holy ground and worship at the shrine where so many noble men laid down their lives in defence of the State and cause. . . . No kings, princes or potentates lie here, but five thousand gallant men, greater than kings, more splendid in their deeds and in their death than any of the princes or great ones who slumber within the fretted walls of Europe's grand old cathedrals – fathers, brothers and kinsmen, men who came from eighteen states to shed their blood on Pennsylvania's soil in defence of the Union and human liberty. No wonder, then, that year by year thousands of Americans visit the field, linger on the long line of battle, dwell on the memories of the fight and meditate upon the heroism displayed in the battle."

¶ Patrick O'Rorke Memorial, on Little Round Top.

This memorial bust of *Colonel Patrick O'Rorke was dedicated in 1889 by veterans of the 140th New York, the regiment which he commanded during its initial ascent of Little Round Top. O'Rorke was shot in the neck, however, just as he prepared his men to fire on the advancing Confederates ("Here they are, men. Commence firing!"). Despite his death, his troops repulsed the enemy charge and captured the summit. (See Rochester, New York.)

¶ Pennsylvania Memorial, at Pleasonton and Sedgwick avenues.

This huge granite structure was erected in 1910 to honor the 34,530

*Memorial bust of
Colonel Patrick O'Rorke.*

*Statues of General George Gordon Meade (left) and Governor Andrew Curtin
on the Pennsylvania Memorial.*

Pennsylvanians who participated in the battle of Gettysburg. The sides of the memorial are adorned with statues of prominent officers and politicians, among them three Irish Americans: Andrew Curtin, George Meade, and John Reynolds. Curtin was the wartime governor of Pennsylvania and the son of an immigrant from County Clare, Ireland.

In his first inaugural address, Curtin proclaimed his state's loyalty to the Union and subsequently aroused such a level of patriotism that 28,000 Pennsylvanians – more than twice the state's quota – responded to Lincoln's call for troops. (The governor obtained funds from the state legislature to maintain the extra forces.) Curtin's subsequent solicitude for his state's soldiers – including caring for them in hospital, retrieving their bodies for burial, and obtaining funds for the support of their orphans – earned him the sobriquet the "Soldier's Friend."

¶ 6th New York Cavalry Memorial, Buford Avenue.

Erected in 1890, this commemorative monument was designed by *James Edward Kelly, who also executed the bas-relief of General Thomas Devin in one of the bronze panels on the memorial.

¶ 66th New York Infantry Monument, Sickles Avenue, east of the Loop.

Because this New York regiment contained a large number of Irish soldiers, this memorial features a shamrock in the representation of Union and Confederate soldiers shaking hands.

¶ 69th Pennsylvania Infantry Monument, at the Angle.

Located where the climax of the three-day battle occurred, this obelisk memorial is adorned with an Irish harp and honors the men in *Colonel Dennis O'Kane's infantry unit. Although he was killed in the fighting, his men pushed back a Confederate charge that hoped to break the Union line.

¶ Soldiers' National Cemetery, Baltimore Road to Taneytown Road.

This seventeen-acre cemetery, which contains the graves of 3,604 soldiers, was established through the efforts of *Governor Andrew Curtin. While visiting the field soon after the battle, he was outraged to find that the bodies of some of the fallen men protruded from the ground because they had been buried in such shallow graves. He ordered that these bodies be reinterred decently.

¶ 28th Massachusetts Infantry Monument, Sickles Avenue, the Loop.

This memorial was dedicated in 1886 to honor the largest unit in the Irish Brigade at Gettysburg. The monument incorporates an Irish harp and the Gaelic phrase *"Faugh A Ballaugh"* ("Clear the Way").

The 224 men in this Massachusetts unit were commanded by Colonel Richard Byrnes, a native of County Cavan, Ireland. Prior to taking command of the 28th in October 1862, Byrnes had enjoyed extensive military experience in the U.S. Cavalry. He led his men into battle at Fredericksburg, Chancellorsville, and Gettysburg before dying of wounds suffered at Cold Harbor in June 1864.

GREENSBURG

¶ **Historic Hanna's Town,** 3 miles northeast on U.S. 119.

This historic reconstruction recreates the first county seat west of the Alleghenies. The reconstructed settlement includes the home of Robert Hanna, a native of northern Ireland; a jail; a storage house; and the stockade fort.

After securing title to this area between Fort Ligonier and Fort Pitt in 1769, Hanna proceeded to erect a log cabin. Within a year additional Irish emigrants settled on the village site he had laid out. As the community grew, Hanna converted his home into a tavern, which, when Westmoreland County was created in 1773, also served as a courthouse. The Irishman was not only a judge on the county court but also one of seven trustees appointed by the Pennsylvania legislature to erect public buildings in the county. He was later elected one of the county's two representatives to the colonial assembly. Hanna's Town was burned by Indians in 1782 and was never rebuilt until the time of the modern reconstruction.

§ Open June-August, Tuesday-Saturday 10-4, Sunday 1-4; May and September-October, Saturday 10-4, Sunday 1-4. Fee. Phone: 724-836-1800.

HANOVER

This city of 14,000 people was founded in 1763 by a Scotch-Irish settler named Richard McAllister. The early settlement was known as "McAllister's Town."

HARMONY

¶ **Legionville,** between Vuss Avenue and State 65. Private.

This was the site of the first training camp for American soldiers during the Revolutionary War. Founded in 1792 by *General Anthony Wayne, the camp was created to teach the troops discipline and combat techniques.

HARRISBURG

¶ **Bishop Shanahan Memorial,** St. Patrick's Cathedral, 212 State Street.

This memorial tablet by *Samuel Aloysius Murray honors *John Shanahan, the third bishop of Harrisburg, who served the diocese for seventeen years before his death in 1916. Prior to his installation, Shanahan had been the superintendent of Philadelphia's Catholic school system.

¶ **Governor Andrew Curtin Statue**, Rotunda, State Capitol.

A statue of *Andrew Curtin, the famous Civil War governor of Pennsylvania, stands on one of the balconies overlooking the marble grand staircase under the dome. (See the Pennsylvania Memorial, Gettysburg.)

§ Capitol open daily 9-4:30. Closed holidays. Phone: 717-787-6810.

¶ **Paxton Presbyterian Church**, Paxtang Avenue and Sharon Street.

Organized in 1732, the congregation of this church erected its first house of worship eight years later, a date that makes this the oldest Presbyterian church in continuous use in the state. *William Maclay is buried in the cemetery adjacent to the church.

In 1763 the minister here at the time – the Reverend John Elder of County Antrim, Ireland – organized the "Paxton Boys," a ranger troop composed predominantly of Scotch-Irish settlers and created to defend against the Indians. In their zeal, however, the "Paxton Boys" murdered several Indians in the area and threatened the authorities in Philadelphia because of their failure to protect the settlers on the frontier. Elder and his rangers laid down their arms only because of the influence of Benjamin Franklin.

¶ **William Maclay House**, 401 North Front Street. Private.

The oldest portion of this structure was built in 1791 by William Maclay, the son of a farmer from northern Ireland who had come to America in 1734. After settling in this area, the younger Maclay was asked by John Harris to survey and lay out what became known as Harrisburg.

Although Maclay was one of Pennsylvania's senators in the first Congress, his role in the new government did not become widely known until 1880 with the publication of the private journal which he had kept during those crucial years. His diary shows him to have been a determined defender of the small farming class against Alexander Hamilton's mercantile and commercial program. The journal vividly portrays the conflict between the Federalists and their opponents over such issues as protective tariffs, excise taxes, a national bank, the interpretation of the Constitution, and the location of the future national capital. He particularly lamented that so many members of Congress were lawyers ("wrangling is their business") and that Hamilton exercised such undue influence over the President ("[W]ould to God this same General Washington were in heaven! We could not then have him brought forward as the constant cover to every unconstitutional and irrepublican act.").

HAZELTON

¶ **Eckley Miners' Village,** 9 miles east off State 940.

This anthracite mining village is representative of the hundreds of such company-owned communities in Pennsylvania during the nineteenth century. Today the village encompasses fifty restored buildings, including a miner's house and two churches, one built in 1862 primarily to serve the Irish. The visitor center features exhibits and slide shows about the mining experience, which was the source of livelihood for thousands of Irish workers and their families. In 1970 Paramount Studios used the village as the setting for its film *The Molly Maguires,* starring Richard Harris and Sean Connery. The "Mollies" were members of a secret organization allegedly responsible for much of the violence against the mine owners.

§ Open Monday-Saturday 9-5, Sunday noon-5. Closed holidays (except Memorial Day, July 4, and Labor Day). Fee. Phone: 717-636-2070.

HERSHEY

¶ **Derry Presbyterian Church,** 248 East Derry Road.

The oldest part of the present church dates from 1884 and was built to serve a congregation that was first formed by Scotch-Irish settlers in 1724. From 1746 to 1791 its pastor was the *Reverend John Elder. The modern addition to the church is known as the John Elder Memorial Chapel.

For his courageous deeds during the French and Indian War and the Revolution, Elder was nicknamed the "Fighting Parson." In 1777, when the Continental Congress met in nearby York, Elder offered this prayer: "O Lord God of the universe, if Thou art unwilling by divine grace to assist us, then stand aside and let us fight it out for ourselves."

• Near the church is the Pastor's Study and Academy (also known as the First Session House), built of logs in 1732 and revered as the first school on this part of the frontier. The structure contains glass windows, the old pulpit, and a pew door from the original church and a wooden beam from Reverend Elder's barn. The entire structure is now enclosed in glass.

HUNTERSTOWN

¶ **Great Conewago Presbyterian Church,** Church Road.

Built in 1787, this Georgian fieldstone structure was one of the area's first churches organized by Scotch-Irish settlers.

JIM THORPE

This area of Pennsylvania was a center of activity by a secret society of Irish and Irish-American miners known as the Molly Maguires. Named for an organization that had used violence against the agents of absentee landlords in Ireland, the Molly Maguires were accused of committing fifty murders in this part of the state. The town of Jim Thorpe was created in the mid 1950s when two small communities merged and adopted the name of the famous Olympic athlete. The new town later erected a memorial in honor of Thorpe, who was of mixed Irish, French, and Indian ancestry.

¶ **Carbon County Jail,** 128 West Broadway.

In 1876 five alleged Molly Maguires were tried in Carbon County on the charge of conspiring to murder a mining company superintendent. Although only one may have been guilty of murder, all five Irishmen were convicted and were hanged in June 1877.

One of those executed was Alexander Campbell, a forty-three-year-old emigrant from Donegal, Ireland. Before leaving Cell 17 in Carbon County Jail, however, he swore his innocence as he placed his hand on the wall of his cell. After his execution his jailers were never able to remove the hand print, despite repeated painting and plastering. Even in modern times the hand print remains visible on the wall. In an unusual "retrial" of his case in December 1993, Campbell's conviction was overturned by a jury in Carbon County. The reenactment of the original 1876 trial took place in Jim Thorpe and was part of the sesquicentennial celebration of the county's court system.

By 1994 the Carbon County Jail had become outdated and after 123 years of use was slated to be razed and replaced by a modern facility. To save the historic jail, Tom McBride, the proprietor of an Irish shop in Jim Thorpe, purchased the structure for $160,000. He plans to open the jail and its fabled Cell 17 to the public.

¶ **Jim Thorpe Memorial,** 0.5 mile east on State 903.

This monumental mausoleum stands in honor of *Jim Thorpe, the winner of the pentathlon and decathlon in the 1912 Olympics. He was later stripped of his medals when he was accused of previous participation in professional sports. In 1982, however, he was reinstated in the Olympic records and his medals were presented to his family. (See Carlisle, Pennsylvania.)

KANE

¶ **Kane Manor Inn,** 230 Clay Street.

This Victorian structure was built in 1870 as the home of General Thomas Kane, whose great-grandfather had emigrated from Ireland about 1750. The inn displays letters to members of the Kane family from five U.S. presidents; Arctic paintings by Elisha Kent Kane, Thomas Kane's brother; and personal belongings of Dr. Evan O'Neill Kane, the first surgeon to perform an operation on himself.

• During his lifetime Thomas Kane was noted for his work on behalf of black slaves and the Mormons. By 1848 he had become an outspoken abolitionist, even going so far as to resign as a U.S. commissioner when he believed that his duty to enforce the Fugitive Slave Law of 1850 conflicted with his moral outrage over slavery. In time he became involved in the effort to spirit African Americans to freedom through the Underground Railroad. His concern for the underdog extended also to the Mormons, for whose westward migration he obtained the help of the U.S. government and whom he accompanied across the continent. He won the confidence of Brigham Young to such a degree that, when the Mormon leader urged his people to prevent the arrival of U.S. troops in Utah, Kane convinced him of the futility of such a course of action.

At the beginning of the Civil War, Kane recruited a regiment of hunters and woodsmen called the "Bucktails." Just before the battle of Gettysburg, he successfully delivered to the Union commander the message that the Confederates had obtained the U.S. military code. He was brevetted major general for "gallant and meritorious services at Gettysburg."

• A graduate of the University of Pennsylvania medical school, Elisha Kent Kane served as physician on various maritime expeditions, among them the unsuccessful search in 1850 for survivors of Sir John Franklin's disastrous attempt to find the Northwest Passage five years before.

In 1853 Kane accompanied a second expedition to the Arctic in search of an open polar sea that many scientists believed existed. After passing into unknown waters now known as Kane Basin, the members of the crew were stricken with scurvy but continued in their search, discovering an ice-free channel which they named for John Pendleton Kennedy, the Scotch-Irish secretary of the navy. (Fifty-four years later Kennedy Channel was used by Robert E. Peary on his trek to the Arctic Circle.) After spending a disastrous second winter in the Arctic, Kane and his crew managed to escape, reaching Upernivik, Greenland, in eighty-eight days. The expedition's astronomical, meteorological, geological, and anthropological investigations provided the foundation for future study of the Arctic.

When Kane died in 1857, he received national acclaim, and his body lay in state in New Orleans, Louisville, Columbus, Baltimore, and Independence Hall in Philadelphia.

• In the 1930s, while in his sixties, Dr. Evan O'Neill Kane performed hernia and gall bladder operations on himself, thereby proving the effectiveness of local anesthesia.

¶ **Kane Memorial Chapel,** 30 Chestnut Street.

This chapel was built in 1878 under the direction of *General Thomas

Kane for the townspeople of the community which he had established here in 1859.

LANCASTER

§ **Edward Hand Burial Site,** St. James Episcopal Church, Duke and Orange streets.

The Revolutionary War general *Edward Hand lies buried in the shaded churchyard. While living at his nearby estate "Rock Ford," he served the church as a warden and vestryman. (See Historic Rock Ford Plantation below.)

• A plaque on an exterior wall of the church honors the members of the congregation who served the Patriot cause during the Revolution, including *George Ross, a signer of the Declaration of Independence, and *Edward Hand, a friend and companion in arms of General Washington.

§ **Fulton Opera House,** 12-14 North Prince Street.

Restored to its nineteenth-century appearance, this 1852 theater was named for *Robert Fulton, a native of nearby Quarryville who proved the commercial viability of steamboat transportation. More than one ghost is said to haunt the interior of the opera house, which is home to local drama and symphony organizations.

§ **Historic Rock Ford Plantation,** 3 miles south on Rock Ford Road, off South Duke Street, in Lancaster County Park.

This large stone farmhouse was the home of General Edward Hand, a physician by profession and a highly regarded officer during the Revolutionary War. Hand purchased 160 acres on this site in 1785 and constructed the Georgian structure in the early 1790s. The house is notable for its porches and ground-level basement.

A native of Clyduff, County Laois, Ireland, Hand had studied medicine at Trinity College in Dublin before enlisting in 1767 as surgeon's mate with the 18th Royal Irish Regiment. He accompanied the regiment to America when it was sent to garrison Fort Pitt in western Pennsylvania. While in that part of the colony, he met the Dubliner George Croghan, the British deputy superintendent of Indian affairs, whom he assisted in the sale of Iroquois lands ceded earlier to the Crown. (Hand seems to have made considerable profit from the transactions.) In 1774, however, Hand resigned from the British military to practice medicine in Lancaster.

With the onset of the Revolution, Hand played a major military role with the American rebels. From heading a battalion of riflemen at the siege of Boston, he went on to serve bravely in the battles of Long Island, White Plains, Trenton, and Princeton. After his promotion to brigadier general, he was sent to mobilize the militia of western Pennsylvania against the

"Rock Ford," the home of General Edward Hand.

Tories and their Indian allies. He also assisted *General John Sullivan in his campaigns against the same threats in central New York. Although a strict disciplinarian, he was respected by his men because of his daring as a soldier and his skill as a horseman. The climax of his career was his appointment as George Washington's adjutant general in 1781.

After the war Hand returned to medical practice and political office. He successively served in the Confederation Congress and the Pennsylvania Assembly and in 1789 urged Congress to select Lancaster as the capital of the newly created federal government. His friendship with Washington led the latter to appoint him major general in the provisional army. An ardent Federalist, Hand adamantly opposed the election of Thomas Jefferson in 1800. The general died at his home two years later.

§ Open April-October, Tuesday-Friday 10-4, Saturday noon-4. Phone: 717-392-7223.

¶ **James Buchanan Burial Site,** Woodward Hill Cemetery, south on State 272 to South Queen Street and then to 538 East Strawberry Street.

A simple monument near the brick chapel marks the grave of *James Buchanan, the fifteenth president of the United States.

§ Open daily sunrise to sunset.

¶ **Wheatland National Historic Landmark,** 1.5 miles west on Route 23 at 1120 Marietta Avenue.

Wheatland, a two-and-a-half-story brick mansion, was the permanent home of *President James Buchanan from 1848 until his death twenty years later. The mansion's seventeen rooms are restored to their appearance when Buchanan lived here and contain much of the president's furniture, silverware, and china.

Prior to becoming the only Pennsylvanian to be elected president of the United States, Buchanan had served in both the U.S. House and the Senate and had been secretary of state and American minister to Russia and Britain. In speaking of his beloved Wheatland, the former president praised "the comforts and tranquility of home as contrasted with the troubles, perplexities, and difficulties" of political life. Here he wrote *Mr. Buchanan's Administration on the Eve of the Rebellion* in defense of his policies toward the seceded Southern states. (See Mercersburg, Pennsylvania.)

§ Open April-November, daily 10-4. Closed Easter and Thanksgiving. Fee. Phone: 717-392-8721.

"Wheatland," the home of President James Buchanan, in Lancaster.

LAUREL

¶ Guinston United Presbyterian Church.

This stone and brick church was erected by Scotch-Irish settlers in 1733.

LIMERICK

This community of 7,000 people was founded in 1716 by members of the Brooke family, who named their settlement after their home in Ireland.

McCONNELLSBURG

¶ **Daniel McConnell House,** 114 Lincoln Way. Private.
This late eighteenth-century dressed log house was the residence of Daniel McConnell, most likely of Irish descent, who founded this community and operated a tavern here.

MERCERSBURG

¶ **James Buchanan Birthplace State Park,** 1 mile northwest off State 16 (Main Street).
A stone pyramid in this eighteen-acre park marks the site of the log cabin in which President James Buchanan was born in 1791. Buchanan's father and paternal grandparents were born in County Donegal, Ireland, while his maternal grandmother had immigrated to Pennsylvania from northern Ireland. Buchanan's father conducted a profitable trade business with Indians and frontiersmen in this area.
§ Open daily dawn-dusk. Phone: 717-485-3948.

¶ The log cabin in which Buchanan was born is on exhibit on the campus of Mercersburg Academy, one mile east on Route 16 (Main Street).

¶ **James Buchanan Hotel,** 17 North Main Street.
This red brick hotel was originally the home and store of *James Buchanan Sr., whose son, the future president, spent his boyhood here from 1796 to 1807, when he entered Dickinson College in Carlisle. The younger Buchanan was expelled from the college, however, for "every sort of extravagance and mischief," although he later returned and was graduated *cum laude*. He later said that he had gone into politics "as a distraction from a great grief," presumably the death of the young woman to whom he had been engaged.

MERION

¶ **General Wayne Inn,** 625 Montgomery Avenue.
In September 1777 this inn was host to the Marquis de Lafayette and American generals George Washington and *Anthony Wayne. The establishment was named for Wayne after he was the honored guest at celebrations here in 1795.

MILESBURG

¶ **Curtin Village,** 3 miles northeast off I-80 exit 23 on State 150.

Curtin Village includes the Federal-style mansion and ironworks operation of Roland Curtin, a native of Dysart, County Clare, Ireland. While attending the Irish College in Paris, he barely escaped the guillotine when the Reign of Terror ravaged the city and prompted him to flee to America. From 1807 until his death in 1850, he was engaged in the manufacture of iron at this site. His son Andrew Curtin was the popular governor of Pennsylvania during the Civil War.

§ Open Memorial Day weekend-Labor Day, Wednesday-Saturday 10-4, Sunday 1-5; day after Labor Day-mid October, Saturday 10-4, Sunday 1-5. Fee. Phone: 814-355-1982.

The Federal-style mansion of Roland Curtin, a native of County Clare.

MOUNT JOY

¶ **Donegal Presbyterian Church,** 1891 Donegal Springs Road.

This church was erected about 1740 for a congregation of Scotch-Irish settlers who had probably come directly from County Donegal, Ireland, twenty years before. The spring near which the church was built is still a source of water.

§ Phone: 717-653-1943.

NEW HOPE

¶ **John Chapman House,** south on State 232 to Eagle Road. Private.

Prior to the battle of Trenton in December 1776, this structure was the headquarters of *General Henry Knox and Alexander Hamilton, captain of artillery in Washington's army. The two-and-a-half-story stone house belonged to Dr. John Chapman.

¶ **Washington Crossing Historic Park,** 6 miles south on State 32.

This 500-acre park honors General George Washington and the 2,400 soldiers of the Continental Army who crossed the Delaware River on Christmas Eve in 1776 to capture Trenton, New Jersey, from its Hessian-held garrison.

• McKonkey Ferry Inn, originally owned by ferryman Samuel McKonkey, an Irish Presbyterian, is believed to have been where General Washington dined before crossing the river from Morrisville. Some of the American commander's men, meanwhile, crossed into New Jersey from Taylorville on boats provided by McKonkey, while other troops were transported across the river with the help of Patrick Colvin, a Catholic Irishman who owned and operated a ferry service on the New Jersey side.

• The Memorial Building houses a copy of the famous painting *Washington Crossing the Delaware* by Emanuel Leutz. During the crossing – says the traditional tale – General Washington noticed that *Henry Knox, whose girth was almost as wide as the boat in which he sat, was causing it to list to one side. The usually taciturn commander-in-chief reportedly said to Knox, "Shift your tail and trim [level off] the boat!" The original painting is in the Metropolitan Museum of Art in New York City.

• Every year a reenactment of the crossing is held at 1 p.m. on December 25.

§ Open Tuesday-Saturday 9-5, Sunday noon-5. Visitor center and historic buildings closed January 1, Martin Luther King Jr.'s Birthday, Columbus Day, and Thanksgiving, and December 24 and 31. Fee. Phone: 215-493-4076.

PAOLI

¶ **Waynesborough,** 1 mile south of U.S. 30 via State 252 at 2049 Waynesborough Road.

This two-and-a-half-story stone house was built in 1724 by the grandfather of *Anthony Wayne, the famous Revolutionary War general. The structure, which was built of stone quarried on the property, displays personal items that belonged to Wayne and other members of his family. The story of the Waynes and Waynesborough is told through a slide presentation.

The elder Wayne was an Englishman who had settled in County Wicklow, Ireland, after fighting for King William at the battle of the Boyne. In 1722 he immigrated to this part of Pennsylvania. Two years later he was followed to America by his son Isaac Wayne, who had been born in Ireland. Isaac's son Anthony was born in this house in 1745. Although the famous American general possessed no Irish blood, he regarded himself as Irish because his father had been born in Ireland and his grandfather had settled there. To prove his sentimental attachment to the land of his father's birth, he always celebrated St. Patrick's Day and in later years became a member of the Friendly Sons of St. Patrick.

§ Open mid March-late December, Tuesday and Thursday 10-4, Sunday 1-4. Closed holidays. Fee. Phone: 610-647-1779.

¶ The nearby Paoli Memorial Ground was the site of a surprise attack by the British against General Wayne and his Continental soldiers, encamped there in September 1777.

PERKASIE

¶ **Deep Run Presbyterian Church,** 16 Irish Meeting House Road.

This congregation was organized in the early 1700s by Scotch-Irish settlers and was a mission station served by *William Tennent after he became pastor at the Neshaminy church in 1726. The original log church at Deep Run was built sometime before 1732. The present church structure on this site is the third, built in 1841 and restored in 1956.

In 1738 the congregation received its first pastor, the Reverend Francis McHenry, a descendant of an old Irish family from County Antrim, northern Ireland. He had immigrated to America only three years before and was ordained the year of his arrival at Deep Run. Since McHenry served here until his death in 1757, he is most likely buried in the cemetery.

§ Phone: 215-249-3689.

PHILADELPHIA

¶ **Balch Institute for Ethnic Studies,** 18 South 7th Street.

The institute's library contains research material on at least seventy ethnic groups, including the Irish, while the museum features photographs, clothing, and other exhibits about America's many immigrants.

§ Museum and library open Monday-Saturday 10-4. Fee. Phone: 215-925-8090.

¶ **Christ Church Burial Ground,** 5th and Arch streets.

Among those interred in the churchyard are three prominent members of the Irish-American community in Philadelphia: Pierce Butler, John

Dunlap, and Philip Syng Physick.

Butler was born in County Carlow, Ireland, and was one of the Irish-born signers of the Constitution. Dunlap, a native of Strabane, County Tyrone, was a well known printer and publisher in the city. In 1784 he began publishing *The Pennsylvania Packet*, the first daily newspaper in the United States. He had the distinction of being the first to print the Declaration of Independence (from Thomas Jefferson's manuscript) and the Constitution of the United States. Physick, meanwhile, is known as the "Father of American Surgery" and was the grandson of an Irish immigrant.

¶ **City Hall,** Penn Square, Broad and Market streets.

• The Irish Founders Memorial, a bronze tablet on the west exterior side of City Hall, was erected in 1926 by the United Irish Societies of Philadelphia to honor men of Irish birth or lineage who risked their lives and fortunes during the American Revolution.

The plaque lists the names of thirteen signers of the Declaration of Independence, including two who are sometimes mistaken for Irish – John Hart and William Whipple. The tablet also includes the names of the following military and naval leaders: John Barry, James Clinton, Arthur Dillon, Edward Hand, William Irvine, Henry Knox, Andrew Lewis, Richard Montgomery, Stephen Moylan, Jeremiah O'Brien, Walter Stewart, John Sullivan, and Anthony Wayne. At the bottom of the memorial plaque is a famous remark which the British statesman Lord Chatham made during the Revolution: "The whole Irish Nation favors America. Ireland is with them to the man."

At the dedication of the memorial, Michael Donohoe, the national president of the Ancient Order of Hibernians, commented that the tablet contains only a very small number of those who sacrificed for the American revolutionary cause. He added that the memorial "could not enumerate the 695 Kellys who fought for America, nor the 494 Murphys, or the 322 Ryans who volunteered on the side of liberty. It has been shown conclusively that twelve of the more familiar Irish family names furnished 3841 enlisted on the rolls of the patriot forces, an average of 320 for each of those good old Celtic names."

• Around City Hall stand three other sites associated with figures in Irish-American history: on the east side a statue of President William McKinley and on the north side a bronze equestrian statue of General John Fulton Reynolds and a sign indicating that Mary "Mother" Jones began her famous Children's March here in 1903. (See Mount Olive, Illinois.)

¶ **Civil War Library and Museum,** 1805 Pine Street.

The museum's collection includes life masks of Abraham Lincoln and uniforms worn by Union generals *George Gordon Meade and *Ulysses S.

Grant.

§ Open Wednesday-Sunday 11-4:30. Closed holidays. Fee. Phone: 215-735-8196.

¶ **Declaration House,** on the southwest corner of 7th and Market streets.

This is a reconstruction of the original house built here in 1775 by Jacob Graff and used by Thomas Jefferson when he drafted the Declaration of Independence. The house was later occupied by the Irishman John Dunlap, in whose printing office the Declaration of Independence and the U.S. Constitution were first set in type and printed.

From 1778 until the capital of the new federal government was moved to New York, Dunlap served as official printer to Congress. About his work the contemporary publisher Isaiah Thomas wrote: "Dunlap executed his printing in a neat and correct manner. It is said that, whilst he conducted a newspaper, he never inserted a paragraph which would wound the feelings of an individual!" The extent of Dunlap's financial success as a publisher is evident in his subscription of £4,000 for the creation of the National Bank of the United States in 1780.

§ Open daily 9-5. Closed January 1 and December 25. Phone: 215-597-1785.

¶ **Edgar Allan Poe National Historic Site,** 532 North 7th Street.

This small building, which *Edgar Allan Poe knew as "Spring Garden Cottage," was his home from 1842 to 1844. Poe did most of his writing in the small first-floor room and in a bedroom upstairs. During this time he wrote "The Gold-Bug," "The Black Cat," "The Tell-Tale Heart," "The Murders in the Rue Morgue," "The Fall of the House of Usher," and the first draft of "The Raven." Poe's mysterious words "Death to the" can still be seen carved in the parlor.

Poe, his dying wife, and his mother-in-law were in such an impoverished condition that his wife's mother sold most of their furnishings to pay the rent and to cover her daughter's medical expenses. When Poe moved from Philadelphia, he reputedly left with only his books and two cats. (See Poe sites in Baltimore, Maryland.)

§ Open June-October, daily 9-5; rest of the year, Wednesday-Sunday 9-5. Closed January 1, Thanksgiving, and December 25. Phone: 215-597-8780.

¶ **Fairmount Park,** accessible by Benjamin Franklin Parkway.

Throughout the park are several sculptures with Irish or Irish-American associations:

• The Catholic Total Abstinence Fountain on Concourse Drive, east of George's Hill, was erected in 1876 and is surrounded by statues of *Bishop John Carroll, *Father Theobald Mathew, *Charles Carroll of Carrollton,

Statues in Fairmount Park (clockwise from top left): Bishop John Carroll, Father Theobald Mathew, Charles Carroll of Carrollton, and Commodore John Barry.

and *Commodore John Barry.

• Erected in 1899, an equestrian statue of Union commander *Ulysses S. Grant stands at East River Drive and Fountain Green Drive.

• A bronze equestrian statue of *General George Gordon Meade, the commander of Union troops at Gettysburg, is on Lansdowne Drive in West Fairmount Park (behind Memorial Hall).

• The Soldiers' Memorial at the 41st Street entrance includes colossal statues of generals *George Gordon Meade, *John Fulton Reynolds, Winfield Scott Hancock, and George McClellan. One of the eight bronze busts on the monument is that of *Andrew Curtin, the wartime governor of Pennsylvania.

• A bronze portrait bust of President James Garfield by *Augustus Saint-Gaudens is located on East River Drive below the Girard Avenue Bridge. The monument was erected in 1896.

• *The Pilgrim* by *Augustus Saint-Gaudens is located along Kelly Drive. This statue is almost identical to Saint-Gaudens' *Puritan*, a likeness of Deacon Samuel Chapin in Springfield, Massachusetts.

• *The Stone Age* by *John Boyle depicts a Native American mother holding a stone hatchet with which she has just killed a bear cub. One of her children is at her feet, while another is clasped in her arms.

Kelly Drive is named for *John ("Jack") Kelly and his son of the same name – both of them native sons renowned for their feats in Olympic rowing competition.

• The Kelly Memorial is located near the rowing grandstands along

The Kelly Memorial in Fairmount Park.

the Schuylkill River, near the intersection of Midvale Avenue and Kelly Drive.

This bronze statue depicting John ("Jack") Kelly in his Olympic rowing scull was erected in 1965 as a tribute to the Philadelphia native whose rowing victories were legendary. Kelly, the grandson of Irish immigrant parents, joined one of the city's rowing clubs at the age of twenty. During the next fifteen years, he scored 126 sculling victories, a record unmatched by an American rower. Following World War I, during which he served in the American Expeditionary Force in France, he established the construction company that eventually made him a millionaire many times over. After taking up rowing again, he promptly became the national single sculls champion for 1919 and 1920 and won the singles competition at the Olympics in that latter year. With his cousin Paul Costello, he won the doubles competition in both the 1920 and the 1924 Olympics. In 1945 Kelly established the John B. Kelly Award, to be given each year to the person who has done the most to promote athletics among young people. Kelly's daughter Grace became a film star and the princess of Monaco, while his namesake son participated in four Olympic rowing competitions.

¶ **Franklin Statue,** College Hall, University of Pennsylvania, bounded by Chestnut, Pine, 32nd, and 40th streets.

This heroic seated bronze statue of Benjamin Franklin in front of College Hall is the work of sculptor *John Boyle. The statue was presented to the city of Philadelphia in 1900 by J. C. Strawbridge and originally stood in front of the U.S. Post Office. When that building was razed in 1938, the statuary was placed on permanent loan with the University of Pennsylvania and was rededicated the next year.

¶ **Free Quaker Meetinghouse,** 5th and Arch streets.

During the American Revolution, the congregation of this church numbered about 100 members, some of Irish birth. This rebuilt 1804 building is the largest Quaker meetinghouse in the world. The diorama inside depicts events from the life of William Penn: writing his "Frame of Government," negotiating a treaty with the Indians, and perusing a map of Philadelphia by his surveyor, Thomas Holme, a native of Ireland. Among those buried in the church cemetery are two other Irish Quakers who were influential in the colonial history of Philadelphia: James Logan and Lydia Darragh.

• Tradition has it that Thomas Holme was born in Waterford, Ireland. He was certainly among the soldiers in Cromwell's army who received a land grant in Ireland about 1655. Holme subsequently joined the Society of Friends and coauthored a pamphlet describing the persecution of fellow Quakers in Ireland.

In 1682 he was appointed surveyor-general of Pennsylvania by that colony's founder and was ordered to select the site of the future Philadelphia. That same year he surveyed and mapped the earliest part of the city, naming the streets for famous personages. When Penn arrived in the City of Brotherly Love later that year, however, he expressed his dislike for such a naming system, considering it "man-worship," and replaced it with numbers and the names of trees and flowers.

Holme was also a member of Pennsylvania's first assembly and its provincial council and was for a time its acting governor. He died on his plantation in Dublin township in Philadelphia County. A copper plate which Holme engraved with his map of the city is in the collection of the Historical Society of Pennsylvania.

• Born in 1674 in County Armagh, Ireland, James Logan began his career in the province as William Penn's secretary, arriving in Philadelphia with the proprietor in 1699. In subsequent years he variously served as member of the provincial council, chief executive of the province, alderman and mayor of Philadelphia, and chief justice of the Pennsylvania Supreme Court.

Although Logan was a member of the Society of Friends and identified with the political interests of the colony's Quaker elite, he was not a "strict professor" of the sect's beliefs. On more than one occasion he demonstrated a belief in aggressive self-defense that alienated his coreligionists. When the ship that first brought him to America was attacked by pirates, for example, Logan defended the vessel with appropriate physical force. Later in his career he suggested that Friends should not be candidates for the colony's legislature unless they could in good conscience bring themselves to vote for measures to defend the citizenry.

Despite Logan's busy public and private life, he was renowned for his scholarship. By age sixteen he had mastered Latin, Greek, Hebrew, Italian, French, and Spanish. In his more mature years he published essays on ethics, science, law, and anatomy and translated Cato's *Moral Distiches* and Cicero's *On Old Age*. He was especially interested in botany and developed a friendship with the Philadelphia botanist John Bartram. Logan's botanical experiments even attracted the attention of Linnaeus, the famous Swedish botanist, who named for Logan an order of thirty genera and over 300 species (*Loganiaceae*). The Philadelphian's most important scientific work was a series of experiments to prove the sexuality of plants. Logan's grave in the Friends' cemetery is unmarked.

• Lydia Barrington Darragh was a woman of unusual daring known for her courage on behalf of the Patriot cause. Born in Dublin in 1729, she married William Darragh, most likely a tutor in her father's household, in a ceremony at the Friends' Meeting House in the Irish capital. By at least 1766 she and her husband had immigrated to Philadelphia, where they joined the congregation of the Monthly Meeting of Friends. Once in America, Lydia became engaged in midwifery and nursing and even expressed a desire to open a mortuary establishment. In carrying out this intention, she placed an advertisement in the *Pennsylvania Gazette* for December 4, 1766, announcing her intention to "make Grave-Clothes, and lay out the Dead, in the Neatest Manner." At her death she left an estate worth more than £1,600.

During their occupation of Philadelphia, the British occasionally held their staff meetings at the Darraghs' house on South Second Street, perhaps because of its proximity to British headquarters. Following one such meeting on the night of December 2, Lydia was presented with an unusual opportunity to help the Patriot cause. Although the British had told the Darraghs to retire for the evening, Lydia eavesdropped on the discussion and learned that General William Howe planned to attack General Washington and his troops at Whitemarsh – just outside the city – two days later. In addition, she discovered that the British were leaving the next day with 5,000 troops, thirteen cannon, a baggage train, and eleven boats on wagon wheels. After overhearing the plans, Lydia returned to her room and pretended to have been asleep by answering a British officer's call at her door only after the third knock.

After the British left the house, Lydia made every effort to inform Washington's troops, among whom was her son, an officer in the Second Pennsylvania Militia Regiment. Using a pass which she had previously obtained, she set out for Whitemarsh on the morning of December 4. Once past the British lines, she headed toward the encamped Americans, thirteen miles away. Along the route she encountered Lieutenant Colonel Thomas Craig of the American Light Horse Cavalry and informed him of the British plans, which he immediately carried to Washington. (Another account tells how either Lydia or a female messenger sent by her also passed the message on to Elias Boudinot, Washington's director of intelligence, while he was dining at a tavern outside Philadelphia. Boudinot rode to Washington's headquarters with the message, concealed in a needlebook which the woman had given him.) As a result of the heroine's actions, the Americans were ready with troops and cannon when the British arrived at Whitemarsh, although several days of skirmishing ensued. On December 8 the British returned to Philadelphia, chastened if not outright defeated.

When a British officer later questioned Lydia whether any of her family had been awake when the British discussed their plans against the Americans, Lydia equivocated. To her statement that they had retired at 8 p.m., the officer naively replied: "I know *you* were asleep, for I knocked at your chamber door three times before you heard me; – I am entirely at a loss to imagine who gave General Washington information of our intended attack, unless the walls of the house could speak. When we arrived near White Marsh, we found all their cannon mounted, and the troops prepared to receive us; and we have marched back like a parcel of fools."

§ Open Memorial Day-Labor Day, Tuesday-Saturday 10-4, Sunday noon-4..

¶ **Hill-Physick-Keith House,** 321 South 4th Street.

For a time beginning in 1815, this four-story brick house was the home of Dr. Philip Syng Physick, the "Father of American Surgery."

Named for his Irish immigrant grandfather (Philip Syng, one of Philadelphia's finest silversmiths), Physick studied medicine in London and was graduated from the University of Edinburgh in 1792. He was subsequently a staff member at the Pennsylvania Hospital and a lecturer in surgery at the University of Pennsylvania. Especially noted for his innovations, he invented needle forceps and the guillotine tonsillotomy, for example, and is reputed to have been the first American physician to use the stomach tube. He promoted the use of animal ligatures in surgery and became famous for his skill in operating for bladder stone. In one celebrated instance, he performed such a procedure on seventy-three-year-old Chief Justice John Marshall, extracting almost 1,000 calculi. Before his own death Physick directed that his grave be guarded to prevent the theft of his body and its subjection to an autopsy.

§ Tours available Thursday-Saturday 12-4, Sunday 1-4. Fee. Phone: 215-925-7866.

¶ **Historical Society of Pennsylvania,** 1300 Locust Street.

Among the society's holdings are paintings by Irish-American artists and a copper plate engraved by *Thomas Holme with his map of Philadelphia.

§ Museum and library open Tuesday and Thursday-Saturday 10-5, Wednesday 1-9. Closed major holidays. Phone: 215-732-6201.

¶ **Independence Hall,** Chestnut Street, between 5th and 6th streets, on Independence Square.

The Declaration of Independence was adopted here in July 1776, although most of the signatures on it were not affixed until the following August. Three signers of the Declaration were natives of Ireland (James Smith, George Taylor, and Matthew Thornton), while five other signers were American-born of Irish or Scotch-Irish descent (Charles Carroll, Thomas Lynch Jr., Thomas McKean, George Read I, and Edward Rutledge). For approximately a month after the adoption of the Declaration, the only two signatures on the document were those of John Hancock and Charles Thomson, the latter the Irish-born secretary of the Continental Congress.

§ Open daily 9-5 (with extended hours in summer). Phone: 215-597-8974.

• The inkstand which was used at the signing of the Declaration of Independence and the Constitution was made by Philip Syng, a native of

*A copy of the Philip Syng inkstand, used in the signing
of the Declaration of Independence.*

Ireland and Philadelphia's famous silversmith. The inkstand, which is on exhibit in Independence Hall, was commissioned by the Pennsylvania Assembly in 1752 and cost £25. After being used by successive Speakers of the Assembly, it was given to the Continental Congress in 1775 and was used by each signer of the Declaration of Independence. When the state capital was transferred to Harrisburg, the inkstand made the move also and was used by the Pennsylvania legislature until 1849, when knowledge of its whereabouts became lost. After its recovery the historic silver piece was restored to Independence Hall on June 7, 1875, the centenary of the day on which a resolution calling for independence from Britain was first introduced in the Continental Congress.

• The Declaration of Independence was first read in public by Colonel John Nixon, the son of Richard Nixon of County Wexford, Ireland. The document was read at noon on July 8, 1776, from an observatory in the yard of Independence Hall.

• Today the yard of Independence Hall is dominated by a bronze statue of Irish-born John Barry, the "Father of the American Navy." Sculpted by *Samuel Aloysius Murray, the statue is nine and a half feet in height and stands atop a twelve-foot granite pedestal. With outstretched arm as if in the act of giving a command, the admiral wears a great coat and carries a naval spy glass in one arm and a sheathed sword by his side. The front of the pedestal bears the name "Barry," while the rear is inscribed with the

Statue of Commodore John Barry,
in the yard of Independence Hall.

words: "Commodore John Barry, U.S.N., Father of the Navy, born in Wexford, Ireland, 1745, died in Philadelphia September 13, 1803. Presented to the City of Philadelphia by the Society of the Friendly Sons of St. Patrick, 1907." (See John Barry Statue, District of Columbia.)

√ A statue of Commodore Barry stands in his native Wexford, Ireland, erected on Crescent Quay by the U.S. government.

¶ John Keating Burial Site, St. John the Baptist Catholic Church, 119 Rector Street, Manayunk district.

Born of Anglo-Norman descent in County Limerick, Ireland, in 1760, John Keating immigrated to France while still a child and was educated at the College of the English Benedictines at Douay, France. After joining the Irish Brigade in the French army, he commanded the Walsh Regiment when in 1792 it accompanied French troops to Santo Domingo to crush a native uprising there. Within a few days of his arrival, he realized the futility of the situation and determined to extricate himself from it. "The blacks were in full insurrection," he wrote. "The whole country was in their power. The plantations had all been burned, the whites and the troops were confined to the town. . . ." Keating left for America almost immediately, ironically with a letter of introduction to George Washington from General

Rochambeau, the new governor of Santo Domingo and the son of Washington's revolutionary comrade-in-arms.

Keating first lived in Wilmington, Delaware, where for a time he was a business associate of the Du Pont family. After moving to Philadelphia, he became involved with land speculators and their colonization efforts along the Susquehanna River. It was during this time that he managed the Ceres Land Company, which owned 300,000 acres in this part of the state. He later became a trustee of the University of Pennsylvania and a manager of the Philadelphia Savings Fund Society.

In 1855, about a year before his death, the Irishman looked back over his career: "In 1783 Napoleon was a lieutenant of the 2nd battalion of the Régiment de la Frères Artillery, and I a captain of the 2nd battalion of the 92nd Regiment of Infantry. Two years afterwards I was captain, and I had the cross of St. Louis given me by Louis XVI. I am, perhaps, the only surviving chevalier created by that unhappy prince. Napoleon, for years master of Europe, but ending his astonishing career on a rock exiled from his country and family, dies immortalized by his triumphs and his misfortunes, and I live in the midst of my children without any ills, manager of a large land company." Keating died at the age of ninety-six.

§ Phone: 215-482-4600.

ℐ John McCullough Burial Site, Mount Moriah Cemetery, Kingsessings Avenue.

An ornate monument erected in 1888 marks the grave site of John McCullough, an Irish-born actor who achieved a national reputation during a twenty-seven-year career. The bust of the actor was sculpted by *William Clark Noble.

Born to peasant parents near Londonderry, northern Ireland, McCullough came to America in 1847 and first worked as a chairmaker in Philadelphia. Although at age fifteen he was unable to read or write, a few years of study prepared him for the stage. His longest acting association was with Edwin Forrest, initially playing supporting roles but then taking the leads in Shakespeare's tragedies as well as in *Richelieu, Damon and Pythias,* and *Virginius.* Midway through his career, he spent two years at McGuire's Theater in San Francisco and then on a series of cross-country tours. His acting was cut prematurely short, however, because of illness.

Although McCullough returned to the stage in the last two years of his life, he suffered a breakdown during a performance in Chicago. The audience, unaware of the reason for his failure to remember his lines, responded to his embarrassment with laughter. His last words to an audience were delivered that night: "Ladies and gentlemen, you are the worst mannered audience I ever saw. If you had suffered tonight as I have, you would never have done this. Good night."

§ Phone: 215-729-1295.

¶ Moylan Park, 25th and Diamond streets.

This park is named in honor of Stephen Moylan, an officer during the Revolutionary War and the first president of the Friendly Sons of St. Patrick. A memorial in the park was dedicated to Moylan in 1922 by the Friendly Sons and is inscribed with the highlights of his military career.

Moylan was born in 1737 in Cork, Ireland, the son of a highly successful merchant and his wife, the Countess of Limerick. (His brother was the Catholic bishop of Cork, while his two sisters were Ursuline nuns. Later in America Stephen Moylan and his two half-brothers were called "the three polite Irishmen.") Because educational opportunities for Catholics were limited in Ireland, Moylan pursued his education in Paris and later spent several years in Lisbon associated with his father's shipping business. In 1771, three years after coming to Philadelphia, he was elected president of the Friendly Sons of St. Patrick even though this charitable society was composed almost entirely of Protestants.

With the outbreak of the Revolution, Moylan joined the Continental Army at Cambridge, Massachusetts. Because of his commercial experience, he was at first assigned to the commissariat department. He quickly became General Washington's secretary and then quartermaster general of the army, with the rank of colonel. After only four months, however, he resigned from the latter position, apparently because of his failure to reorganize the army. Now back in the field, he was easily recognized by his unusual uniform: red waistcoat, bright green coat, bearskin hat, and buckskin breeches. After serving with distinction in the battle of Princeton, he rhapsodized: "I know I never felt so much like one of Homer's Deities before. We trod on air -- it was a glorious day!"

Moylan subsequently raised and led a cavalry unit known as the Fourth Pennsylvania Light Dragoon under the overall command of Casimir Pulaski. When Moylan and his Polish superior quarreled, the Irishman was court-martialed for insubordination but was later acquitted. (After the Polish officer resigned his command, Moylan was appointed in his place.) Toward the end of the war, Moylan and his dragoons assisted Lafayette in forcing Cornwallis's surrender at Yorktown.

¶ Museum of American Art of the Pennsylvania Academy of the Fine Arts, 118 North Broad Street at Cherry Street.

This Victorian Gothic structure houses a collection that spans three centuries of American art and includes works by Mary Cassatt, Thomas Eakins, *Georgia O'Keeffe, Katherine Porter, and Benjamin West.

§ Open Monday-Saturday 10-5, Sunday 11-5. Closed holidays. Fee. Phone: 215-972-7600.

¶ **Nathaniel Irish House,** 704 South Front Street. Private.

This three-and-a-half-story house with dormer windows was the home of Nathaniel Irish, a carpenter of most probably Irish descent who built it for himself about 1769. This Flemish bond brick house was one of several Georgian row houses built by Nathaniel Irish, a member of the Carpenters Company of Philadelphia.

¶ **North Laurel Hill Cemetery,** 4th and Pine streets.

Memorial monuments mark the graves of three famous Americans of Irish birth or descent: Thomas McKean, a signer of the Declaration of Independence; George Gordon Meade, the Union commander at the battle of Gettysburg; and Charles Thomson, the secretary of the Continental Congress. (See Wilmington, Delaware; Gettysburg and Bryn Mawr, Pennsylvania.)

Charles Thomson's grave is adorned with a sixteen-foot obelisk inscribed with these words: "This monument covers the remains of the honourable Charles Thomson, the first, and long the confidential secretary of the Continental Congress and the enlightened benefactor of his country in its day of peril and need. As a patriot, his memorial and just honours are inscribed on the pages of his country's history. As a Christian, his piety was sincere and enduring. His Biblical learning was profound, as is shown by his translation of the Septuagint. As a man He was honoured, loved and wept. Erected to the memory of an honoured uncle and benefactor by his nephew, John Thomson of Delaware. Hic jacet homo veritatis et gratiae."

¶ **Old St. Mary's Catholic Church**, 4th Street, above Spruce Street.

The graveyard of Philadelphia's second oldest Catholic church is the final resting place of several illustrious Irishmen who played significant roles in early American history: John Barry, Mathew Carey, Thomas FitzSimons, George Meade, and Stephen Moylan.

In 1876 the tomb of John Barry was rededicated with the following inscription: "Sacred to the memory of Commodore John Barry, Father of the American Navy. Let the Christian, patriot and soldier who visits these mansions of the dead view this monument with respect and veneration. Beneath it rests the remains of John Barry, who was born in County Wexford, Ireland, in the year 1745. America was the object of his patriotism and the aim of his usefulness and ambition. At the beginning of the Revolutionary War he held the commission of captain in the then limited navy of the Colonies. His achievements in battle and his renowned naval tactics merited for him the position of Commodore, and to be justly regarded as the Father of the American Navy. He fought often, and bled in the cause of freedom. But his deeds of valor did not diminish in him the virtues which adorned his private life. He was eminently gentle, kind,

*One of several memorials
in honor of John Barry
at Old St. Mary's Church.*

just and charitable, and no less beloved by his family and friends than by his grateful country. Firm in the faith and practice of the Catholic Church, he departed this life on the 13th day of September, 1803, in the fifty-ninth year of his age. In grateful remembrance a few of his countrymen, members of St. Mary's Church, and others, have contributed toward this second monument. Erected July 1, 1876. *Requiescat in pace.*"

• Born in Dublin in 1760, Mathew Carey early determined on a career in printing and bookselling. When at age nineteen he published an anonymous pamphlet against British mistreatment of Irish Catholics, he wisely left Ireland for Paris. While in the French capital, he made the acquaintance of Benjamin Franklin and found employment for several months in the famous American's printing office in France. By 1783 Carey had returned to Dublin and, with his father's patronage, assumed the ownership of the *Volunteer's Journal*. While carrying out the paper's purpose of defending the Irish against English oppression, Carey was arrested for a verbal attack on the Prime Minister and the House of Commons. Following his release, he prudently sailed for the United States, disguised as a woman.

Once in Philadelphia, Carey began his career as a publisher, thanks to a $400 gift from the Marquis de Lafayette. (Carey returned the gift forty years later, when the Frenchman revisited the United States.) As editor of the *Pennsylvania Herald*, Carey introduced a novelty in American journalism by reporting almost verbatim the debates of the Pennsylvania Assembly, using a shorthand of his own invention. An unfortunate duel with a rival editor, however, left him permanently crippled.

In 1786, with five partners, Carey began publication of the *Columbian Magazine*, the first successful American production of that genre. In the magazine's first issue, the Irishman made a number of predictions about America sixty years into the future: the thirtieth state would have been admitted, 10,000 blacks would have been transported from Virginia to a settlement in Africa, "very few" African Americans would remain in the United States, and a canal across the Isthmus of Panama would have been completed. Before long, however, Carey left the partnership to found the rival *American Museum*, which published such articles as medical and educational essays, antislavery tracts, and serials like the *Federalist Papers*, Paine's *Common Sense* and *Crisis*, and Dickinson's *Letters from a Pennsylvania Farmer*. One selection – the reprint of a poem recounting the dialogue between a dead cat and a dog lying in the filth of Philadelphia's streets – led to the creation of the city's first street-sweeping brigade. In related civic activity, he founded the Hibernian Society for the relief of Irish immigrants and helped establish the first nonsectarian Sunday School in America.

Because of financial difficulties, Carey abandoned the *American Museum* and devoted himself to publishing and selling books. By 1824 he had published more works by American authors than any other publisher, and he was the first person in America to publish the works of Charles Dickens and Sir Walter Scott. He also published the first Catholic edition of the Bible in the United States. His trade eventually expanded to all parts of the country, and he had agents and exchange agreements with publishers in Europe and South America. One of Carey's most regular customers was Thomas Jefferson, who, in a letter of 1820, acknowledged receipt of a chemistry book from Carey's bookselling business. At the height of his career, Carey did business amounting to $300,000 and frequently employed as many as 150 workers.

Carey himself was a prolific writer on many of the urgent issues of the day. He composed almost sixty pamphlets advocating a protective tariff and a series of pamphlets calling for reconciliation between the Federalists and the Democratic Republicans over sectional differences that threatened the Union. In the face of the 1832 tariff nullification crisis between the federal government and South Carolina, he wrote and issued *The Crisis; An Appeal to the good sense of the nation against the spirit of resistance and dissolution of the Union*. He ended the work with a monitory epitaph: "Here to the ineffable joy of the Despots, and Friends of Despotism, throughout the world, and the universal distress and mortification of the friends of human liberty, lie the shattered remains of the noblest fabric of Government ever devised by man, the Constitution of the United States."

• Thomas FitzSimons, George Meade, and Stephen Moylan were among the twenty-four founding members of the Friendly Sons of St. Patrick at its creation in Philadelphia on March 17, 1771. According to the rules of the society, each member had to provide for himself a gold medal inscribed accordingly: "On the right HIBERNIA. On the left AMERICA. In the center LIBERTY joining the Hands of HIBERNIA and AMERICA, to be represented by the usual figures of a Female supported by a Harp for HIBERNIA – an Indian with his quiver on his back and his bow slung for AMERICA. Underneath UNITE. On the reverse ST. PATRICK trampling on a snake, a Cross in his hand, dressed in his Pontifical robes."

§ Cemetery open daily 9-5. Phone: 215-923-7930.

❡ **Penn's Landing,** between Market and Lombard streets, along the Delaware River.

This thirty-seven-acre area marks the landing site of William Penn in 1682. Seventeen years later Penn returned to the city aboard the *Canterbury,* accompanied by his Irish secretary, James Logan, a native of County Armagh. Today the park features a sculpture garden, several historic ships, and concerts and festivals during the year.

Although Penn was of English ancestry, his father owned Macroom Castle in County Cork, and it was there that the younger Penn, while in his twenties, was converted to a new sect known as Quakers or Friends. Almost immediately, however, Penn and some of his Irish coreligionists were imprisoned for nonconformity.

❡ **Philadelphia Club,** 13th and Walnut streets.

This private club is the former home of Thomas Butler, whose father, Pierce Butler, was one of the Irish-born signers of the Constitution. (See National Archives, District of Columbia.)

❡ **Philadelphia Museum of Art,** Benjamin Franklin Parkway at 26th Street.

Besides its collection of Renaissance and contemporary American paintings, the museum has extensive holdings of Irish and Irish-American paintings, furniture, and silver. Its most treasured silver pieces are by the Irishman Philip Syng.

A native of Cork, Syng learned the silversmith trade from his father, who had brought his family to Philadelphia sometime before 1720. The younger Syng eventually became known as one of Philadelphia's finest craftsmen. His most famous work is the inkstand which he made for the Pennsylvania Assembly and which was used at the signing of the Declaration of Independence and the Constitution. (See Independence Hall, Philadelphia.) His hallmark consisted of his initials in Roman capitals enclosed by a rectangle.

Probably through his acquaintance with Benjamin Franklin, Syng developed a machine which helped generate electricity. He was also the treasurer of the American Philosophical Society, a founder of the University of Pennsylvania, and a vestryman of Philadelphia's Christ Church. He and his wife had twenty-one children. One of his grandsons was Philip Syng Physick, the "Father of American Surgery." (See Hill-Physick-Keith House, Philadelphia.)

§ Open Tuesday-Sunday 10-5, Wednesday 10-9. Closed holidays. Fee. Phone: 215-763-8100.

¶ In the park to the west of the museum is a statue of Richard Montgomery, one of the Irish-born generals in George Washington's Continental Army. (See St. Paul's Chapel, New York City.) The larger-than-life bronze statue is one of several likenesses of famous figures from the Revolutionary War (Lafayette, Nathaniel Greene, Thaddeus Kosciuszko, John Paul Jones, and Baron von Steuben) in the park.

¶ **Presbyterian Historical Society,** 425 Lombard Street, at 3rd Street.

Three of the six stone statues outside the entrance to the society's headquarters are representations of Presbyterian ministers of Scotch-Irish descent: Francis Makemie, the founder of Presbyterianism in the United

Statues of Gen. Richard Montgomery (left) and Rev. Francis Makemie.

States; James Caldwell, the "Soldier Parson" known for his active military support for the American Revolution; and John McMillan, the "Father of Education in Western Pennsylvania."

§ Open Monday-Friday 8:30-4:30. Closed holidays. Phone: 215-627-1852.

¶ St. Peter's Church, 3rd and Pine streets.

In the peaceful cemetery surrounding the church lie the graves of the Irish-Americans John Nixon and Stephen Decatur.

• The son of an Irishman from County Wexford, Nixon had followed his father into the shipping business and became a prominent figure in the political affairs of Philadelphia. In addition to serving as a manager of the Pennsylvania Hospital and as a trustee of the University of Pennsylvania, he was a founder of the Friendly Sons of St. Patrick and a member of the Hibernia Fire Company. During the strife with Britain, he was active on several revolutionary committees and was a colonel with a Philadelphia battalion that served under General Washington. Toward the end of the war he subscribed £5,000 to the formation of the Bank of Pennsylvania, created to supply the Continental army with provisions.

It was Nixon's connection with the new nation's founding documents, however, that assured his place in the annals of American history. Not only did he render the first public reading of the Declaration of Independence (on July 8, 1776), but he also played a prominent role in the grand procession twelve years later celebrating the adoption of the Constitution. In that national fete he represented Independence "on horseback, bearing the staff and cap of Liberty; under the cap a white and silk flag, with these words, 'Fourth of July, 1776,' in large letters."

• Decatur, whose maternal grandparents were Irish, had fought his first duel at the age of twenty, as a handsome, athletic midshipman. He achieved later fame for an incident during the Tripolitan War in which, armed with a cutlass, he fought in hand-to-hand combat with a pike-wielding pirate. While commanding the *United States* at the start of the second war with England, he captured the frigate *Macedonia*, in the fray suffering only a dozen losses to the Britons' 104. After the war he led a squadron to Algiers, offering the Dey the choice of war or peace on American terms. With the treaty in his hands, he proceeded to Tunis and Tripoli to exact payment for injuries sustained during the recent war with Britain. Upon his return to the Norfolk Navy Yard, he was feted as one of the nation's greatest heroes. It was to a toast in his honor that he replied with his famous response: "Our country! In her intercourse with foreign nations may she always be in the right; but our country, right or wrong."

¶ South Front Street Historic District, 700-712 South Front Street.

This is a continuous block of eighteenth-century Georgian row houses built before 1769 by such craftsmen as Daniel Harrison, Nathaniel Irish, and Samuel Smith, all of whom were most likely Irish.

¶ **Stenton Mansion,** 18th and Windrim streets, Germantown.

This Georgian colonial brick house was built in 1728 by James Logan, William Penn's Irish-born secretary, on what was originally a 500-acre estate. The mansion's second-floor library once housed Logan's collection of more than 3,000 books, at one time the finest private collection in America and now part of the holdings of the Library Company of Philadelphia (on Broad Street between Christian and Carpenter Streets).

Despite his busy public life, Logan was able to acquire a fortune through land speculation and trade with the Indians. His relation with the Native Americans was so good that they were often his guests at Stenton. As many as 400 at a time visited for several weeks, some sleeping on the mansion's interior staircase. In 1742 the chief of the Onondagas saluted Logan as "a wise man and a fast friend to the Indians." Stenton was visited twice by General Washington: once on his way to the battle of Brandywine in 1777 and again during the Constitutional Convention, when he witnessed some farm experiments on the estate. The mansion was used by the British general Sir William Howe as his headquarters during the battle of Germantown. (See Free Quaker Meetinghouse, Philadelphia.)

§ Open mid March-mid December, Tuesday-Saturday 1-4. Fee. Phone: 215-329-7312.

"Stenton," the home of Irish-born James Logan.

¶ **Thomas FitzSimons Statue,** Logan Circle.

This statue of one of the Irish signers of the Constitution was presented to the city of Philadelphia on Constitution Day, September 17, 1946, by the Society of the Friendly Sons of St. Patrick. The eight-foot bronze statue depicts FitzSimons in the act of stepping forward – with quill pen in hand – to sign the famous document. The inscription on the front pedestal reads: "Thomas FitzSimons. Born in Ireland 1741. Died in Philadelphia in 1811. Member of the Continental Congress. Signer of the Constitution of the United States. Member of the 1st, 2nd & 3rd Congresses." He was the only Catholic signer of the Constitution.

While still a relative newcomer to Philadelphia, the Irish-born FitzSimons had formed a mercantile partnership with his brother-in-law, George Meade (whose father was an Irish refugee from County Limerick.) During the Revolution, FitzSimons contributed liberally in ships, supplies, and money to the Patriot cause. As a member of the first Congress under the new Constitution, he urged passage of a bill creating a protective tariff for America's developing industries.

In addition, FitzSimons was instrumental in creating the first bank in America, was a founder and director of the Insurance Company of North America, and served for many years as president of the Philadelphia Chamber of Commerce. He was also a trustee of the University of Pennsylvania,

Statue of Thomas FitzSimons, an Irish-born signer of the Declaration of Independence.

a member of the Hibernia Society in Philadelphia, and a benefactor of St. Augustine's Catholic Church. At the height of his commercial success, FitzSimons owned a fleet of fourteen ships. Because of imprudent loans and attacks upon American shipping during the Napoleonic era, however, he suffered financial failure.

¶ **Todd-Moylan House,** on the northeast corner of 4th and Walnut streets.

This house was the home of John Todd and his wife *Dolley Payne from 1791 to 1793, when both he and the couple's young son died during a fever epidemic. It was here that Aaron Burr introduced the young widow to James Madison, then a member of the House of Representatives and later president of the United States. The two were married in September 1794.

Between 1796 and 1807 this brick row house was the home of *Stephen Moylan, the Revolutionary War officer and aide-de-camp to General George Washington. (See Moylan Park, Philadelphia.)

§ Hours vary. Closed January 1 and December 25. Fee. Phone: 215-597-8974.

¶ **Woodmere Art Museum,** 4 miles south of I-276, exit 25, at 9201 Germantown Avenue.

The museum's collection includes works from the eighteenth through the twentieth centuries, including paintings by Benjamin West and the Anglo-Irish painter Edward Moran.

§ Open Tuesday-Saturday 10-5, Sunday 1-5. Closed major holidays. Phone: 215-247-0476.

PITTSBURGH

¶ **Allegheny Cemetery,** 4734 Butler Street, Lawrenceville.

This is the final resting place of Pittsburgh pioneer *James O'Hara, renowned songwriter *Stephen Collins Foster, and financier and philanthropist *Andrew Mellon.

¶ **Croghan House,** Stanton Heights Golf Course, opposite 4424 Stanton Avenue.

This Classic Revival mansion was built about 1835 by William Croghan Jr., whose Irish-born father had distinguished himself as a soldier during the Revolutionary War.

The younger Croghan attended Litchfield Law School and Dickinson College and studied medicine at the University of Pennsylvania. His wife, Mary O'Hara, was the daughter of *James O'Hara, an Indian trader, a member of *General Anthony Wayne's campaign against the Indians, and one of the founders of Pittsburgh's first glassworks. (His home in Pittsburgh had some of the first carpets found west of the Alleghenies.) When the Croghans' daughter Mary was only fourteen years old, she ran away from the boarding school she was attending and married Captain Edward Schenley, a British soldier three times her age. Many years later, as a widow in England, Mary Croghan Schenley became a generous benefactor of the city of Pittsburgh.

¶ **John O'Hara Study,** Pattee Library, Pennsylvania State University.

Originally located in Princeton, New Jersey, the study displays several manuscripts of one of America's most popular novelists, who, like his contemporary *F. Scott Fitzgerald, resented the fact that his Irish roots prevented him from entering the ranks of America's WASP elite.

The grandson of an emigrant from Famine-era Ireland, O'Hara was born in 1905 in Pottsville, Pennsylvania, an area that served as the locale for a cycle of autobiographical works centered on the character James Malloy. Even the social prominence which O'Hara's father enjoyed as a physician could not overcome the son's sense of social inferiority, an oppression that caused him to feel prouder of his mother's descent from established American stock than of his father's Celtic roots. "I go through some cheap shame," O'Hara once wrote to Fitzgerald, "when the O'Hara side gets too close for comfort." O'Hara later expressed this sense of exclusion from the mainstream of American life through the character Malloy in *Butterfield 8*: For all his refined table manners and Brooks Brothers clothes, Malloy – like O'Hara – will always be just a "Mick" to WASP Americans.

[Ironically, this psychological inferiority gave way to its opposite when O'Hara visited Dublin. The author described the phenomena in a letter to Fitzgerald: "When Sister and I were in Dublin a few years ago my friend Geraldine Fitzgerald explained to me that the gentry were not so much in awe of me as an author as of one of 'the real thing,' O'Hara being one of the seven or eight ancient Irish names. Well, I believe that, if only for two reasons: whenever I am in the company of the Irish (and this has been true all my life) I instantly get a feeling of being a little bit superior to the other ones – and they in turn look at me as though whatever I had to say was going to be important. There is a sort of resentful respect to them . . . ."]

The young O'Hara's embarrassment about his father's origins led to tension between the two, a situation that was worsened when the son was expelled from three schools. Frustrated in his desire to attend Yale, O'Hara instead found employment as a reporter on the *Pottsville Journal*, the first of many journalistic jobs, many of which he lost because of his drinking and uncontrollable temper.

With the publication of *Appointment in Samarra* in 1934, O'Hara emerged a serious literary figure. This work and most of the other novels that followed earned O'Hara critical praise for his ability to portray the habits and speech of the upper-class American characters whom he both admired and despised. His detractors, however, pointed out the moral vacuity of his major characters, most of them Irish Americans depicted as vulgar parvenus (Harry Reilly in *Samarra*), conniving social climbers (Joseph Chapin in *Ten North Frederick*), or venal political manipulators (Creighton Duffy in *From the Terrace*). Whatever his attitude toward his characters may have been, O'Hara's themes were consistent – what Matthew Bruccoli describes as "the cruelty of human conduct and the pain of loneliness."

During the 1960s O'Hara published thirteen volumes of fiction. In doing so he seems to have fulfilled a task that he described at the beginning of the decade: "The Twenties, the Thirties, and the Forties are already history, but I cannot be content to leave their story in the hands of the historians and the editors of picture books. I want to record the way people talked and thought and felt, and to do it with complete honesty and variety." Although during the 1960s he was probably the nation's best-selling serious author, he was denied the critical acclaim – and the Nobel Prize – which he craved. As a result he scorned the literary establishment which overlooked him and which came to denigrate what they regarded as his outdated material and political conservatism. In the end, his wife had the last word through the epitaph which she selected: "Better than anyone else, he told the truth about his time, the first half of the twentieth century. He was a professional. He wrote honestly and well."

§ Library open Monday-Friday 8-5, Saturday 9-1. O'Hara Study open by appointment only. Phone: 814-865-1793.

¶ Magee Memorial, near the Carnegie entrance to Schenley Park.

This monument to Christopher Lyman Magee, the grandson of an immigrant from County Derry, Ireland, is adorned by a bronze cornucopia bas-relief by *Augustus Saint-Gaudens. Although Magee held various political positions in Pittsburgh, he was more renowned as a business entrepreneur who owned newspaper and real estate interests as well as stock in more than fifty enterprises. He once wished the children of Pittsburgh a Merry Christmas by donating $100,000 for a zoological garden. He left most of his $4 million estate for the foundation of the Elizabeth Steele Magee Hospital.

¶ Mellon Institute, 4400 5th Avenue.

Although now part of Carnegie Mellon University, this massive Greek Revival structure was dedicated in 1937 as a gift of *Andrew Mellon, longtime U.S. secretary of the treasury. The research center takes up a city block and consists of nine floors and 335 rooms. Under Mellon's guidance, Pittsburgh's aluminum and cokemaking industries were developed. (See Andrew Mellon Memorial Fountain, District of Columbia.)

§ Phone: 412-268-4960.

♫ Schenley Park, Schenley Drive, north of I-376.

This 456-acre expanse grew from a 300-acre donation to the city made in 1889 by *Mary Croghan Schenley, the daughter and granddaughter, respectively, of two prominent names in the history of Pittsburgh – *William Croghan Jr. and *James O'Hara. At the time of her bequest, Mrs. Schenley had been living in London for forty years. In 1918 a statue in her honor was erected at the entrance to the park.

♫ Stephen Foster Memorial, University of Pittsburgh, Forbes Avenue and Bigelow Boulevard.

This Gothic memorial to Stephen Collins Foster, the famous song writer, was built in 1937 with $500,000 in donations from music clubs throughout the United States. Murals illustrate many of Foster's songs, while a museum on the main floor exhibits Foster memorabilia. A statue of Foster stands in a small park across Forbes Street.

Foster was born in Pittsburgh in 1826 of Scotch-Irish parentage on both sides. The popularity of his early Negro ballads – "O Susanna," "Louisiana Belle," "Uncle Ned," and "Away Down South" – led him to consider musical composition as a full-time career and to determine to be-

Statue of Stephen Collins Foster.

come "the best Ethiopian song writer." Beginning in 1852, some of his ballads became part of the repertory of the minstrel companies of the day, including the famous Christy's. His fame increased with the appearance of "The Old Folks at Home," "Massa's in the Cold Ground," "My Old Kentucky Home," and "Old Black Joe." Following an unhappy marriage and excessive drinking, however, he died in poverty in New York City in 1864.

§ Open Monday-Friday 9-4. Closed university holidays. Fee for guided tour. Phone: 412-624-4100.

¶ **University of Pittsburgh,** 5th Avenue and Bigelow Boulevard.

The university's forty-two-story Cathedral of Learning houses twenty-three nationality classrooms, each contributed by the host country and reflecting its particular cultural and ethnic characteristics.

The Irish Classroom resembles a sixth-century Irish stone chapel or oratory, while its vestibule entrance is copied from Killeshin Chapel in County Laois, Ireland. Limestone arches are carved with intricate designs, some from the Church of Clonkeen, near Limerick, and others from Cormac's Chapel on the Rock of Cashel. The stained-glass windows bear medallions depicting famous teachers from the three major Irish schools during the early Christian period: St. Finian at Clonard, St. Columkille at Derry, and St. Carthagh at Lismore. The cornerstone comes from Abbey Clonmacnoise near Athlone, Ireland; behind it is a metal container holding earth from Navan Fort, County Armagh, and from the Hill of Tara, County Meath. The Gaelic lettering on the cornerstone translates as, "For the Glory of God and the Honor of Ireland." Other typically Celtic ornamentation includes carvings of long locks of hair, wild dogs and cats, and birds with twisted bodies.

During the last three weeks in December each room is decorated in the traditional holiday manner of its host country.

§ Tours Monday-Saturday 9:30-3, Sunday 11-3. Reservations and fee for tour. Phone: 412-624-6000.

POTTSVILLE

Pottsville was a center of activity by a secret society of miners known as the Molly Maguires, modeled after an organization in Ireland that used violence against the agents of absentee landlords. Ironically, the Mollies' chief antagonists were both Irishmen. During a sensational trial of accused Mollies at Pottsville in June 1877, the prosecution's key witness was James McParlan, a redheaded, Irish-born Catholic who had worked as a lumberman, a policeman, a teamster, and a saloonkeeper before becoming a Pinkerton detective. He was subsequently hired to infiltrate the Mollies by Franklin Gowan, the son of Irish immigrant parents and the president of the Philadelphia and Reading Railroad Company, the largest mine operator in the anthracite region. As a result of the trial, ten Molly Maguires were hanged and fourteen were sentenced to prison.

QUARRYVILLE

¶ Robert Fulton Birthplace National Historic Landmark, 8 miles south on U.S. 222 to Swift Road.

This two-and-a-half-story structure was built from the ruins of the house in which Robert Fulton was born in 1765. Fulton, whose father had probably come from Kilkenny, Ireland, before settling in Lancaster, Pennsylvania, by 1735, proved the commercial viability of steamboat transportation.

§ Open Memorial Day-Labor Day, Saturday and Sunday. Phone: 717-548-2679.

SCRANTON

¶ Terence Powderly House, 614 North Main Street. Private.

This was the home of Terence Vincent Powderly, an early labor leader who was born in 1827 in Carbondale, Pennsylvania, to immigrant parents from County Meath, Ireland.

After working at various railroad jobs as a teenager, Powderly joined the Machinists' and Blacksmiths' Union and later became a labor organizer for the Industrial Brotherhood. Beginning in 1874 with his induction into the Knights of Labor, he held various leadership positions in that organization, including the post of Grand Master Workman from 1879 to 1893. Although he championed the Knights' call for abolition of child labor, government ownership of public utilities, and regulation of trusts and monopolies, he opposed the use of strikes. His ultimate goal was to abolish the wage system through creation of producers' cooperatives. Toward the end of his life he was appointed U.S. commissioner-general of immigration. The author of many works on labor issues, he is most remembered for *Thirty Years of Labor, 1859 to 1889,* a book that is not only an autobiography but also a history of the national labor struggle in which he played such a prominent role.

VALLEY FORGE

¶ Freedoms Foundation at Valley Forge, State 23.

Founded to encourage responsible citizenship, this 105-acre campus features several points of interest:

• The Medal of Honor Grove honors the recipients of the nation's highest award for military valor.

• The Henry Knox Building – named for the famous Revolutionary War general of Irish descent – houses archives and photographs of many Medal of Honor recipients.

• The Obelisk of Honor commemorates the foreign-born recipients of the Medal of Honor, including the 202 Irish-born recipients (the largest group of immigrants to be so honored). These soldiers were recognized for valor in the Civil War, the Indian campaigns, the Korean campaign of 1871, the Spanish-American War, the Philippine Insurrection, the China Relief Expedition (during the Boxer Rebellion), World War I, and various interim periods. The obelisk is made of granite from Wicklow, Ireland, and was donated in 1985 by the Ancient Order of Hibernians in America.

• The Faith of Our Fathers Chapel.

• The Credo Monument.

§ Open Monday-Friday 9-5. Fee. Phone: 610-933-8825.

¶ Valley Forge National Historical Park.

From mid December 1777 to mid June of the following year, this 3,600-acre park was the site of the winter encampment of General George Washington and the 12,000 men of his Continental Army.

On St. Patrick's Day in 1778, wrangling broke out between Irish and German troops over the making of a "stuffed Paddy." The conflict arose, apparently, when the Germans – threadbare and suffering tremendously from the cold – resented what they regarded as the waste of clothing in the outfitting of an effigy of St. Patrick. When General Washington was informed of the row, he quieted things down with a Solomon-like decision. To placate the Irishmen, he said that "I too am a lover of St. Patrick and must settle the affair by making the whole army keep the day." And to satisfy the Germans, he ordered that all the men be given an extra allowance of grog that day.

• The National Memorial Arch, which is dedicated to the "incomparable patience and fidelity" of the American soldiers who were encamped here, is adorned with bronze tablets listing the names of the officers who served here under Washington, among them *General John Sullivan.

• West of the National Memorial Arch is a bronze equestrian statue of *General Anthony Wayne. The statue was dedicated in 1908 and is located in the area where his Pennsylvania troops were encamped. A plaque on the pedestal summarizes his career: He was born in Pennsylvania, was a member of various Pennsylvania legislative bodies (the provincial convention, the state assembly, and the convention called to ratify the U.S. Constitution), and served at the battles of Brandywine, Germantown, Monmouth, Stony Point, and Yorktown.

• In the headquarters area is the home of Samuel Brown, where *General Henry Knox and his wife lived during the army's encampment here. The troops and artillery pieces under Knox's command were located in

what is now Artillery Park.
   • The star-shaped redoubt overlooking the Schuylkill River is a re-construction of the original built by army engineers under the supervision of *General John Sullivan. It was the largest of the fortifications at Valley Forge.
   § Open daily 9-5. Closed December 25. Phone: 610-783-1077.

WAYNE

¶ **Anthony Wayne Burial Site,** St. David's Episcopal Church, 763 Valley Forge Road.
   A monument in the church cemetery marks the tomb of *Anthony Wayne, the famous Revolutionary War general.

WARMINSTER

¶ **Log College Monument,** York Road.
   This granite memorial marks the location of "Log College," founded in 1737 by the Reverend William Tennent as the first educational institution of higher learning in America affiliated with the Presbyterian Church. The monument lists the names of the sixty-three schools which were founded by Log College graduates.
   Tennent, a native of Ireland, was a graduate of the University of Edinburgh and was ordained a priest of the Church of Ireland in 1706. After coming to Philadelphia, however, he petitioned to be admitted to the Presbyterian ministry.
   The famous revivalist preacher George Whitefield described Tennent's "college" as "a little log house about 20 feet long and nearly as many broad," resembling "the school of the old prophets." The college was closed when its successor, the College of New Jersey (now Princeton), was established in 1747.

¶ **Neshaminy Warwick Presbyterian Church,** 1401 Meetinghouse Road.
   Erected in 1743, this stone structure was preceded by a log church built by the *Reverend William Tennent, its first pastor. Although his grave is located in the adjacent graveyard, his original tombstone is embedded in a wall of the church.
   § Phone: 215-343-6060.

WYOMING

¶ **Wyoming Massacre Monument,** 4th Street and Wyoming Avenue.
   This memorial marks the burial place of the victims of the Wyoming

Massacre, a series of raids carried out in the summer of 1778 by bands of Native Americans.

The massacre was the culmination of a campaign by Tories and American Indians to destroy the region's importance as a granary for Patriot troops during the Revolutionary War. On July 3, 1778, approximately 1,200 Indians and renegade whites – under the command of the Tory leader *Guy Johnson – defeated 300 frontiersman near Forty Fort (north of Kingston). The victory left the Wyoming Valley defenseless, and the next day the Native Americans attacked the white settlements in that region. The Indians' victory was short-lived, however. In reprisal *General John Sullivan led an expedition up the Susquehanna River, during which his troops devastated the area and broke the Indians' hegemony in the area. (See Sullivan Monument, Elmira, New York.)

YORK

¶ **James Smith Burial Site,** First Presbyterian Church, on the northeast corner of Market and Queen streets.

In the cemetery next to the church is the grave of James Smith, one of the Irish-born signers of the Declaration of Independence.

Smith was born in northern Ireland about 1719 and came to Pennsyl-

Grave of James Smith, an Irish-born signer of the Declaration of Independence.

vania when he was approximately ten years old. He studied Greek, Latin, and surveying at the school in Philadelphia conducted by the *Reverend Francis Alison and later read law in Lancaster.

Beginning in 1774, Smith took an active part in Pennsylvania's response to British policies. After raising the first company of volunteers for the defense of the colony, he was elected to various extralegal conventions held in Philadelphia. At one he read an essay surveying the constitutional relationship between Britain and America, called for a policy of nonimportation against the mother country, and urged the convening of a general congress of the colonies to deal with Britain from a common position.

In June 1776 Smith was a member of the committee which drafted a resolution asking the Continental Congress to declare independence. Although he was not a member of the Congress when it voted for such a step, he was among the delegates who signed the document the following August.

¶ **General Gates House,** 157 West Market Street.

Here in 1778 the Marquis de Lafayette toasted George Washington, thereby expressing his loyalty to his commander-in-chief and frustrating a plot to replace him with General Horatio Gates. Gates and others had been part of the "Conway Cabal," a conspiracy named after Thomas Conway, an Irish mercenary who had enjoyed rapid advancement in the Continental Army.

Because of his previous experience in the French army, Conway had been made a brigadier general immediately after his arrival in America in 1777. His animus against Washington may have been due to the latter's refusal to promote him to major general on the premise that to do so would have been unfair to veteran American officers. When Congress gave Conway the desired promotion, he proceeded to criticize Washington in letters to Gates, perhaps confident that congressional dissatisfaction with the commander-in-chief would result in Washington's dismissal. Conway was accordingly embarrassed when Washington confronted him over the issue and when Lafayette refused to accept him as his second in command for the proposed invasion of Canada. Even one of Conway's supporters in Congress wrote that his "conduct respecting General Washington is criminal and unpardonable, severely censured by all the foreign officers."

In a subsequent duel related to this unfortunate episode, Conway suffered a wound to the mouth. During his recuperation he penned an apology to Washington for all the harm his indiscretion had caused. After his return to France, he was appointed governor-general of the French possessions in India.

§ Open Monday-Saturday 10-4, Sunday 1-4. Closed major holidays. Fee. Phone: 717-848-1587.

RHODE ISLAND

CRANSTON

¶ **Cranston Print Works,** Cranston Street, west of Dyer Avenue. .

Originally founded in 1824 as the A. and W. Sprague Company, this early industrial enterprise printed finished textiles by machine. The operation was part of a company town known as Sprague's Village, whose "feudal lord" was Amasa Sprague (the "A" in the company's name).

One of the Irish immigrants who developed for Sprague a reciprocated hatred was Nicholas Gordon, who had emigrated from Ireland in the mid 1830s and had set himself up as the owner of a small store in Cranston. Gordon was described as "a man of much talk, a sportive, swearing little Irishman, beneath the size of an ordinary man," but "more genteel than the run of factory workers." Although his business flourished even more after he was issued a liquor license, his trade in *aqua vitae* apparently affected the productivity of some of the workers at the print shop. As a result, Sprague blocked renewal of the license in June 1843. Gordon's subsequent threat to take revenge on Sprague before the year was out seemed to have come true when the factory owner's bludgeoned body was found in a secluded spot outside the village. Gordon's brothers John and William were charged with murder, while Nicholas Gordon was indicted as an accessory before the fact, allegedly as the instigator of the crime.

As events unfolded, it became evident that a fair trial for the three brothers would be highly doubtful, given the prejudice against Catholics and the Irish at the time. According to a newspaper report, a red-stained shirt found in the Gordon house was covered with Sprague's blood. (The "blood" later proved to be dye from a factory in which John Gordon had worked.) Even the chief justice, in his charge to the jury, made a distinction between testimony by native-born witnesses and by "the countrymen of William Gordon."

Luckily, however, the testimony of a Yankee corroborated that of Irish witnesses who had claimed that William had been in Providence on the day of the murder. Although no direct testimony placed John at the scene of the crime, circumstantial testimony by a prostitute and the village idiot proved effective on the jury, which convicted John but acquitted William. Despite a petition for reprieve to the General Assembly, John was hanged in February 1845. Subsequent uncertainty about the fairness of his trial eventually led to the abolition of capital punishment in Rhode Island in 1852.

§ Open to visitors by arrangement.

MIDDLETOWN

¶ Berkeley Memorial Chapel, at the corner of Vauclause Avenue.

This English Gothic structure was consecrated in 1887 in honor of George Berkeley, the famous Anglo-Irish philosopher, educator, and bishop of Cloyne, Ireland, who had lived in this area between 1729 and 1731. Stones from Cloyne Cathedral and the isle of Iona adorn the porch.

¶ Whitehall Museum House, 311 Berkeley Avenue, near Green End Avenue.

Following his arrival in Newport in 1729, George Berkeley erected this house and made it the centerpiece of his ninety-acre farm. He named the estate "Whitehall" after the royal palace in London.

Berkeley was a native of County Kilkenny, Ireland, where he was born in 1685. After attending Kilkenny College, he began a lengthy career as a teacher of Hebrew, logic, classics, and theology at Trinity College, Dublin. While in the Irish capital, he wrote a number of works expounding his philosophy of immaterialism, including a pioneering essay on the psychology of perception published in 1709, the year of his ordination as a priest in the Church of Ireland.

Following his appointment as dean of the cathedral in Londonderry in 1724, Berkeley proposed the creation of a university in Bermuda to educate pastors for colonial parishes and train missionaries to the Native Americans. Prospects for the project seemed promising when many English notables – including Jonathan Swift – supported the idea and when

"Whitehall House," the home of the Irish-born missionary George Berkeley.

the Parliament pledged £20,000. Berkeley resigned his deanery and sailed for Bermuda in September 1728, but his ship lost its direction and landed instead in Newport, Rhode Island, the following January. For the next two years he resided at Whitehall, whose farm he hoped would supply the new university with produce. It was while living here that he wrote the first chapter of *Alciphron*, a book in defense of Christianity against the criticism of freethinkers.

After realizing that his educational proposal would never receive the financial support he had expected from England, Berkeley returned to Ireland and bequeathed Whitehall to Yale College. The income from Berkeley's farm was subsequently a source of scholarship funds for Yale students, among them Eleazer Wheelock, founder and first president of Dartmouth College; Aaron Burr Sr., president of Princeton University; Timothy Dwight, president of Yale College; and Daniel Coit Gilman, president of the University of California and of Johns Hopkins University. In 1733 Berkeley donated 880 volumes to Yale, a gift that has been described as "the finest collection of books that ever came at one time into America." Though he had resisted requests to become the first bishop in the British colonies, he did accept appointment as bishop of Cloyne in County Cork. In 1985 the Irish government honored Berkeley with a postage stamp on the three-hundreth anniversary of his birth.

A century later Frederick Billings, one of the trustees of the University of California, suggested the name "Berkeley" for the proposed site of California's new university. He said that the city's location on the western perimeter of the country reminded him of George Berkeley's prophetic lines about a golden age in the New World: "There shall be sung another golden Age, / The rise of Empire and of Arts, / The Good and Great inspiring epic Rage, / The Wisest Heads and Noblest Hearts .... / Westward the Course of Empire takes its Way; / The four first Acts already past, / A fifth shall close the Drama with the Day; / Time's noblest Offering is the last."

§ Open July-Labor Day, daily 10-5; rest of the year, by appointment. Fee. Phone: 401-846-3116 or 847-7951.

NARRAGANSETT PIER

¶ **St. Peter-by-the-Sea Church,** 72 Central Street.

The church has a stained-glass window in memory of Varina Anne (Winnie) Davis, the daughter of Confederate president *Jefferson Davis. (The elder Davis's mother was of Scotch-Irish descent.)

Born in the final year of the Civil War, Winnie spent her teenage years at a school in Germany and returned to America fluent in both French and German. During her father's last years, she was his constant companion, either at "Beauvoir" in Biloxi, Mississippi, or on his journeys through the

South. At one of his appearances, she was dubbed "The Daughter of the Confederacy" by a Confederate veterans' group.

Her status as the symbol of the "Lost Cause" was compromised, however, when she became engaged to the grandson of a New York abolitionist. In the end, her mother blocked the marriage, probably because of the fiancé's less than promising financial prospects rather than because of his Northern connections. Winnie subsequently continued to support herself and her mother through her writing – magazine articles, two novels, and a biography of *Robert Emmet (*An Irish Knight of the Nineteenth Century*). She died in Narragansett Pier at the age of thirty-four.

§ Phone: 401-783-4623.

NEWPORT

ℐ Belcourt Castle, 657 Bellevue Avenue.

Designed in 1891, this French Renaissance-style castle was the summer residence of *Oliver Hazard Perry Belmont and his wife. The house is noted for its antiques, stained glass collection, and coronation coach.

Belmont, whose maternal grandfather was the naval hero *Matthew C. Perry, served in the U.S. House of Representatives during the 1880s, notably as a member of the Foreign Relations Committee. His father was August Belmont, the New York banker and financier.

§ Open Memorial Day-mid October, daily 9-5; mid October-November 30, daily 10-4; rest of the year, variable times. Closed Thanksgiving and December 25. Fee. 401-846-0669.

ℐ Hammersmith Farm, Ocean Drive.

Following their marriage in Newport in 1953, John F. Kennedy and his new wife, Jacqueline Bouvier, held their wedding reception here. During the next decade they were frequent guests at the twenty-eight-room shingled "cottage" on this 500-acre estate. (The "farm" was known as the "Summer White House" during the Kennedy presidency.) The property was originally owned by John Auchincloss, whose son had married Jacqueline Bouvier's mother, Janet Lee Bouvier, after the latter's divorce from Jack Bouvier.

Despite the French blood which Jacqueline Bouvier inherited from her father, her mother was 100 percent Irish, the family's first American ancestor having come from Ireland to New York City in the 1840s. Jacqueline's grandfather – James Thomas Lee – was vice president of Chase Manhattan Bank and president and chairman of the board of New York Central Savings Bank. When he died at the age of ninety-five, he left a $12 million estate.

When J.F.K. and Jackie celebrated their tenth wedding anniversary in 1963 at Hammersmith Farm, the president gave his wife the inventory of a New York art dealer with permission to buy anything on the list. The First Lady, in turn, presented her husband with a leather scrapbook containing photographs of the newly landscaped White House Rose Garden. She also gave him a St. Christopher medal to replace the one which he had buried with their prematurely born son, Patrick Bouvier Kennedy, who had died the month before.

§ Guided tours April-mid November, daily 10-5. Fee. Phone: 401-846-7346.

¶ **Irish Servant Memorial,** along Cliff Walk (at the bottom of the Forty Steps at the end of Narragansett Avenue).

This marker is located in the area where many Irish servants met to socialize at the end of their working day in the Newport mansions.

The early nineteenth-century prejudice against Irish-Catholic female servants was gradually dispelled as more and more prosperous American families sought domestic help and as the Irish "biddy" or "Bridie" (both diminutives of "Bridget") earned a reputation for honesty and ability.

Contemporaries could not have missed the irony in the fact that domestic service jobs in America were offered to young Irish girls totally unfamiliar with the "common duties of servants in respectable positions." To the visiting observer Dr. Daniel Cahill, "They can neither wash nor iron clothes. They don't understand the cleaning of glass or silver plate. They cannot make fires expeditiously, or dust the carpets, or polish the furniture." (An awareness of Irish naiveté was evident in the story of the Irish servant girl who always walked down the stairs backwards because in Ireland she had never climbed anything but a barn ladder.) Nor, of course, were young girls who had most likely never seen a leg of mutton boiled or roasted in their homeland ideal candidates for the chef's hat in an American kitchen.

Yet what they lacked in skill they made up for in willingness to learn and in their reputation for honesty. As early as 1829 a Boston placement office required that each applicant for a domestic service position exhibit "a Testimonial of moral conduct" from previous families or from a Catholic clergyman for "honesty, sobriety, and the practical observances of the Duties which the Holy, Catholic Religion enjoins and enforces." (Again self-deprecation was evident in the Irish girl who explained to her employer: "Sure I had a splendid character when I left the ould country, but I lost it on the ship coming over.") No matter how anti-papist in their views, many Protestant employers preferred young Irish girls precisely because of their moral upbringing. By 1860 such girls enjoyed a near monopoly in Yankee households in Boston and New England and in most hotels throughout the country.

¶ **Island Cemetery,** Farewell and Warner streets.

A monument here marks the graves of Newport heroes *Matthew C. Perry and *Oliver H. Perry. *The Standing Angel*, a statue by the Irish-born sculptor Augustus Saint-Gaudens, is in the Alfred Smith plot toward the back of the cemetery.

¶ **Matthew C. Perry Birthplace,** 31 Walnut Street. Private.

This small, gambrel-roofed house was the birthplace in 1794 of *Matthew C. Perry, known chiefly for his successful efforts in opening Japan to American trade. He lived here until about 1810.

Perry was the son of Christopher Perry, who had seen service on both land and sea during the Revolutionary War and four times had been taken prisoner by the British. During his confinement in Ireland, he met Sarah Wallace Alexander, a blue-eyed Irish beauty whom he vowed to make his wife. In 1784 she accompanied him to America, where they were soon married. Matthew, the couple's fourth child, was given the middle name "Calbraith" for an Irish fellow passenger on his parents' voyage to America. Another of the couple's sons was Oliver H. Perry.

Prior to his mission to Japan, Matthew C. Perry enjoyed a varied career in the U.S. Navy. His brief service in the War of 1812 was followed by an assignment in 1820 as executive officer of a naval vessel that escorted the first group of African Americans to be settled in Liberia. In 1843 he commanded a squadron that helped suppress the slave trade and protect the African-American colonies on the west coast of Africa. During the Mexican War he rose to commander-in-chief of the squadron cruising the east coast of Mexico and commanded the naval forces that helped General Winfield Scott force the surrender of Vera Cruz.

Despite his reputation for gruffness and strict discipline, "Old Bruin" was at the forefront of reform efforts within the Navy. Early in his career he stressed the importance of proper hygiene among his men in order to prevent diseases. On one voyage he ordered that the men be required to wear flannel and be forbidden to sleep on deck, wear wet clothes, or be turned out at night unnecessarily. He also insisted that the deck be fumigated and whitewashed every day. Always interested in improving naval education, in 1824 he proposed and lobbied for a naval apprenticeship system until it was adopted by Congress thirteen years later. Upon his appointment as second in charge at the New York Navy Yard, he led the way to creation of the U.S. Naval Lyceum for the further education of naval officers. In addition, he helped prepare the first curriculum for the Naval Academy at Annapolis.

¶ **Naval War College Museum,** Founders Hall, Coasters Harbor Island.

Founders Hall is the original site of the U.S. Naval War College, created in 1884. The second president of the college was Captain Alfred Thayer

Mahan, whose famous work *The Influence of Sea Power upon History, 1660-1783* influenced the thinking of *Theodore Roosevelt when the latter was assistant secretary of the navy.

Mahan, whose grandparents had fled Ireland after the unsuccessful uprising in 1798, chose a naval career, even though his father was an instructor at the U.S. Military Academy at West Point. Following his graduation from the Naval Academy in 1859, Mahan began a career that alternated between sea and shore duty. Cruises to Japan, Rio de Janeiro, Capetown, Aden, and Bombay were interrupted by blockade duty during the Civil War. While sailing along the west coast of South America, he received an invitation to lecture on tactics and naval history at the War College.

After delivering his first lectures in 1886, Mahan was appointed president of the college, a position that required him to defend its role in the face of opposition from the secretary of the navy. In 1890 his lectures were published as the famous *Influence of Sea Power*, in which he surveyed the waxing and waning of the world's great maritime nations, examined the factors which contributed to a nation's sea power, and analyzed the relationship between naval and political history. Two years later Mahan published a companion work on the influence of sea power on the French Revolution and the French Empire. The two works made their debut at an opportune time, almost as if to justify the naval buildup that had been occurring in Britain, Germany, and the United States. *Theodore Roosevelt predicted that the first work would become a classic, while Kaiser Wilhelm II announced that he was "devouring" both books and had made them standard reading on all his ships. The British, meanwhile, lionized Mahan and his works, hosting him at a dinner attended by the Queen and awarding him honorary degrees from both Cambridge and Oxford.

Despite his retirement from the Navy in 1896, Mahan continued to write and to influence American policy. His ideas undoubtedly played a significant role in promoting and sanctioning American expansionism in the Caribbean and the Pacific. To an earlier biography about Admiral Farragut, he added one on Nelson and authored additional works on naval strategy and sea power in the American Revolution and the War of 1812. His autobiography, *From Sail to Steam*, appeared in 1907.

§ Open Monday-Friday 10-4 (also Saturday and Sunday noon-4, June-September). Closed holidays. Phone: 401-841-4052 or 841-1317.

¶ **Newport Casino,** 194 Bellevue Avenue.

One of the first country clubs in the nation, the Casino was founded by *James Gordon Bennett Jr. following his expulsion from the Newport Reading Room, the town's premiere social club.

Bennett, the publisher of the *New York Herald*, had already made a name for himself in the world of sports. In his youth he had become a well known yachtsman, boasting a crew of 100 on the largest steam yacht ever built on the River Clyde in Scotland. In the 1870s he introduced polo among the upper classes in Newport and later sponsored various international competitions involving airplanes, automobiles, and balloons.

¶ Oliver H. Perry Statue, Washington Square.

This tree-shaded statue honors the American naval commander whose unprecedented victory over a British fleet gave the United States control of Lake Erie until the end of the War of 1812. (See Put-in-Bay, Ohio.)

¶ Redwood Library and Athenaeum, 50 Bellevue Avenue.

The library, which dates from 1750, contains a fine collection of books and early American paintings, including seven by Gilbert Stuart. The library evolved from a suggestion by *George Berkeley that Newport establish a literary society.

§ Open Monday-Saturday 9:30-5:30. Closed holidays. Phone: 401-847-0292.

¶ Rosecliff, Bellevue Avenue.

Designed after Louis XIV's Grand Trianon palace at Versailles, Rosecliff was built by Hermann Oelrichs and his wife, Theresa Fair Oelrichs, at the turn of the century. The mansion, notable for its forty-by-eighty-foot ballroom, was featured in the 1974 film *The Great Gatsby*. Rosecliff's billiard room reflects Oelrichs' tastes: the wooden mantelpiece is carved with the heads of Irish kings and reputedly was saved from the wreck of a ship that was bringing it from Ireland. The garden ornamentation, including the *Court of Love*, is the work of *Augustus Saint-Gaudens.

Mrs. Oelrichs was the daughter of James Fair, an Irish immigrant who had struck it rich in the Nevada Comstock silver lode. (See Virginia City, Nevada, in *Irish America*, Volume 2.) Fair was one of a group of young Irishmen known as the "Silver Kings" because of their success in developing the Comstock Lode, which yielded more than $500 million of ore before it was exhausted in 1898. Fair served as a U.S. senator from Nevada from 1881 to 1887. In 1883, however, after twenty-one years of marriage, his wife divorced him on the grounds of habitual adultery. The ex-Mrs. Fair received a $5 million divorce settlement, the largest in American history until that time. After the divorce Theresa lived with her two daughters in the magnificent Fair Mansion in San Francisco. It was there that one of the girls – Theresa, or Tessie – married Hermann Oelrichs, a German whose family was in the steamship business.

As mistress of Rosecliff, Tessie Oelrichs was known for her unconventionality and the magnificence of her fetes. Although distinguished by her white lace dresses and "towering picture hats," she was not above wielding a mop herself to make up for the deficiencies of her domestic staff. In addition, she regularly shocked and amused her acquaintances with her racy monologues and "up-to-the-minute profanity." In 1904 Tessie dazzled Newport society with her "Bal Blanc" and reflected the white motif of the dance with an elegant lace dress embroidered with silver. One of the fountains on the property was stocked with white swans that evening, and the guests were treated to the sight of a mock fleet of white ships in the surf below the house.

§ Open April-October, daily 10-5. Fee. Phone: 401-847-1000.

¶ **St. Mary's Catholic Church,** 250 Spring Street, at Memorial Boulevard.

This brownstone Gothic Revival church was designed by *Patrick Keely and was built between 1848 and 1852. A hundred years later – on September 12, 1953 – John F. Kennedy and *Jacqueline Bouvier were married here. Almost 3,000 people broke through the police lines outside the church that morning, nearly crushing the bride.

When Jackie became engaged to J.F.K., her friend John White bet her that she wouldn't go through with the planned marriage. She promised to give him two dollars if she didn't marry Kennedy, and White in turn promised to give her one dollar if she did marry him. White arrived late at the wedding, but just in time to see the bride walk down the aisle. Realizing that he had lost the bet, he waved his dollar bill at his friend as people around him laughed. Jackie acknowledged his sportsmanship with a big smile.

¶ **Soldiers' and Sailors' Monument,** Niantonomi Park.

This memorial to the veterans and victims of World War I is the work of *William Clark Noble.

¶ **Touro Park,** Bellevue Avenue and Mill Street.

• The statue of Dr. William Ellery Channing is the work of *William Clark Noble.

• The pedestal on which the statue of *Matthew C. Perry stands is faced with bas-reliefs depicting episodes in his career and captioned with the words "Africa, 1843," "Mexico, 1846," and "Treaty with Japan, 1854." (See Matthew C. Perry Birthplace, Newport, Rhode Island.)

In January 1852 Perry was chosen to lead a historic diplomatic mission to Japan. He was commissioned to negotiate with that isolated nation a treaty that would ensure the protection of American sailors and property in Japan and bring about the opening of Japanese ports to American trade. About his assignment Perry wrote: "We pray God that our present attempt to bring a singular and isolated people into the family of civilized nations may succeed without resort to bloodshed." After anchoring in Yedo Harbor in July 1853, Perry proceeded to insist that he be greeted by a Japa-

*Statue of Commodore
Matthew C. Perry.*

nese emissary equal to his own rank. Perry's bluster finally won for him an elaborate welcome by representatives of the Emperor. Almost immediately Perry wrote his wife: "This achievement of mine I consider an important event in my life. The Pageant was magnificent and I am the only Christian that has ever before landed peacefully [in Japan] without submitting to the most humiliating degradation."

Although a full-scale commercial treaty was not negotiated until 1858, Perry and his men had given the Japanese their first introduction to Americans and western technology. The Japanese were amused and delighted by Perry's crew – by the African Americans who entertained their hosts with a minstrel show and by the other Americans' light hair, fair complexions, and regrettable table manners. The Americans, in turn, examined an enormous sumo wrestling champion, demonstrated the telegraph wire, and presented the Japanese with clocks, a small-scale locomotive, a telescope, and a barrel of whiskey. From these first encounters Perry concluded that the Japanese "are in most respects a refined and rational people . . . . I have never met in any part of the world, even in Europe, with a people of more unaffected grace and dignity. . . ." The American commander was equally complimentary about Japanese resourcefulness: "Their curiosity to learn the results of the material progress of other people, and their readiness in adapting them to their own uses, would soon . . . raise them to a level with the most favored countries." The Japanese, he predicted correctly, "would enter as powerful competitors in the race for mechanical success in the future."

¶ Trinity Church, Queen Anne Square.

Constructed in 1726, the church boasts a wine glass (three-tiered) pulpit, the only one of its kind in New England and the only remaining pulpit used by George Berkeley, the eighteenth-century Irish-born philosopher. The central part of the organ in the church was presented by Berkeley in 1733. His gift had been refused by the town of Berkeley, Massachusetts, "as an instrument of the devil for the entrapping of men's souls." His daughter Lucia is buried in the churchyard.

Berkeley was impressed by the degree of religious toleration in Rhode Island and wrote to a Dublin friend: "Here are four sorts of Anabaptists, besides Presbyterians, Quakers, Independents and many of no profession at all. Notwithstanding so many differences here are fewer quarrels about religion than elsewhere, the people living peaceable with their neighbors of whatsoever permission." (See Middletown, Rhode Island.)

§ Open early July-Labor Day, daily 10-4; day after Labor Day-Columbus Day, Monday-Friday 10-4; rest of the year, Monday-Friday 10-1. Phone: 402-846-0660.

NORTH KINGSTON

¶ James MacSparran Burial Site, Old St. Paul's churchyard, Shermantown Road, between Pendar and Congdon Hill roads.

Although Old St. Paul's (Old Narragansett) Church was removed to Wickford in 1800, the church's cemetery still remains (though poorly marked) and is the final resting place of the Reverend James MacSparran, the Anglican rector of the church for thirty-seven years. A large cross marks his grave.

Born in 1693 in County Londonderry, Ireland, MacSparran was graduated from the University of Glasgow and took preparatory steps toward ordination in the Presbyterian ministry before sailing to America. While in Boston, however, he came into conflict with the Puritan minister Cotton Mather, who proceeded publicly to challenge the newcomer's credentials and otherwise to delay his ordination. After returning to Ireland, MacSparran carried out his intention to seek ordination, but to the Anglican priesthood instead. Within a year of his ordination he had returned to the American colonies, this time as a missionary of the Society for the Propagation of the Gospel in Foreign Parts.

One of MacSparran's most important published works was *America Dissected*, a 1753 account of the British colonies which he composed in the form of letters to friends in Ireland. In that work he expressed his opposi-

Grave of Rev. James MacSparran.

tion to any political union of Ireland and England: "You [Irish] are greater slaves already than our negroes, and an union of that kind would make you more underlings than you are now. The accounts of the open irreligion on the greater island inclines me to imagine, that Ireland is on the brink of obtaining . . . its ancient name of Insula Sanctorum [Isle of Saints]." While the rector at St. Paul's, he baptized Gilbert Stuart, the future artist, and entertained the philosopher George Berkeley, another native of Ireland and the future bishop of Cloyne, Ireland. (During their visits the two clergymen conversed in the Irish language.)

PROVIDENCE

¶ Ambrose Burnside Statue, City Hall Park.

This equestrian statue of the Civil War general Ambrose Burnside was sculpted by *Launt Thompson.

¶ Brown University, College Hill, College Street.

Originally founded as Rhode Island College in 1764, the school was renamed in 1804 when Nicholas Brown Jr. created a $5,000 endowment for a professorship in oratory and belles lettres. His subsequent benefactions to the university totaled $160,000.

Brown belonged to the city's most illustrious merchant family and was descended from Nicholas Power, a native of Ireland who had served in the Rhode Island General Assembly. In 1791 Nicholas Brown Jr. married Ann Carter, the granddaughter of an Irish naval officer who had died in the service of the Crown.

• The John Carter Brown Library on the campus was named for the son of Nicholas Brown Jr. and Ann Carter. The library contains one of the best collections of Americana printed before 1825. Brown's collection of about 7,500 volumes formed the nucleus of the library's holdings.

§ Library open during the academic year, Monday-Friday 8:30-5, Saturday 9-noon; rest of the year, variable times. Closed holidays. Phone: 401-863-2725.

¶ John Brown House, 52 Power Street.

This large brick Georgian mansion was built in 1786 by John Brown, a China trade merchant and a member of the famous mercantile family that dominated the city's history. (Brown's maternal grandfather was Nicholas Power, a native of Ireland.) Abigail Adams once described the house as "one of the grandest I have seen in the country. Everything in and about it wore the marks of magnificence and taste." John Quincy Adams later spoke of the mansion in even more superlative terms, calling it "the most magnificent and elegant private mansion I have ever seen on this continent." Today the John Brown House is furnished with colonial antiques, decorative arts, and silver and pewter collections.

§ Open March-December, Tuesday-Saturday 10-4:30, Sunday noon-4:30; rest of the year, Saturday 10-4:30, Sunday noon-4:30. Closed holi-

The John Brown House, the home of a wealthy China trade merchant.

days. Fee. Phone 401-331-8575.

℘ John Reynolds House, 88 Benefit Street. Private.

Between 1803 and 1878 this was the home of Sarah Helen Whitman, a woman with whom *Edgar Allan Poe fell in love and to whom he wrote his famous poem "To Helen." Miss Whitman had first attracted Poe's attention when he saw her standing in her garden on a moonlit evening in 1845. After corresponding with her for four years, the poet returned to Providence and proposed to her in the churchyard behind her house. Although she accepted his offer of marriage, she later broke the engagement. Poe died a month later.

℘ Kennedy Plaza, between Exchange and Dorrance streets.

This public square in the center of Providence was named for *President John F. Kennedy.

℘ St. Joseph Catholic Church, 86 Hope Street.

Constructed from 1851 to 1853 by architect *Patrick Keely, this is the oldest standing Catholic church in the state. It was erected to minister to the Irish immigrants who had come to work on the Providence and Worcester Railroad. The famous showman *George M. Cohan was the son of Irish immigrants who lived in this area.

• Keely also designed the Cathedral of Saints Peter and Paul (1889) in Cathedral Square.

℘ State Capitol, Smith Street, between Gaspee and Francis streets.

A tablet at the entrance to the capitol commemorates *General John Sullivan, the American commander during the battle of Rhode Island, when the Americans besieging British-held Newport in 1778 were driven back. (See Durham, New Hampshire.)

§ Open Monday-Friday 8:30-4:30. Closed holidays. Phone: 401-277-2357.

WAKEFIELD

℘ Oliver H. Perry Birthplace, 2 miles south on U.S. 1, at 184 Post Road.

This two-story gambrel house is located on land owned by the Perry family since 1702. The residence has been called the "house that launched a fleet of ships." From here *Oliver Hazard Perry went to take command of the American inland fleet on Lake Erie. The house contains memorabilia associated with Perry as well as with his younger brother, *Commodore Matthew C. Perry.

WICKFORD

¶ **Old Narragansett Church,** Church Lane, off Main Street.

This church, one of the oldest Episcopal churches in the nation, was moved to this site in 1800 from North Kingston, Rhode Island, where it was built in 1707 and where the *Reverend James MacSparran had served as pastor.

§ Guided tours July and August, Friday-Sunday 11-4. Phone: 401-294-4357.

VERMONT

FAIRFIELD

¶ **Chester A. Arthur Historic Site,** 6 miles northeast on a county road.

The site features a replica of the parsonage in which Chester A. Arthur, the twenty-first president of the United States, lived as an infant. Arthur's father, a Baptist minister, had moved to the parsonage a year after his son's birth in a cabin in North Fairfield in 1829. The parsonage contains an exhibit on President Arthur's life and political career. The brick church where Arthur's father preached stands nearby.

The president's father, William Arthur, was a native of Ballymena, County Antrim, Ireland, and a graduate of Belfast College. After immigrating in 1816 to Durham, Quebec, where he taught school for a time, the elder man became a Baptist preacher, ministering to eleven parishes in New York and Vermont. He and his wife and their four daughters moved to Fairfield in 1828, a year before Chester's birth. After moving his family to New York State in 1835, William Arthur became an outspoken abolitionist and the cofounder of an antislavery society.

Eleven years later Chester Arthur was admitted to the New York bar and continued his father's commitment to securing civil rights for African Americans. In the "Lemmon Slave Case" he successfully argued that slaves brought into New York while in transit to a slave state were legally free. In

A replica of the house in which Chester Arthur lived as an infant.
(Courtesy of the Vermont Division for Historic Preservation.)

another case he obtained a judgment that recognized equal rights for blacks and whites on public transportation within the state.

§ Open Memorial Day-Columbus Day, Wednesday-Sunday 10-4. Fee. Phone: 802-828-3226.

√ The thatched cottage which William Arthur left behind in Ireland is still located on its original site in Cullybackey, near Ballymena. The one-story cottage has the traditional split door, a clay floor, and a flax-straw thatch roof.

FAIR HAVEN

¶ **Zenas Ellis House,** South Main Street. Private.

This house is reputed by some authorities to have been the home of Matthew Lyon, a native of County Wicklow, Ireland, known for a variety of firsts.

Lyon arrived in New York in 1755, indentured to the Connecticut farmer who had paid the cost of his transatlantic passage. Following the outbreak of hostilities at the battle of Lexington, the Irishman enlisted in the Patriot army and was soon commissioned as a lieutenant in the "Green Mountain Boys." After the war Lyon built Fair Haven's first sawmill, first meetinghouse, and first gristmill, established its first printing press, and published its first newspaper. He also began several manufacturing enterprises in New England, among them iron casting and paper making. He combined the two processes by casting the type and manufacturing the paper for a thoroughly democratic newspaper which he published under the name *The Scourge of Aristocracy*.

Following his election to Congress in 1797, Lyon became the object of attack and ridicule by the Federalists and their allies in the press. After receiving repeated insults from a Connecticut congressman, Lyon spat in his antagonist's face – on the very floor of the House of Representatives. When that chamber failed to expel Lyon for "the first breach of decorum in Congress," the Connecticut Federalist physically attacked him on the floor of the House and beat him with a cane. The hot-tempered Lyon responded in kind. He later defended himself by saying that he had "not come here to have my ___ kicked by everybody."

In 1798 Congress passed the Sedition Act, a broadly worded piece of legislation intended to silence criticism of the new government by foreign-born journalists and the anti-Federalist press in general. The Irish-born Mathew Carey, editor of the *Pennsylvania Herald*, declared that under "the execrable law, . . . to laugh at the cut of a congressman's coat . . . will be treason." John Daly Burk, the Irish editor of a journal in New York, escaped prosecution by promising to leave the country. Meanwhile, the libel action against the Irishman William Duane, the editor of the most prominent Republican newspaper in Philadelphia, failed to result in a conviction.

The first conviction under the new law was obtained against Matthew Lyon, still a congressman from Vermont. The fiery Irishman was fined $1,000 and jailed for four months for making libelous remarks about President Adams. On one occasion the congressman had referred to Adams and his Puritan ancestors as "the bastards of Oliver Cromwell" and as the "witch-hunting Puritans of New England who persecuted the Quakers and despised all joy." At another opportunity to antagonize his opponents, Lyon had said that "the pomp of the White House better became the court of a king than the residence of the President of a Republic!" From prison Lyon had the last laugh: In 1799 he was easily reelected to Congress.

Lyon also enjoyed the distinction of being "the man who elected Jefferson" and the first person to be elected to Congress by the people of three different states. In 1801, when the House of Representatives had failed in thirty-five ballots to break the Electoral College tie between Jefferson and Aaron Burr, Lyon cast the deciding vote. That same year Lyon moved to Kentucky, which he represented in Congress from 1804 to 1812. After heading west to Arkansas, he was elected to Congress from that state, but he died before he was able to take his seat.

FRANKLIN

¶ **Fenian Monument,** near the border of Vermont and Quebec.

This memorial commemorates the Fenians' unsuccessful attempt in 1870 to invade Canada and hold it hostage to their demand for Irish independence from Britain.

Colonel John O'Neill, an Irish-born veteran of a failed incursion four years earlier, led a force of 200 men across the border, only to see them retreat in the face of stiff Canadian resistance near the village of Eccles Hill in Quebec. While riding to the rear for reinforcements, O'Neill was arrested by a U.S. marshal sent to enforce the neutrality laws.

Although sentenced to two years' imprisonment, O'Neill was released in three months after obtaining a pardon from *President Ulysses S. Grant. (During a visit to St. Louis, the President had received a ten-foot-long petition with two columns of signatures seeking O'Neill's release from prison.)

Following this second Fenian disaster, an editorial in the *New York Times* remarked that even if the Fenians had been successful "nobody believes it would produce the liberation of Ireland from British rule. It would be just as sensible to expect Russia to liberate Poland if she heard that our Polish fellow-citizens had overpowered the garrisons of Alaska."

Despite the folly of the Fenians' efforts, O'Neill attempted another invasion of Canada. In September 1871, without the support of the Fenian council, he and a few followers seized the Hudson's Bay post in what is now Manitoba before being arrested by American troops. He later became an agent for a group of land speculators who attempted to attract Irish settlers to Nebraska. The town of O'Neill in Holt County, Nebraska, is named for him.

NORTH BENNINGTON

¶ **Park-McCullough Mansion,** Park and West streets, 1 block west off State 67A.

Built in 1865, this thirty-five room Victorian house was the home of John McCullough, governor of Vermont from 1902 to 1904. Members of his family lived here until 1965.

McCullough, whose Scotch-Irish grandfather had immigrated to America in 1701, received a degree from the University of Pennsylvania law school in 1858. His early practice in Philadelphia was interrupted, however, by a pulmonary attack, which caused him to seek a change of climate in California. Following the outbreak of the Civil War soon after his arrival on the West Coast, the twenty-five-year-old lawyer made a name for himself with his speeches in defense of the Union. Beginning in 1862, he was elected successively to the state assembly, the state senate, and the post of attorney general. Between 1867 and 1872 he carried on a lucrative legal practice in San Francisco before settling in southern Vermont.

This second phase of McCullough's life revolved around his commercial, financial, and railroad interests. In 1873 he became vice president of the Panama Railway until assuming the presidency in 1882 at the urging of Ferdinand de Lesseps. At various times over the next decade, he served as president of the Bennington & Rutland Railroad and the Chicago & Erie Railroad before being elected governor of Vermont. During his tenure the state abandoned the prohibition of liquor for a policy of licensing and local option. Once out of political office, McCullough served either as president or director of numerous enterprises, including the Lackawanna Steel Company and the Atcheson, Topeka & Santa Fe Railroad Company.

§ Open late May-late October, Thursday-Monday 10-3. (Inquire about hours in December.) Fee. Phone: 802-442-5441.

ST. ALBANS

¶ **The Common,** in the center of town.

In June 1866 about a thousand Fenians were massed at St. Albans in preparation for an invasion of Canada, the first in a series of steps which they hoped would lead to the creation of an independent Irish republic. As many as 300 volunteers arrived on a single train, and many of them slept on the St. Albans Common.

Although the Fenians advanced six miles into Canada, they were forced to turn back, their only accomplishment being the capture of a British flag. Before long, U.S. troops under *General George Gordon Meade arrived in St. Albans to put an end to the Fenians' violation of American neutrality. During their two-week stay on the Common, the U.S. troops dispatched the demoralized Fenians south by train and entertained the residents of St. Albans with band concerts.

SHELDON JUNCTION

¶ **Fenian Marker,** on the bridge across the Black River along State 105 just west of State 78.

This marker takes note of the raids and other Fenian activity which took place in northern Vermont in 1866 and 1870. (See Franklin and St. Albans, Vermont.)

VERGENNES

¶ **Thomas Macdonough Monument,** in the town square.

This memorial to *Thomas Macdonough commemorates the fact that the famous naval officer's flagship, the twenty-six-gun *Saratoga*, and the rest of his flotilla were constructed here in the record time of forty days during the winter of 1813-14. With this superior fleet Macdonough challenged the British navy's control of Lake Champlain. On September 11, 1814, in an engagement that lasted only a few hours, he and his flotilla captured every major British warship. Macdonough's victory dramatically changed the course of the peace negotiations with the British and resulted in a treaty more favorable to American interests. (See Plattsburgh, New York.)

WISCONSIN

APPLETON

¶ Joseph McCarthy Bust, Outagamie County Courthouse, 410 South Walnut Street.

The courthouse foyer contains a bust of Joseph McCarthy, the controversial senator who during the 1950s launched a crusade against what he described as Communist influence in the U.S. government.

McCarthy was born in 1908 in a farming area known as the "Irish settlement" near Grand Chute, Wisconsin. His father was of German and Irish background, while his mother – Bridget Tierney – was a native of Ireland. At age twenty he enrolled in a local high school and completed the four-year curriculum in a year. In 1935 he was graduated from Marquette University with a law degree. After his admission to the Wisconsin bar, he won election as a state circuit court judge. During his tenure he was reprimanded by the state supreme court for destroying court records before they could be used in an appeals case. (Other critics castigated him for turning his court into a divorce mill.) At the beginning of World War II, he took a leave of absence from the bench to accept a commission as a first lieutenant in the Marines. Although he served in the Pacific as an intelligence officer, he later claimed that he had been a tail gunner and that he had been wounded in action.

In 1946 McCarthy easily won election to the U.S. Senate as a Republican. During the campaign he had stressed his opposition to the New Deal in general and to farm price controls and national health care in particular and attacked his opponent as "communistically inclined." As a senator he generally opposed price controls and social welfare programs and was dubbed the "Pepsi Cola Kid" because of his lobbying efforts for the soft drink industry.

But it was McCarthy's anti-Communist fervor which brought him nationwide attention. His charge in 1950 that American foreign policy was being shaped by 205 members of the Communist Party who worked for the State Department came soon after the Communist victory in China and the conviction of Alger Hiss as a Soviet spy. Although a congressional investigation found no evidence to substantiate the senator's charges, he continued his attacks on the Truman administration. In 1954, as chairman of a Senate investigating committee of his own, McCarthy sought to ferret out alleged Communists in the U.S. Army. During the nationally televised hearings, he continued to attack the army and even began to assail the Eisenhower administration, a move which ultimately alienated most of the Republican leadership and increasing numbers of the public. Toward the end of that year the Senate censured McCarthy for behavior that was "contemptuous, contumacious, and denunciatory." Calling the 67-22 vote a farce, McCarthy issued his own challenge: "I'm happy to have this circus ended so I can get back to the real work of digging out communism, crime and corruption. That job will start officially Monday morning after ten months of inaction."

CUDAHY

This town of 20,000 population dates from 1893, when Patrick Cudahy relocated his meat-packing plant from Milwaukee to a 700-acre tract he had acquired here. In laying out the city, he named the first streets after well known Midwestern meat packers – Armour, Layton, Plankinton, and Swift.

Born in County Kilkenny, Ireland, Cudahy and his brothers Michael and John came to America in 1849 with their parents, who eventually settled in Milwaukee. At one time or another each of the sons worked for the meat-packing houses in the city as those firms combined and recombined under various names. Of the three brothers, Michael seems to have made the most rapid advance in the industry. After advancing to the position of meat inspector on the Milwaukee Board of Trade, in 1875 he accepted a partnership with Armour & Company of Chicago. His most important contribution to the industry was the curing of meats under refrigeration, a process which permitted the consumption of meat during the entire year. He was also instrumental in applying refrigeration to the transportation phase of the business, an innovation that was perfected in the 1870s with the invention of the refrigerated railroad car. In 1887 he and his younger brother, Edward, joined with Philip D. Armour in acquiring a small packing plant in South Omaha, Nebraska, which they conducted under the name Armour-Cudahy Packing Company. Three years later Michael Cudahy bought out Armour's interests and changed the name of the company to the Cudahy Packing Company.

In the meantime, Patrick Cudahy had entered into a partnership with his brother Edward to operate a meat-packing company in Milwaukee under the name the Cudahy Brothers. It was this business which he relocated to the newly established town of Cudahy in 1893. After serving as vice president of the company, Patrick's son John was the American ambassador to Poland and minister to Ireland and Belgium.

EAGLE

¶ **Old World Wisconsin,** 1 mile south on State 67.

This 576-acre outdoor "living museum" consists of fifty restored and furnished structures built by nineteenth-century immigrants. One of the buildings on display is a house erected in 1885 in Hubbleton, Wisconsin, for Mary Hafford, an Irish-born widow. The Ramsey Barn Visitor Center offers a slide presentation about early Wisconsin.

§ Open May-June and September-October, Monday-Friday 10-4, Saturday-Sunday 10-5; July-August, daily 10-5; late December-early March, Saturday-Sunday 9-4. Fee. Phone: 414-594-6300.

ERIN

Erin Township was largely settled by Irish immigrants, who first came here in 1841. The area may have attracted the Irish because its kettle moraine landscape is similar to the land formations in Ireland.

FOND DU LAC

¶ **Galloway House and Village,** 1 mile north on State 175 and then 1 mile east on Pioneer Road to 336 Old Pioneer Road.

Although the original portion of this structure was built in 1868, it was remodeled into a thirty-room Victorian-Italianate mansion by Edwin Galloway. The mansion is surrounded by gardens, a log cabin, and a carriage house. The nearby village includes the following structures: schoolhouse, general store, church, gristmill, pharmacy, doctor's office, law office, court room, blacksmith shop, and print shop. The village sponsors

The thirty-room Victorian-Italianate Galloway House.
(Photo courtesy of the Fond du Lac County Historical Society.)

several special events during the year: a crafts day, an ice cream social, and Christmas at Galloway House.

Edwin Galloway was most likely descended from William Galloway, who had accompanied other Scotch-Irish families into southern Wisconsin in the early 1800s. The younger Galloway arrived in the Fond du Lac area in 1848 and became active in banking, lumbering, and dairy farming. His grandson, Edwin P. Galloway, donated the family residence to the Fond du Lac County Historical Society in 1954.

§ Open Memorial Day-Labor Day, daily 10-5; day after Labor Day-September 30, Saturday and Sunday 10-5. Fee. Phone: 920-922-6390.

GREENDALE

¶ Jeremiah Curtin House, 8685 West Grange Avenue.

Built in 1846-47, this residence was the birthplace of Jeremiah Curtin, linguist, author, and student of comparative mythology.

This son of Irish immigrants was early attracted to the study of foreign languages, beginning with those spoken by Norwegian, Polish, and German immigrants in nearby Milwaukee. Soon after graduating from Harvard, he accepted an invitation from the admiral of a visiting Russian fleet to come to St. Petersburg, where he served as a translator and then as an assistant secretary at the American Legation.

To acquaint himself with the Slavonic languages, he traveled through eastern Europe and Asia, even living for three months among the last Mongol tribe to practice the traditional horse sacrifice. After spending time in the British Isles collecting myths and legends, he began to study the customs and languages of the Iroquois, Shawnee, and other Native American tribes. Although he was renowned as a translator of many European works (including Sienkiewicz's *Quo Vadis*), he is chiefly remembered for his numerous ethnological works about Celtic, Slavonic, Mongolian, and American Indian peoples. He was reputed to have had either a working knowledge of or an acquaintance with seventy languages and dialects.

§ Open July and August, Sunday 1-5.

MADISON

¶ Old Executive Mansion, 130 East Gilman Street.

Now the home of the state's governors, this house was purchased in 1882 by Governor Jeremiah Rusk, the first chief executive to live here and popularly referred to as "Uncle Jerry."

Rusk was descended from Scotch-Irish grandfathers who had fought in the Revolutionary War soon after coming to America from Ireland. After managing his widowed mother's farm and working as a stage driver and a railway construction foreman, he moved in 1853 with his wife and children – Charity and Lycurgus – to Viroqua, Wisconsin.

With his earnings from the operation of a public house, Rusk bought a farm, a stage line, and part ownership of a bank. His capture of a horse thief earned him the respect of the voters of Bad Axe County, who elected him sheriff in his first foray into politics. At the beginning of the Civil War, he resigned his seat in the state assembly to recruit and command the 25th Wisconsin Infantry, which participated in the sieges of Vicksburg and Atlanta. Beginning in 1871, he served three terms in the U.S. House of Representatives.

During his record seven years as governor, Rusk faced two major crises that could have sabotaged his political career. When a bankrupt railway company left 1,700 of its workers stranded in a remote area without food and pay, property owners asked the governor for military protection against expected violence and rioting. The governor responded by sending supplies to the workers, saying that "These men need bread, not bayonets." He also refused to allow the bankrupt company to liquidate its other debts until it had paid the workers in full.

In the second crisis Rusk acted in accord with public opinion when, after repeatedly warning that violence and the destruction of property by rioting strikers in Milwaukee would not be tolerated, he dispatched a militia unit to the city. He gained national recognition when the rioting ended, although with the death of five people killed by the militia. His comment after this latter episode – "I seen my duty and I done it" – reflected most people's expectations from the governor.

¶ Studio of the Artist in Residence, University of Wisconsin, 1645 Linden Drive, between Babcock Hall and Stock Pavilion.

The Studio of the Artist in Residence was built in 1937 for John Steuart Curry, the first such artist appointed by the university. Curry, who traced his lineage to an eighteenth-century ancestor from County Tyrone, Ireland, amused his students with the informality of his dress. While at the university, he initiated the Rural Arts Project to encourage local artistic talent.

Having studied at the Art Institute of Chicago, Curry received his first commissions from Wild West journals that expected him to capture the spirit of that most characteristic of American regions. After further study in Paris and Russia and at the New York Art Students' League, he was accepted as a serious artist with the exhibition of his *Baptism in Kansas* in Washington, D.C., in 1928. With *State Fair, Hogs Killing a Rattlesnake,* and *Tornado,* he became a leading exemplar of Regionalism and the darling of eastern critics eager for purely American representational art. His other major pieces are *Kansas Stockman, The Line Storm, Spring Shower, The Gospel Train,* and *Return of Private Davis.*

MARINETTE

❡ Isaac Stephenson Monument, along Riverside Drive.

This memorial honors Isaac Stephenson, a wealthy pioneer lumber-man who represented Wisconsin in Congress for many years.

Of Scotch-Irish ancestry, Stephenson was born in New Brunswick, Canada, but moved to Milwaukee at the age of sixteen. After laboring at odd jobs in eastern Wisconsin, he began to acquire property in Michigan, hired himself out to move logs up Lake Michigan, and invested in steam-ships on the lake.

By 1858 Stephenson had joined N. Ludington & Company and had settled in Marinette. He supplied Chicago and Milwaukee not only with logs and lumber but also with a variety of wood products from his facto-ries at Peshtigo, the profits of which he invested in mining companies, railroads, and banks. Sadly, however, his factories were destroyed by for-est fires that swept the northeastern section of the state in 1871, on the first day, ironically, of the Great Chicago Fire. Within only four hours the flames had killed 600 people and deforested a strip of land forty miles long and ten miles wide.

Like many other venture capitalists of his time, Stephenson tried his luck in the political arena. He was twice elected to the Wisconsin Assem-bly and three times to the House of Representatives during the 1880s. Af-ter falling victim to the state machine, he threw in his lot with Democratic Party rebels, helping to finance not only the successful gubernatorial can-didacy of Robert M. LaFollette in 1900 but also the creation of the Milwau-kee *Free Press.*

In 1907 Stephenson was chosen to fill a resigned seat in the U.S. Sen-ate but came under attack for disbursing $107,000 in his reelection pri-mary campaign. A fellow politician pointed out the sinister influence of money upon the political process by complaining that "through the agency of the primary the state of Wisconsin offers its rich old men an opportu-nity to buy the senatorship as sort of a floral tribute to themselves." Stephenson was elected by the state legislature in 1909, but his right to remain in the Senate was challenged by members of the next legislature, although unsuccessfully.

MILWAUKEE

❡ Milwaukee Art Museum, War Memorial Building, 750 North Lin-coln Memorial Drive.

The museum's 20,000 pieces include works of the Old Masters, Ger-man Expressionism, and nineteenth- and twentieth-century European and American art. *Georgia O'Keeffe, Picasso, and Warhol are among the mod-ernists whose work is on display.

§ Open Tuesday-Wednesday and Friday-Saturday 10-5, Thursday noon-9, Sunday noon-5. Closed January 1, Thanksgiving, and December 25. Fee. Phone: 414-224-3200.

¶ Milwaukee County Historical Center, 910 North 3rd Street.

Among the center's holdings is a door from the *Lady Elgin,* an excursion steamer which collided with a lumber schooner and sank near Winnetka, Illinois, in 1860. Of its 400 passengers, 295 drowned, many – if not most – of them of Irish descent.

§ Open Monday-Friday 9:30-5, Saturday 10-5, Sunday 1-5. Phone: 414-273-8288.

¶ Patrick and Beatrice Haggerty Museum of Art, Marquette University campus, east mall, 13th and Clybourn streets.

The museum was named for Patrick Haggerty and his wife, Beatrice Menne Haggerty, who in 1980 donated to the museum their collection of 105 hand-colored biblical etchings by Marc Chagall. Among the museum's more than 6,000 *objets d'art* are Renaissance, Baroque, and modern paintings; Asian decorative arts; and sculpture and photography.

Of Irish ancestry, Patrick Haggerty was a 1936 graduate of Marquette University and a cofounder of Texas Instruments, Inc. Between 1945 and 1976 he held a variety of positions with that enterprise, including those of chief executive officer and chairman. Under his direction Texas Instruments moved into the manufacture of transistors, a development which made possible the first pocket radio and the application of semiconductor technology to military and space electronic systems. These advances were followed in 1958 with the invention of the integrated circuit. During his tenure as president, Texas Instrument's annual sales grew from $92 million to $1.3 billion.

Before his death in 1980, Haggerty had been a trustee of the University of Dallas, a member of the President's Science Advisory Committee, and the recipient of the 1970 Brotherhood Award of the National Conference of Christians and Jews. He had also received honorary degrees from eight universities, including Brooklyn Polytechnic and Rensselaer Polytechnic institutes, as well as the papal decoration of the Equestrian Order of the Holy Sepulchre.

§ Open Monday-Saturday 10-4:30 (also Thursday 4:30-8), Sunday noon-5. Closed January 1, Easter, Thanksgiving, and December 25. Phone: 414-288-1669.

WEST SALEM

¶ Hamlin Garland Homestead, 357 West Garland Street.

This restored structure pays tribute to *Hamlin Garland, who won the 1921 Pulitzer Prize for Literature for *A Daughter of the Middle Border*. (See Aberdeen, South Dakota, in *Irish America*, Volume 2.)

§ Open Memorial Day weekend-Labor Day, Monday-Saturday 10-4:30, Sunday 1-4:30; rest of the year, by appointment. Fee. Phone: 608-786-1399 or 786-1675.

ALBERTA

CALGARY

¶ **The Burns Building,** 237 8th Avenue S.E.

Named for *Patrick Burns, the famous cattle king, this structure was built between 1911 and 1912 as an office building and retail market for the P. Burns Company. The original interior had marble columns and was equipped with the most advanced lighting, heating, and ventilation systems available at the time. Although the structure was scheduled to be demolished in the early 1980s, it was rescued and renovated at a cost of $4.5 million. Reopened in 1984, it now houses a restaurant and office and retail space. (See Patrick Burns Memorial Gardens below.)

¶ The areas of Burns Avenue and Burnsland are both named for Patrick Burns, whose stock yards and meat packing plant were located in this section of the city.

¶ **Carleton Street,** Mount Royal, S.W.

This street commemorates *Sir Guy Carleton, the most famous eighteenth-century governor of Quebec. (See Rue Carleton, Quebec City, Quebec.)

¶ **The Palliser Hotel,** 9th Avenue S.W. at 1st Street S.W.

This four-star establishment in the heart of Calgary perpetuates the memory of John Palliser, an Irish aristocrat who explored western Canada between the 49th Parallel and the North Saskatchewan River and between the Red River and the Rocky Mountains. The hotel was constructed by the Canadian Pacific Railroad and opened in 1914.

Palliser was born in Dublin in 1817, the scion of a distinguished family that traced its Irish roots to an ancestor who had emigrated from England to Dublin in 1660. John Palliser received his early education abroad and was fluent in French, German, and Italian. Although he entered Trinity College in 1834, he eventually withdrew to assume the duties of high sheriff and justice of the peace, obligations which fell to him because of his family's social position. For a time he commanded a detachment of militia at Duncannon Barracks in County Waterford.

Young Palliser's real passion, however, was to travel "in search of adventure and heavy game." In this pursuit he journeyed to the "Grand Prairies of the Missouri," where for almost a year he hunted buffalo and grizzly bear and learned about the Indians and fur-traders who peopled those plains. After his return to London, he wrote an account of his sojourn in the heart of the North American continent. For his contributions he was elected to the Royal Geographical Society.

Eager to return to the New World, Palliser in 1856 succeeded in persuading the society to sponsor an expedition to the southern prairies of British North America. After arriving in New York the next year, the members of the expedition proceeded to Lake Superior, with Palliser in command. There they began what turned out to be three years traversing southern Manitoba and Saskatchewan and parts of Washington and Idaho. Along the way Palliser determined topographically the present boundary between Canada and the United States from the western end of Lake Superior to the Pacific. In the opinion of his companions on this expedition, Palliser disliked rows, was fond of a good joke, and treated them like colleagues rather than subordinates.

Once returned to Britain, the members of the expedition shared their reports with various scientific societies. These reports – and the great map which the men prepared – provided the first compendium of accurate information about the southern prairies and the Rocky Mountains in Canada. One of the most significant pieces of information which the explorers brought back was the fact that the semi-arid land of the south was bordered by an extensive "fertile belt" that promised successful cultivation and stock-raising in the future. With regard to a possible railroad route to the Pacific, the reports concluded that the cost of construction through the passes in the Rockies by a route completely within British territory would be prohibitive, although the feat itself was possible.

❡ The Captain John Palliser Elementary School is located at 1484 Northmount Drive N.W.

❡ In recognition of Palliser's explorations in western Canada, a river in southeastern British Columbia bears his name.

❡ **Patrick Burns Memorial Gardens,** Riley Park, 10th Street N.W. and 7th Avenue N.W.

These hillside gardens are named for Patrick Burns, the famous Calgary cattle king. Sandstone from his dismantled home is used in the walls and the walkways throughout the grounds.

The son of Irish emigrants, the pioneer cattleman was born in Oshawa, Ontario, in 1856. After settling briefly in Manitoba, he was drawn even farther west, in 1878 walking 155 miles from Winnipeg to Minnesota, where he decided to homestead. By the mid 1880s he was buying cattle full time and had obtained his first contract to supply beef to a railroad construction crew.

The growth of his business paralleled that of the railroads, and it was not long before he branched out into ranching and then into packing and retailing meat. So successful were his operations that in 1890 he established in Calgary the meat-packing firm of P. Burns and Company, one of the world's largest businesses of its kind, with branches in Liverpool, London, and Yokohama. By 1912 he owned a dozen ranches and operated retail shops in almost thirty communities throughout British Columbia and the Yukon. At the end of the 1920s he sold his packing business for $15 million.

Burns also served as director of several major insurance, banking, and engineering companies. He accepted an appointment to the Canadian Senate in 1931 and was one of the "Big Four" western cattle kings who started the Calgary Stampede. His obituary in the *New York Herald* referred to him as the "Cattle King of the British North-West."

¶ **Samuel Livingston Building,** 4th Street and 12th Avenue S.W.

This federal government office building is located on a portion of the ranch owned by Sam Livingston, one of western Canada's most famous prospectors and traders.

Born in 1831 in Avoca, Ireland, Livingston emigrated about 1848 and for the next two decades prospected in the gold fields of California, present-day Idaho and Montana, southern British Columbia, and Fort Edmondton, Saskatchewan. Following his marriage in 1865, however, the Irishman became a trader in buffalo skins. By the middle of the 1870s he had moved his business operations to the south so as to be able to trade directly with the Plains Indians. In 1876 he moved with his family to Fort Calgary, a newly established post for the North West Mounted Police.

It was at this time that Livingston took up farming, becoming one of the first farmers in the Calgary area. His attempts at cultivation were so fruitful that his farm became an example of the area's agricultural potential, attracting visitors who marveled at the fecundity of his soil and the innovations which he introduced. Besides bringing the first threshing machine and the first binder into the area, he introduced new grasses and 350 fruit trees from Minnesota as well as the raising of cattle.

Known for his grizzled beard and hair and his wide-brimmed hat and fringed buckskin coat, Livingston was equally renowned for the eight sons and the six daughters whom his wife bore him. Mary Dowler, one of those children, attended the ceremony that marked the opening of this federal office building in 1966.

¶ The Samuel Livingston School is located at 10211 Bonaventura Drive S.E.

EDMONTON

¶ **Emily Murphy Plaque,** Emily Murphy Park, Emily Murphy and Groute roads, on the south side of the Groute Road Bridge.

This memorial celebrates the life and career of Emily Ferguson Murphy, a truly exceptional woman in Canadian history: the first female police magistrate in the British Empire, the instigator of a crusade to recognize women as legal persons, the author of the first comprehensive book on drug addiction, and a prominent literary figure known for her travel sketches.

The granddaughter of Ogle Gowan, a native of County Wexford, Ireland, Emily Ferguson was born in Cookstown, Ontario, in 1868. She seems to have taken up travel writing when she accompanied her husband, Arthur Murphy, an Anglican priest, on a preaching tour to England and Germany. Her account of this experience was published in 1902 under the title *The Impressions of Janey Canuck Abroad*. (The author adapted her fictional name from the Canadian cartoon figure Jack Canuck.) Although the book conveys a generally favorable attitude toward British culture, it betrays the author's uneasiness about the pervasive poverty she encountered in England and raises questions about how to alleviate it. After moving to Winnipeg, she wrote *Janey Canuck in the West*, a paean to the region's wide-open spaces which contrasts the artificial life experienced by Easterners with the challenges of the frontier.

When the Murphys took up residence in Edmonton in 1907, Emily directed her attention to various social and political issues. She spearheaded efforts, for instance, to create municipal hospitals, to elect women to local school boards, and to win female suffrage. When she suggested that female offenders be tried in the presence of women, the authorities appointed her a police magistrate in 1916. From the bench she stressed compassion and rehabilitation, and her horror at realizing the link between crime and the use of illegal drugs led her to undertake what became the definitive study on drug addiction. Her findings caused several Canadian provinces to adopt her recommendations for the control of drugs and the treatment of addicts. She was stunned, however, to find that her jurisdiction as a judge was challenged on the grounds that she was not legally a "person." As a result, she launched a campaign that lasted thirteen years before achieving legal personhood for Canadian women. To the end she maintained that "The only truly contented women are those who have both a home and a profession."

MOUNT TYRRELL

Standing almost 9,000 feet high, this peak commemorates the career of *Joseph Burr Tyrrell, a nineteenth-century geologist, explorer, and historian. The mountain was christened in 1885 by George Dawson, on one of whose expeditions Tyrrell was an assistant. (See Dawson City, Yukon.)

PINCHER CREEK

⚓ Kootenai Brown Historical Park and Museum, James Avenue.

One of the twelve historical buildings in the park is the restored log cabin of George "Kootenai" Brown, among the first settlers in this part of Canada. The structures display more than 14,000 items, including farming equipment, clothing, jewelry, military uniforms, and books on local history.

This Irish adventurer was born in 1839 in Ennistymon, County Clare, the grandson of a British army officer. After military service in India, he sold his commission and immigrated to British Columbia. Although his prospecting efforts in the gold fields there were a failure, one incident which occurred during this period showed his pluck. Though not yet twenty-six, Brown was assigned the task of arresting three men who had passed several thousand dollars worth of "bogus gold dust" in Wild Horse, British Columbia. While trying to flush out one of the counterfeiters, Brown cried, "Throw up your hands or I'll make a lead mine of your carcass."

Brown and several companions later made the momentous trek from Wild Horse across the Rocky Mountains through the South Kootenay Pass and into Indian territory. It was then that he first caught a glimpse of the Kootenay (now Waterton) Lakes, which he would later be instrumental in preserving as a national treasure. Before long, Brown had his first encounter with the Blackfeet. Struck in the back with an arrow, the Irishman thought the end had come but managed to extract the flint. He described the primitive treatment of the time: "I had a bottle of turpentine and, opening up the wound[,] one of my companions inserted the neck of the bottle and[,] when I bent over, about half a pint ran into the opening made by the arrowhead. This was all the doctoring I ever got and in a few days I was well again."

Ever restless and on the move, Brown next tried his luck in Dakota Territory, where he was employed by the U.S. Army to carry mail and dispatches between several frontier forts. Almost immediately, though, he was captured by Sitting Bull and barely escaped with his life. To the chief's questions Brown replied in Sioux, "My father was a white man and my mother a Santee Sioux woman." (Brown himself married a Métis girl, who bore him two daughters and a son.) When his postal contract ended in 1874, he joined a band of Métis and hunted buffalo and wolves. About the lucrativeness of wolfing, he wrote: "We got $2.50 a piece for [wolf hides]. . . . We averaged about one thousand wolves in a winter and as we were living on buffalo meat which didn't cost us anything and using tents or cabins we built with our own hands, our only expense was the ammunition we used for killing buffalo and the strychnine for poisoning wolves."

While attending the annual rendezvous at Fort Benton, Montana Territory, in 1877, Brown became involved in an especially unfortunate incident. During a quarrel with the trader Louis Ell, Brown went into an uncontrollable fury and killed the man. The May 4 edition of the Fort Benton *Record* reported the episode: "Ell had attached some furs belonging to Brown for a debt which the latter refused to pay. On the day following the seizure the two men met on a hill near the Government Coulee, where

Brown plunged a sharp edged butcher knife into Ell's abdomen, and wrenching the weapon sideways almost severed the unfortunate man in two, killing him instantly." Although the homicide fled the scene, he was quickly captured and imprisoned to await trial. During his confinement, however, he attempted suicide, using a small knife to cut himself on the left breast and causing a flesh wound that bled profusely. For reasons unknown, Brown was acquitted when his case was heard before a jury.

Changed forever by this last experience, Brown sought solace in the beautiful surroundings at Waterton Lakes. During the 1880s he worked either as a scout for the Rocky Mountain Rangers or as a packer and guide for the North West Mounted Police. A visitor who was entertained at Brown's ranch in 1890 described the legendary but reclusive "Kootenai": "dressed in buckskin & had long white hair which came down to his shoulders. As far as I can remember he had keen eyes and was a first class packer, trapper & hunter. He sometimes brought Latin quotations into his talk & had been previously something of a scholar, but he never spoke to me of his past . . . ."

When the Kootenay Lakes Forest Reserve was created in 1895, Brown was made game guardian, and when the reserve was named a national park in 1910, he became acting superintendent. Following his death in 1916, Brown was buried beside his wife, Olive Lyonnais, on the western shore of the Lower Waterton Lake. Robert Cooper, who succeeded Brown as superintendent of the park, acknowledged the Irishman's role in the region: "[T]he existence of the park is largely due to his efforts to have protection afforded the game, as he realized that with the number of settlers in the country its destruction was certain."

§ Open mid May-mid September, daily 10-8; rest of the year, Sunday and Wednesday 1-5, or by appointment. Fee. Phone: 403-627-3684.

ROCKY MOUNTAIN HOUSE NATIONAL HISTORIC PARK

¶ **Paul Kane Plaque,** 300 yards along the "Short Trail" from the information center.

The son of an Irish mother and an English corporal in the British army, Paul Kane was born in Mallow, County Cork, Ireland, in 1810. At the age of nine he immigrated with his parents to York (Toronto), where he later received painting lessons. Beginning in the mid 1830s, he lived a rather peripatetic life, traveling around the United States as a portrait painter. In 1841 he embarked for Europe, primarily to study at the art academies in Rome and to sketch works by the Old Masters in Florence and Venice. While visiting London he met the American artist George Catlin, whose depiction of Native American culture was prompted by a desire to preserve that way of life before its eventual extinction.

Kane returned to Toronto in 1845, intent upon devoting himself to a similar task in Canada. Either alone or in the company of fur traders, the artist traveled thousands of miles – by canoe, horse, or snowshoe – to record the lives of his subjects throughout Canada. His works constitute a veritable catalogue of Native Americans – Chippewas, Ojibwas, Ottawas, Potawatomis, Saulteux, Métis, Sioux, Clackama, Cayuse, Nez Percés, and Crees. On one occasion he sketched an assembly at Mackinac Island where government officials made a payment to the Indians for lands ceded to the United States. On another he limned the erupting Mount St. Helens. And at every turn he was fascinated by the particulars of Indian culture, whether they be canoe burials, head deformation practices, or medicine pipe-stem dances. In only three years he made more than 700 sketches, some of which appeared in *Wanderings of an Artist among the Indians of North America*, the first published account of his peregrinations. (See National Gallery of Canada, Ottawa; and Royal Ontario Museum, Toronto.)

❡ Kane's career has been memorialized in the name of Mount Kane, a 10,000-foot-high peak in the Rocky Mountains of Alberta.

BRITISH COLUMBIA

ANARCHIST MOUNTAIN

This 4,000-foot peak east of Osoyoos is named for Richard Sidley, an Irishman who arrived in this region about 1889. For his extremist political views, his appointments as justice of the peace and customs officer at Sidley were revoked.

BURKE CHANNEL

This offshoot of Fitz-Hugh Sound north of Vancouver Island was named for Edmund Burke (1729-97), the famous Irish parliamentary orator, as was Edmund Point, at the southwest entrance to the channel.

BURNS LAKE

Despite its misspelling, this body of water near Prince George was named for Michael Byrnes, most likely of Irish birth, who passed this way while surveying a route from Fort Fraser to Hagwilget. The community of Burns Lake began as a tent town, founded in 1914 by a trapper named Trygarn Pelham Lyster Mulvaney.

Born in 1876 at Carrying Place, Ontario, "Barney" – as Mulvaney was popularly known – was the son of an Anglican clergyman of Irish origin. The young Mulvaney had originally intended to study law, but, when presented with a chance to head for British Columbia, he eagerly took it. In 1897 he signed on to a sealing schooner, and during the next dozen years he packed supplies for prospectors, did a little prospecting of his own, and carried the mail by dog team. He betrayed his natural wanderlust by saying that his "first ambition was to start at the mouth of every river in B.C. [British Columbia] and go to the head of it to see what was on the other side of the summit."

Although Mulvaney had first camped at Burns Lake in 1906, it was not until about seven years later that he put down roots there. He must have been quite a sight as he arrived bearing a variety of tents and assorted equipment (which he had won in a poker game, by the way). One of the two tents that he pitched at Burns Lake boasted a floor and contained twelve rooms and a dining hall. The other tent did service as a kitchen after the chance arrival of a Chinese cook. Mulvaney soon added five or six more tents to his establishment and began to rent them as sleeping accommodations.

Eager to promote the commercial possibilities at Burns Lake, Mulvaney pressed the authorities to survey the townsite. Although the Irish-Canadian wanted the main street to be laid out parallel to the railroad track, the surveyor ignored that route and instead ran the street around Mulvaney's barn and his corral. The thoroughfare's resulting meandering led him to charge that the surveyor had been drunk and had followed the trail of the last cow that went over the road. With the surveying completed in 1917, Mulvaney proceeded to sell lots. That same year he was appointed a notary public, perhaps in anticipation of his doing a "land-office business" in registering land purchases.

In the meantime, Mulvaney had replaced his tents with a hotel, the first in Burns Lake and in 1919 the scene of a mammoth rendezvous. The harvest in martin pelts that year was the largest in years, and the going rate of $75 per pelt broke all previous records. Because of the large number of trappers and buyers who descended on Burns Lake, the only place able to accommodate them was Mulvaney's hotel. For three days the trappers conducted business, slept on the floor, and savored 350-proof rum. Mulvaney died in 1961 at the age of 85.

CAMPBELL RIVER

¶ **John Hart Dam,** west of town on Highway 28.

This power development is named for John Hart, the former premier of British Columbia, who started the province's publicly owned hydroelectric system.

Hart, who was born in County Leitrim, Ireland, in 1879, came to Victoria, British Columbia, at the age of nineteen and began what became a successful business career. For many years he was the president of Gillespie, Hart, and Todd, Ltd., financial agents and brokers.

In his mid thirties Hart tried his hand at politics. He was first elected to the British Columbia legislature in the Liberal landslide of 1916 and served as finance minister for two of the next three decades. In 1941 he became the leader of the Liberal party and subsequently premier, the first Catholic to be selected for that post. Under his leadership the British Columbia Power Commission was established to undertake rural electrification throughout the province. He also promoted a program of highway construction, including the Hart Highway from Prince George to Dawson Creek.

HAYNES POINT PROVINCIAL PARK

Located south of Osoyoos on Highway 97, this small park commemorates John Carmichael Haynes, an early lawman in the "Wild Northwest" and a prominent cattle baron in the Okanagan Valley.

A native of Landscape, County Cork, Ireland, Haynes immigrated to British Columbia in 1858 in hopes of joining the police force. His first assignment was to accompany an expedition to restore order among the miners in the goldfields at Hills Bar. He did subsequent duty as customs collector at several locations, the chief being in the Okanagan Valley and the Osoyoos Lake regions. There in 1862 he collected more than £2,200 in revenue from duties on livestock transported through the area.

Haynes's most challenging assignment, however, was as justice of the peace and assistant gold commissioner in Wild Horse Creek (now River). Arriving there soon after a brawl in which one man was killed, the Irishman learned that 20 percent of the 1,000 men in the camp were "bad." "[H]orrified," as he said, "to think of such a thing happening in Her Majesty's Domain," he vigorously enforced the government's mining and revenue laws. After only six weeks a visiting official reported "no pistols to be seen, and everything as quiet and orderly as it could possibly be in the most civilized district of the colony." For his successful law enforcement, Haynes was appointed to the Legislative Council.

In his private life Haynes concentrated on expanding his land holdings in the vicinity of Osoyoos Lake, where he had settled in 1866. One of the visitors to Haynes's ten-room log house was William Sherman. The famous American Civil War general left a record of his impression: "Unlike the custom-house on the other side of the line [between Canada and the United States], this is a neat, comfortable frame building with brick chimneys and broad piazzas. It occupies a beautiful site on the shore of the lake, which is here a clean sandy beach. Judge Hayne[s] received us most hospitably. . . ."

Within two decades the Irishman had acquired almost 21,000 acres, 4,000 head of cattle, and the title "The Cattle-King of the South Okanagan." In the words of his granddaughter, Haynes was "an expert horseman, and to him a good mount was one of the necessities of life. . . . On horseback he invariably appeared as if 'riding in the Row' with his Irish tweed coat, riding breeches, and English riding boots. An army helmet was part of the picture in summer; a felt hat at other seasons – never a Stetson or a 'cowboy [hat].'"

❡ The ruins of some of the buildings on the Haynes ranch are located between the towns of Osoyoos and Oliver (on Road 18 off Highway 97).

KENNEDY LAKE

The largest lake on Vancouver Island is named for Sir Arthur Kennedy, the governor of the island from 1864 to 1866, just prior to its union with British Columbia.

Kennedy was born in County Down, Ireland, in 1809. After matriculating at Trinity College, Dublin, he entered the British army but resigned two decades later to become a poor law inspector in Ireland. During the subsequent famine, he was a member of a relief mission in County Clare that attempted to provide relief to almost half of the 82,000 inhabitants in the Kilrush Union district. Years after the famine he still recalled that "there were days in that western county when I came back from some scene of eviction so maddened by the sights of hunger and misery . . . that I felt disposed to take the gun from behind my door and shoot the first landlord I met."

In 1851 Kennedy entered the colonial service. During the next decade he served as governor – successively – of Gambia, Sierra Leone, and Western Australia. By 1862 he was regarded as one of the best governors in the empire. About him a contemporary wrote: ". . . Kennedy's career rather supports the opinion that many Irish . . . gentlemen have certain innate personal qualifications for the governing of colonies and dependencies. . . . [T]he high sense of honour, quickness of apprehension, and courtesy of the Celt, together with his devotion to duty and general powers of entertainment, make him a formidable competitor" to the Englishman.

Following his appointment as governor of Vancouver Island two years later, Kennedy found himself embroiled in controversy with the islanders' elected representatives. The ensuing political deadlock caused the exasperated executive to remark that there were only two classes of people on Vancouver Island: "those who are convicts and those who ought to be convicts." Even his efforts to stimulate the economy failed to deflect unpopular opinion. The public remembered only his attempt to purchase Carey Castle (for $40,000) as his official residence. (See Government House, Victoria, British Columbia.)

The governor and the Assembly disagreed over other major issues as well. Believing that the native peoples of Vancouver were being victimized by the illegal trade in alcohol, he proposed a tightening of the prohibition against the alcohol trade. Predictably, the Assembly blocked these measures. The conflict continued over the possible unification of Vancouver Island with British Columbia. In general, the Assembly favored federation (rather than legislative union), the retention of representative government, and fiscal independence. Equally predictably, the governor – as the imperial representative – generally opposed those terms. In the end, the union was completed according to the imperial design: a complete incorporation of Vancouver Island into British Columbia.

As a result of this incorporation, Kennedy's position was abolished and he prepared to sail for England. So unpopular had he become that a contemporary wrote that Kennedy "is disliked in his official capacity & his family in their domestic capacity, in about the same ratio." An official tried to describe the irony of the final leave-taking: "The Governor's family departed in a shower of tears; 't was most affecting – entre nous, only an Irish family could have got up such a scene. One would have thought they had been beloved & revered all the time." Kennedy later served successively as governor of the West African Settlements, Hong Kong, and Queensland.

❡ Kennedy's name is also memorialized in a mountain range on Vancouver Island and in an island off the coast. A statue of Kennedy is located in Hong Kong, in the government gardens on Kennedy Island.

KIMBERLEY

❡ Sullivan Mine. Not open to the public.

The story of the Sullivan Mine began in the early 1890s, when tales of the North Star Mine attracted the attention of four prospectors to the region. After their arrival in the vicinity of St. Mary's River and Mark Creek, the miners – Walter Burchett, Ed Smith, John Cleaver, and *Pat Sullivan – staked two claims, which, in a nod to Shakespeare, they named Hamlet and Shylock. When preliminary prospecting promised little success, the miners appear to have lost interest in the site.

Ironically, though, when the four returned to the scene to retrieve a $9 compass left there by Smith, they uncovered a hedge of rather low-grade lead-zinc ore. Because the men had insufficient capital to develop their property – which they had named after Sullivan, a tall red head from Bantry Bay, Ireland – they decided to work elsewhere for day wages so they could maintain one of their number at the site. They continued this arrangement for four years, during which time Sullivan was reportedly killed in a cave-in in Idaho. In 1896 the three surviving partners sold their mine for $24,000 to a Spokane syndicate, sending their dead partner's $6,000 share to his relatives in Ireland.

McBRIDE

This small town along Highway 16 east of Bowron Lake Provincial Park bears the name of *Sir Richard McBride, the youngest premier in the history of British Columbia. (See New Westminster, British Columbia.)

MONCK PROVINCIAL PARK

North of Merritt along the Coquihalla Highway, this provincial park commemorates *Charles Monck, Canada's first governor general. (See Government House, Ottawa, Ontario.)

MOUNT BREW

Located south of Lillooet, this 7,500-foot peak bears the name of Chartres Brew, a gold commissioner and judge and the first police inspector for British Columbia.

A veteran of the Crimean War, Brew was born in County Clare, Ireland, in 1815. Both before and after the war, he served in the Royal Irish

Constabulary, and by his early forties he was the inspector of constabulary in Cork. After being recommended for the post of chief inspector of police in British Columbia, the Irishman sailed for Canada, surviving a shipwreck en route and arriving in Victoria at the end of 1858.

Brew's first assignment was to create a force which would ensure law and order among the thousands of miners pouring into the Fraser River goldfields. At first he recommended a police force of 150 men recruited locally and subject to a centralized control, but the governor objected to the use of miners and preferred the employment of sixty members of the Irish Constabulary. The governor's attention was diverted from the issue, however, by a violent dispute in the Hills Bar goldfields. In response the chief executive appointed Brew chief gold commissioner and sent him to the Yale district with two other constables, one of them *John Carmichael Haynes. (See Haynes Point Provincial Park above.) After the trouble either subsided or was squelched, Brew was accorded unexpected praise from eighty local miners, who acknowledged his ability to administer justice while maintaining "the kind feelings and respect of all."

Despite the pacific ending to this episode, both Brew and the governor agreed on the need for 150 Irish constabulary for the colony, but the refusal of the British government to fund such a force doomed the plan. Brew spent the remainder of his career serving unwillingly – though competently – in a variety of judicial and administrative posts. The epitaph on his tombstone in Barkerville records the estimation of his friend Judge Matthew Begbie: "A man imperturbable in courage and temper, endowed with a great and varied administrative capacity, a most ready wit, a must pure integrity and a most humane heart."

MOUNT SCRIVEN

Located in the Coast Mountains north of Vancouver Island, this 4,300-foot peak honors Joseph Medlicott Scriven, the Irish-born composer of the hymn "What a Friend We Have in Jesus." (See Bewdley, Ontario.)

MOUNT SHAUGHNESSY

This 9,380-foot peak in the Hermit Range of the Selkirk Mountains was named in honor of *Thomas Shaughnessy, the president of the Canadian Pacific Railroad from 1890 to 1918. The mountain is in the Kootenay district of British Columbia, north of Glacier. (See Shaughnessy House, Montreal.)

NEW WESTMINSTER

❡ Richard McBride Plaque, Richard McBride Elementary School, 331

Richmond Street.

This commemorative marker honors Sir Richard McBride, the youngest premier in the history of British Columbia.

The grandson of a native of County Down, Ireland, McBride was born in New Westminster in 1870. After graduating from Dalhousie University, he studied law and engaged in its practice during the 1890s. In 1898 he was elected to the British Columbia legislature and two years later was appointed minister of mines. Following the narrow Conservative victory in 1903, he became premier, committed to a program of reducing taxes. The prosperity which the province experienced during the next decade prompted the government to make plans for a provincial university and to support continued railroad construction. In the elections of 1909 and 1912, the Conservatives almost eliminated the opposition from the legislature.

Like his friend Winston Churchill, McBride was an ardent imperialist. As premier he supported the idea that the Canadian government should contribute a force to the imperial navy. When British Columbia was virtually defenseless at the outbreak of World War I, he persuaded the province to purchase two submarines. Perhaps because of the economic depression which hit British Columbia at the beginning of the war, he resigned in 1915 and became the province's agent-general in London.

¶ McBride Lake is located in the Hazelton Mountains north of Tweedsmuir Provincial Park.

PALLISER RIVER

This river in the southeastern portion of British Columbia bears the name of *John Palliser, who explored western Canada from the Cypress Hills to the Rocky Mountains. (See the Palliser Hotel, Calgary, Alberta.)

PEMBERTON

This community north of Garibaldi Provincial Park commemorates Joseph Despard Pemberton, an engineer, politician, and businessman, and the author of the 1867 resolution calling for the admission of British Columbia to the Canadian Confederation.

Born in Dublin in 1821 into an Anglo-Irish family, Pemberton was the grandson of a lord mayor of Dublin. After a year at Trinity College in the Irish capital, he accepted a succession of engineering jobs with four different railway lines in England and Ireland, including the Dublin & Drogheda Railway. He interrupted a brief stint as a professor of engineering and surveying to accept a practical position in those fields with the Hudson's Bay Company.

During the following decade Pemberton laid out town sites and surveyed lands on Vancouver Island and throughout British Columbia. In 1857, upon landing on the west coast of Vancouver Island, he was confronted by a band of Nitinat Indians just returned from a victory. Unintimidated by the bloody heads of their victims impaled on poles, Pemberton proceeded – in Queen Victoria's name – to demand food and canoes from the natives. He paid for the items with vouchers scribbled on pages torn from his notebook.

Despite his status as a member of the landowning elite of the Hudson's Bay Company, Pemberton in 1859 resigned to become surveyor general of Vancouver Island. Early in this new position he wrote a handbook for "emigrants, merchants, or capitalists" intending to seek their fortunes in Vancouver Island or British Columbia. The work is significant for its proposal that a transcontinental railway be constructed as a way to unite eastern Canada, the Red River settlement in Manitoba, and the colonies on the Pacific Coast.

As surveyor general, Pemberton moved easily within the colony's political circles. In 1856 he was elected a member of the first House of Assembly to meet on British soil west of the Great Lakes, a prelude to his appointment to the legislative and executive councils of Vancouver Island. When the island was united politically with British Columbia in 1866, he served on the Legislative Council of the new colony. It was in this capacity that he supported the efforts of British Columbia to be incorporated into the Canadian Confederation. A friend of forty-two years described Pemberton as "always cheery, bright, and sanguine."

❡ Pemberton's name can be found in several other locations throughout the province: Pemberton Meadows (north of the town of Pemberton), Pemberton Point and 900-foot-high Despard Cone (on Broughton Island in Fife Sound), and Pemberton Road and Despard Avenue (in Victoria).

PENTICTON

❡ **Penticton (R. N. Atkinson) Museum,** 785 Main Street.

Among the exhibits in the museum are the diary and other personal effects of Thomas Ellis, who settled in the Okanagan Valley in 1866 and planted the area's first orchard eight years later. The valley is still known for its fruit, especially peaches.

One of seventeen children, Thomas Ellis was a native of Omagh, County Tyrone, Ireland. After immigrating to Canada, he had made his way to Osoyoos Lake, British Columbia, to visit John Carmichael Haynes, a fellow Irishman. (See Haynes Point Provincial Park above.) It was from him that Ellis learned of a vast tract of land surrounding Okanagan Lake, about forty miles from his friend's ranch. During the next three decades, Ellis acquired more than 30,000 acres – and several thousand head of cattle – in a swath between the two lakes. (The cattle were identified by Ellis's

"69" brand.) He also financed the construction of the first power-driven boat on Okanagan Lake and was a major shareholder in the Okanagan Mine along the lakefront north of town.

To the immediate location of his home Ellis gave the name "Penticton," derived from the Indian word "Pen-tak-tin," meaning "a permanent abode." His first house – built in 1872 – was a frequent stopping place for surveyors, government officials, and local dignitaries and friends, including Ellis's Irish neighbors John Carmichael Haynes, Peter O'Reilly, Charles Houghton, and Charles and Forbes Vernon. It was to this house that he brought his wife, *Wilhelmina Wade, after the two were married in Ireland in 1872. Of the couple's nine children, all lived to adulthood except their youngest son, who was killed by a bucking horse.

In 1892 Ellis replaced his first house with a larger one, which stood near Windsor Park until the 1940s. In 1892 he also helped construct with his own hands Penticton's Anglican church, still located at Winnipeg Street and Orchard Avenue. The church contains a stained-glass memorial to the Ellis family.

§ Open Monday-Saturday 10-5 (to 8:30 on Tuesday July-August). Phone: 250-490-2451.

⚑ Thomas Ellis Memorial Plaque, Windsor Park.

This aluminum plaque replaces an earlier wooden one dedicated in 1956 by Dr. Kathleen Ellis, one of Thomas Ellis's nine children. (See entry above.)

VERNON

This town of 20,000 inhabitants bears the name of Forbes George Vernon, one of the city's pioneers and the chief commissioner of lands and works in British Columbia.

Born at Clontarf Castle, Dublin, in 1843, Vernon was descended from an Anglo-Norman family that had settled in Ireland in the fifteenth century. Although his education in England prepared him for a career as a military engineer, he soon resigned his first commission and immigrated to British Columbia in 1863. After settling in the Okanagan Valley, he and his brother became financially successful traders and miners. In 1869 they purchased the Coldstream Ranch from Charles Houghton, who had emigrated with them from Ireland.

In 1875 Vernon was elected to the provincial legislature and two years later was named chief commissioner of land and works in the cabinet. He retained this position in several governments until at least 1890. His colorful electioneering technique is described by C. W. Holliday: "Forbes George, a big genial Irishman with a merry twinkle in his eye, sized up his audience, and mounted a barroom chair . . . and, had a representative of the press been present[,] he would have had little trouble reporting the speech, for, holding up his hand to silence the applause, 'Gentlemen,' he said, 'you boys all know me and know all about me, and I am quite sure none of you want to hear me make a speech, so all I will say at present is: Let us all go and have a drink.'"

¶ **O'Keefe Historic Ranch,** 7 miles north on Highway 97.

The site of one of the first cattle ranches in the Okanagan Valley, the homestead was established in 1867 by Cornelius O'Keefe. The property features several original structures, among them the family mansion, a church, and a general store.

The "O'Keefe of O'Kan-i-gan" entered this world in 1837 on a farm in Fallowfield, Ontario, one of ten children born to his Irish father and his wife. Fortified with a $300 gift from his parents, the ambitious young man headed west – via the Panama Canal and San Francisco – to Victoria, British Columbia, and from there to the mouth of the Fraser River and beyond to Yale. (He walked the final 450 miles to the Cariboo.) He must have had some initial luck in the gold fields, since he claimed that he was swindled out of a $2,000 interest which he had acquired in a mine. Thrown back on his own devices, he was forced to hire himself out as a surveyor for $100 a month. By the end of his five years in the Cariboo, though, he had managed to save $3,000.

Apparently intending to begin a new career, O'Keefe in 1866 traveled

The Cornelius O'Keefe Mansion. (Photo courtesy of Historic O'Keefe Ranch.)

to Oregon to buy cattle. Along the way at Little Shuswap, he met Thomas Wood at the head of a cattle drive. After forming some kind of partnership, the two men proceeded to Big Bend, where they found a ready market for their beef among the 2,000 miners there. With their handsome profits, the two cattle drivers went south, stopping at Oregon City to purchase 176 head of cattle. After a drive of three months, they arrived at Okanagan Lake, British Columbia, in June 1867, having lost but a single steer.

Although they had originally planned only to rest at the lake, the three men were so pleased with the area that they decided to stay. They built a cabin just west of where the O'Keefe ranch house now stands. For the next four years they lived there together, farming, operating a store, trading with the Indians, and guiding hunters who came to the area. On one occasion, when Governor Trutch and his party visited the ranch, he asked O'Keefe to be his gun bearer. "Carry your own damn gun," O'Keefe replied testily. "I intend to do some shooting, too."

In 1876 O'Keefe returned to his birthplace with the intention of marrying. After what must have been the briefest of courtships, he returned with his bride, Mary Ann McKenna. Twenty-seven years old at the time, she was the daughter of Irish immigrants who had lived and farmed not far from the O'Keefe homestead. When his wife showed some hesitancy about moving west, the new husband persuaded his niece, Elizabeth Coughlin, to accompany them. After the three arrived at Okanagan Lake in 1877, O'Keefe built a larger house on the ranch. (This structure is now part of the historic site.) By 1907 the estate had grown to 5,700 acres.

§ Open Mothers Day-Thanksgiving, daily 9-5. Fee. Phone: 250-542-7868.

VICTORIA

¶ **Government House,** 1401 Rockland Avenue. Closed to the public.

The present residence of the lieutenant governor is a reconstruction of Carey House (or Castle), purchased by *Governor Arthur Kennedy as his official residence and destroyed by fire in 1897. (See Kennedy Lake, British Columbia.)

§ Gardens open daily dawn-dusk.

¶ **John Work Burial Site,** Pioneer Square, Quadra Street and Rockland Avenue.

Located in the shadow of Christ Church Cathedral, the square contains the prominent tomb of John Work, an explorer, officer of the Hudson's Bay Company, and legislative councillor of British Columbia.

Born near Londonderry, Ireland, about 1792, Work (originally Wark) was hired by the Hudson's Bay Company as a clerk and a fur trader. While trekking to a new assignment in the Columbia River district, he began the first of what would become fifteen journals detailing his widespread explorations and trapping expeditions over the next decade. From that first base on the Columbia, he trapped and explored as far as the Fraser River in British Columbia.

Between 1830 and 1833 Work headed three major expeditions through what is now the American Northwest and the Northern Plains. On the first he led his fur-trapping companions over some 2,000 miles, eastward from Walla Walla into central Idaho and then southward to the Humboldt River Valley. The second went in the opposite direction – into the upper reaches of the Missouri River in western Montana – until attacks by Blackfeet forced the trappers to leave the area. The final expedition went south through Oregon territory to the Sacramento Valley and the California coast. Along the way Work and his men stopped at San Francisco Bay and the Russian settlement at Fort Ross to the north.

In 1834 Work was placed in charge of the coasting trade at Fort (now Port) Simpson, British Columbia. His first months there were spent in supervising the construction of a fort, which, when completed, was his residence for the next decade. He complained about the isolation and the "treacherous . . . and ferocious" Indians but more so about the fact that his efforts seemed to be unappreciated. His letters are full of complaints about his lack of advancement and expressions of his desire to return to Ireland or to immigrate to Ontario. In addition, he suffered from a very serious lip-sore, probably due to his persistent pipe smoking and requiring four operations before it was completely removed (as was more than half his upper lip). A contemporary described Work at the end of his tenure at Fort Simpson as "a queer looking old chap – of his hair there remains but three small elfs of locks which protrude, far between over his Coat neck[,] and the point of his nose is actually coming in contact with that of his chin. . . ."

Work's professional situation improved when he was named chief factor in 1846. Now in charge of the coastal area, he established Fort Rupert to exploit the local coal beds. By 1849 he had settled his large family at Fort Victoria, where he regularized his common-law marriage of more than two decades to a Spokane half-breed. By 1860 the largest landholder on Vancouver Island, Work was appointed to that colony's Legislative Council. When the imperial government instructed the governor to create a popular assembly for the island, Work objected to "representation without taxation." "I have always considered such a Colony & such a government where there are so few people as little better than a farce," he wrote, "and this last scene of a house of representation the most absurd of the whole. . . . The principle of representation is good, but there are too few people and no body to pay taxes. . . . "

❡ The Irish fur trader is memorialized in the following locations in Victoria: Wark Street; Work Point (in the harbor); and John, Henry, and

David streets (named after his sons). Work Channel, north of Prince Rupert, is also named for him.

¶ Pemberton Road and Despard Avenue.
These two cross streets are named for *Joseph Despard Pemberton, a prominent engineer and politician who was responsible for surveying large areas of Vancouver Island and British Columbia. These two streets – as well as Mountjoy Avenue – either adjoin or cross property that was originally part of Pemberton's estate. Pemberton gave the name "Mountjoy" to his residence on Foul Bay Road to remind himself of Mountjoy Square, Dublin, where his father had lived. (See Pemberton, British Columbia.)

MANITOBA

KILLARNEY

Situated in the southwestern part of the province, this town of 2,200 inhabitants was originally known as Oak Lake. When a settler by the name of John Sidney O'Brien noticed the area's resemblance to the Lakes of Killarney in Ireland, he gave the town and its lake their present names. Erin Park is noted for its replica of the Blarney Stone and for a fountain shaped like a shamrock and adorned with a statue of a leprechaun on a turtle. The small town also boasts green fire trucks.

MANITOU

¶ **Nellie McClung Plaque,** Nellie McClung Collegiate School, Carrie Street.

A commemorative tablet at the school recalls the career of Nellie Mooney McClung, one of Canada's foremost writers and a leader in the temperance and women's rights movements.

Nellie was born in 1873 near Chatsworth, Ontario, where her Irish father, John Mooney, had settled after working as a logger in Bytown (Ottawa). After completing her education in Winnipeg, Nellie entered the teaching profession, armed with the advice to "Demand decent salaries and wear clean linen." She later married Wesley McClung, a Manitoba pharmacist. As an author Mrs. McClung is best remembered for *Sowing Seeds in Danny* (1902), *The Second Chance* (1910), and *Clearing in the West*, the last work written in her sixtieth year.

McClung's campaign for prohibition and women's rights, however, gained her even greater fame as a lecturer. At one presentation her temperance message had an unexpected result. After placing a limp worm into a vase of water, and another worm into a receptacle of liquor, she pointed out that the first worm perked up while the other one sank to the bottom. To her question about the experiment's lesson, a young boy in the audience quipped, "If you drink whiskey, you'll never get worms." In another incident designed to make a political statement, she played the role of premier in a production of *Women's Parliament*, a burlesque of the male-dominated government probably based on Aristophanes' *Ecclesiazusae*. About that experience she later wrote in her autobiography: "We had one desire to make the government ridiculous and set the whole province laughing at the old concept of chivalry, when it takes the form of hat lifting, giving up seats in street cars, opening doors and picking up handkerchiefs, pretending that this can ever be a substitute for common, old-fashioned justice." The government finally granted female suffrage in 1916.

While serving as a representative for Edmonton in the Alberta legislature (1921-1926), McClung supported a wide array of social legislation, including old age pensions, better working conditions, a minimum wage, access to birth control, and more liberal divorce. She later devoted her energies to the "Parson's Case," a minor cause célèbre that arose over the question of whether women were considered "persons" under the British North American Act. The controversy was finally settled when the Privy Council ruled in the affirmative. McClung greeted that legal decision with characteristic wit, saying that the ruling "came as a surprise to many women in Canada . . . who had not known that they were not persons until they heard it stated that they were." She later became the first female member of the Canadian Broadcasting Company's board of governors (1936-1942). (See Chatsworth and Ottawa, Ontario.)

¶ Six miles west in the town of La Riviere, the Archibald Historical Museum features exhibits on Nellie McClung. The museum property is home to several restored structures, some of them associated with McClung: the log house where she boarded while teaching at Hazel School in 1890-91 and the house in which she and her husband, Wesley, lived.

§ Open mid May-early September, Friday-Tuesday noon-8. Phone: 204-242-2825 or 242-2554.

NEW BRUNSWICK

CHATHAM

J Celtic Cross, Middle Island Park, east on Route 117.

This memorial honors about 200 Irish immigrants buried in unmarked graves. The immigrants had arrived in 1847 on two ships carrying famine victims and had been quarantined here to prevent the spread of typhoid.

DRUMMOND

Drummond and the surrounding area have prospered from potato farming since the 1860s. The first bushel of potatoes grown here was planted by Barney McLaughlin, an Irishman. Today the crop is stored in potato cellars partly buried in the ground to protect against frost.

FREDERICTON

J Beaverbrook Art Gallery, on Queen Street, opposite the Legislative Assembly Building.

Named in honor of William Maxwell Aitken, Lord Beaverbrook, the gallery is one of the famous publisher's gifts to the city. The museum is known for its collection of British art, much of it from Beaverbrook's initial bequest of a collection worth $2 million. Despite the quality of the art pieces, Beaverbrook believed that the best "picture" in the building was the view of the Saint John River from the great window in the main gallery.

Aitken was born in 1879 in Maple, Ontario, where his maternal grandfather, Joseph Noble, had settled after emigrating from County Tyrone, Ireland. According to biographers Anne Chisholm and Michael Davie, Beaverbrook used to maintain that "whereas the dour side of his character came from the Aitkens, it was his Celtic strain, inherited from his Irish mother, that gave him the side that 'gets up and dances.' This mixture, he claimed, was a clue to his character."

After attending school in Newcastle (now Miramichi), New Brunswick, young Aitken briefly studied law at the University of New Brunswick. His excursion into the law was followed by an even briefer stint as publisher of a four-page newspaper in Newcastle – with the motto "We lead, let those follow who can." In his mid twenties, Aitken turned his sights on a career in business. He was subsequently influential in either organizing or reorganizing numerous companies in Canada and the West Indies, chief among them the Steel Company of Canada, the Canadian Car and Foundry Company, and the Nova Scotia Steel and Coal Company.

By 1910 Aitken was living in England and had won a seat in Parliament as a Unionist free trader. With regard to the issue of home rule for Ireland, he opposed denying national freedom for the Irish if they wanted it. In fact, from Tom Healy, an Independent Irish Nationalist and his closest friend in Parliament at the time, Aitken learned to admire the Irish. But as willing as he was to grant some measure of home rule to Ireland, as a Presbyterian he was more determined to prevent the Protestants in Ulster from becoming subject to "Rome rule," or the dominance of the Catholic Church, as he believed was the case in the rest of Ireland.

Most of Aitken's political career coincided with the special demands imposed by two world wars. During the first great conflict, for instance, the young politician served as special correspondent for the Canadian Expeditionary Force and as the Canadian government's representative at the front. After the war he was the British minister of information. Perhaps because of the unique advantage which this last position afforded him, many of the nine books which he wrote during his lifetime dealt with issues and personalities prominent during the war, including *The Decline and Fall of Lloyd George*. In the beginning years of the Second World War, he played a prominent role in the British cabinet as minister for aircraft production. In the meantime he had been knighted and raised to the peerage, taking the title "Beaverbrook" from a small stream near his home in Canada where he used to fish.

Although in Britain Beaverbrook was known primarily as a politician and a business mogul, Canadians associated him with the worlds of publishing and philanthropy. As early as 1917 he had purchased the London *Daily Express*, the first of four news publications in Britain which he was to own and which ultimately boasted a circulation of eight million. In addition, during his lifetime he gave an estimated $16 million to numerous causes or institutions in his native province, particularly the University of New Brunswick and the city of Newcastle (now Miramichi). That many of the objects of Beaverbrook's philanthropy were named for their benefactor caused the journalist Malcolm Muggeridge to write that Beaverbrook had memorialized himself during his lifetime "to a degree which might have been considered excessive if accorded to Napoleon in Corsica or Shakespeare in Stratford-upon-Avon."

• A bronze bust of Beaverbrook is located on the terrace of the art gallery.

§ Open July-August, Monday-Friday 9-6, Saturday-Sunday 10-5; rest of the year, Tuesday-Friday 9-5, Saturday 10-5, Sunday noon-5. Fee. Phone: 506-458-8545.

❡ **Beaverbrook Statue,** Officer's Square, between King Street and Waterloo Row near Regent Street.

JACQUET RIVER

This town was probably named after James 'Jock' Doyle – most likely an Irishman – who, despite threats and harassment by local Indians, settled near here in 1790. For many years he was the area's only white inhabitant.

JOHNVILLE

This Irish farming community northeast of Bathurst dates from 1861, when *Father Thomas Connolly purchased 10,000 acres of land and named the settlement for John Sweeney, the bishop of Saint John, New Brunswick.

Sweeney was a native of Clones, Ireland, where he was born in 1821. While still a child, he immigrated with his parents to New Brunswick and received his early education at St. Andrew's College on Prince Edward Island. After attending the Quebec Seminary, he was ordained a priest in 1844. Sweeney was consecrated bishop of Saint John, New Brunswick, in 1860 and presided over that diocese until his death in 1901.

Numerous other communities with an Irish name or association are scattered throughout the province: Irish River, Irish Settlement, and Irishtown (all along the coast near Moncton); Cork (southwest of Fredericton); Ennishowen (for Inishowen, County Donegal); Londonderry and Waterford (near Sussex); Losier Settlement (for an Irish settler named Samuel Losier); Shannon (for a settler named Shanahan); Vinegar Hill (for the scene of a battle in 1798 in County Wexford); and Youghall Beach Provincial Park (named for a town in County Waterford).

MOUNT CARLETON

Located in Mount Carleton Provincial Park, this highest peak in Atlantic Canada measures 2,693 feet and honors Thomas Carleton, the first governor of New Brunswick.

Born in Ireland in 1735, Carleton advanced through the ranks of the British army and served on the Continent during the Seven Years' War. After coming to Canada in 1776, he became quartermaster general of the troops under the command of Sir Guy Carleton, his more famous brother. In 1784 Thomas Carleton was named the first governor of the newly created colony of New Brunswick. (He had unsuccessfully suggested that the new colony be named New Ireland.) Although his instructions required him to allow the election of a representative assembly as soon as possible, he waited a year before doing so, preferring to govern the colony with an executive council of Loyalist gentry. In fact, in Carleton's view New Brunswick was to be a Loyalist refuge quite different from the society emerging in the American states to the south.

When an assembly was finally elected, it came into frequent conflict with Carleton. The major points of contention were salary issues, a weakening economy, and the desire of the mercantile interests to move the capital from Fredericton to Saint John. Such disputes brought political deadlock and caused the governor to complain that his plans were being frustrated by "a few Members, who evidently have a predilection for the Republican Systems formerly prevalent in the chartered Colonies of New England." In addition, when Carleton's military authority in the colony continued to be eroded and when Halifax was made the military center of British defenses, he requested a leave of absence. Although he served as governor until his death in 1817, he lived in England during the last thirteen years of his tenure, leaving the government in the hands of colonial administrators.

MIRAMICHI

¶ **Beaverbrook Bust,** Beaverbrook Town Square.

A larger-than-life bronze bust of *William Maxwell Aitken (Lord Beaverbrook) stands atop a pedestal, into the base of which the famous philanthropist's ashes were placed following his death. The bust, by Oscar Nemon, depicts a frowning Beaverbrook staring into space, his neck protected by his turned-up collar.

Beaverbrook Town Square, so familiar to its namesake as a boy, was presented to him in 1958 in recognition of his many benefactions to Newcastle (now Miramichi). One of the other attractions in the square is the monument of a sailing ship which Beaverbrook erected to honor Peter Mitchell, his youthful hero. At the side of the square is the Beaverbrook Theatre and Town Hall. (See Fredericton, New Brunswick.)

¶ **Beaverbrook House,** 225 Mary Street, near Sts. John and James Church.

This structure was originally known as the Old Manse, the parish house where *William Maxwell Aitken (Lord Beaverbrook) grew up while his father, a Presbyterian minister, served at St. John's Church. Miramichi was formerly known as Newcastle. (See Fredericton, New Brunswick.)

SACKVILLE

¶ **Mount Allison University,** York and Salem streets.

This well-known institution was founded in 1839 by Charles Allison, a local merchant and philanthropist. The first degree ever awarded to a woman in the British Empire was granted here in 1875.

Of Scotch-Irish descent, Allison received his early education in Cornwallis, Nova Scotia, where he was born in 1795. After working for several years as a store clerk, at the age of twenty-one he joined his cousin in the operation of a successful mercantile firm. The company, Crane and Allison, exported timber to Liverpool and distributed imported goods and local farm produce. Because of its extensive trading connections and its need for sailing vessels, the firm was influential in developing the shipbuilding industry in the Sackville area. Unlike his business partner, however, Allison preferred conservative investments, being inclined, as one contemporary phrased it, "to pursue safe rather than rapid modes of acquiring wealth."

Allison's desire to foster education seems to have been the result of a religious experience he underwent in the mid 1830s. Although originally a member of the Church of England, he was converted to Methodism after attending a series of revival meetings in Sackville in 1836. Three years later he helped the Methodists fulfill their hope of establishing a school in the Maritimes by offering funds to buy suitable land in Sackville, to erect a building, and to provide a £100 annuity for each of the next ten years. During the meeting at which Allison made his generous proposal to create a boys' preparatory school, he self-effacingly attributed his motivation to the divine will. "The Lord hath put it into my heart to give this sum towards building a Wesleyan Academy," he said. After a pause the benefactor admitted that only God could have moved him to part with his money: "I know the impression [on my heart] is from the Lord, for I am naturally fond of money."

The following year, in 1840, the former businessman laid the foundation stone for the Mount Allison Wesleyan Academy. Not only did he serve as its treasurer until his death in 1858, but he was also instrumental in establishing a female academy. His desire to see the creation of a degree-granting institution was fulfilled with the creation of Mount Allison Wesleyan College four years later. The present university traces its ancestry to these earlier institutions.

¶ A full-length oil portrait of Charles Allison by the English artist William Gush hangs in the Owens Art Gallery on the campus of the university.

§ Art gallery open Monday-Friday 10-5, Saturday-Sunday 1-5. Closed holidays. Phone: 506-364-2574.

ST. ANDREWS

¶ **Pagan-O'Neill House,** 235 Queen Street. Private.

In 1783, when the Loyalist founders of St. Andrews fled Castine, Maine, after the American Revolution, some of them used barges to transport their houses, section by section, to this location. One such house belonged to Robert Pagan until it was purchased by Henry O'Neill in the 1830s, not long after he and his brother had come from Ireland. Henry, a butcher, established a grocery and general store – H. O'Neill & Son – that was a fixture on Water Street until it was torn down in 1968. O'Neill owned a large amount of property in the area and helped established the Catholic church in St. Andrews. O'Neill's four maiden granddaughters were the last family members to live in the house.

SAINT JOHN

❡ Cathedral of the Immaculate Conception, 91 Waterloo St.

The foundation stone of this imposing structure was laid in 1853 under the direction of Bishop Thomas Connolly, a native of Cork, Ireland. Construction of the church was completed by a force of mostly Irish laborers.

Born in 1814, Connolly came under the influence of the Irish temperance crusader Father Theobald Mathew and entered the Capuchin Order. After ordination the young priest worked as a prison chaplain and at the Capuchin Mission House in Dublin. In 1842 he accompanied the newly appointed bishop of Halifax to Nova Scotia as his secretary. A decade later Connolly was appointed bishop of Saint John. As bishop, and later as archbishop, he was a strong supporter of Canadian confederation and was able to win many other Maritime bishops to his position. Besides emphasizing the commercial advantages that confederation would bring to the Maritimes, he hoped that it would lead to the legal recognition of separate schools for Maritime Catholics. He also believed that confederation would protect eastern Canada from the Fenians – "that pitiable knot of knaves and fools" – from whom, he insisted, Irish Catholics in Canada had nothing to gain.

❡ Celtic Cross, St. Mary's Cemetery, Loch Lomond Road.

Just inside the entrance to this historic burial ground is a memorial Celtic Cross erected in 1995 by the Saint John-Irish Canadian Cultural Association. The cemetery dates from 1853 and contains the remains of 15,000 people buried in both marked and unmarked graves. The base of the cross is inscribed thus: "Nineteenth century Saint John was utterly transformed by the arrival during the first half of that century of tens of thousands of Irish immigrants though many merely passed through. The impact of the thousands who stayed and put down roots in the community was profound. We remember and we celebrate the 15,000 who lie buried here, many of the nameless and forgotten, many of them once prominent citizens but for the most part ordinary men and women with no particular claim to fame but whose offspring still comprise a major portion of the population of modern day Saint John. The enduring Irish presence in the city is a testament to the courage and tenacity of the immigrant generation and to the commitment of their descendants to preserving their legacy."

Celtic Cross in honor of Saint John's 19th-century Irish immigrants.
(Photo courtesy of Heritage Resources, Saint John.)

¶ **David Lynch Shipyard Site,** at the foot of Main Street.

It was in this area that David Lynch, a prominent shipbuilder from Londonderry, Ireland, launched some of the largest wooden ships ever constructed in New Brunswick.

¶ **Fort Howe Lookout,** Magazine Street.

The blockhouse on this site today is a replica of the original one constructed in 1777-78 by Captain Gilfred Studholme, a native of Dublin, Ireland, to protect the local inhabitants from incursions by American privateers. The site provides a panoramic view of Saint John.

Prior to the American Revolution, Studholme had completed two tours of duty in Canada with British infantry units. The first posting was in Halifax, Nova Scotia, while he was an ensign of only sixteen or seventeen years of age. During the second assignment, he commanded a company stationed in Fort Frederick (now Saint John, New Brunswick). Although commanded to order the Acadians living in the Fredericton area to move to other parts of the province, he took no action against them when they refused to comply.

At the outbreak of the American Revolution, Studholme played an important role in protecting New Brunswick. As a brigade-major in the Royal Fencible Americans, he helped frustrate an attempt by rebel troops to capture Fort Cumberland (near Sackville). In the face of continued attacks by Indians and American privateers, he decided to erect a new fortification in Saint John to replace the earlier one damaged by rebels the year before. Studholme's command of the completed Fort Howe contributed to the safety of the region and maintained communications between Halifax and Quebec. It was also from here that he helped carry out the British policy toward the Indians, playing a major role at the Indian conference in 1780 that neutralized the Micmacs and the Malecites.

With the conclusion of the war, Studholme directed his attention to acquiring land, both for himself and for the Loyalist refugees who flooded the province. He eventually acquired 7,000 acres, some for his service in the Seven Years' War and the rest as the nucleus of a community which he named "Studville." At the request of *Governor John Parr, Studholme superintended the settlement of the Loyalists on the Saint John River, assigning them land and providing them with construction material. For his efforts he was appointed to the first executive council of the new province of New Brunswick. His last years were marked by ill health and by efforts to keep his creditors at bay.

ℐ King Edward VII Memorial Bandstand, King's Square.

This ornate bandstand was donated to the people of Saint John by the City Cornet Band. Considered an Irish musical group, this marching troop was formed in 1847, was composed mostly of Roman Catholics, and remained in existence until 1986.

ℐ The New Brunswick Museum, Market Square

In addition to natural history displays, this upscale structure contains exhibits on the history and decorative arts of the Irish in Saint John. The museum's archives (on Douglas Avenue) have numerous original documents and other research materials related to Saint John's Irish heritage.

§ Museum open Monday-Friday 9-9, Saturday 10-6, Sunday noon-5. Archives open Monday-Friday 10-4:30 or by appointment. Closed Good Friday and December 25. Fee. Phone: 506-643-2300.

ℐ Numbers 1 and 5, Chapman Hill.

These two residential structures were erected for Robert Armstrong and Aaron Hastings, two Saint John merchants of northern Irish ancestry. The buildings are notable for their *trompe l'oeil* interior fresco paintings.

ℐ Partridge Island, in the harbor.

Visible from almost any vantage point along the waterfront, this twenty-four-acre island was designated a quarantine station as early as 1785. The primary historic feature of the island is a traditional Celtic Cross, erected in 1927 to honor the Irish immigrants who arrived here eighty years earlier, refugees from the Great Famine. The text on the cross reads as follows: "This monument was erected in memory of more than 2,000 Irish immigrants who died of typhus fever, contracted on shipboard, during the voyage from Ireland, in the famine year 1847, and of whom 600 were buried in this island. This Cross also commemorates the devotion and sacrifice of Dr. James Patrick Collins, who, after ministering to the victims of the disease, himself contracted it and died."

The first sizable numbers of Irish arrived in New Brunswick with the Loyalists – refugees from the American Revolution– and continued arriving in the half century after the Napoleonic Wars. Between 1819 and 1829, for instance, almost 18,000 immigrants, mostly Irish, landed at Saint John. In fact, at least two-thirds of the immigrants between 1815 and 1865 were Irish, a fact that gave Saint John its reputation as Canada's "Most Irish City."

Partridge Island did extra duty as a quarantine station when in 1830 Irish immigrants infected with typhus and smallpox arrived aboard the brigs *Feronia* and *Leslie Gault*. When the passengers were landed, their clothes and bedding were washed and their children vaccinated. At first the immigrants were sheltered in army tents until a pest house – measuring eighty by sixty feet – could be constructed. Within days, however, the island saw its first casualties, when Agnes Murphy and William Marks, two Irish teenagers, succumbed to smallpox. Theirs were the first recorded immigrant deaths and burials on the island.

Irish immigration into Saint John peaked during the 1840s. The numbers increased dramatically from 6,569 immigrants in the first year of that decade to 16,251 at the end of the 1847 season. Unfortunately, most of the immigrants who arrived between 1845 and 1847 were afflicted with smallpox and typhus. By that latter year 2,115 had died in New Brunswick, about half of them in Saint John and on Partridge Island. In fact in June of that year Dr. George Harding, one of three physicians who ministered to the sick and dying on the island, wrote that more than 2,500 sick immigrants lay ill in quarantine, some in tents and more on the ground.

One of the two other local doctors who served the afflicted Irish during the 1847 epidemic was James Patrick Collins. This native of County Cork, Ireland, had emigrated in 1837 at the age of thirteen, settling in Saint John with his family. After completing an apprenticeship with a local physician, Collins continued his medical studies in Paris and London. He had only recently returned to Saint John and opened a practice in his family's residence on Mill Street when the typhus epidemic struck the city.

Collins seems to have offered himself as a medical assistant at the Partridge Island quarantine station for a variety of reasons. He was no doubt grieved by "the sufferings of his countrymen," and he agreed to assume the risks involved despite the warnings of his family. In addition, he believed that helping Dr. George Harding, the health officer, would redound to the benefit of his medical career. It is also possible that he was encouraged to accept the challenge by his wife's brothers, James and Edmond Quinn, both of whom were priests already active in charitable work for the immigrants.

After only a month on the island, however, Collins fell victim to the disease. The authorities granted special permission for his body to be brought from the island to the Catholic cemetery in Indiantown. (Out of fear of contagion, his corpse was sealed in a lead coffin.) The crowd of 4,000 mourners who swelled the ranks of his funeral procession was the largest ever seen in the city. Several years later Collins's body was removed to St. Peter's Cemetery near Fort Howe; in 1949 it was placed in a common grave in St. Joseph's Cemetery.

¶ Saint John Regional Library, Market Street.

The library's first-floor reading area features the St. Patrick's Society exhibit case, a collection of historical artifacts. The holdings of this modern library also include research and genealogical materials about the city's Irish history and population.

The St. Patrick's Society was founded in 1819 "for gentlemen of Irish descent." During its early history, its members provided financial and charitable assistance to the increasing numbers of Irish immigrants coming to Saint John. Although the original society dissolved in the 1880s, it was revived in 1929. Since then the presidency of the all-male organization has alternated between a Protestant and a Catholic. Today the society sponsors charitable fund-raising events and hosts an annual St. Patrick's Day banquet.

¶ St. Patrick's Square, on Reed's Point, at the foot of Prince William Street.

Renamed in 1967 to honor citizens of Irish heritage, this small grassy plot is noted for its Celtic Cross, a replica of the one on Partridge Island. (The text on both crosses is the same. See Partridge Island above.) In 1997 a memorial marker erected in the square by Famine 150 and the St. Patrick's Society was unveiled by Mary Robinson, the president of Ireland.

¶ St. Patrick Street.

Originally located in the old East End section of the city, this street disappeared in the urban redevelopment of the late 1960s. The saint's name reappeared in 1989 when the former Dock Street (fronting City Hall) was renamed for the Irish patron in a ceremony attended by the famous entertainer Carmel Quinn.

¶ Verner Lodge Site, Germain Street.

Though now a law office, this historic structure was once the headquarters of the Verner Lodge, established in 1843 as a unit of the Loyal Orange Order. Still active in Saint John, the Orange Order was named for the Protestant leader William of Orange, who defeated James II, the Catholic king of Great Britain, at the battle of the Boyne in 1690. Originally established in Britain to advance the cause of Protestantism there, the Order was introduced into New Brunswick to protect the interests of Protestants and Loyalists during the heavy Irish Catholic immigration. Today the organization's lodges carry out a variety of charitable purposes.

¶ York Point, at the foot of Union Street.

Although today belied by its Hilton Hotel, waterfront development, and modern high-rises, this area was the Irish Catholic district of the nineteenth century. It was here that the Orange and Green Riots of 1847 and 1849 broke out. The great fire of June 20, 1877, started here and went on to destroy half the city.

NEWFOUNDLAND

CARBONEAR

¶ **"Irish Princess" Burial Site,** in a private garden at the west end of the village.

Beneath the tombstone are the remains of an Irish princess named Sheila Na Geira, the daughter of John Na Geira, the king of County Down. Sheila was reputedly captured in the English Channel by a pirate named Gilbert Pike during the time of Elizabeth I. According to tradition, the pair fell in love and settled in Newfoundland, but only after the princess had prevailed upon Pike to abandon his piratical ways. While making their home in Carbonear, Sheila gave birth to the couple's child, claimed by some to be the first European born in Newfoundland. Pike, whose descendants continue to live in town, is said to be buried with his wife.

GREENLEY ISLAND

This island off the coast of Labrador witnessed the crash-landing of the German aircraft *Bremen* on April 13, 1928. The crew – two Germans and one Irishman (Colonel James Fitzmaurice) – thereby completed the first successful nonstop flight from Europe to North America. The flight was the fourth attempt to cross the Atlantic by plane.

The *Bremen* had left Baldonnel, Ireland, on April 12, intending to make a nonstop flight to Mitchell Field on Long Island, New York. For more than half of the thirty-six-hour flight, however, visibility was severely hampered by rain, fog, and snow. After sighting what they thought was the smokestack of a ship, the crew discovered that they were approaching a lighthouse and decided to land. The historic site was one mile from the Labrador mainland on the north side of Belle Isle Strait. (The two copies of the *Irish Times* which Fitzmaurice carried with him became the first European newspapers to cross the Atlantic.) A rescue party of three Newfoundlanders set out almost immediately. They crossed the strait in a fishing boat (which they had to drag and push through drifting ice for fifteen miles) and reached the crew on the following night (April 14).

The three pilots arrived in New York City thirteen days later and were accorded a tumultuous welcome. In his comments to the press, Fitzmaurice remarked: "Certainly there is no other city in the world where such a thing could be done. It could not be equalled in Europe. They don't let go so much over there. Such receptions as you have given transatlantic fliers have not been since the days of ancient Rome. It is not that we liken ourselves to Roman conquerors, but in its mass and enthusiasm there has been nothing like these welcomes in the modern world."

Born in Dublin in 1898, Fitzmaurice had served in France with British forces during World War I, sustaining wounds twice before being transferred to the Royal Flying Corps in 1917. Two years later his reputation as a competent pilot caused him to be selected to fly the first mail flight from Folkestone, England, to Cologne. For the next eight years he was a lieutenant in the Army Air Corps. He did transport duty during the Irish civil war and was sent to Baldonnel Field, outside Dublin, to take charge of flight training. Because he found this latter assignment boring, he eagerly agreed to join the *Bremen* crew in its transatlantic flight.

Following this historic accomplishment, Fitzmaurice tried to interest the British government in establishing air service between Great Britain and Ireland, but he resigned when his efforts failed. He spent a number of years in the United States, but he was again in England during World War II, when he operated a club in London for servicemen. He returned to his native Ireland in 1951 and attended the twenty-fifth anniversary celebration of his flight in Bremen, Germany. He died in 1965.

HARBOUR GRACE

¶ **Rev. Laurence Coughlan Plaque,** Water Street, across from the Conception Bay Museum.

This commemorative marker honors Laurence Coughlan, who established North America's first Wesleyan mission here in 1766 and was the first Anglican priest to serve in the Conception Bay area. He was the third Anglican priest then resident in Newfoundland.

Most likely born in Drummersnave (now Drumsna), Ireland, at an unknown date, Coughlan was raised a Catholic but converted to Methodism in 1753. Although John Wesley referred to Coughlan as having "no learning at all," the Irishman was accepted as an itinerant preacher in the Methodist movement, originally an offshoot of Anglicanism. For a number of years he carried on his ministry in Waterford, Ireland, until his ordination by a Greek Orthodox bishop angered Wesley, who thought the uneducated Coughlan unworthy of ordination.

Coughlan's connection with Newfoundland began when the residents of Harbour Grace and Carbonear requested the Board of Trade to send them a Protestant minister. Within a matter of days in April 1766, Coughlan was raised to the diaconate and ordained an Anglican priest. Having arrived in Harbour Grace, Coughlan lived an unusual double religious life. As an Anglican priest he held regular services and administered the sacraments according to the rites of the Church of England. On occasion he even preached in Irish to Irish fishermen in order to make them see "the Errors of Popery."

But Coughlan's real interest was to lead people to a personal evangelical conversion. To this end he went from house to house, exhorting his hearers and using the new "methodism" employed by Wesley. It took the

Irish clergyman three years, however, to make his first Methodist con-
verts. Although he was finally successful in creating Methodist societies
beyond Harbour Grace, his desire to spread the Gospel along the coast
was frustrated by his fear of having to do so in small boats.

Almost from the beginning Coughlan came into conflict with some of
his influential parishioners. On one occasion he publicly condemned a
merchant for adultery and later used physical force to prevent some of the
merchant's workers from violating the Sabbath. In another unfortunate
episode the minister refused to allow a merchant to stand as godfather to
two children on the grounds that the man led an immoral life. In each
instance some of the local merchants petitioned the governor to silence
and remove the "meddling" minister, whom they accused of "being Ignorant of the Laws of his Country & a Person of no Education." In the end
Coughlan lost his commission as justice of the peace and later requested
the Society for the Propagation of the Gospel to accept his resignation.
After returning to England, he seems to have served as minister to a chapel
in London for an unknown length of time. According to a contemporary,
he died "utterly broken in pieces."

ST. JOHN'S

¶ **Basilica of St. John the Baptist,** Military Road at Harvey and
Bonaventure streets.

Designed by John Jones, a Protestant architect from Clonmel, Ireland,
this landmark church was constructed between 1841 and 1850 of Newfoundland granite and Irish limestone. The building follows the traditional
Romanesque plan of a Latin cross and at the time of its completion was
the largest house of worship in North America and the largest structure in
British North America. It was raised to the rank of a minor basilica in
1950, the centenary of the cathedral's completion.

The interior of the church is noted for its ornate decoration. The
ceiling's moulding and pendant drops are adorned with gold leaf, and the
pulpit was erected in memory of *Michael Francis Howley, appointed the
first archbishop of Newfoundland in 1904. Near the altar is a marble carv-
ing entitled *The Dead Christ,* the work of John Hogan, Ireland's greatest
sculptor. Among the memorials in memory of the city's bishops are tablets by Hogan in honor of *Thomas Scallan and *Michael Fleming.

The memorial to Bishop Scallan depicts the aged cleric on his death-
bed receiving the last rites from his successor. His funeral was marked by
the attendance of 7,000 people of every religious persuasion and most
notably by the presence of Methodist and Anglican clergy. His obituary in
the *St. John's Newfoundlander* paid Scallan a fitting tribute: "With his various accomplishments, he combined a lofty zeal for the advancement of
religion, wholly free, however, from that bias of intolerance which is some-

times found in minds deeply imbued with religious feelings."

Numerous statues can also be found throughout the church. The largest are the seven-foot-high likenesses of St. Patrick, St. Brigid, St. Anthony, and St. Joseph. The Fatima statuary group (under the gallery stairs) was donated by Portugal in 1955 to commemorate three Portuguese "firsts": the discovery of the Grand Banks in 1455, the discovery of Newfoundland by Corte Real in 1500, and the beginning of organized fishing in Newfoundland in 1555.

§ Open Monday-Friday 8:30-8, Saturday 8:30-6, Sunday 8:30-noon. Phone: 709-754-2170.

• John Hogan was born in County Waterford, Ireland, in 1800. After two years as a lawyer's clerk in Cork, he became apprenticed to the architect Thomas Deane. Although he initially worked as a carpenter, he took up sculpture at the urging of Deane and was soon granted commissions by the bishop of Cork. Through the help of a public subscription, he was able to travel to Rome, where he studied at the Galleries of the Vatican and the School of St. Luke. While still in Italy, he was elected a member of the prestigious Virtuosi del Pantheon, married an Italian woman, and worked on many commissions received from Ireland. He prudently returned home after the Revolution of 1848 rocked Italy. His best-known Irish works are statues of Father Theobald Mathew (Cork), Daniel O'Connell (Limerick and the Dublin city hall), the *Dead Christ* (Clarendon Street Church, Dublin), and the *Drunken Faun* (University Church, Dublin).

• Thomas Scallan was a native of Churchtown, County Wexford, Ireland, where he was born about 1766. After receiving a classical education at the Franciscan friary in Wexford, he completed his studies for the priesthood at St. Isidore's College in Rome. He returned to Wexford in 1794 to take up a succession of duties as seminary professor, principal, and superior. In 1812, however, he was named a curate in St. John's. Within four years he was appointed coadjutor bishop of that city, and by the end of 1816 he was vicar apostolic of Newfoundland. As bishop he did his best to recruit more priests for the thousands of Irish who had immigrated to Newfoundland in the previous five years.

One of the notable features of Scallan's episcopate was the cordial relationship between the island's Catholics and Protestants. He not only allowed his clergy to attend non-Catholic funerals but he himself attended services in the Anglican church and was one of the first to pay a courtesy call on the Anglican bishop of Nova Scotia when that gentleman visited Newfoundland. According to Governor Thomas Cochrane, Scallan's great desire was "to live in peace and harmony with the members of every religious denomination."

• Michael Fleming was born in Carrick on Suir, County Tipperary, about 1792. Following the encouragement of his uncle, he entered the

Franciscan friary in Wexford, where he was ordained in 1815 and served for eight years. At the invitation of *Thomas Scallan, the bishop of St. John's, the young priest sailed for Newfoundland. His advance from curate to coadjutor bishop to vicar apostolic took only seven years.

The first decade of Fleming's episcopate was marked by sectarian and political conflicts. As of 1830 the British government had not yet granted to Catholics in Newfoundland the civil rights which their coreligionists in Britain had so recently won. Fleming and many of the young priests whom he imported from Ireland, however, were intent upon asserting those rights. In the remarkably short period of two years, Fleming succeeded in winning from the government his primary objective – an end to the civil disabilities that applied to Newfoundland's Catholics. The British also allowed male suffrage and representative government.

Almost immediately, though, Fleming and one of his more outspoken priests were accused by the British of using their influence to sway the subsequent election, a charge that would be repeated frequently during Fleming's tenure. As early as 1834 the British government began to pressure the Vatican to censure the outspoken bishop for his political "meddling." When an official of the Vatican secretariat of state asked Fleming to prevent activities "which debase the sacerdotal character," the Irish bishop replied that he had thrown his political support behind candidates whose election would be "advantageous to the Country." In the campaign of 1840, Fleming and his clergy used their influence to win the election of a Catholic candidate over a Presbyterian political liberal. (The governor of Newfoundland remarked that Fleming's intervention was due to "a pure love of dissension.")

Despite this Church-State conflict, Fleming thought he could obtain from the government the property on which he hoped to build a new cathedral. Six times he crossed the Atlantic to press his case, and he even wrote to Daniel O'Connell, describing the superb site overlooking the city and perhaps hoping that the Irish patriot would exert his own pressure on the British. When permission to build was finally granted, Fleming personally supervised the cutting of the stone and enlisted the thousands of volunteer men, women, and children who excavated 79,000 cubic feet of earth for the cathedral's foundations. At his death in 1850 he was buried in the cathedral.

¶ On Military Road, near the basilica, is the motherhouse of the Presentation Sisters, an order of Catholic nuns whom Bishop Fleming brought to St. John's from Galway, Ireland, in 1833. The nuns are the oldest order of sisters in English-speaking Canada and the third oldest in English-speaking North America. The nuns opened their first school – the island's first officially Catholic educational institution – in a converted tavern on Duckworth Street. By 1846 the convent had eight nuns, and a new school could accommodate 2,000 girls. The motherhouse has a small museum, which is open to visitors by appointment.

¶ **Confederation Building,** on Prince Philip Drive in C. A. Pippy Park.
The main lobby is dominated by Harold Goodridge's mural chroni-
cling the history of Newfoundland. The artwork depicts various historical figures, some with interesting Irish associations: a Viking (whose face
is that of Philip Little, the son of Irish immigrants and Newfoundland's
first prime minister), *James Wolfe (the general who defeated the French
in Quebec in 1759), *Ambrose Shea (one of Canada's "Fathers of Confederation"), and *Patrick Morris (a champion of self-government for the province).

The other figures in the mural are those of a Beothuck Indian, John
Cabot (who discovered the island in 1457), Humphrey Gilbert (who
founded the British Empire at St. John's in 1583), the explorers Champlain
and La Salle and Cook, David Kirke (who defeated Champlain in 1629),
Frederick Carter (a "Father of Canadian Confederation"), Joe Smallwood
(who led Newfoundland into the Confederation), Leonard Outerbridge
(the first governor of the province after Confederation), William Carson
(an advocate of self-government), and Wilfred Laurier and Mackenzie King
(Canadian prime ministers).

Around the lobby are busts of Newfoundland's speakers and prime
ministers before it joined the Confederation, including at least three of
Irish birth or ancestry: Philip Little, John Kent, and Edward Patrick Morris.
A historical marker in the Confederation Building honors the Irish-Canadian Ambrose Shea.

• Patrick Morris – the most versatile of Newfoundland's early leaders
– was born in Waterford, Ireland, about 1789 and was working as a trader's
clerk in St. John's by 1804. He later went into business for himself, importing products and emigrants from Waterford and exporting cod and seal-
skins in return. As he came to believe that many of the colony's govern-
mental structures were outmoded, Morris took the lead in petitioning the
imperial government for an elected local legislature and the abolition of
laws forbidding Catholics to practice law and hold office. In this early
reform movement Morris was supported by an overwhelming number of
the city's middle-class Irish.

During a five-year period during which he lived in Waterford, Morris
attacked the disabilities that applied to Catholics in Ireland and agitated
for the repeal of the political union between that colony and Britain. On
this latter issue he disagreed with Daniel O'Connell's approach, a difference that prompted a minor episode at a large repeal meeting near
Waterford. When Morris tried to address the gathered throng, O'Connell
called out in his Kerry brogue: "Well, Pat, when did you come across, was
there much fog on the Banks?" And then with his finger to his nose,

O'Connell asked: "Boys, do you smell the fish?"

While still in the British Isles, Morris wrote a pamphlet urging the creation of a Newfoundland legislature. In this work he argued that New-foundland – "the oldest and most valuable of the British possessions in North America" – was entitled to the same constitutional privileges which had been bestowed on the neighboring colonies. In the end, Catholic "emancipation" in Newfoundland was granted in 1832, and a popular assembly was elected that year.

Upon his return to St. John's in 1833, Morris continued his assault upon the colony's "despotic" judiciary by engaging in a public dispute with the new chief justice, Henry Boulton. Determined that the Protestant merchant class and the colonial administration maintain political control, Boulton had – in Morris's words – trampled "on the rights and privileges and immunities of the British subject!" When Boulton jailed a local news-paper editor, Morris and others led the overwhelmingly Irish populace in the collection of 5,000 signatures on a petition for the journalist's release. Morris's role in this incident and his presidency of the Benevolent Irish Society helped secure his election to the Assembly in 1836. From that van-tage point he led the reformers' assault against the power of the Protes-tant Council and their merchant allies, who viewed politicians like Morris as demagogues, "ignorant, besotted [Irish] Catholics . . . so bound by the magic spell of Popery they are quite incapable of properly exercising po-litical power."

• The son of Irish immigrants, Philip Little was born in Charlottetown, Prince Edward Island, in 1824. After training for the law, he moved to St. John's, Newfoundland, drawn perhaps by the chance to become the first Catholic lawyer in that predominantly Catholic community. He quickly became the beneficiary of a successful practice and just as rapidly emerged as a leader in Catholic social circles. In fact, his association with the Be-nevolent Irish Society helped cement his political alliance with the reform-ers in St. John's – primarily Catholic Irish – who had begun to demand a greater degree of self-government.

It was inevitable that a leader with Little's ambition and strong views should come to lead the Assembly. As the official Liberal candidate in the 1850 election, he promised to work for "responsible government," as home rule was then known. For good measure he attacked absentee landlords and the Protestant domination of Newfoundland's government – themes bound to attract the Irish Catholic vote. Although Little won the contest, it was not until the next election – in 1852 – that he became the undisputed leader of the party. From this position he led the Liberals in their refusal to pass any legislation until the Colonial Office granted "responsible gov-ernment." Word of the imperial government's favorable decision arrived in St. John's in March 1854. The Liberal victory a year later resulted in Little's selection as prime minister and attorney general. Besides spending more money on health, roads, and education, his administration passed legislation to allow Newfoundland to enjoy the advantages of free trade with the United States.

Little resigned from the government in 1858 on the grounds of ill health but with the intention of accepting a seat on the Supreme Court. A decade later he left the bench and moved permanently to Ireland. There he lived near the farms of relatives and managed property which he subsequently acquired as well as estates which his wife's Anglo-Irish family owned. His earlier experiences in Newfoundland served him well in his efforts to obtain home rule for Ireland.

• John Kent was a native of Waterford, Ireland, and, like his uncle Patrick Morris, enjoyed a successful commercial career in St. John's before entering politics. Kent's election to the first Newfoundland assembly in 1832 was facilitated by his relationship with *Bishop Michael Fleming, his brother-in-law. Since the population of the colony was almost evenly divided between Catholics and Protestants, such episcopal connections were extremely helpful, although Kent was not above roiling "the storm of religious rancour" if he had to in order to get reelected. When London granted responsible government to Newfoundland in the mid 1850s, Kent was made colonial secretary in the administration of *Philip Little, the province's first prime minister. As a member of the Liberal government, Kent led the fight against an Anglo-French agreement that would have extended French fishing rights in Newfoundland.

Kent's succession to the premiership in 1858 was followed by an economic downturn and by especially acrimonious political wrangling. A decline in government revenues was exacerbated by failures in the fishery and the potato crop. When the issue of how best to handle poor relief came to the forefront, Kent came under attack by a cabal led, he claimed, by *Ambrose Shea, "a designing, cozening, cunning rogue." When the prime minister imprudently said that Governor Bannerman was in league with Kent's political opponents, the governor dismissed the ministry. In a scenario reminiscent of Patrick Morris's duel with Chief Justice Boulton, Kent carried a resolution in the Assembly protesting that his dismissal was a "gross act of treachery" to the people of Newfoundland. In retaliation, Bannerman dismissed the Assembly. The subsequent election campaign was marred by rioting and loss of life, and in the end the Liberal party was defeated. Although the former prime minister was reelected from St. John's East, he was soon eclipsed as leader of the opposition by Shea.

• Edward Patrick Morris was born in St. John's, the son of an immigrant father from Waterford, Ireland. Like his brother Father Michael Morris (mentioned in the next site entry), he attended St. Bonaventure's College in St. John's. Upon graduation from the University of Ottawa, he studied law and was called to the bar in 1885, the same year in which he was elected to the Newfoundland House of Assembly. For two decades he served in the legislature and was a member of several Liberal governments. He introduced legislation to establish life insurance for fishermen, promote higher education, and create an employers' liability system.

Perhaps his most important – though unsuccessful – work during this time was as a negotiator in the effort to bring Newfoundland into the Canadian Confederation. By 1895 the idea of confederation had become particularly attractive to some Newfoundlanders after a disastrous fire in St. John's, a bad fishing season, and a banking collapse had struck the colony in the previous three years. As events played out, however, the terms which the Confederation offered Newfoundland were not generous, and negotiations ended in the face of strong opposition to confederation among Newfoundlanders.

In 1907 Morris broke with his former political colleagues to form the People's Party. Two years later, when the new party won a majority in the legislature, Morris became prime minister and his government proceeded to introduce an old-age pension. During World War I, Morris was a leading figure in efforts to create the Royal Newfoundland Regiment and to enlist Newfoundlanders in the Royal Navy. He was also a member of the Imperial War Cabinet. He resigned as prime minister in 1918, soon after being made Baron of St. John's and of Waterford.

• [For information about James Wolfe and Ambrose Shea, see other entries.]

¶ Father Morris Monument, at the south end of Bannerman Park.

This ten-foot-high granite shaft is surmounted by a bust of Father Michael Morris, who established the first orphanage in St. John's and died from an outbreak of typhoid fever at the institution.

A native of St. John's, Morris was one of three sons born to Edward and Catherine (Fitzgerald) Morris, Irish emigrants from Waterford and Tipperary, respectively. After attending St. Bonaventure's College in St. John's, he studied for the priesthood at All Hallows in Dublin. His brother Edward Patrick was prime minister of Newfoundland from 1909 to 1918 and was awarded the title 1st Baron Morris.

The inscription on the monument reads: "Reverend Michael P. Morris, Born at St. John's, July 12th, 1852, Guardian of the orphanage of Villa Nova, contracted Typhoid Fever while nursing the orphanage boys under his care and died, August 1st, 1889."

¶ James J. O'Mara Pharmacy Museum, Apothecary Hall, 488 Water Street.

Located in the administrative offices of the Newfoundland Pharmaceutical Association, the James J. O'Mara Pharmacy Museum honors a pioneer in the development of pharmacy in the province. Among the pe-

Bust of Father Michael Morris. (Photo courtesy of the Archives of the Roman Catholic Archdiocese, St. John's.)

riod displays in the museum are pharmacy equipment, medicine bottles, and scales.

The great-grandson of John O'Mara, an emigrant from Waterford, Ireland, James O'Mara was born in St. John's in 1938. He attended St. Bonaventure's College and was employed in the family business, the O'Mara-Martin Drug Company in St. John's, from 1962 to 1981, the last seven years as president. He was also president of the Canadian Academy of the History of Pharmacy and a member of more than thirty other boards, committees, and community groups during his career.

O'Mara was instrumental in establishing a degree program for pharmacists at Memorial University of Newfoundland. (A dispensing lab in the School of Pharmacy there is named in his honor.) For many years he was either a member or a director of St. Patrick's Mercy Home for the Aged. He also belonged to the Irish Club and the Benevolent Irish Society and was the recipient of the Robin Bowl Hygenia Award for service to the community. At the time of his death in 1990, he was secretary-treasurer of the Newfoundland Pharmaceutical Association.

§ Open June 15-Labour Day, daily 10-5; rest of the year by appointment. Closed major holidays. Phone: 709-753-5877.

¶ **Kent's Pond,** along Confederation Parkway.

This aquatic landmark is named for Robert Kent, a prominent lawyer and politician and the older brother of Newfoundland's second prime minister. (Another brother was mayor of Waterford, Ireland.)

Born in Waterford in 1835, Robert Kent came from a family which had long been involved in trade between that Irish city and Newfoundland. He most likely attended St. John's College in Waterford before sailing in 1863 for Newfoundland, where he worked as a clerk in an uncle's business. After studying law, he was admitted to the Newfoundland bar and then entered a partnership with *Joseph Ignatius Little, the brother of a former prime minister of Newfoundland.

During the 1870s and 1880s, Kent represented a district of St. John's in the provincial legislature. Although he opposed Canadian confederation, he supported a transinsular railway. His tenure as speaker of the Assembly and later as the leader of the Liberal party was eclipsed, unfortunately, by sectarian strife that plagued St. John's in the 1880s.

The proximate cause of his political demise was a riot between Catholics and Orangemen which occurred at Harbour Grace in 1883. Five persons were killed, and nineteen Catholics were arrested for the murders. The fact that Kent successfully defended some of the accused at two subsequent trials caused the Protestants to turn against him, thereby splitting the Assembly along sectarian lines. He resigned the speakership in 1885, although he continued to serve as president of the Benevolent Irish Society for six more years. He died in 1893, probably because of distress caused when his office was destroyed by the great St. John's fire.

¶ **The Littledale Complex,** Waterford Bridge Road, near Bowring Park.

Now used for retreats, classroom space, and nursing staff offices, this center had its origins in St. Bride's Academy, Littledale, founded in 1884 by Sister Bernard Clune as a residential educational institution for Catholic women. At a later period in its history, the school was a junior college. The property on which the complex is located was originally the estate of *Philip Little, the first prime minister of Newfoundland. (See Confederation Building above.)

Sister Bernard (née Mary Bridget Clune) was born in Limerick, Ireland, in 1837. At the age of twenty-one she sailed to Newfoundland, where she entered the Sisters of Mercy and two years later professed her vows. Soon after becoming superior of the motherhouse in 1880, she concluded that the order's boarding school no longer served the needs of young women in Newfoundland. With the intention of redirecting the order's efforts into a broader educational function, Mother Bernard purchased Little's estate in Waterford Valley. There she opened St. Bride's, at first both a convent of four sisters and an academy for young Catholic women, under the patronage of St. Bridget of Ireland. With Sister Theresa O'Halleran, Mother Bernard visited Halifax to become acquainted with other boarding schools and the pedagogical techniques which they employed.

In the annals of the Sisters of Mercy, Mother Bernard is remembered as an exemplary religious, a talented teacher, a wise administrator, a polyglot, and a soloist of note. She continued as superior until 1884, when she died "after eight years of most intense suffering borne with saintly patience and perseverance."

¶ **Thomas Meagher & Sons Site,** between Adelaide and Holdsworth streets.

This is the former site of Thomas Meagher & Sons, a commercial company based in Waterford, Ireland. *Thomas Francis Meagher, a grandson of the founder, lived in St. John's during the summer and later became one of the most famous generals in the American Civil War. (He organized and commanded the Irish Brigade.) When the Meagher firm in St. John's went bankrupt after a fire in 1818, the family returned to Ireland. (See Irish Brigade Monument, Antietam National Battlefield, Sharpsburg, Maryland.)

¶ **Timothy O'Brien's Barn Site,** at the junction of Freshwater, Pennywell, and Cookstown roads.

On this site on July 8, 1892, a fire broke out in the barn of *Timothy O'Brien when *Tommy Fitzpatrick, one of his drivers, stumbled while smoking a pipe, a misstep which ignited some hay in the barn. Within a half hour high winds had fanned the flames in easterly and westerly directions until about two-thirds of the city was destroyed. Efforts to put out the conflagration were almost impossible because the city's water supply had been shut off that day while new mains were being laid at Rawlins Cross. A total of 2,000 buildings (including many churches, the law courts, business offices, and theaters) were destroyed, and 12,000 people were without homes.

¶ **United Irishmen Mutiny Site,** 2 Belvedere Street.

A plaque at this location commemorates the abortive attempt of Lord Edward Fitzgerald's United Irishmen to overthrow British authority in Newfoundland and join the colony to the United States.

The historical marker reads: "An army powder shed which occupied this site was chosen as a place of rendezvous by 50 United Irish mutineers of the Royal Newfoundland Regiment on the night of April 25, 1800. Nineteen men stationed on Signal Hill deserted their posts and met as planned. But others from Fort William and Fort Townshend were prevented from joining. In June, 1800, five of the mutineers were hanged on gallows erected on the site after being found guilty of Mutiny by a general Court Martial."

That troops from Fort William and Fort Townshend did not join the mutiny was due to *James O'Donel, the Catholic bishop of the city, who informed the commander of the British garrison about the planned uprising. O'Donel, born near Knocklofty, Ireland, in 1737, was so horrified that the excesses of the French Revolution might be repeated in St. John's that he was intent upon bolstering the lawful authorities in the colony. Other convicted conspirators were transported to Halifax for execution.

NOVA SCOTIA

AUBURN

¶ **Charles Inglis Plaque,** St. Mary's Anglican Church, Morden Road.
A tablet at the church commemorates the life of *Charles Inglis, the first bishop of Nova Scotia, who lived for many years at "Clermont," his nearby estate. (See St. Paul's Church, Halifax.)

BADDECK

Baddeck Bay, adjacent to St. Patrick's Channel, was the scene on February 23, 1909, of the first airplane flight in the British Empire. It was here that John Alexander McCurdy, piloting his own plane, *The Silver Dart*, made the historic flight above the frozen waters of the Bras d'Or Lakes.

The pioneer airman was born in Baddeck in 1886, the son of a Cape Breton newspaper publisher and his wife, Lucy O'Brien, the latter most likely of Irish ancestry. After graduating from the University of Toronto with a degree in mechanical engineering, McCurdy joined the Aerial Experiment Association, which numbered among its members Alexander Graham Bell, a resident of Baddeck. Two years later McCurdy entered the history books with his epochal flight.

Following that event the famous pilot went into the aviation-supply business in Toronto, forming in 1928 the Reid Aircraft Company. After a merger he was president of Curtiss-Reid Aircraft Limited from 1929 to 1939 but resigned to take a position as assistant director of aircraft production in Ottawa. He attended the reenactment of his historic flight in 1959, at which time he was made an honorary air commodore.

CANSO

¶ **Historical Marker,** School Street.
A tablet affixed to a cairn describes Canso's role in the duel for empire between England and France in the middle of the eighteenth century, particularly as the site of the rendezvous for the expedition against Louisbourg in 1745. It was here that New England volunteers under Colonel William Pepperell joined forces with an English fleet commanded by Commodore Peter Warren, an Irishman, for the assault on the famous fortress. (See Greenwich Village, New York City, and Louisbourg, Nova Scotia.)

DARTMOUTH

¶ **Meager Sisters Grave,** Woodlawn Cemetery.
A marker identifies the common grave of Jane and Margaret Meager,

sisters of most likely Irish ancestry who at the respective ages of four and six wandered away from their home in 1842 and died of exposure in a forest. The story of these 'babes in the woods' became part of local folklore."

GUYSBOROUGH

Originally settled by disbanded soldiers and Loyalists from the United States, this town of 500 residents was named for *Sir Guy Carleton, the commander-in-chief of British forces in North America. (See Cape Diamond, Quebec City, Quebec.)

¶ **Burke-Gaffney Observatory,** Loyola Building, Saint Mary's University, Inglis Street.

This observatory on the roof of the Loyola Building, a twenty-three-story academic and residential structure, commemorates the career of Father Michael Burke-Gaffney, the founder of the astronomy program at Saint Mary's. Completed in 1971, the observatory has an aluminum revolving door twenty feet in diameter and is 425 feet above sea level. The facility's telescope is the most powerful in eastern Canada and, in accord with Burke-Gaffney's wishes, has always been available for student instruction as well as research purposes.

Burke-Gaffney was born in Dublin in 1896 and received a bachelor's degree in civil engineering from the National University of Ireland. During World War I, he worked for the War Office and the Air Ministry in London. Following his emigration from Ireland in 1920, he at first worked with his brother Patrick – another engineer – in constructing bridges for the Manitoba government.

Within a year, however, Burke-Gaffney joined the Society of Jesus and proceeded to earn a master's degree in mathematics from the University of Montreal and a doctorate in astronomy from Georgetown University. A brief teaching stint at Paul's College in Winnipeg in 1939 ended when he joined the faculty of Saint Mary's College (now University) in Halifax. For the next quarter century he served successively as dean of engineering, dean of science, and professor of astronomy. (Saint Mary's was founded by Father Richard O'Brien, an Irish priest, and was later administered by the Irish Christian Brothers.)

The astronomy program at Saint Mary's dates from 1957, when Burke-Gaffney, then almost sixty years old, began to teach the school's first courses in that subject. Although his personal interest lay in the history of astronomy, he did his best to popularize the scientific aspect of the discipline through articles and interviews in the media. He was a founding member of the Nova Scotia Astronomical Society and the recipient of numerous professional awards.

¶ Carleton House, 1685 Argyle Street.

The large residential and commercial complex on this site surrounds the mansion erected by Richard Bulkeley, an Irishman whose prominence in the political life of Nova Scotia earned him the title "Father of the Province." The mansion, which was built of stone brought from the ruins of the fortress at Louisbourg, played host to much of the city's social life. The dining room could seat fifty guests and was the scene of Bulkeley's annual levees on New Year's Day, the royal birthday, St. Patrick's Day, and St. George's Day. Part of the first floor of the restored house is now a museum.

Although Bulkeley's paternal ancestors had originally lived in Chester, England, his great-grandfather had begun the Irish line of the family by accepting an appointment as archbishop of Dublin in the middle of the seventeenth century. Bulkeley himself was born in Dublin in 1717 and received a commission in the Dragoon Guards stationed in that city. His exceptional horsemanship and knowledge of German and French earned him a post at Whitehall as the king's messenger.

Bulkeley's association with Canada began in 1749, when he accompanied Edward Cornwallis, the newly appointed governor of Nova Scotia, to the province as an aide-de-camp. (Bulkeley brought a butler, a valet, and a groom with him aboard ship.) While employed in the task of assisting Cornwallis establish the new city of Halifax, the Irishman served as director of public works. Although he took no active part in the expulsion of the Acadians from the province in 1755, he supported the decision as a military necessity.

Bulkeley's prominent role in Nova Scotian political life began in 1758, when the royal governor appointed him provincial secretary. In that capacity he conducted the government's correspondence and was in charge of issuing commissions, land grants, and letters patent. For a time he edited the *Halifax Gazette*, the city's first newspaper, and he is believed to have written a tract to draw settlers and investors to the province and to encourage agriculture and the export trade. He also served as a judge of the Court of Admiralty (for thirty years) and a member of the governor's advisory council (for forty years). In the latter capacity Bulkeley assisted *Governor John Parr in dealing with a tremendous influx of Loyalists into Nova Scotia after the American Revolution. Bulkeley's correspondence contains references to tools and rations for the Loyalists as well as efforts to settle the immigrants on land grants throughout the province.

Bulkeley's private life was as varied as his political career. Besides being Grand Master of the Freemasons in Halifax, he was the first organist at St. Paul's Church and a vestryman there for four decades. He also helped organize the Charitable Irish Society of the city and served as its president for two terms. He showed the traditional Irish love of equines and in 1767 imported three blood horses for purposes of stock breeding.

At the first horse race held in Halifax the next year, one of his entries won first prize on a mile-and-a-half course.

§ Museum open Tuesday-Saturday 11-3. Phone: 902-422-1439.

¶ Inglis Street.

This street is named for either *Bishop Charles Inglis or his son Sir John Inglis, the "Hero of Lucknow." (See St. Paul's Church, Halifax.)

¶ Inglis House Site, 1334 Barrington Street. Private.

A tablet at this location notes its association with *Charles Inglis, the first bishop of Nova Scotia. The tablet reads: "The site of the house of Charles and John Inglis, 1st and 3rd Bishops of the Diocese of Nova Scotia, and the birthplace of Sir John Eardley Wilmot Inglis 1814-1862, 'The Hero of Lucknow.'"

¶ St. Paul's Church, Barrington and Prince streets.

Reputedly the oldest Protestant church in Canada, this white clapboard structure is notable for the memorial tablets which adorn its interior walls. Three of the tablets honor Charles Inglis, Richard John Uniacke, and Norman Fitzgerald Uniacke, men of Irish birth or ancestry who played significant roles in the history of the province. The hatchments of two other Irish-born political leaders – Bryan Finucane and John Parr – hang in the gallery of the church. Each of these men is buried in the church crypt.

§ Open June-August, Monday-Saturday 9-4:30; rest of the year, Monday-Friday 9-5. Phone: 902-429-2240.

• A tablet on the interior south wall of the church pays tribute to Charles Inglis: "Sacred to the Memory of The Right Reverend and Honourable Charles Inglis, D.D. Third son of the Rev. Archibald Inglis, of Glen and Kilcar, in Ireland. Bishop of Nova Scotia and its Dependencies, whose Sound Learning and Fervent Piety, directed by Zeal according to Knowledge and Supported by Fortitude unshaken amidst peculiar trials Eminently qualified him for the arduous labor of the First Bishop Appointed to a British Colony. This Stone is raised by Filial Duty and Affection in grateful Remembrance of every Private Virtue that could endear a Father and a Friend of the Ability, Fidelity, and Success, with which he was Enabled, by the Divine blessing, to discharge all his Public Duties. The general prosperity of the Church in his Diocese, the increase of his Clergy, and the provision for their support, the establishment of a Chartered College, and the erection of more than twenty Churches, are the best monument."

• Charles Inglis, the first Anglican bishop of Nova Scotia, was born in 1734 in Glencolumbkille, Ireland, the scion of a clerical family of Scottish descent that had settled in Ireland at the end of the previous century. After his ordination in England in 1758, he sailed for New York City, where he eventually became rector – and "Catechist to the Negroes" – at Trinity Church. On at least one occasion he visited the Mohawk Indians in the state, and he used his influence to secure an English missionary to work among them. During the American Revolution he was a staunch Loyalist and the object of Patriot hostility until the British occupied New York in the fall of 1776.

Soon after his appointment as the first bishop of Nova Scotia, the new prelate lamented the immensity of the challenge which faced him. "The state of religion is truly deplorable in this province," he wrote. "[T]he lamp of true national piety is almost extinguished. Ignorance and lukewarmness on the one hand; fanaticism and irreligion on the other; and the natural consequences of the former have left few traces of genuine Christianity among us."

Despite what he regarded as an extreme situation, Inglis adopted a generally laissez-faire attitude toward the personnel in his diocese. This approach was understandable, if only because of the vast extent of his diocese – originally encompassing Nova Scotia, Newfoundland, St. John's (Prince Edward) Island, Quebec, and Bermuda. In addition, he came into immediate conflict with the local clergy, primarily because they were unaccustomed to episcopal authority and resentful that they had been allowed no voice in Inglis's appointment. He was also forced to share leadership over the church with the lieutenant governor, John Parr, a fellow Irishman. In the end, Inglis was careful to consult as much as possible with his clergy and to conduct himself as *primus inter pares*.

While reluctant to interfere in local parish affairs, Inglis took steps to improve the overall condition of the church in his diocese. He succeeded in obtaining additional financial support from the British Parliament, the Society for the Propagation of the Gospel, and the colonial legislature to improve clerical salaries and to complete a modest church-building program. In helping establish King's College in Windsor, he hoped to educate and train a native clergy.

By 1796 Inglis had retired to "Clermont," his country estate near Aylesford. There he pursued the life of a gentleman farmer, delighting especially in experimenting with new species of apples. (On a single day he transplanted thirty-two apple trees from his nursery.) Following his death in 1816, his son and two daughters inherited the estate and more than 12,000 additional acres in the Annapolis valley.

• A marble tablet memorializes Richard Uniacke: "Sacred to the memory of Richard John Uniacke, Fourth Son of Norman Uniacke of Castletown, in the County of Cork, Ireland: Many years member of His Majesty's Council and Attorney General of this Province. He died at Mount Uniacke, October 11th, 1830, in the 77th Year of his age. His Remains were removed and deposited in a Vault beneath this Church." (See Mount

Uniacke, Nova Scotia.)

• Born in 1737 at Ennis, County Clare, Ireland, Bryan Finucane practiced at the Irish bar until he was appointed chief justice of Nova Scotia in 1778. He was also a member of the governor's council, serving in both capacities until his death in 1785.

• John Parr, a native of Dublin, was selected in 1782 to become governor of Nova Scotia. Almost immediately he was faced with a chaotic situation when the population of the province was doubled by the arrival of 35,000 Loyalists from the recently independent United States. That very first winter Parr commandeered every warehouse, church, and ship in Halifax to accommodate the 10,000 refugees and disbanded soldiers who flooded the city. When the immediacy of the crisis subsided, the governor busied himself in securing for the newcomers land grants in the unoccupied portions of the province. In a letter to Lord North at the beginning of 1784, Parr detailed the plight of the refugees: "I cannot better describe, the wretched situation of these people than by enclosing a list of those just arrived in the transport *Clinton*, chiefly women and children, scarcely clothed, utterly destitute, still on board the transport, crowded like a sheep-pen as I am totally unable to find any sort of place for them, and we cannot move them by reason of the ice and snow."

Despite the skill which he exhibited in coping with the refugee problem, Parr saw his authority diminished as the result of policies adopted by the British government. First, Nova Scotia's territory was considerably reduced with the creation of the province of New Brunswick. Then, with the appointment of the Anglo-Irishman Guy Carleton as governor general of British North America, Parr was demoted to lieutenant governor. In addition, his authority over the Anglican Church in Nova Scotia was reduced when *Charles Inglis was appointed the first bishop of the province. And his frustration with trying to mediate between the Loyalist newcomers and the earlier colonists led him to complain to a British bureaucrat in an especially adjectival way: "I am surrounded with a number of Fanatical, diabolical, unprincipled, expecting, disappointed, deceitful, lying Scoundrels, who . . . [are] eternally finding fault with, and complaining against their Superiours in Office."

¶ One of the most interesting grave stones in St. Paul's Cemetery is that of Major General Robert Ross, whose maternal great-grandfather was from Castle Bernard, County Cork. The stone is inscribed as follows: "Here on the 21st Sept. 1814, was consigned to the earth the body of Major General Ross, who, having distinguished himself in all ranks as an officer in Egypt, Italy, Portugal, Spain and America, was killed at the commencement of an action which resulted in the defeat and flight of the troops of the United States near Baltimore, on the 12th Sept. 1814. At Rostrevor, the seat of the family in Ireland, a monument more worthy of his memory has been erected by the noblemen and gentlemen of his county, and the officers of a gallant army which, under his conduct, attacked and dispersed the Americans at Bladensburg, on the 24th Aug. 1814, and on the same day victoriously entered Washington, the capital of the U.S. In St. Paul's [in London] a monument has also been erected to his memory by his country."

During the final six months of the War of 1812, Ross led an infantry brigade against the coast of the United States. The force, which consisted of about 4,500 men by the time of its arrival in the Chesapeake, was launched "to retaliate upon the Americans for the outrages which they had committed upon the frontiers," specifically the burning of York (now Toronto), the capital of Upper Canada. On August 24, 1814, Ross's troops marched on Washington, D.C., by way of Bladensburg, where they found an American force of about 6,500 men. After three hours of fighting – during which Ross's horse was shot from under him – the Americans broke ranks and fled, but not before killing 250 British.

Emboldened by the American retreat, Ross and his men proceeded to Washington itself. (En route the British commander again narrowly escaped when his horse was killed.) "So unexpected was our entry and capture of Washington," Ross wrote, "and so confident was Madison of the defeat of our troops, that he had prepared a supper for the expected [American] conquerors; and when our advanced party entered the President's house, they found a table laid with forty covers [sets of utensils]." During the night the British torched the public buildings in the American capital city – including the Capitol and its library, the treasury building, and the executive mansion. Ross later told the Washington physician whose house he commandeered that night that he regretted burning the library and would not have set the presidential mansion on fire if the First Lady had not fled the building. ("I make war neither against letters nor ladies," he said.)

After returning unopposed to his ships, the British general set his sights on Baltimore. With a reduced force of less than 4,000 men, Ross marched a dozen miles to the city, where 6,000 militia had taken their stand. This time Ross's earlier luck was missing, and he was killed when a bullet passed through his right arm into his breast. Although the militia were routed, the British gave up the attack when their naval forces were unable to provide cover. Ross's body was brought to Halifax aboard H.M.S. *Tonnant* and was laid to rest in St. Paul's Cemetery on September 29 of that year. To commemorate Ross's part in the American campaign, a royal warrant a year later granted to his widow and their descendants the title "Ross of Bladensburg."

¶ The unrelated Captain William Ross, a Corkonian who established a colony for disbanded soldiers in the province, is also buried in the churchyard. (See New Ross, Nova Scotia.)

¶ **Samuel Cunard Plaque,** Point Pleasant Park.

This commemorative marker in the lower parking lot honors Samuel Cunard, a native of Halifax and the founder of the famous steamship line. Cunard's mother, Margaret Murphy, traced her roots to Ireland, her family having emigrated from that country in 1773. Murphy's ancestors settled in South Carolina before fleeing to Nova Scotia with other Loyalists after the American Revolution.

For many years Samuel Cunard was a merchant in Halifax and the owner of whalers that plied the seas from Nova Scotia to the Pacific. In 1839 he and two partners formed the British and American Royal Mail Steam Packet Company, an enterprise that boasted four steamships (each 1,200 tons burden) recently constructed in England. That same year Cunard contracted with the British government to deliver mail between Liverpool and Halifax and between Boston and Quebec. The contract was to last seven years (at £60,000 a year) and stipulated that the original six steamships be large enough to carry troops.

Cunard launched his mail service for the government on July 4, 1840, when the *Britannia* – with Cunard himself aboard – left Liverpool. After a voyage of fourteen days and eight hours, the vessel arrived in Boston, where Cunard was lionized with a public banquet celebrating the new postal service. Three years later Cunard expanded his fleet with four more ships when the government decided to begin weekly delivery service. Cunard was later elected to the Royal Geographical Society and received a baronetcy from the Queen.

¶ Cunard Street honors the famous steamship entrepreneur and his prominent Halifax family.

LOUISBOURG

¶ **Fortress of Louisbourg National Historic Site,** on Cape Breton Island, 22 miles south of Sydney.

The central attraction of this twenty-five-acre historic site is a reconstruction of the sprawling stone fortress erected by the French between 1720 and 1745 to defend their North American colonies.

In that latter year, after a seven-week siege, the fortress was captured by New England volunteers under Colonel William Pepperell and by an English fleet commanded by Commodore Peter Warren, a native of County Meath, Ireland. (See Greenwich Village, New York City.) Although Louisbourg was returned to France in 1748, it again fell to the British a decade later, this time to a force led by *James Wolfe. (See Wolfe-Montcalm Monument, Quebec.) In 1760 the British government ordered the stronghold to be demolished. Some of the stones were used in the construction of St. Patrick's Church in nearby Sydney in 1828.

Today fifty of the fortress's eighty original buildings – as well as ramparts and fortifications – have been rebuilt to their appearance prior to the siege of 1745. A number of the reconstructed buildings are open to visitors. Costumed interpreters explain the history of the site and provide demonstrations of colonial music, gardening, and cooking.

§ Park open July-August, daily 9-7; June and September, daily 9:30-5. Additional times in May and October. Fee. Phone: 902-733-2280 or 800-213-7275.

MAITLAND

¶ **William Lawrence House Museum,** 0.5 mile northwest on Highway 215.

This is the former home of the shipbuilder William Lawrence, who constructed the largest wooden ship ever built in the Maritimes. Built about 1870, the Victorian house overlooks the former site of the owner's shipyard. The structure contains memorabilia and furnishings of Lawrence's family, as well as shipbuilding artifacts and a cross-section model of Lawrence's famous vessel. The portico on the two-and-a-half-story house resembles the bridge of a ship.

Born in 1817 in Banbridge, northern Ireland, Lawrence accompanied his parents to Nova Scotia when he was an infant. At the age of ten or eleven he began an apprenticeship in the Lyle and Chappel shipyards in Dartmouth. By 1852, however, he was designing, building, and operating his own ships, although usually in partnership with other investors. Over the next decade and a half, he either built or launched seven barques or brigantines, each ranging in tonnage from 117 to 1,120.

His largest ship, however, was the *William D. Lawrence*, a three-master of 2,459 tons and 259 feet in length that cost $107,452 to construct. (The builder mortgaged his house to raise the necessary capital.) Lawrence himself sailed aboard the ship during a voyage of almost three years, returning with enough gold to pay off his debts. Upon his arrival in Nova Scotia, he published an account of the people and places he had encountered. The vessel was sold to a group of Norwegians in 1883.

To his career as a shipbuilder and shipowner, Lawrence added a less distinguished one as a politician. During the 1860s he served variously as a justice of the peace or a representative for Hants County in the provincial legislature. In that latter position he opposed Canadian confederation but was a strong advocate of free public education.

§ Open June 1-mid October, Monday-Saturday 9:30-5:30, Sunday 1-5. Phone: 902-261-2628.

MOUNT UNIACKE

¶ **Uniacke Estate Museum Park,** off Route 101 at exit 3 to Route 1.

The Georgian mansion on this 2,300-acre estate was built between 1813 and 1815 for Richard John Uniacke, an Irishman who had become Nova Scotia's attorney general in 1797. He selected this site because the terrain reminded him of his ancestral home in Ireland. He named his residence "Uniacke House" after the home of his Irish grandfather.

The two-story, eight-bedroom white wooden house later became the summer home of Richard Uniacke's son, James Boyle Uniacke, a Tory leader who resigned from the Legislative Council in 1837 to join Joseph Howe's reform party. In 1848 the younger Uniacke became Nova Scotia's prime minister and attorney general.

According to tradition the family name was derived from the Latin word *unicus* ("the only one"), an appellation given an ancestor – an Irish knight named Fitzgerald – for a singularly brave deed performed, no doubt, for the honor of the family.

Born in Castletownroche, Ireland, in 1753, Richard Uniacke was descended from a formerly Roman Catholic family whose repression during the Tudor and Cromwellian regimes had forced its members to adopt Protestantism. As irony would have it, however, Uniacke seems to have been sympathetic to the plight of Catholics in his native land. He particularly

"Uniacke House," the home of Richard John Uniacke.
(Photo courtesy of Uniacke Estate Museum Park, a part of the Nova Scotia Museum.)

angered his father by his involvement in agitation on behalf of the civil rights of Catholics. Feeling the sting of parental disapproval, the son sailed for America and arrived in Philadelphia in 1774. After forming a partnership with a Nova Scotian trader, the Irishman married his associate's twelve-year-old daughter.

Even after moving to New Brunswick, Uniacke continued to flirt with sedition. In 1776, when Canadians in sympathy with the American rebels tried to capture Fort Cumberland in Nova Scotia, Uniacke was arrested on suspicion of being involved in the uprising. His release was perhaps due to the influence of Irish officers in the garrison at Halifax. Whatever the case, Uniacke decided to return to Ireland to complete his legal studies in Dublin. Following his return to Nova Scotia, he was admitted to the bar and was soon elected to the provincial House of Assembly and to its speakership.

Although Uniacke's ambitions propelled him to seek the position of attorney general, the newly arrived Loyalists were as equally determined to deny him that preferment. (One Loyalist newcomer labeled him "a great lubberly insolent irish [sic] rebel.") Thus between 1784 and 1797 he bided his time in the Assembly and as advocate general of the Vice Admiralty Court. In this latter position he amassed a considerable fortune, primarily from the fees he collected during the Napoleonic Wars. With this wealth he was able to educate his twelve surviving children (six of them sons) and to build a large townhouse in Halifax and his country home at Mount Uniacke (originally an estate of 11,000 acres).

Finally appointed attorney general at the end of the century, Uniacke proceeded to make a name for himself as a constitutional scholar and theorist. In 1805 he published a compilation of Nova Scotian laws for the previous half century. He likewise challenged the attempts of the provincial governor to deprive the Assembly of its right to supervise provincial finances. He early advocated colonial self-government and the repeal of imperial policies against free trade for the colonies.

In the 1820s Uniacke came to fear that atheism and democracy – unleashed by the French Revolution – would spread to Canada. From his perspective these twin evils would infect his adopted land after the "hoards of semi-barbarians" in the southern and western United States had succumbed to their sway. To defend against this contamination, Uniacke drafted a plan for the confederation of the British North American colonies. (Two decades earlier he had proposed a union of the Maritime provinces with Upper and Lower Canada.) The British government, however, looked with disfavor on plans for any type of Canadian union. Failing to stem the tide of atheism and democracy via constitutional change, Uniacke placed his hopes in the ability of the established Anglican Church to help maintain a Christian civilization and serve as a bulwark of the British constitution.

Despite his exalted position in the community, Uniacke was not above indulging in a playful escapade. One such incident, recorded by a contemporary scribe, had its origin during an evening party at the residence of a gentleman in Halifax. Discovering that the host's lack of musical instruments frustrated the guests' desire to dance, Uniacke volunteered to find a solution. He accordingly proceeded to the nearby home of two unmarried women who, he knew, owned a spinet. After knocking and pounding on the door, he heard a female voice waft down from a window above. "What do you want, waking ladies up in the middle of the night?" the voice asked. "Is there a fire in the town?" The disturber of the peace responded with mock seriousness: "I'm Mr. Uniacke, the Attorney General. In the King's name open the door, or I'll break it in!" The scribe concluded the story: "The ladies laughed, and when they had attired themselves after a fashion, stepped down and opened the door. Mr. Uniacke explained the purport of his visit; and being good natured people, the ladies willingly entrusted the instrument to his care. He was . . . a tall, powerful man; so putting it on his shoulders, he carried it over to the party; and they danced to their hearts' content . . . ."

§ Open June- mid October, Monday-Saturday 9:30-5:30, Sunday 1-5:30. Phone: 902-866-2560 or 866-0032.

NEW ROSS

¶ Ross Farm Museum, on Highway 12.

Now a living-history museum, Ross Farm chronicles the way of life experienced by five generations of the Ross family since their Irish-born ancestors, Captain William Ross and his wife, settled here in 1816.

Today the Ross Farm features several types of livestock as well as a variety of structures, including Ross's two-story farmhouse, a school house, a peddler's shop, a general store, a cooperage, a barn, a blacksmith shop, and a stave mill. Visitors can engage in various husbandry chores, including milking and butter churning.

The family cottage, known as "Rosebank," was built by Captain Ross in 1817 to replace an earlier log cabin. The present house, constructed of hand-sawn boards, has five fireplaces and boasts a piano which four soldiers transported here from Chester, fifteen miles away.

Prior to their arrival in Canada, William Ross and his wife had been stationed – presumably with the British army – in Ireland, South America, England, and Quebec. (Each of their first four children was born in one of Ross's far-flung postings.) A native of Cork, Ross arrived in this part of Canada as captain of 172 former soldiers of the Nova Scotia Fencibles. He had come at the request of the Earl of Dalhousie, the governor of the colony, who promised a land grant to each of the soldiers. Ross himself was granted 800 acres, sixty of which comprise the modern Ross Farm Museum. Ross's two youngest children were born in Sherbrooke, the original name of Ross's settlement until it was later rechristened in his honor.

In the fall of 1821, the Irishman and a guide attempted to lay out a route for a proposed road to Halifax. After exposure during a violent storm, however, Ross became ill and died the next spring at the age of thirty-nine. He was buried with military honors in the churchyard of St. Paul's Church in Halifax [*q.v.*].

§ Open June-mid October, daily 9:30-5:30; January-March, Saturday-Sunday 9:30-4:30. Fee. Phone: 902-689-2210.

SHELBURNE

§ **Loyalist Settlers Plaque,** near the Tourist Office at Dock and King streets.

Attached to a large boulder, this bronze tablet relates the founding of Shelburne by Loyalists from the United States and notes the part played in the town's naming by John Parr, the Irish-born governor of Nova Scotia at the time.

The marker reads: "Shelburne, A Loyalist Town. Settled in the years following the close of the American Revolution by men and women determined to remain under the flag and rule of Great Britain rather than become citizens of the United States. The harbour, once known as Port Razoir, and then as Port Roseway, was the site chosen by the Port Roseway Associates of New York. The first Loyalist settlers arrived 4th May 1783. Laid out the same year, the town was officially named Shelburne, 22nd July, by John Parr, Governor of Nova Scotia."

§ **McNutt Island,** at the entrance to Shelburne Harbor.

Named for Alexander McNutt, an enterprising colonizer, this island was originally part of a 100,000-acre land grant made to the Irish immigrant in 1765.

McNutt, probably born in Londonderry, Ireland, in 1725, had immigrated to Virginia with his parents sometime before his thirtieth birthday. After serving under Major Andrew Lewis, a fellow Irishman, on a campaign against the Shawnees on the Ohio River, McNutt seems to have taken up residence in Londonderry, New Hampshire. He later served with militia units in Maine and Nova Scotia.

Soon after his arrival in Halifax in 1759, McNutt was granted land in present-day Colchester and Shelburne counties. When the British expulsion of the Acadians severely reduced the population of Nova Scotia, he saw an opportunity to better his own circumstances while helping to re-colonize the province. After establishing a colonization company, he obtained title to two million acres and began to recruit colonists for this vast domain. He himself visited Ireland to launch an advertising campaign offering 200 acres to the head of each family that emigrated.

Between 1761 and 1765, Scotch-Irish settlers from New Hampshire established Truro, Nova Scotia, and McNutt resettled 420 emigrants from Ireland. These newcomers were invariably indigent and required assistance from the government as well as private charity. In time, though, the imperial government began to fear the consequences of massive emigration of Protestants from Ireland and took steps to make it harder for Irish settlers in Nova Scotia to acquire land.

This new policy somewhat dampened McNutt's colonization schemes, but the situation improved in 1765 when he received title to 100,000 acres in Port Roseway (now Shelburne). In this latest venture he seems to have combined a religious fervor with a practicality for making money, hoping to turn Port Roseway into "a city by the name of Jerusalem on the Cape Sable shore, that being the best harbor for carrying on the fishery." Although this quasi-utopian scheme failed, McNutt continued to live on the island which bears his name and on which he constructed a house.

Despite McNutt's apparent sympathies for the American Revolution, his house was robbed of £300 by "armed ruffians" from an American privateer in 1778. To make a claim for compensation, he traveled to Boston to plead his case before the Massachusetts council. Rebuffed in his suit, he went to Philadelphia to request the Continental Congress to urge the people of Nova Scotia to cast off their loyalty to the Crown and side with the American revolutionists.

McNutt was nevertheless allowed to return to Halifax, but only to obtain documents that would verify his claim for compensation. The authorities prudently watched the Irishman's movements, especially after rumors surfaced that he had tried to circulate several "dangerous pamphlets" throughout the province. One of these tracts may have been a constitution for an independent state of New Ireland, to be created out of an area in present-day Maine between the Saco and St. Croix rivers. According to the document, New Ireland was to be a theocratic state based on puritanical principles. Plays, balls, gambling, horseracing, and cockfighting were forbidden, and only Christians in good standing were eligible for public office. (Lawyers were expressly excluded from election.)

SYDNEY

ℐ St. Patrick's Museum, 87 Esplanade.

Constructed in 1828, this Gothic-style former church is the oldest Catholic sanctuary on Cape Breton Island. The museum features exhibits about the history of Sydney and the local area.

§ Open mid June-October 1, Monday-Saturday 9:30-5:30, Sunday 1-5:30. Phone: 902-562-8237.

ONTARIO

BEWDLEY

❡ **Joseph Medlicott Scriven Monument,** Pengelly Cemetery, north from town on Highway 28.

This impressive memorial marks the grave of the Irish-born composer of the hymn "What a Friend We Have in Jesus." The monument, erected in 1920, is inscribed with three verses of the hymn, regarded by at least one authority as the "best-known piece of Canadian literature."

Born in Banbridge, County Down, in 1819, Joseph Scriven received a bachelor's degree from Trinity College, Dublin, at the age of twenty-three. After becoming a member of the Plymouth Brethren, a sect whose theology was essentially Lutheran, he immigrated to Ontario, where he taught school and engaged in preaching. About 1857 he moved to Bewdley to accept a position as tutor in the household of Robert Pengelly, a retired naval officer.

Through his religious zeal and numerous acts of charity, Scriven gathered a faithful if uninfluential following. He was a familiar figure in the vicinity, whether distributing poems and tracts of his own composition or preaching in the streets and taverns. In his sermons he employed simple language and an equally unaffected delivery. He frequently visited the men on a railroad construction gang to read them the Bible, for years he carried the milk from a widow's cow to her customers, and he once sold his watch to replace someone's lost bovine.

Scriven's last days were marked by ill health and an untimely death. Apparently ravaged by fever or by the heat of an August night in 1886, the evangelist rose from his bed in order to drink at a nearby spring. It is conjectured that he either fainted or fell on his way to the spring, since he was later found dead – "in an attitude of prayer" – in the spillway of Sackville's grist mill.

§ Take Highway 28 north to the Hamilton-South Monaghan line and then turn right. Follow the road to Rice Lake and turn left. The cemetery is 1,000 feet farther.

CHATSWORTH

❡ **Nellie McClung Cairn,** south on Route 6 toward Sullivan Township.

The plaque on this memorial summarizes the career of *Nellie Mooney McClung: "Lecturer, Legislator, Teacher and Writer. Ardent advocate of Women's Rights in Canada. Author of 'Sowing Seeds in Danny' and other works. Born near Chatsworth, 20th October 1873. Died in Victoria, B.C., 1st September 1951." (See Manitou, Manitoba.)

HAMILTON

J McMaster University, Main Street West.

Established in 1887, this private institution is named for William McMaster, whose substantial financial support formed the nucleus of the university's original endowment.

McMaster, who was born in County Tyrone, Ireland, in 1811, was the son of a linen merchant and at the age of ten joined the Baptist Church in Omagh. After immigrating to Canada in 1833, he established a wholesale dry goods business in York (now Toronto). He eventually became head of the prosperous firm of William McMaster and Nephews, by 1860 the largest dry goods firm in western Canada. (His wealth the year before was estimated at between $600,000 and $800,000.)

Sometime in the 1860s the Toronto businessman became allied with George Brown's reform movement. McMaster seems to have been attracted to the cause of political reform because of its opposition to the Church of England and its conservative allies. In joining the reformers, the Irishman hoped to challenge Montreal's control of the western economy and to improve the situation of religious nonconformists like the Baptists. Believing that his coreligionists were "a people of destiny," he remained in the Baptist denomination for the rest of his life, even though connection with a more "prestigious" church would have helped his social and business advancement.

McMaster was first elected to the Legislative Council of United Canada in 1862, where he represented the Midland until his appointment to the Canadian Senate in 1867. In the latter year he played a major role in establishing the Canadian Bank of Commerce, of which he was president for almost two decades. Because he was childless in both his marriages, he left $1 million – most of his estate – to McMaster University, in whose founding he had been one of the chief promoters.

LONDON

J Middlesex County Administration Building, 399 Ridout Street North, at Dundas Street.

This crenelated, fortress-like structure was built in 1831 as the county courthouse and was modeled on Malahide Castle in Ireland, the ancestral home of Thomas Talbot, an enthusiastic promoter of settlement in this part of Canada.

Talbot, the offspring of an Anglo-Irish family that had lived in Ireland since the twelfth century, was born in County Dublin in 1771. At the age of eleven he received a commission in a British infantry unit but retired only four months later as a lieutenant. His subsequent military career brought him a variety of posts: aide-de-camp to the lord lieutenant of Ire-

The Middlesex County Building, modeled after Malahide Castle in Ireland.
(Photo courtesy of the London Regional Art and Historical Museums.)

land, regimental commander in Quebec, and private secretary to the first lieutenant governor of Canada. In 1800, however, he sold his commission and took the unexpected step of removing to Upper Canada as a settler. What motivated the twenty-nine-year-old aristocrat to make such a decision remains unclear, but various theories have suggested unrequited love and frustrated military and political ambitions.

Whatever the case, by the next year Talbot had taken up the unlikely roles of farmer and land promoter on the north shore of Lake Erie. Within a few years he obtained a land grant of 5,000 acres and settled at Port Talbot, his home for the next half century. In a short time he acquired for himself numerous public offices, including county lieutenant, legislative councillor, district magistrate, township constable, and school trustee. His reputation for acquisitiveness was only enhanced by his remark that he preferred appointment to the Legislative Council rather than to the Executive Council because he did "not like working for nothing, and . . . the £100 is as well to have as not."

Talbot's land grant was extremely generous and afforded him the opportunity to create his subsequent "empire." For every fifty acres of his original 5,000 which he granted to the head of a family he received an additional 200 acres. In 1807, however, he decided to ignore the terms of his grant and allow settlers to locate outside his own domain. His motivation for doing so seems to have been his desire to isolate himself from the increasing numbers of incoming settlers. "[W]ithin my home Belt, . . ." he wrote, "I do not like to have settlers, as I find too near Neighbors a great nuisance." Yet it was precisely this isolation that caused him to press the authorities for the construction of more roads. After securing his own appointment as road commissioner, he was instrumental in planning three new roadways, each denominated "Talbot Road" but differentiated by its direction from York (now Toronto). At the height of his power, he held 65,000 acres and controlled settlements extending over 130 miles from east to west and including portions of twenty-nine townships in the southwestern region of Upper Canada. (Talbot's "capital" was located at St. Thomas, near Talbotville.)

Never on the best of terms with the authorities because of his snobbery and hard drinking, the "Baron of Lake Erie" came into serious conflict with the provincial government because he refused to grant his settlers full title to their land until they had paid him their settlement dues. When this policy prevented the government from collecting its various fees, the authorities terminated Talbot's "palatinate" powers and forced him to cede control over his lands. Thus chastened and financially weakened, Talbot applied for a government pension and the remission of fees he had paid on his own lands. With a £400 annual pension and the proceeds from the sale of cattle, he was able in 1832 to build a new house on his estate, which still boasted approximately 60,000 acres. He continued despondent, however, and in 1836 expressed his wish to be "possessed of a sufficiency to enable me [to] remove to the *Moon* or some other more wholesome place of residence." After his death at the age of eighty-one, the lifelong bachelor was buried in the Anglican cemetery at Tyrconnell, a few miles west of Port Talbot.

§ Open Monday-Friday 8:30-4:30. Phone: 519-434-7321.

LUCAN

ℐ Donnelly Gravesite, St. Patrick Cemetery, east off Route 4 at Roman Line.

Erected in the 1960s, this granite stone marks the graves of five members of the local Donnelly family: James and Johannah, their sons John and Thomas, and their niece Bridget. The five were killed on February 4, 1880, the climax to a forty-year-old feud that had begun in County Tipperary, Ireland. Because of the testimony of two eyewitnesses – eleven-year-old Johnny O'Connor and the Donnelly's eldest son, William – six men were indicted for the murders. The accused were eventually acquitted, however.

MADOC

¶ **O'Hara Mill Museum and Conservation Area,** northwest of town, following signs from Highway 62 or Highway 7.

The site contains a number of restored structures dating from the nineteenth century, including a farmhouse and a water-powered sawmill erected by James O'Hara Sr. A carriage house, a log blacksmith shop, a schoolhouse, and a museum are also on the eighty-five-acre property. The farmhouse was built in 1848 and remained in the O'Hara family until 1965, when a great-granddaughter of James O'Hara Sr. sold it to the Moira River Conservation Authority.

O'Hara was one of twelve children born to Patrick O'Hara, a native of Londonderry, Ireland, and his wife. About 1789, at the age of twenty, the older O'Hara had come to Canada with a regiment of the British army. He seems to have deserted sometime before 1794, however, because in that year he was in Vermont, where he married Cynthia Prindle.

The couple's second child, James O'Hara, was born in Vermont but also lived in New York State, at least after his marriage in 1818 to Mary Healey, perhaps of Irish ancestry also. Five years later the couple and their first child, Elizabeth, moved to Modoc Township, drawn apparently by the prospect of land in Ontario newly opened up by the British government. According to Minnie O'Hara Maines, James's great-granddaughter, O'Hara enjoyed good relations with the local Native Americans, who of-

The O'Hara House, built in 1848 by James O'Hara Sr.
(Photo courtesy of Moira River Conservation Authority.)

ten stole into his house at night to take advantage of the warm fireplace.

As Modoc Township's first justice of the peace, O'Hara was given the nickname "Squire." In that capacity he was called upon to judge a case involving a young man whose father had punished him for his frequent swearing. Maines tells the story as follows: "There was a man named 'Carman' in the vicinity who lived just up the road from the Squire. He had a son who would swear and whose father very positively objected to the habit. He [the father] used to punish his son severely. The young man waited until he was twenty-one years of age and then decided his father would be made aware he had attained his majority. He swore as much as he pleased. This led to altercations between father and son, the latter thrashing the young fellow well. So enraged was the young man that he decided to go down the road to the Squire and to swear out a warrant against his father. The squire listened to his complaint, asked a few questions and gave his decisions: 'I know of no one who has better right to thrash you [than your father] for taking the name of God in vain. I will issue no warrant against your father. Go home and quit swearing.' There was no other Justice of the Peace to appeal to and the matter was thus settled."

In May 1850 O'Hara and his own son, James Jr., entered into a partnership to construct a sawmill on their property. Although the arrangement was to expire after twenty years, the water-powered mill was still cutting lumber commercially until 1908. Known as a frame or gate saw, the mill is reputedly the only such water-powered saw in Ontario.

§ Open June-Labour Day, daily 10-45 Fee. Phone: 613-968-3434.

MAITLAND

¶ **Barbara Heck Gravesite,** Blue Church.

Among the graves of the many Ontario settlers buried here is the grave of Barbara Heck, the founder of Methodism in North America. After emigrating from Ireland in 1760, she settled in New York, where she established a Methodist society and the first Wesleyan church on the continent. She moved to this part of Canada after the American Revolution, forming Ontario's first Methodist society and living here until her death.

OSHAWA

¶ **Parkwood,** off Highway 401 exit 417 to 270 Simcoe Street North.

The centerpiece of this twelve-acre estate is a fifty-five-room mansion owned by Colonel Robert Samuel McLaughlin, a pioneer in the Canadian automobile industry. The house, now a National Historic Site, is decorated with lavish original furnishings and artwork and stands on landscaped grounds that feature greenhouses and garden spaces ranging from the serene to the spectacular.

"Parkwood," the 55-room mansion owned by Robert Samuel McLaughlin.
(Photo by Anthony Randall and courtesy of The Parkwood Estate and Gardens.)

McLaughlin was born in Enniskillen, Ontario, in 1871, the grandson of a cobbler who had emigrated from County Tyrone, Ireland, almost forty years before. The emigrant – John McLaughlin (nicknamed "Broghie") – had arrived by ship at Montreal in the company of 140 other Irish newcomers. At Montreal the emigrants boarded river boats for the journey to Lake Ontario, but along the way McLaughlin's boat capsized on the St. Lawrence River. The Irishman escaped with little more than his wallet and his Bible. After settling with some of his compatriots in an area which they named Tyrone, McLaughlin took possession of a 160-acre grant of Crown land. There he married Eliza Rusk, an Irishwoman, who gave birth to their first child – Robert – in 1836.

As he grew older, Robert McLaughlin began to use his woodworking talents in the production of axe handles, but he soon branched off into the manufacture of horse-drawn sleighs or cutters. One of his earliest cutters was made for a local Irish Protestant who wanted it decorated with a painting of King William of Orange crossing the Boyne on his white horse – the traditional symbol of triumphant Protestantism. With the help of an upholsterer and a blacksmith, McLaughlin constructed the cutter and, although he was not an Orangeman, added the desired artwork.

As McLaughin's business continued to expand, he moved his operations to a succession of new locations. In Enniskillen, for example, he continued to build his earlier line of products, but he also began to manufacture carriages, doing business as the McLaughlin Carriage Company with the motto "One Grade only and that the Best." Enniskillen's long distance from a railway depot and its lack of banking facilities, however, finally caused McLaughlin to move his family and the enterprise to Oshawa in 1877. Three years later he revolutionized the carriage-making business by inventing a new chassis that combined a fifth wheel with flexible springs, couplings of Norwegian iron, and brass and rubber washers. These innovations provided greater flexibility in turning as well as added strength and safety. And, of course, he continued to insist on the highest quality. His son Robert Samuel wrote admiringly of his father: "People called him a 'crank for quality,' and he took it as a compliment. No workman would dare skimp a job, or rush it through, because my father inspected everything and poor workmanship was the one sure way of calling down his wrath." Although young "Sam" had ideas of becoming a lawyer, he eventually joined his father's firm, though not before doing yeoman work as a journeyman upholsterer.

In 1896 the McLaughlin Carriage Company opened a branch in Saint John, New Brunswick, the first of several outlets. In time the enterprise had offices in Montreal, London, Winnipeg, Regina, and Calgary. The company suffered a major setback, however, when its Oshawa factory was completely destroyed in 1899. Although fifteen municipalities offered financial incentives to relocate the company near them, the firm remained in Oshawa when the city offered a $50,000 loan to be repaid "as convenient." By the turn of the century the company was producing 143 separate body designs of carriages and sleighs.

It was not long before the McLaughlins entered the automobile age as well as the lucrative American market. After creating the McLaughlin Motor Car Company, Sam began to manufacture car bodies, first for Buick Motor Company in Flint, Michigan, and then for Chevrolet. It was at this time that McLaughlin became director of the Chevrolet Motor Car Company of Canada. Three years later the family sold out to General Motors, although Sam remained as president of the newly incorporated General Motors of Canada and vice president of its American parent company. By the mid 1920s the Oshawa plant employed 3,000 people and manufactured more cars for the Canadian and Commonwealth markets than the rest of Canada combined.

§ Open June-Labour Day, Tuesday-Sunday and holidays 10:30-4; rest of the year, Tuesday-Sunday 1:30-4. Fee. Phone: 905-433-1311.

¶ **Robert McLaughlin Gallery,** in the Civic Center at the foot of Bagot Street, via Highway 401 exit 417 and Simcoe Street.

Named for *Colonel Robert Samuel McLaughlin, a pioneer in the Canadian automobile industry, the gallery presents changing exhibits of artwork by contemporary Canadian artists. (See preceding entry.)

§ Open Tuesday-Friday 10-5 (to 9 on Thursday), Saturday-Sunday noon-4. Closed January 1 and December 25. Phone: 905-576-3000.

OTTAWA

¶ **Bytown Museum,** at the bottom of Ottawa Locks behind the Chateau Laurier.

Among the museum's exhibits on the history of Bytown and Ottawa are some personal effects belonging to *Thomas D'Arcy McGee, the only Canadian political leader to be assassinated.

§ Open mid May-mid October, Monday-Saturday 10-5, Sunday 1-5; April 1-mid May and mid October-November 30, Monday-Friday 10-4; rest of the year by appointment. Fee. Phone: 613-234-4570.

¶ **Edward Hanlan Statue,** in Exhibition Place (along Lake Shore Boulevard), on the north side of the Marine Museum in the vicinity of Princes' Boulevard and Newfoundland Drive.

This giant bronze statue was unveiled in 1926 in honor of Canada's most famous oarsman, Edward Hanlan. The statue depicts Hanlan holding a pair of oars, one knee resting on a granite base. The base is shaped like the stern of a rowing shell and supports a bronze seagull with outstretched wings. The memorial bears this inscription: "Most renowned oarsman of any age, whose victorious career has no parallel in the annals of sport. Victor in three hundred consecutive races. His achievements are all the more worthy of commemoration by his display of that spirit of true sportsmanship, which is held in honour in all fields of sport."

The son of Irish parents, Hanlan (properly Hanlon) was born in 1855 in Toronto, where his father was a hotel proprietor. The son achieved his first important distinction as an oarsman at the age of eighteen, when he became the amateur champion of Toronto Bay. After turning professional, he beat all challengers at the centennial international exhibition in Philadelphia in 1876. During the next three years he rowed to successive victories as champion oarsman of Canada, the United States, and England, the last triumph achieved on the River Tyne in a record time of twenty minutes and twenty-one seconds. In 1880 he won the world's championship by beating Australia's best in a race on the Thames. In four subsequent matches Hanlan defeated challengers to his title but finally succumbed in 1884 to William Beach. Hanlan suffered four additional defeats between 1885 and 1888.

Hanlan's record of wins is particularly impressive because of his relatively slight physical build and his unique style as a sculler. In height he stood about five feet nine inches and weighed just over 155 pounds. Unlike his English rivals, he used the slide and the swing motions simultaneously, kept his body well back, and held his arms straight long past the

Statue of Edward Hanlan,
Canada's most famous sculler.
(Photo courtesy of Canadian
National Exhibition Archives.)

perpendicular before bending them to row the stroke. Though several times offered a fortune for "throwing a race," he resisted the temptation and continued to maintain his reputation for honesty.

Following his retirement, the citizens of Toronto presented him with an honorarium of £4,000, and the government granted him that section of Toronto Island now known as Hanlan's Point. There he operated a hotel and raised his family until moving to a house on Beverly Street. He died in 1908 and was buried in the Necropolis Cemetery in Toronto. The famous athlete was the subject of *The Boy in Blue*, a 1986 Canadian motion picture starring Nicholas Cage.

Canada's preeminent sculler was eulogized in verse especially written for the dedication of his memorial statue in 1926:

No more we'll trust to fickle fame / The honour due to Hanlan's name,
The champion sculler of his time, / His laurels won in every clime.
No victor with Olympic crown / Brought his country such renown;
As if propelled by magic grace / His boat was foremost in the race.
The thrilling cheer we hear anew – / "Hanlan Wins – The Boy in Blue – "

The shout resounds from shore to shore / To hail the champion of the oar.
No more again let it be said, / "Canada forgets her glorious dead."

In sculpted bronze he'll live again / And take a place once more 'mong
men.
O'er island lake, lagoon and bay, / His noble spirit holds its sway
Like some Greek god returned to earth / To mark the place that gave
him birth.
By Lake Ontario's surging foam, / By his beloved island home:
But more than in the sculptor's art, / He lives in each Canadian's
heart.

❡ A large portrait of Hanlan painted in 1879 hangs in the Toronto City
Hall, on the northwest corner of Queen and Bay streets.

❡ **Embassy of Ireland,** 130 Albert Street, #1105.

❡ **Government House (Rideau Hall),** 1 Sussex Drive, at the entrance
to Rockcliffe Park.

This is the official residence of the Queen's representative, the governor general of Canada. Originally built as a villa in 1838, the house was
selected as an official residence by Charles Monck, Canada's first governor general, in 1864. Two years later Monck moved into the villa with his
family and supervised the subsequent construction, renovation, and furnishing which took place. The residence is surrounded by eighty-eight
acres of lawns, woods, and formal gardens.

Charles Monck was born in Templemore, Ireland, in 1819, the son of
the 3rd Viscount Monck. He received his education at Trinity College,
Dublin, and at the Inns of Court. Even before he was called to the bar, he
had become active in Irish politics, winning election to the House of Commons in 1852 as a Liberal. He later served as lord of the treasury in
Palmerston's administration. In the meantime he had succeeded to the
Monck viscountcy at the death of his father in 1849. Having inherited large
debts as well as titled estates, the thirty-year-old Monck was in need of
additional income, a problem which Palmerston helped solve by offering
the young aristocrat the governor generalship of British North America in
1861. (Monck later acknowledged that he had accepted the post "for the
money.")

Newly arrived in Quebec, Monck found the British colonies beset with
problems which he believed could be solved only through confederation.
The United States threatened war over the *Trent* affair and the use of Canadian territory by Confederate spies and agents, while the Fenian inva-
sions of 1866 threatened Canadian territorial integrity. To deal with these
challenges, Monck urged the government in London to create a unified
military system for the British colonies and worked for the eventual political confederation of the Canadian colonies. He accordingly attended
the confederation conferences in Charlottetown and Quebec in 1864 and

had the pleasure of participating in the debate on the British North American Act in the House of Lords three years later. He also took the lead in the surprisingly subdued ceremonies marking the new nation's inaugural on July 1, 1867, during which he took his oath of office and swore in the prime minister and the lieutenant governors.

After returning to Ireland, Monck served in several government posts as a member of the Church Temporalities and the National Education commissions, a commissioner of the new Irish Lands Acts, and lord lieutenant of County Dublin. When his wife died in 1892, he retired to his estates in Charville, County Wicklow.

§ Gardens open varied times April-October. Phone: 613-998-7113.

¶ National Gallery of Canada, 380 Sussex Drive.

Besides works by the European masters, this strikingly contemporary museum features eleven canvasses by *Paul Kane, whose work, according to J. Russell Harper, stands alone as a record of the early Canadian northwest. The works were commissioned by the Library of Parliament in 1851. (See Rocky Mountain House National Historic Park, Alberta.)

§ Open Victoria Day weekend-Thanksgiving, daily 10-6 (to 8 on Thursday); rest of the year, Wednesday-Sunday 10-5 (to 8 on Thursday). Phone: 613-990-1985 or 800-319-2787.

¶ Nellie McClung Plaque, Parliament Buildings, Parliament Hill.

The efforts of *Nellie Mooney McClung to open the Canadian Senate to women are commemorated by a plaque outside that chamber. (See Manitou, Manitoba.)

¶ O'Connor Street.

This street honors Daniel O'Connor, an emigrant from Wexford, Ireland, who arrived in Ottawa in 1827 and was treasurer of Carleton County from 1842 to 1858.

¶ O'Meara Street.

This street is named for *John O'Meara, a justice of the peace of Carleton County.

¶ Thomas D'Arcy McGee Memorial, on the west side of the Parliamentary Library on Parliament Hill.

The statue of this famous journalist, poet, and politician captures the Irish-born McGee in an oratorical pose, a fitting representation for the finest public speaker in Canadian politics in his time. The statue was sculpted by George William Hill. Cast in Belgium, the art work was prevented from being shipped to Canada by the German invasion of that small neutral country in World War I and was buried to prevent its capture. The statue was sent to Ottawa after the war.

Thomas D'Arcy McGee was born in 1825 in Carlingford, County Louth, Ireland. Because his only formal education was limited to what he received in a Catholic "hedge school," he relied heavily for his intellectual development on the major contemporary events and figures in Irish history. He was particularly stirred by Daniel O'Connell's campaign to repeal the union between Ireland and Britain and by the temperance crusade of Father Theobald Mathew (from whom he took the pledge, although he repeatedly failed in its observance).

Following his mother's death, the teenager embarked for North America, sailing from Wexford to Quebec aboard the *Leo*. Even as a boy of seventeen, he showed poetic promise in a composition he wrote en route. With a mixture of regret and hope, he apostrophized Wexford, his childhood haunt:

> Friend of my early days, my happiest hours,
> No more among the rocky wilds we'll stray,
> Or in the sunny meadows cull the flow'rs,
> Or while[,] with wondrous tales, the time away;
> With riper years come care and sorrow's sense,
> Yet meet we may again, please Providence!

After making his way to Boston, a chance circumstance conspired to bring the lad a convenient podium for his views. When asked to address the Boston Friends of Ireland during a Fourth of July celebration, he used the occasion to remind them of continued British tyranny in his native land. "The sufferings which the people of that unhappy country have endured at the hands of a heartless, bigoted, despotic government are well known to you. . . ," he orated. "Her people are born slaves, and bred in slavery from the cradle; they know not what freedom is." His remarks were received so well that the seventeen year old was offered a job on the *Boston Pilot*, the foremost Catholic newspaper in New England.

Although originally hired as the paper's traveling agent, within two years the young Irishman was made editor. While on the circuit collecting subscription fees and signing up subscribers, he gave lectures describing the repeal and temperance movements in Ireland. He also penned forty articles for the *Pilot* on the history of Irish literature. As editor he became a forceful defender of immigrant Irish Catholics against nativists and Protestants and urged his readers to support the cause of Irish nationality. With regard to the British North American colonies, he predicted that they would some day join their American neighbor in a political union. "One vast Federal Union will stretch from Labrador to Panama," he wrote. "A river like the St. Lawrence cannot safely be left in European hands. . . . Either by purchase, conquest, or stipulation, Canada must be yielded by Great Britain to this Republic."

Soon after he accepted a position with the *Freeman's Journal* in Dublin in 1845, McGee became involved with the Young Ireland movement. These Irish nationalists were attempting to make the people of Ireland aware of their unique cultural heritage as a prelude to self-government. In 1848 the newly married McGee was drawn into a plan for an Irish uprising and was arrested for sedition. Freed when charges were dropped, he fled to Scotland, hoping – but failing – to raise an army. After being recognized in Glasgow, he again fled for his life – first to England and then to Derry, where he embarked for the United States, disguised as a priest.

Once arrived in Philadelphia, McGee lost no time in publicizing the recent unrest in Ireland and Europe. In a public letter he laid the blame for the rebellion's failure at the feet of the Irish clergy and even went so far as to sign his name and the proud epithet "A Traitor to the British Government." He soon moved on to New York, where he started the *Nation*, a newspaper devoted to generating American support for the nationalist and liberal revolutions that had recently erupted in Europe. He quickly lost the support of his natural constituency, though, when he seemed to abandon his crusade for immediate Irish nationhood in favor of gradual reform. When two Irish republicans challenged him to a duel, the editor wisely left the city.

After moving to Boston and starting another newspaper, McGee made an additional reversal in his political expression. Through the pages of the

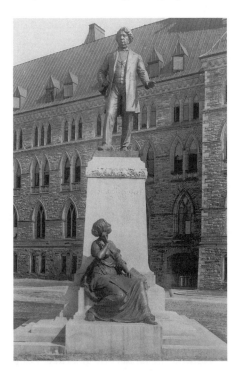

Thomas D'Arcy
McGee Memorial.
(Photo courtesy of the National
Archives of Canada. PA-034427.)

American Celt, he emphasized issues that affected the Irish in America and supported a campaign to naturalize Irish throughout New England. It was during this phase of his life that he wrote *A History of the Irish Settlers in North America*, a work that chronicled the contributions of the Irish to North American history. It was also at this time that he abandoned his anticlerical attacks, primarily because they were helping fuel the anti-Catholic campaign of American nativists. For the next four years he accordingly promoted Catholic interests in the United States and condemned the nationalism and revolutionary liberalism that he had so recently championed, branding them as threats to civilization and Christianity. By 1855 he had become a leader in the colonization movement that encouraged Irish Catholic immigrants to settle in the western United States, where it was hoped they would be able to retain their distinctive Catholic and Celtic culture.

When his colonization efforts were thwarted by the American hierarchy, McGee moved to Montreal. No longer an advocate of American annexation, he championed Canada as a place where the rights of Catholics were recognized. He also urged Irish emigrants to settle in Canada rather than in the United States. Through his editorials in the *New Era*, yet another of his publications, McGee insisted that the Irish had a right to representation in the Quebec Assembly, denounced the influence of the Orange Order, and outlined a program for what he called "a new nationality." In addition to economic development, a protective tariff, and the encouragement of immigration, he advocated economic cooperation between Canada and the Maritimes and envisioned a possible Canadian confederation in the future. In a unique constitutional proposal that allowed for Canadian sovereignty while maintaining a tie to Great Britain, he suggested that one of Queen Victoria's sons establish a Canadian dynasty in a "kingdom of the St. Lawrence."

McGee argued for his vision of Canada's future with his usual oratorical skill. "I look to the future of my adopted country with hope, though not without anxiety," he said in a speech to the legislative assembly. "I see in the not remote distance, one great nationality bound, like the shield of Achilles, by the blue rim of Ocean. I see it quartered into many communities, each disposing of its internal affairs, but all bound together by free institutions, free intercourse, and free commerce. I see within the rounds of that shield the peaks of the Western Mountains and the crests of the Eastern waves, the winding Assinibone, the five-fold lakes, the St. Lawrence, the Ottawa, the Saguenay, the St. John, and the basin of Minas. By all these flowing waters in all the valleys they fertilize, in all the cities they visit in their courses, I see a generation of industrious, contented, moral men, free in name and in fact – men capable of maintaining, in peace and in war, a constitution worthy of such a country!"

McGee's literary skills were also evident in the large number of poems which he composed. Written as either ballads or lyrics, many of them told about Irish heroes and saints or expressed his personal feelings about his native land. In tone the lyrics ranged from pride to anger to despair. In "The Exile's Request," for instance, he boasted and mourned at the same time ("For I was born in Ireland – I glory in the name – / I weep for all her sorrows, I remember well her fame!"). But in "The Parting from Ireland" the tone is hopeless:

> God! it is a maddening prospect thus to see this storied land
> Like some wretched culprit writhing in a strong avenger's hand –
> Kneeling, foaming, weeping, shrieking, woman-weak and woman-
>   loud –
> Better, better, Mother Ireland! we had laid you in your shroud!

By 1864 McGee was a leader in the confederation movement and a determined opponent of the Irish Republican Brotherhood. While minister of agriculture and immigration in the Conservative government, he was a delegate to the Charlottetown and Quebec conferences that proposed Canadian confederation. His animosity to the I.R.B., meanwhile, was based not only on his opposition to the Fenians' plan to invade Canada but also on his preference for Irish self-government within the British Empire rather than outright independence. His comment during a visit to Ireland that his earlier career as a rebel had been "the follies of one and twenty" caused him to be branded a traitor to his native land. He was subsequently expelled from the St. Patrick's Society in Montreal and lost the Irish vote in his successful bid for a seat in the provincial legislature. And it was generally believed that his assassination on April 7, 1868, was part of a Fenian conspiracy. Yet, although Patrick James Whelan, an Irish immigrant, was found guilty of the assassination and hanged, he was never accused by the Crown of being a Fenian.

¶ A plaque noting the assassination is located on Sparks Street. McGee lived in a boarding house at #71 Sparks Street and was killed by a .32-calibre bullet in the neck while opening the door with his key. (The original site is now a pedestrian mall.)

Patrick James Whelan, the convicted assassin, had been born in Ireland in 1840 and had been apprenticed to a tailor at the age of fourteen. About ten years later he had emigrated to Canada and proceeded to work for a succession of tailoring companies in Quebec, Montreal, and Ottawa. Along the way he had acquired a fondness for drinking, dancing, and shooting.

Within twenty hours of the assassination, Whelan was arrested when he was found to be in possession of a .32-calibre revolver. The case was prosecuted by Peter O'Reilly, a friend of McGee's and a native of Westport, County Mayo. O'Reilly expressed his determination: "God forbid that the man who committed the foul deed should not suffer the just punishment consequent upon his crime. The people of this country desire to see the murderer punished; the press unanimously agree that every effort should be made to lay bare the murder, and if I have been instrumental in drawing it to light I shall go down in my grave satisfied that I have tracked the felon who killed D'Arcy McGee."

Newspaper coverage of the subsequent trial received international attention and was noted for its details. It was reported, for example, that Whelan – the "tailor with the red whiskers" – made his first court appearance wearing a white vest, garnet cuff links, and a small green rosette. To the expected verdict of guilty, he replied: "Now I am held to be a black assassin. And my blood runs cold. But I am innocent. I never took that man's blood."

Although the verdict was carried to two appellate courts, each appeal was rejected. To the end Whelan denied that he was the assassin, but shortly before his execution he admitted that he did "know that man who shot Mr. McGee." On the day of his execution (February 11, 1869), Whelan addressed a crowd of about 5,000 spectators from the scaffold.

PETERBOROUGH

¶ **Irish Settlers Monument,** east of Water Street near Peterborough Square Mall and the Ministry of Natural Resources.

The plaque on this large stone monument commemorates the arrival in 1825 of a group of Irish settlers to what is now Peterborough, named after the Canadian official who arranged for their emigration. The memorial was unveiled in 1975 by James Flavin, the Irish ambassador to Canada at the time, and Fred O'Grady, a descendant of one of the families that arrived in 1825.

The marker reads: "This plaque erected in honour of nearly 2000 Irish settlers who sailed from Cork Harbour, under the leadership of the Honourable Peter Robinson, and arrived in this area in the Autumn of 1825, settling in the Town of Peterborough and the surrounding townships."

Robinson, who himself was not of Irish ancestry, had been enlisted in this emigration project by the British undersecretary of state for the colonies. The latter believed that ridding Ireland of its dispossessed tenant farmers would be the first step in implementing agricultural reforms throughout that island country. Robinson had led his first group out of Ireland in 1823, when 568 émigrés sailed from Cork bound either for enlistment in the Canadian military or for the Lanark settlements in Upper Canada. Although the members of the Ontario government publicly supported the undersecretary's plan, they privately regarded the Irish Catholics as the least desirable of British subjects.

The second phase of Robinson's emigration plan occurred in 1825, when 2,024 settlers embarked from Ireland in nine ships. Some of the emigrants died either en route or soon after their arrival in Quebec. The newcomers – usually in small groups – sailed by steamer to Montreal and then traveled overland to Lachine, where bateaux awaited to take them to Prescott. After arriving in Kingston, they lived in a tent village while they waited for Robinson. With the help of a guide, their leader had in the meantime selected a site at the head of Otonabee River, a location which offered excellent land for cultivation and was accessible by a navigable river. After additional hardships en route, the emigrants at last settled in this area, originally known as Scott's Plains but renamed Peterborough for Robinson.

¶ **Robinson Headquarters Site,** the corner of Water and Simcoe streets.

A circular plaque on the exterior of the Bank of Montreal notes that Peter Robinson's headquarters stood on this site during the early days of the Irish settlement.

¶ **Robinson Settlement Marker,** Water Street near Simcoe Street.

This historic sign summarizes the history of Peterborough's founding as a colony of Irish emigrants: "The Robinson Settlement 1825. In an effort to alleviate poverty and unemployment in Ireland, the British government in 1825 sponsored a settlement of Irish emigrants in the Newcastle District of Upper Canada. Peter Robinson, later that province's Commissioner of Crown Lands, was appointed superintendent and, in May, 2024 persons sailed from Cork. A few settled elsewhere and disease thinned their numbers, but by September the remainder were gathered in temporary shelters on the site of Peterborough. Under Robinson's supervision, free rations were distributed until November, 1826, cabins erected and 1878 settlers successfully established on land in the Peterborough region."

Some of these Irish immigrants went on to settle the townships of Ennismore, Emily, Douro, Smith, Asphodel, and Otonabee. The homes of several of these early settlers can still be seen throughout Peterborough and Victoria counties: the Dan Cadigan House, the John Scollard House, the Bernard Harrington House, the Jerry Gorman House, the Maurice O'Connor House, and the Pat and Michael Crough houses (all in Ennismore Township); the Michael Costelo House, the Thomas Flynn House, the Edward Morrissey House, and the John Scully House (all in Emily Township).

¶ A historical marker next to St. James Anglican Church in East Emily honors the memory of Thomas and Esther Carew and the other Irish immigrants who came to this area in 1825. The plaque reads: "In Memory of Thomas and Esther Carew of Farrahy, County Cork, Ireland, who with their eight children settled immediately west of this place on lot 21, concession 6, Emily Township in 1825 and are buried in this cemetery, and also of the company of over 2000 men, women and children of which they were part, mainly from counties Cork and Tipperary, Ireland, known as the Robinson immigration, who settled in the townships of Emily and Ennismore, helping to found the counties of Victoria and Peterborough." The plaque was placed here in 1968 by the Honourable Leslie Frost, the premier of Ontario, whose wife was a descendant of the Carews.

RIDGEWAY

¶ **Fort Erie Historical Museum,** 402 Ridge Road (west of Fort Erie)

One of the museum's most important exhibits is a collection of twenty-two watercolor paintings depicting the battle of Ridgeway, the climax of the Fenian invasion of Canada in June 1866. The paintings are the work of Alexander von Erikson, a Civil War artist who observed the battle first hand. The museum has other exhibits on the Fenians and their efforts to gain Irish independence.

§ Open mid June-Labour Day, daily 9-5. Fee. Phone: 905-894-5322.

¶ **Ridgeway Battlefield Museum,** Highway 3 (Garrison Road), east of Ridge Road.

The museum is located in a cabin that stood on the edge of the battle-field during the military encounter between local Canadians and invading Fenian troops in June 1866. The exhibits in the museum include displays about the Fenian raid. At the time of the battle, Ridgeway was a village of twenty houses, two taverns, a flour mill, and a few stores.

The initial Fenian invasion force was led by John O'Neill, a native of County Monaghan, Ireland. During the Civil War he had moved up the ranks in the Union army and left the service as captain of the 17th U.S. Colored Infantry. Early on the morning of June 1, 1866, two Fenian detachments of 600 men crossed the Niagara River from a point north of Buffalo, New York. (Another 200 were too drunk to get into the boats.) Within thirty minutes they had raised the green Fenian standards on Canadian soil. In the meantime 20,000 Canadians were assembling in response to the government's call for 14,000 volunteers.

The second prong of the Fenian assault was under the command of Colonel Owen Starr, who led a force to capture Fort Erie, a town of about 600 inhabitants. Starr's intention to seize the Erie & Ontario Railroad as well as the local livestock was frustrated, however, when the residents scattered their animals (including the horses which the invaders had hoped to use) and alerted the railroad about the invaders. Railroad officials quickly combined all rolling stock into a single train and ordered it moved west, away from the expected encounter. Although the Fenians found a few horses and received additional weapons, the arrival of more men and supplies was prevented by the sudden appearance of a U.S. gunboat.

Despite their setback the Fenians issued a proclamation to the people of British North America: "We come among you as foes of British rule in

Ireland," it announced. "We have taken up the sword to strike down the oppressor's rod, to deliver Ireland from the tyrant, the despoiler, the robber. . . . We have no issue with the people of these Provinces, and we wish to have none but the most friendly relations. Our weapons are for the oppressors of Ireland. Our bows shall be directed only against the power of England. . . . We do not propose to divest you of a solitary right you now enjoy. . . . We are here neither as murderers, nor robbers, for plunder and spoliation. We are here as the Irish army of liberation. . . . To Irishmen throughout these Provinces we appeal in the name of seven centuries of British iniquity and Irish misery and suffering . . . to stretch forth the hand of brotherhood in the holy cause of fatherland, and smite the tyrant where we can. . . ."

The Canadian military command, meanwhile, had decided that its forces were to meet at Stephensville the next morning. En route to that location Lieutenant Colonel Alfred Booker arrived at Ridgeway with 840 Canadians. As Booker began to lead his poorly provisioned men north to Stephensville for the planned rendezvous, they were surprised by O'Neill and his men but succeeded in forcing them to retreat.

The Canadian advantage that morning slipped away when the appearance of several mounted Fenians along Ridge Road caused the Canadian vanguard to fear a cavalry attack. When the Canadians formed a square in order to repel the expected Fenian charge, they came under a barrage of enemy bullets from O'Neill's troops. The Canadians retreated a mile and a half south, pursued to Ridgeway by Fenians under Starr. One eyewitness compared the Canadian rout to the Union retreat at Bull Run seven years before. The Canadians lost ten killed and thirty-seven wounded, compared to the Fenians' eight dead and sixteen wounded. It was perhaps during this engagement that Patrick O'Reilly, a Fenian from Buffalo, was wounded and sought aid at a nearby farmhouse. The owner's daughter cleaned and bandaged the man's wounds and hid him in a barn until he could escape. O'Reilly later returned – disguised as a peddler – and eloped with the farmer's daughter.

Fearful that the larger Canadian unit would arrive, O'Neill retreated east to Fort Erie and attacked a small Canadian force that had arrived there. When the invaders charged with fixed bayonets, the Canadians retreated to the steam tug that had transported them to Fort Erie. The Fenians encamped in the ruins of Old Fort Erie that night and waited for promised reinforcements from Buffalo. When it appeared that they would not be rescued, the Fenians abandoned their camp early on June 3 and recrossed the Niagara River on two canal boats. An armed U.S. tug overtook the returning raiders and forced them to surrender. The glorious adventure came to an inglorious end when 700 Fenians were taken into custody by American authorities.

Editorial reaction to the Fenian raids was predictably harsh, even from newspapers sympathetic to the cause of Irish freedom. On June 5 the *St. Paul Pioneer* editorialized: "However much we may delight to see the English ox gored . . . justice demands that the United States authorities shall prevent further movements in our borders to attack a nation with whom we are at peace." The *New York Times* was more direct, expressing the hope that "every ruffian that crossed the frontier might be straightway caught and hung." Even the *Irish Canadian* – Toronto's pro-Fenian publication – admitted the absurdity of recent events and concluded that the possession of Canada by the Fenians "could not advance an iota the cause of Ireland's freedom from misrule."

The invasion of Ontario in 1866 was part of a larger plan devised by *Thomas Sweeny, a Civil War major general and the Fenian commander-in-chief. According to this strategy, the attacks in Ontario would divert the British from Quebec, thereby allowing a Fenian force of 16,000 troops to cross into Canada from Vermont and seize Quebec. Such attempts were made in 1866 and 1870, although they were even more disastrous than those in Ontario. (See Franklin, St. Albans, and Sheldon Junction, Vermont.)

§ Open mid June-Labour Day, daily 12:30-5. Fee. Phone: 905-894-3433.

TORONTO

¶ Carling O'Keefe Breweries of Canada Ltd., 175 Bloor Street East.

Until 1973 this Toronto beer factory was known as Canadian Breweries Ltd., created in the 1930s with the merger of the O'Keefe Brewing Company and Carling's Brewery. The former enterprise had been founded in 1862 by Eugene O'Keefe as the first in Canada to produce lager beer.

O'Keefe was a native of Bandon, County Cork, and had come to Canada with his parents in 1832, at the age of five. After the family settled in Toronto, Eugene began a career in the banking industry, working first as a bookkeeper for the Toronto Savings Bank and becoming by 1901 the president of the Home Savings and Loan Association. Three years later he was elected a member of the Toronto branch of the United Irish League. For his philanthropy toward numerous Catholic institutions in the city – including gifts of $180,000 toward the construction of St. Monica's Church and St. Augustine's Seminary – he was appointed a papal chamberlain.

Until 1996 O'Keefe's name was perpetuated in the O'Keefe Centre for the Performing Arts in Toronto, a 3,000-seat auditorium that was the home of the Canadian Opera Company and the National Ballet of Canada. Originally built by the O'Keefe Brewing Company, the center opened in 1960 and was operated by the company until 1968, when it was turned over to the Metropolitan Toronto Council. The center's name was changed in 1996 to the Hummingbird Centre (1 Front Street East).

¶ Enoch Turner Schoolhouse, 106 Trinity Street, 1 block south of King

Street.

Constructed in 1848 by a brewer named Enoch Turner, this was the city's first free school and was attended for the most part by poor Irish immigrants. The building is part of a living-history program.

§ Open Monday-Friday 10-4. Closed holidays. Fee. Inquire about accessibility to the public at 416-863-0010.

℥ Royal Ontario Museum, 100 Queen's Park.

Among the six million pieces in Canada's largest museum are 100 paintings by *Paul Kane. The canvasses represent a cycle of works commissioned by George William Allan for $20,000. The museum also holds most of the sketches that Kane made during his field trips. Some modern art critics declare Kane's sketches superior to his completed canvasses, primarily because of the former's greater intimacy and brilliance of color. (See Rocky Mountain House National Historic Park, Alberta.)

§ Open Monday-Saturday 10-6 (to 8 on Tuesday), Sunday 11-6. Closed January 1 and December 25. Fee. Phone: 416-586-8000.

WILLIAMSTOWN

℥ Williamstown County Library, off Main Street

The east wing of the library dates from about 1790, when it was built as the home of *Sir John Johnson, one of the Loyalists who settled here in 1784 after leaving New York. The original wing is a log structure with a red roof and five bays. In 1814 Johnson presented the people of the district with twelve acres of land to be used as a fairground. The property is still used for the Williamstown Fair, the oldest regularly operated county fair in Canada. The annual event is held in August.

Johnson, an army officer, colonial official, and landowner, was born in 1741 near Amsterdam, New York, where his father, a native of Ireland, had a manor house. (See Fort Johnson, New York.) At thirteen the son served under his father, Britain's agent to the Six Nation Indians, in the battle against the French at Lake George, New York. He attended most of his father's conferences with the natives and in 1764 led an Indian expedition into the Ohio Valley following Pontiac's uprising. During a grand tour of the British Isles the next two years, he visited his father's brother at the family seat in Smithtown, County Meath, Ireland. In letters home he wrote that he liked Ireland better than England and that he spent four weeks at Newtown Castle Byrne, four miles from Dublin and sixty yards from the seashore. "[W]ee have a Very pretty Garden to walk in . . . ," he wrote, "Which is directly over the Sea & about Seventy foot high, with pretty Zig-Zag Gravel Walks, down to the Sea Shore & a Couple of handsome Grotto's in the face of the Bank, in Which I spend many an hour in Contemplation, & from which I often descend to Bath[e] in the Sea, for

Which purpose Numbers from Dublin and other places resort here. . . ."
While in Britain he was knighted by George III.

After returning to his father's estate at Fort Johnson, New York, the
"American Knight" assumed the life of a seigneur. At first he lived with
his common-law wife and their two children, but he eventually followed
his father's wish that he marry into the New York aristocracy. On the elder Johnson's death in 1774, the son inherited his father's baronetcy and
almost 200,000 acres of land. It was then that he and his wife, Mary Watts,
took up residence at Johnson Hall in Johnstown, New York [*q.v.*].

During the American Revolution Johnson's sympathies naturally lay
with the British cause, and as major general of the district militia he did
his best to keep the Mohawk Valley loyal. Failing in this attempt and fleeing American troops sent to arrest him, he escaped to Montreal, where he
proceeded to recruit a battalion of the King's Royal Regiment of New York.
He and his troops later defeated the Americans at Oriskany and denied
supplies to the Continental Army by laying waste the Mohawk Valley. He
paid a huge price for his loyalty to the Crown, however, seeing all his
American estates confiscated.

After the war Johnson was named to two major positions: brigadier
general and superintendent of Indian Affairs for British North America.
In this latter post he was an unfailing advocate of the Indians' rights and
a protector of their interests. When the Native Americans feared that the
British were about to sacrifice them in peace negotiations with the Americans, for instance, Johnson allayed their fears and prevented them from
engaging in hostilities that would have only worsened their situation.
Johnson was also in charge of allocating land to the Loyalist veterans and
refugees in Upper Canada.

Toward the end of the century Johnson moved into the palatial Chateau de Longueuil on Rue St. Paul in Montreal. On his 84,000-acre seigneury
at Monnoir, meanwhile, he built a beautiful manor house. He was once
described as "very lively in countenance & speaks rapidly Very
gentlemanlike manners, & with all that a kind of wildness, as if he wished
to appear a character tinctured with the habits and the intercourse he has
had with the Indian tribes." Johnson's funeral in 1830 was attended by
300 Indians, one of whom eulogized him as a "friend and fellow warrior."
He was buried on his estate at Monnoir.

WOODSTOCK

¶ **Joseph Boyle Burial Site,** Presbyterian Cemetery, Vansittart Avenue
at Devonshire Street.

This large monument marks the grave of *Joseph Boyle, one of the
Yukon's early entrepreneurs and a military adventurer known as the "Savior of Romania." (See Dawson City, The Yukon.)

PRINCE EDWARD ISLAND

Prior to the mid nineteenth century, Irish immigrants to Prince Edward Island had arrived in three successive waves. The first – between 1767 and 1810 – paralleled the first Scottish settlement of the island, while the next influx (1810-1835) brought emigrants from Kilkenny, Tipperary, and Waterford counties. Between 1830 and 1850, approximately 4,000 Irish arrived from Donegal, Monaghan, and Tyrone, until by the middle of the century the island counted 6,400 Irish natives among its residents.

ALBERTON

¶ **Alberton Museum,** Highway 12 (Church Street).

Among the museum's exhibits are items relating to the silver fox fur industry, including a plaque commemorating Charles Dalton and Robert Oulton, pioneers in the fox-breeding industry in this area. After thriving for four decades, the industry declined during the depression of the 1930s.

Dalton, who was born in 1850 in Norway, Prince Edward Island, was the son of Patrick and Margaret (McCarthy) Dalton. Although Charles's interest in hunting and trapping dated from his youth, it was not until the 1870s that he bought a pair of silver foxes with the intention of breeding them. After selling the family homestead at Norway, he bought a house and ranch in Tignish, where he established a drug store. When this business failed, he formed a partnership in 1900 with Robert Oulton of New Brunswick, hoping to breed foxes on a small island which the latter man owned in Cascumpeque Harbour. Despite the success of their venture, the partnership was dissolved in 1911 when Oulton decided to return to New Brunswick.

With his share of the enterprise's foxes, Dalton moved back to his Tignish ranch, where he served as president of the Charles Dalton Silver Black Fox Company. Within two years, perhaps anticipating the collapse of the fox-breeding industry, he sold his ranch as well as the remainder of his holdings, a move that allowed him to retire as a self-professed "millionaire." With the considerable wealth which he had accumulated in the fur business, he was a generous patron of educational and medical facilities throughout the province. Besides donating $55,000 to St. Dunstan's University for the completion of Dalton Hall, he contributed $60,000 for the erection of the tuberculosis sanitarium at North Wiltshire.

Dalton's first attempt to win elective office failed, but in 1912 he was elected as a Conservative to represent Prince County in the local legislature. At one point he served as a member without portfolio in the Mathieson ministry. Although a Roman Catholic, he was irregular in his observance. (When asked why he did not attend mass regularly, he replied: "See that tallest tree over there. Well, that's my church.") Nevertheless, he received a papal knighthood in the Order of St. Gregory the Great for his "great benevolence towards Catholic institutions." He was also a member of the Knights of Columbus and the Ancient Order of Hibernians. From 1930 to 1933 – while in his eighties – he was the lieutenant governor of Prince Edward Island but died before completing his term.

Dalton's obituary noted his interest in literature and mathematics and his penchant for devising mathematical problems for his friends to solve. The obituary also highlighted his proverbial kindness of heart: "He was one of nature's gentlemen, and never would willingly hurt the feelings of anyone, or permit an unkindness or discourtesy to be committed in his presence."

§ Open mid June-Labour Day, Monday-Saturday 9:30-5:30, Sunday 1-5; rest of the year, by appointment. Fee. Phone: 902-853-4048 or 853-3372 (off season).

CARLETON COVE

This sheltered recess was named for *Sir Guy Carleton, the commander-in-chief of British forces in North America. (See Cape Diamond, Quebec City.)

CHARLOTTETOWN

¶ Province House National Historic Site, at University and Grafton streets.

This sandstone neoclassical structure was erected in 1847 to accommodate the island's colonial legislature. Here in September 1864 delegates from Prince Edward Island, New Brunswick, Nova Scotia, and Upper and Lower Canada (now Quebec and Ontario) met to consider the formation of a Canadian confederation. One of the delegates, Thomas D'Arcy McGee, was a native of Ireland. (See Thomas D'Arcy McGee Memorial, Ottawa.)

The Charlottetown Conference, as the meeting was known, was followed by a similar gathering in Quebec the next month. McGee also attended that second conference, as did Edward Whelan (another Irishman) and Ambrose Shea (the son of an Irish immigrant). A plaque in Whelan's memory is located on the grounds of the Province House.

The two conferences led to the signing of the British North American Act in London in 1867 and the birth of modern Canada on July 1 of that year. Although New Brunswick, Nova Scotia, Quebec, and Ontario joined the Confederation upon its creation, Prince Edward Island did not become a member until 1873.

Today the Confederation Chamber, where Canada's "Fathers of Confederation" deliberated in 1864, contains original furnishings. During July and August local actors known as the Fathers of Confederation Players present "living history" tableaux at Province House. The building is still the seat of the provincial legislature.

§ Open to visitors July-August, daily 9-8; June and September-mid October, daily 9-6; rest of the year, Monday-Friday 9-5. Phone: 902-566-7626.

• Edward Whelan was born in Ballina, County Mayo, in 1824 and at the age of six immigrated to Halifax, Nova Scotia, with his mother. His first employment there seems to have been as a printer's devil for Joseph Howe. By 1842 the young Irishman was editor of the *Register*, a Liberal newspaper that appealed to its Irish Catholic readership by calling for the repeal of the political union between Ireland and Britain. After only a year, though, he left the *Register* and moved to Charlottetown, where he announced his intention to publish semiweekly. In the pages of the *Palladium* he continued his advocacy of repeal but broadened his appeal by attacking the injustice of the land tenure system, or what he called the "Landocracy System." Severe financial problems caused him to discontinue the paper two years later. In 1846, at the age of only twenty-two, he was elected to the Assembly, a position to which he was reelected over the next two decades.

Fresh from his electoral victory, Whelan took steps to inaugurate the *Examiner*, a newspaper that was noticeably milder in tone but no less dedicated to the Liberal reform agenda. He accordingly used his paper to urge passage of legislation extending the franchise, providing for free public education, and reforming the land laws. On one major issue, however, Whelan disagreed with his Liberal allies. Although he had earlier expressed doubts about the prospects for Canadian confederation, by 1863 he was an enthusiastic advocate, claiming that "a union will relieve us from the provoking intermeddling of the Colonial Office in our local legislation. . . ." In 1865 he published *The Union of the British Provinces*, an account of the Charlottetown and Quebec conferences of 1864.

Although Whelan's denunciation of Fenianism and his support for confederation were probably the major reasons for his electoral defeat in 1867, he himself attributed it to the influence of Bishop Peter MacIntyre. According to this interpretation, Whelan had fallen out of the prelate's graces for several reasons. One of them was the fact that in advocating confederation Whelan had allied himself with the island's most notorious anti-Catholic politician. In addition, Whelan's fondness for "the drink" and his marriage in the presence of an Anglican clergyman antagonized the bishop. And, finally, in promoting a secular educational system for the island, Whelan blamed denominational schools for perpetuating national and religious prejudices. He had also imprudently said that "clergymen are generally the most incompetent persons in the world to have anything to do with the administration of secular affairs."

• Ambrose Shea was born in St. John's, Newfoundland, in 1811, the son of a mercantile agent from Carrick on Sur, Ireland. The son followed in his father's commercial footsteps and enjoyed a successful business career. In 1850 he entered the Newfoundland Assembly, which he led as Speaker from 1855 to 1861. As mentioned above, he was sent as a provincial delegate to the Quebec Conference in 1864. Three decades later he was the Newfoundland commissioner to the Fisheries Exchange in London. The *Halifax Herald* at one time called him "the ablest politician in Newfoundland." Following his selection as Knight of the Cross of St. Michael and St. George, Sir Ambrose became governor and commander-in-chief of the Bahama Islands in 1887.

CONNOLLY ISLAND

This island in Malpeque Bay was named for the Irish politician Thomas Connolly (1738-1803), the son of the first member of Parliament elected for Ballyshannon, Ireland. From 1759 to 1784 the younger Connolly was a member of the British House of Commons. He also represented County Londonderry in the Irish Commons for three decades.

FINLEY POINT

This prominence bears the name of Patrick Finley, a native of County Kilkenny, Ireland, who came to Prince Edward Island from Newfoundland about 1832. He died in 1875.

O'LEARY

This village of fewer than 1,000 inhabitants (fifty minutes from Summerside) is reputedly named for Michael O'Leary, an Irish farmer who settled in this area in the 1830s. After failing to find any of his relatives when he visited Ireland in 1858, he returned to Canada. He reportedly drowned after being accidentally pushed off a wharf in Halifax.

To residents of Prince Edward Island, the village is famous as Canada's largest producer of potatoes. Today, if the autumn harvest is threatened by an early frost, local farmers can be seen gathering their crop at night, their tractor headlights illuminating the fields.

¶ **Prince Edward Island Potato Museum,** 22 Parkview Drive (in Centennial Park, off Main Street).

Visitors interested in the impact of the potato on both Irish and local Canadian history should find a stop at this museum especially worthwhile.

§ Open mid June-August, Monday-Friday 9-4, Saturday 11-4, Sunday

2-4. Fee. Phone: 902-859-2039.

SUMMERSIDE

¶ **International Fox Museum and Hall of Fame,** 286 Fitzroy Street.
   Through photographs and exhibits the museum details the story of fox farming, at one time the main industry on Prince Edward Island. The Hall of Fame honors pioneers in the industry, including *Charles Dalton and Robert Oulton. (See Alberton, Prince Edward Island.)
   § Open May-September, Monday-Saturday 9-5. Fee. Phone: 902-436-2400.

TIGNISH

¶ **Tignish Museum,** School and Maple streets.
   Originally a school built in 1930 through the beneficence of *Charles Dalton, a lieutenant governor of Prince Edward Island, the museum commemorates his career as a political leader and a pioneer in the island's silver fox fur industry. (See Alberton, Prince Edward Island.)
   § Open July-August, Monday-Friday 10-6, Sunday 1-6. Fee. Phone: 902-882-2488.

   ¶ Dalton is buried in the Catholic cemetery across the road from Sts. Simon and Jude Catholic Church (at Church and Maple streets).

WEST POINT

¶ **Cape Wolfe,** north on Highway 14, on the western end of the island.
   According to a disputed tradition, it was here that the British commander *General James Wolfe landed in 1759 during his campaign to dislodge the French from Canada. (See James Wolfe Statue, Quebec City, Quebec.)

QUEBEC

BAIE-COMEAU

❡ **Robert R. McCormick Statue,** Place la Salle, near the Donahue Paper Company.

This community of 26,000 was initially settled as a pulp and newsprint milling town. The mill was erected in 1936 by publisher *Robert R. McCormick as a source of paper for his New York and Chicago newspapers. The statue in his honor depicts him exploring the area by canoe. McCormick was the grandnephew of the famous inventor *Cyrus McCormick. (See Wheaton, Illinois.)

CARLETON

The name of this town of almost 3,000 residents was originally a Micmac Indian word meaning "place of many herons," but it was changed to honor Sir Guy Carleton, the Irish-born governor of Canada during the second half of the eighteenth century. (See Rue Carleton, Quebec City.)

DANVILLE

❡ **Timothy O'Hea Memorial,** Daniel Johnson Street (in front of the town hall).

The plaque on this stone memorial recalls the heroism of Timothy O'Hea, a soldier who single-handedly averted an explosive situation and for his valor received the Victoria Cross.

Although little is known of O'Hea's early life, he was born in Bantry, County Cork, Ireland, and in 1866 accompanied his military unit, the Prince Consort's Own Rifle Brigade, to Canada. During the Fenian uprising that year, he and three other soldiers were guarding a shipment of munitions attached to a passenger train carrying 800 German immigrants. When the train passed through Danville on its way to the site of military action on Lake Erie, someone discovered that the munitions car was on fire. Immediately seizing the keys to the car from the sergeant in charge, O'Hea opened the door and for almost an hour fought the blaze by himself until it was extinguished. When he received the Victoria Cross six months later, his was the first instance in which that honor was bestowed for service within Canada and for an act of bravery in peacetime. He later moved to Australia, where he died of thirst while trying to locate possible survivors of an earlier expedition. His body is buried at Nockatunga station in Queensland.

MONTMAGNY

¶ **Grosse Ile and the Irish Memorial,** in the St. Lawrence River.

Between 1815 and 1937 this isolated island was the major quarantine station for European immigrants suffering from infectious diseases. It is also the burial site of thousands of Irish immigrants who died of cholera in 1832 and of typhus, ship fever, and starvation while fleeing the Great Famine in 1847. Future development of the site will highlight its Irish connection and will focus on the mass graves of the Irish famine victims, the Celtic Cross (erected in 1909), and the Lazaretto, a long wooden shed that is the only remaining hospital from 1847. Some of the other historic buildings on the site are being restored.

The tragedy of 1847 unfolded as 110,000 Irish emigrants sailed up the St. Lawrence River in an armada of merchantmen appropriately dubbed "coffin ships." Thousands of refugees had already died en route, and thousands more perished either aboard ship while the vessels were in quarantine at Grosse Ile or in the hastily erected tents and sheds that served as hospitals. Despite the efforts of Dr. George Douglas and a team of clergymen, lay workers, and other physicians, the death rate was staggering. (Between 5,000 and 15,000 Irish victims are buried in the mass grave on the island.) Douglas himself contracted typhus, and among the dead were four other doctors, five Catholic priests, three Anglican clergymen, and forty-two lay volunteers.

Celtic Cross in honor of the Irish typhoid victims of 1847-48. (Photo courtesy of Grosse Ile and the Irish Memorial National Historic Site.)

In testimony before a committee of the Assembly, Dr. Douglas described the harrowing conditions at Grosse Ile during that fateful summer of 1847. An English translation of the French transcript follows: "Doctor Douglas declared that the bodies were dragged from the hold of the ships by means of hooks and that the authorities had to pay [$4.86] for each corpse thus dragged and carried to the cemetery located a few steps from the bank, on the west side of Grosse Ile. There they dug trenches three feet in depth . . . and placed the coffins – two of one upon the other – of those who died while ascending the river or at the hospitals on the island. With this double range of coffins, there remained no more than six or seven inches of earth to cover them. An army of rats, having come down from the ships in the roadstead, took possession of the field of the dead, dug thousands of holes, and began to gnaw at the dead bodies. The authorities on the island, fearing with reason that these thousands of bodies covered only by a light coating of earth, and of whom several were rendered almost naked by the rats, would produce a pestilence, ordered that thousands of cart-loads of earth gathered on the surrounding hills be carried [to the graves]. Thus one avoids a new epidemic and the bodies of the poor Irish were sheltered from the attacks of the rodents."

In the fall of 1847, Dr. Douglas and eighteen of the medical officers who had assisted him the previous summer erected a monument to the victims of the typhus, both the Irish emigrants and the physicians who also succumbed to the fever "in the faithful discharge of their duty upon the sick." The names of the medical officers are inscribed on the south side of the monument: Dr. Benson (of Dublin), Dr. Alex. Pinet, Dr. Alfred Malihiot, and Dr. John Jameson.

Sixty years later, in 1909, the Ancient Order of Hibernians erected a Celtic cross in honor of the Irish victims of typhoid fever in 1847-48. The granite cross, almost thirty feet in height, stands atop a seventeen-foot-high pedestal. An inscription on the south side of the pedestal reads: "Sacred to the memory of thousands of Irish immigrants, who, to preserve the faith, suffered hunger and exile in 1847-48 and stricken with fever ended here their sorrowful pilgrimage." The north side records the names of the priests who ministered to the typhus victims. The clerical list is a mixture of both French and Irish names, the latter being Moylan, McGauran, Nelligan, Bailey, McQuire, O'Reilly, Kerrigan, O'Grady, Horan, Dunn, and Power. Besides the five priests who died of the fever, another thirteen contracted the disease.

§ Guided tours are available May-October. Phone: 418-248-9196 or 800-463-5643. The island is accessible only by commercial boat. Phone: 418-259-2140 or 418-248-7977 (late September-late June) or 888-476-7734.

MONTREAL

During the early 1820s the Irish population in the city increased considerably, as workmen arrived to take jobs on the docks or on construction sites in the city. At that early date they lived in Griffintown, an area to the west of Old Montreal that was often flooded when the St. Lawrence River was blocked by ice jams. By 1831 the increased numbers required the use of a second church, a necessity that led to the reopening of the Récollet church on Notre Dame Street for the use of Irish Catholics in the western and central sections of the city. A few years later the Irish organized the St. Patrick's Society, founded for benevolent and national purposes and originally including Irishmen of all religious denominations. When the enlarged Récollet church became inadequate, plans were launched to erect St. Patrick's Church, which was dedicated in 1847. (See St. Patrick's Church below.)

The Irish generally found themselves in politically uncomfortable surroundings, tugged for their loyalty by the Catholic French and the Protestant British. In December 1857 the city's Irish Catholics gathered to elect a representative to the Assembly of Lower Canada. The Irish, whose numbers in the recent census entitled them to name one of Montreal's three legislative delegates, duly selected *Thomas D'Arcy McGee. While some of the Irish later supported the efforts of the mostly American Fenians to invade Canada – and thereby force Britain to grant Irish independence – most followed McGee's lead and favored the confederation of the British North America colonies into the country of Canada.

❡ **Basilica of Notre-Dame-de-Montréal,** on the Place d'Armes at 116 Rue Notre-Dame.

Regarded as one of the most outstanding churches in French Canada, Notre Dame was completed in 1829, shortly after the death of its designer, James O'Donnell. The basilica reflects the English Gothic style favored by O'Donnell, whose remains are buried under the church.

Born in County Wexford in 1774, O'Donnell moved to Dublin to apprentice himself to an architect (most likely Francis Johnston). After a European Grand Tour to study the Continent's finest architectural structures, O'Donnell took up residence in New York City. During his early architectural career in that city, he designed the Bloomingdale Asylum, the Fulton Street Market, Christ Church, and several residential structures that resembled the Regency townhouses on Merrion Square in Dublin. In 1817 he was elected to the American Academy of Fine Arts. He was described by one New Yorker as "a very retiring man, entirely devoted to his profession, and having in consequence found few friendships in this city."

By 1823 O'Donnell's reputation had preceded him to Montreal, where the churchwardens of the parish of Notre-Dame were planning to erect a new church that could accommodate 9,000 people. His final plans called for a structure 150 feet by 258 feet erected on a floor supported by forty-two pillars. In May 1824 the Irishman moved to Montreal to supervise construction and ultimately to provide the contractors with more than 100 drawings and plans. At the height of the summer construction season, about 250 workmen were engaged on the site. The cost of just the stone for the five-foot-thick walls was £18,000.

Because of pressures to complete the structure on schedule, O'Donnell forced the chief contractor to make the work gangs keep longer hours. Despite this accommodation, the architect continued to complain of the workers' lack of discipline: "Not a man of them appears the least interested in the building[;] all they care for is to get their pay, and to do as little work for it as they can. They are determined[,] too, to slight the work, and do it their own way whenever my back [is] turned." By 1832 the cost of constructing the church had swelled to £47,446, fifteen percent more than the original estimate. Although O'Donnell's original plans had called for twin towers 196 feet in height, they were never erected until 1841, eleven years after his death.

In the meantime, O'Donnell had been suffering for some time from edema. Toward the end of 1829 he made his will and converted to Catholicism, the latter decision perhaps due to pressure from the Sulpicians. In accordance with his wishes, his remains were buried under the church. A marble tablet indicates the location of his grave. Translated from the French, the marker reads: "James O'Donnell, Esquire, Architect, born in Ireland and died in this City, January 28, 1830, aged 56 years. He worked for five years on this church, for which he provided the design and directed the workers with zeal and intelligence. After embracing the Catholic faith, he desired that his ashes be interred in this place. His impartiality, his talents, and his probity earned for him the esteem of this parish."

§ Open daily 7-6 (to 8 p.m. June 24-Labour Day). Phone: 514-842-2925.

¶ Black Stone (Ship Fever Monument), Bridge Street (Highway 112), near the west entrance to the Victoria Bridge.

A plaque on this ten-foot-high boulder marks the cemetery where as many as 6,000 Irish immigrants, victims of the typhus epidemic of 1847-48, were buried. The boulder was placed at its original site by workmen who uncovered the cemetery in 1859 while building the Victoria Bridge.

• St. Patrick Square and St. Columban Street are located near the western end of Bridge Street.

¶ Catholic Firefighters Monument, Cemetery of Notre-Dame-des-Neiges.

Erected in 1875, this memorial honors Catholic firefighters who gave their lives in service to the Montreal community. Three of the men listed on the monument had Irish names:

• "Patrick Kelly, of No. 7 Station, killed by the falling of the Skinner ladder on exhibition grounds – 18 Sept. 1876 – aged 25 years."

• "Michael Barry, of No. 3 Station, aged 25 years, killed at the Oil Cabinet and Novelty Works Fire in St. Urbain St. 29 April 1877."

• "John O'Rourke of No. 4 Salvage Corps killed at a fire in Lemoine St. May 11, 1893 aged 33 years."

¶ **Chateau Ramezay,** 280 Notre-Dame.

This rubble- and cut-stone structure was erected in 1705 for Claude de Ramezay, the eleventh governor of French Canada. During the occupation of the city by troops of the Continental Army in 1775, the house was used as the headquarters of the two American commanders – Benedict Arnold and Irish-born Richard Montgomery. (See St. Paul's Chapel, New York City.) Today the building is a museum depicting life in eighteenth-century New France.

§ Open early June-September, daily 10-6; rest of the year (except for the last week of December and the first week of January), Tuesday-Sunday, 10-4:30. Fee. Phone: 514-861-3708.

¶ **Lett Hackett Monument,** Mount Royal Cemetery, on the north side of Chemin Camillien-Houde (north of Mount Royal Park).

This monument over the grave of Lett Hackett recalls an unfortunate incident of sectarian violence that rocked the city of Montreal in the summer of 1877.

Hackett had been a member of the Orangemen, an organization that annually celebrated the victory of the Protestant King William of Orange over the Catholic King James II in Ireland in 1690. Although the Montreal Orangemen had originally planned to carry out their traditional march in July on the anniversary of the victory, they canceled the parade at the last minute. Hackett was either unaware of the change of plans or arrogantly imprudent. Whatever the case, when he unwisely wore the Orange insignia in the streets of the city that day, he was chased by a crowd of outraged Irish Catholics. In the brawl that ensued, Hackett was shot in the head. A few days after his death, the *London Times* editorialized about the incident:

"We have no desire to put forward the slightest excuse or extenuation on behalf of the Roman Catholic rowdies, whether Irish or French-Canadians, who carried their brutal intolerance and lawless violence to the extent of murder. But what are we to say of the Orangemen, who thrust the lighted torch of their organized and openly paraded fanaticism into such a magazine of combustibles. No good end was to be gained, no intelligible principle was ever to be asserted, by the public defiance of Roman Catholic traditions in a Roman Catholic city. . . . The Orangemen of Canada are reproducing in the full light of modern day the most discreditable episodes of the Ascendancy period in Irish history. They have been less extreme because Orange intolerance had in Ireland a historical root and a natural growth, while in Canada it is an imported plant, nurtured by a calculating bigotry and propagated by the labours of a misdirected zeal."

The monument was erected over Hackett's tomb in 1886 and carries the following inscription: "In memory of Brother Lett Hackett, L.O.A., who was barbarously murdered . . . . on Victoria Square when quietly returning from divine service on the 12th of July 1877. This monument was erected by the Orangemen and Protestants of the Dominion as a last tribute to his memory and to mark their detestation of this murdering." [The line attributing the murder to Catholics has been effaced.]

¶ McCord Museum of Canadian History, 690 Rue de Sherbrooke (across from McGill University).

The McCord, one of the foremost history museums in the country, was founded by David Ross McCord, both of whose parents were descended from a common Scotch-Irish ancestor. The McCords were of Scottish origins but had lived in County Antrim, Ireland, since at least 1677. The family's first émigré to Canada was John McCord of Newry, Ireland, a merchant who arrived in Quebec in 1760.

David Ross McCord was born in Montreal in 1844. After completing his education at McGill University (B.A., M.A., and B.C.L.), he was admitted to the bar of Lower Canada in 1868. During his spare time he was an avid collector of Canadiana. In 1919 he presented his collection to his alma mater with the hope that the items would form the nucleus of a national museum on Canadian history. The collection was first put on public display in 1921.

The collection includes 700,000 historical photographs and 80,000 objects and encompasses seven categories: costume and textiles, ethnology and archaeology, photographic archives, decorative arts, archives, prints and drawings, and the library. The museum's holdings include material and memorabilia relating to *General James Wolfe. (See James Wolfe Statue, Quebec City, Quebec.)

§ Open Tuesday-Friday and Monday holidays 10-6 (to 9 on Thursday), Saturday-Sunday 10-5. Closed January 1 and December 25. Fee. Phone: 514-398-7100.

¶ Notre Dame-de-Bonsecours Chapel, 400 Rue St. Paul East.

The story of the Irish in Montreal began in 1817, when a Sulpician priest discovered that a group of Irish regularly gathered to worship at an earlier church of the same name on this site. A directory of 1819 lists only about thirty presumably Irish names, and a visitor to the church the next year stated that he could have "covered with a good-sized parlor carpet" all the Irish Catholics worshipping there on Sundays. Yet by 1823 the number of Irish orphans was so great that a ward was opened at the Grey

Nuns' hospital exclusively for *"les Petites Irlandaises."* On the ceiling under the choir loft in the present church is a painting of Catholic nuns from Montreal ministering to Irish immigrants suffering and dying of typhus. The malady was introduced into the city in 1847 by Irish refugees who had become contaminated at the quarantine station on Grosse Ile in the St. Lawrence River. (See Montmagny, Quebec.)

¶ **St. Patrick's Basilica,** 454 Boulevard René Lévesque.
     Since its opening on St. Patrick's Day in 1847, this neo-Gothic structure has been the largest English-language Catholic church in the city. The basilica was built by Montreal's Irish community and is located in an area once known as "Little Dublin," a neighborhood particularly devastated during the typhus epidemic of 1847. The church's first pastor, *Father Joseph Connolly, unselfishly served his typhus-stricken parishioners, seeing them die at the rate of fifty a day for six weeks. (See Black Stone above.) Connolly was succeeded by *Father Patrick Dowd, who established such local institutions as St. Patrick's Orphan Asylum, St. Bridget's Home for the Old and Infirm, and St. Patrick's School for Girls.
     Designed by P. L. Morin and Father Felix Martin, the basilica is topped by a steeple 228 feet tall and boasts a bell cast in 1774. The cavernous interior of the church is dominated by its columns, each carved from an eighty-foot pine tree. The Irish heritage of the church's parishioners is reflected in an interior decor of Celtic crosses and shamrocks. The fleurs-de-lys salute the French Sulpicians, who helped the Irish acquire the church site and who ministered to the city's Irish for 138 years. The basilica's other notable features are 150 oil-painted figures of saints, stained-glass windows, Stations of the Cross, a gold mural in the sanctuary, a lamp weighing 1,800 pounds, and its wooden floors, pews, and wainscoting.
     In 1868 the church was the scene of the funeral of *Thomas D'Arcy McGee, a longtime parishioner at St. Patrick's, one of Canada's "Fathers of Confederation," and the victim of an assassin's bullet. (See Thomas D'Arcy McGee Memorial, Ottawa, Ontario.) A plaque in the church honors his memory; his pew in the pulpit aisle still bears the number "240."
     Another plaque (in the vestibule of the main entrance) commemorates Emile Nelligan, Quebec's noted Irish- and French-Canadian poet. He was baptized here on St. Patrick's Day in 1879.
     § Open Monday-Friday 10-6, Saturday 8-6, Sunday 9-6. Phone: 514-866-7379.

Nelligan's father, a volatile Irishman, came to Canada at the age of twelve. The older man's job as a postal inspector in the Gaspé region took him away from Montreal for lengthy periods of time, absences that caused his son to ask his French-Canadian mother, "Is that Irish man coming to visit us tomorrow?" In a poem entitled "Le Voyageur," the young Nelligan described his father as an absent phantom: "He can be seen no more on his native sod. / He disappeared in the night, a phantom cast / On the mortal breath of a wintry blast."

In 1896 Nelligan entered the Collège de Sainte-Marie, where he devoted most of his time to the study and composition of poetry. His efforts met with success when nine of his poems were published in local journals or newspapers, the first of approximately 160 poems that he wrote between the ages of sixteen and nineteen. The next year, however, he abandoned his studies to join the Ecole Littéraire de Montréal, a group of rather Bohemian writers and intellectuals. He quickly abandoned the more traditional poetic subjects that had preoccupied Canadian poets (e.g., devotion to country and the soil, the glories of Old France, and fidelity to the Church) in favor of a more personal expression. He even began to fancy himself a romantic rebel artist, describing himself in "Un poète" as "a dreamer passing by, / An angel soul, open to infinity, / Bearing his own dawn of celestial spring."

In 1898 Nelligan's father, hoping that his son would abandon what he regarded as a directionless life, dispatched him on a sea voyage to Liverpool and Belfast and then obtained employment for him as a bookkeeper. As one would expect, the son disliked the job and returned to his poetic flights, finding consolation and validation when several more poems were acknowledged with publication. It was probably at this time that the generally stormy relationship with his father reached a climax. The younger Nelligan eventually denied his Irish heritage, going so far as to insist that his name be pronounced à la français and even spelling it "Nelighan."

Following a public reading of his poems in early 1899, Nelligan began to show serious mental instability. He reacted to a reviewer's harsh criticism of his work by withdrawing into a shell and replying to his attacker: "I have a heart but am not understood / Except in moonlight and in great nights of storm." In August of that year Nelligan's mental state was so fragile that he suffered a breakdown of sorts, running from his garret and climbing a tree in Saint-Louis Square and threatening suicide. He was straightaway admitted to a retreat facility, where he remained for a quarter century before being transferred to Saint-Jean-de-Dieu Hospital. Diagnosed as schizophrenic, he died there in 1941. According to Kathy Mezei, Nelligan's schizophrenia "symbolically captures the tension between the French and the English, the uneasy dual heritage of Quebec so tragically manifested in his own family."

Many of Nelligan's poems are suffused with the imagery of childhood, music, death, and a desire to escape the material world for an ideal existence, often represented as a garden. And despite his objection to what he regarded as the oppressive rigidity of Roman Catholicism, his poetry is replete with Catholic images and themes – stained-glass windows, prayer, damnation, priests, and chapels. As his mental condition deterio-

rated, though, his works seemed more and more to show the influence of
*Edgar Allan Poe, especially in their use of phantoms, macabre music, and
haunted castles. In summing up Nelligan's career, Mezei has remarked
that his poems expressed themes that seem "to obsess Quebec artists: en-
trapment, isolation, alienation, exile, and ambivalence toward one's Catholic heritage, so rich but so oppressive. He was the first Quebec poet to
portray the state of his soul and to reveal the often divided images of the
self. . . ."

Following his death, Nelligan achieved added fame through the artistic expression of others. He has been, for example, the subject of a painting by Jean-Paul Lemieux, images in his poems have been depicted in
watercolors by Louis Pelletier, and his name graces both a ballet and an
opera. He has continued to be a subject of other poets' works and he appears as either a symbol or a figure in novels. In 1979 Le Prix Emile Nelligan
was first awarded to an outstanding poet.

¶ **Shaughnessy House,** part of the Canadian Centre for Architecture at
1920 Rue Baile.

This Second Empire-style mansion was completed in 1874 and was at
one time the home of Thomas Shaughnessy, a general manager of the Canadian Pacific Railway. The center is the world's largest museum devoted
solely to architecture. Its sculpture garden – across Boulevard René
Lévesque – is located on a bluff overlooking an old Irish working-class
neighborhood known as Little Burgundy.

Shaughnessy was a native of Milwaukee, Wisconsin, where his father
had settled after arriving almost penniless from Limerick, Ireland, his
money having been stolen on the transatlantic voyage. The son took a
combined commercial and classical course of studies at St. Aloysius Academy before accepting a job as a clerk in the purchasing department of the
Milwaukee & St. Paul Railway. His advancement was extremely slow,
however, until William Van Horne, the railroad's new general superintendent, made Shaughnessy railroad storekeeper. In this new position
Shaughnessy supervised the purchase of all materials and the disbursement of payroll.

When Van Horne left the Milwaukee & St. Paul to become general
manager of the Canadian Pacific Railroad, he persuaded Shaughnessy to
join him as purchasing agent for the entire CPR system. It was at this time
that Shaughnessy moved with his wife and daughter to Montreal, where
he subsequently earned a reputation as a shrew buyer. In January 1884 he
became Van Horne's assistant. A year later, however, the Canadian Pacific
experienced a severe financial crisis, which Walter Vaughn, Van Horne's
biographer, credits Shaughnessy with helping the company weather.

Shaughnessy was also able to help redeem an unfortunate situation
on a more personal level, as a tale from CPR lore shows. It seems that a

young employee who was also an amateur pugilist had staged a fight in an anteroom of the company's headquarters. When David McNicoll, the vice president, heard the commotion, he fired the young man. Shaughnessy became involved in the situation when the young offender's Catholic mother appealed to him, asking him to get the son his job back and claiming that he was her only support. In an interview with the erring pugilist, Shaughnessy said: "Well, my lad, you have only yourself to blame. It was a breach of good order in the office, and Mr. McNicoll was right in disciplining you. You are a clerk in his department, and I cannot ask him to take you back. The only thing I can do is take you into my own office. Report to me tomorrow."

The period of Shaughnessy's presidency of the Canadian Pacific (1899-1918) coincided with the height of the company's renown and prosperity. One of his most notable achievements was the creation of CPR's Atlantic fleet, a development which brought large numbers of passengers to the St. Lawrence region for the first time. In addition, the railroad's trackage increased by almost 50 percent, and dividends to stockholders were almost consistently around 10 percent per year. Under Shaughnessy's direction Consolidated Mining and Smelting became an important producer of lead and zinc. And in an extremely forwardlooking move, he sent an agent over the Trans-Siberian Railway to Vladivostok in order to investigate the possibilities of passenger and freight traffic with CPR steamships at that port.

As if in recognition of his services to the Canadian Pacific, Shaughnessy received a knighthood after the Duke and Duchess of York showed that the railroad was a truly first-class transcontinental line by riding its rails from sea to sea. In his telegram informing his parents in Milwaukee about his knighthood, the former railroad clerk remarked, "One owes a great deal to a good father and mother." In 1916 he was created 1st Baron Shaughnessy of Montreal, Canada, and Ashford, County Limerick. Milwaukeeans henceforth referred to their native son as "the Peer that made Milwaukee famous," a punning allusion to the city's Schlitz beer. From that date he used his influence to settle the Irish question, and in 1921 he was proposed as the first governor general of the Irish Free State.

Shaughnessy was encouraged in his romantic thinking about railroads by Jeremiah Curtin, an Irish-American who had worked for a time in St. Petersburg and who had translated the works of several Slavic writers into English. (See Greendale, Wisconsin.) Curtin dedicated his translation of Sienkiewicz's *Field of Glory* to Shaughnessy with the following words: "My Dear Sir Thomas: Railroads are to nations what arteries and veins are to each individual. Every part of a nation enjoys a common life with every other through railroads. Books bring remote ages to the present, and assemble the thoughts of mankind and of God in one divine company. I find great pleasure in railroads in the day and the night, at all seasons. You enjoy books with a keen and true judgment. Let me inscribe to you, therefore, this volume."

§ The center is open June-September, Tuesday-Sunday 11-6 (to 8 on Thursday); rest of the year, Wednesday-Friday 11-6 (to 8 on Thursday), Saturday-Sunday 11-5. Fee. Phone: 514-939-7026.

¶ **Thomas D'Arcy McGee Burial Site,** Cote-des-Neiges Cemetery, on the north side of Chemin Remembrance (north of Mount Royal Park). (See Thomas D'Arcy McGee Memorial, Ottawa, Ontario.)

QUEBEC CITY

¶ **Cape Diamond,** the eastern tip of the Old City (now occupied by the Citadel).

This formidable promontory witnessed one of the most consequential military engagements in the history of North America in December 1775. A six-foot-high tablet affixed to the rock facing Champlain Street below commemorates the Canadians' historic defense of the city against an invading American force under *General Richard Montgomery. The tablet is thus inscribed: "Here stood the Undaunted Fifty safeguarding Canada, defeating Montgomery at the Près-de-Ville Barricade on the last day of 1775, Guy Carleton Commanding at Quebec."

The chain of events leading to the Canadian victory began when the Continental Congress in Philadelphia ordered an invasion of Canada as part of the Americans' offensive against the British during the Revolutionary War. An American force under Montgomery, an Irish native who had served at Louisbourg in 1757, headed north via Lake Champlain. When he swept aside all opposition at Sorel, Montreal, and Three Rivers, *General Guy Carleton, the British governor, abandoned Montreal in order to focus his defense at the more strategically located Quebec. (As youngsters, Carleton and Montgomery had been neighbors in Ireland, where both were members of the Anglo-Irish gentry. They had also served together in the British army.) (See St. Paul's Episcopal Chapel, New York City.)

After arriving in Quebec on November 30, 1775, Carleton discovered that the garrison there contained only 127 British regulars. That meagre number swelled to 1,800 men, however, when 230 Royal Emigrants as well as loyal inhabitants and the crews of several ships placed themselves under Carleton's command. The Canadian defenses were strengthened, and barricades were erected in the Lower Town (in Sault-au-Matelot Street) and at Près-de-Ville, just below the center of the Citadel cliff.

Montgomery reached Quebec with his army on December 1, thereby bringing the attack force to 2,000 men. An eyewitness described his first review of his troops: "It was lowering and cold, but the appearance of the general here gave us warmth and animation. He was well-limbed, tall, and handsome, though his face was much pock-marked. His air and manner designated the real soldier. He made us a short, but energetic and elegant speech, the burden of which was in applause of our spirit in crossing the wilderness; a hope our perseverance in that spirit would continue; and a promise of warm clothing; the latter was a most comfortable assurance. A few huzzas from our freezing bodies were returned to this address of the gallant hero. New life was infused into the whole corps." Montgomery subsequently erected batteries on the high ground commanding the St. John and the St. Louis gates, but the ensuing American bombardment produced few results.

Deciding to storm the town by night, Montgomery and his men set out at 2 a.m. on December 31, crossed the Plains of Abraham, and descended into what is now Champlain Street. By 4 a.m., however, a blinding northeast snowstorm was raging as Montgomery descended the cliff and advanced along a ledge flanked by the crags of Cape Diamond. Although the Americans' objective – the Près-de-Ville barricade – was defended by only fifty Canadian seamen and militiamen, the defenders peppered Montgomery's advancing column with cannon and musket fire. Montgomery, two of his aides, and ten of his men were killed in the first discharge, a surprising turn of events that caused the remaining 700 Americans to turn and flee. The bodies of the slain Americans were covered under the driving snow; their bodies were dug out the next morning by a detachment from the British garrison. Montgomery was buried under the bastion.

A second American assault – led by Benedict Arnold – broke through the barricade across Sous-le-Cap Street but was stopped near the present site of Molson's Bank. A historic tablet at that location describes the Canadian victory against Arnold: "Here stood her old and new defenders, uniting, guarding, saving Canada, defeating Arnold at the Sault-au-Matelot Barricade on the last day of 1775, Guy Carleton Commanding at Quebec."

When a British man-of-war arrived in May 1776, the garrison in Quebec made a sortie, only to discover that the besieging Americans had already left the city. Following the arrival of more ships and troops, Carleton marched to Three Rivers, defeated the Americans again, and proceeded to Montreal without opposition. Within a few more days Carleton succeeded in driving the rest of the invaders from Canada. (See Rue Carleton below.)

Not long after these historic encounters, General Montgomery appeared as a character in an unusual work written by Thomas Paine and entitled *A Dialogue Between the Ghost of General Montgomery and an American Delegate*. Not surprisingly, Paine used Montgomery as a mouthpiece for some of his (Paine's) most vehement remarks against aristocracy. "I maintain that it is your interest to be independent of Great Britain," Montgomery's ghost advised, "but I do not recommend any new form of

government for you. I should think it strange that a people who have virtue enough to defend themselves against the most powerful nation in the
world should want [lack] wisdom to contrive a perfect and free form of
government. . . . I would only beg leave to observe to you, that monarchy
and aristocracy have in all ages been the vehicles of slavery." Elsewhere in
the dialogue Montgomery's ghost contrasts his youthful regret that he
had not suffered a glorious death on the Plains of Abraham while trying
to extend the British empire with his later attempt to free Canada from
British "despotism." "It was no small mortification to me when I fell upon
the plains of Abraham," he recalls, "to reflect that I did not expire like the
brave General Wolfe, in the arms of victory. But I now no longer envy him
his victory. I would rather die in *attempting* to obtain permanent freedom
for a handful of people, than survive a conquest which would serve only
to extend the empire of despotism."

¶ **The General's House,** 72 Rue St. Louis.
This historic site is named for Richard Montgomery, the Irish-born
American general whose body was brought to the house after his death
while trying to capture Quebec in 1775. He was originally buried near the
St. Louis Gate, but his body was returned to the United States in 1818. (See
previous entry and St. Paul's Chapel, New York City.)

¶ **James Wolfe Statue,** Library of the Literary and Historical Society of
Quebec, 44 Rue St. Stanislas.
The library's collection of historic items includes a wooden statue of
*General James Wolfe and a desk belonging to George Etienne Cartier,
one of the Fathers of Canadian Confederation. (See next entry.)
§ Library open Monday-Friday 9:30-4:30, Saturday 10-4. Phone: 418-
694-9147.

¶ **James Wolfe Statue,** on the façade of the Parliament Buildings (Hotel du Parlement), on Grande Allée.
One of the many statues depicting heroic figures in the history of
Canada is that of General James Wolfe. Installed in 1894, the likeness is
the work of the sculptor Philippe Hébert and is located in a niche directly
above the main entrance.
Although Wolfe was born in England in 1727, his ancestors had lived
in Ireland since the fifteenth century. In Ireland some members of the family had acquired considerable influence, particularly in County Limerick.
One ancestor (James Woulfe) was bailiff in Limerick as early as 1605, another served as sheriff of that city in 1613, and the most famous (Captain
George Woulfe) led the unsuccessful resistance to Ireton's siege of the city
in 1651.
The young James Wolfe advanced so rapidly in the military that at the

age of eighteen he was a major and a deputy quartermaster under his father during the latter's campaign against Scottish rebels. The young soldier spent the following decade in either garrison duty or active service in the Netherlands, Scotland, Ireland, and England. A contemporary described him as "5 feet 11 or six in height, very straight, his air and carriage perfectly military, his action free, his gestures open to those of an actor who feels no constraint – his hair red, generally worn in a queue, his face of a long oval, complexion very fair and much freckled."

In 1752 Wolfe visited Belfast, Londonderry, and Dublin and probably his ancestral seat in Limerick. He recorded his impressions of his ancestors' adopted land: "The north of Ireland and the neighborhood of this city [Dublin] are very little inferior for beauty and fertility to any parts of England that I have seen, and others they exceed in both. . . . They have fine clear streams . . . and very large timber where it is encouraged; but I am told that the best estates are deeply in debt, the tenants racked and plundered, and consequently industry and good husbandry disappointed or destroyed. This [Dublin] appears to be a prodigious city, and they continue to build; the streets are crowded with people of a large size and well limbed, and the women very handsome. They have clearer skins and fairer complexions than the women of England or Scotland, and are exceedingly straight and well made." By 1758, however, Wolfe was in America, a brigadier general in command of a division under General Amherst at the siege of Louisbourg. (See Louisbourg, Nova Scotia.)

In June 1759 Wolfe was en route to Quebec for the final act in the epochal struggle against the French for control of Canada. Arriving at the head of a large fleet and a force of 8,000 men, Wolfe, now a major general, erected batteries at Point Lévis and on the island of Orleans. After an unsuccessful attack on the French position at Montmorency, Wolfe ordered his troops to retire to the island. Disappointed by his failure and suffering from fever, the British commander at first urged the government to abandon the venture but soon changed his mind and decided on another attack. He accordingly landed his troops above the city and – by scaling a precipice – gained the heights behind the town, where it was less fortified. On the night of September 12, as Wolfe and his 5,000 men stood in the boats that carried them a mile above Cape Diamond, the British general recited portions of Gray's "Elegy in a Country Churchyard." (He then turned to his companions and declared that he would rather have been the author of those lines than the recipient of any military honors.)

After effecting their landing, the British gained the heights of Abraham, where they soon faced the Marquis de Montcalm and the French, who had in the meantime crossed the St. Charles River. Toward the beginning of the ensuing battle, Wolfe sustained two severe wounds, one in the wrist and the other in the groin. He continued to lead his men, however, until struck again, this time in the chest. Informed that the enemy was retreating, Wolfe ordered that a regiment be sent to cut off the retreat. He then murmured his last words: "Now God be praised, I will die in peace." The French surrendered five days later.

Wolfe's body was carried to England, where a memorial to his honor was erected in Westminster Abbey. Horace Walpole eulogized him thus: "Ambition, industry, passion for the service were conspicuous in him. He seemed to breathe for nothing but fame, and lost no moments in qualifying himself to compass that object. Presumption in himself was necessary for his object, and he had it. He was formed to execute the designs of such a master as Pitt."

In commemorating the historic battles that occurred in Quebec, the Irish-born Canadian patriot Thomas D'Arcy McGee eulogized Wolfe and Montgomery, the sons of Anglo-Irish aristocrats: "Three generals have fallen at Quebec under three different flags. All were brave, all merciful, all young. Montcalm, with blood ardent as the wine of his own France; Wolfe, with courage as indomitable as the enterprise of his island, which can wring a prize from every rock; Montgomery, the last and best of all, with soul as noble as his cause, and honor bright as his own sword. Three deaths, Quebec, do consecrate this rock; three glories crown it, like a tiara! Of the three, his death was the saddest, and even so has his glory become brightest of them all."

¶ Montmorency Falls Park, 7 miles east via Autoroute 440, at the confluence of the St. Lawrence and Montmorency rivers.

One of the historic sites in the park is a fortification built by the army of *General James Wolfe in July 1759. (See previous entry.)

§ Park open late June-early August, daily 9 a.m.-11 p.m.; mid August-Labour Day, daily 9-9; day after Labour Day-late October and mid April-late June, daily 9-6; rest of the year, Saturday-Sunday 9-4. Phone: 418-663-2877.

¶ National Battlefields Park, between the St. Louis Gate and Rue Bougainville.

The park includes the Plains of Abraham, where one of the decisive battles for empire took place between the British and the French in 1759. After a siege of the city, the British general *James Wolfe and his troops scaled the city's natural defenses to reach the Plains of Abraham – an accomplishment previously thought impossible. The British surprised the French that September day and within twenty minutes defeated the Marquis de Montcalm and his troops. The battle ended in the death of both commanders and the fall of Quebec to the British.

• Near the Quebec Museum, at the southern end of the park, stands the James Wolfe Monument. This thirty-eight-foot obelisk was erected to honor the victor against the French. The column is surmounted by a sword and a helmet. The legend on the base of the monument describes its history: "The first memorial was the stone that Wolfe's own army rolled here to mark the spot on which he died 1759. A second monument was placed in position 1832. The third memorial was set up by the British army stationed in Canada 1849. This fourth memorial reproduces the column of the third, preserves its crowning piece and two inscriptions and was set up by the National Battlefield Commission 1913." The fourth monument was dynamited in 1963 by the Front de Libération de Québec. The present monument was erected in 1965.

¶ **Rue Carleton,** near Artillery Park National Historic Site.

Named for Guy Carleton, this short street memorializes the Irish-born military officer who served as governor of Canada from 1768 to 1778 and again from 1786 to 1796.

Born in Strabane, County Tyrone, in 1724, Carleton was descended from a family which had originally haled from England but which had resided in Ireland since the beginning of the seventeenth century. His father and mother were from counties Down and Donegal, respectively.

In 1759 Carleton took part in the British expedition against Quebec as quartermaster general under *General James Wolfe. He was wounded during the crucial military engagement that year on the Plains of Abraham, a British victory which effectively ended French control of the colony. After becoming governor, he adopted a conciliatory stance toward the French-Canadian clergy and landowners. This policy was formalized when the British Parliament passed the Quebec Act, which allowed Britain's new subjects to retain their former rights and privileges.

When the Americans under *General Richard Montgomery and Benedict Arnold invaded Montreal in 1775, Carleton fled the city disguised as a peasant. He later defeated Montgomery's army at Quebec, however, and pursued the Americans as far as Lake Champlain. (See Cape Diamond, Quebec City.) After the American Revolution, Carleton was appointed both commander-in-chief and governor-in-chief of British North America. Created Baron Dorchester in 1786, he promoted passage of the Constitution Act of 1791, adopted by Parliament to foster the development of representative institutions in Canada. During his tenure as governor, he proposed the federation of all British North America, a suggestion which the home government at the time found unacceptable but which became a reality in 1867.

¶ **Rue McMahon,** near Artillery Park National Historic Site.

Leading east through the old city walls into the Irish Quarter, this street honors the memory of Abbé Patrick McMahon, the first chaplain of St. Patrick's Church.

McMahon was born in 1796, probably in Abbeyleix, Ireland, and completed classical studies most likely at St. Patrick's College in Carlow. After immigrating to Lower Canada about 1817, he found employment as an English teacher at Collège de Saint-Hyacinthe, where he also studied for the priesthood. He was ordained at Notre Dame Cathedral in Quebec in 1822.

Except for a three-year assignment in Saint John, New Brunswick, McMahon served the English-speaking and mostly Irish parishioners of Quebec for almost three decades. He performed his priestly duties first at the cathedral but then at St. Patrick's, built when the Anglophone Catholics wanted a church of their own. The new building was completed in 1833 and served approximately 6,000 people.

McMahon's tenure at St. Patrick's coincided with a tremendous influx of Irish immigrants into the city and the occurrence of several natural disasters. As an executive member of the Quebec Emigrant Society, the priest was influential as a spokesman for the Irish newcomers. He was also called upon to minister to them during the frequent outbreaks of cholera that struck the city. Despite championing the cause of his Irish parishioners, he was known for his loyalty and attachment to the British government. His conservative stance led him on several occasions to use the pulpit to denounce so-called reformers from the French-Canadian community. On the occasion of his silver jubilee as a priest, McMahon was presented with a full-length portrait by Théophile Hamel, showing the cleric with his hand resting on the plans for St. Patrick's Church. After his death in 1851, he was buried under the pulpit of the church.

¶ The ruins of St. Patrick's Church are located along Rue McMahon, in an area still known as the Irish Quarter. The church was renovated in 1846 to accommodate the increasing numbers of Irish Catholics, who by then represented fully 20 percent of the city's population. The church was closed in 1970, after most of the Irish had left this neighborhood. The structure burned down soon later, although its stone walls are still standing.

¶ **Taschereau Monument,** Place de l'Hotel-de-Ville.

For people of Irish descent, this statue of Elzéar-Alexandre Taschereau recalls the French priest's ministry to the Irish immigrants who, stricken with typhoid, were quarantined on Grosse Ile [q.v.] in 1847. At the time, Taschereau was teaching philosophy, astronomy, architecture, theology, and Sacred Scripture at Grand Séminaire de Québec. Because he spoke English, he was called upon to serve the afflicted Irish. After a week with the desperate immigrants, though, he contracted the dread malady and was confined to the hospital for three weeks, close to death. After recovering, he went on to become archbishop of Quebec (1871) and Canada's first cardinal (1886).

¶ **Wolfe-Montcalm Monument,** in the Governor's Garden behind Chateau Frontenac.

This fifty-foot memorial obelisk honors the two military commanders who fought on the Plains of Abraham in 1759 – the Anglo-Irish general James Wolfe and the French Marquis de Montcalm. The monument's cenotaph bears a famous Latin inscription: "Mortem virtus communem / Famam historia / Monumentum posteritas dedit." ("Courage gave them the same death; history, the same renown; posterity, the same monument.")

§ Garden open all year.

RIVIERE-DU-LOUP

¶ **John McLoughlin Plaque,** on a monolith to the left of the City Hall entrance, 65 Rue de l'Hôtel-de-Ville.

The inscription on this historical marker summarizes the career of one of the most prominent figures in Irish-Canadian history: "Born in Rivière-du-Loup, McLoughlin was a physician before joining the North West Company in 1806. In 1814 he became a wintering partner and in 1820 led a group of dissident Nor'Westers seeking union with the Hudson's Bay Company. Although McLoughlin was ignored in the formal negotiations, he became Chief Factor when the companies merged. He was placed in charge of the Columbia District and established his headquarters on the lower Columbia River where he spent the rest of his life. After retirement he remained in what became American territory and is known as the 'Father of Oregon.'" (See Statuary Hall, District of Columbia; and Oregon City, Oregon, in *Irish America*, Volume 2.)

SASKATCHEWAN

CYPRESS HILLS

¶ **Fort Walsh National Historic Park,** 34 miles southwest of Maple
Creek by Highway 271.

The fort in this historic park is a reconstruction of an earlier Fort Walsh,
built in 1875 by men under the command of James Walsh, an inspector
with the North West Mounted Police. Until the fort was dismantled in
1883, the police stationed here brought law and order to the region and
maintained the peace with the thousands of Sioux who fled to Canada
after confrontations with the U.S. Cavalry.

The extensive reconstruction includes workshops, a stable, a powder
magazine, a guardroom, barracks, and the commanding officer's residence.
The interpretive center provides information about the Plains Indians and
their way of life, the fur and whiskey trades, and a policeman's life at the
fort.

Walsh, the son of Irish Presbyterian immigrants, was born in Prescott,
Upper Canada, in 1840. The young man early exhibited leadership skills
in a variety of positions in Prescott: captain of the volunteer fire company,
organizer of a championship lacrosse team, and lieutenant in a rifle company. All the while he held an even more varied number of jobs as machinist, railwayman, dry goods clerk, and exchange broker.

In 1873, when plans were being made to create the North West
Mounted Police, Walsh eagerly applied for admission. By the spring of
1875 he had been sent to an area near the site of the Cypress Hills Massacre with orders to construct a fort. (According to Henry McKay, a squatter
in the area, the site was selected when the mounted police learned that
McKay had five daughters "who were all considered pretty and respectable girls.") Although a soldier who helped build the fort remembered
Walsh as a cold, quick-tempered man, the subinspector effectively put an
end to the whiskey trade in the area and laid the foundation for a remark-
able network of informants who kept him advised about the local native
peoples.

Only eighteen months after the fort was completed, however, Walsh
was stricken with a severe streptococcal infection. The superior officer
who granted Walsh a medical leave filed a glowing report about him, describing him as "an excellent Officer, untiring in his exertions to do his
work. He understands the working of men and has I believe got his Division into very good order. He has occupied an important and somewhat
difficult position at Cypress Hills on account of the different tribes of Indians and Halfbreeds who frequent the neighborhood, and he has done
his duty well."

Walsh returned to Cypress Hills in August 1876 just before the Sioux, pursued by American troops after the Indians' victory at the Little Big-horn, crossed into Canada. The following spring he met with Sitting Bull, who impressed him a great deal and who promised to refrain from hostile activity. To a newspaper reporter Walsh expressed his belief that the Sioux would be persuaded to return south but that negotiations might take a year. Walsh continued to press the Sioux to leave Canada, but his unwill-ingness to use force eventually lost him the confidence of his military and political superiors. As it turned out, the threat of starvation caused by the disappearance of the buffalo finally caused many of the Sioux to return to the United States. In addition, when Walsh was reassigned in 1880, the Sioux who were still in Canada abandoned hope of remaining there. As a gesture of respect and friendship, Sitting Bull presented Walsh with his war bonnet, now in the collection of the Royal Ontario Museum.

Although Walsh interpreted his transfer as the act of ungrateful supe-riors, his past and future conduct may have warranted such a decision. In a report at the end of 1880, for instance, the new commissioner opined that Walsh was "prone to act on his own authority in a manner that can-not be considered subordinate, with a view of making his own name con-spicuous." In addition, although married, Walsh seems to have been in-discreet in his liaisons with at least two native women, abandoning one woman for another with whom he had a daughter. Walsh compounded his problem by keeping in contact with the Sioux leaders after his transfer, thereby leading the prime minister to believe that the officer was trying to

Fort Walsh, named for one of the first men to volunteer for the North West Mounted Police. (Photo courtesy of Fort Walsh National Historic Site.)

undermine the government's policy. After leaving the mounted police, Walsh enjoyed a successful business career as a coal dealer.

Walsh's commercial activities were briefly interrupted by a less successful stint as commissioner of the Yukon. When gold prospectors had made a major strike in the Yukon in 1896, the North West Mounted Police set up headquarters in Dawson. To oversee this operation, the government decided to appoint Walsh commissioner of the Yukon and commander of the 285 mounted police there. To some observers Walsh seemed an unlikely choice, especially since only a year before he had urged the new prime minister to reduce the size of the force drastically. At least one historian of the force regards Walsh's advice as an attempt "to repair his self-esteem by humbling the organization which had rejected him."

Whatever Walsh's motivation in accepting the position, his tenure in the Yukon was short-lived. He quickly made enemies by imposing a 10 percent tax on gold output, limiting the importation of liquor, and ruling on claims disputes. After clashes with the superintendent of the North West Mounted Police, Walsh's authority was limited to the performance of menial duties. He was dismissed after only three months, his reputation besmirched and his soul even more embittered. A few years later, though, the editor of the *Dawson Daily News* wrote that Walsh's influence in the Yukon had for the most part been beneficial. (Mount Walsh in the Yukon's St. Elias range is named in his honor.) Walsh's obituary described him as "one of the most genial of men – one with whom it was always a pleasure to meet. He was well read, and a most interesting conversationalist, and few had a greater fund of information, especially about Western Canada, than he."

§ Open daily Victoria Day weekend-Thanksgiving, 9-5:30. Cafeteria and picnic sites available. Fee. Phone: 306-662-3590.

THE YUKON

DAWSON CITY

¶ **Joseph Boyle Plaque,** outside of town at Dredge #4 on Bonanza Creek.

This commemorative plaque was unveiled in 1986 to honor "Klondike Joe" Boyle, one of the Yukon's legendary early promoters and entrepreneurs. It was on Bonanza Creek that Boyle's mining company – Canadian Klondyke – operated the largest wooden-hull bucket dredge in the world.

Boyle was born in Toronto in 1867 and lived as a youngster in Woodstock, Ontario. He traced his ancestry to an emigrant from Balllymena, Ireland, who had arrived in Canada three decades earlier. At the age of seventeen Boyle joined the merchant marine, where he distinguished himself for rescuing a sailor from a shark and for saving his vessel during a typhoon.

When Boyle's marriage ended in failure in 1896, he was operating a boxing club in New Jersey. There he met Frank Slavin, the Australian heavyweight, and agreed to become his manager and sparring partner. Almost immediately, though, the pair headed north to seek their fortune in the Klondike gold strike. After blazing a trail over the unmapped White Pass from British Columbia into the Yukon, they soon acquired four jointly held individual claims. By 1907 Boyle had gained control of the Canadian Klondyke Mining Company, which within seven years made him a millionaire – the "King of the Klondike." One of his holdings was a power plant that provided electricity for Dawson City.

With the start of World War I, however, Canadian Klondyke fell upon hard times and Boyle decided to join the military. Although he created and financed a fifty-man machine gun unit, the Canadian government refused to accept him for active service. After moving to Britain, he joined the American Committee of Engineers, formed to support the Allied war effort. He was immediately placed in command of a mission to Russia to improve the chaotic conditions in that country's railway system. He finally saw the military action he so desperately sought when he led the defense of Tarnopol against German attack. His role in the siege won him a medal from the Russian High Command.

It was Boyle's wartime efforts on behalf of Romania that earned him recognition as the savior of that Balkan country. Besides organizing a relief train to save a starving Romanian army, he played a major role in guaranteeing the safety of the country's crown jewels and national archives. These treasures had earlier been transferred to the presumed safety of Moscow, but the Bolshevik takeover of Russia caused the Romanian royal family to fear for the items' safe return. As a result, Boyle was en-

listed in a successful plan to spirit the jewels and the archives out of the
new Soviet capital. He escorted the treasures 800 miles to Jassy, just inside
the Romanian border, from where he later operated a spy ring of almost
500 agents. In addition to helping sixty Romanian dignitaries escape from
Soviet troops, Boyle arranged a peace treaty between the Soviet giant and
its neighbor to the south. After the war he attended the Versailles Peace
Conference as part of the Romanian delegation and helped the country
obtain $25 million in aid from Canada.

Sir Robert Borden, the Canadian prime minister during World War I,
left an interesting summary of Boyle's attitude toward the Bolsheviks.
According to one of Borden's diary entries, Boyle "says that triumph of
Bolshevism in Russia means that it will overrun Germany and that Germany and Russia will overrun the world or reduce organized society to
anarchy. He insists that it must be put down or that worse will come and
he declares that an army of a million men can do it. He says it will be a
fraud and a sham if Peace Conference concludes its labours without ter-
minating the war and that cannot be done until anarchy is ended in Russia."

While making a name for himself as a Romanian national hero, Boyle
had become a personal confidant of Queen Marie. In fact, after suffering a
stroke in 1918, the Canadian was nursed back to health by the Romanian
monarch, whose lover he was reputed to be. Boyle died in England in
1923 and was buried on the grounds of St. James Church, Hampton Hill,
Middlesex. Next to his grave stood a ground stone and an ancient cross,
gifts of the Romanian queen. The granite slab on the grave bears the inscription: "Man with the heart of a Viking / And the simple faith of a
child." The epitaph was adapted by Marie from lines in "The Law of the
Yukon," a poem by Robert Service, whose works Boyle often read to her.
Sixty years later Boyle's body was transported to Canada for burial in
Woodstock, Ontario [*q.v.*].

¶ Joseph Tyrrell Plaque, Front Street, between St. Paul Church and
the Royal Canadian Mounted Police Headquarters.

This historical marker honors the memory of Joseph Burr Tyrrell, a
nineteenth-century geologist, explorer, and historian.

Born in 1858 in Weston, Ontario, Tyrrell was the son of an emigrant
from County Kildare who had settled near Toronto about twenty years
earlier. The younger Tyrrell enjoyed a lengthy career with the Geological
Survey of Canada, for which he explored vast regions of the western and
northern areas of the country. His work added immeasurable knowledge
to the geography, mammalogy, ornithology, entomology, and botany of
many regions. He was also responsible for discovering rich dinosaur beds
and important coal fields in Alberta.

The considerable wealth which Tyrrell acquired as a mining consultant and a miner in northern Ontario and the Klondike allowed him to pursue other interests. He not only served as president of the Champlain Society but also was involved in the production of several historical publications, most notably in editing the diaries of the explorers Samuel Hearne and David Thompson. In 1927 Tyrrell endowed a $1,000 prize to be awarded on a regular basis by the Royal Society of Canada for the furtherance of knowledge about Canadian history.

MOUNT WALSH

This peak in the St. Elias range was named for *James Walsh, a controversial inspector with the North West Mounted Police during the 1870s. (See Fort Walsh, Cypress Hills, Saskatchewan.)

WHITEHORSE

¶ **Sam McGee Cabin,** Macbride Museum, 1st Avenue and Wood Street.
This renovated cabin was constructed in 1899 by William Samuel McGee, a prospector of most likely Irish ancestry because of his birth in Peterborough, Ontario, a community of colonists from Ireland created in 1825. The cabin, originally located on 5th Avenue, was acquired and renovated in 1940 by the Imperial Daughters of the Empire. In 1954 the structure was given to the Yukon Historical Society and was moved to its present location.

McGee had come to Whitehorse via San Francisco in 1898, drawn to the area by news of the gold strikes. His prospecting efforts proved fruitless, however, and he spent most of his first two years in Whitehorse packing supplies and working as a construction engineer. He later operated several roadhouses or taverns, including one at Canyon Creek. Before returning to Ontario to attend his mother's funeral in 1900, he staked a claim on a cooper belt and acquired an interest in the War Eagle and the LeRoi fields. When McGee returned to Whitehorse, he brought his new wife, Ruth Warnes, with him. The couple left the area in 1909 and spent the next three decades at various localities in British Columbia, Alberta, and Montana. McGee made one final visit to the Yukon two years before his death in 1940 in Calgary.

McGee's name was immortalized in "The Cremation of Sam McGee," a poem by Robert Service, the "Bard of the Yukon," who lived in Dawson City between 1909 and 1912. The poem, which is set at nearby Lake Laberge, presents a highly fictionalized picture of its title character.

§ Open June-Labour Day, daily 10-6; rest of the year, varied times. Phone: 867-667-2709.

NORTHWEST TERRITORIES

KANE BASIN

Located on the northern continuation of Baffin Bay between Ellesmere
Island and Greenland, this body of water bears the name of *Dr. Elisha Kent
Kane (1820-1857), the commander of the second Grinnell expedition (1853-
1855). (See Kane, Pennsylvania.)

Works Consulted

Ahern, Patrick Henry. *The Catholic University of America 1887-1896: The Rectorship of John J. Keane.* Washington, D.C.: The Catholic University of America Press, 1948.

Akrigg, G. P. V. *1001 British Columbia Place Names.* Vancouver: Discovery Press,   1970.

Alden, Carroll Storrs. *Lawrence Kearny: Sailor Diplomat.* Princeton: Princeton University Press, 1936.

Allen, Gay Wilson. *William James: A Biography.* New York: The Viking Press, 1967.

Allen, Hervey. *Israfel: The Life and Times of Edgar Allan Poe.* New York: Farrar & Rinehart, Inc., 1934.

Alper, M. Victor. *America's Freedom Trail: A Tour Guide to Historical Sites of the Colonial and Revolutionary War Period.* New York: Macmillan Publishing Company, Inc., 1976.

Alsberg, Henry G., ed. *Delaware: A Guide to the First State.* American Guide Series. New rev. ed. New York: Hastings House, 1955.

American Automobile Association Tour Books.

"The American Cardinal." *New York Times* 28 April 1875: 10.

"Andrew O'Connor, Noted Sculptor, 67." *New York Times* 11 June 1941: 21.

Andrews, Matthew Page. *The Founding of Maryland.* Baltimore: The Williams & Wilkins Company, 1933.

Architect of the Capitol. *Compilation of Works of Art and Other Objects in the United States Capitol.* Washington, D.C.: Joint Committee on the Library, 1965.

Arnebeck, Bob. *Through a Fiery Trial: Building Washington 1790-1800.* New York: Madison Books, 1991.

Atherton, William Henry. *Montreal 1535-1914.* Vol. 2. Montreal: The S. J. Clarke Publishing Company, 1914.

Avery, Elroy McKendree. *A History of Cleveland and its Environs.* Chicago: The Lewis Publishing Company, 1918.

Avrich, Paul. *The Haymarket Tragedy.* Princeton: University Press, 1984.

Baedeker's Ireland. New York: Prentice Hall Press, n.d.

Bailyn, Bernard, et al., eds. *The Great Republic: A History of the American People.* 3rd ed. Lexington, Mass.: D.C. Heath and Company, 1985.

Bakeless, John E. and Katherine L. *Signers of the Declaration.* Boston: Houghton Mifflin, 1969.

Banning, Kendall. *West Point Today.* New York: Funk & Wagnalls Company, 1937. Reprint 1943.

Barbour, Hugh, and J. William Frost. *The Quakers*. New York: Greenwood Press, 1988.

Barnes, Jack A. *Irish-American Landmarks: A Traveler's Guide*. Detroit: Visible Ink Press, 1995.

Barton, George. *Angels of the Battlefield: A History of the Labors of the Catholic Sisterhoods in the Late Civil War*. 2nd rev. ed. Philadelphia: The Catholic Art Publishing Company, 1898.

Bateman, Newton, et al. *Historical Encyclopedia of Illinois*. Vol. 1. Chicago: Munsell Publishing Company, 1925.

Bearse, Ray, ed. *Maine: A Guide to the Vacation State*. The New American Guide Series. Boston: Houghton Mifflin Company, 1969.

———, ed. *Massachusetts: A Guide to the Pilgrim State*. The New American Guide Series. 2nd ed. rev. Boston: Houghton Mifflin Company, 1971.

———, ed. *Vermont: A Guide to the Green Mountain State*. The New American Guide Series. Boston: Houghton Mifflin Company, 1968.

Bennett, Carol. *Peter Robinson's Settlers*. Ontario: Juniper Books, 1987.

Bennett, William Harper. *Catholic Footsteps in Old New York: A Chronicle of Catholicity in the City of New York from 1524 to 1808*. New York: Schwartz, Kirwin and Fauss, 1909.

Bergman, Edward R. *Woodlawn Remembers: Cemetery of American History*. Utica, N. Y.: North County Books, Inc., 1988.

Berton, Pierre. *Flames Across the Border: The Canadian-American Tragedy, 1813-1814*. Boston: Little, Brown and Company, 1981.

———. *The Impossible Railway: The Building of the Canadian Pacific*. New York: Alfred A. Knopf, 1972.

Bicknell, Thomas Williams. "Major General Anthony Wayne." *The Journal of the American Irish Historical Society* 10 (1910-11): 277-300.

Bigelow, E. Victor. *A Narrative History of the Town of Cohasset, Massachusetts*. Cohasset: The Committee on Town History, 1898.

Bigelow, Francis Hill. *Historic Silver of the Colonies and its Makers*. New York: The Macmillan Company, 1917.

Bilby, Joseph G. *Remember Fontenoy!* Hightstown, N.J.: Longstreet House, 1995.

Biographical Dictionary of the American Congress 1774-1927. Washington, D.C.: U.S. Government Printing Office, 1928.

Biographical Sketches of American Artists. 5th ed. rev. Lansing: Michigan State Library, 1924.

Birmingham, Stephen. *Real Lace: America's Irish Rich*. New York: Harper & Row, 1973.

Birnbaum, Alexandra Mayes. *Birnbaum's Montreal & Quebec City 1993*. New York: Harper Perennial, 1993.

Bishop, Joseph Bucklin. *Theodore Roosevelt and His Times*. Vol. 1. New York: Charles Scribner's Sons, 1920.

"Bishop McLaughlin, Many Others, Join in Eulogizing McBride." *Pater-*

son Morning Call 4 January 1946: 1.

Blade, Robert E. "Pioneer Presbyterian Congregations." *American Presbyterians, Journal of Presbyterian History* 67 (1989).

Blanco, Richard, ed. *The American Revolution 1775-1783: An Encyclopedia.* 2 vols. New York: Garland Publishing, Inc., 1993.

Boatner, Mark Mayo, III. *The Civil War Dictionary.* New York: David McKay Company, Inc., 1959.

——. *Encyclopedia of the American Revolution.* New York: David McKay Company, Inc., 1974.

Bogue, Margaret Beattie, and Virginia A. Palmer. *Around the Shores of Lake Superior: A Guide to Historic Sites.* N.p.: The University of Wisconsin Sea Grant College Program, 1979.

Boisgilbert, Edmund. [pseud. for Ignatius Donnelly]. *Caesar's Column: A Story of the Twentieth Century.* Chicago: The Garden Vity Book Company, 1890.

Bolino, August C. *The Ellis Island Source Book.* 2nd ed. Washington, D.C.: Kensington Historical Press, 1990.

Bothwell, Margaret Pearson. "The Astonishing Croghans." *The Western Pennsylvania Historical Magazine* 48 (April 1965): 119-144.

Bottigheimer, Karl S. *Ireland and the Irish: A Short History.* New York: Columbia University Press, 1982.

Boucher, John N. *History of Westmoreland County, Pennsylvania.* Vol. 1. New York: The Lewis Publishing Company, 1906.

Boylan, Henry. *A Dictionary of Irish Biography.* New York: Barnes & Nobles Books, 1978.

Brasher, Earl L. *Mathew Carey: Editor, Author and Publisher.* New York: The Columbia University Press, 1912.

Brault, Lucien. *Ottawa Old and New.* Ottawa: Ottawa Historical Information Institute, 1946.

Brown, John Howard, ed. *Lamb's Biographical Dictionary of the United States.* 7 vols. Boston: James H. Lamb Company, 1900-1903.

Bruce, Robert. *Art and Sculpture of James Edward Kelly 1855-1933.* New York: n.p., 1934.

Bryan, Wilhelmus Bogart. *A History of the National Capitol.* Vol. 1. New York: The Macmillan Company, 1914.

Bryan, William Jennings, and Mary Baird Bryan. *The Memoirs of William Jennings Bryan.* Philadelphia: The United Publishers of America, 1925.

Busbey, L. White. *Uncle Joe Cannon: The Story of a Pioneer American.* New York: Henry Holt and Company, 1927.

Byers, A. R., ed. *Canadian Book of the Road.* N.p.: The Reader's Digest Association (Canada) Ltd., 1979.

Callahan, North. *Henry Knox: General Washington's General.* New York: Rienhart & Company, Inc., 1958.

Campbell, John H. *History of the Friendly Sons of St. Patrick and of the Hiber-*

nian Society for the Relief of Emigrants from Ireland. Philadelphia: Hibernian Society, 1892.

Carey, Mathew. *Autobiography of Mathew Carey*. Brooklyn: Research Classics, 1942.

Carr, William H. A. *The du Ponts of Delaware*. New York: Dodd, Mead & Company, 1964.

Castle, Henry A. "General James Shields, Soldier, Orator, Statesman." *Collections of the Minnesota Historical Society* 15 (1915): 711-730.

Catholic University of America. *New Catholic Encyclopedia*. 17 vols. New York: McGraw-Hill, 1967-79.

"Central Bridge Named for Outstanding Hero." *The (Lawrence, Mass.) Evening Tribune* 29 January 1940: 1.

Champlin, John Denison. *Cyclopedia of Painters and Painting*. New York: C. Scribner's Sons, 1886-87.

Chapman, Charles H. "The Historic Johnston Family of the 'Soo.'" *Collections of the Michigan Pioneer and Historical Society* 32 (1903): 305-353.

Charlesworth, Hector, ed. *A Cyclopedia of Canadian Biography*. National Biographical Series III. Toronto: The Hunter-Rose Company Ltd., 1919.

Chase, Robert P. *Property and Progress: Concord Township, Pennsylvania, 1683-1983*. Vol. 1 of *The Colonial Legacy*. N.p.: Concord Township Historical Society, 1983.

Chidsey, Donald Barr. *The Siege of Boston*. New York: Crown Publishers, Inc., 1966.

Chisholm, Anne, and Michael Davie. *Lord Beaverbrook: A Life*. New York: Alfred Knopf, 1995.

Churchyards of Trinity Parish 1697-1947. New York: Corporation of Trinity Church, 1948.

Claghorn, Charles Eugene. *Biographical Dictionary of American Music*. West Nyack, N.Y.: Parker Publishing Company, Inc., 1973.

———. *Woman Patriots of the American Revolution*. Metuchen, N.J.: The Scarecrow Press, Inc., 1991.

Clarke, Joseph I. C. "Unveiling the Sullivan Monument." *The Journal of the American Irish Historical Society* 12 (1913): 217-237.

Clarke, William J. "John Barry – Poem." *The Journal of the American Irish Historical Society* 13 (1914): 307-308.

Cleaves, Freeman. *Meade of Gettysburg*. Norman: University of Oklahoma Press, 1960.

Clement, J., ed. *Noble Deeds of American Women*. Buffalo: George H. Derby and Company, 1852.

Cohalan, Florence D. *Popular History of the Archdiocese of New York*. Yonkers: U.S. Catholic Historical Society, 1983.

Cohn, Victor. *Sister Kenny: The Woman Who Challenged the Doctors*. Minneapolis: The University of Minnesota Press, 1975.

Collar, Helen. "Irish Immigrants to Beaver Island." *The Journal of Beaver*

Island History 1 (1976): 27-49.

Colombo, John Robert. *Colombo's Canadian References*. Toronto: Oxford University Press, 1976.

Condon, Edward O'Meagher. *The Irish Race in America*. Glasgow: Cameron & Ferguson, n.d.

Condon, William H. *Life of Major-General James Shields*. Chicago: Press of the Blakely Printing Company, 1900.

Conley, Patrick T. *The Irish in Rhode Island: A Historical Appreciation*. Providence: The Rhode Island Heritage Commission and The Rhode Island Publications Society, 1986.

Conover, Charlotte Reeve, ed. *Dayton and Montgomery County*. Vol. 3. New York: Lewis Historical Publishing Company, Inc., 1932.

Conyngham, D. P. *The Irish Brigade and Its Campaigns*. Boston: William McSorley & Company, 1867.

Cooper, Brian, ed. *The Irish-American Almanac and Green Pages*. Rev. ed. New York: Harper & Row, 1990.

Cooper, J. Fenimore. *History of the Navy of the United States of America*. New York: G. P. Putnam & Company, 1854.

Corby, William, C.S.C. *Memoirs of Chaplain Life: Three Years with the Irish Brigade in the Army of the Potomac*. Chicago: La Monte, O'Donnell & Company, 1893.

Cosentino, Frank. "Ned Hanlan – Canada's Premier Oarsman: A Case Study in 19th Century Professionalism." *Ontario History* 66:241-250.

Cottman, George S. *Centennial History and Handbook of Indiana*. Indianapolis: Max R. Hyman, 1915.

Couper, Colonel William. *One Hundred Years at V.M.I.* Vol. 4. Richmond: Garrett and Massie, Incorporated, 1939.

Craig, Michel Williams. *General Edward Hand: Winter's Doctor*. Lancaster, Pa.: Rock Ford Foundation, 1984.

Craven, Bvt. Lieut.-Col. John J., M.D. *Prison Life of Jefferson Davis*. New York: Carleton, 1866.

Crimmins, John D. *Irish-American Miscellany*. New York: Published by the author, 1905.

Crofut, Florence S. Marcy. *Guide to the History and the Historic Sites of Connecticut*. Vol. 1. New Haven: Yale University Press, 1937.

Cromie, Alice Hamilton. *Restored America: A Tour Guide*. New York: American Legacy Press, 1979.

———. A Tour Guide to the Civil War. Chicago: Quadrangle Books, 1965.

Culbertson, Judi, and Tom Randall. *Permanent New Yorkers: A Biographical Guide to the Cemeteries of New York*. Chelsea, Vt.: Chelsea Green Publishing Company, 1987.

Cullen, Virginia. *History of Lewes, Delaware*. N.p.: Lewes and Rehoboth Hundred, Colonel David Hall Chapter, National Society, Daughters of the American Revolution, 1956.

Cushman, Clare, ed. *The Supreme Court Justices: Illustrated Biographies, 1789-1993*. Washington, D.C.: Congressional Quarterly, 1993.

Crew, H. W. *Centennial History of the City of Washington, D. C.* Dayton, Ohio: United Brethren Publishing House, 1892.

Cullen, James Bernard, ed. *The Story of the Irish in Boston*. Boston: James B. Cullen & Company, 1889.

Cutter, Elizabeth F., and Walter Hirthe. *Six Fitzgeralds – Lake Captains All*. Milwaukee: Wisconsin Marine Historical Society, 1983.

D'Arcy, Mary Ryan. *The Saints of Ireland*. St. Paul, Minn.: The Irish American Cultural Institute, 1974.

David, Henry. *The History of the Haymarket Affair*. New York: Russell & Russell, 1958.

Davie, Michael. *Titanic: The Death and Life of a Legend*. New York: Alfred A. Knopf, 1986.

Davin, Nicholas Flood. *The Irishman in Canada*. London: Sampson Low, Marston & Co., 1877.

Davis, John H. *The Kennedys: Dynasty and Disaster, 1848-1983*. New York: McGraw-Hill, 1984.

Davis, Kenneth S. *The Hero: Charles A. Lindbergh and the American Dream*. Garden City: Doubleday & Company, Inc., 1959.

Davis, Perry R. "Butch O'Hare, Chicago's Borrowed Hero." *Chicago History* (Fall and Winter 1988-89): 103-110.

Davis, W. W. H. *The History of Bucks County, Pennsylvania*. Doylestown, Pa.: Democrat Book and Job Office Prints, 1876.

Day, Catharina. *Ireland*. Cadogan Guides. Chester, Conn.: The Globe Pequot Press, 1991.

"Death of a Venerable Irish Priest." *Freeman's Journal* 12 December 1898.

"Dedicate New Bridge in Memory of Sgt. O'Leary." *The (Lawrence, Mass.) Evening Tribune* 1 July 1935: 8.

Dee, Henry Drummon. "An Irishman in the Fur Trade." *British Columbia Historical Quarterly* 7 (October 1943): 229-268.

DeGregorio, William. *The Complete Book of U.S. Presidents*. 4th ed. New York: Barricade Books, Inc., 1993.

Delaney, John J. *Dictionary of American Catholic Biography*. Garden City, N.Y.: Doubleday & Company, Inc., 1984.

de Mare, Marie. *G. P. A. Healy: An American Artist*. New York: David McKay Company, Inc., 1954.

"Denis B. Sheahan, Famed Sculptor." *The Journal of the American Irish Historical Society* 23 (1924): 220-221.

Descriptive Catalogue of Painting and Sculpture in the National Museum of American Art. Boston: G. K. Hall & Company, 1983.

Dickie, Anna Adams. "Scotch-Irish Presbyterian Settlers in Southern Wisconsin." *Wisconsin Magazine of History* 31 (March 1948): 291-304.

Dictionary of Canadian Biography. 13 vols. Toronto: University of Toronto

Press, 1966-94.

Dijon, Harold. "Goody Glover, an Irish Victim of the Witch Craze, Boston, Mass., 1688." *The Journal of the American Irish Historical Society* 5 (1905): 16-22.

Dinen, Joseph. *The Purple Shamrock: The Hon. James Michael Curley of Boston.* New York: W. W. Norton & Company, Inc., 1949.

Documentary History of the Construction and Development of the United States Capitol Building and Grounds. Washington, D.C.: Government Printing Office, 1904.

Dolin, Mary C. "American Irish Women 'Firsts.'" *The Journal of the American Irish Historical Society* 24 (1925): 215-221.

Donovan, Herbert D. A. "William C. Kinsella." *The Journal of the American Irish Historical Society* 21 (1922): 146-153.

Dougherty, Daniel J. *History of the Society of the Friendly Sons of St. Patrick.* Philadelphia: Friendly Sons of St. Patrick, 1952.

Douglas, R. *Place-Names of Prince Edward Island.* Ottawa: F. A. Acland, 1925.

Downs, Robert, et al. *Memorable Americans 1750-1950.* Littleton, Colo.: Libraries Unlimited Inc., 1983.

Drosdick, Nan, and Mark Morris. *Atlantic Canada Handbook.* Chico, Calif.: Moon Publications, 1995.

Drury, Clifford Merrill. *The History of the Chaplain Corps, United States Navy.* Vol 1 (1778-1939). Washington, D.C.: U.S. Government Printing Office, 1948-1950.

Drury, John. *Old Chicago Houses.* Chicago: The University of Chicago Press, 1941.

Dunne, Edward F. *Illinois: The Heart of the Nation.* Vol. 5. Chicago: The Lewis Publishing Company, 1933.

Durham, Michael S. *The Smithsonian Guide to Historic America: The Mid-Atlantic States.* New York: Stewart, Tabori & Chang, 1989.

Durkin, Joseph T., S.J. *William Matthews: Priest and Citizen.* New York: Benziger Brothers, Inc., 1963.

Eastman, John. *Who Lived Where: A Biographical Guide to Homes and Museums.* New York: Facts on File Publications, 1983.

Eaton, Diane, and Sheila Urbanek. *Paul Kane's Great Nor-West.* Vancouver: University of British Columbia Press, 1995.

Eberlein, Harold Donaldson, and Cortlandt Van Dyke Hubbard. *Portrait of a Colonial City: Philadelphia 1670-1838.* Philadelphia: J. B. Lippincott and Company, 1939.

"Edmund Fitzgerald, Insurance Executive." *New York Times* 9 January 1986: D15.

Egle, William H., ed. *Andrew Gregg Curtin: His Life and Services.* Philadelphia: Avil Printing Company, 1895.

Eleuterio-Connor, Susan K. *Irish American Material Culture.* New York: Greenwood Press, 1988.

Eliot, Alexander. *Three Hundred Years of American Painting*. New York: Time Incorporated, 1957.

Ellis, Nancy, and Parker Hayden. *Here Lies America: A Collection of Notable Graves*. New York: Hawthorne Books, Inc., 1978.

Emmet, Thomas Addis. *Memoir of Thomas Addis and Robert Emmet with Their Ancestors and Immediate Family*. Vol. 1. New York: The Emmet Press, 1915.

Estes, J. Worth. "Honest Dr. Thornton: The Path to Rebellion." *Physician Signers of the Declaration of Independence*. New York: Science History Publications, 1976.

Fairman, Charles. Art and Artists of the Capitol of the United States. Washington, D.C.: U.S. Government Printing Office, 1927.

Falk, Peter Hastings, ed. *Who Was Who in American Art*. Madison, Conn.: Sound View Press, 1985.

Fetherling, Dale. *Mother Jones: The Miners' Angel*. Carbondale, Ill.: Southern Illinois University Press, 1974.

Federal Writers' Project of the Work Projects Administration. *Chicago and Suburbs 1939*. Evanston, Ill.: Chicago Historical Bookworks, 1991.

———. Connecticut: A Guide to its Roads, Lore, and People. American Guide Series. Boston: Houghton Mifflin Company, 1938.

———. *Kansas: A Guide to the Sunflower State*. American Guide Series. New York: The Viking Press, 1939. 141-142.

———. *Maryland: A Guide to the Old Line State*. American Guide Series. New York: Oxford University Press, 1940.

———. *Massachusetts: A Guide to its Places and People*. American Guide Series. Boston: Houghton Mifflin Company, 1937.

———. *New Hampshire: A Guide to the Granite State*. American Guide Series. Boston: Houghton Mifflin Company, 1938.

———. *New Jersey: A Guide to its Present and Past*. American Guide Series. New York: Viking Press, 1939.

———. *The Ohio Guide*. American Guide Series. New York: Oxford University Press, 1940.

———. *Philadelphia: A Guide to the Nation's Birthplace*. American Guide Series. Philadelphia: William Penn Association of Philadelphia, Inc., 1937.

———. *Rhode Island: A Guide to the Smallest State*. American Guide Series. Boston: Houghton Mifflin Company, 1937.

———. *Washington: City and Capital*. American Guide Series. Washington, D.C.: Government Printing Office, 1937.

Fell, Thomas, ed. *Some Historical Accounts of the Founding of King William's School and its Subsequent Establishment as St. John's College*. Annapolis: Friendenwald Company, 1894.

Ferguson, C. Bruce, ed. *Uniacke's Sketches of Cape Breton*. Halifax: The Public Archives of Nova Scotia, 1958.

Ferrier, William Warren. *The Story of the Naming of Berkeley*. Berkeley: n.p.,

1929.

Ferris, Robert G., ed. *Signers of the Constitution.* Washington, D.C.: U.S. Department of the Interior, 1976.

Fielding, Mantle. *Dictionary of American Painters, Sculptors and Engravers.* New York: James F. Carr, 1965.

Fink, Gary M., ed. *Biographical Dictionary of American Labor Leaders.* Westport, Conn.: Greenwood Press, 1974.

Finley, Pepper Rae. "The Molly Maguires Are Still Polarizing Historians!" *Irish American Celebration.* Fall 1994: 6.

Fitzgerald, Margaret E., and Joseph A. King. *The Uncounted Irish in Canada and the United States.* Toronto: P. D. Meany Publishers, 1990.

"Five Iowa Brothers Lost in Pacific Battles." *New York Times* 13 January 1943: 10.

"5 Sullivans Died, Survivor Writes." *New York Times* 15 January 1943: 7.

Foley, Dylan. "Destination: Ellis Island." *Irish Echo* 14-20 July, 1993: 27.

"Foley in Politics for the Love of it." *New York Times* 16 January 1925: 2.

Formisano, Ronald P., and Constance K. Burns, eds. *Boston 1700-1980: The Evolution of Urban Politics.* Westport, Conn.: Greenwood Press, 1984.

Foner, Philip S., ed. *Mother Jones Speaks: Collected Writings and Speeches.* New York: Monad Press, 1983.

Forbes, Allan. *Towns of New England and Old England, Ireland and Scotland.* Vol. 1. Boston: State Street Trust Company, 1920.

Forbes, Allan, and Ralph M. Eastman. *Some Statues of Boston.* Boston: State Street Trust Company, 1946.

Ford, Worthington Chauncey, ed. *The Writings of George Washington.* Vol. 9. New York: G. P. Putnam's Sons, 1891.

Foster, Morrison. *Biography, Songs and Musical Compositions of Stephen C. Foster.* Pittsburgh: Morrison Foster, 1896.

Foster, R. F. *Modern Ireland 1600-1972.* London: Allen Lane, The Penguin Press, 1988.

Freely, John. *Blue Guide: Boston and Cambridge.* New York: W. W. Norton & Company, Inc., 1984.

Fried, Frederick. *New York Civic Sculpture: A Pictorial Guide.* New York: Dover Publications, Inc., 1976.

Froncek, Thomas, ed. *The City of Washington.* New York: Alfred A. Knopf, 1979.

Frueh, Erne R., and Florence. *Chicago Stained Glass.* Chicago: Loyola University Press, 1983.

Fullerton, Laurie. *Vacations in the Maritimes.* N.p. Yankee Publishing Inc., 1993.

Galbreath, Charles B. *History of Ohio.* Vol. 3. Chicago: The American Historical Society, 1925.

Gallagher, H. S. "An Irish Island Colony." *The Journal of the American Irish Historical Society* 28 (1929-30): 198-203.

Galvin, Clare. *The Holy Land: A History of Ennismore Township*. N.p.: The History of Ennismore Research Committee, 1978.

Gannon, Robert J., S.J. *The Cardinal Spellman Story*. New York: Doubleday & Company, 1962.

Gardner, Martin, ed. *The Annotated Casey at the Bat: A Collection of Ballads About the Mighty Casey*. New York: Clarkson N. Potter, 1967.

Germain, Aidan Henry. *Catholic Military and Naval Chaplains 1776-1917*. Dissertation, Catholic University of America, 1929.

Gibbon, John Murray. *The Romantic History of the Canadian Pacific: The Northwest Passage of Today*. New York: Tudor Publishing Company, 1937.

Gibson, Florence E. *The Attitudes of the New York Irish Toward State and National Affairs 1848-1892*. New York: Columbia University Press, 1951.

Gilbert, Mrs. Thomas D. "Memories of the 'Soo.'" *Collections of the Michigan Pioneer and Historical Society* 30 (1905): 623-633.

Glaspell, Susan. *The Road to the Temple*. New York: Stokes, 1927.

Gleeson, John. *The Book of Irish Lists and Trivia*. Dublin: Gill and Macmillan Ltd., 1989.

Goldman, John J. "Rose Kennedy, 104, Dies; Matriarch of a Dynasty." *Los Angeles Times* 23 January 1995: A1+.

Golin, Steve. "The Unity and Strategy of the Paterson Silk Manufacturers during the 1913 Strike." *Silk City: Studies on the Paterson Silk Industry, 1860-1940*. Edited by Philip B. Scranton. Newark: New Jersey Historical Society, 1985.

Goode, James M. *The Outdoor Sculpture of Washington, D.C.* Washington, D.C.: Smithsonian Institution Press, 1974.

Goodwin, Doris Kearns. *The Fitzgeralds and the Kennedys*. New York: Simon and Schuster, 1987.

"Governor Shaken by Friend's Death." *New York Times* 16 January 1925: 2.

Graham, Clara. *This was the Kootenay*. Vancouver: Evergreen Press Ltd., 1963.

Grant, Gay. "W. Clark Noble: Maine Sculptor." *The Kennebec Proprietor* 6 (Summer 1989): 20-25.

Greenberg, Ronald M, ed. *The National Register of Historic Places 1976*. 2 vols. Washington D.C.: U.S. Department of the Interior, 1976.

Greenbie, Sydney, and Marjorie Barstow Greenbie. *Anna Ella Carroll and Abraham Lincoln*. Tampa, Fla.: University of Florida Press, 1952.

Greenhow, Rose O'Neal. *My Imprisonment and the First Year of Abolition Rule at Washington*. London: Richard Bentley, 1863.

Griffin, Martin J. "Capt. Jeremiah O'Brien of Machias, Me." *American Catholic Historical Researches* 20 (1903): 80-81.

———. *Commodore John Barry, "The Father of the American Navy": The Record of His Services for Our Country*. Philadelphia: Published by the author, 1903.

———. "The First American Catholic Bible." *American Catholic Historical*

Researches 4 (April 1887): 64-68.

———. *The History of Commodore John Barry*. Philadelphia: The American Catholic Historical Society, 1897.

———. "James Hoban, the Architect and Builder of the White House and the Superintendent of the Building of the Capitol." *American Catholic Historical Researches* 24 (1907): 35-52.

———. "James Reed Dermott, the Planner of the City of Washington." *American Catholic Historical Researches* 27 (1910): 356-357.

Griffin, William D. *The Book of Irish Americans*. New York: Times Books, 1990.

A Guidebook to Newport Mansions. Newport, R.I.: The Preservation Society of Newport County, 1984.

Guelcher, Leslie A. *The History of Nininger . . . More than Just a Dream*. Stillwater, Minn.: The Croixside Press, 1982.

Guffey, Alexander. "The First Courts in Western Pennsylvania." *Western Pennsylvania Historical Magazine* 7 (July 1924): 145-177.

Gurn, Joseph. *Commodore John Barry: Father of the American Navy*. New York: P. J. Kenedy & Sons, 1933.

Hall, David D., ed. *Witch-hunting in Seventeenth-Century New England: A Documentary History, 1638-1692*. Boston: Northwestern University Press, 1991.

Haltigan, Patrick J. *The Irish in the American Revolution and their Early Influence in the Colonies*. Washington, D.C.: Patrick J. Haltigan, 1908.

Hamilton, William B. *The Nova Scotia Traveller*. Toronto: The Macmillan Company of Canada, 1981.

Hammond, John Martin. *Colonial Mansions of Maryland and Delaware*. Philadelphia: J. B. Lippincott Company, 1914.

Hanchett, William. *Lincoln Murder Conspiracies*. Chicago: University of Illinois Press, 1983.

The Handbook of Private Schools. 75th ed. Boston: Porter Sargent Publishers, Inc., 1994.

Hanna, Charles A. *The Scotch-Irish or The Scot in North Britain, North Ireland, and North America*. Vol. 1. New York: G. P. Putnam's Sons, 1902.

———, ed. *The Wilderness Trail*. Vol. 1. New York: G. P. Putnam's Sons, 1911.

Hansen, Harry, ed. *Illinois: A Descriptive and Historical Guide*. American Guide Series. New rev. ed. New York: Hastings House, 1974.

Harris, John. *Historic Walks in Old Boston*. Chester, Conn.: The Globe Pequot Press, 1982.

Harris, Reginald V. *Charles Inglis: Missionary, Loyalist, Bishop (1734-1816)*. Toronto: General Board of Religious Education, 1937.

———. *The Church of Saint Paul in Halifax, Nova Scotia*. N.p.: Ryerson, 1949.

Hart, Charles Henry. "Colonel John Nixon." *The Pennsylvania Magazine of History and Biography* 1 (1877): 188-202.

Harting, Emilie C. *A Literary Tour of the United States: Northeast*. New York:

William Morrow and Company, Inc., 1978.

Hatfield, Edwin F. *History of Elizabeth, New Jersey*. New York: Carlton & Lanahan, 1868.

Healy, George P. A. *Reminiscences of a Portrait Painter*. Chicago: A. C. McClurg and Company, 1894.

Hearst, William Randolph Jr. *The Hearsts, Father and Son*. Niwot, Colo.: Roberts Rinehart Publishers, 1991.

Hedlund, Nancy M. "The Buckley Homestead." Crown Point, Ind.: Lake County Parks and Recreation Department, n.d.

Heise, Kenan, and Mark Frazel. *Hands on Chicago*. Chicago: Bonus Books, 1987.

Henderson, Dorothy. *Robert McLaughlin: Carriage Builder*. Toronto: Griffin House, 1972.

Herbermann, Charles George, et al. *Catholic Encyclopedia*. 15 vols. New York: Appleton, 1907-12.

Hergesheimer, Joseph. *Sheridan: A Military Narrative*. Boston: Houghton Mifflin Company, 1931.

Herlihy, Elizabeth M., ed. *Fifty Years of Boston*. Boston: Boston Tercentenary Committee, 1932.

Heymann, C. David. *A Woman Named Jackie*. New York: A Lyle Stuart Book, 1989.

Highsmith, Carol M., and Ted Landphair. *Embassies of Washington*. Washington, D.C.: The Preservation Press, 1992.

Hill, George W. "Nomenclature of the Streets of Halifax." *Nova Scotia Historical Society Collections* 15 (1911): 1-22.

Hill, Sarah, and Harry B. *Yankee City . . . Faces from Our Past*. Vol. 1. Newburyport, Mass.: The Newburyport Five Cents Savings Bank, 1982.

"Historic Tablets." *Nova Scotia Historical Society Collections* 18 (1914): xxxi-xxxv.

History of Dayton, Ohio. Dayton: United Brethren Publishing House, 1889.

The History of Peoria County, Illinois. Chicago: Johnson & Company, 1880.

History of St. Clair County, Michigan. Chicago: A. T. Andreas and Company, 1883.

Hogarth Paul. *Walking Tours of Old Philadelphia*. Barre, Mass.: Barre Publishing, 1976.

Holli, Melvin G. and Peter d'A. Jones, eds. *Biographical Dictionary of American Mayors, 1820-1980*. Westport, Conn.: Greenwood Press, 1981.

Holt, Glen E., and Dominic A. Pacyga. *Chicago: A Historical Guide to the Neighborhoods: The Loop and South Side*. Chicago: Chicago Historical Society, 1979.

Hood, M. McIntyre. *Oshawa: Canada's Motor City*. [Oshawa, Ont.]: McLaughlin Public Library, 1968.

Horan, James D. *Mathew Brady: Historian with a Camera*. New York: Bonanza Books, 1955.

Horle, Craig W., et al. *Lawmaking and Legislators in Pennsylvania: A Biographical Dictionary*. Vol. 1. Philadelphia: University of Pennsylvania Press, 1991.

Howe, Henry. *Historical Collections of Ohio*. Cincinnati: Henry Howe, 1851.

Hughes, Rupert. *George Washington, The Savior of the States 1777-1781*. New York: William Morrow & Company, 1930.

Hunter, W. H. "The Pathfinders of Jefferson County." *Ohio Archaeological and Historical Publications* 6 (1898): 95-313.

Illustrated Guide to the Treasures of America. Pleasantville, N.Y.: The Readers' Digest Association, Inc., 1974.

"Ireland's New Envoy Received by Truman." *New York Times* 18 April 1950: 10.

Irwin, Robert, ed. *Baltimore: 200th Anniversary 1729-1929*. Baltimore: Baltimore Municipal Journal, 1929.

Jackson, Joseph. *Encyclopedia of Philadelphia*. Harrisburg: The National Historical Association, 1933.

Jackson, Ronald Vern, and Altha Polson. *American Patriots*. N.p.: n.p., 1981.

"Jeremiah Sullivan House." Madison, Ind.: Historic Madison, Inc., n.d.

"John Gibbons and the Gibbons House." Wilmington, Del.: Hagley Museum and Library, 1970.

Johnson, Allen, et al., eds. *Dictionary of American Biography*. 28 vols. New York: C. Scribner's Sons, 1928-88.

Johnson, James E. *The Scots and Scotch-Irish in America*. Minneapolis: Lerner Publications Company, 1966.

Johnson, Robert Underwood. *Saint-Gaudens: An Ode and Other Verse*. New York: The Century Company, 1910.

Jolly, Ellen Ryan. *Nuns of the Battlefield*. Providence: The Providence Visitor Press, 1927.

Jones, Louis C. *Cooperstown*. Cooperstown, N.Y.: New York State Historical Association, 1982.

Jones, Maldwyn Allen. *American Immigration*. 2nd ed. Chicago: The University of Chicago Press, 1992.

Jones, Thomas C., ed. *The Halls of Fame*. Chicago: J. G. Ferguson Publishing Company, 1977.

Jordan, John W. "Bishop J. C. F. Carmmeroff's Narrative of a Journey to Shamokin, Pennsylvania, in the Winter of 1748." *The Pennsylvania Magazine of History and Biography* 19 (April 1905): 160-179.

Journal of the Illinois State Historical Society 50 (Spring 1957): 74.

Karlsen, Carol F. *The Devil in the Shape of a Woman: Witchcraft in Colonial New England*. New York: W. W. Norton & Company, 1987.

Karpel, Bernard, ed. *Arts in America: A Bibliography*. Vol. 1. Washington, D.C.: Smithsonian Institution Press, 1979.

Keany, Harry. "Molly Maguire' Found Not Guilty." *Irish Echo* 22-28 December 1992.

———. "Sainthood Beckons for Ordinary Irish American." *Irish Echo* 23-29 August 1995.

Kearny, Thomas. *General Philip Kearny: Battle Soldier of Five Wars*. New York: G. P. Putnam's Sons, 1937.

Keating, Percy. "John Keating and His Forebears." *Records of the American Catholic Historical Society* 29 (December 1918): 289-335.

Kenneally, James J. *The History of American Catholic Women*. New York: Crowrood, 1990.

Kennedy, J. H. "Governor Dongan and Religious Liberty in New York 1683-1688." *The Journal of the American Irish Historical Society* 28 (1929-30): 100-106.

Kerr, J. B. *Biographical Dictionary of Well-Known British Columbians*. Vancouver: Kerr & Begg, 1890.

Kevan, Martin. *The Best of Montreal & Quebec City: A Guide to the Places, Peoples and Pleasures of French Canada*. New York: Crown Publishers, Inc., 1992.

Kobles, John J. *F. Scott Fitzgerald's Minnesota: His Homes and Haunts*. St. Paul, Minn.: Minnesota Historical Society Press, 1978.

Koenig, Louis W. *Bryan: A Political Biography of William Jennings Bryan*. New York: G. P. Putnam's Sons, 1971.

Kohl, Lawrence Frederick, ed. *Memoirs of Chaplain Life: Three Years with the Irish Brigade in the Army of the Potomac by William Corby, C.S.C.* New York: Fordham University Press, 1992.

Kruh, David, and Louis Kruh. *Presidential Landmarks*. New York: Hippocrene Books Inc., 1992.

Kussart, Mrs. S. "One Hundredth Anniversary of the Birth of Mrs. Mary E. Schenley." *Western Pennsylvania Historical Magazine* 9 (October 1926): 209-220.

Lake, Benjamin J. *The Story of the Presbyterian Church in the United States of America*. Philadelphia: Westminster Press, 1956.

Lathrop, H. W. *The Life and Times of Samuel J. Kirkwood*. Iowa City: Published by the author, 1893.

Leacock, Stephen. *Montreal: Seaport and City*. Garden City: Doubleday, Doran & Company, Inc., 1942.

Lee, Thomas Amory. "The Tracy Family of Newburyport. *Historical Collections of the Essex Institute* 57 (January 1921): 57-74.

Lee, Thomas Z. "American Irish Historical Notes." *The Journal of the American Irish Historical Society* 25 (1926): 218-222.

Leviero, Anthony. "U.S., Ireland Raise Envoys' Status to Top Rank – Thanks to a Woman." *New York Times* 25 February 1950: 1.

Levingston, Steven E. *Historic Ships of San Francisco*. San Francisco: Chronicle Books, 1984.

LeVot, Andre. *F. Scott Fitzgerald: A Biography*. Garden City: Doubleday & Company, Inc., 1983.

"Lewis and Loretta Glucksman Honor the Irish." *New York Times* 17 May 1991: B6.

Lewis, Charles Lee. *The Romantic Decatur*. Philadelphia: University of Pennsylvania Press, 1937.

Lewis, R. W. B. *The Jameses: A Family Narrative*. New York: Farrar, Straus and Giroux, 1991.

Linden-Ward, Blanche. *Silent City on a Hill: Landscapes of Memory and Boston's Mount Auburn Cemetery*. Columbus: Ohio State University Press, 1989.

Livermore, Mary A. *My Story of the War: A Woman's Narrative of Four Years Personal Experience*. Hartford: A. D. Worthington and Company, 1888.

Lockwood, George B. *The New Harmony Movement*. New York: D. Appleton and Company, 1905.

Logan, Rayford W., and Michael R. Winston, eds. *Dictionary of American Negro Biography*. New York: W. W. Norton & Company, Inc., 1982.

Lonn, Ella. *Foreigners in the Union Army and Navy*. New York: Greenwood Press, 1951.

Macdonald, James S. "Memoirs of Governor John Parr." *Nova Scotia Historical Society Collections* 14 (1910) 41-78.

———. "Richard Bulkeley." *Nova Scotia Historical Society Collections* 12 (1905): 59-87.

"The MacGahan Monument." *Ohio Archaeological and Historical Quarterly* 21 (April-July 1912): 215-244.

Mackenzie, Alexander Slidell. *Life of Stephen Decatur*. Boston: Charles C. Little & James Brown, 1846.

MacKenzie, Margaret and Rod. *Toronto: The Ultimate Guide*. San Francisco: Chronicle Books, 1992.

MacNutt, Francis Augustus. *Six Decades of My Life*. Vol. 1. Brixen, Italy: Weigers Press, 1927.

Madden, R. R., M. D. *The United Irishmen: Their Lives and Times*. Vol. 2 (2nd series). London: J. Madden & Company, 1843.

Madison, James. *Notes of Debates in the Federal Convention of 1787*. Edited by Adrienne Koch. Athens, Ohio: Ohio University Press, 1984.

Maginniss, Thomas Hobbs. "General Edward Hand." *The Journal of the American Irish Historical Society* 23 (1924): 124-126.

Mahoney, William H. "Franklin Murphy, Governor of New Jersey." *The Journal of the American Irish Historical Society* 24 (1925): 175-177.

———. "The Irish Element in Newark." *The Journal of the American Irish Historical Society* 21 (1922): 131-146.

Maier, Eugene F. J. "Mathew Carey, Publicist and Politician." *Records of the American Catholic Historical Society* 39 (June 1928): 71-154.

Makers of History in Washington 1800-1950. Washington, D.C.: National Gallery of Art, 1950.

Malone, Russ. *Hippocrene U.S.A. Guide to Irish America*. New York:

Hippocrene Books, 1994.

Marsh, James H., ed. *The Canadian Encyclopedia*. Edmonton: Hurtig Publishers, 1985.

Mather, Cotton. *Memorable Providences, Relating to Witchcraft and Possessions*. Reprinted in *Narratives of the Witchcraft Cases, 1648-1706*. Edited by George L. Burr. New York: C. Scribner's Sons, 1914.

McCaffrey, Lawrence J., et al. *The Irish in Chicago*. Urbana, Ill.: University of Illinois Press, 1987.

McCann, James H. "Towers of Silence Speak." *The Journal of the American Irish Historical Society* 30 (1932): 134-163.

McClure, Paul, ed. *Washington Information Directory 1996-1997*. Washington, D.C.: Congressional Quarterly Inc., 1996.

McGee, Thomas D'Arcy. *A History of the Irish Settlers in North America from the Earliest Period to the Census of 1850*. Boston: Patrick Donahue, 1852.

McKane, Frank E. *General Sullivan: New Hampshire Patriot*. Vol. 1. New York: Vantage Press, 1977.

McKean, Dayton David. *The Boss: The Hague Machine in Action*. Boston: Houghton Mifflin Company, 1940.

A Memorial of Crispus Attucks, Samuel Maverick, Jonas Caldwell, Samuel Gray, and Patrick Carr. Boston: City of Boston, 1889.

A Memorial of John Boyle O'Reilly from the City of Boston. Boston: The Board of Aldermen, 1891.

"Memorial to Jeffrey Roche." *The Journal of the American Irish Historical Society* 9 (1910): 441.

Meyers, Albert Cook. *Immigration of the Irish Quakers into Pennsylvania 1682-1750*. Swarthmore, Pa.: Published by the author, 1902.

Michelin Green Guide to Ireland. 1992 ed.

Miller, Pamela, et al. *The McCord Family: A Passionate Vision*. N.p.: McCord Museum of Canadian History, n.d.

Mintz, Max M. *The Generals of Saratoga*. New Haven: Yale University Press, 1990.

Mitchell, Brian C. *The Paddy Camp: The Irish of Lowell 1821-61*. Urbana, Ill.: University of Illinois Press, 1988.

Mitchell, Broadus. *Alexander Hamilton: Youth to Maturity 1755-1788*. New York: The Macmillan Company, 1957.

Mizener, Arthur. *Scott Fitzgerald and His World*. New York: G. P. Putnam's Sons, 1972.

Mobile Travel Guide: Great Lakes. New York: Prentice Hall General Reference and Travel, 1993.

Mobile Travel Guide: Middle Atlantic. New York: Prentice Hall General Reference and Travel, 1994.

Morgan, Henry James, ed. *The Canadian Men and Women of the Time*. 2nd ed. Toronto: William Briggs, 1912.

Morison, Samuel Eliot. *Admiral of the Ocean Sea: A Life of Christopher Co-*

lumbus. Boston: Little, Brown and Company, 1942.

———. *The European Discovery of America: The Northern Voyages A.D. 500-1600*. New York: Oxford University Press, 1971.

———. *"Old Bruin": Commodore Matthew C. Perry 1794-1858*. Boston: Little, Brown and Company, 1967.

Mosier, Richard D. *Making the American Mind: Social and Moral Influences in the McGuffey Readers*. New York: King's Crown Press, 1947.

Mosley, Leonard. *Lindbergh: A Biography*. Garden City: Doubleday & Company, Inc., 1976.

"A 'Most Magnificent' Mansion." Providence: The Rhode Island Historical Society, 1985.

"Mother's Tears for Her Five Heroic Sons Christen New Destroyer 'The Sullivans.'" *New York Times* 5 April 1943: 11.

Mott, Frank Luther. *A History of American Magazines 1741-1850*. New York: D. Appleton and Company, 1930.

Mulholland, St. Clair A. *The Story of the 116th Regiment Pennsylvania Volunteers in the War of the Rebellion*. Philadelphia: F. McManus, Jr., & Company, 1903.

Mulligan, Hercules. "Narrative of Hercules Mulligan." In *Hercules Mulligan: Confidential Correspondent of General Washington* by Michael J. O'Brien. New York: P. J. Kenedy & Sons, 1937.

Murdock, Myrtle Cheney. *National Statuary Hall in the Nation's Capitol*. Washington, D.C.: Monumental Press, Inc., 1955.

Murphy, Robert T. "Keely, Patrick Charles." Vol. 2. *Macmillan Encyclopedia of Architects*. Edited by Adolf K. Placzek. New York: The Free Press, 1982.

Murphy, T. L. *Kelly's Heroes: The Irish Brigade at Gettysburg*. Gettysburg: Farnsworth House Military Impressions, 1997.

Murray, Thomas Hamilton. "Rev. James MacSparran, Irishman, Scholar, Preacher and Philosopher, 1680-1757." *The Journal of the American Irish Historical Society* 3 (1900): 52-61.

Muse, Vance. *The Smithsonian Guide to Historic America: Northern New England*. New York: Stewart, Tabori & Chang, 1989.

Naden, Corinne J. *The Haymaket Affair, Chicago, 1886*. New York: Franklin Watts, Inc., 1968.

"Name 'The Sullivans' Set for Destroyer." *New York Times* 10 February 1943: 16.

National Cyclopaedia of American Biography. 81 vols. New York: J. T. White Company, 1893-1978.

National Gallery of Art. *Makers of History in Washington 1800-1950*. Washington, D.C.: National Gallery of Art, 1950.

National Portrait Gallery, Smithsonian Institution, Permanent Collection Illustrated Checklist. Washington, D.C.: National Portrait Gallery, 1987.

Neidhardt, W. S. *Fenians in North America*. University Park: The Penn State

University Press, 1975.

Nelson, Paul David. *Anthony Wayne: Soldier of the Early Republic*. Bloomington, Ill.: Illinois University Press, 1985.

Nevins, Allan. *Grover Cleveland: A Study in Courage*. New York: Dodd, Mead & Company, 1933.

Nevins, Allan, and Frank Ernest Hill. *Ford: Expansion and Challenge 1915-1933*. New York: Charles Scribner's Sons, 1957.

New, W. H., ed. *Canadian Writers, 1890-1920*. Volume 92 of *Dictionary of Literary Biography*. Detroit: Gale Research Inc., 1990.

Newberry, Linda, ed. *New Jersey: A Guide to its Present and Past*. American Guide Series. New York: Hastings House, 1977.

Norris, Walter B. *Annapolis: Its Colonial and Naval Story*. New York: Thomas Y. Crowell Company, 1925.

North, S. W. D. "The Story of a Monument." *Magazine of American History* 12 (July-December 1884): 97-112.

Notman, William, and Fennings Taylor. *Portraits of British Americans, with Biographical Sketches*. Vol. 2. Montreal: William Notman, 1867.

O'Brien, Michael J. *George Washington's Associations with the Irish*. New York: P. J. Kenedy & Sons, 1937.

———. "Hercules Mulligan." *The Journal of the American Irish Historical Society* 26 (1927): 96-104.

———. *Hercules Mulligan: Confidential Correspondent of General Washington*. New York: P. J. Kenedy & Sons, 1937.

———. *In Old New York: The Irish Dead in Trinity and St. Paul's Churchyards*. New York: The American Irish Historical Society, 1928.

———. "The Irish Ancestors of Theodore Roosevelt." *The Journal of the American Irish Historical Society* 17 (1918): 144-145.

———. *The Irish at Bunker Hill*. Shannon, Ireland: Irish University Press, 1968.

———. *Irish Settlers in America. A Consolidation of Articles from The Journal of the American Irish Historical Society*. 2 vols. Baltimore: Genealogical Publishing Company, Inc., 1979.

———. "Washington's Irish Friends." *The Journal of the American Irish Historical Society* 25 (1926): 344-369.

O'Conor, Charles. *"Negro Slavery Not Unjust": Speech of Charles O'Conor, Esq., at the Union Meeting at the Academy of Music, New York City, December 19th, 1859*. New York: Van Evrie, Horton & Company, [1859].

O'Hanlon, Ray. "Antietam Irish to Get Memorial." *Irish Echo* 12-18 July 1995: 4.

Olcott, Charles S. *The Life of William McKinley*. Vol. 1. Boston: Houghton Mifflin Company, 1916.

O'Neill, Eugene. *Long Day's Journey into Night*. New Haven: Yale University Press, 1955.

O'Neill, James L. "Rev. James Caldwell, a Patriot of the American Revolution." *The Journal of the American Irish Historical Society* 3 (1900): 89-94.

O'Neill, Paul. *Everyman's Complete St. John's Guide.* St. John's: Valhalla Press, 1975.

Orear, Leslie F. *Our Castle on the Hill.* Chicago: Beverly Unitarian Church, 1980.

O'Reilly, John Boyle. *Selected Poems.* New York: P. J. Kenedy & Sons, 1913.

O'Reilly, Vincent Fleming. "Major-General Richard Montgomery." *The Journal of the American Irish Historical Society* 25 (1926): 179-194.

Ormsby, Margaret. *British Columbia: A History.* Vancouver: The Macmillans in Canada, 1958.

———. "Some Irish Figures in Colonial Days." *British Columbia Historical Quarterly* 14 (January-April 1950): 61-82.

O'Sheel, Shaemus. "Breakfast with Hercules Mulligan." In *Hercules Mulligan: Confidential Correspondent of General Washington* by Michael J. O'Brien. New York: P. J. Kenedy & Sons, 1937.

Paine, Thomas. *A Dialogue Between the Ghost of General Montgomery and an American Delegate.* New York: Privately reprinted, 1865.

Parmet, Herbert S., and Marie B. Hecht. *Aaron Burr: Portrait of an Ambitious Man.* New York: The Macmillan Company, 1967.

Phelan, Thomas P. "Thomas Dongan, Colonial Governor of New York." *The Journal of the American Irish Historical Society* 16 (1917): 22-36.

Pidgeon, Paul. "The Black Stone on Bridge Street." *Irish America* (January/February 1996): 34-35.

Piggott, Michael. "Irish Pioneers of the Upper Mississippi Valley." *The Journal of the American Irish Historical Society* 9 (1910): 301-330.

Pilcher, Edith. The Constables: First Family of the Adirondacks. Utica, N.Y.: North Country Books, Inc., 1992.

Plummer, Mary H., and Gerald W. Gillette, eds. *On Holy Ground: American Presbyterian/Reformed Historical Sites.* Philadelphia: Presbyterian Historical Society, 1982.

The Poetical Works of T. Buchanan Read. New rev. ed. Philadelphia: J. B. Lippincott & Company, 1883.

Pollack, Queena. "An Irish Innkeeper and His Internationally Known 'Innkeeper's Daughter.'" *The Journal of the American Irish Historical Society* 28 (1929-30): 94.

The Postal Service Guide to U.S. Stamps. 19th ed. Washington, D.C.: U.S. Postal Service, 1993.

Potter, George. *To the Golden Door: The Story of the Irish in Ireland and America.* Boston: Little, Brown and Company, 1960.

Powell, Walter Louis. *The Alexander Dobbin House: A Short History.* N.p.: Published by the author, 1986.

Power, L. G. "Richard John Uniacke." *Nova Scotia Historical Society Collections* 9 (1895): 73-118.

"President Wilson's Speech." *The Journal of the American Irish Historical*

Society 13 (1913-14): 300-302.

Prouse, D. W. *A History of Newfoundland*. London: Macmillan and Company, 1895.

Punch, Terrence M. "Finding Our Irish." *The Nova Scotia Historical Review* 6 (1986).

Purcell, L. Edward. *Who Was Who in the American Revolution*. New York: Facts on File, Inc., 1993.

Pusey, Merlo J. *Charles Evans Hughes*. Vol. 1. New York: The Macmillan Company, 1951.

Putnam, Carleton. *Theodore Roosevelt*. Vol. 1. New York: Charles Scribner's Sons, 1858.

Quigley, Michael. "Irish Famine Memorial." *Irish America* (May / June 1996): 44-46.

Quinn, C. Edward, F.S.C. *The Signers of the Constitution of the United States*. The Bronx: The Bronx County Historical Society, 1987.

Quinon, Stephen. "Careers of the Croghans." *Western Pennsylvania Historical Magazine* 5 (July 1922): 215-219.

Reagan, Ronald. *An American Life*. New York: Simon and Schuster, 1990.

Ridge, Martin. *Ignatius Donnelly: The Portrait of a Politician*. St. Paul, Minn.: Minnesota Historical Society Press, 1991.

Roberts, Charles G. D., and Arthur L. Tunnell, eds. *A Standard Dictionary of Canadian Biography*. Toronto: Trans-Canada Press, 1938.

Roberts, Gary Boyd. *Ancestors of American Presidents*. Santa Clarita, Calif.: Carl Boyer III, 1995.

Roche, James Jeffrey. *Life of John Boyle O'Reilly*. Chicago: J. S. Hyland & Company, 1891.

Rodney, William. *Joe Boyle: King of the Klondike*. Toronto: McGraw-Hill Ryerson Limited, 1974.

———. *Kootenai Brown: His Life and Times 1939-1916*. Sidney, B.C.: Gray's Publishing Ltd., 1969.

Rose, William Ganson. *Cleveland: The Making of a City*. Cleveland: The World Publishing Company, 1950.

Ross, A. H. D. *Ottawa Past and Present*. Toronto: The Musson Book Company, 1927.

Ross, Betty. *A Museum Guide to Washington, D.C.* Washington, D.C.: Americana Press, 1986.

Ross, David. *Superintendent James Morrow Walsh: An Interpretative & Biographical Study*. [Unpublished] 1996.

Ross, Ishbel. *Charmers and Cranks*. New York: Harper & Row, 1965.

Rowe, G. S. *Thomas McKean: The Shaping of an American Republicanism*. Boulder: Colorado Associated University Press, 1978.

Roy, Pierre-Georges. *Les Monuments Commémoratifs de la Province de Québec*. Vol. 1. Québec: La Commission des Monuments Historiques de la Province de Québec, 1923.

A Rush County Retrospect. Vol. 1. Rushville, Ind.: Rush County Historical Society, 1984.

Ryan, Leo Raymond. *The Mother Church of Catholic New York (1785-1935)*. New York: The United States Catholic Historical Society, 1935.

Sadie, Stanley, ed. *The New Grove Dictionary of Music and Musicians*. 20 vols. London: Macmillan Publishers Limited, 1980.

Sadlier, Mary Anne, ed. *The Poems of Thomas D'Arcy McGee*. New York: D. & J. Sadlier & Company, 1869.

Salwen, Peter. *Upper West Side Story*. New York: Abbeville Press, 1989.

Sampson, Harriet Susan. "My Father, Joseph Despard Pemberton: 1821-93." *British Columbia Historical Quarterly* 8 (1944) 111-125.

Samuels, Edward A., and Henry H. Kimball. *Somerville Past & Present: An Illustrated Historical Souvenir*. Boston: N.p., 1897.

Scales, John. "Master John Sullivan." *The Journal of the American Irish Historical Society* 5 (1905): 63-81.

Scharf, J. Thomas. *History of Delaware 1609-1888*. Vol. 1. Philadelphia: L. J. Richards & Company, 1888.

Schauinger, Joseph Herman. "Jeremiah C. Sullivan, Hoosier Jurist." *Indiana Magazine of History* 37 (September 1941): 217-237.

Schlesinger, Arthur M., Jr., ed. *The Almanac of American History*. New York: Bramhall House, 1986.

Scholefield, E. O. S., and F. W. Howay. *British Columbia: From the Earliest Times to the Present*. Vol. 4. Vancouver: The S. J. Clarke Publishing Company, 1914.

Schoolcraft, Henry Rowe. "Memoir of John Johnston." *Collections of the Michigan Pioneer and Historical Society* 36 (1908): 53-90.

Seale, William. *The President's House*. Vol. 1. Washington, D.C.: White House Historical Association, 1986.

Semmes, Rafael. *Captains and Mariners of Early Maryland*. Baltimore: The Johns Hopkins Press, 1937.

Shannon, William V. *The American Irish*. Rev. ed. New York: The Macmillan Company, 1966.

Shapiro, Mary J. *Ellis Island: An Illustrated History of the Immigrant Experience*. New York: Macmillan Publishing Company, 1991.

Shea, John Gilmary. *"History of Georgetown University": Memorial of the First Centenary of Georgetown College, D.C.* Washington, D.C.: Published by the College, 1891.

———. *History of the Catholic Church in the United States 1808-15 to 1843*. New York: Published by the author, 1890.

———. *The Life and Times of the Most Rev. John Carroll*. New York: Published by the author, 1888.

Sheaffer, Louis. *O'Neill: Son and Playwright*. Boston: Little, Brown and Company, 1968.

Sheahan, James W., and George P. Upton. *Chicago: Its Past, Present and Fu-*

ture. Chicago: Union Publishing Company, 1871.

Shenkman, Richard, and Kurt Reiger. *One-Night Stands with American History*. New York: William Morrow & Company, Inc., 1980.

Sheppard, J. Havergal. "Colonel John Binns." *The Journal of the American Irish Historical Society* 29 (1930-31): 55-66.

Shipman, David. *Judy Garland: The Secret Life of an American Legend*. New York: Hyperion, 1992.

Siegel, Beatrice. *Sam Ellis's Island*. New York: Four Winds Press, 1985.

Sifakis, Stewart. *Who Was Who in the Civil War*. New York: Facts on File Publications, 1988.

"Sister of 5 Sullivans in Waves." *New York Times* 7 April 1943: 22.

Smallwood, J. R., ed. *The Book of Newfoundland*. Vol. 1. St. John's: Newfoundland Book Publishers, Ltd., 1937.

Smith, George. *History of Delaware County, Pennsylvania*. Philadelphia: Henry B. Asgmead, 1862.

Smith, Page. *The Nation Comes of Age: A People's History of the Ante-Bellum Years*. New York: McGraw-Hill Book Company, 1981.

———. *A New Age Now Begins. A People's History of the American Revolution*. New York: McGraw-Hill Book Company, 1976.

———. *The Rise of Industrial America*. New York: McGraw-Hill Book Company, 1984.

———. *The Shaping of America: A People's History of the Young Republic*. New York: McGraw-Hill Book Company, 1980.

Smylie, James H. *American Presbyterianism: A Pictorial History*. Philadelphia: Presbyterian Historical Society, 1985.

Sobel, Robert, and John Raimo, eds. *Biographical Dictionary of the Governors of the United States 1789-1978*. 4 vols. Westport, Conn.: Meckler Books, 1978.

Soderberg, Paul, et al. *The Big Book of Halls of Fames in the United States and Canada*. New York: R. R. Bowker Company, 1977.

Sorensen, Theodore C. *Kennedy*. New York: Harper & Row, 1965.

Spry, Irene M, ed. "The Papers of The Palliser Expedition, 1857-1860." Volume 44 of *The Publications of the Champlain Society*. Toronto: The Champlain Society, 1968.

Steinberg, Sheila, and Cathleen McGuigan. *Rhode Island: An Historical Guide*. Providence: Rhode Island Bicentennial Foundation, 1976.

Stewart, James. *The DuPont Company and Irish Immigration 1800-1857: A Study of the Company's Efforts to Arrange Passages for the Families of its Workmen*. Unpublished work, 1976.

Stewart, William Rhinelander. *Grace Church and Old New York*. New York: E. P. Dutton & Company, 1924.

Stonehouse, Frederick. *The Wreck of the Edmund Fitzgerald*. Au Train, Mich.: Avery Color Studios, 1977.

"Sullivans Typify War Spirit of U.S." *New York Times* 8 February 1943: 21.

"Sunny Jim." *The Blood Horse* 83 (July 13, 1963): 108-111; 85 (July 20, 1963): 220-225; 91 (March 19, 1966): 714-715.

Sylvester, Lorna Lutes. "Conner Prairie Pioneer Settlement and Museum." *Indiana Magazine of History* 65 (March 1969): 1-24.

Taormina, Francis R. *William Johnson: Who He Was, What He Did.* Schenectady: Published by the author, 1993.

Taylor, A. J. P. *Beaverbrook.* New York: Simon and Schuster, 1972.

Taylor, Robert M. et al. *Indiana: A New Historical Guide.* Indianapolis: Indiana Historical Society, 1989.

Thatcher, John Boyd. *Christopher Columbus: His Life, His Work, His Remains.* Vol. 1. New York: G. P. Putnam's Sons, 1903.

Thavis, John. "U.S. Capuchin Solanus Casey Declared Venerable by Vatican." *Tidings* 14 July 1995.

Thayer, Theodore. *As We Were: The Story of Old Elizabethport.* Elizabeth, N.J.: The Grassman Publishing Company, Inc., 1964.

Thomas, Samuel W. "William Croghan, Jr. (1794-1850): A Prominent Pittsburgh Lawyer from Kentucky." *Western Pennsylvania Historical Magazine* 51 (July 1868): 213-227.

Thompson, Charles N. "Sons of the Wilderness: John and William Conner." *Indiana Historical Society Publications* 12 (1937).

Thompson, Ray. *Washington at Whitemarsh: Prelude to Valley Forge.* Fort Washington, Pa.: The Bicentennial Press, 1974.

Thoreau, Henry David. *Cape Cod.* New York: Literary Classics of the United States, 1985.

Thornton, Francis Beauchesne. *Our American Princes: The Story of the Seventeen American Cardinals.* New York: G. P. Putnam's Sons, 1963.

Toker, Francis. "James O'Donnell: An Irish Georgian in America." *Journal of the Society of Architectural Historians* 29 (1970): 132-143.

Tolchin, Martin. "Thomas P. O'Neill Jr., a Democratic Power in the House for Decades, Dies at 81." *New York Times* 7 January 1994: A21.

"Top 100 Irish Americans of 1997." *Irish America* March/April 1997: 26-72.

Truett, Randall Bond, ed. *Washington, D.C.: A Guide to the Nation's Capital.* American Guide Series. New rev. ed. New York: Hastings House, 1968.

Tucker, Glenn. *Dawn Like Thunder: The Barbary Wars and the Birth of the U.S. Navy.* Indianapolis: The Bobbs-Merrill Company, Inc., 1963.

Turkki, Pat. *Burns Lake & District.* Burns Lake, B.C.: Burns Lake Historical Society, 1973.

Turnbull, Andrew. *Scott Fitzgerald.* London: The Bodley Head, 1962.

Tyler, Samuel. *Memoir of Roger Brooke Taney.* Baltimore: John Murphy & Company, 1876.

"'Typhoid Mary' Dies of a Stroke." *New York Times* 13 November 1938: 30.

"Uncle to Sail on The Sullivan." *New York Times* 22 April 1943: 5.

Van Doren, Carl. *Mutiny in January.* New York: The Viking Press, 1943.

Varble, Rachel M. *Jane Clemens: The Story of Mark Twain's Mother.* Garden

City, N.Y.: Doubleday & Company, 1964.

Villard, Oswald Garrison. *John Brown 1800-1859: A Biography Fifty Years After*. New York: Alfred A. Knopf, 1943.

Volwiler, Albert T. *George Croghan and the Westward Movement*. Cleveland: The Arthur H. Clarke Company, 1926.

von Pressentin Wright, Carl. *Blue Guide: New York*. 2nd ed. New York: W. W. Norton & Company Inc., 1991.

Vroom, F. W. "Charles Inglis – An Appreciation." *Nova Scotia Historical Society Collections* 22 (1933): 25-42.

Waggoner, Hyatt H., ed. *The Poetical Works of Whittier*. Boston: Houghton Mifflin Company, 1975.

Wakin, Edward. *Enter the Irish-American*. New York: Thomas Y. Crowell Company, 1976.

Walbran, John T. *British Columbia Coast Names 1592-1906*. Ottawa: Government Printing Bureau, 1909.

Waldman, Carl, and Alan Wexler. *Who Was Who in World Exploration*. New York: Facts on File, 1992.

Walke, Mrs. Edwin S. "Soldiers of the American Revolution Buried in Illinois." *Journal of the Illinois State Historical Society* 8 (April 1915): 46-54.

Wallace, W. Stewart, ed. *Dictionary of Canadian Biography*. Toronto: The Macmillan Company of Canada, 1926.

———, ed. *The Encyclopedia of Canada*. Toronto: University Associates of Canada, 1936.

Waller, George. *Saratoga: Saga of an Impious Era*. Englewood Cliffs, N.J.: Prentice-Hall, Inc., 1966.

Waln, Robert Jr. *The Biographies of the Signers of the Declaration of Independence*. 9 vols. Philadelphia: R. W. Pomeroy, 1824.

Walsh, Alice. *A Sketch of the Life and Labors of the Rev. James T. O'Reilly, O.S.A.* Lawrence, Mass.: Free Press Printing Company, 1928.

Walsh, J. C. "Charles O'Conor." *The Journal of the American Irish Historical Society* 27 (1928): 285-313.

Walworth, Arthur. *Woodrow Wilson: World Prophet*. Vol. 2. New York: Longmans, Green and Company, 1958.

Walz, Jay and Audrey. *Portrait of Canada*. New York: American Heritage Press, 1970.

Ward, Geoffrey C. *Baseball: An Illustrated History*. New York: Alfred A. Knopf, 1994.

"A Warm Welcome for N.Y.U.'s Irish Center." *New York Times* 27 April 1993: C12.

Warsaw, Michael P. *The National Shrine of the Immaculate Conception: America's Church*. Washington, D.C.: The National Shrine of the Immaculate Conception, 1990.

Waters, Edward N. *Victor Herbert: A Life in Music*. New York: The Macmillan Company, 1955.

Watson, John F. *Annals of Philadelphia and Pennsylvania*. Philadelphia: Edwin S. Stuart, 1899.

Weber, Francis J. *America's Catholic Heritage*. N.p.: St. Paul Editions, 1976.

———. "These Immortal Chaplains." San Buenaventura, Calif.: Junipero Serra Press, 1976.

Webster, Daniel. "An Address delivered at the Laying of the Corner-Stone of the Bunker Hill Monument at Charlestown, Massachusetts, on the 17th of June 1825." *The Writings and Speeches of Daniel Webster*. Vol. 1. Boston: Little, Brown, & Company, 1903.

Webster's American Military Biographies. Springfield, Mass.: G. & C. Merriam Company, 1978.

Wecter, Dixon. *Sam Clemens of Hannibal*. Boston: Houghton Mifflin Company, 1952.

Weichmann, Louis J. *A True History of the Assassination of Abraham Lincoln and of the Conspiracy of 1865*. Edited by Floyd E. Risvold. New York: Alfred A. Knopf, 1975.

Westerhoff, John H. III. *McGuffey and His Readers: Piety, Morality, and Education in Nineteenth-Century America*. Nashville: Abingdon, 1978.

Whalen, Richard J. *The Founding Father: The Story of Joseph P. Kennedy*. New York: The New American Library, 1964.

White, Hester E. "John Carmichael Haynes: Pioneer of the Okanagan and Kootenay." *British Columbia Historical Quarterly* 4 (1940): 183-201.

Whitehill, Walter Muir. *Boston Statues*. Barre, Mass.: Barre Publishers, 1970.

Whitney, David C. *Founders of Freedom in America: Signers of the Declaration of Independence*. Chicago: J. G. Ferguson Publishing Company, 1964.

Who Was Who in American History: Arts and Letters. Chicago: Marquis Who's Who, Inc., 1975.

Wibberly, Leonard Patrick O'Connor. *The Coming of the Green*. New York: Henry Holt and Company, 1958.

Wiencek, Henry. *The Smithsonian Guide to Historic America: Southern New England*. New York: Stewart, Tabori & Chang, 1989.

———. *The Smithsonian Guide to Historic America: Virginia and the Capital Region*. New York: Stewart, Tabori & Chang, 1989.

Wildes, Harry Emerson. *Anthony Wayne: Troubler Shooter of the American Revolution*. New York: Harcourt, Brace and Company, 1941.

Wilkinson, Burke. *Uncommon Clay: The Life and Works of Augustus Saint-Gaudens*. New York: Harcourt Brace Jovanovich, 1985.

Willcox, Joseph. "Biography of Rev. Patrick Kenny." *Records of the American Catholic Historical Society of Philadelphia* 7 (1896): 27-79.

———, ed. "Extracts from the Diary of Rev. Patrick Kenny, from June 23, 1827, to February 6, 1829." *Records of the American Catholic Historical Society of Philadelphia* 9 (June 1898): 223-256.

Willson, Beckles. *The Life and Letters of James Wolfe*. London: William Heineman, 1909.

Wilson, James Grant, and John Fiske, eds. *Appleton's Cyclopaedia of American Biography*. 8 vols. New York: D. Appleton and Company, 1887-1918.

Wilson, Mary Poe. "Dr. William Beattie Laughlin." *Rush County Sesquicentennial*. Shelbyville, Ind.: Tippecanoe Press, 1972.

Winckler, Suzanne. *The Smithsonian Guide to Historic America: The Great Lakes States*. New York: Stewart, Tabori & Chang, 1989.

Winson, Justin. *Narrative and Critical History of America*. Boston: n.p., 1890.

Wirt, William. *The Two Principal Arguments of William Wirt, Esquire, on the Trial of Aaron Burr, for High Treason, and on the Motion to Commit Aaron Burr and Others, for Trial in Kentucky*. Richmond: Samuel Pleasants, Jr., 1808.

Wittke, Carl. *The Irish in America*. Baton Rouge: Louisiana State University Press, 1956.

———. *We Who Built America: The Saga of the Immigrant*. Rev. ed. Cleveland: The Press of Western Reserve University, 1964.

Wolfe, Gerard R. *New York: A Guide to the Metropolis*. New rev. ed. New York: McGraw-Hill Book Company, 1988.

"A Woman's Trip Around the Globe." *New York Times* 26 January 1890: 8.

Wood, William. *The Father of British Canada*. Vol. 12 of *Chronicles of Canada*, edited by George M. Wrong and H. H. Langton. Toronto: Glasgow, Brook & Company, 1920.

Writers' Program of the Work Projects Administration. *Indiana: A Guide to the Hoosier State*. American Guide Series. New York: Oxford University Press, 1945.

———. *Michigan: A Guide to the Wolverine State*. American Guide Series. New York: Oxford University Press, 1941.

———. *Missouri: A Guide to the "Show Me" State*. American Guide Series. New York: Duell, Sloan and Pearce, 1041.

———. *New York: A Guide to the Empire State*. American Guide Series. New York: Oxford University Press, 1940.

———. *Pennsylvania: A Guide to the Keystone State*. American Guide Series. New York: Oxford University Press, 1940.

———. *Wisconsin: A Guide to the Badger State*. American Guide Series. New York: Duell, Sloan and Pearce, 1941.

Würtele, Fred. C., ed. *Blockade of Quebec in 1775-1776 by the American Revolutionists (Les Bastonnais)*. Series 7. Quebec: Literary and Historical Society of Quebec, 1905.

Young, Agatha. *The Women and the Crisis: Women of the North in the Civil War*. New York: McDowell, Obolensky, 1959.

Young, William, ed. *A Dictionary of American Artists, Sculptors and Engravers*. Cambridge: William Young and Company, 1968.

Zobel, Hiller B. *The Boston Massacre*. New York: W. W. Norton & Company, Inc., 1970.

Site Index

¶ Although some of the statues and monuments in this list do not honor Irish or Irish Americans, they are included because they were created by sculptors of Irish descent.

United States

A

B

603

Subject Index

United States

A

Alexander, Sarah Wallace 444
Alison, Francis 26, 27, 376, 434
Arthur, Chester A. 45, 57, 74, 210, 257, 292, 301, 450
Arthur, William 450

B

Barnwell, John 335
Barrett, John 83
Barry, D. F. 55
Barry, John 52, 53, 58, 118, 160, 210, 250, 405, 408, 413, 414, 417
Beckett, Samuel 294
Belmont, Oliver H. Perry, Jr. 438
Bennett, James Gordon, Jr. 295, 441
Berkeley, George 21, 436, 437, 442, 445, 446
Blaine, James G. 40, 61, 75
Blair, Francis Preston 41, 70, 72
Bly, Nellie 339, 340
Borah, William Edgar 70
Bouvier, Jacqueline 54, 438, 443
Bouvier, Janet Lee 438
Boyle, John 52, 54, 87, 408, 409
Brady, James "Diamond Jim" 139, 316
Brady, Mathew 43, 55, 58, 61, 322
Brennan, Patrick 304
Brennan, William 67
Bresnahan, Roger 279
Brown, Alexander 143
Brown, George 143
Brown, John 447
Brown, Margaret Tobin 209
Brown, Nicholas, Jr. 446
Browne, Margery 129
Bryan, William Jennings 70, 102, 103, 210, 217
Buchanan, James 45, 51, 57, 74, 210, 399-401
Buchanan, James, Sr. 401
Buckley, Dennis 113
Burk, John Daly 451
Burke, Edmund 46, 294
Burke, John 70
Bush, George 58
Butler, Pierce 67, 404, 420
Butler, Richard 37, 258
Butler, Thomas 420
Byrnes, James 67
Byrnes, Thomas 325

C

Caffrey, Anthony 63
Cairnes, Elizabeth 137
Caldwell, James 252, 269, 272, 309, 422
Calhoun, John C. 21, 45, 70
Callahan, William F. 167
Callan, Nicholas 74
Campbell, Alexander 396
Campbell, John 66
Cannon, Joseph 41
Carey, Mathew 418, 419, 451
Carlin, Thomas 78
Carr, Patrick 162, 165, 175
Carroll, Anna Ella 143, 149
Carroll, Charles ("Barrister") 131, 132, 135
Carroll, Charles (of Bellevue) 73
Carroll, Charles (of Carrollton) 70, 130, 134, 136, 140, 141, 142, 144, 155, 156, 406, 412
Carroll, Charles (of Ireland) 130
Carroll, Charles, Jr. 139
Carroll, Daniel (of Annapolis) 63
Carroll, Daniel (of Duddington) 35, 56,

619

Canada

DATE DUE
